Netherlands Yearbook of International Law

Volume 47

More information about this series at http://www.springer.com/series/8913

Martin Kuijer · Wouter Werner
Volume Editors

Netherlands Yearbook of International Law 2016

The Changing Nature of Territoriality in International Law

ASSER PRESS

Springer

Volume Editors
Martin Kuijer
Ministry of Security and Justice of the Netherlands
The Hague
The Netherlands

and

VU University Amsterdam
Amsterdam
The Netherlands

Wouter Werner
Faculty of Law
VU University Amsterdam
Amsterdam
The Netherlands

ISSN 0167-6768 ISSN 1574-0951 (electronic)
Netherlands Yearbook of International Law
ISBN 978-94-6265-206-4 ISBN 978-94-6265-207-1 (eBook)
DOI 10.1007/978-94-6265-207-1

Library of Congress Control Number: 2017944369

Published by T.M.C. ASSER PRESS, The Hague, The Netherlands www.asserpress.nl
Produced and distributed for T.M.C. ASSER PRESS by Springer-Verlag Berlin Heidelberg

Printed on acid-free paper

This T.M.C. ASSER PRESS imprint is published by Springer Nature
The registered company is Springer-Verlag GmbH Germany
The registered company address is: Heidelberger Platz 3, 14197 Berlin, Germany

Board of Editors

Aims and Scope

The Netherlands Yearbook of International Law (NYIL) was first published in 1970. As a double-blind peer-reviewed publication, the NYIL offers a forum for the publication of scholarly articles of a conceptual nature in a varying thematic area of public international law. In addition, each Yearbook includes a section *Dutch Practice in International Law*. The NYIL is published under the auspices of the T.M.C. Asser Instituut.

T.M.C. Asser Instituut

Located in the 'international zone' of The Hague—the City of Justice, Peace and Security, the T.M.C. Asser Instituut is a leading, inter-university research institute operating in the broad field of international law.

Founded in 1965, the Institute's international community of scholars is engaged in research, postgraduate training and dissemination of knowledge in furtherance of the purposes and principles of international law. This inter-university institute cooperates closely with and supports the Dutch universities' activities in the relevant disciplines. The academic fields covered by the Institute are Private International Law, Public International Law, Law of the European Union, International Commercial Arbitration, International Humanitarian Law, International Criminal Law and International Sports Law.

The Institute enjoys an excellent reputation at both a national and an international level for its development, organisation and hosting of conferences and academic meetings, demand-driven postgraduate programmes and training. Its ancillary websites and data collections all contribute to a coherent and integral strategy in the area of knowledge transfer.

The Institute has its own publishing house, T.M.C. Asser Press. T.M.C. Asser Press not only serves the publishing needs of the T.M.C. Asser Instituut, but also those of academics and practitioners worldwide in the fields of International and European Law.

T.M.C. Asser Instituut
Institute for Private and Public International Law
International Commercial Arbitration and European Law

Institute Address:
R. J. Schimmelpennincklaan 20–22
2517 JN The Hague
The Netherlands

Postal Address:
P.O. Box 30461
2500 GL The Hague
The Netherlands
Tel.: +3170 342 0300
Fax: +3170 342 0359
Email: NYIL@asser.nl
Internet: www.asser.nl

Contents

Part I
The Changing Nature of Territoriality in International Law

Chapter 1
The Paradoxical Place of Territory in International Law

Martin Kuijer and Wouter Werner

Abstract This introductory chapter presents some of the key issues and developments surrounding the relationship between territory and international law. While most rules of international law are traditionally based on the notion of State territory, new developments have challenged territory as the main organising principle in international relations. In particular, three trends have affected the role of territoriality in international law: the move towards functional regimes, the rise of cosmopolitan projects claiming to transgress state boundaries, and the development of technologies resulting in the need to address intangible, non-territorial, phenomena. Yet, notwithstanding some profound changes, it remains impossible to think of international law without a territorial locus. The contributions to this Volume demonstrate that, if international law is undergoing changes, this implies a reconfiguration of territory, but not a move beyond it.

Keywords Territory · Territoriality · Jurisdiction · Sovereignty · Functionalism · Cosmopolitanism · Technology

---

Martin Kuijer is the Legal Adviser of the Netherlands Ministry of Security and Justice, (substitute) member of the Venice Commission, and Professor of human rights law at the VU University Amsterdam. Wouter Werner is Professor public international law and co-director of the Centre for the Politics of Transnational Law, VU University Amsterdam.

M. Kuijer (✉)
Ministry of Security and Justice of the Netherlands, The Hague, The Netherlands
e-mail: m.kuijer@minvenj.nl

M. Kuijer · W. Werner
VU University Amsterdam, Amsterdam, The Netherlands
e-mail: w.g.werner@vu.nl

M. Kuijer and W. Werner (eds.), *Netherlands Yearbook of International Law 2016*, Netherlands Yearbook of International Law 47,
DOI 10.1007/978-94-6265-207-1_1

Contents

1.1 Introduction

International law holds a paradoxical position when it comes to territory. On the one hand, international law is predicated on the idea that the world is made up of territorially bounded, sovereign entities. While the historical bond of sovereigns over 'their people' is considerably older than the jurisdiction of sovereigns over their territory, the allegiance of subjects to their ruler was gradually replaced by an allegiance to an abstract entity: the State.[1] With the emergence of the State, the significance of borders grew simultaneously. Even though borders between States were frequently redrawn after wars and peace negotiations, they gradually became more permanent. Since the twentieth century, all over the world borders have been more stable than ever before. The whole surface of the earth is nowadays divided among politically distinct entities, States, and res communis belonging to humanity as a whole. By contrast to orders such as the *Respublica Christiana*, that took the moral and political unity of the world as their starting point, international law departs from the notion that the world is *pluriverse*; a world divided up in political, territorially delimited units.[2] The State remains central to modern-day public international law and contemporary international relations, and territoriality is one of the most characteristic features, if not the most characteristic feature, of the State. Territoriality still significantly shapes our contemporary legal system. Most treaties still take State territory as the spatial application, but more importantly in the absence of a centralised international authority the functioning and enforcement of international law is largely dependent on effective territorial control to avoid a situation in which no entity responds to infringements of rules of international law.

As Ryngaert wrote in this Volume, international lawyers have come to think of 'territory as pre-given political knowledge.'[3] One of the traditional tasks of international law has been to translate this 'pre-given political knowledge' into issues of jurisdictional borders, to set out how 'territory' functions as a dividing line between

[1] See also Hirsch Ballin 2017, Chap. 10 in this Volume.
[2] The contradiction between 'universe' and 'pluriverse' is taken from Schmitt 1950.
[3] Ryngaert 2017, Chap. 3 in this Volume.

the exercise of legal powers. Not surprisingly, therefore, the issue of borders has always been at the centre of international law. International law not only contains rules that separate sovereign States (to keep them 'peacefully apart' as Wolfgang Friedman put it),[4] it also contains rules delimitating territory under sovereign jurisdiction from areas beyond the (exclusive) control of States, such as the high seas, or outer space. Where sovereign territory is treated as the exclusive realm of the State, non-sovereign spaces are often regarded as belonging to 'human society' or 'mankind'.[5] International law thus assumes, protects and delimits territorial divisions between territorial units among themselves, as well as between sovereign and non-sovereign territories.

On the other hand, international law is predicated on the idea that social interactions transcend territorial States; on the idea that borders are never able to seal off territories completely. If States were able to regulate their affairs solely on the basis of domestic law, there would be no place left for international law. International legal regulation is sometimes necessary, precisely because certain forms of social interaction cross and challenge territorial boundaries. This then leads to the construction of legal regimes whose territorial scope transgresses State borders. In addition, international law sometimes relies on conceptions of international society that are difficult to square with the idea of a pluriverse of territorially bounded, sovereign communities. Human rights law, for example, also presupposes the existence of some form of cosmopolitanism, some form of unity and universality. The preamble to the International Covenant on Civil and Political Rights, for instance, holds that 'freedom, justice and peace in the world' is founded upon the 'recognition of the inherent dignity and of the equal and inalienable rights of all members of the human family', while '[r]ecognizing that these rights derive from the inherent dignity of the human person'.[6]

The paradoxical place of territory in international law has structured many debates on the nature, position and direction of the international legal order. From at least the nineteenth century on, the territorial order of international law has been questioned as 'outdated' and in need of revision. Writing in 1864, the French international lawyer Charles Vergé witnessed increasing interdependence between States, a growing web of transnational economic relations, accelerating technological developments and an ever-stronger humanitarian sensibility across the world. Taken together, they were 'signs of a new period, symbols of a universal law'.[7] The idea that territoriality constitutes an outdated mode of legal regulation

---

[4] Friedman 1964.

[5] The term 'human society' is taken from de Vattel 1758, para 283. References to 'mankind' can be found in several legal instruments regulating non-sovereign territories. One of the most beautiful expressions is contained in Article V of the Outer Space Treaty, which labels astronauts as 'envoys of mankind' (1967 Treaty on Principles Governing the Activities of States in the Exploration and Use of Outer Space, including the Moon and Other Celestial Bodies, A/RES/21/2222 Annex).

[6] 1966 International Covenant on Civil and Political Rights, 999 UNTS 171 (ICCPR), Preamble.

[7] As cited by Koskenniemi 2004, at 27.

has been repeated ever since, both in international law and in adjacent fields such as international relations.[8] And yet, it proved difficult, if not impossible, to do away with the notion of territory as ordering principle in international law. Partly this had to do with the fact that the increase in transboundary transactions and relations went hand in hand with the rise of State power and different forms of nationalism. The era described by Vergé was not only a period of globalization, it was also the time when nationalism spurred the creation of new States in the heart of Europe. This combination of interdependence and nationalism was not unique to the 1860s. A century later, international law witnessed new forms of international cooperation and mutual dependencies, but also the rise of a norm of national self-determination, with newly independent States jealously guarding their territorial boundaries.[9] In addition, it proved difficult to regulate transboundary relations without the involvement of States at different levels. Humanitarian sentiments and transboundary economic transactions, for example, were translated into forms of extra-territorial jurisdiction; linking the territorial State to the protection of a core of universal values.

1.2 Reshaping the Notion of Territory in International Law

However, this is not to say that the role of 'territory' in international law has remained basically the same over the past 150 years or so. The extension of State jurisdiction beyond its borders, for example, has given rise to a series of new questions regarding the relation between territory, jurisdiction and sovereignty. In the past few decades, questions of territoriality have gained renewed meaning and significance for international law due to at least three developments: (a) the (further) specialization of international law; (b) the (further) rise of cosmopolitan values and institutions (c) the (further) development of technology.

1.2.1 Territoriality and Functionalism

International law has not proven immune to processes of specialization and compartmentalization that seem inherent to complex social systems.[10] By now, international law consists of a series of highly specialized fields, such as environmental law, human rights law, economic and trade law, investment law, international

[8] An example are the 'interdependence theories' as developed since the 1970s. See for example the seminal article by Keohane and Nye 1987.

[9] See for example how UNGA Resolution 2625 (1970) combines a plea for self-determination with an emphasis on the sanctity of the borders of newly independent States.

[10] See, e.g., Luhmann 1997.

criminal law, et cetera. This has given rise to anxieties about the 'fragmentation' of international law: the splitting up of international law into a series of functional regimes, each with their own forms of expertise, rules and institutions.[11] One of the questions that kept popping up in these debates is whether the division of the world in territorial units has been replaced by a division of the world into separate functional regimes. In other words, the question is whether we have moved 'from territoriality to functionality'.[12] As several chapters in this volume attest, the move to more specialized regimes has indeed affected international law's treatment of territory. However, it has proven impossible to bypass territory altogether: specialized regimes still need a territorial scope of applicability and often still heavily rely on the cooperation of territorially defined States. The specialization of international law has thus resulted in important transfigurations of territory, not in the abandonment of the notion as such.

1.2.2 Territoriality and Cosmopolitanism

The same goes for the rise of cosmopolitan rules and institutions in international law. Since the late 1990s there have been renewed attempts to ground international law in universalistic principles that transcend the rights, interests and boundaries of individual States. Liberal-cosmopolitan thinkers such as Thomas Pogge, Alan Buchanan or Fernando Teson proposed new foundations for international law along these lines. According to them, international law should not take States, but rather individuals and their basic rights and interests as its starting point.[13] In similar fashion, the Appeals Chamber of the International Criminal Tribunal for the Former Yugoslavia witnessed a trend in international law, where '[a] State-sovereignty-oriented approach has been gradually supplanted by a human-being-oriented approach'.[14] In international legal theory, cosmopolitan ideas found their way into theories of international or global constitutionalism. Several authors argued that international law has progressed from solely an order between territorially bounded States towards an order based on core constitutional values,[15] foundational documents or institutions[16] that protect the interests of the international community as a whole. And indeed, it would be difficult to deny that

[11] The literature on the topic of fragmentation in international law is vast. For an overview of some of the core topics, see the report of the study group of the International Law Commission, 'Fragmentation of International Law: Difficulties Arising From the Diversification and Expansion of International Law', finalised by Martti Koskenniemi, A/CN.4/L.682, 13 April 2006.

[12] Paulus 2004.

[13] See, among other works: Pogge 2002; Buchanan 2003; Teson 2001.

[14] *Prosecutor v Tadić*, ICTY Appeals Chamber, Decision on the Defence Motion for Interlocutory Appeal on Jurisdiction, Case No. IT-94-1-AR72, 2 October 1995, para 97.

[15] de Wet 2006.

[16] Fassbender 2009. For a somewhat more cautious approach, see Franck 2002 and MacDonald 1999. For a critique, see Werner 2007.

international law underwent significant transformations due to the rise of cosmopolitan values and supranational institutions. The question remains, however, what these transformations imply for the role of territory in international law. On the one hand, they challenge the idea that the best way to make legal sense of the world is to split it up in separate territorial units. On the other hand, they are still in many ways bound up with the powers of the very same States they seek to transgress. The main addressee of human rights obligations, for example, remains the territorially bounded State; the main parties involved in the (dis)functioning of the International Criminal Court are territorial States, the human-being-oriented approach that the ICTY witnessed in the field of humanitarian law is tied to the inter-State logic of the laws of armed conflict, etc. As Martti Koskenniemi has set out in relation to cosmopolitanism generally: 'A deep-structured cosmopolitanism maintains that deep down the world is already united. The problem is that the claimed deep-structural principles vary, are conflicting, indeterminate and receive meaning and applicability only through formal decision-making structures. Re-enter government to make the choice; re-enter intergovernmental negotiations to set the balance. Cosmopolis must wait.'[17]

1.2.3 *Territoriality and Technology*

Finally, the development of technology has affected and questioned the territorial make-up of the world. One example is the opening up of new 'spaces' that call for regulation, such as outer space or cyberspace. These spaces differ in some important respects from 'earthly' spaces such as the high seas or Antarctica, for example in terms of their limits and their tangibility. In addition, technological developments have contributed to what sociologists have called 'social acceleration',[18] the development of 'high speed societies'[19] or the 'contraction of the present'.[20] One of the main driving forces of social acceleration has been the development of technology, in particular the speeding up of goal-oriented processes in areas such as transportation, production and communication.[21] Since the Industrial Revolution, the acceleration of technology (and the acceleration of the *pace* of technological development) has been quite spectacular, as is evidenced by for example the increased speed of transportation. Where in 1750 a stagecoach travelled at 5.5 miles an hour,[22] today extensive railway network connect countries, whereas the globe can be crossed by using passenger airplanes at an average speed of 600 miles per

[17] Koskenniemi 2003.

[18] Rosa 2015.

[19] Rosa and Scheuerman 2008.

[20] Lübbe 2008.

[21] Rosa 2015, at 71.

[22] Rodrigue 2013, Chapter 2.2, para 3.

hour.[23] As Harmut Rosa has set out, technological acceleration is not an isolated process. It is tied to different societal sectors such as the economy, the military and family life, which often turn to technology for ways to enhance efficiency and to speed up goal-oriented processes.[24] Processes of acceleration have had significant impact on the role of territory in social life. In this context, sociologists have used terms such as 'time-space compression',[25] or even the 'annihilation of place by time'.[26] With technology and societies speeding up, territory becomes less and less of an obstacle to human interaction. Just think of the speed with which financial transactions take place across the globe, the time it takes to communicate, to travel or to launch military attacks over a long distance. In today's world, it is often more important to control speed than to control territory.

Technology has not only produced social acceleration. It has also contributed to the rise of new forms of risk associated with phenomena such as climate change, nuclear energy and weaponry, or bio-engineering.[27] One of the characteristics of these risks is that they transcend temporal and geographical boundaries. Nuclear melt-downs, for example, produce intergenerational effects and could cause harmful effects for societies living thousands of miles away. Risks associated with climate change are global in nature, although their negative effects are spread unevenly across communities. Bio-engineering could affect the make-up of the human being itself, and thus produce long-term changes for the world population.[28] Regulating such risks requires institutions and mechanisms that transcend the territorial boundaries of individual States. Yet, even the regulation of these risks cannot get around the cooperation of sovereign States, the adoption of laws binding within particular territories and the formulation of territorial scopes of application for normative instruments. Again, what these risks induce is not an abandonment of the notion of territory, but a reconfiguration of its role in legal regulation.

1.3 Overview of Chapters

The chapters in this volume all deal with the question if and how the notion of territory is reshaped in light of the developments described above.

In her contribution, Bílková describes territoriality as the default legal status in the current system of international law. She does not deny that the concept of a deterritorialised State may be conceivable. The international community has in the

[23] Rosa 2015, at 100.

[24] Rosa 2015.

[25] Harvey 1990, at 260 et seq.

[26] Rosa 2015, at 99, links this term to the work of Koselleck 2000.

[27] The literature on risk in late modernity is vast. Some of the core writings include Beck 1992; Beck 2006; Giddens 1991, 1999; Beck et al. 1994; Ewald 1991, 2002.

[28] Ewald 2002.

past shown willingness to accommodate certain anomalous entities (States *in statu nascendi*, governments-in-exile, sui generis entities such as the Holy See), but the author argues that this does not entail that the Montevideo criteria have ceased to reflect the default setting. Ordinarily the lack of territory has either been treated as a temporary phenomenon caused by foreign occupation or annexation that should sooner or later end, resulting in the full restoration or creation of statehood (national liberation movements, governments-in-exile). Or it has been accepted as a permanent phenomenon and then, the entity has changed its status from 'State' to a 'sui generis legal person' (the Holy See, the Order of Malta). The latter scenario could possibly be applied to disappearing States as a result of the rising sea level.[29]

In search of a viable alternative approach to territoriality, Ryngaert recalls that territoriality is a relatively recent invention and that 'community' was the jurisdictional alternative in the pre-territory era. Another jurisdictional alternative could be temporality. Apart from community and temporality, justice could be an alternative conception of jurisdiction. This would be an ethics-based jurisdiction of conscience (of common humanity). The author acknowledges that all of these non-territorial theoretical conceptualizations of jurisdiction struggle to take root in actual legal praxis. While non-territorial transnational communities have, at least to a certain extent, developed their own regulatory capacities, it is important to realise that such systems are usually embedded within the territorial State-based system, as States are the very creators of the systemic autonomy of non-State systems, through delegation, facilitation, orchestration, and management.[30]

Territoriality therefore undeniably remains a pivotal concept. However, territorial sovereignty is affected by globalization and the increased importance of new technologies. Various chapters in this volume discuss the impact of new technologies on the primacy of territorial sovereignty.

The chapter by Kendall analyses how drone technology and the practice of targeted killings has led to a reshaping of the notion of territorial sovereignty in relation to the use of force. She observes how drone warfare leads to a vertical, mobile, and shifting battlespace that transgresses state borders, and analyses how justifications that have been advanced for these incursions question our understanding of territory. In the trend observed towards 'contingent sovereignty', territorial sovereignty can only be asserted as long as effective territorial control is exercised. Thus territory remains the framework of reference, but, with regards to the use of force, some States are increasingly invoking it in conditional terms to justify limitations to the territorial integrity of others. While this rhetoric remains controversial, it nonetheless points out at a possible reconfiguration of the relationship between sovereignty and territory.[31]

The effects of the development of new technologies on the role of territory in international law are further discussed in the contributions by Johns, Kleijssen and

[29] Bílková 2017, Chap. 2 in this Volume.

[30] Ryngaert 2017, Chap. 3 in this Volume.

[31] Kendall 2017, Chap. 4 in this Volume.

Perri, and Boer. Technological developments, such as the emergence of a 'data society' and the rise of cyber warfare and cybercrime, are intrinsically linked to a deterritorialisation of notions and relationships. The dematerialized nature of the online world raises new questions on how international law can operate in a non-geographical context.

The chapter by Johns analyses in general terms the implications of the rise of data for territory. She offers a conceptual analysis of the 'datafication' of territory, that is, the representation of territory as information, and the parallel phenomenon of territorialisation of data. Global data flows resulting from automated collection and analysis of data are reshaping the global landscape and possibly leading to a reconfiguration of territoriality. The analysis identifies 'datafication' as a rule of association with the potential to fundamentally reshape territoriality, yet at the same time points out at the persistence of territoriality, which remains the guide of data flows.[32]

Turning to cyber warfare, the contribution by Boer analyses more specifically how the notion of territory is reflected in the Tallinn Manual on the International Law Applicable to Cyber Warfare. She discusses the inherent conceptual difficulties of grasping what territory can mean in the cyberspace, and how this has resulted on the use of metaphors to describe a non-physical space. Such metaphors are used to attribute a physical location to virtual phenomena, for instance by relying on the physical location of cyber infrastructures. However, this type of analogies with relatable geographical concepts do not always allow to grasp the reality of cyberspace, and thus hinges on the possible need for new jurisdictional concepts to address the cyberspace.[33]

Finally, Kleijssen and Perri offer a practical perspective on the issues raised by the deterritorialisation of data in the context of cybercrime. Their contribution enquires into how territoriality and jurisdiction can operate with respect to dematerialised evidence which is located 'in the cloud'. In view of 'the switch of almost every human activity into a digital form', cybercrime constitutes a threat affecting individuals as much as private and public institutions, but the prosecution of such crimes is hampered by the difficulty of applying principles of jurisdiction to volatile and intangible data. The authors do not however argue for a move away from territoriality and jurisdiction. Rather, they suggest that, in order to provide operational solutions to the jurisdictional hurdles encountered with regards to cybercrime, efforts should focus on developing principles and procedures within the existing legal framework.[34]

The rise of new technologies has undoubtedly affected the primacy of territorial sovereignty. The principle of territoriality in public international law has lost its exclusive role and a shift towards functionality can be discerned. Authority is increasingly exercised on the basis of regimes specifically set up to attain certain

[32] Johns 2017, Chap. 5 in this Volume.

[33] Boer 2017, Chap. 6 in this Volume.

[34] Kleijssen and Perri 2017, Chap. 7 in this Volume.

goals. Functionalism allocates 'authority' to actors, independently of their formal position. The contributions by Arcuri and Violi, Skogly and Hirsch Ballin all describe this process from different viewpoints. Interestingly, while all of them describe a certain level of deterritorialisation in their respective fields, all of them underline the remaining significance of territoriality.

In their contribution, Arcuri and Violi focus on the international trade regime and international investment law. With regard to international investment law for example, functionalism dictates that 'authority' is attributed to investors. Contractual provisions relating to choice of law and stabilization clauses contribute most significantly to the phenomenon of deterritorialisation. The authors' hypothesis is however that territoriality and functionality are no substitutes or competitors, but impart meaning to each other. Functionality is co-determined by territoriality. It is States that perceive a certain law as in violation of WTO law and decide that it should be challenged, it is States that implement global law, it is States that will be arguing for and against certain interpretations and it is States that can mutually agree on how to eventually manage a specific conflict. States thus remain critical actors in determining how the rules of the international trade system are applied, interpreted and enforced. At the same time, the authors demonstrate that the concept of territoriality has transformed over the last decades. A multiplication of territorial units has emerged. Next to the nation State, customs unions and free trade areas have gained a unique legal status.[35]

In international human rights law, the one-sided focus on 'territoriality' has never existed to the same extent as in other fields of public international law. Both the texts of the European Convention on Human Rights (1950) as the International Covenant on Civil and Political Rights (1966) refer to the notion of 'jurisdiction'. The notion of 'jurisdiction' has originally been interpreted as essentially territorial. However, the territoriality of human rights obligations has been questioned as individuals' lives become increasingly affected by the actions of foreign actors (whether another State, an international organisation or a transnational corporation). In an increasing body of case law, the European Court of Human Rights acknowledged that States may be held accountable for situations over which they exercise 'effective control'. Similarly, United Nations treaty bodies have accepted that State Parties have a duty to ensure respect for the rights laid down in the Covenant as long as they exercise de jure or de facto effective control. Skogly demonstrates in his contribution that these considerations—by means of indirect horizontal effect and the doctrine of positive obligations—will have an impact on the regulation of activities of transnational corporations and other business enterprises.[36]

Hirsch Ballin focuses on the effects of globalisation and the consequent need to rethink the relation between territoriality and citizenship. Traditionally, citizenship is the default legal status of individuals who belong to the nation State. However,

[35] Arcuri and Violi 2017, Chap. 8 in this Volume.

[36] Skogly 2017, Chap. 9 in this Volume.

the rule that the State's authority over people is limited to its territory and the territorial principle of international jurisdiction is less convincing then before. In times of (rapidly growing) migration, extraterritorial citizenship (the continued presence of nationals as a result of emigration in a different State who wish to maintain a bond with the State where they came from), border-crossing relations, and an intensively connected world, the traditional approach is under pressure. A more functional approach dictates that people who participate in the social, economic and cultural life of a society regardless of nationality should be entitled to have their voice in public affairs, i.e. the right to participate in decision-making on public affairs. But again, States remain critical actors as long as the democratic meaning of citizenship finds its fulfilment within the territoriality of States. The territorial State provides the constitutional setting for citizenship free from ethnic privileges and prejudices.[37]

The shift towards functionality has raised a number of new concerns. One of them is that an issue-specific approach leads by definition to fragmentation resulting in a need to make these regimes more compatible in order to avoid 'regime collisions'. Another issue is that not all regimes are equally well developed. One could argue that trade and investment regimes are more developed than for example international environment and human rights regimes. A third issue is that the shift towards functionality has also resulted in a detachment from the democratic principle intrinsic in political territoriality. There is therefore a need to make these regimes legitimate and (more) accountable.

What is more, the inclination towards an alternative approach to territoriality is perhaps fading itself. People still tend to demonstrate strong attachment to the territory they see as theirs. This attachment might be getting weaker in some parts of the world or in some social classes, but in other quarters we can discern a revival of the nation State and the accompanying focus on territoriality. While it might be more difficult for States to defend their territory in the era of globalization, the territory of the State clearly remains the main unity of security. We have witnessed this in the recent 'refugee crisis'. The point of departure in asylum law is, as is demonstrated in the contribution of Battjes, that sovereign States have the right to determine who is offered protection on their territory. The importance States still attach to the concept of territoriality is demonstrated by some attempts to escape responsibility under the Refugee Convention, for example by attempting to redefine the 'border' or by establishing control schemes outside the territory of the State concerned.[38]

A similar trend is described in the contribution by Burke, Hannesson and Bangsund. The fact that certain special regimes provided for the direct enforceability of rights prescribed by international treaties by individuals or legal persons

[37] Hirsch Ballin 2017, Chap. 10 in this Volume.

[38] Battjes 2017, Chap. 11 in this Volume.

in (domestic) courts, had the effect of elevating individuals and economic entities to the extent that they could challenge the actions of sovereign States with regard to domestic governance measures that clashed with international obligations. This led in certain quarters to a feeling of losing sovereignty, self-determination and economic independence without feeling any 'ownership' vis-à-vis the newly established international legal order. Using Brexit as a case-study, they elaborate on these propositions.[39]

1.4 Conclusion

The various chapters in this Volume show that territory takes on a variety of meanings, depending on the functional field under discussion. Different functional fields have carved out different territories to organize the application and delimitation of law and jurisdiction. The role of territory in asylum law, for example, is quite different from the role of territory in international economic law, and from its role in relation to the use of force or to the risks of climate change. The chapters thereby clearly show how the increased specialization (fragmentation) of international law has led to a reconfiguration of territory, partly driven by the way in which specific functional fields are organized. Besides, several chapters discuss the impact of cosmopolitan ideas on the role of territory in international law. Skogly's chapter, for example, discusses the place of extra-territorial jurisdiction in order to protect human rights,[40] Battjes analyses how States and human rights organizations have reframed territory in light of supposedly universal obligations,[41] and Hirsch Ballin looks into new ways to conceive the right to citizenship.[42]

While the chapters thus differ in their field of application, they all build on similar, overlapping trends that affect the role of territory in international law. What is more, they all deal with reconfigurations of two core functions of territory in international law. In the first place, territory sets boundaries between different spheres of jurisdiction, and thus determines what can be regarded as illegal 'incursions' from one jurisdictional sphere into another. In international law, the traditional way of framing this was in terms of inter-State interventions, but it is of course also possible to think of these delimitations in different terms (e.g. in terms of the protection of specific functional regimes from incursions of other regimes). Secondly, the delimitation of territory marks out who is included and who is excluded from specific legal communities and what counts as the 'internal affairs' of a territorially delimited unit (see also the chapters by Hirsch Ballin and Kendall).

[39] Burke et al. 2017, Chap. 12 in this Volume.

[40] Skogly 2017, Chap. 9 in this Volume.

[41] Battjes 2017, Chap. 11 in this Volume.

[42] Hirsch Ballin 2017, Chap. 10 in this Volume.

Traditionally, this aspect of territory was discussed almost exclusively in terms of the internal dimension of State sovereignty (or in terms of 'civilized territories' in relation to 'uncivilized' and 'barbaric communities').[43] However, the development of international law has by now created a multitude of different and often overlapping legal communities, each with their own 'internal affairs'. The territorial scope of the WTO, for example, overlaps with that of the European Union, and partly with that of the ICC, the ASEAN, the parties to the ICCPR, etc.

Unsurprisingly, the line between territoriality and the (nation) State has been a thin one in this Volume. As there is 'no realistic and practical alternative [to the state] even on the horizon',[44] it may come as no surprise that all authors have stressed the fact that territoriality remains an essential regulating principle. Our politics still center around the nation State and the principle of subsidiarity in relation to the development of international instruments. Undoubtedly, territorial sovereignty is affected by globalization and the increased importance of new technologies which have led to an empowerment of non-State actors and a dematerialisation of legal relationships. However, an alternative approach to territoriality —such as functionality—has not yet matured. One concern is the absence of a mechanism to avoid 'regime collisions', but even more importantly there is currently no mechanism to ensure the democratic legitimacy and accountability of those regimes.

References

Anghie A (2004) Imperialism, Sovereignty and the Making of International Law. Cambridge University Press, Cambridge

Arcuri A, Violi F (2017) Reconfiguring Territoriality in International Economic Law. Netherlands Yearbook of International Law 47:175–215

Battjes H (2017) Territoriality and Asylum Law: The Use of Territorial Jurisdiction to Circumvent Legal Obligations and Human Rights Law Responses. Netherlands Yearbook of International Law 47:263–286

Beck U (1992) Risk Society: Towards a New Modernity. Sage Publishing

Beck U (2006) Living in the World Risk Society. Economy and Society 35(3):329

Beck U, Giddens A, Lash S (eds) (1994) Reflexive Modernization: Politics, Tradition and Aesthetics in the Modern Social Order. Polity Press

Bílková V (2017) A State Without Territory? Netherlands Yearbook of International Law 47:19–47

Boer LJM (2017) 'Spoofed Presence Does Not Suffice': On Territoriality in the Tallinn Manual. Netherlands Yearbook of International Law 47:131–145

Buchanan A (2003) Justice, Legitimacy and Self-Determination, Moral Foundations for International Law. Oxford University Press, Oxford

Burke C, Hannesson ÓÍ, Bangsund K (2017) Schrödinger's Cake? Territorial Truths for Post-Brexit Britain. Netherlands Yearbook of International Law 47:287–312

[43] For a more elaborate discussion on the division of the legal world into spheres of civilization, see Koskenniemi 2004; Anghie 2004; Gong 1984.

[44] Jackson 2007, at 315, as cited by Ryngaert 2017, Chap. 3 in this Volume.

de Vattel E (1758) The Law of Nations or the Principles of Natural Law. Available at: http://lonang.com/library/reference/vattel-law-of-nations. Accessed 19 February 2017
de Wet E (2006) The International Constitutional Order. International and Comparative Law Quarterly 55:51–76.
Ewald F (1991) Insurance and Risk. In: Burchell G, Gordon C, Miller P (eds) The Foucault Effect: Studies in Governmentality. University of Chicago Press
Ewald F (2002) The Return of Descartes's Malicious Demon: An Outline of a Philosophy of Precaution. In: Baker T, Simon J (eds) Embracing Risk. University of Chicago Press, pp 273–298
Fassbender B (2009) The U.N. Charter As Constitution of The International Community. Martinus Nijhoff, Leiden/Boston
Franck T (2002) Recourse to Force, State Action Against Threats and Armed Attacks. Cambridge University Press, Cambridge
Friedman W (1964) The Changing Structure of International Law. Columbia University Press, New York
Giddens A (1991) Modernity and Self-Identity: Self and Society in the Late Modern Age. Polity Press
Giddens A (1999) Risk and Responsibility. Modern Law Review 62(1):1–10
Gong GW (1984) The Standard of Civilization in International Society. Clarendon Press, Oxford
Harvey D (1990) The Post-Modern Condition: An Enquiry into the Origins of Cultural Change. Blackwell, Cambridge
Hirsch Ballin EMH (2017) Citizenship at Home and Across Borders. Netherlands Yearbook of International Law 47:245–262
Jackson R (2007) Sovereignty and its Presuppositions: Before 9/11 and After. Political Studies 55 (2):297–317
Johns F (2017) Data Territories: Changing Architectures of Association in International Law. Netherlands Yearbook of International Law 47:107–129
Kendall S (2017) Cartographies of the Present: 'Contingent Sovereignty' and Territorial Integrity. Netherlands Yearbook of International Law 47:83–105
Keohane RO, Nye JS (1987) Power and Interdependence Revisited. International Organization 41 (4):725–753
Kleijssen J, Perri P (2017) Cybercrime, Evidence and Territoriality: Issues and Options. Netherlands Yearbook of International Law 47:147–173
Koselleck R (2000) Zeitschichten: Studien zur Historik. Suhrkamp Verlag, Frankfurt
Koskenniemi M (2003) Legal Cosmopolitanism: Tom Franck's Messianic World. New York University Journal of International Law and Politics 35:471–486
Koskenniemi M (2004) The Gentle Civilizer of Nations: The Rise and Fall of International Law 1870–1960. Cambridge University Press, Cambridge
Lübbe H (2008) The Contraction of the Present. In: Rosa H, Scheuerman W (eds) High-Speed Society: Social Acceleration, Power, and Modernity. Penn State University Press, pp 159–178
Luhmann N (1997) Die Gesellschaft der Gesellschaft. Suhrkamp Verlag, Frankfurt
MacDonald R (1999) The Charter of the United Nations in Constitutional Perspective. Australian Yearbook of International Law 20:205–231
Paulus A (2004) From Territoriality to Functionality? Towards a Legal Methodology of Globalization. In: Dekker I, Werner W (eds) Governance and International Legal Theory. Martinus Nijhoff, Leiden, pp 59–96
Pogge P (2002) World Poverty and Human Rights. Polity Press, Cambridge
Rodrigue J-P (2013) The Geography of Transport Systems. https://people.hofstra.edu/geotrans/eng/ch2en/conc2en/ch2c1en.html. Accessed 20 January 2017
Rosa H (2015) Social Acceleration: A New Theory of Modernity. Columbia University Press, New York
Rosa H, Scheuerman W (2008) (eds) High-Speed Society: Social Acceleration, Power, and Modernity. Penn State University Press

Ryngaert C (2017) Territory in The Law of Jurisdiction: Imagining Alternatives. Netherlands Yearbook of International Law 47:49–82
Schmitt C (1950) Der Nomos der Erde im Völkerrecht des Jus Publicum Europaeum. Duncker & Humblot, Berlin
Skogly S (2017) Extraterritorial Obligations and the Obligation to Protect. Netherlands Yearbook of International Law 47:217–244
Teson F (2001) The Liberal Case for Humanitarian Intervention. FSU College of Law, Public Law Research Paper 39.
Werner W (2007) The Never-Ending Closure: Constitutionalism and International Law. In: Tsagourias N (ed) Transnational Constitutionalism, International and European Perspectives. Cambridge University Press, Cambridge, pp 329–368

Chapter 2
A State Without Territory?

Veronika Bílková

Abstract The chapter considers whether a State can exist without territory. It argues that if the functional theory of territory is accepted, then the concept of a deterritorialized State may indeed be conceivable. The chapter however cautions against embracing this concept hastily, drawing attention to four caveats. First, the functional theory requires solid justification that is so far lacking. It is not so evident that territory is nothing more than a special tool people use and would be ready to abandon. Secondly, even if the theory is accepted, doubts arise as to whether all the traditional functions of territory can, in the current state of affairs, be assumed by a substitute and what this substitute would be. Thirdly, there are no historical 'precedents' of deterritorialized States to demonstrate the viability of the concept. Fourthly, other options are available to respond to the problems that the concept of deterritorialized State is supposed to resolve, especially the problem of disappearing States. As long as the concept remains insufficiently developed, these other options may seem preferable.

Keywords Deterritorialization · Disappearing States · Montevideo Definition · Territory · State

---

Associate Professor at the Charles University of Prague, Coordinator of the Centre for International Law of the Institute of International Relations in Prague. I would like to thank the University of Helsinki, on whose premises the research for this paper was conducted. I would also like to thank the two anonymous reviewers whose constructive comments have helped improve the manuscript. All the usual caveats apply.

V. Bílková (✉)
Faculty of Law, Charles University, Prague, Czech Republic
e-mail: bilkova@prf.cuni.cz

M. Kuijer and W. Werner (eds.), *Netherlands Yearbook of International Law 2016*, Netherlands Yearbook of International Law 47,
DOI 10.1007/978-94-6265-207-1_2

Contents

2.1 Introduction

The State is traditionally defined as an entity possessing, in addition to permanent population, government, and the capacity to enter into relations with other States, a defined territory. In fact, territory has traditionally been considered as the most characteristic feature of the State, making it different from other entities, such as international organizations or various non-state actors. States are by their very nature territorial units. They control a certain territory, exercising territorial supremacy—and they are the only ones to do so. Speaking about a de-territorialized State might therefore appear as a *contradictio in adjecto.* And yet, attempts have been made to establish new 'States' which, although (allegedly) possessing some territory, exist more in a virtual than in a real space.[1] At the same time, the discussions about the future of States which might lose their territory as a result of the rising sea level also suggest that for some, a State without territory could be an option.[2]

This chapter argues that the concept of a deterritorialized State might indeed be conceivable. If we accept that territory has merely a functional value, providing simply and solely a space in which members of a political community live together, governed by a central authority, then once this function is assumed in another way, territory loses its centrality. Existing States could thus survive a complete loss of their

[1] See D Nolan (2015) Liberland: Hundreds of Thousands Apply to Live in World's Newest 'Country', The Guardian, 24 April 2015, https://www.theguardian.com/world/2015/apr/24/liberland-hundreds-of-thousands-apply-to-live-in-worlds-newest-country, accessed 13 May 2016.

[2] See Stoutenburg 2015.

territory. And new States could potentially be established in the absence of territory. This argument, however, comes with four caveats. First, the functional theory requires more solid justification than so far provided in scholarly literature. It is not so evident that territory is nothing more than a special tool people use and would be ready to replace with another tool. Secondly, even if the functional theory is accepted, doubts may arise as to whether all the traditional functions of territory can, in the current state of affairs, be assumed by a substitute. Thirdly, contrary to what certain authors claim, there are no historical 'precedents' of deterritorialized States that could be invoked to demonstrate the viability of the concept. Fourthly, other options may be available to respond to the problems that the concept of deterritorialized State is supposed to resolve, especially the problem of disappearing States. As long as the concept remains insufficiently developed, these other options may seem preferable.

The chapter proceeds in three steps. First, it shows that the State has traditionally been conceptualized as a territorial unit. Very few scholars have however given deeper thought to what this actually implies. Functional theory of territory of the State has been promoted by some authors but it is far from clear whether this theory gives a full account of the importance territory has for communities and individuals. The second section discusses, and refutes, historical examples of deterritorialized States that are propounded in scholarly literature. The third section focuses on the arguments in favour of the concept of deterritorialized State raised within the recent debate on the so-called disappearing or sinking States. It reveals that these arguments fail to demonstrate that territory is, in the current state of affairs, fully dispensable and that its functions could be assumed in other ways. It also shows that arguments in support of the concept of deterritorialized State, aimed at finding an innovative solution to the problem of disappearing States, may have unintended consequences. The chapter comes to the conclusion that while the idea of a State without territory is interesting, embracing it prematurely might do more harm than good.

2.2 State as a Territorial Unit?

Territory of the State is a part of geographic space which is under the control and sovereignty of the State. It encompasses land territory with internal waters and territorial sea, the airspace and the subsoil.[3] The territory is surrounded by boundaries—an imaginary line that separates the State from other States and from *res communis* (high seas, outer space). As an 'an area of bounded space',[4] the territory of the State is the main spatial unit of contemporary international relations. That States have a territory over which they exercise supremacy is also the main assumption on which the system of international law is predicated. International law is (still) primarily the law created by and for States. And what makes States different

---

[3] Shaw 1982.

[4] Storey 2001, at 1.

from other entities operating at the international scene, including international organizations, armed opposition groups or non-governmental organizations, is the possession of and control over a certain portion of the Earth's surface.[5]

It thus should not come as a surprise that the very concept of territory pervaded international law at the period of the formation of modern national States. Based on the Latin word *territorium,*[6] which under the Roman law had been associated with a geographical space as well as a community living in this space, the word *territory* came to common use in late feudalism, where small decentralized feudal domains were replaced by larger centralized States. '[T]he idea of owing allegiance to territory', as Storey notes, 'began to supersede allegiance to lord or to God. [...] Territory has become the mobilizing force and, to a considerable extent, control of territory became the geographical expression of political power'.[7] Ever since, territoriality has been the main organizing principle of international relations. The whole surface of the Earth and, in fact, the whole universe is nowadays divided among politically distinct entities, States, and *res communis* belonging to the humanity as a whole. Although the centrality of States is increasingly challenged, 'it still makes a great difference whether an entity is or is not a State'.[8] Only States are considered full legal persons with a rich set of rights and duties under international law. 'Loss of statehood implies a loss of [the] preferential treatment and consequently a significant degradation of international legal personality.'[9] This explains why some entities may strive to get or maintain statehood even if they clearly do not, or have ceased to, meet the definition of a State.

2.2.1 *The Montevideo Definition of the State*

This definition has traditionally reflected the territorial nature of the State. The 1933 Montevideo Convention on the Rights and Duties of States[10] defines the State as a person of international law which possesses, in addition to a permanent population, government, and capacity to enter into relations with the other States, 'a defined territory' (Article 1).[11] This definition is still largely accepted as valid. In 1991, the Arbitration Commission of the Conference on Yugoslavia (also known as the Badinter Arbitration Commission) confirmed that 'the State is commonly defined as a community which consists of a territory and a population subject to an organized

[5] See Alston 2005, at 3.

[6] The word probably comes from the combination of *terra*—earth or land, with the suffix *-orium* denoting place.

[7] Storey 2001, at 1.

[8] Crawford 2006, at 31.

[9] Jain 2014, at 6.

[10] 1933 Montevideo Convention on the Rights and Duties of States, 165 LNTS 19.

[11] See Grant 1999.

political authority'.[12] The definition of the State has also been, in two instances, discussed in the UN International Law Commission—in the 1940s, during the preparation of the Draft Declaration on Rights and Duties of States,[13] and in the 1950s, in the course of the codification of the law of treaties.[14] Although neither of these cases resulted in the adoption of a definition of the State, the two drafts both listed territory as one of the necessary requirements for a State.

The territory requirement also regularly appears in definitions of the State proposed by scholars. In the pre-Montevideo period, Hall argued that '[t]he marks of an independent State are, that the community constituting it is permanently established for a political end, that it possesses a defined territory, and that it is independent of external control'.[15] Scelle saw the State as 'a juridically organized collectivity fixed on a delimited territory'.[16] Lawrence went so far as to declare that 'as the rules of modern International Law are so permeated from end to end with the idea of territorial sovereignty that they would be entirely inapplicable to any body politic that was not permanently settled upon a portion of the earth's surface'.[17] In the post-Montevideo period, scholars have often taken the definition in the Convention as the starting point.[18] Although this definition has not been accepted without reservations,[19] the territory requirement has provoked only limited criticism. Most scholars would probably still share the view that Jessup expressed in 1948, that 'one cannot contemplate a State as a kind of disembodied spirit. [...] [T]here must be some portion of the earth's surface which its people inhabit and over which its Government exercises authority'.[20]

International law sets few conditions as to what the territory of the State should be like. No minimal extent is required: States with large territory, for instance Russia or China, can exist alongside those with minimal territory, such as Andorra or Monaco. While doubts have been expressed as to whether so-called microstates are truly States,[21] the membership of these entities in the UN suggests that the

[12] Badinter Arbitration Commission, Yugoslavia Peace Conference Opinion No 1, 92 ILR 162, 29 November 1991, at 165.

[13] 'The Commission concluded that no useful purpose would be served by an effort to define the term "State", though this course had been suggested by the Governments of the United Kingdom and of India. In the Commission's draft, the term "State" is used in the sense commonly accepted in international practice.' ILC, Yearbook of the International Law Commission 1949, Vol II, UN Doc A/CN.4/SER.A/1949, 1949, at 289, para 49.

[14] ILC, Yearbook of the International Law Commission 1956, Vol II, UN Doc A/CN.4/SER. A/1956/Add.l, 1956, at 107.

[15] Hall 1924, at 18.

[16] Scelle 1932, at 74.

[17] Lawrence 1895, at 59.

[18] See, for instance, Crawford 2006, at 37–95; and Shaw 2008, at 197–204.

[19] See Crawford 2012, at 128; Craven 2010, at 220; Grant 1999.

[20] US Ambassador Jessup, UNSCOR 383rd meeting (2 December 1948), at 11, cit. in Crawford 2006, at 48.

[21] Higgins 1963, at 34–35.

international community in its majority answers the question in the affirmative.[22] By virtue of the principle of sovereign equality, enshrined in Article 2(1) of the UN Charter, all States notwithstanding their political, economic and social system and also their size, have equal rights and duties.[23] Although no minimal size is required, territory must be natural in origin. 'Only those parts of the surface of the earth which have come into existence in a natural way can be recognized as constituting State territory'.[24] Man-made land can be part of the territory of a State but it cannot constitute the whole of this territory.[25] International law does not require that the territory be contiguous or that it have undisputed defined borders.[26] As Wong puts it, '[t]erritory does not have to be defined with absolute certainty, but there must still be a territorial base from which to operate [...] In short, territory is a leg upon which the state must be created; the leg may be bent, but it must exist'.[27]

2.2.2 The Concept of a Deterritorialized State

But must this leg—territory—really exist? Or could there be a deterritorialized State, a State without territory, a State consisting solely of a population governed by some authority and capable of entering into international relations? The concept of deterritorialization is not all that new. Coined by Deleuze and Guattari in their book *Anti-Oedipus: Capitalism and Schizophrenia* published in 1972,[28] the term originally referred to a move away from a rigidly imposed hierarchy of capitalist society toward an order based on multiple identities. It soon penetrated social sciences, including international law. Scholars such as Brölmann have discussed the deterritorialization of international law, defining it as 'detachment of social and cultural practices from specific places'[29] and showing that 'function [...] is the most recent and the most powerful competitor for territoriality as an organising principle for authority, legal or otherwise'.[30] Deterritorialization is often associated with globalization,[31] which strengthens the status of non-state actors at the expense of that of

22 See also Mendelson 1972, at 609–630.

23 UNGA, Declaration on Principles of International Law concerning Friendly Relations and Co-operation among States in accordance with the Charter of the United Nations, UN Doc. A/RES/25/2625, 24 October 1970.

24 *In re Duchy of Sealand*, Federal Republic of Germany, Administrative Court of Cologne, Case No. 9 K 2565/77, 3 May 1978.

25 See also *Re Hartmann and Pude*, Italy, Constitutional Court, 71 ILR 258, 18 April 1967; *United States v Ray*, United States Court of Appeals, Fifth Circuit, 51 ILR 225, 1970.

26 *Sovereignty over Certain Frontier Land (Belgium v Netherlands)*, ICJ, Judgment, 20 June 1959.

27 Wong 2013, at 354.

28 Deleuze and Guattari 1972.

29 Brölmann 2007, at 92.

30 Ibid.

31 Mégret 2009; and Michaels 2013. See also Allott 1990.

States and 'changes individuals' sense of community by reconstructing it along both more local and cosmopolitan lines'.[32] In a globalized world regulated by deterritorialized international (or transnational) law, the State loses its centrality. Could it lose its territory as well, getting decentralized itself?

The answer to this question depends largely on the legal status of the definition of the State and the role that is assigned to territory within this definition. Surprisingly few authors have dealt with these two issues. In his seminal book on the Creation of States in International Law, Crawford describes the Montevideo definition simply as 'the best known formulation of the basic criteria for statehood'.[33] He adds, however, that 'the criteria of statehood are of special character, in that their application conditions the application of most other international law rules'.[34] Does that suggest that the definition of the State constitutes some kind of a Kelsenian basic norm (*Grundnorm*) that lies at the core of the international legal system and cannot be changed without putting this system into jeopardy?

In his overview of the definitions of statehood put forward by scholars, Grant shows that while the *existence* of the State is often considered to be such a basic norm, a concrete *definition* is not. Giving examples of alternative definitions used throughout history (based on legitimism, contiguity doctrine and effectiveness-population-territoriality), he concludes that 'the notion of statehood and sovereignty is, at least in part, historically contingent. What may be counted as a source of sovereignty or as a basis to a claim to statehood at a particular time may not be counted as such at a later date'.[35] Bederman opines that the Montevideo definition, though not uncontested, 'remains the customary international law standard of statehood'.[36] Customary international law, as is well known, is not set in stone (not even in paper) and can evolve over time. If the Montevideo definition is customary in nature, then any of the criteria it is based on—including territory—could potentially be modified or abandoned.

2.2.3 *The Functional Theory of the State Territory*

There are indeed authors, albeit in a minority, who do not consider territory as a necessary condition of statehood. Kelsen, for instance, identifies the State with the legal order. For him, territorial supremacy is a reflection of the existence of a State rather than a condition for this existence.[37] Out of the authors who adhere to the Montevideo definition, Starke and Shearer opine that territory is not really

[32] Mégret 2009, at 495.

[33] Crawford 2006, at 45.

[34] Ibid.

[35] Grant 1999, at 456.

[36] Bederman 2010, at 53.

[37] Kelsen 1941–1942.

necessary for statehood, at least for entities whose statehood has already been established.[38] Crawford, also embracing the Montevideo definition, notes that 'the State must consist of a certain coherent territory effectively governed—a formula that suggests that the requirement of territory is rather a constituent of government and independence than a distinct criterion of its own'.[39]

This view is shared by Jain who argues that 'the territory requirement has its roots in the idea that territory is necessary for effective governance'.[40] The territory requirement is therefore justified on the basis of the functional utility of territory. This justification applies both at the creation of a State and for its continuity. In the former situation, the functional theory is further complemented by the desirable barrier argument, which serves as a check on the creation of new States. Thus, 'the territory requirement for the continuity of statehood is justified on the basis of the functional utility of territory, while the territory requirement for the creation of statehood is justified on the basis of functional utility and the desirable barrier argument'.[41]

Developing further his functional theory of territory, Jain distinguishes four main functions that territory assumes. First, territory is a source of security. It creates a physical divide between 'us' and 'them' and protects 'us' against threats from both inside and outside.[42] Secondly, territory is a source of economic resources. Thirdly, territory facilitates the effective exercise of jurisdiction. And fourthly, territory is a source of historical and cultural resources. Jain sums up all these functions by saying that 'territory is a critical constituent of statehood because it provides security, economic and cultural resources and delimits and protects the jurisdiction and sovereignty of the state'.[43] As we will see later, Jain is persuaded that neither of the four functions necessarily has to be assumed by territory. The desirable barrier argument relies on a pragmatic consideration that the territory requirement allows to quash claims for statehood by entities not exercising effective control over any substantial area of land, thus preventing an uncontrolled proliferation of new States.

The functional theory of territory has been, albeit mostly implicitly, embraced by other scholars as well.[44] The functions of territory they have identified partly overlap with and partly complement those described by Jain. Three functions with a direct link to international law are particularly worth mentioning. First, territory determines the space that is subject to the sovereignty of a concrete State. While the

---

38 Starke and Shearer 1994, at 85.

39 Crawford 2006, at 52.

40 Jain 2014, at 18.

41 Jain 2014, at 27.

42 As Herz notes, the State is 'an ultimate unit of protection for those within its boundaries'. See Herz 1957, at 474.

43 Jain 2014, at 23.

44 See Crawford 2006, at 45–46; Shaw 2008, at 487–489.

State might occasionally exercise its sovereign rights outside its territory, the thrust of its activities takes place on it. Territory is the *'domaine reservé'* of the State and as the PCIJ held in 1928, 'failing the existence of a permissive rule to the contrary [a State] may not exercise its power in any form in the territory of another State'.[45] Secondly, territory sets the divide between national and international law. National law applies within a State, international law among States. 'The state's territorial boundary delimitates its political and legal power, and vice versa, and constitutes its border with international law'.[46] Thirdly, most concepts of international law reflect the territorial principle. The jurisdiction of the State is primarily territorial.[47] The rules applicable to State responsibility, for instance, are premised on the assumption that States control their territory and the extent of the obligations they have within it is broader than that applicable outside.[48] Similarly, while it is now largely recognized that human rights apply extra-territorially, the extent of obligations States have outside their territory is much narrower than the one they have inside it.[49]

There can thus be no doubts that territory of the State assumes many functions. This, however, does not necessarily entail that its value is merely functional. In his separate opinion to the ICJ advisory opinion in the Western Sahara Case, Judge Dillard held that 'it is for the people to determine the destiny of the territory and not the territory the destiny of the people'.[50] While this is true, it might be difficult to separate the two, provided that the destiny of the people and that of a concrete territory are often intertwined. Both the people as a collective unity and concrete individuals may see, and often do see, their link to a specific territory as an important part of their identity.[51] From that perspective, human beings are probably not only political animals, as Aristotle famously held, but also territorial animals. People live not only *on* a certain piece of land, but also *for* a certain piece of land for which they are often ready to fight and, if need be, die.[52] This makes it difficult to argue that territory is nothing more than a 'spatial tool' that can be easily replaced by other instruments assuming the same function. It is also hard to say what these other instruments could be.[53] The functional theory of territory, while interesting, is thus not self-evident. Were it to be embraced, more solid justification would have to be provided that would both demonstrate that territory has merely a

---

[45] *The Case of the S.S. Lotus (France v Turkey),* PCIJ, Judgment, 7 September 1927, at 18.

[46] Brölmann 2007, at 85.

[47] See Ryngaert 2015.

[48] See Szigeti 2010.

[49] See *Loizidou v Turkey,* ECtHR Grand Chamber, Judgment, No. 15318/89, 18 December 1996, para 56; and *Ilaşcu and Others v Moldova and Russia,* ECtHR Grand Chamber, No. 48787/99, 8 July 2004, para 333.

[50] *Western Sahara,* ICJ, Advisory Opinion, 16 October 1975, Separate Opinion of Judge Dillard, at 114. See also Sumner 2004.

[51] See Knight 1982.

[52] See Herb and Kaplan 1999.

[53] See, for instance, Schnapper 2001.

functional value and elaborate on what its functions are and how they can be assumed in alternative ways.

2.3 Historical Examples of Deterritorialized States?

It is sometimes argued that the concept of deterritorialized State is nothing new at the international scene.[54] There are, allegedly, historical precedents of States lacking territory. In some instances, entities that did not possess territory were recognized as States. In other instances, entities which lost their territory, on a temporary or permanent basis, continued to be treated as States. The interpretation of these cases is, however, controversial. In most of them, the absence of territory was considered as an unfortunate, provisional and curable state of affairs related to the fact that the territory that the entity would claim as its own was controlled by another State. In cases where the absence of territory turned out to be permanent, the entity typically ceased to be considered as a State, though it could in some instances keep legal personality. Finally, that some entities are or continue to be *recognized* as States does not necessarily mean that they meet the objective Montevideo definition of a State.[55]

2.3.1 New States Established Without Territory?

A canonical example of an entity allegedly established or, at least, recognized as a State in the absence of territory was Czechoslovakia in the early twentieth century. In the pre-1914 period, the Czech and Slovak nations lived in the Austro-Hungarian Empire. Not considering this empire as their own country, the two nations sought independence. In 1916, in the midst of World War I, a Czechoslovak National Council was set up in Paris by the Czech and Slovak émigrés. In summer of 1918, several months before the end of the war and the dissolution of the Austro-Hungarian empire, the Council was recognized first as 'the trustee of the future Czecho-Slovak Government'[56] by the United Kingdom and then as a 'de facto *government*'[57] by the United States and France. Yet, the Council only transformed itself into a Provisional Government in October 1918 and the creation

[54] See Kittel 2014, at 1228.

[55] As Jain notes, 'statehood and recognition are two distinct but related facets of the rules of international law that define its primary subjects. In modern international law, statehood is an objective status—if entities meet certain criteria [...] Recognition, on the other hand, refers to the political act of acceptance of a state into the international community by states that are already members of the international community'. Jain 2014, at 43.

[56] Cit. in Mueggenberg 2014, at 186.

[57] Mueggenberg 2014, at 187–188.

of a new independent State, the Czechoslovak Republic, was only announced on 28 October 1918.

According to Crawford, the government is the most important single criterion of statehood, 'since all the others depend upon it'.[58] The recognition of a government should therefore logically imply the recognition of a State. And since at the time of the recognition, the Czechoslovak National Council did not exercise control over any territory, it could be argued that Czechoslovakia was originally recognized as a State without territory. Yet, such an argument might go too far. When the relations with Czechoslovakia were discussed in the French Parliament, the view was expressed that:

> The Czech State did not exist during the war. The territories which historically and geographically formed it were incorporated as mere provinces in the Austro-Hungarian Empire [...] The Government of the Republic, being unable to deal with a not yet existing State, dealt with the Czecho-Slovak nation. [...] France, adopting a new practice without precedence in legal history, has taken the initiative of recognizing as a nation a country which it could not recognize as a State, because it lacked a territory and frontiers, i.e. the two essential attributes of sovereignty.[59]

Even the Czech authors writing at the time or in the subsequent decades did not claim that Czechoslovakia existed prior to 28 October 1918, speaking at best about a State 'in statu renascendi'.[60] The recognition of the Czechoslovak National Council could thus hardly be considered as a precedent of a deterritorialized State.

The situation is more complicated with respect to certain Cold War cases in which a new independent State was proclaimed by a national liberation movement, without the consent of the country exercising control over the relevant territory. This happened in 1958, when the Front de libération nationale (FLN) proclaimed the independence of Algeria, in 1976, when the Frente Polisario announced the creation of the Saharan Arab Democratic Republic, or in 1988, when the Organization for the Liberation of Palestine (OLP) proclaimed the State of Palestine. The three movements were recognized by a number of countries as representatives of their (Algerian, Saharian, Palestinian) people or, alternatively, as governments. The recognition sometimes explicitly extended to the new States, although the FLN, Polisario and the OLP clearly did not control any portion of territory at the time. Algeria got formal independence on 5 July 1962 and it considers itself a State since that date (not since 1958). The status of the other entities remains disputed. One of the factors taken into account when granting or denying recognition of statehood to Western Sahara and Palestine is the presence or absence of a territory under the effective control of the movement.[61] Instead of providing examples of deterritorialized States, the practice thus largely confirms the territorial bias of international law.

---

[58] Crawford 2006, at 56.

[59] Kiss 1965, at 28, cit. in Talmon 2001, at 78.

[60] Táborský 1946, at 129. See also Hobza 1922.

[61] Quigley 2012 (arguing that Palestine has territory and is a State); and Ash 2012 (arguing that Palestine does not have a territory and is not a State).

2.3.2 States Surviving the Loss of Their Territory?

With the entities that lost their territory but continued, or have continued, to be treated as States, the practice is richer and more diverse. It encompasses, first, cases of governments-in-exile claiming to represent a certain State. Unlike governments *in situ*, governments-in-exile are outside the territory of the State and fail to exercise control over this territory, though they intend to return and re-establish this control in future. The classical impediment preventing them from doing so is the occupation or annexation of the territory by another State. There are many instances, where governments-in-exile were recognized as legitimate governments.[62] Since, as Talmon notes, 'there can [...] logically be no "government", either in exile or *in situ*, without the legal existence of State which the government represents',[63] the recognition of the government-in-exile implies the recognition of the State. Governments-in-exile continue to exercise the usual governmental functions to the extent that their absence from the territory allows them to. Some authors consider that there is an element of deterritorialization present in these situations.[64] This claim, however, is controversial.

The status of governments-in-exile and of the States they claim to represent first got larger attention during World War II (WWII), when several countries occupied by the Nazi Germany had their governments-in-exile settled in allied countries, mostly the United Kingdom. This was the case of Czechoslovakia, France, Greece, Luxembourg, the Netherlands, Norway, Poland and Yugoslavia. These Germany had their governments-in-exile were, sooner or later, recognized as *de facto* and *de jure* governments of the occupied States. Recognition was on the contrary denied to entities that were not considered to represent a State. For instance, the UK refused to recognize an Albanian governments-in-exile on the ground that 'while we shall endeavour to re-establish an independent Albanian State after the war we do not regard an Albanian State as now existing. Thus no question of recognizing any Albanian government in exile arises at present'.[65] The statement suggests that when *a contrario* the question of recognizing a certain governments-in-exile arose, i.e. recognition was granted, this implied the confirmation of the existence of the State represented by this government.

This WWII precedent has been followed in many other instances during the Cold War and even after 1990. Governments-in-exile have been repeatedly treated as governments of a State despite the lack of territorial control. Talmon gives the examples of the Coalition Government of Democratic Kampuchea—CGDK (1979–1990), the Delvalle Government of Panama (1988–1989), the Sabah Government of

[62] According to Talmon, in the course of the twentieth century, some 75 authorities in exile claimed to be governments in exile and in about a half of these cases, they were recognized as such. See Talmon 1999.

[63] Talmon 1999, at 500.

[64] See Stoutenburg 2015, at 377.

[65] As cited in Fischer 1999, at 145.

Kuwait (1990–1991), the Aristide Government of Haiti (1991–1994), the Kinigi Government of Burundi (1993) or the Kabbah Government of Sierra Leone (1997–1998).[66] Analysing this practice, McAdam states that 'the fact that governments can operate in exile suggests that the existence of territory, while essential to the original constitution of that entity as a State, is not integral to the exercise of certain governmental functions'.[67] The statement is carefully formulated to suggest that the presence of territory remains crucial for the establishment of a State but that its absence or, rather, inaccessibility, does not necessarily mean the immediate disappearance of the State. McAdam also notes that the status of governments-in-exile 'is a time-bound mechanism which enables a government to operate outside its territory until it once again becomes possible for that government to reassert its control there'.[68] Governments-in-exile thus do not represent a State without territory. They represent a State whose territory (and population, who normally stay in its majority on this territory) is temporarily controlled by another State.

Such is also the case with States, which, while having their territory occupied or annexed by another country, do not have a (recognized) governments-in-exile to represent them. Once the occupation or annexation is over, these States are restored rather than re-established—the term suggests that they have never ceased to be States, even when they missed three out of the four Montevideo conditions (territory, government, capacity to enter into international relations). This is what happened with respect to Ethiopia, after its liberation from the Italian occupation in the 1940s, or to the three Baltic States—Estonia, Latvia, and Lithuania—after the dissolution of the Soviet Union in 1991.[69] Again, it is difficult to argue that Ethiopia in the 1930s or the Baltic States in 1944–1991 constituted deterritorialized States. Temporary control of the territory by another State is not identical to the disappearance of this territory. And the very fact that with the end of the occupation or annexation, the statehood has to be restored, suggests that full statehood is conditioned on the possession of, and control over, territory.

Yet another controversial example of deterritorialized States is that of the Holy See and of the Sovereign Military Hospitaller Order of St John of Jerusalem of Rhodes and of Malta (Order of Malta).[70] The Holy See is qualified either as a *sui generis* entity or as a State or as both. Historically, the Holy See controlled a large portion of territory known as the Papal State. After this State ceased to exist in 1870, the Holy See had no territory until the Lateran Treaty was concluded with Italy in 1929. This, as Wong notes, 'led to the suggestions that the Holy See was a

[66] Talmon 1999, at 499.

[67] McAdam 2016.

[68] Ibid.

[69] See Mälksoo 2003 and Ziemele 2005.

[70] Kittel, for instance, argues that 'the notion of a deterritorialized state is already accepted in international law. Two prominent deterritorialized states—Knights of Malta and the Holy See—are recognized as states despite lacking a defined territory'. Kittel 2014, at 1228; see also Jain 2014, at 44–45.

sovereign power unaffected by the loss of its territory'.[71] These suggestions however are disputable. In 1937, the status of the Holy See was considered by the Court of the First Instance in Rome, which held that it could not qualify as a State prior to 1929 due to the absence of territory.[72] This view finds support in the doctrine with most scholars either considering that the Holy See has been a State except for the period 1870–1929,[73] or concluding that the Holy See has not been a State since the fall of the Papal State at all.[74]

The Order of Malta also used to possess territory. Established in the early eleventh century, the Order first controlled the island of Rhodes and then, in 1530–1798, it ruled the island of Malta. It lost the territorial control over the latter island following the French invasion at the end of the eighteenth century and, unlike the Holy See/Vatican, it has never regained it. While it remains one of the largest landowners in Italy, the Order has no independent territory of its own. Despite that, it maintains diplomatic relations with more than a hundred of States and it can conclude treaties. Yet, as several scholars have noted, this does not turn it into a State.[75] The Order of Malta itself does not claim to be a State; it describes itself as 'a sovereign subject of international law'.[76] Thus, rather than a deterritorialized State, the Order of Malta—similarly as the Holy See/Vatican—should be considered as a legal person *sui generis,* 'an international body that has some legal personality'.[77]

2.3.3 The Lack of Historical Precedents

This section has shown that history does not provide us with any conclusive examples of deterritorialized States. Whereas recognition was sometimes granted to, or not withdrawn from, entities claiming to represent a certain State—i.e. national liberation movements or governments-in-exile –, this happened on the assumption that such entities would, sooner or later, gain or regain control over their territory. When this did not happen, for instance in the case of the CGDK in Cambodia, recognition was later reconsidered. The Holy See/Vatican and the Order of Malta are not deterritorialized States either. It is true that these entities were or have been 'deterritorialized', i.e. deprived of territory, on a temporary (Holy See/Vatican) or

---

[71] Wong 2013, at 357.

[72] *Thome Guadalupe v Associazione Italiana di S. Cecilia,* Italy, Court of First Instance of Rome (1945) 8 ILR 151, 27 February 1937.

[73] See Arangio-Ruiz 1996.

[74] See Ryngaert 2011 and Morss 2015.

[75] See D'Olivier 1954 and Cox 2006.

[76] What is the Sovereign Order of Malta? http://www.orderofmalta.int/sovereign-order-of-malta/faq, accessed 4 June 2016.

[77] Wong 2013, at 357.

permanent (Order of Malta) basis. It is also true that despite the loss of territory, they have maintained the capacity to conclude treaties or have diplomatic missions. Yet, as the ICJ held in the *Reparations for Injury Case*,[78] States are not the only subjects of international law. Most scholars support the view that the Holy See/Vatican and the Order of Malta are legal persons under international law but cannot be considered as States. In the absence of any historical precedents, a deterritorialized State, were it to exist, would need to be a rather recent phenomenon.

2.4 Recent Examples of Deterritorialized States?

Recently, the concept of deterritorialized State has been the most frequently invoked within the debate on the so-called disappearing (or sinking) States. The Atlantis-style scenario has kept the imagination of many scholars. It is indeed an undeniable fact that the sea level is rising and that, as a consequence, certain States—especially small island States—may see a part or even the whole of their territory sink below the sea level. It has been rightly stressed that the islands 'will become uninhabitable long before they physically disappear'[79] and that, consequently, permanent population will be gone long before the territory is fully submersed. Despite that, it is the territorial element of the State that is primarily at stake, because unlike population and government, it cannot be easily transferred somewhere else. Moreover, it is the natural processes affecting the territory that are the cause of the *exodus* of the population and the relocation of the government structures.

2.4.1 The Phenomenon of Disappearing States

The risks ensuing from the rising sea level have been widely acknowledged.[80] In the report on climate change and its possible security implications published in 2009, the UN Secretary General noted that 'many island States face the prospect of loss of significant amounts of territory to sea-level rise and inundation, and some face the prospect of complete submersion'.[81] Among the most threatened States are the Maldives, the flattest country in the world with no ground surface higher than 3 meters and 80% of the land area lying below 1 m above average sea level, and

[78] *Reparation for Injuries Suffered in the Service of the United Nations*, ICJ, Advisory Opinion, 11 April 1949.

[79] McAdam 2016, at 2

[80] See also International Law Association, International Law and Sea Level Rise, Draft Committee Report, ILA 77th Biennial Conference, Johannesburg, South Africa, 7–12 August 2016.

[81] UN Secretary-General, Climate change and its possible security implications, Report of the Secretary-General, UN Doc. A/64/350, 11 September 2009, para 71.

some of the Pacific Ocean Islands, especially Kiribati, Nauru and Tuvalu (with an average height of 3–4 m).[82] These countries are well aware of the threat they face and have sought to draw attention to it for years.[83] While no State has been completely submerged so far, some islands have already had to be evacuated. In 2005, the Carteret Islands, belonging to Papua New Guinea, had their inhabitants resettled to the neighbouring Bougainville Island.[84] The resettlement was a preventative measures: the Islands are still above the sea level but the scientists have indicated that they would become uninhabitable by 2020.[85] In 2006, the Lohachara Island in India became the first island to sink under the sea level[86] (though it, according to some sources, re-emerged again in 2009).[87]

The disappearance of a State is not unknown in international law. Yet, the ways of disappearance that international law foresees and regulates—the unification with another State, the absorption by another State, the dissolution into several new States and, in the past, the annexation of a State defeated in a war—all presuppose the continuing existence of the State territory. The State disappears but its territory remains—it just becomes part of the territory of another State (or States). Legal issues arising from the disappearance of the State are addressed within the regime of succession, symptomatically defined as 'the replacement of one State by another in the responsibility for the international relations of *territory*' (emphasis added).[88] Crawford identified seven instances of a disappearance of States in the post-1945 period: Hyderabad, Somaliland, Tanganyika, Republic of Vietnam, Yemen Arab Republic, German Democratic Republic, Yugoslavia and Czechoslovakia.[89] None of these instances resulted from the physical loss of the territory. No precedent in

[82] See Church et al. 2006.

[83] For instance in September 2009, the government of Maldives held an underwater Cabinet meeting to manifest the urgency of the problem. See Daily Mail (2009) Maldives government highlights the impact of climate change… by meeting underwater, 20 October 2009, http://www.dailymail.co.uk/news/article-1221021/Maldives-underwater-cabinet-meeting-held-highlight-impact-climate-change.html, accessed 6 June 2016.

[84] B Merchant (2009) First Official Climate Change Refugees Evacuate Their Island Homes for Good, Treehugger, 8 May 2009, http://www.treehugger.com/corporate-responsibility/first-official-climate-change-refugees-evacuate-their-island-homes-for-good.html, accessed 6 June 2016.

[85] W Flannery (2012) 'We Can't Walk on Water'—small island communities, climate change and human rights, Right Now—Human Rights in Australia, 27 August 2012, http://rightnow.org.au/opinion-3/%E2%80%9Cwe-can%E2%80%99t-walk-on-water%E2%80%9D-%E2%80%93-small-island-communities-climate-change-and-human-rights/, accessed 6 June 2016.

[86] The Independent (2006) Disappearing world: Global warming claims tropical island, 24 December 2006, http://www.independent.co.uk/environment/climate-change/disappearing-world-global-warming-claims-tropical-island-5331748.html, accessed 6 June 2016.

[87] A Ray (2009) Lohachara rises from waters again, The Times of India, 3 April 2009, http://timesofindia.indiatimes.com/city/kolkata/Lohachara-rises-from-waters-again/articleshow/4352475.cms, accessed 6 June 2016.

[88] 1978 Vienna Convention on Succession of States in respect of Treaties, 1946 UNTS 3, Article 1 (2)(b).

[89] Crawford 2006, at 716.

this regard, with the exception of the mythical Atlantis, is known from the pre-1945 period either.

One may wonder whether it could be argued that 'submerged territory meets the territory requirement'.[90] After all, this territory does not physically 'disappear'. It is just made inaccessible or, rather, incapable to sustain human habitation. Yet, a careful reading of the UN Convention on the Law of the Sea (UNCLOS)[91] suggests that on the legal plan, there is no difference between non-existent and inaccessible territory. In its Articles 40(5) and 57Art. 40(5), the UNCLOS makes it clear that submerged territory does not give rise to any claims to maritime spaces or resources. In its Article 121(1), it defines an island as 'a naturally formed area of land, surrounded by water, which is *above water* at high tide' (emphasis added). This regulation reflects the fact that international law has traditionally conditioned the claims to territory on the functional ability to control and use such territory. Yet, 'as technology stands today, life and economic activity cannot be sustained underwater'[92] and, consequently, submerged territory can hardly be considered as 'territory' under the Montevideo definition. The question as to what happens to States whose territory is fully submerged thus arises.

2.4.2 Possible Legal Responses to the Phenomenon of Disappearing States

The submersion of the whole territory of State is a new situation or, rather, a new prospect and it thus calls for innovative legal solutions. Various proposals have been put forward both by scholars and by representatives of the sinking islands themselves. Whereas some of these proposals anticipate the 'transfer' of the State to a new territory, others, more radical, suggest that the State could continue its existence without territory. The former proposals rely on several main options to procure new territory, each linked to some challenges.[93] Occupying *terra nullius* or a part of *res communis* is theoretically sound but practically impossible since there is currently no territory falling under one of those categories that would be suitable for long-term human habitation. Constructing artificial islands may be more realistic and, indeed, the Maldives have made some projects in this respect.[94] Yet, the costs of the projects together with the uncertain prospects of their sustainability[95] made

---

[90] Jain 2014, at 35.

[91] 1982 United Nations Convention on the Law of the Sea, 1833 UNTS 3.

[92] Jain 2014, at 38.

[93] Jain 2014, at 47–49.

[94] See Gagain 2007, at 77–120.

[95] See R Spencer (2011) The World is Sinking: Dubai Islands 'Falling into the Sea', The Telegraph, 20 January 2011, http://www.telegraph.co.uk/news/worldnews/middleeast/dubai/8271643/The-World-is-sinking-Dubai-islands-falling-into-the-sea.html, accessed 12 May 2016.

this option hard to implement. Procuring land from another State—through sale or long-term lease—is, at least *prima facie,* more feasible.[96]

This option has already been contemplated and, in fact, explored, by some of the sinking islands. In 2008, the Maldives begun to divert a portion of its annual tourist revenue into buying a new land for the potential relocation of its population.[97] Negotiation started with Australia but so far they have not brought any tangible results.[98] This is not surprising, provided that States can hardly be expected to willingly sell or lease a part of their territory to another State, especially with the prospect that the sale or lease would be for good. There are some precedents of the sale of territory (France selling Louisiana to the United States in 1803, Russia selling Alaska to the United States in 1867, etc.). Yet, they all date back to the pre-1945 period. From the legal perspective, moreover, it is not clear whether a sovereign State could exist on leased territory. A lease does not entail transfer of ownership, let alone of sovereignty. The leased land would therefore continue to belong to the lessor. The lessee might be entitled to use it but it would not exercise sovereign rights in this (or any other) land. The option of procuring new land from another State therefore does not offer an optimal solution to the problem of the sinking island either. The 'transfer' of the State, while theoretically conceivable, is difficult to carry out in practice. That makes some authors opt for a more innovative solution and propose the concept of deterritorialized State.

2.4.3 Deterritorialized State as a Response to the Phenomenon of Disappearing States

The idea of turning toward the concept of deterritorialized State to solve the problem of disappearing States is inspired by the model of governments-in-exile. A deterritorialized State

> would have a population in states (host states) spread across the globe. Its government could be located anywhere in the world—inside the territory of another state [...] Its government would exercise its internal sovereignty remotely and would continue to engage in international relations as before.[99]

Several authors find this idea appealing, adding details as to how such an entity could come about. Kittel, for instance, suggests the conclusion of a new treaty that

---

[96] Oliver 2009.

[97] R Ramesh (2008) Paradise Almost Lost: Maldives Seek to Buy a New Homeland, The Guardian, 10 November 2008, https://www.theguardian.com/environment/2008/nov/10/maldives-climate-change, accessed 12 May 2016.

[98] B Doherty (2012) Climate Change Castaways Consider Move to Australia, The Sydney Morning Herald, 7 January 2012, http://www.smh.com.au/environment/climate-change/climate-change-castaways-consider-move-to-australia-20120106-1pobf.html, accessed 12 May 2016.

[99] Jain 2014, at 49.

she labels as a Global 'Disappearing Act'. In this treaty, States would pledge to address root causes of climate change, lowering their greenhouse emissions. Those the most responsible for the emissions would, moreover, have to agree to host the government-in-exile and the population of the sinking islands.[100] Burkett speaks about *ex situ* nationhood,[101] which would consist of 'a virtual nation-state, held together by a social network',[102] governed by an interim body composed of elected representatives of the nation. The model takes inspiration from the UN Trusteeship system with the difference that the trustees would be members of the *ex situ* nation. Rayfuse explains that the primary task of the authority governing the deterritorialized State would be to 'act as a trustee of the assets of the state for the benefit of its citizens wherever they might now be located',[103] especially with respect to the maritime zone.

Scholars writing in support of the concept of a deterritorialized State acknowledge practical difficulties that would be involved in its realisation. States might be reluctant to accept inhabitants of the sinking States and host their governments-in-exile; inhabitants of the relocated State may assimilate into the host nation, bringing about the disappearance of the State due to the loss of population; the relocation might be extremely expensive, etc. Recent practice shows that these difficulties are indeed real. In the early 2000s, Tuvalu approached Australia and New Zealand to discuss the possibility of relocating its population. Australia refused outright, New Zealand offered a 30-year programme of relocation with the maximum of 75 (!) Tuvaluans accepted a year.[104] As early as in the 1960s, the Nauru Local Government Council rejected a similar plan aimed at relocating the Nauruans to Australia, fearing that it 'would lead to the assimilation of the Nauruans into the metropolitan communities where they settled'.[105] The establishment of a deterritorialized State therefore faces at least as many practical challenged as the transfer of the State to a new territory.

Yet, it is interesting to note that at the theoretical level, many scholars consider the concept of deterritorialized State feasible. Some argue that 'the notion of a deterritorialized state is already accepted in international law',[106] invoking historical 'precedents' analysed in the previous section. Others rely on the new and unprecedented nature of the sinking States phenomena, which in their view calls for 'a novel but justified interpretation of the state'.[107] All concord in recalling a

[100] Kittel 2014, at 1237–1250.

[101] Burkett 2011.

[102] Ibid., at 361.

[103] Rayfuse 2009, at 11; and Rayfuse 2011.

[104] Harman G (2014) Has the great climate change migration already begun? The Guardian, 15 September 2014, https://www.theguardian.com/vital-signs/2014/sep/15/climate-change-refugees-un-storms-natural-disasters-sea-levels-environment, accessed 12 May 2016.

[105] As cited in *Certain Phosphate Lands in Nauru (Nauru v Australia)*, ICJ, Preliminary Objections of the Government of Australia, December 1990, para 60.

[106] Kittel 2014, at 1228.

[107] Burkett 2011, at 346.

presumption of continuity that exists in international law[108] and under which 'once a state is established, the lack of one or more factors may not necessarily indicate extinction of a state'.[109] Further arguments made in support of the concept relate to fairness and stability in international relations.[110] Allowing sinking States to survive the loss of their territory would be fair, because they are not among the most responsible for the climate change. Having to endure the consequences of irresponsible behaviour of other States is bad enough already; withering away because of such behaviour would be unjustifiably severe. Moreover, the disappearance of sinking States could prompt a need to redraw the maritime boundaries, thus threatening international stability and, even, international peace and security.

While all these arguments are relevant for the debate on the future of disappearing States, they do not help us decide whether a State actually *could,* and not simply *should,* exist as a deterritorialized entity. Would it be able to assume all the functions that have traditionally been linked to territory? Out of all the scholars, only Jain comments on this issue, claiming that 'it is possible to defend the continuing statehood [...] on the basis of technological developments that have diminished the value of functions served by territory'.[111] Each of the four functions of territory that he identifies could allegedly be assumed by other means today. Or, rather, none of them can be served by territory any longer. The security function has been compromised by non-state actors, such as terrorist groups, operating freely across borders. Economy is no longer confined within these borders and the State has a limited role in it. Jurisdiction can be exercised extra-territorially. And cultural ties do not require territory to survive and thrive.[112]

This account, while certainly interesting, is somewhat too concise to be persuading. Although it is true that globalization has made the attachment to territory less crucial, it does not necessarily mean that all the functions assumed by territory can be easily transferred to other entities. It is symptomatic that scholars largely fail to indicate what these other entities might be, simply noting that territory has somewhat change its relevance. This however is not the same as demonstrating that territory has lost all its value and has become totally dispensable. The practice in Jain's four areas is far from unambiguous in this respect. While it might be more difficult for States to defend their territory in the era of globalization, the territory of the State clearly remains the main unity of security. We have witnessed this in the recent refugee crisis, which has brought about claims—and attempts—to re-establish national borders and toughen the conditions under which 'they' are allowed to come to 'us'. While some may argue that this move has been driven by

[108] See Crawford 2006, at 715; Burkett 2011, at 354; Jain 2014, at 28; Kittel 2014, at 1220; McAdam 2016, at 6; Wong 2013, at 360.

[109] Kittel 2014, at 1220.

[110] See Burkett 2011, at 362.

[111] Jain 2014, at 24.

[112] Ibid., at 24–25.

unrealistic nostalgia of times that have already passed, the very fact that in times of crisis people turn back to territory should not be dismissed as irrelevant.

Similarly, States may not be able to control the economic activity on their territory and, in fact, this activity may have become detached from any concrete territory. Yet, this again does not mean that territory has lost all its value. Economic activities have to take place somewhere, natural resources are found somewhere, etc. In a globalised world, economic autarky—i.e. the capacity of a State to produce everything its population needs within its borders—is a myth. Yet, the irrelevance of territory—i.e. the capacity of a State to exist without territory—may be another myth. The same applies in the third area, that of jurisdiction. It is correct to notice that jurisdiction is not strictly territorial. It is also correct to emphasise that the concept of extraterritorial jurisdiction has recently gained in prominence, particularly in some areas (human rights law). Accepting that jurisdiction can be extraterritorial is, however, not the same as saying that it is only extraterritorial or that territory does not matter any longer. Finally, the cultural and symbolic function of territory should not be underestimated. If this function is to be discarded as 'the least immediately critical',[113] then some solid evidence must be given in support of this claim. Other disciplines, especially cultural anthropology, should be consulted, as their conclusions seem to confirm the 'territorial bias' of human beings.[114]

2.4.4 *Creation of New Deterritorialized States*

In the debate relating to disappearing States, the concept of deterritorialized State is used solely with respect to entities which originally met the Montevideo criteria, including that of territory, but later have ceased (or might cease) to do so due to climate change. Yet, if an established State could continue to exist in the absence of territory, what would be there to prevent a new State from being created without territory? Although this question might seem wholly theoretical, it is not. Over the past decades and especially since 2010, there have been attempts to establish 'States' which, though claiming to possess and control some minor territory (formerly *terra nullius* in the opinion of the 'founders'), resemble more a decentralized or even a virtual entity. Such entities encompass the Principality of Sealand,[115] proclaimed in

[113] Jain 2014, at 25.

[114] See, for instance, Basso 1996, at 86.

[115] The so-called Principality of Sealand was established in September 1967 by the UK citizen Roy Bates on Roughs Tower, an offshore platform located in the North Sea, off the coast of Suffolk, the UK. See the 'official' website of the Principality at http://www.sealandgov.org/, accessed 4 June 2016.

the 1960s, or the Kingdom of North Sudan[116] and Liberland,[117] established in the 2010s. All the three 'States' have a self-proclaimed 'government' and some 'population', made up of nationals of other countries having asked for the citizenship of these entities (in case of Liberland, the number of such 'citizens' amounts to some 250 000. Neither the members of the 'government' nor a single 'citizen' lives in the territory of their 'States'. Thus, the entities primarily, if at all, operate on a virtual basis, with people connected through Facebook and e-mail.

The phenomenon of 'virtual States' has so far largely escaped scholarly attention. The few scholars writing about it have mostly considered them in light of the Montevideo criteria.[118] The discussion is then centred around such questions as to whether a State can be established on a man-made land (Sealand)[119] or whether a certain territory is truly *terra nullius* (North Sudan, Liberland).[120] The questions are usually not answered in any conclusive way, because, as Dennis puts it, 'the creation of new states by individuals is such a rare event it has simply not been adequately addressed by the international community'.[121] If we moreover accept that the Montevideo criteria, including that of territory, do not necessarily need to apply, the situation gets even more complicated. How would we then recognize that we have to do with a State? In case of continuing deterritorialized States, the distinctive feature would be, as a minimum, their past statehood. In case of new deterritorialized States, no similar common feature exists. It would therefore become rather difficult to distinguish between deterritorialized State and various non-state entities.

These intricacies are what makes most scholars quite sceptical about the prospects of new (virtual) States. Klabbers, for instance, notes that 'the idea of a cyberstate then, a state without territory, is difficult to conceive of under the requirements of international law'.[122] Even those scholars who generally support the concept of deterritorialized State and advocate its use with respect to disappearing States, are reluctant to apply this concept to new (virtual) States. Jain, for instance, stresses that his 'argument, rooted in recognition of the diminishing utility and importance of the territory requirement, is [...] limited to the continuation rather than the creation of states'.[123] The creation of a State and its continuity are two distinct legal phenomena for him. During the creation of a State, the territory

---

[116] The so-called Kingdom of North Sudan was established by the US citizen Jeremiah Heaton in June 2014 in an uninhabited and unclaimed area (around 2000 km^2) on the borders between Egypt and Sudan. See the 'official' website of the Kingdom at https://kingdomsudan.org/, accessed 4 June 2016.

[117] The so-called Liberland was established by the Czech Republic's citizen Vít Jedlička in April 2015 in the area called Gornja Siga (around 6,5 km^2) at the borders between Croatia and Serbia. See the 'official' website of Liberland at https://liberland.org/en/main/, accessed 4 June 2016.

[118] Dennis 2002; Lyon 2015; Rossman 2016.

[119] Lyon 2015, at 663–670.

[120] Rossman 2016, at 329–330.

[121] Dennis 2002, at 296.

[122] Klabbers 2013, at 70.

[123] Jain 2014, at 26.

requirement acts not only as a source of functional utility but also as 'a desirable barrier to statehood'.[124] It is a barrier, because the finite nature of global territorial reserves together with the requirement that territory be big enough to allow the State to exercise effective governance, serves as a check on proliferation of States. It is desirable, because such proliferation would increase the complexity of international relations beyond any control. New deterritorialized States would also, as any States, acquire a range of territorial rights that they, however, could hardly exercise.

This desirable barrier argument certainly has some merit, especially when the classical Montevideo definition is applied. After all, this definition was introduced to provide States with objective criteria on the basis of which to assess whether a certain entity could quality as their peer. Once this assessment has been made with a positive outcome, a temporary failure by the already established State to meet all the requirements of the Montevideo definition does not necessarily have to entail the extinction of such a State. The international community has repeatedly shown a willingness to continue to treat as States entities that have for some time lacked effective government as well as, as we saw in Sect. 2.3.2, entities that could temporarily not control their own territory (occupied States during WWII, etc.). Yet, the distinction between the creation of a State and its continuity becomes less (if at all) relevant, when the failure to meet some of the Montevideo criteria becomes permanent and/or when the functional theory of the State is accepted. If an entity can operate as a State in the total absence of territory, i.e. if all the functions linked to territory can be assumed otherwise, should it really matter whether such an entity has lost its territory forever or has never had one in the first place? And if the entity is 'operational', why should it be desirable to prevent it from joining the international community by setting a barrier that would require it to originally possess something that is can lose forever later on and that is not necessary for its existence? These questions remain largely unaddressed in the scholarly literature.

2.4.5 *Alternatives to the Concept of Deterritorialized State*

The previous sections have shown that while the concept of deterritorialized State might be theoretically conceivable, there are still a lot of uncertainties relating to its actual content and operation. It is not clear whether all the functions traditionally assumed by territory can be assumed by other tools and if so, what these tools would be. It is also disputable, whether a deterritorialized State could only exist as an *a posteriori* entity that would develop out of an existing territorial State, or whether it could be an *a priori* entity that would come into being in the absence of territory straightaway. The lack of a more extensive debate on these issues cannot certainly be interpreted as a result of a general consensus among scholars over the concept of deterritorialized States. Rather, it stems from the fact that so far, this

[124] Ibid., at 27.

concept has been almost exclusively considered, and advocated for, in the context of a case-specific discussion, that relating to disappearing (sinking) States.

The tragic prospects of these States—having its territory submerged by rising sea level due to irresponsible behaviour of other States—provokes, quite understandably, sympathy among scholars. Those scholars then, again understandably, seek to come up with innovative legal solutions that would allow disappearing States to legally survive their own 'death', keeping rights they have had up to now. Since under international law, such rights have traditionally been granted only to States, emphasis is placed on proving that even a complete and permanent loss of territory does not necessarily entail the extinction of the State and that a State can exist—or continue to exist—as a deterritorialized entity. This certainly is a *bona fide* construction that aims at mitigating the rigidity of legal rules where they would cut too deep (and into an innocent body).

One may however wonder whether with the bathwater, the baby is not thrown as well. Accepting that a State can exist without territory might have implications going far beyond the case of disappearing States. It would cast serious doubts on how we can recognize a State, what makes States different from various non-state actors, where the borders between the sovereign spaces (and jurisdictions) of various States lie, what makes international law different from national law, etc. Having the concept of State revisited by scholars in light of new developments at the international scene might indeed be useful. Rejecting the traditional definition of the State without having a new one, revealing sufficient degree of quality, to replace it, might on the contrary be dangerous.

One may also wonder whether doing so is in any way necessary even in the context of the disappearing States. After all, turning these entities into deterritorialized States is not the only plausible legal answer to the challenges that they face. They could, for instance, be granted a wholly new legal status of *sui generis* entities similar to that the Holy See or the Order of Malta possess. This status would allow them to keep some rights after they cease to qualify as States *stricto* sensu. Presenting a detailed analysis of what such entities could look like is beyond the remit of this chapter. Yet, some of the proposals aimed at introducing the concept of deterritorialized State, such as Kitell's idea of a Global 'Disappearing Act',[125] could be rather easily altered to fit the new model. They might even have better chances to materialize within this model, as trying to introduce a new *sui generis* entity, designed for very specific and rather narrow circumstances, can be less controversial to the international community than seeking to modify the general definition of one of the fundamental concepts of international law, the State.

[125] Kittel 2014, at 1237–1250.

2.5 Concluding Remarks

State is a human, social construction. It is 'not a tangible phenomenon of the physical world, but a construction of the human mind which has joined all these elements into a single and separate whole'.[126] These elements encompass, in addition to population, government and the capacity to enter into international relations, also a defined territory. Ever since the fall of medieval empires, States have been conceptualized as territorial unit. The Montevideo definition has been repeatedly confirmed in legal scholarship. It might be said that territory represents the single most characteristic feature of the State, making it different from other legal persons under international law. As one scholar has noted, 'international law uses territory as a factor to determine statehood and then uses statehood to recognize and legitimize territory and its control'.[127] That States possess and control territory is also one of the most important assumptions that international law stems from.

This, however, does not mean that the State could not be conceptualized otherwise, for instance as an entity fulfilling—through territorial control or otherwise—certain functions for its population. As Burkett noted, 'the substrate of the State is not property, it is the people of the State seen as a collective'.[128] So far, the people has organized itself on the territorial principle. With the process of globalization, the spread of modern technology and the virtualization of human life, this may change. It has already been suggested that the State might be living its Grotian moment—'an instance in which a fundamental change in the exiting international system happens, thereby provoking the emergence of a new principle of customary law with outstanding speed'.[129] As we saw in Sect. 2.4, an increasing number of scholars think that this moment could bring about a change in the definition of the State itself. Such a change is not, indeed, theoretically unconceivable. As Henkin once held, the Montevideo criteria might be 'not requisite qualifications but descriptions of states as we know them'.[130] If the reality changes, the criteria for and the definition of statehood might change as well.

Yet, we should caution before proclaiming that the change has already occurred and that from now on, Jessup's disembodied spirit is no longer a ghostly presence but a fact of life. First, despite all the announcement of the end of the territorial bias in international relations, people still tend to demonstrate strong attachment to the territory they see as theirs. This attachment might be getting weaker in some parts of the world or in some social classes.[131] Yet, no conclusive evidence has been put forward to prove it has ceased to exist.[132] At the same time, the competing theory,

[126] Marek 1968, at 588.

[127] Harrington 2016, at 67.

[128] Burkett 2011, at 346.

[129] Sterio 2011, at 211.

[130] Henkin 1995, at 13.

[131] Sassen 2006.

[132] See, for instance, Nevola 2011.

based on the functional approach, has not been elaborated in sufficient detail. Territory of the State certainly serves various purposes and assumes various functions. What these purposes and functions exactly are and whether they are linked to territory or could be assumed through other tools remains however unclear. As Basso rightly noted, 'placeless events are an impossibility; everything which happens must happen somewhere'.[133] The development of technologies might have deprived territory of some of its roles. Yet, whether it has made it completely unnecessary remains questionable. Were all territory to disappear, would human beings be able to survive in some kind of 'virtual reality'?

Some scholars, as we saw in Sect. 2.3, argue that a deterritorialized State is not a new phenomenon. Historical 'precedents' are invoked to demonstrate that the Montevideo definition has never been applied strictly, always leaving space for deterritorialized States. This is controversial. While it is true that the international community has always shown willingness to accommodate certain anomalous entities (States *in statu nascendi,* governments-in-exile, *sui generis* entities such as the Holy See and the Order or Malta), there are no cogent reasons to believe that this practice amounts to the abandonment of the Montevideo criteria. The lack of territory has either been treated as a temporary phenomenon caused by foreign occupation or annexation that should sooner or later end, resulting in the full restoration or creation of statehood (national liberation movements, governments-in-exile). Or it has been accepted as a permanent phenomenon and then, the entity has changed its status from 'State' to a '*sui generis* legal person' (the Holy See, the Order of Malta).

The latter scenario could also be used with respect to disappearing States, whose tragic prospects have given rise to the recent increase of the interest in the concept of deterritorialized State. These prospects are truly worrisome and call for an innovative solution that would allow disappearing States to legally survive their physical death. Yet, it is well known that hard cases make bad law. We may thus wonder whether the right solution to the phenomenon of disappearing States really lies in the redefinition of statehood and the abandonment of the territory requirement. Once the concept of a deterritorialized State is accepted, it becomes difficult to reserve it for disappearing States only. A lot of practical questions relating to the functioning of a deterritorialized State also remain open and, often, unaddressed. Thus, while we might be heading towards the era of deterritorialization, asserting that this era has already come and the territory requirement in the definition of the State does not apply any longer, could not only be premature but it could also do more harm than good.

[133] Basso 1996, at 86.

References

Allott P (1990) Eunomia, New Order for a New World. Oxford University Press, Oxford
Alston P (2005) Non-State Actors and Human Rights. Oxford University Press, Oxford
Ash RW (2012) Is Palestine a 'State'? A Response to Professor John Quigley's Article, 'The Palestine Declaration to the International Criminal Court: The Statehood Issue'. In Meloni C, Tognoni G (eds) Is There a Court for Gaza? A Test Bench for International Justice. TMC Asser Press, The Hague, pp 441–460
Arangio-Ruiz G (1996) On the Nature of the International Personality of the Holy See. Revue Belge de Droit International 32(2):355–369
Basso KH (1996) Wisdom Sits in Places: Landscape and Language Among the Western Apache. University of New Mexico Press, Mexico
Bederman DJ (2010) International Law Frameworks, 3rd edn. Thomson Reuters and Foundation Press, New York
Brölmann C (2007) Deterritorializing International Law: Moving Away from the Divide between National and International Law. In: Nollkaemper A, Nijman J (eds) New Perspectives on the Divide between National and International Law. Oxford University Press, Oxford, pp 84–109
Burkett M (2011) The Nation *Ex-Situ:* On Climate Change, Deterritorialized Nationhood and the Post-Climate Era. Climate Law 2:345–374
Church JA, White NJ, Hunter JR (2006) Sea-Level Rise at Tropical Pacific and Indian Ocean Islands. Global and Planetary Change 53:155–168
Cox N (2006) The Continuing Question of Sovereignty and the Sovereign Military Order of Jerusalem, of Rhodes and of Malta. Australian International Law Journal 13:211–232
Craven M (2010) Statehood, Self-Determination, and Recognition. In: Evans MD (ed) International Law, 3rd edn. Oxford University Press, Oxford, pp 203–251
Crawford J (2006) The Creation of States in International Law, 2nd edn. Oxford University Press, Oxford
Crawford J (2012) Brownlie's Principles of Public International Law, 8th edn. Oxford University Press, Oxford
D'Olivier FC (1954) The Sovereign Order of Malta in International Law. International and Comparative Law Quarterly 3(2):217–232
Deleuze G, Guattari F (1972) L'Anti-Oedipe. Capitalisme et Schizophrénie. Editions de Minuit, Paris
Dennis TA (2002) The Principality of Sealand: Nation Building by Individuals. Tulsa Journal of Comparative and International Law 10(1):261–296
Fischer BJ (1999) Albania at War, 1939–1945. Hurst & Company, London
Gagain M (2007) Climate Change, Sea Level Rise, and Artificial Islands: Saving the Maldives' Statehood and Maritime Claims Through the 'Constitution of the Oceans'. Colorado Journal of International Environmental Law and Policy 23(1):77–120
Grant TD (1999) Defining Statehood: The Montevideo Convention and Its Discontents. Columbia Journal of Transnational Law 37:403–457
Hall W (1924) A Treatise on International Law. Clarendon Press, Oxford
Harrington AR (2016) Is there a Right to Territory in International Law? In: Smith JC (ed) Property and Sovereignty: Legal and Cultural Perspectives. Routledge, London, pp 59–79
Herz JD (1957) Rise and Demise of the Territorial State. World Politics 9(4):473–493
Henkin L (1995) International Law: Politics and Values (Developments in International Law, Vol 18). Martinus Nijhoff Publishers, Leiden
Herb GH, Kaplan DH (eds) (1999) Nested Identities: Nationalism, Territory, and Scale. Rowman & Littlefield, Lanham/Oxford
Higgins R (1963) Development of International Law through the Political Organs of the United Nations. Oxford University Press, Oxford
Hobza A (1922) La République Tchécoslovaque et le Droit International. Revue Générale de Droit International public 29: 385–409

Jain AG (2014) The 21st Century Atlantis: The International Law of Statehood and Climate Change-Induced Loss of Territory. Stanford Journal of International Law 50:1–50

Kelsen H (1941–1942) The Pure Theory of Law and Analytical Jurisprudence. Harvard Law Review 55:44-70

Kiss AC (1965) Répertoire de la Pratique Française en Matière de Droit International Public, Vol III. Centre National de la Recherche Scientifique (CNRS), Paris

Kittel J (2014) The Global 'Disappearing Act': How Island States Can Maintain Statehood in the Face of Disappearing Territory. Michigan State Law Review 5:1207–1250

Klabbers J (2013) International Law. Cambridge University Press, Cambridge

Knight DB (1982) Identity and Territory: Geographical Perspectives on Nationalism and Regionalism. Annals of the Association of American Geographers 72(4):514–531

Lawrence T (1895) The Principles of International Law. MacMillan, London

Lyon AHE (2015) The Principality of Sealand, and Its Case for Sovereign Recognition. Emory International Law Review 29:637–671

Mälksoo L (2003) Illegal Annexation and State Continuity: The Case of the Incorporation of the Baltic States by the USSR. A Study of the Tension between Normativity and Power in International Law. Martinus Nijhoff Publishers, Leiden

Marek K (1968) Identity and Continuity of States in Public International Law. Librairie Droz, Geneva

McAdam J (2016) 'Disappearing States', Statelessness and the Boundaries of International Law. University of New South Wales Faculty of Law Legal Studies Research Paper Series No. 2010-2. https://papers.ssrn.com/sol3/papers2.cfm?abstract_id=1539766. Accessed 21 February 2017

Mégret F (2009) Globalization. In: Wolfrum R (ed) Max Planck Encyclopedia of Public International Law, Vol VI. Oxford University Press, Oxford, pp 493–503

Mendelson MH (1972) States in the United Nations. International and Comparative Law Quarterly 21:609–630

Michaels R (2013) Globalisation and Law: Law Beyond the State. In: Banakar R, Travers M (eds) Law and Social Theory, 2nd edn. Hart Publishing, Oxford, pp 287–304

Morss JR (2015) The International Legal Status of the Vatican/Holy See Complex. European Journal of International Law 26(4):927–946

Mueggenberg B (2014) The Czecho-Slovak Struggle for Independence, 1914–1920. McFarland & Company, Jefferson

Nevola G (2011) Politics, Identity, Territory. The 'Strength' and 'Value' of Nation-State, the Weakness of Regional Challenge. Universita dgli studi di Trento. Quaderno 58. http://web.unitn.it/files/download/8701/quaderno58.pdf. Accessed 21 February 2017

Oliver S (2009) A New Challenge to International Law: The Disappearance of the Entire Territory of a State. International Journal on Minority and Group Rights 16:209–243

Quigley J (2012) The Palestine Declaration to the International Criminal Court: The Statehood Issue. In: Meloni C, Tognoni G (eds) Is there a Court for Gaza? A Test Bench for International Justice. TMC Asser Press, The Hague, pp 429–440

Rayfuse R (2009) W(h)ither Tuvalu? Oceans Governance and Disappearing States, Ocean Policy Research Foundation. Proceedings of the International Symposium on Islands and Oceans. https://www.spf.org/opri/publication/pdf/200903_ISBN978-4-88404-217-2.pdf, pp 91–103. Accessed 21 February 2017

Rayfuse R (2011) International Law and Disappearing States – Maritime Zones and the Criteria for Statehood. Environmental Policy and Law 41(6):281–287

Rossman G (2016) Extremely Loud and Incredibly Close (But Still So Far): Assessing Liberland's Claim of Statehood. Chicago Journal of International Law 17(1):306–339

Ryngaert C (2011) The Legal Status of the Holy See. Goettingen Journal of International Law 3 (3):829–859

Ryngaert C (2015) Jurisdiction in International Law. 2nd edn. Oxford University Press, Oxford

Sassen S (2006) Territory, Authority, Rights. From Medieval to Global Assemblages. Princeton University Press, Princeton

Scelle G (1932) Précis de Droit des Gens: Principes et Systématique. Sirey, Paris
Schnapper D (2001) De l'Etat-nation au Monde Transnational. Du Sens et de l'Utilité du Concept de Diaspora. Revue Européenne des Migrations Internationales 17:9–34
Shaw MN (1982) Territory in International Law. Netherlands Yearbook of International Law 13:61–91
Shaw MN (2008) International Law, 6th edn. Cambridge University Press, Cambridge
Starke JG, Shearer IA (eds) (1994) Starke's International Law, 11th edn. Butterworth, London
Sterio M (2011) A Grotian Moment: Changes in the Legal Theory of Statehood. Denver Journal of International Law and Policy 39(2):209–237
Storey D (2001) Territory. The Claiming of Space. Pearson Education Limited, London
Stoutenburg JG (2015) Disappearing Island States in International Law. Brill Nijhoff, Leiden/Boston
Sumner BT (2004) Territorial Disputes at the International Court of Justice. Duke Law Journal 53:1779–1812
Szigeti PD (2010) Territorial Bias in International Law: Attribution in State and Corporate Responsibility. Journal of Transnational Law and Policy 19(2):311–355
Táborský E (1946) Naše věc (Our Cause). Melantrich, Prague
Talmon S (1999) Who is a Legitimate Government in Exile? Towards Normative Criteria for Governmental Legitimacy in International Law. In: Goodwin-Gill G, Talmon S (eds) The Reality of International Law. Essays in Honour of Ian Brownlie. Oxford University Press, Oxford, pp 499–537
Talmon S (2001) Recognition of Governments in International Law: With Particular Reference to Governments in Exile. Oxford University Press, Oxford
Wong D (2013) Sovereignty Sunk? The Position of 'Sinking States' at International Law. Melbourne Journal of International Law 14:346–391
Ziemele I (2005) State Continuity and Nationality: The Baltic States and Russia. Martinus Nijhoff Publishers, Leiden

Chapter 3
Territory in the Law of Jurisdiction: Imagining Alternatives

Cedric Ryngaert

Abstract Territory is central to the doctrine of international jurisdiction. However, the use of territory as the jurisdictional linchpin is a political choice, the result of a confluence of historically specific political, material, epistemic, and above all mapping practices. The political contingency of territory begs the question whether alternative, non-territorial jurisdictional concepts could be contemplated. In this contribution, community, temporality, and justice are explored. The territorial imbrications of these jurisdictional alternatives are acknowledged, but it is highlighted how territory can in fact be re-conceptualized in the service of 'its others'. Opting for the 'others' and for a novel conceptualization of territory remains a political choice. However, the political character of jurisdiction is not something to lament, but rather to celebrate, as it creates opportunities for a variety of political actors to have an impact on the actual application and construction of the un(der)determined notions of jurisdiction and territory, and ultimately on the modes of exercise of public authority. The salience of these theoretical ideas is exemplified by applying them to the case of transnational human rights litigation against corporations, a manifestation of socio-legal globalization that encapsulates the key role played by jurisdiction in negotiating claims of authority.

Keywords Territory · Jurisdiction · Space · Community · Time · Justice · Legal theory · Human rights · Litigation

---

Professor of Public International Law, Utrecht University. The research which resulted in this publication has been funded by the European Research Council under the Starting Grant Scheme (Proposal 336230—UNIJURIS) and the Dutch Organization for Scientific Research (NWO) under the VIDI Scheme (No. 016.135.322).

C. Ryngaert (✉)
Utrecht University, Utrecht, The Netherlands
e-mail: C.M.J.Ryngaert@uu.nl

M. Kuijer and W. Werner (eds.), *Netherlands Yearbook of International Law 2016*, Netherlands Yearbook of International Law 47,
DOI 10.1007/978-94-6265-207-1_3

Contents

3.1 Introduction

In 2014, an author writing in the *European Journal of International Law* characterized this author as 'one of the border guards of borders'.[1] I take it that he did not necessarily mean this disparagingly. Implicitly, however, he may have accused me of believing that territoriality continued to call the shots in the law of jurisdiction, while neglecting its shifting foundations in theory and practice. I am not a person to staunchly defend earlier work or to crusade against perceived slights. Rather, I have taken this characterization—which in fact, given the centrality of territoriality in my earlier (largely doctrinal) work, I am ready to acknowledge as largely accurate—as an invitation to indeed problematize territoriality and to take seriously the ominous warnings of 'the end of geography'.[2] After all, as Shakespeare wrote in *King Lear*, '[t]here is nothing so confining as the prison of our perceptions.'[3]

To problematize and perhaps eventually change perceptions, we should first try to understand them at a deeper level and to explore how we have acquired and continue to hold them in the first place. This is not very different from how a doctor tries to understand and remedy an ailment. Using a range of diagnostic techniques, she aims to determine what disease explains a patient's symptoms; on the basis of

[1] Landauer 2014, at 32.

[2] Landauer was in fact responding to a published lecture delivered by Daniel Bethlehem, titled 'The End of Geography: The Changing Nature of the International System and the Challenge to International Law', in which Bethlehem, while observing that state jurisdiction 'is largely manifested in territorial terms' (Bethlehem 2014, at 14), called for a more flexible conception of jurisdiction termed 'deemed jurisdiction', which, especially in cyberspace, would 'move the competence that is asserted closer to the technical and away from the political'. Note that the notion of 'the end of geography', as a consequence of globalization, has been around in political science circles for some time. See, notably, Greig 2002.

[3] Shakespeare 1623. See also John H Patterson: 'Only fools and dead men do not change their minds. Fools will not and dead men cannot'.

the diagnostic opinion reached, the doctor proposes treatment.[4] As I am supposed to be a learned doctor myself, there is even more merit in auto-applying this medical approach to a patient suffering from the affliction of territorial bias.[5]

The obstinacy of territoriality in the law of jurisdiction is obviously related to the spell that the political concept of state sovereignty, and its legal overtones of regulatory exclusivity, has cast over our legal imagination. Jurisdiction has come to be seen as the practical, legal instantiation of political power and authority over a given territory, with territorial jurisdiction giving spatial form and meaning to legal relations.[6] Jurisdiction is the 'quotidian' and instrumental reflection of the political-theological concept of sovereignty,[7] which, inextricably tied up as it is with 'the state', suffers from its own territorial bias.

Precisely because lawyers consider territory as pre-given political knowledge, they have difficulties in imagining jurisdiction in non-territorial terms. They may even refrain from trying in the first place, believing it to be beyond their epistemic domain. Imagination may not be the preserve of lawyers indeed. As Douzinas and Nead wrote in 1999, '[l]awyers live by the text and love the past, they hate novelty and misunderstand new languages.'[8] They do not like 'imagining', as (artistic) imagery 'breaks away from conventions and rules and expresses creative freedom and imagination' and thus forms the antithesis of law.[9] Imagination is, however, precisely what is needed to breathe new life into the stale, territory-based concept of jurisdiction.

Lawyers would do well to take some inspiration from political scientists in this respect, who have demonstrated daring in reconceiving of jurisdiction's sister concept sovereignty. Jens Bartelson, for instance, has argued that, thanks to the linguistic turn in philosophy and the social sciences, 'sovereignty is what we make of it through our linguistic practices, given the contextual constraints at hand',[10] and thus that sovereignty should not be considered as necessarily territorially bounded. Accordingly, sovereignty may have no meaning apart from its actual function, which might be being an instrument of global governance.[11] When we agree that jurisdictional representations should track evolutions in the political representation of sovereignty, and that lawyers are the class of technicians giving concrete societal shape to political change, also lawyers cannot escape imagination. In this process of imagination, legal experts dealing more specifically with issues of

---

[4] See more at length Treasure 2011.

[5] There is in fact a lively literature on what we can learn from doctors, especially in business studies. See, e.g., Nohria 2012.

[6] Cf. Dorsett and McVeigh 2012, at 40 (submitting that 'sovereign territorial jurisdictions provide the means of organizing relations between laws').

[7] Kaushal 2015, at 781 (arguing that 'jurisdiction locates questions about state power in quotidian legal practice while sovereignty locates them in political theology').

[8] Douzinas and Nead 1999, at 1.

[9] Ibid.

[10] Bartelson 2014, at 10.

[11] Ibid., at 69.

jurisdiction should realize the crucial role they play as 'constitutors' of the law. After all, jurisdiction is 'the political heart of the juridical order';[12] it inaugurates law and governance by producing the latter's authority. Unless an actor has jurisdiction in the first place, it cannot produce law.[13]

In this contribution, imagination is precisely what is endeavored. I prepare the field by outlining the centrality of territory in the dominant doctrine of international jurisdiction, espoused by leading writers and practitioners (Sect. 3.2). I go on to unpack the epistemic bias towards territory in the international legal profession, exploring what underlies our preference for a physical boundary-based jurisdictional system (Sect. 3.3). Having laid bare the implicit *political* choice to propel territory to such prominence, I try to imagine some alternative, non-territorial jurisdictional beginnings, based on community (a principle with its own history), temporality, and justice (Sect. 3.4). I acknowledge the territorial imbrications of these alternatives, but I highlight how territory can in fact be re-conceptualized in the service of 'its others', set out in Sect. 3.5. It is true that opting for the 'others' and for a novel conceptualization of territory remains a political choice. However, the political character of jurisdiction is not something to lament, but rather to celebrate. Acknowledging it makes transparent that jurisdiction and territory are sites in which various political imaginations of global jurisdictional order, including non-territorial ones, are, and can be advanced and mediated (Sect. 3.6). This creates opportunities for a variety of political actors to have an impact on the actual application and construction of the un(der)determined notions of jurisdiction and territory, and ultimately on the modes of exercise of public authority. The salience of these theoretical ideas is exemplified by applying them to the case of transnational human rights litigation against corporations, a manifestation of socio-legal globalization that encapsulates the key role played by jurisdiction in negotiating claims of authority (Sect. 3.7). Section 3.8 concludes.

In this contribution 'territory' and 'territoriality' are used as slightly distinct concepts. However, the reductionist temptation is avoided to conceive of 'territory' as just physically bordered land or to conceive of 'territoriality' as just denoting a relationship with, or quality of territory (the Latin suffix '-alis'). Rather, relying on geographer Stuart Elden, territory is approached in more conceptual terms, as a historical, geographical, and political question.[14] Relying on another geographer, Robert Sack, territoriality is defined as 'the attempt to affect, influence, or control actions, interactions [...] by asserting and attempting to enforce control over a geographic area'.[15]

[12] Kaushal 2015, at 788.

[13] Valverde 2009, at 141 and 144 (writing that 'the governance of legal governance is the work of jurisdiction', and that 'jurisdiction sorts the where, the who, the what, and the how of governance').

[14] Elden 2013, at 328.

[15] Sack 1983, at 55.

The theoretical argument made in this contribution is that the concepts of jurisdiction, spatiality, and territoriality are socially and politically constructed. Methodologically speaking, constructivism, critical legal studies, and critical geography are resorted to. Taking the cue from the constructivist tradition in international relations, the contribution posits that our ideas, norms and beliefs affect how we conceive of material space, territory, and 'the state'.[16] From a critical legal studies perspective, such ideas, norms and beliefs are assumed to be politically contingent, volatile, and subject to constant contestation, with every equilibrium reached being open to challenge by a variety of actors propounding different interpretations. Like critical geographers, the nature of territory as political technology is acknowledged, and alternative spatial and non-spatial representations of authority are explored.

3.2 The Centrality of Territory in the Modern Legal Doctrine of Jurisdiction

It is stating the obvious that the practice and theory of modern international law is centered around state sovereignty and territory.[17] Without much hesitation, contemporary writers and practitioners on international law and jurisdiction consider the principle of territoriality to be the bedrock of the law of jurisdiction.[18]

The primacy of territoriality is arguably derived from the principles of sovereign equality and non-intervention.[19] These principles, most clearly enunciated in the 1928 *Island of Palmas* arbitral award,[20] go to the very heart of the international legal system, and consider territorially delimited states as equal subjects of international law whose territorial sovereignty is not to be encroached upon by their peers.[21] Thus, as FA Mann held, '[s]tate legislation as would have the effect of regulating the conduct of foreigners in foreign countries', would be unlawful.[22] In essence, the law of jurisdiction ensures that state competences are properly allocated, with the most

---

[16] E.g., Wendt 1999.

[17] Dorsett and McVeigh 2012, at 40: 'The traditional formulations of international law are both conceptually and institutionally organized around the forms of the sovereign territorial state.'

[18] E.g., Hirst 2003, at 45; Ryngaert 2015a, at 49. In its *Report on Extraterritorial Jurisdiction* (2009), the International Bar Association rather unambiguously stated that '[t]he starting point for jurisdiction is that all States have competence over events occurring and persons ... present in their territory.' International Bar Association 2009. On occasion, writers may reserve some room for the nationality principle as well. Oxman 2007, para 11.

[19] Compare Mann 1984, at 20 (arguing that there exists merely a terminological difference between sovereignty, territoriality, and the principle of non-intervention).

[20] *Island of Palmas Case* (*Netherlands v United States of America*), Permanent Court of Arbitration, Arbitral Award, Case No. 1925-01, 4 April 1928, at 838 ('Sovereignty in the relations between States signifies independence. Independence in regard to a portion of the globe is the right to exercise therein, to the exclusion of any other State, the functions of a State').

[21] Ryngaert 2015a, at 36; Buxbaum 2009, at 668.

[22] Mann 1964, at 47.

natural allocative principle being the physical, clear boundary-based principle of territoriality. Ordinarily, in order to preserve the *status quo* of competence allocation, states will tend to protest other states' assertions of *extraterritorial* jurisdiction, thereby further cementing the exclusivity of territoriality.[23]

Key is that, at a *meta*-level, the doctrine does not question the legitimacy of the principle of territoriality. Controversy merely focuses on the exact scope of application of the principle, in its objective and subjective iterations. Indeed, the dominant theory of ubiquity, pursuant to which territorial jurisdiction obtains as soon as one of the constituent elements of the wrongful activity are located on a state's territory, the legal inquiry turns on the intensity of territorial effects and territorial acts required to trigger application of the territoriality principle.[24] Thus, for instance, in *Morrison* (2010), the US Supreme Court ruled that the *focus* of a statute has to be determined for purposes of determining whether a particular application of the statute is or is not extraterritorial.[25] The Court did not doubt the validity of the congressional presumption against extraterritoriality, however, nor do courts and legislators more generally question territory as the ordering principle (in spite of the at times artificial reliance on territory).

It is observed that at a more doctrinal level, the spatial knowledge regarding territoriality in the law of jurisdiction was consecrated rather late. It is recalled that in the 1927 *Lotus* (*France v Turkey*) judgment, the Permanent Court of International Justice (PCIJ) famously held that '[f]ar from laying down a general prohibition to the effect that States may not extend the application of their laws and the jurisdiction of their courts to persons, property and acts outside their territory, it leaves them in this respect a wide measure of discretion, which is only limited in certain cases by prohibitive rules; as regards other cases, every State remains free to adopt the principles which it regards as best and most suitable.'[26] On its face, *Lotus* considered the exercise of *extraterritorial* jurisdiction to be presumptively lawful, at least absent a prohibitive customary or treaty rule to the contrary, and thus to cast doubt on the pre-eminence of territoriality.[27] The PCIJ's stance in *Lotus* represents the high-water mark of jurisdictional liberalism. Importantly, it has not explicitly

---

[23] The law of jurisdiction evolves on the basis of action and reactions, with the latter—or the absence thereof—determining the legality of the former. See Akehurst 1975, at 176. Protest is typically couched in the language of extraterritoriality. E.g., comment c to para 442(1)(c) of the Restatement (Third) of US Foreign Relations Law (1987), discussing European states' reactions to US discovery orders for the production of documents located within European states' territory (American Law Institute 1987).

[24] Vagias 2014, at 6–7; Lowe and Staker 2010, at 322; Ryngaert 2009.

[25] *Morrison* et al. *v National Australia Bank Ltd.* et al., Supreme Court of the United States, Opinion, 561 U.S. 247, 24 June 2010, at 266–269.

[26] *Case of the SS Lotus (France v Turkey)*, PCIJ, Judgment, 27 September 1927 (*'Lotus'*), para 46.

[27] A close reading of the judgment reveals, however, that this may not be what the Court actually intended. Indeed, it also held that 'in all systems of law the principle of the territorial character of criminal law is fundamental', and that 'the exclusively territorial character of law relating to this domain constitutes a principle which, except as otherwise provided, would *ipso facto*, prevent States from extending the criminal jurisdiction of their courts beyond their frontiers'). *Lotus*, at 20.

been repudiated by the PCIJ's successor, the International Court of Justice (ICJ). Nevertheless, in the 1970 *Barcelona Traction* case, the ICJ recognized that the principles of states sovereignty and non-intervention required the imposition of limits on the exercise of jurisdiction.[28]

By 1970, in any event, the *Lotus*-based jurisdictional free-for-all had been largely abandoned in the doctrine, and territoriality had risen to prominence as the chief principle of jurisdiction. Notably the influential 1935 Harvard Research Draft Convention on Jurisdiction with respect to Crime has been instrumental in this respect.[29] The Harvard Draft Convention, which was admittedly never formally adopted by states but can partly be read as an indictment of the *Lotus* liberalism, backed *territoriality* as the basic principle of jurisdiction. In so doing, it harked back to Vattel, who as the first modern international law writer emphasized the centrality of territory in the law of jurisdiction,[30] and even to Baldus, who as early as the late Middle Ages poetically posited that territory and jurisdiction 'go together as mist to a swamp'.[31] The Draft Convention, exceptionally, and in limited circumstances, also allowed the exercise of jurisdiction on some other grounds (personality, security, universality) on the basis of prevailing (and still current) state practice. Most of these exceptions, while formally 'extraterritorial', have their roots in territoriality after all, however.[32] The personality principle operates on the basis of the perpetrator or victim's nationality of a *territorially* delimited state, and the security or protective principles operates on the basis of threats to the political sovereignty and independence of, again, such a state. Universality does not (necessarily) refer back to territorial state interests, but its practical importance is negligible, as only a limited number of offenses are amenable to universal jurisdiction, and only a handful of cases arising under the universality principle have made it to the trial case.[33] Yet even the exercise of universal jurisdiction has a

[28] *Barcelona Traction, Light and Power Company, Limited (Belgium v Spain)*, ICJ, Judgment, 5 February 1970, para 105. Compare *Case concerning the Arrest Warrant (Democratic Republic of the Congo v Belgium)*, ICJ, Merits, Judgment, 14 February 2002, Separate Opinion of President Guillaume, para 15 ('The adoption of the United Nations Charter proclaiming the sovereign equality of States, and the appearance on the international scene of new States, born of decolonization, have strengthened the territorial principle').

[29] American Society of International Law (1935) Draft Convention on Jurisdiction with Respect to Crime, American Journal of International Law 29:439–442 ('Harvard Draft Convention')

[30] de Vattel 1710, para 84 (emphasis added) ('The sovereignty united to the domain establishes the jurisdiction of the nation *in her territories*, or the country that belongs to her. It is her province, or that of her sovereign, to exercise justice in all the places under her jurisdiction, to take cognisance of the crimes committed, and the differences that arise in the country').

[31] Elden 2013, at 36, fn 149, also writing that 'jurisdiction inheres in a *territorio* [...] but a territorium has its own boundaries' (fn 148). Note that in Baldus' time—characterized by city-states - the concept of state sovereignty was not fully developed yet, so that Baldus may possibly not be considered as the 'father' of the contemporary paradigm of exclusive jurisdictional sovereignty of the state.

[32] Maier 1996, at 65.

[33] See Langer 2011.

territorial dimension, in that the territorial presence of the presumed offender is normally required as a trigger.[34]

The territorial bias of the Harvard Draft Convention has cast a long shadow in the practice of states.[35] At the same time, it has become a lightning rod for critics of the jurisdictional—territorial—*status quo*.[36] In this contribution, I join this chorus of critics. Importantly, I develop a theoretical rather than doctrinal argument. In the next section, I start with unpacking the international legal profession's epistemic bias in favor of territoriality.

3.3 Unpacking the Epistemic Bias Toward Territory

The doctrinal pre-eminence of territory in the law of jurisdiction elicits the obvious question as to how come territory ultimately carried the day as the jurisdictional linchpin, sidelining and eliminating alternative jurisdictional concepts, particularly those based on personality and community.[37] A variety of explanations have been proffered in this regard, ranging from the rediscovery of Roman law in the twelfth century, economic evolutions, centralizing tendencies in burgeoning governmental administrations, and epistemic changes.[38] These explanations are valid in their own right, but what has really propelled territory as *the* principle of jurisdictional order, is arguably the rise of cartography and grid-based, Ptolemaic maps, developed from the sixteenth century onwards. Geometrical maps gave each place on the map equal prominence and clearly demarcated boundaries between territories. These new cartographic practices gradually led to changing ideas about appropriate and legitimate governance, finally ushering in novel political practices that presented

[34] E.g., Article 2(1)(a) of the Dutch International Crimes Act. Territory also informs the operation of the principle of *aut dedere aut judicare*, which often constitutes the treaty basis for 'universal jurisdiction'. E.g., Article 5(2) ('Each State Party shall likewise take such measures as may be necessary to establish its jurisdiction over such offences in cases where the alleged offender is present in any territory under its jurisdiction and it does not extradite him pursuant to article 8 to any of the States mentioned in paragraph I of this article [these are the States who can exercise jurisdiction on the basis of another permissive principle].' The operation of this principle—extradite or prosecute—logically requires territorial presence, as the custodial state cannot extradite a person whom it has not first arrested on its territory.

[35] See Ryngaert 2015a, at 77–99, for an overview of the variety of assertions made by states under the territoriality principle.

[36] This argument is made more in particular by authors dealing with transnational computer crime and data protection violations, which take place in a largely virtual, de-territorialized sphere. Svantesson 2015.

[37] Grotius, for instance, defined jurisdiction as the authority exercised over 'two subjects, primarily persons', and only secondarily refer to 'the place, which is called territory' as the relevant jurisdictional nexus. Elden 2013, at 238, fn 230.

[38] Ruggie 1993.

territorially bounded political space and the attendant exclusive territorial jurisdiction of the State as logical and natural phenomena.[39] These practices are variously grounded on the need for global order (international lawyers), on the domestic social contract (constitutional theorists), or simply on the visual features of the natural environment (all), even if these justifications have considerable shortcomings.

A territory-based jurisdictional order is inherently attractive to the international lawyer, since it does away with overlapping jurisdictional allegiance. Thereby, it arguably creates international order, stability, predictability, peace and security. These are the traditional goals of international law itself.[40] Admittedly, this idea of territoriality as order and predictability has inched closer to an ideal type as, in reality, acts and events cannot be located in just one place, in our current interconnected world; instead, they have worldwide effects. In an age of increasing digitalization, and de-territorialized cloud computing, territory, or its 'territorial effects' iteration, may even have become nonsensical.[41] Nevertheless, it remains that, even in respect of borderless phenomena, regulators continue to rely on territoriality with its connotation of regulatory exclusivity, and have no qualms feigning the principle's ordering potential.[42]

---

[39] Branch 2011, 2013.

[40] Abass 2014, at 18–20. This classic idea of allocating acts and events to just one sovereign can notably be found in the 1908 US Supreme Court judgment in the *American Banana* antitrust case, where the Court held that '[t]he general and almost universal rule is that the character of an act as lawful or unlawful must be determined wholly by the law of the country where the act is done', citing in this respect the principles of justice and non-interference. *American Banana Co. v United Fruit Co.*, 213 US 347, 26 April 1909, at 356.

[41] Svantesson 2015, at 69–70, suggesting as jurisdictional principles, instead of territoriality, connections, interests, and reasonableness (at 74), but reasoning mainly from a cyberspace perspective. See also Schultz 2008, at 815 (rejecting the application of the territorial effects doctrine to cyberspace).

[42] Ryngaert 2015b; E.g., in accordance with its Aviation Directive (Directive 2008/101/EC of the European Parliament and of the Council of 19 November 2008 amending Directive 2003/87/EC so as to include aviation activities in the scheme for greenhouse gas emission allowance trading within the Community, [2009] OJ L 8/3 ('Aviation Directive')), the EU considers a foreign aircraft's departing from, or landing at an aerodrome located within its territory, as a sufficient territorial nexus for the application of EU law to the entire flight trajectory, including outside EU airspace. The Court of Justice of the European Union has found the approach to be in keeping with the territoriality principle under customary international law, see *Case C-366/10: (Air Transport Association of America and Others v Secretary of State for Energy and Climate Change)*, ECJ Grand Chamber, Judgment, ECR I-13755, 21 December 2011 (*'Air Transport Association of America and Others')*. Also, in accordance with the 1982 United Nations Convention on the Law of the Sea, 1833 UNTS 3, it is the port state, meaning the state whose ports are visited by a vessel, who may exercise specific legislative and enforcement powers over the vessel, in accordance with Articles 211(3), 218, and 219 of the Convention. Furthermore, Article 4(1)(a) of Directive 95/46/EC of the European Parliament and of the Council of 24 October 1995 on the protection of individuals with regard to the processing of personal data and on the free movement of such data [1995] OJ L 281/31 provides that 'Each Member State shall apply the national provisions it adopts pursuant to this directive to the processing of personal data where: (a) the processing is carried out in the context of the activities of an establishment of the controller *on the territory* of the Member State [...]' (emphasis added).

Territory has not only cast a jurisdictional spell on international lawyers but also on constitutional lawyers and theorists. Seemingly, territory offers a rationale for the very authority of the law, insofar as the social contract is seen as revolving around territory. By their very act of entering or residing in the sovereign's territory, individuals can be presumed to consent to the law, thereby legitimating governmental coercion. This territorial aspect of the social contract theory was most clearly enunciated by John Locke in his Second Treatise of Government (1689), where he wrote as follows: 'If a man owns or enjoys some part of the land under a given government, while that enjoyment lasts he gives his tacit consent to the laws of that government and is obliged to obey them [...]. It holds indeed if he is only travelling freely on the highway; and in effect it holds as long as he is merely in the territories of the government in question.'[43] Accordingly, Locke considered *voluntary territorial presence* as tacit consent to governmental coercion, thereby transforming such coercion into legitimate authority and jurisdiction. This rationale later came to underlie the due process-based doctrine of personal jurisdiction in the United States, pursuant to which minimum (territorial) contacts with the US suffice for a person to be put on notice of being subject to US jurisdiction.[44] It has also legitimated the application of a host of import/export requirements imposed on goods crossing the border.[45] In the eighteenth century, the principle of *democracy* was grafted onto the already constructed nexus between sovereignty and territory, thereby reinforcing the latter's inevitability as the *nec plus ultra* of legitimate governance. Democracy and popular sovereignty were considered as realizable only in polities with recognizable physical boundaries,[46] and the nation-state based community became the primary, and even quasi-exclusive, political community. However, *why* the social contract should be cast in territorial terms remains unexplained by these theories. After all, decisions on drawing the territorial boundaries themselves, or on the use of the concept of territoriality as the very mode of governance, have not been taken on the basis of consent.[47] Accordingly, these theories suffer from a *petitio principii* as they simply posit or accept the inevitability of territory as a mode of governance.[48]

---

[43] Locke 2012, para 119.

[44] Brilmayer 1987; *World-Wide Volkswagen Corp. v Woodson*, Supreme Court of the United States, Opinion, 444 US 286, 21 January 1980; *International Shoe v State of Washington*, Supreme Court of the United States, Opinion, 326 US 310, 3 December 1945; *Goodyear Dunlop Tires Operations, S.A., et al. v Brown et UX., co-administrators of the Estate of Brown et al.*, Supreme Court of the United States, Opinion, 564 U.S. 915, 27 June 2011; *Daimler AG v Bauman*, Supreme Court of the United States, Opinion, 134 S. Ct. 746, 14 January 2014.

[45] Howse and Regan 2000, at 374.

[46] Radon 2004, at 199.

[47] Bartelson 2014, at 30 (questioning whether boundaries and the restrictions they pose are democratic and noting that 'everyone is subjected to some sovereignty authority simply by virtue of inhabiting some portion of planetary space, irrespective of whether they have consented to subjection or not').

[48] Brilmayer 1987, at 309 (submitting that 'the tacit consent argument turns on prior notions that a state has a right to regulate within its own boundaries').

In spite of the apparent practical and theoretical shortcomings of the concept of territoriality, the intellectual prison which territory has created, remains also *intuitively* hard to escape. This is so for two reasons. First, territory's visual representation on a map, containing unambiguous boundaries, makes territorial jurisdiction straightforward and easy to comprehend (see also the next section). Second, territory has an undeniable natural and physical character. In this respect, the reduction of the juridical conception of the 'bordered territory' to 'a brute, physical landscape' 'effaces but reinforces the normative assumption that territory is the fixed and eternal site of politics'.[49] The naturalization or 'physicalization' of territory may thus render the 'territorial trap',[50] which refers to the epistemic bias of international relations theory, seemingly unavoidable.

3.4 Non-Spatial Alternatives to Territory

In spite of the extant, hard-to-escape, epistemic basis in favor of territory, critical scholars—especially outside, or on the fringes of legal scholarship—have not given up on imagining alternatives to jurisdictional territoriality. Shah, for instance, called on scholars to study conceptions of spatiality other than territory and notably to explore 'the global' as political theory. In her view, 'global' as a constitutive spatial-political category could reshape how we normatively conceive of legitimate authority.[51] This would allow us to imagine jurisdiction beyond the confines of the territorial State, and give us the analytical tools to jurisdictionally address de-territorialized, global or transnational problems that cannot easily be tied down to the territory of just one or only a handful of states.

One should admit that for geographically-minded scholars—which most of us are—properly representing the non- or extra-territorial in space is an uphill struggle, as non-territorial or even non-state political authority is not easily (cartographically) mapped and represented. Nevertheless, digital technology may possibly enable us to depict nonlinear jurisdictional spaces, e.g., transnational functionally differentiated epistemic or other communities living by their own norms, such as game-centered communities governed by bylaws. After all, even without such technology, our late-medieval forebears were somehow able to map complex jurisdictional loyalties through itinerary maps, *mappaemundi*, and item-based lists.[52] Non-state authority may not easily map onto a geometric grid-based map, but such authority still inhabits a space and has certain boundaries. As Hans Lindahl observed, '[t]he law governs human behavior, and human behavior takes place in space', and spatial boundedness also holds for transnational private authority and

[49] Shah 2012, at 67.

[50] Agnew 1994.

[51] Shah 2012, at 71.

[52] Branch 2011, at 9–10 and 30.

regulation.[53] If one is indeed willing to accept that a regulatory community necessarily has boundaries, even if non-geographical ones, depiction of these boundaries may not be impossible.

Alternatively, one could simply forego spatiality as a useful category to capture the jurisdictional complexities of our current era—and thus abandon political geography as a discipline that can relevantly analyze non-cartographic political and legal realities. This should not equal epistemic defeat but rather invite us to consider other analytical and disciplinary lenses to behold a changed world. Note in this respect that complex allegiances in the Middle Ages were not mapped either, at least not in the strict sense of the word; item-based lists simply described jurisdictional rights, obligations, and places, and did not depict extended geographic spaces over which jurisdiction would be exercised.[54] In this section, I explore and imagine 'community', 'temporality', and 'justice' as promising alternative, non-spatial concepts of jurisdiction.

3.4.1 Community

If we take medieval allegiances as our jurisdictional point of departure, recalling that contemporary history is never made *ex nihilo*, it may be worthwhile to study *membership in a community* as a historically tried counterpoint to territoriality. Until the Modern Age, governance and law were indeed based on personal, sometimes tribal allegiances rather than territorial location.[55] Some decades ago, sociologists have already predicted a return to this 'tribalism', as people grow disenchanted with a dehumanizing modernity, and look for identity within communities rather than territory-based institutions.[56] In contemporary scholarship, Paul Schiff Berman, drawing also on ethnographic research with respect to identity-formation, has picked up this disenchantment, and suggested *community* as the relevant jurisdictional linchpin. Arguably, a changing social context characterized by multiple identifications has yielded unified but overlapping communities that can be non-territorial and decoupled from physical location; hence, jurisdiction should become a function of which community, including transnational community,

[53] Lindahl 2010, at 34 and 39. See also ibid., at 36 ('A legal space is never only a geographical surface [...] but rather a concrete articulation of normative and physical dimensions').

[54] E.g., the division of Charlemagne's empire into three parts in the early medieval Treaty of Verdun (843 AD) 'was framed in terms of jurisdictions and revenues, not territory per se'. Branch 2013, at 25.

[55] Kassan 1935, at 240. We can find the roots of the personality principle in these allegiances. One could thus safely state that the personality principle is older than the territoriality principle. See also Lowe and Staker 2010, at 323. Note that Morgan, one of the fathers of modern anthropology, traces only two sorts of human governance: governance based on *territory*, and governance based on *community* (Morgan 1877).

[56] E.g., Maffesoli 1995.

rather than territorially delimited state, has ties with a dispute.[57] This theory is both descriptively and normatively attractive: trying to break free from a self-sustaining territorial paradigm, Berman identifies entry-points for his community-based jurisdictional ideal in actual 'hybrid' (state/non-state) socio-legal practices (e.g., corporate self-regulation) on which future worlds could be built.[58] Berman's theory may have been criticized as *social* rather than *political*,[59] but he should surely be credited for highlighting the decreasing relevance of territory, and for foregrounding individuals' non-state community affiliations in the law of jurisdiction.

3.4.2 Temporality

Another jurisdictional alternative to address the current regulatory challenges is to move from the time-worn jurisdictional concepts of spatiality/territoriality and community, to *temporality* as a novel theoretical premise of jurisdiction. Mariana Valverde has usefully observed in this respect that '[t]he machinery of jurisdiction is not tethered to or limited by spatial analysis', and that 'each mode of governance has one or more distinct *temporalities*'.[60] She does not give clear suggestions as to how temporality could, in more practical terms, ground jurisdictional practices in the international field.[61] Still, by highlighting the orientation of risk management strategies, notably in the environmental field, to *future* prevention,[62] she gives at least an empirical indication.

It is known that in some functional domains of international law, the imperative to prevent future harm has informed temporal concepts such as intergenerational equity (pursuant to which resources should be responsibly managed now in the interest of future generations)[63] or the precautionary principle (pursuant to which, even in the absence of a scientific consensus, regulatory action can be taken to avert dangers to health or the environment).[64] 'Temporariness' has even been the theme of this Yearbook in 2014, with eleven contributions addressing various international law dimensions of the concept of time.[65] None of these contributions addressed jurisdiction in particular. It is submitted here, however, that

[57] Berman 2005.

[58] See, at length, Berman 2012.

[59] E.g., Kaushal 2015, at 773.

[60] Valverde 2009, at 154 (emphasis added).

[61] In her *Chronotopes* monograph, she does apply temporality however to a number of municipal case studies, notably 'the honour of the Crown' in Canadian law (in respect of indigenous rights), feminism, and security. Valverde 2015, Chaps. 4–6.

[62] Valverde 2009, at 155.

[63] See, e.g., Brown Weiss 2007; Churchill and Freestone 1991.

[64] See, e.g., Cameron and Abouchar 1991; McIntyre and Mosedale 1997.

[65] Ambrus and Wessel 2015.

temporality-based reasoning could play an innovative, although largely unexplored role in the law of *jurisdiction*.

For instance, the *future risk* of a global climate catastrophe could be invoked to buttress more expansive, non-territorial jurisdictional practices, where a state or regional organization such as the EU includes foreign operators and foreign emissions within its regulatory net, irrespective of territorial borders. Arguably, the currently suspended 'extraterritorial dimension' of the EU Aviation Directive, which required foreign airlines to surrender emissions allowances to the EU also in respect of mileage beyond the EU's borders,[66] could be legitimated on the basis of a temporal version of jurisdiction—even if the CJEU famously justified the Directive's reach in territorial terms.[67]

Temporality is not only a useful analytical lens to jurisdictionally make sense of *future risk* but also of *simultaneous occurrences*, i.e., events occurring at the same time in different places. A classic spatial logic struggles to conceive of simultaneity in jurisdictional terms, as territoriality carries with it the assumption that an event takes place in one bounded space to the exclusion of other spaces. Admittedly, territorial jurisdiction could accommodate *subsequent events* in different places, notably via the continuous offense doctrine, by virtue of which multiple territorial sovereigns can exercise jurisdiction over an offence that has spatiotemporal continuity (*e.g.*, conspiracy to commit fraud).[68] However, territoriality cannot account for the same event arising simultaneously in different places. Technological changes have brought about just that: the advent of the Internet has allowed a multitude of geographically dispersed users to simultaneously experience the same activity, or

[66] The application of the EU's Aviation Directive was limited to emissions generated within EU airspace, see Regulation (EU) No 421/2014 of the European Parliament and of the Council amending Directive 03/87/EC establishing a scheme for greenhouse gas emission allowance trading within the Community, in view of the implementation by 2020 of an international agreement applying a single global market-based measure to international aviation emissions, [2014] OJ L 129/1.

[67] *Air Transport Association of America and Others*, para 125 ('In laying down a criterion for Directive 2008/101 to be applicable to operators of aircraft registered in a Member State or in a third State that is founded on the fact that those aircraft perform a flight which departs from or arrives at an aerodrome situated in the territory of one of the Member States, Directive 2008/101, inasmuch as it extends application of the scheme laid down by Directive 2003/87 to aviation, *does not infringe the principle of territoriality or the sovereignty which the third States from or to which such flights are performed have over the airspace above their territory, since those aircraft are physically in the territory of one of the Member States of the European Union and are thus subject on that basis to the unlimited jurisdiction of the European Union*') (emphasis added).

[68] Each state would have territorial jurisdiction as soon as a significant portion of the activities constituting that offence takes place on its territory. See *Libman v The Queen*, Supreme Court of Canada, Judgment, 2 SCR 178, 10 October 2015 (establishing jurisdiction over conspiracy to commit fraud arising out of the conduct of an individual's Toronto telephone sales solicitation room, from which sales personnel telephoned U.S. residents and attempted to induce them to buy shares in two Central American mining companies, with promotional material being mailed from Central America). For a US due process analysis of transnational conspiracy and territorial jurisdiction, see Althouse 1983.

suffer harm arising from just one source. States may have used the cannon of territoriality to respond to online threats, but there is no denying that the instantaneous nature of the Internet is at loggerheads with a territorial logic. Conceiving of Internet offences in temporal terms surely does not solve the jurisdictional conundrum, but at least it draws attention to the obsolescence of territory, with its connotations of spatial exclusivity. It may allow us to reflect on the permissibility of 'extraterritorial' computer network searches by law-enforcement agencies, the rationale of which is to secure foreign evidence that with the click of a mouse, or even through automated processes may switch geographical location in a split second, without territorial sovereigns being even aware of the presence of the data on their territory.[69] It may similarly invite us to ponder the legality of criminal warrants for the production of email account data stored by technology companies on a server located physically in a State's territory, bearing in mind that such data may just 'happen' to be located there, and may at will be geographically moved by the company or its automated processes.[70]

3.4.3 *Justice*

Finally, apart from community and temporality, justice, however construed, may also usefully inform alternative conceptions of jurisdiction which are not tethered to territoriality. Thus, Dorsett and McVeigh suggest an ethics-based 'jurisdiction of events that shapes the form of responsibility for freedom'.[71] This is a jurisdiction of conscience (of common humanity), the roots of which can be situated in Hannah Arendt's reflections on the Eichmann trial in *Eichmann in Jerusalem*.[72] In this book, Arendt suggested jurisdiction as giving form to a new beginning in respect of genocide prosecutions.[73]

Truth be told, invoking *Eichmann in Jerusalem* as inaugurating a new conscience- or freedom-based form of jurisdiction replacing territoriality, may appear

[69] *Wijziging van het Wetboek van Strafrecht en het Wetboek van Strafvordering in verband met de verbetering en versterking van de opsporing en vervolging van computercriminaliteit (computercriminaliteit III)* (Proposal of Amendment of the Dutch Criminal Code and the Code of Criminal Procedure relating to the improvement and strengthening of the investigation and prosecution of cybercrime), https://www.eerstekamer.nl/9370000/1/j9vvhwtbnzpbzzc/vk0992hkwnxq/f=y.pdf, accessed 16 February 2016.

[70] *In re Warrant to Search a Certain Email Account Controlled and Maintained by Microsoft Corporation (Microsoft Corporation v United States of America)*, United States District Court for the Southern District of New York (S.D.N.Y.), 15 F. Supp. 3d 466, 2014 (allowing such warrants), United States Court of Appeal for the Second Circuit, No. 14-2985, 14 July 2016 (disallowing them).

[71] Dorsett and McVeigh 2012, at 137.

[72] Arendt 1964.

[73] Note that Arendt also theorized 'new beginnings' in other settings, notably as regards constitutional institutions. See Palonen 2012.

to be somewhat incongruous, as in respect of the atrocities of which Eichmann was accused, Arendt oddly suggested precisely *territory* as the appropriate principle of jurisdiction:

> Israel could easily have claimed territorial jurisdiction if she had only explained that 'territory,' as the law understands it, is a political and a legal concept, and not merely a geographical term. It relates not so much, and not primarily, to a piece of land as to the space between individuals in a group whose members are bound to, and at the same time separated and protected from, each other by all kinds of relationships, based on a common language, religion, a common history, customs, and laws.[74]

Justifying Eichmann's trial on the basis of territorial jurisdiction, however, is farfetched in the absence of a territorial nexus, and also unnecessary.[75] What Arendt really meant was basing jurisdiction on the *injustice done to a community.*[76] In *Eichmann in Jerusalem*, this community was defined in a rather particularized manner as a community of Jews to which injustice was done, as she patently rejected universal jurisdiction on the legal ground that it was not incorporated in the Genocide Convention.[77]

However that may be, insofar as Arendt suggested that, in the *Eichmann* trial, *justice* had to be meted out and that jurisdictional principles should thus be oriented towards *justice*, her reflections on jurisdiction can be considered as signaling a new beginning indeed: one that is not necessarily based on territorial connections, nor even on personal links, but on the *substantive wrongfulness* of the act. Her stance ushered in a critical approach to the law of jurisdiction which is geared toward providing 'forms of jurisdiction adequate to the experience of those who engage with jurisdiction' and 'considering whether a jurisdiction was adequate to those who suffered the wrong of [an] event'.[78] Obviously, a perception of *injustice* has *already* grounded instantiations of universal criminal jurisdiction over a number of crimes, but it could be used to underwrite more extensive corrective justice-based assertions of jurisdiction to remedy the undersupply of global public goods (e.g., environmental goods).[79]

---

[74] Arendt 1964, at 262–263.

[75] Luban 2011, at 633.

[76] In this sense, Arendt's jurisdictional principle can be characterized as a hybrid of the passive personality and protective principle. See also ibid. ('What Arendt had in mind was a connection entirely unique to the Jews and the state of Israel ... The fanciful part is the claim that such jurisdiction is in any sense territorial').

[77] Arendt 1964, at 262. The community takes on a universal form, however, in her correspondence with fellow philosopher Karl Jaspers in 1960, i.e., prior to *Eichmann in Jerusalem.* (Arendt to Jaspers, 23 December 1960: 'The only possibility seems to be to attach to the International Court at The Hague a criminal court for hostes generis humani that would be competent to try individuals regardless of nationality. As long as such a court does not exist, international law holds that any court in the world is competent—so why not Israel? Legally, Israel couldn't even claim it isn't competent.'), cited in Luban 2011, at 631–632; 1948 Convention on the Prevention and Punishment of the Crime of Genocide, 78 UNTS 277.

[78] Dorsett and McVeigh 2012, at 128

[79] Compare Krisch 2014.

Recalling that visual attractiveness is what draws us to territoriality, it may be argued that justice-based, non-territorial jurisdiction can in fact measure up to territorial jurisdiction and has representational advantages that the other alternatives to territory may lack. True, justice-based jurisdiction cannot be visualized as a colored, bounded space on a cartographic map, but '[p]eople *seeing injustice* as governed by law, no matter where it is, will give meaning to universal jurisdiction'[80] over atrocities. Pictures of injustice may galvanize public opinion support for universal jurisdiction. Moreover, the political imagery attendant to the actual exercise and visualization through the arrest of the presumed offender, as well as the screening of the trial may further harness the political power and authority of such jurisdiction. Accordingly, the concept of injustice could easily be paired with representational techniques that enhance its intuitive pull, thereby making it, at least in respect of a number of events, a palatable alternative to territory. Proponents of other 'extraterritorial' conceptions, such as community and temporality, would do well to explore more visual representations of their new jurisdictional beginnings with a view to becoming ingrained in the human *psyche*.[81]

3.5 Reconceptualizing Territory

Whatever the merits of the novel, non-territorial theoretical conceptualizations of jurisdiction set out in Sect. 3.4, there is no denying that they struggle to take root in actual legal praxis. This is largely because the territorial state, for better or worse, largely remains the sun around which the law's planets revolve. To be true, non-territorial transnational communities have, to a certain extent, developed their own regulatory capacities—witness transnational private regulation or the *lex mercatoria*—[82]and thus seem to have carved out a jurisdictional space that enjoys autonomy *vis-à-vis* the state. In a sort of throwback to medieval times, members of such (functional) communities pledge allegiance to non-state, private governance systems,[83] which sideline territoriality as a principle of jurisdictional order.[84] Nonetheless, and this is an important point, such systems are usually *embedded within the territorial state-based system*, as *states* are the very creators of the systemic autonomy of non-state systems, through delegation, facilitation,

[80] Brigham 2009, at 401 (emphasis added).

[81] As neuroscientists have pointed out, human beings are *visual beings* indeed. Koch 2004, at 1107.

[82] Cafaggi et al. 2013; Berman and Kaufmann 1978.

[83] See more at length Callies and Zumbansen 2010.

[84] Backer 2012, at 122 (arguing that non-state actor governance, while having a limited scope, cross national boundaries, thus yielding the consequence that 'the old foundational notion of territoriality loses coherence as the marker *par excellence* of jurisdiction').

orchestration, and management.[85] A similar argument is made by Saskia Sassen in her acclaimed *Territory, Authority, and Rights*, where she argues that the novel spatio-temporal order results from new global assemblages being inserted in, or arising from the national/territorial.[86] Reflecting on global financial markets, she observes that such markets make use of the capabilities entailed by territoriality. After all, such markets inhabit national territories, e.g., the City of London,[87] while at the same time spanning them. This 'multi-sited territoriality' cannot be compared to the classic territoriality of the nation-state, but relies on state authority 'in the service of a global regime'.[88]

Such an observation does not mean that territorial state regulation is necessarily being captured by private actors who simply use it as a device to further their own interests (although at times this may be part of the truth).[89] The state may still have its own agency but may not just use its power to the benefit of a territorially delimited sphere. Rather, disposing of a monopoly on legal coercion and force, it remains a regulatory arbiter of political claims made by various actors and communities. Possibly, it cannot be otherwise, as plurality will almost inevitably lead to chaos in the absence of an overall normative-institutional framework that arbitrates between various conceptions of jurisdiction. In this sense, the time-honored *territorial state*, in spite of its defects and limitations, may remain the primary political community that 'pulls on other communities and repels other states', as a result of which jurisdiction is actually *confluent* (although not necessarily co-extensive) with the nation-state.[90] Robert Jackson similarly believes that there is 'no realistic and practical alternative [to the state] even on the horizon'.[91] But then again, the role of the state has changed. As Jens Bartelson reminds us in respect of sovereignty, while sovereignty is a fetish of political theory, it is *mutable* and 'no longer best understood as a constitutive attribute of states, but rather as something akin to a grant contingent upon its responsible exercise in accordance with the norms of the international community'.[92] Accordingly, to paraphrase Mark Twain, the reports of territory's death can be said to have been greatly exaggerated.

In the actual practice of state jurisdiction, there is no denying of this (re-)territorialization, understood not as the sort of bordered territoriality *cum* jurisdictional exclusivity of yesteryear, but as the redefinition of territory as a site for legal-political struggles which are informed by community, temporality, or justice-based arguments,

[85] Cf. ibid., at 98–100 (arguing that non-state actors cannot escape government, which keeps them like a dog on a leash, and thus that such actors operate in the shadow of hierarchy). See on state orchestration and facilitation of non-state regulation notably Abott and Snidal 2000.

[86] Sassen 2006, at 378.

[87] Sassen 2006, at 386. See on global cities also Sassen's earlier work: Sassen 1991, 1994.

[88] Sassen 2006, at 418.

[89] Carpenter and Moss 2013.

[90] Kaushal 2015, at 774.

[91] Jackson 2007, at 315.

[92] Bartelson 2014, at 69.

and which are *multi-scalar*, i.e., not limiting themselves to the scale of the national, but extending to the regional and global. As Hannah Buxbaum has pointed out, 'activists, legislative reformers, and plaintiffs seeking recovery for harm suffered, are attempting to create a broader area of engagement for domestic courts through methods that rescale regulatory challenges'.[93] Domestic courts, which are invariably imbricated with the territorial legal order of the state, then become arenas where *global problems* are fought over.[94]

At the same time, national or regional political authorities, unsatisfied with the slow pace of progress at the multilateral level, may take power in their own hands,[95] and use territorial, border-based jurisdiction over foreign economic operators wishing to access a profitable territorial consumer or industrial market, with a view to pushing the international regulatory envelope. Recent EU measures of climate change unilateralism come to mind here, e.g., the aforementioned Aviation Directive, but also the recently adopted global emissions monitoring, reporting, and verification system imposed on foreign vessels docking in EU ports.[96] Ideas floated for carbon-related border-adjustment taxes to mitigate climate change can be cited as well.[97]

The latter use of jurisdiction has attracted the attention of legal scholars recently, with Joanne Scott identifying it as a novel form of jurisdiction, named 'territorial extension'.[98] This label of 'novel' may be exaggerated to the extent that the imposition, at the border, of national requirements on the bringing of goods or services within the territory goes to the heart of what jurisdiction in the modern era is all about: the regulation and limitation of *movement*, movement and mobility defining our modern condition.[99] One of the characteristics of the new 'unilateral'

---

[93] Buxbaum 2004, at 173.

[94] Ibid., at 167: 'a global problem can be recast in local terms, in order to take advantage of local political or social resources. The concept of scale is therefore a useful analytical tool in examining how global economic misconduct is situated before the courts of one particular country.' Territorial courts are attractive as global dispute-resolution mechanisms especially when they are located in well-functioning states that have considerable regulatory and enforcement capacity, and are willing to construe their jurisdiction broadly. Such courts may exercise different forms of jurisdiction (territorial, personal, universal), but the important point is that they may offer an accessible, 'downscaled' forum where global legal-political struggles over jurisdiction can take place, in the absence of competent international courts.

[95] Cf. Hakimi 2014.

[96] Regulation (EU) 2015/757 of the European Parliament and of the Council of 29 April 2015 on the monitoring, reporting and verification of carbon dioxide emissions from maritime transport, and amending Directive 2009/16/EC [2015] OJ L 123/55.

[97] Kaufmann and Weber 2011.

[98] Scott 2014, at 90 (defining a measure as territorial extension where its 'application depends upon the existence of a relevant territorial connection, but where the relevant regulatory determination will be shaped as a matter of law, by conduct or circumstances abroad').

[99] As John Brigham observed: 'Jurisdiction regulates movement, where movement is the characteristic of modernity, first on foot, then by train, plane, and automobile over the countryside [...]. Jurisdiction is about stasis or at least limitations on movement. It is about the reach of law, and it suggests the more physical qualities of place that law defines.' Brigham 2009, at 382. In John

territoriality is, however, that it does not only regulate movement (notably import of goods in the case) merely in the interest of the territorial state but also *in the international interest*, such as combating global climate change or furthering the fundamental rights of non-citizens. Territory accordingly becomes a managerial instrument[100] to reach for universal justice and protect global public goods. A global operator or a global problem's contact with a state's territory is seen to trigger the latter's territorial jurisdiction, but its effects are inevitably extraterritorial; they may affect foreign operators' global process and production methods, lead to modifications of foreign regulation (the term 'Brussels effect' is used to describe the impact of EU law on foreign regulation),[101] and up the ante for better multilateral regulation.[102] This process of redeploying territory is a fine example of a legal achievement resulting from using 'a social machinery geared to other ends'.[103]

3.6 Acknowledging the Political Nature of the 'New Territoriality'

The 'new territoriality', in particular the grafting of *alternative* jurisdictional concepts onto the time-honored territoriality principle, sketched in the previous sections, is not a stable category or process, because its nature and functioning is inherently political. This may not appear to be very different from any jurisdictional form. However, the political nature of the new territoriality is even more pronounced in that the blending of territory and 'its others' may yield a particularly undetermined and content-empty cocktail. It is then only through *politicization* that a concrete, although brittle shape can be given to these jurisdictional concepts. I understand politicization as the advancement of interest-based arguments by a

(Footnote 99 continued)

Locke's *Second Treatise of Government* (1689), we find one of the earliest modern expressions of this connection between movement and territorial jurisdiction: 'anyone who comes to enjoy [the] land—whether through inheritance, purchase, permission, or whatever—must take it with the condition it is already under, namely, submission to the government of the commonwealth under whose jurisdiction it falls'. Locke 2012, para 120.

[100] On the managerial approach to international law: Koskenniemi 2009, at 16–17 (characterizing 'managerialism' as a governance rationality which suggests that international problems should be resolved by developing increasingly complicated technical vocabularies for institutional policy-making).

[101] Bradford 2012; Kleizen 2015.

[102] E.g., the European Commission has 'stopped the clock' as regards the immediate application of the Aviation Directive to foreign operators in the order to give a multilateral emissions reduction solution within the International Civil Aviation Organization a chance. See European Commission (2012) Stopping the clock of ETS and aviation emissions following last week's International Civil Aviation Organisation (ICAO) Council, MEMO/12/854, 12 November 2012, http://europa.eu/rapid/press-release_MEMO-12-854_en.htm, accessed 9 January 2017.

[103] Llewellyn 1930, at 251.

variety of societal actors (such as states, individuals, corporations, NGOs, international organizations) through given but open-ended jurisdictional categories. In both legal and political processes, these actors suggest rival jurisdictional interpretations in the hope of ultimately carrying the day by convincing their interlocutors,[104] or relevant dispute-settlement mechanisms that are called upon to determine the law's jurisdictional reach. In this section I unpack and celebrate this 'politics of jurisdiction' that is central to the actual workings of the jurisdictional alternatives/new beginnings suggested above. In the next section, I apply these insights to the particular case of transnational human rights litigation, in which domestic courts arbitrate rival jurisdictional interpretations regarding the geographical reach of human rights protections.

The political character of the exercise of jurisdiction has lately gained the interest from legal theorists, who have so far largely shunned jurisdiction as an interesting field of research. Somehow, they may have relegated it to 'the technical' that is not amenable to theory formation. In part inspired by the anthropologist Annelise Riles's highlighting of the political character of even the seemingly most technical legal rules,[105] theorists try to 'retrieve the space for the political in the study of jurisdiction'.[106] A theorist would draw attention to the inaugural character of jurisdiction, jurisdiction being 'a means or instrument through which law asserts or withdraws its authority.[107] Jurisdiction is, quite literally, the site of law speaking to itself, drawing attention to itself.[108] For (substantive) law to apply, the regulator needs to have jurisdiction first. Accordingly, exploring jurisdiction more theoretically allows us to shed light on the moment just before law and governance comes into being. It allows us to draw the contours of the political community that sees itself as having jurisdiction over a particular space, event, group, etc., and being entitled to apply its particular laws. Sure enough, states and courts may apply seemingly technical rules of jurisdiction, as they are recognized in international law and laid down in domestic statutes. However, one should not overlook that these

[104] E.g., the Air Transport Association of America's direct challenge of the EU Aviation Directive before the Court of Justice of the EU (*Air Transport Association of America and Others*); foreign states' political protests against the reach of the Directive also after the CJEU's handed down its judgment (e.g., US European Emissions Trading Scheme Prohibition Act 2011 (HR 2494); Joint Declaration of the Moscow Meeting on the Inclusion of International Civil Aviation in the EU-ETS; China and India also condemned the action as not respecting the principle of common but differentiated responsibilities, this protest however appears to be informed by the desire to protect trade interests rather than by the opinion that the jurisdictional assertion violates international law, in particular the principle of non-intervention, see de Baere and Ryngaert 2013.

[105] Rilcs 2005.

[106] Kaushal 2015, at 760.

[107] Ibid., at 779.

[108] Brigham 2009, at 382.

rules are in themselves political technology, and, moreover, that they cannot, as such, settle jurisdictional conflicts through straightforward categorization.[109]

As regards the character of jurisdictional rules as instantiations of political technology, it is recalled, as discussed above, that, in our Modern Age, political considerations, strengthened by the development of the science of cartography, have propelled territory to a dominant position in the law of jurisdiction, with some limited exceptions. Territoriality rose to power simply because it was deemed rational and strategically useful by political powers intent on entrenching and expanding their position of authority. It remains, though, that territorial jurisdiction is a historically contingent, socially constructed invention that is the result of unique historical circumstances in Western Europe.[110] The organization of societal life could as well have been, and could become non-territorial.[111] In Sect. 3.4, we have suggested a number of alternatives in this respect. However, even as territoriality has become the dominant mode of jurisdictional reasoning, or as territory has become the concept through which jurisdictional alternatives are filtered (cf. Sect. 3.5), politics does not recede. Territoriality suffers from, or more neutrally and accurately is characterized by its *indeterminacy*, just like other international law concepts. Koskenniemi famously explained in this respect that sovereignty, and with it the set of territorial rights and duties are not just something *external* to the law, which the law must recognize but cannot control (which he terms the 'pure fact view'), but also 'part of the law's substance, determined and constantly determinable within the legal system, just like any other norms' (which he terms the 'legal view').[112] This well-known indeterminacy critique reminds us, to paraphrase the Portuguese poet Fernando Pessoa, that '[territory] is what we make of it [...]. What we see is not what we see but what we are'.[113] Thus, particular interpretations of territoriality, or extraterritoriality for that matter, are invoked by situated actors bent on furthering their own political, or other, interests,[114] hoping to persuade

---

[109] Valverde 2008, at 14 (submitting that a 'merely technical analysis—such as those produced by appellate courts engaging in the work of allocating jurisdiction or policing its exercise—tends to reduce conflicts among competing powers/knowledges to a classificatory exercise of deciding what governing activity belongs in what drawer, a sorting process that obscures the incommensurabilities and the conflicts that see the under the surface in the most mundane of jurisdiction cases'). See also Liste 2014, at 14 (drawing attention to the 'perspective on the *little litigation nothings* that renders that hidden politics of space visible').

[110] See, *inter alia*, Ford 1999, at 929.

[111] 'Almost anything that is organized territorially could be organized in some other way.' Ford 2012, at 133; See also Berman 2005, at 1108 (arguing that nation-states with fixed territorial borders are not the only relevant jurisdictional entities).

[112] Koskenniemi 1990, at 14.

[113] Cf. Pessoa 2002: 'Life is what we make of it. Travel is the traveler. What we see isn't what we see but what we are'.

[114] Cf. Buxbaum 2009, at 635: '"Territoriality" and "extraterritoriality" [...] are legal constructs. They are claims of authority, or of resistance to authority, that are made by particular actors with particular substantive interests to promote'.

courts, other actors, or simply the invisible college of lawyers, of the superiority of their claim.

The inherent *politicization* of jurisdiction is not something to regret. Referring to *politics* in the context of the *prima facie* technical law of jurisdiction need not smack of bare-knuckle power politics in which authority is a function of money or brute force. Instead, it is simply an acknowledgement of the critical instability of the law of jurisdiction. Viewed in a positive light, politics in law allows for the (re-) constitution of the relevant political community,[115] by creating an arena in which underlying normative conflicts come to the surface, and give rise to potential innovative solutions.[116] This positive assessment of the role (to be) played by politics in international law, is by no means unique to the law of jurisdiction. Notably as regards international development, David Kennedy has suggested law as a 'terrain for the inquiry', a 'field of contestation', a complex of norms that renders more precise the political, distributional consequences of particular choices to be made.[117] Partly drawing on Kennedy, Sundhya Pahuja has highlighted the political quality of international law, including its self-deconstructive character and its capacity for responsive change, which arguably makes law something more than just regulation, bare rules, and violence, a field that accommodates the possibility of difference.[118] The open-ended, capacious character of international legal concepts may make them amenable to anti-hegemonic and subversive discourses, leading to a repositioning and redefinition of the original concept. However, there is no denying that a ruling rationality presented as universal and self-evident, but which is in fact driven by dominant political interests, may at times be difficult to overcome.[119]

In the law of jurisdiction, this ruling rationality is obviously state-based territoriality, but the capaciousness of jurisdiction may, as suggested above, allow for other expressions of political authority, e.g., based on transnational, global, or cosmopolitan[120] conceptions of space, community, time, or justice. At the same

---

[115] Kaushal 2015, at 786 ('[J]urisdiction is not apolitical … It is robustly implicated in politics and sovereignty, part of the original constitution of the *polis* as well as its ongoing reconstitution'). (emphasis in the original).

[116] Berman 2005, at 1126 (conceiving of jurisdiction as 'the locus for debates about the appropriate definition of community and the articulation of norms', constant search for balance).

[117] Kennedy 2003, at 20 and 26.

[118] Pahuja 2011, at 245–246 and 252.

[119] Ibid., at 250–251 (submitting that the 'critical instability of international law creates the possibility for a level of resistance and redefinition within the bounds of an international legality but is repeatedly contained by a rationality that operates in terms of a claim for the universality of particular categories, terms, and ideas').

[120] Cosmopolitanism can either refer to a jurisdictional order based on transnational community affiliation (e.g., technology-based or commercial communities, diasporas), as advanced by Paul Schiff Berman (see Berman 2012), or to an order referring to a global community, in which actors strive for humanity's common good (justice).

time, the capaciousness of territoriality itself, in its various dimensions (objective/subjective territoriality, quasi-territoriality, territorial extension, effects doctrine), may enable considerable political engagement. As highlighted above, territoriality may be explored to fulfill global objectives that are not spatially delimited. Moreover, in the globally interconnected world in which we live, events in one place may have 'butterfly' effects in far-flung places,[121] thereby allowing multiple sovereigns to claim 'territorial' jurisdiction on the basis of minor connections, and often for political reasons (in the process, for that matter, diluting the *ordering* power of the principle of territoriality).

3.7 Beholding Transnational Human Rights Claims: Donning Spatial and Non-Territorial Lenses

In this last section, I move from the abstract to the concrete, and conduct a more grounded analysis of jurisdictional new beginnings, bearing in mind that normative arguments about jurisdiction need a specific empirical context lest they vanish into thin air.[122] I have chosen to focus on transnational human rights litigation against corporations,[123] as such litigation nicely teases out the political tug-of-war of the imbrications of alternative jurisdictional conceptions with the inherent territoriality of the domestic dispute-resolution forum offered. This focus also allows me to engage with some interesting interdisciplinary work recently published by Philip Liste regarding the case of *Kiobel v Royal Dutch Petroleum*.[124] In this—by now famous case, which many readers may already be familiar with—the US Supreme Court ruled that the US Alien Tort Statute (ATS) barred US federal courts from hearing foreign-to-foreign claims alleging corporate torts in violation of the law of nations, on the grounds that the ATS should be presumed not to apply extraterritorially.[125] As a result, the Supreme Court refused to exercise jurisdiction over a

---

[121] The term 'butterfly effect' was coined by mathematician/meteorologist Lorenz to denote that small causes can have major (meteorological, e.g., hurricane) effects; see Lorenz 1963.

[122] Cf. Valverde 2009, at 146 ('Normative arguments about which scale is best make sense in concrete governance situations, in which one might indeed foresee the actual effects of choosing one scale over another, and thus make choices on the basis of concrete information. Without a specific, situated social/political issue whose practical implications can be examined, debates about scale can only be battles of abstractions').

[123] Transnational human rights litigation could be defined as litigation where victims and activists call on foreign courts to exercise their jurisdiction over violations committed overseas, sometimes by and against foreigners.

[124] Liste 2014, 2016.

[125] *Kiobel v Royal Dutch Petroleum Co.*, Supreme Court of the United States, Opinion, 133 S.Ct. 1659, 17 April 2013 ('*Kiobel*'). The presumption against extraterritoriality is a long-standing canon of statutory construction in the United States. See for the seminal case: *Equal Employment Opportunity Commission v Arabian American Oil Co. et al.*, Supreme Court of the United States, Opinion, 499 U.S. 244, 26 March 1991.

claim brought by Nigerian citizens alleging that the oil corporation Royal Dutch Petroleum (Shell) had aided and abetted the government of Nigeria in committing violations of international law (in particular arbitrary arrest and detention, crimes against humanity, and torture or cruel, inhuman, and degrading treatment).

This final section does not purport to give a detailed overview of the role of territoriality in transnational human rights tort litigation. Such overviews, also from a comparative law perspective, have been offered elsewhere.[126] Doctrinal analyses of *Kiobel* and the post-*Kiobel* era are also abundantly available in other publications.[127] In this section, my only ambition is to engage at a *theoretical* level with the US Supreme Court's reasoning in *Kiobel*, and in particular to problematize territoriality, which was, via the presumption against extraterritoriality, so central to the solution of the dispute. I take Philip Liste's theoretical work on *Kiobel* as a foil to apply my own theoretical argument.

In his first publication on *Kiobel*, Liste highlights how the Supreme Court, relying on the presumption against extraterritoriality, *naturalized* territory, and obscured the political nature of social space—which may well have yielded alternative knowledge of spatial normativity, e.g., universal jurisdiction based on a transnational space.[128] In his second publication, which consists mainly of an analysis of arguments centered on spatial normativity made in the various *amicus curiae* briefs in the *Kiobel* litigation, he demonstrates how various actors—states, multinational corporations, non-governmental organizations—conceive differently of the contours of territoriality and spatiality, depending on their social and political preferences. Most interestingly, he draws attention to how *transnational* corporations, somewhat counterintuitively perhaps, 'reproduce a highly *territorialized* knowledge of state jurisdiction',[129] whereas (at least a number of) *territorial states*, including the forum state itself (the United States), make arguments that nuance territoriality, foreground the human rights interests of the aggrieved individual, and tentatively construct a *global or transnational space*.[130] Liste's analysis shows that a territorially delimited actor (the state) does not, as a matter of course, espouse a territory-based spatial discourse, and conversely, that a transnational actor (the corporation) does not *per se* develop transnational jurisdictional arguments.

As signaled above, states may well prove to be an enlightened trustee of mankind, willing to further the global public interest, and ready—within certain bounds obviously—to offer a territorial forum, or enact local legislation to address global problems. Private actors, for their part, may well turn to concepts almost belonging

[126] Enneking 2012.

[127] E.g., Alford 2014; Blaine 2014; Mora 2014.

[128] Liste 2014, at 17 and 19.

[129] Liste 2016, at 14–15 (citing the *amicus* briefs by Chevron et al., and BP America et al.) (emphasis added).

[130] Ibid., at 11–14, discussing the *amicus* briefs of the US, Germany, and Argentina. Note that The Netherlands and the United Kingdom, by contrast, formulate a more conservative territorial argument in their *amicus* brief, which is undeniably informed by their being the home countries of the defendant Royal Dutch Shell.

to a bygone age, e.g., territorial exclusivity, that nevertheless remain part of the jurisdictional toolbox of states, thereby using, and in fact cherry-picking territorial state institutions that still command some authority, for their own private profit-making purposes. This recalls Sassen's observation that these territorial insertions—in the case the invocation of territorial sovereignty by a corporation—are not constitutive of, or strengthen, state authority, unlike before, but rather articulate state authority in the service of a global, denationalized legal and political regime.[131]

In *Kiobel*, the US Supreme Court ultimately experienced difficulties in conceiving of a global or transnational space, and could not escape from its self-imposed intellectual prison of territoriality. Despite the criticism that has been leveled at the 'conservative' *Kiobel* judgment, at a deeper conceptual level one should also concede, as indicated above, that imagining and representing the extra- or non-territorial in spatial terms is hardly obvious given the enduring attractiveness of the territorial paradigm as world public order's cognitive script. Since 'space' is readily confused with physical 'place' and 'territory', proponents of 'global space' may perhaps expect too much from our human imagination. As suggested above, while I do think that it is not impossible to conceive of spatiality in non-territorial terms, possibly only a clear break with the existing geographic paradigm in imaging 'the global' can give rise to a veritable 'new jurisdictional beginning'. In this respect, I have suggested the alternative analytical lenses of justice, community, and temporality. I propose to don those lenses when having another look at *Kiobel*, and transnational human rights litigation against corporations more generally.

Donning the lens of *justice* in *Kiobel*, the US Supreme Court could have focused on the *nature of the underlying violations* alleged (Shell's alleged aiding and assisting the Nigerian government in committing acts of violence against local Ogoni people peacefully protesting against oil exploration projects). Put differently, it could have zeroed in on the Statute's jurisdiction *ratione materiae* rather than on its geographic reach, and could thus have established jurisdiction on the mere basis that gross injustice was alleged, possibly in combination with the conceptualization of space as 'global'. After all, going by its language, the ATS itself provides a cause of action for violations of *the law of nations*,[132] which include gross human rights violations doing *injustice* to individuals.[133]

---

[131] Sassen 2006, at 418–420 (submitting that 'territorial insertions in a foreign country denationalize rather than produce an extension of national territorial authority' and describing 'partial and often highly specialized formations centered in particular utilities and purposes').

[132] Alien Tort Statute, 28 U.S.C. § 1350 ('ATS') ('The district courts shall have original jurisdiction of any civil action by an alien for a tort only, committed in violation of the law of nations or a treaty of the United States').

[133] In *Sosa v Alvarez-Machain*, the Supreme Court found that the ATS did not create a cause of action, but instead merely 'furnish[ed] jurisdiction for a relatively modest set of actions alleging violations of the law of nations' (*Sosa v Alvarez-Machain*, Supreme Court of the United States, Opinion, 542 U.S. 692, 29 June 2004, at 720). Such actions must 'rest on a norm of international character accepted by the civilized world and defined with a specificity *comparable to* the features of the 18th-century paradigms we have recognized' (ibid., at 725) (emphasis added).

In addition, donning the lens of *community membership*, one could argue that the Nigerian Ogoni people affected by Shell's oil exploration project formed part of the same community as Shell. It is recalled in this respect that the United Nations Global Compact coined the term *sphere of influence* 'to establish the scope of corporate responsibility for human rights issues based on the extent of a particular business' influence'.[134] The idea is that a business can be considered to exercise influence over a variety of stakeholders, an influence that radiates beyond its premises and reaches not only its employees, but also suppliers, governments, and the wider community. While the UN Special Representative for Transnational Corporations and Human Rights has indicted the concept of sphere of influence as 'too broad and ambiguous a concept to define the scope of due diligence required to fulfil the [corporate] responsibility to respect',[135] it remains a promising concept to delimit a relevant community for jurisdictional purposes.[136] Accordingly, irrespective of the nature of the violation and irrespective of geographical location, the US Supreme Court in *Kiobel* could have decided to offer a jurisdictional forum to settle the dispute simply based on the joint community membership of plaintiff and defendant.[137]

An alternative outcome in transnational human rights cases of the sort of *Kiobel* could finally be ensured by donning the lens of *temporality*. More in particular, in such cases involving linked corporate actors and activities, the simultaneity iteration of the concept of temporality may allow for jurisdiction to be simultaneously established over a multitude of geographically dispersed actors who caused the same harm. This approach may yield jurisdiction over related claims brought against a variety of organizationally linked corporate wrongdoers. A temporal perspective may possibly not have changed the outcome in the Supreme Court case, as this case concerned just one actor—the Royal Dutch Shell parent corporation. However, it could have widened the number of defendants appearing in front of the Court. It is recalled in this respect that a lower court hearing the *Kiobel* case had refused to exercise personal jurisdiction over Shell's Nigerian subsidiary for lack of minimum contacts with the United States, as a result of which the case continued

[134] United Nations Office of the High Commissioner for Human Rights (2013) United Nations Global Compact, E-Learning, Module 2. http://human-rights-and-business-learning-tool.unglobalcompact.org/site/, accessed 17 February 2016.

[135] Ruggie J (2008) Clarifying the Concepts of 'Sphere of influence' and 'Complicity', Report of the Special Representative of the Secretary-General on the Issue of Human Rights and Transnational Corporations and other Business Enterprises, Eight Session of the Human Rights Council, UN Doc. A/HRC/8/16, 15 May 2008.

[136] The concept for that matter echoes the medieval concept of 'place', viewed as jurisdictional influence radiating outward from a geographic center (a town, a fortress) to outlying areas and their inhabitants (Branch 2013).

[137] This is provided that the US could establish personal jurisdiction over the defendant, on the basis of the latter's minimum contacts with the US.

only against Shell's parent.[138] Temporal sensitivity would instead have allowed the court to draw a link between the claims brought simultaneously against parent and subsidiary, in respect of the same harm, and exercise jurisdiction over the subsidiary, despite the latter not having minimum contacts with the US.[139]

An instructive precedent of purported temporal jurisdiction is offered by Dutch courts' jurisdictional rulings in *Akpan v Shell* (2013, 2015), in a tort case related to Shell's oil operations in Nigeria (in the case concerning oil spills causing environmental damage).[140] The main jurisdictional issue in *Akpan v Shell* was whether Shell's Nigerian *subsidiary* was amenable to suit in the Netherlands—apart from Shell itself, which was incorporated in the Netherlands and accordingly unambiguously subject to suit before Dutch courts under the domicile principle.[141] Ordinary rules of jurisdiction did not provide for jurisdiction over alleged torts committed by foreign corporations against other foreigners on foreign soil, but regardless, Dutch courts ruled that the suits brought against the parent and subsidiary corporation were so much related that *joint treatment*—and thus extension of Dutch jurisdiction over the Nigerian subsidiary—was justified for reasons of procedural economy (efficiency).[142] In so doing, the courts acknowledged that the complexity of international business transactions and corporate structures in a globalized world could be reduced by injecting *simultaneity* into the response offered by the law; where victims struggle to identify the responsible party among multiple potential defendants, it is advisable for courts to extend their jurisdiction to entertain claims against *all* defendants, including those of foreign origin, and thus to entertain the claims *at the same time*, in order to prevent inconsistent outcomes.[143]

A full acknowledgment of the drastic spatiotemporal changes in the global corporate value-chain could possibly have led to another jurisdictional outcome in

---

[138] *Kiobel v Royal Dutch Petroleum Company*, United States District Court for the Southern District of New York (S.D.N.Y.), No. 02 Civ. 7618 (KMW) (HBP), 2010 WL 2507025, 21 June 2010. Shell's parent corporation, however, operated an office in New York to manage its New York Stock Exchange listing. This was deemed sufficient to establish personal jurisdiction. The issue of personal jurisdiction was ultimately not before the US Supreme Court.

[139] Note also that the international law of responsibility has taken a particular interest in the responsibility consequences of multiple tortfeasors causing the same harm; notably the concept of 'shared responsibility'. See on this notion Nollkaemper and Jacobs 2012.

[140] See for the relevant jurisdictional judgments: *Friday Alfred Akpan and Vereniging Milieudefensie v Royal Dutch Shell PLC and Shell Petroleum Development Company of Nigeria LTD,* Hague District Court, ECLI:NL:RBDHA:2013:BY9854, 30 January 2013; and Hague Court of Appeal, ECLI:NL:GHDHA:2015:3587, 18 December 2015 ('*Akpan v Shell*').

[141] Articles 2(1) and 60(1) of Council Regulation (EC) No 44/2001 of 22 December 2000 on jurisdiction and the recognition and enforcement of judgments in civil and commercial matters, [2001] OJ L12/1.

[142] The courts applied Article 7 of the Dutch Code of Civil Procedure, which indeed provides for the joinder of cases in case of unity ('samenhang') of claims.

[143] This does not mean that territoriality disappears entirely. It only implies that one claim can piggyback on another claim over which uncontroversial jurisdiction can be exercised, such as on grounds of territoriality or domicile.

Kiobel as well. In particular, it could have brought US courts to establish personal jurisdiction over Shell's Nigerian subsidiary alongside the Shell parent. True, in the Supreme Court, the case against the subsidiary would still have stranded on the ground of subject-matter jurisdiction under the ATS being absent.[144] But then, when pondering the scope of ATS jurisdiction, the Court could have espoused an (admittedly unlikely) radical understanding of temporality with respect to the subject-matter jurisdiction it could exercise over both Shell and its Nigerian subsidiary, e.g., that the communication revolution had made corporate decision-making nearly instantaneous, thereby making a mockery of geography and territoriality. At any rate, in states that do not draw a precise distinction between personal and subject-matter jurisdiction—continental European states for instance—the form of temporality constituted by the connected claims doctrine may redefine and expand the exercise of jurisdiction over transnational torts.

This section has accordingly demonstrated that imagining jurisdiction using alternative conceptual lenses than the tired category of territory—global space, justice, community, temporality—may drastically change jurisdictional outcomes in transnational human rights litigation. Nevertheless, it bears emphasis that, however dramatic these re-conceptualizations of jurisdiction may appear, they do not necessarily do away with the state territory-based global order. Rather they invite us to imagine how new jurisdictional beginnings could be grafted onto the enduring institutions of the territorially bounded state, such as its domestic courts. They allow us to conceive of domestic institutions as fora for the resolution of global, rather than purely territorial, political and social conflicts.

3.8 Concluding Observations

International law's dominant positivist epistemology almost inevitably leads to 'territorial bias' on the part of its practitioners and scholars. This privileging of territory as the jurisdictional linchpin is indeed the logical outcome of a law-identification methodology that only takes seriously *what states actually do and say*. Territory being one of the basic features of statehood,[145] it is not expected that states, in their legal practice and discourse, will abandon territory.

A critical scholar, however, denaturalizes the world-view and power relations that are reified by positivist, doctrinal scholarship. In particular, he critiques *state*

[144] The temporality lens donned here does not automatically make the claims actionable under the ATS, nor does it displace the presumption against extraterritoriality, as under US law, unlike under Dutch or European, courts should not only establish due process-based personal jurisdiction based on minimum links, but also subject-matter jurisdiction (does the claim fall within the substantive scope of the relevant statute?).

[145] 1933 Montevideo Convention on Rights and Duties of States, 165 LNTS 19, Article 1.

power-based scholarship.[146] Historicizing territory is helpful in this respect, as it shows that 'territory' is a relatively recent 'invention'—the product of historically specific political, material, epistemic, and above all mapping practices—that points to the existence of a prior jurisdictional alternative: community. Drawing on *inter alia* Mariana Valverde's work, I have noted that critical analysis should go beyond the merely historical, however. This is why I have explored non-historical temporality[147] as well as ethics as resources allowing us to imagine forms of non- or extra-territorial jurisdiction that are based on time or justice, and not only on space.

Sure enough, such imagining may risk never leaving the ivory towers of academic philosophy. The task of the lawyer, however, is to inscribe bold governance ideas into the inevitable path dependency of our legal institutions, so that these ideas could inform actual decision-making. These institutions—e.g., the courts—remain largely territorial state-based, but they could repurpose themselves in the service of non-territorial jurisdictional aims, by inventively exploring the interstices of positive law. This 'new territoriality' holds promise for considerable political engagement through the law, as it enables non- or extra-territorial interests to take on a valid legal form. The example of transnational human rights litigation shows how such engagement can lead to legal outcomes that are quite surprising, but not necessarily less legitimate than those reached under the territorial paradigm.

References

Abass A (2014) International Law: Test, Cases, and Materials. Oxford University Press, Oxford

Abbott KW, Snidal D (2000) Hard and Soft Law in International Governance. International Organization 54(3):421–456

Agnew J (1994) The Territorial Trap: the Geographical Assumptions of International Relations Theory. Review of International Political Economy 1(1):53–80

Akehurst M (1975) Jurisdiction in International Law. British Yearbook of International Law 46:145–257

Alford RP (2014) Human Rights After Kiobel: Choice of Law and the Rise of Transnational Tort Litigation. Emory Law Journal 63:1089–1161

Althouse A (1983) The Use of Conspiracy Theory to Establish *in Personam* Jurisdiction: A Due Process Analysis. Fordham Law Review 52:234–260

Ambrus M, Wessel RA (eds) (2015) Between Pragmatism and Predictability: Temporariness in International Law. Netherlands Yearbook of International Law 2014, vol 45. TMC Asser Press, The Hague

American Law Institute (1987) Restatement of the Law (Third): The Foreign Relations Law of the United States. American Law Institute Publishers, St Paul

Arendt H (1964) Eichmann in Jerusalem: A Report on the Banality of Evil. Penguin Books, London

[146] Valverde 2015, at 31 (defining critical theory as 'distancing oneself from that scholarship which is imbricated with state power').

[147] I am particularly indebted to Mariana Valverde in this respect, who in *Chronotopes* magisterially argued that time should not be reduced to history, and drew attention to the temporal dimension of 'human experience'. Valverde 2015, at 38.

Backer LC (2012) Governance Without a Government: An Overview. In: Handl G, Zekoll J, Zumbansen P (eds) Beyond Territoriality: Transnational Legal Authority in an Age of Globalization. Martinus Nijhoff Publishers, Leiden, pp 87–126
Bartelson J (2014) Sovereignty as Symbolic Form. Routledge, London
Berman HJ, Kaufmann C (1978) Law of International Commercial Transactions (Lex Mercatoria). Harvard International Law Journal 19:221–277
Berman PS (2005) Conflict of Laws, Globalization, and Cosmopolitan Pluralism. Wayne Law Review 51:1105–1146
Berman PS (2012) Global Legal Pluralism: a Jurisprudence of Law Beyond Borders. Cambridge University Press, Cambridge
Bethlehem D (2014) The End of Geography: the Changing Nature of the International System and the Challenge to International Law. European Journal of International Law 25(1):9–24
Blaine JHL (2014) Sosa, Kiobel and Pirates Inc.: Defining the 'Modern' Parameters of the Archaic Alien Tort Statute. Hague Yearbook of International Law 26:116–140
Bradford A (2012) The Brussels Effect. Northwestern University Law Review 107:1–67
Branch J (2011) Mapping the Sovereign State: Technology, Authority, and Systemic Change. International Organization 65(1):1–36
Branch J (2013) The Cartographic State: Maps, Territory, and the Origins of Sovereignty. Cambridge University Press, Cambridge
Brigham J (2009) Seeing Jurisdiction: Some Jurisprudential Issues Arising from Law Being '… All Over'. Law & Policy 31(4):381–404
Brilmayer L (1987) Jurisdictional Due Process and Political Theory. University of Florida Law Review 39:293–314
Brown Weiss E (2007) Climate Change, Intergenerational Equity, and International Law. Vermont Journal of Environmental Law 9:615–627
Buxbaum HL (2004) From Empire to Globalization…and Back? A Post-Colonial View of Transjudicialism. Indiana Journal of Global Legal Studies 11(1):183–189
Buxbaum HL (2009) Territory, Territoriality, and the Resolution of Jurisdictional Conflict. The American Journal of Comparative Law 57:631–675
Cafaggi F, Renda A, Schmidt R (2013) Transnational Private Regulation. In: OECD, International Regulatory Co-operation: Case Studies, vol 3. Transnational Private Regulation and Water Management. OECD Publishing, Paris, pp 9–58
Callies G, Zumbansen P (2010) Rough Consensus and Running Code: A Theory of Transnational Private Law. Bloomsbury Publishing, London
Cameron J, Abouchar J (1991) The Precautionary Principle: A Fundamental Principle of Law and Policy for the Protection of the Global Environment. Boston College International and Comparative Law Review 14(1):1–27
Carpenter D, Moss DA (2013) Preventing Regulatory Capture: Special Interest Influence and How to Limit It. Cambridge University Press, Cambridge
Churchill R, Freestone D (1991) International law and Global Climate Change. Graham & Trotman, London
de Baere G, Ryngaert C (2013) The ECJ's Judgment in Air Transport Association of America and the International Legal Context of the EU's Climate Change Policy. European Foreign Affairs Review 18:389–409
de Vattel E (1834) The Law of Nations; or Principles of the Law of Nature Applied to the Conduct and Affairs of Nations and Sovereigns, Book II: Of a Nation Considered in Her Relation to Other States (edited by Chitty J). Cambridge University Press, New York
Dorsett S, McVeigh S (2012) Jurisdiction. Routledge, London
Douzinas C, Nead L (1999) Introduction. In: Douinas C, Nead L (eds) Law and the Image: The Authority of Art and the Aesthetics of Law. University of Chicago Press, Chicago, pp 1–15
Elden S (2013) The Birth of Territory. University of Chicago Press, Chicago
Enneking L (2012) Foreign Direct Liability and Beyond: Exploring the Role of Tort Law in Promoting International Corporate Social Responsibility and Accountability. Eleven International Publishing, The Hague

Ford RT (1999) Law's Territory (A History of Jurisdiction). Michigan Law Review 97(4):843–930
Ford RT (2012) Law and Borders. Alabama Law Review 64:123
Greig JM (2002) The End of Geography? Globalization, Communications, and Culture in the International System. Journal of Conflict Resolution 46(2):225–243
Hakimi M (2014) Unfriendly Unilateralism. Harvard International Law Journal 55(1):105–150
Hirst M (2003) Jurisdiction and the Ambit of the Criminal Law. Oxford University Press, Oxford
Howse R, Regan D (2000) The Product/Process Distinction – An Illusory Basis for Disciplining 'Unilateralism' in Trade Policy. European Journal of International Law 11:249–289
International Bar Association (2009) Report of the Task Force on Extraterritorial Jurisdiction. International Bar Association, London
Jackson R (2007) Sovereignty and its Presuppositions: Before 9/11 and After. Political Studies 55 (2):297–317
Kassan S (1935) Extraterritorial Jurisdiction in the Ancient World. American Journal of International Law 29:237–247
Kaufmann C, Weber RH (2011) Carbon-Related Border Tax Adjustment: Mitigating Climate Change or Restricting International Trade? World Trade Review 10(4):497–525
Kaushal A (2015) The Politics of Jurisdiction. The Modern Law Review 78(5):759–792
Kennedy D (2003) Laws and Developments. In: Hatchard J, Perry-Kessaris A (eds) Law and Development: Facing Complexity in the 21st Century. Cavendish Publishing Limited, London/Portland, pp 17–26
Kleizen B (2015) Externalizing EU Law, Policy and Values: Europe's Global Identity, Mechanisms of Rule Transfer and Case Studies on Illegal Logging and Bosnia and Herzegovina. http://papers.ssrn.com/sol3/papers.cfm?abstract_id=2706564. Accessed 16 February 2016
Koch C (2004) Consciousness: Introduction. In: Gazzaniga MS (ed) The Cognitive Neurosciences III, 3rd edn. MIT Press, Cambridge/London, pp 1107–1110
Koskenniemi M (1990) The Politics of International Law. European Journal of International Law 1:4–32
Koskenniemi M (2009) The Politics of International Law – 20 Years Later. European Journal of International Law 20(1):7–19
Krisch N (2014) The Decay of Consent: International Law in an Age of Global Public Goods. American Journal of International Law 108(1):1–40
Landauer C (2014) The Ever-Ending Geography of International Law: The Changing Nature of the International System and the Challenge to International Law: A Reply to Daniel Bethlehem. European Journal of International Law 25(1):31–34
Langer M (2011) The Diplomacy of Universal Jurisdiction: The Political Branches and the Transnational Prosecution of International Crimes. American Journal of International Law 105:1–55
Lindahl H (2010) A-Legality: Postnationalism and the Question of Legal Boundaries. The Modern Law Review 73(1):30–56
Liste P (2014) Transnational Human Rights Litigation and Territorialised Knowledge: Kiobel and the 'Politics of Space'. Transnational Legal Theory 5(1):1–19
Liste P (2016) Geographical Knowledge at Work: Human Rights Litigation and Transnational Territoriality. European Journal of International Relations 22(1):217–239
Llewellyn KN (1930) Case Law. In: Seligman ERA, Johnson A (eds) Encyclopedia of the Social Sciences. MacMillan, New York
Locke J (2012) Second Treatise of Government: An Essay Concerning the True Original, Extent and End of Civil Government. John Wiley & Sons, New Jersey
Lorenz EN (1963) Deterministic Nonperiodic Flow. Journal of the Atmospheric Sciences 20 (2):130–141
Lowe V, Staker C (2010) Jurisdiction. In: Evans MD (ed) International Law, 3rd edn. Oxford University Press, Oxford, pp 313–339
Luban D (2011) Hannah Arendt as a Theorist of International Criminal Law. International Criminal Law Review 11(3):621–641

Maffesoli M (1995) The Time of the Tribes: The Decline of Individualism in Mass Society. Sage, London
Maier HG (1996) Jurisdictional Rules in Customary International Law. In: Meessen KM (ed) Extraterritorial Jurisdiction in Theory and Practice. Kluwer Law International, London, pp 64–102
Mann FA (1964) The Doctrine of Jurisdiction in International Law. Recueil des Cours 111:1–162
Mann FA (1984) The Doctrine of Jurisdiction Revisited after Twenty Years. Recueil des Cours 186:9–116
McIntyre, Mosedale T (1997) The Precautionary Principle as a Norm of Customary International Law. Journal of Environmental Law 9:221–242
Mora PD (2014) The Alien Tort Statute After 'Kiobel': The Possibility for Unlawful Assertions of Universal Civil Jurisdiction Still Remains. International & Comparative Law Quarterly 63:699–719
Morgan LH (1877) Ancient society; Or, Researches in the Lines of Human Progress from Savagery, Through Barbarism to Civilization. Henry Holt and Company, New York
Nohria N (2012) What Business Schools Can Learn from the Medical Profession. Harvard Business Review 90(1–2):38-38
Nollkaemper PA, Jacobs D (2012) Shared Responsibility in International Law: A Conceptual Framework. Michigan Journal of International Law 34:359–438
Oxman BH (2007) Jurisdiction of States. Max Planck Encyclopedia of Public International Law. http://opil.ouplaw.com/view/10.1093/law:epil/9780199231690/law-9780199231690-e1436. Accessed 9 January 2017
Pahuja S (2011) Decolonising International Law: Development, Economic Growth and the Politics of Universality. Cambridge University Press, Cambridge
Palonen K (2012) The Search for a New Beginning: Hannah Arendt and Karl Jaspers as Critics of West German Parliamentarism. In: Goldoni M, McCorkindale C (eds) Hannah Arendt and the Law. Bloomsbury Publishing, London, pp 151–170
Pessoa F (2002) The Book of Disquiet. Penguin Books, London
Radon J (2004) Sovereignty: A Political Emotion, Not a Concept. Stanford Journal of International Law 40(2):195–209
Riles A (2005) A New Agenda for the Cultural Study of Law: Taking on the Technicalities. Buffalo Law Review 53:973–1033
Ruggie JG (1993) Territoriality and Beyond: Problematizing Modernity in International Relations. International Organization 47(1):139–174
Ryngaert C (2009) Territorial Jurisdiction Over Cross-Frontier Offences: Revisiting a Classic Problem of International Criminal Law. International Criminal Law Review 9:187–209
Ryngaert C (2015a) Jurisdiction in International Law, 2nd edn. Oxford University Press, Oxford
Ryngaert C (2015b) Whither Territoriality? The European Union's Use of Territoriality to Set Norms with Universal Effects. In: Ryngaert C, Molenaar EJ, Nouwen SMH (eds) What's Wrong with International Law? Liber Amicorum A.H.A Soons. Brill, The Hague, pp 434–448
Sack RD (1983) Human territoriality: A Theory. Annals of the Association of American Geographers 73(1):55–74
Sassen S (1991) The Global City. Princeton University Press, Princeton
Sassen S (1994) Cities in a World Economy. Pine Forge Press, Thousand Oaks
Sassen S (2006) Territory, Authority, Rights: From Medieval to Global Assemblages. Princeton University Press, Princeton
Schultz T (2008) Carving up the Internet: Jurisdiction, Legal Orders, and the Private/Public International Law Interface. European Journal of International Law 19(4):799–839
Scott J (2014) Extraterritoriality and Territorial Extension in EU law. American Journal of Comparative Law 62(1):87–125
Shah N (2012) The Territorial Trap of the Territorial Trap: Global Transformation and the Problem of the State's Two Territories. International Political Sociology 6(1):57–76
Shakespeare W (1623) Mr. William Shakespeares Comedies, Histories, & Tragedies. Edward Blount and William and Isaac Jaggard, London

Svantesson D (2015) A New Jurisprudential Framework for Jurisdiction: Beyond the Harvard Draft. American Journal of International Law Unbound 109:69–74

Treasure W (2011) Diagnosis and Risk Management in Primary Care: Words That Count, Numbers That Speak. Radcliffe Publishing, Oxford

Twain M (1907) Chapters from My Autobiography. The North American Review 185(618):465–474

Vagias M (2014) The Territorial Jurisdiction of the International Criminal Court. Cambridge University Press, Cambridge

Valverde M (2008) Analyzing the Governance of Security: Jurisdiction and Scale. Behemoth A Journal on Civilisation 1(1):3–15

Valverde M (2009) Jurisdiction and Scale: 'Legal Technicalities' as Resources for Theory. Social & Legal Studies 18(2):139–157

Valverde M (2015) Chronotopes of Law: Jurisdiction and Scale. Routledge, London

Wendt A (1999) Social Theory of International Politics. Cambridge University Press, Cambridge

Chapter 4
Cartographies of the Present: 'Contingent Sovereignty' and Territorial Integrity

Sara Kendall

Abstract Sovereignty as territorial integrity has been recast by state legal advisors, diplomats and scholars, who employ terms and principles from international law while disregarding the content of the law. This chapter takes up the apparent permeability of borders in contemporary discourses and practices of military intervention. In spaces of alleged terrorist activity the relationship between state and territory has been called into question, and the global legal imaginary of sovereign states is separated *de facto* into actual sovereigns and 'contingent' sovereigns. The claim that ineffective internal sovereignty may justify intervention forms part of a broader reconfiguration of the relationship between sovereignty and territory. Drawing upon insights from political geography, this chapter uses 'contingent sovereignty' as a critical diagnosis. It focuses on contemporary practices of drone warfare and emerging justifications for intervention that are premised upon a state's unwillingness or inability to confront internal threats. It argues that the international legal order is recast in these cartographic projections, where territory operates as a political technology for preserving certain populations.

Keywords Territory · Sovereignty · Drones · Asymmetrical warfare · Biopolitics

Contents

S. Kendall (✉)
University of Kent, Canterbury, UK
e-mail: S.Kendall@kent.ac.uk

M. Kuijer and W. Werner (eds.), *Netherlands Yearbook of International Law 2016*, Netherlands Yearbook of International Law 47,
DOI 10.1007/978-94-6265-207-1_4

4.1 Introduction

Writing in the Netherlands Yearbook of International Law in the early 1980s, Malcolm Shaw began from sovereign equality and territorial integrity as cornerstones of the international order. Shaw claimed that

> Territory is, of course, itself a geographical conception relating to physical areas of the globe, but its centrality in law and international law in particular derives from the fact that it constitutes the tangible framework for the manifestation of power by the accepted authorities of the state in question. The principle whereby such a state is deemed to exercise exclusive power over its territory can be seen as a fundamental axiom of classical international law.[1]

For Shaw, territory appears first as a geographical and spatial form, as is the case in other disciplines. It then becomes significant for international law through its relationship to sovereignty, with the exclusive exercise of power over a territory that the term implies. More recent scholarship has noted that the international order has drifted from this Westphalian presumption, suggesting a shift that was already foregrounded in Shaw's own claims over thirty years ago regarding the decline of territorial sovereignty, and in turn, of the role of territory itself: '[i]t thus appears that trends are emerging in international relations challenging or at least restraining the dominant territorial conception of world affairs'.[2]

In the intervening decades, scholarship addressing the dynamic of globalization has problematized conceptions of territory as well as sovereignty. For sociologist Saskia Sassen, globalization brought 'multiple relations between territory and institutional encasement' beyond the traditional relationship between national territory and sovereign rule.[3] Sub- and supra-state actors, both public and private, have decentred the role of the nation-state. Some scholars have broadly asserted that state power has waned in relation to transnational economic forces.[4] International relations theorists have called into question their field's persistent thinking in terms of the territorial state.[5] Within legal scholarship, transnational—as distinct from international—approaches have sought to recognize the role of economic actors as well as non-state entities in producing regimes of global governance, further contesting the centrality of the sovereign state.[6]

[1] Shaw 1982, at 61.

[2] Ibid., at 66.

[3] Sassen 2009, at 574.

[4] Brown 2010. Some critical international legal scholarship has noted the shift from sovereign control over natural resources to the protection of foreign investors; see Pahuja 2011.

[5] Agnew 1994. For a contemporary revisiting of this post-Cold War critique, see Agnew 2010, Elden 2010, and McConnell 2010.

[6] Handl et al. 2012.

In spite of these reorientations, the Westphalian nexus between territory and sovereignty remains central within the field of international law, where territory operates as a 'state of mind' undergirding countless international legal doctrines.[7] This may be a product of the constitutive force of territory in the international order, whether colonial-era conceptions of uninhabited territory (*terra nullius*) as a justification for colonial possession or the administration of territory through trusteeships following the cessation of the League of Nations. Conceptions of territory appear within foundational texts such as the UN Charter as well as in subsequent General Assembly resolutions on decolonisation and self-determination.[8] Sovereign equality and territorial integrity remain touchstones of a more optimistic vision of the contemporary international legal order, which is thought to constrain recourses to force and to promote respect for the territorial boundaries of sovereign states.

Yet shifts in security discourse and state practices in the past fifteen years have unsettled these conceptions, re-casting how sovereignty is understood and, in turn, how territorial incursions are justified. Commentators proclaim that '[t]he geography of conflict has evolved.'[9] Unprecedented lines of argument emerged from state actors, such as 'pre-emptive' self-defence as a basis for the 2003 invasion of Iraq, the 'responsibility to protect' claims undergirding the 2011 Libyan intervention, and the 'unwilling or unable' theory as a means of expanding the scope of Article 51 self-defence claims for intervening in Pakistan and Syria. Meanwhile, practices such as targeted killing through drone strikes have posed challenges for international lawyers, who have extensively debated their humanitarian merits and their legality under the laws of armed conflict.

The field of international law tends to address these phenomena through existing categories, applying legal frameworks to make determinations about compliance and non-compliance with *jus ad bellum* and *jus in bello*, for example, rather than attempting to diagnose the shifting discursive frames through which these incursions are justified.[10] In this sense, as some reflexive scholars of international law have noted, the field operates as its own language, with its particular structures and

---

[7] Kritsiotis 2009, at 547. For an account of the ongoing resilience of sovereignty as an organizing category in international law and international relations in spite of contemporary challenges, see Aalberts 2012.

[8] See for example UN GA Resolution 1514 (XV) on 14 December 1960, 'Declaration on the Granting of Independence to Colonial Countries and Peoples', and UN GA Resolution 2625 (XXV) on 24 October 1970, 'Declaration on Principles of International Law Concerning Friendly Relations and Co-operation Among States', recognizing the importance of sovereign equality and territorial integrity.

[9] Schmitt 2013, at 97

[10] See the 2016 'Symposium on the Fight Against ISIL and International Law' in the *Leiden Journal of International Law* 29, which largely employs the UN Charter based recourse to force and international humanitarian law frameworks.

modes of expression.[11] Yet the social phenomena to which these forms refer may not fit within the confines of available structures of argument: the existing technical legal vocabulary addressing the recourse to force and the law of armed conflict may fail to capture the plurality of contemporary expressions justifying armed interventions.[12] An internal reading that takes international law as the given backdrop often ends within an either/or frame, where an intervention is either lawful or unlawful; alternatively, it ends with identifying a gap in law that can presumably be resolved through extending existing legal logics. What it tends not to do is diagnose the phenomena themselves, whether discourses or practices, that it attempts to fit within its frame.

This chapter contends that in order to grasp these alternate modes of territoriality appearing through contemporary lines of argument and practice, international law can benefit from insights from other disciplines, such as political geography and critical security studies.[13] Political theorist and geographer Stuart Elden referred to 'contingent sovereignty' a decade ago to describe 'the idea that in certain key circumstances—in particular, when states harbour terrorists or seek to acquire weapons of mass destruction—norms of sovereignty do not apply.'[14] This critical diagnosis has grown even more relevant in light of recent uses of the 'unwilling or unable' theory, which claims that a state that has suffered an armed attack may lawfully use force in the territory of another state if its government is incapable of suppressing the threat. More recently, critical geographer Derek Gregory diagnosed what he termed the 'everywhere war', where the contours of 'the battlespace' are indefinite and uncontained.[15] When these two insights are taken together, the pliant territoriality of the 'everywhere war' is extended through the logic of 'contingent sovereignty', challenging orthodox international legal conceptions of the relationship between sovereignty and territorial integrity.

---

[11] Koskenniemi 2006.

[12] Put another way, the *parole* in which political justifications are spoken may point back to a background *langue* other than international law. This structuralist terminology, employed by some contemporary international legal thinkers following Koskenniemi, draws upon the work of structural linguist Ferdinand de Saussure. For an account of structuralism in legal scholarship, see Desautels-Stein 2015.

[13] This claim assumes a position within existing debates in international legal scholarship regarding the role and value of interdisciplinary research. On the challenges of interdisciplinarity, in particular concerning international relations, see Klabbers 2009 and Kratochwil 2012. For an argument supporting interdisciplinarity in international legal scholarship, see Kendall 2016.

[14] Elden 2006, at 14. While this idea was developed during the Bush administration, Elden claims in a subsequent publication that it continued through the Obama administration; see Elden 2009.

[15] Gregory 2011, at 248. Scholars in other fields have observed that the post-9/11 security paradigm has blurred the boundaries between internal and external; see for example Beck 2002, who argues that a world risk society emerged from these shifts.

4.2 Territorial Narratives and Techniques

Conceptions of territory emerged together with the international legal order, designating the space where sovereignty is enacted. In Shaw's 1982 NYIL article, territory appears epiphenomenal to sovereignty in the international legal order, at least in the frame of international legal scholarship. As a geographical form, it is relevant to modern law to the extent that it is seen as the space where state power extends. Tracing the emergence of territory in the canon of Western political thought, Stuart Elden has shown that modern accounts of territory view it as an extension of a state's power. Yet territory has been understood otherwise: '[t]he idea of a territory as a bounded space under the control of a group of people, usually a state', with exclusive internal sovereignty and equal external status, is 'historically produced.'[16] This narrative is produced, Elden claims, from out of an amalgam of elements from earlier accounts that imagined different relationships between place and power, reminding us of our contingent inheritance of this modern explanation.

Alternate possibilities for understanding the relationship between power and place can be seen in the archive of texts and laws from antiquity to the seventeenth century, the period of the Peace of Westphalia from which modern international law is often said to originate. They form a diverse body of source material, 'techniques' of territory that include 'legal systems and arguments; political debates, theories, concepts, and practices; colonization and military excursions; works of literature and dictionaries; historical studies, myths, and—the technical in the narrower sense—geometrical instruments, statistical handbooks, maps, land-surveying instruments, and population controls.'[17] This forms a far broader and more eclectic story than international law's own archive of the production of territory, where the Peace of Westphalia is seen to mark 'a crucial point towards the creation of modern international law, based as it has been upon defined territorial units.'[18] As Jacques Derrida observed, the concept of archive operates etymologically as both an authoritative origin (commencement) and as a place from which order is given (commandment)[19]; in this sense 'Westphalia' archives one of international law's persistent origin myths, locating its emergence in Europe in the seventeenth century and its ordering role through the principles of sovereign equality and territorial integrity.

---

[16] Elden 2013, at 322.

[17] Ibid., at 17. We can add insights from interdisciplinary legal scholarship that draws upon critical theory, philosophy, and history, as Jothie Rajah does in her account of law as a record that appears not only in legal doctrine, but also in '[i]mages, sound, gesture, affect, and feeling' that help in tracing the limited and largely unofficial archive of Osama bin Laden's death. Rajah 2016, at 46.

[18] Shaw 1982, at 62.

[19] Derrida 1998. Building on Derrida's work, Renisa Mawani explains that '[l]aw's archive is a site from which law derives its meanings, authority, and legitimacy, a proliferation of documents that obscures its originary violence and its ongoing force, and a trace that holds the potential to reveal its foundations as (il)legitimate.' Mawani 2012, at 337.

International legal scholarship often builds upon Westphalia as a historical point of origin and, frequently, as a structuring grammar containing these two central presumptions—sovereign equality and territorial integrity—that are thought to undergird the international order, in theory if not in practice.[20] Critical scholars have shown how this operates as a fiction sustaining the order in its present constellation.[21] Westphalia itself was a uniquely European phenomenon that focused on creating a balance of power between European states while sidelining the vast colonial holdings of those powers elsewhere. Its iconic status in international law serves as a reminder of the field's colonial origins and their iterations in the present, as noted by critics across multiple fields. Yet some doctrinal scholarship continues to treat the regulative ideals of sovereign equality and territorial integrity as ahistorical and decontextualized givens.

An alternate approach is to undertake a 'history of the present', in Michel Foucault's terms, where genealogical inquiry uncovers the conflicts and contingencies that unsettle the givenness of the contemporary order.[22] As an orientation towards history that begins from 'a diagnosis of the current situation',[23] it reveals how historical processes continue to shape present modes of reasoning. This approach also opens a broader archive beyond positive law, including political theories, treaty texts, maps, and other techniques of governance. Such an approach not only reveals continuities with the past but also what is distinct about the present. For example, Gregory's characterization of U.S. counterinsurgency campaigns in Afghanistan and Iraq as an 'old-new paradigm' of orientalism explores continuities with colonial practices of rendering space visible, or what Gregory terms 'scopic regimes', in addition to historically shared presumptions about fundamental differences between liberal democratic states and 'tribal societies'. At the same time, he acknowledges the distinct technological shifts and changing notions of the battlespace 'in which the contours of the enemy are indeterminate and fluid', distinguishing the present from the past.[24] Similarly, Elden shows how the contingency of territorial sovereignty preceded the geopolitical events of 2001: 'many states have long had their sovereignty compromised, and the United States is no stranger to making claims for the contingency of sovereignty, undertaking many interventions within both the Cold War and the "war on drugs" in Central America

---

[20] Shaw elaborates: 'Territory therefore plays not only a definitional role, but a constitutive one historically as well. It is the link between a people, its identity as a state and its international role. It has thus been of crucial importance in Westphalian international law'; see Shaw 1982, at 63.

[21] For a growing body of literature, a key orienting text is Antony Anghie's *Imperialism Sovereignty and the Making of International Law*; see Anghie 2005. Michel Foucault also notes the relationship between Westphalia and *jus gentium* in his lectures entitled 'Security, Territory, Population'; see Foucault 2007.

[22] Foucault 1977. For an explanation of Foucault's genealogical approach as a historiographic method for scholarship in law and criminology, see Garland 2014.

[23] Dreyfus and Rabinow 1982, at 119.

[24] Gregory 2013, at 158.

in the 1980s and 1990s.'[25] Yet contemporary interventions operate through different rhetorical logics and military practices. The conceptions of 'contingent sovereignty', 'earned sovereignty',[26] and the contested 'unwilling and unable' theory of intervention are novel ways in which territorial incursions are justified.

A growing body of interdisciplinary scholarship is undertaking this diagnostic work in order to better grasp the role of international law in distinct historical and political contexts. For example, work on the notion of sovereign equality has shown how it relies upon a standard of civilization that continues into contemporary international legal forms.[27] Sovereign equality operates as a norm, in the Foucaultian sense as both a measure as well as as a means of managing deviance, through its implicit standard of civilization. As Aalberts observes, 'the principle of sovereign equality itself provides the parameters for ordering and making distinctions between states and disciplining of those that do not adhere to the rules and norms of contemporary international society.'[28] These rules and norms are products of a broader history of inclusion and exclusion, from the pre-modern and colonial periods to present distinctions between liberal and illiberal states. Other critical work on the relationship between sovereignty and territory through the phenomenon of drone warfare has shown continuities with historical projects at the 'imperial periphery', revealing how colonial logics persist in the contemporary 'vertical battlespace' of drone warfare.[29] Munro argues that the spatial incursions performed through military drone use amount to a new form of 'aerial sovereignty', where 'each of the target zones is haunted by the continuities of a differentiated and ambiguous sovereign status that is indexed to their imperial past, and arguably produces tangible legal effects in the present.'[30] Among the tangible legal effects is the sustained violation of territorial integrity performed by hovering drones, where the terrain underneath is subjected to an on-going *de facto* form of occupation.

---

[25] Elden 2009, at 139. Elden notes an early articulation of contingent sovereignty in a 1998 U.S. policy document, where the authors argue that states ought to be obliged to reassure the international community that they are not developing weapons of mass destruction, and '[f]ailure to supply such proof, or prosecute the criminals living in their borders, should entitle worried nations to take all necessary actions for their self-defence.' Elden 2006, at 14. Not only a security-related concept, 'contingent sovereignty' has also been used in humanitarian discourses. Mark Duffield has noted how the aid industry in the Cold War period became a way of routing political influence through humanitarianism as part of the 'emergence of contingent sovereignty', as well as its relationship to the 'responsibility to protect'. Duffield 2007, at 70–81.

[26] Elden attributes this language of 'earned sovereignty' to the Washington, D.C.-based Public International Law and Policy Group (PILPG), defined by Michael Scharf as 'a concept that seeks to reconcile the principles of self-determination and humanitarian intervention with the principles of sovereignty and territorial integrity.' Scharf 2003, at 374, as noted in Elden 2009, at 166.

[27] Aalberts 2014.

[28] Ibid., at 783.

[29] Munro 2014.

[30] Ibid., at 260.

Taken together, these interdisciplinary approaches to international law illustrate how sovereign equality in practice operates as a kind of 'conditional equality'.[31] Conditionality is tied to historical power differentials as well as to present practices such as '"interventions" in the territory or air space of another state, which, at worst, renders the sovereignty of that state contingent.'[32] As Aalberts and Werner observe, 'sovereignty is a dynamic concept that has always been used for the creation of disciplined, responsible sovereign subjects within the international legal order', where discipline is meted out through institutional mechanisms that oblige states to prevent possible terrorist activities.[33] The ability to exercise territorial control has been invoked as a standard for evaluating whether a state is properly sovereign, from the mandate system of the League of Nations to present 'unwilling or unable' arguments discussed in more detail below.[34]

It would seem that, *pace* Shaw, territory operates in the international legal order as more than merely 'a geographical conception relating to physical areas of the globe'.[35] Here it helps to think of territory not as an inert terrain in relation to the dynamic conception of sovereignty, but rather as a political technology itself, as Elden suggests:

> Territory should be understood as a political technology, or perhaps better as a bundle of political technologies. Territory is not simply land, in the political-economic sense of rights of use appropriation, and possession attached to a place; nor is it a narrowly political-strategic question that is closer to a notion of terrain. Territory comprises techniques for measuring land and controlling terrain. Measure and control – the technical and the legal – need to be thought alongside land and terrain.[36]

Here Elden is concerned with unveiling historical forms of territorial technologies, from cartographic practices and means of surveying to conceptual ways of seeing territory. Elsewhere he addresses the territorial dimensions of the 'war on terror', claiming that '[s]overeignty over territory became both a privilege and a liability: a privilege for dominant powers who invoke it as a legitimation for self-defence; a liability for states that have nonstate actors operating within their boundaries.'[37] The seemingly de-territorialized 'everywhere war' is *re*-territorialized in specific locations: Afghanistan and Iraq, and later Pakistan, Libya, Yemen and Syria, among others. As Elden observes, the relationship between territory and sovereignty appears to unfold on two different registers. In spaces of alleged terrorist activity the relationship between state and territory is called into question, whereas the sovereign 'homeland' continues to shore up its own borders. In this

[31] Aalberts 2014, at 787.

[32] Munro 2014, at 234.

[33] Aalberts and Werner 2011, at 2185. Their article addresses the UN Counterterrorism Committee as one institutional site where state disciplining takes place.

[34] For an account of the mandate system in relation to African decolonization, see Grovogui 1996.

[35] Shaw 1982, at 61.

[36] Elden 2013, 322–323.

[37] Elden 2009, at 3.

way the global legal imaginary of sovereign states is separated *de facto* into actual sovereigns, on the one hand, and contingent sovereigns on the other.

This chapter's central concern lies with the apparent permeability of borders in contemporary discourses and practices of intervention, especially among Western powers. Here sovereignty as territorial integrity is invoked and recast by state legal advisors, diplomats, and scholars, who employ terms and principles from international law even while disregarding the content of the law itself. Some critical commentators have termed this 'lawfare', or 'the waging of war by law'.[38] Yet legal language is not self-executing as a form of war; as philosopher J.L. Austin observed, speech acts require uptake and the meeting of certain 'felicity conditions' in order to take effect.[39] Furthermore, the legal status of some of these expressions remains in dispute, and are often aspirational rather than settled law. 'Normfare' may be a less compelling but more accurate term. Indeed, many of the rhetorical efforts that seek to unsettle conventional understandings of territory for political aims are not international law as such, but they ape its signifiers, logics, and material expressions of practice—such as diplomatic communications, legal memoranda, and argumentative structures—in order to appear more authoritative.

The phrase 'contingent sovereignty' is one such claim that confusingly operates as both a policy prescription or aspiring legal norm as well as a critical description or diagnosis. On the one hand, the phrase has an aspirational life as a legal form. A U.S. State Department official explained it in 2004 as an emerging doctrine:

> Historically, the main obstacle to armed intervention – humanitarian or otherwise – has been the doctrine of sovereignty, which prohibits violating the territorial integrity of another state. One of the striking developments of the past decade has been an erosion of this non-intervention norm and the rise of a nascent doctrine of 'contingent sovereignty.' This school of thought holds that sovereign rights and immunities are not absolute. They depend on the observance of fundamental state obligations.[40]

On the other hand, the phrase is used critically to describe efforts to undermine territorial integrity. In diagnosing this affront to territorial sovereignty as traditionally understood, Elden traces these conceptions not only through the arguments of U.S. neoconservatives concerning security objectives, but also shows their emergence in the language of U.N. actors on humanitarian grounds, arguing that "'contingent sovereignty', in both its humanitarian and security guises, profoundly affects the question of territorial integrity'.[41] Building upon these insights from political geography, where contingent sovereignty is used as a critical diagnosis, the following section explores arguments about security within the international legal imaginary: the broader discursive field in which international law operates, not only appearing in legal doctrine but also in the various ways in which the international legal order is envisioned and invoked.

---

[38] Kennedy 2006, at 12. On the different framings of the concept, see Werner 2011.

[39] Austin 1962.

[40] Patrick 2004, as noted in Elden 2006, at 15.

[41] Elden 2006, at 21.

4.3 Drone Warfare, Targeted Killing, and Territorial Incursions

> The drone counters the terrestrial forms of territorial sovereignty, founded upon the enclosure of land, with the continuity of the air above. [...] By becoming stratospheric, an imperial power alters its relationship to space. It now becomes a matter not so much of occupying a territory as of controlling it from above by ensuring its mastery of the skies.[42]

In *Drone Theory*, philosopher Grégoire Chamayou traces the historical emergence of the drone in aerial warfare, from its use as a reconnaissance technology to its deployment in targeted killing. The text contends that the spatial aspect of sovereignty must now be understood not only territorially, but also as three-dimensional and volumetric. Military practices such as the U.S. conception of the 'kill box' enable air-based elements to interact with terrestrial targets within a cube structure that can be opened or closed within a territory. Chamayou argues that this conceptual structure 'makes it possible to envisage extending such a model beyond the zones of declared conflict. Depending on the contingencies of the moment, temporary lethal microcubes could be opened up anywhere in the world if an individual who qualifies as a legitimate target has been located there.'[43]

Because the kill box's zone of armed conflict can be reduced to the body of a targeted individual, the battlespace becomes a mobile and shifting terrain that transgresses state borders, at times without state consent. As the U.S. maintains that its continuing non-international armed conflict with al-Qaeda and its affiliates extends to where participants travel, the kill box can pierce the veil of sovereignty, with material effects on a state's territory. It may be opened within sovereign territory through the targeting state's assertion of a direct relationship with the targeted individual, unmediated by concerns with their nationality and location. As one critic recently observed, 'targeted killing is deployed in an American homeland which is the planet'.[44]

This recasting of the territorial relationship emerged through a number of shifts in U.S. military and political policy that prefigured the congressional authorisation of force in September 2001. For example, a 1998 report by two lieutenant colonels in the U.S. army and army reserve, then security fellows at MIT and Harvard University, argued that '[t]o win in the twenty-first century battlespace', the army needed to shift to the vertical dimension to foster 'mobility across inhospitable

---

[42] Chamayou 2015, at 53.

[43] Ibid., at 56.

[44] Gunneflo 2016, at 82. In its December 2016 Report on the Legal and Policy Frameworks Guiding the United States' Use of Military Force and Related National Security Operations', the U.S. government contends by contrast that '[t]he unable or unwilling standard is not a license to wage war globally or to disregard the borders and territorial integrity of other States.' Available at https://www.justsecurity.org/wp-content/uploads/2016/12/framework.Report_Final.pdf, accessed 17 January 2017, at 10.

terrain, the ability to observe the enemy with exceptional clarity, and the ability to maneuver and strike with great precision over ranges beyond those of our current tank and gun tube artillery systems.'[45] Claiming this shift would provide an asymmetrical advantage over ground-bound armies, the report's authors present terrestrial space as an obstacle to be overcome through moving to three-dimensional battlespace. The text is an artefact of a particular political dream: that the gaze of the army, the military's most terrestrial form, would be broadened through verticality, developing techniques that enable it to 'observe the enemy with exceptional clarity'. Contemporary drone-mounted technologies of visualisation such as the 'Gorgon Stare' system, developed to produce a view of an entire area through multiple cameras operating at the same time, suggest a prospective fulfilment of this dream.[46] The weaponised drone brings surveillance together with the capacity for lethal force, which is translated into military practice through targeted killing, the sanitised term used to designate extrajudicial assassination.

Much has been written about the international legal implications of the rise of targeted killing through drone warfare, particularly in relation to IHL and human rights.[47] The academic literature is far too extensive to review for the purposes of this chapter. Yet it is noteworthy that prevailing approaches tend to address the territorial dimensions of targeted killing as an aside to more overtly legal questions, such as lawfulness of the recourse to force under the UN Charter, determining the nature of the armed conflict and the status of combatants, and the rights and duties of different parties.[48] Where geographical dimensions appear, they are framed in relation to these questions, as when Schmitt argues for a geographically unrestricted approach to the applicability of IHL.[49] Some debates focus on the extent to which drone warfare amounts to a new form of violence or whether it forms part of a historical continuum;[50] others have argued that there are 'few issues unique' to this technological form that are not already covered by IHL.[51] Sociolegal scholarship has noted the agentic role of drones as actants and their effect on the production of legal expertise, as well as the mutually constitutive relationship between the practice of

[45] Halblieb and Earley 1998, at 2 and 3.

[46] As envisioned, the Gorgon Stare would enable a four kilometre square picture capable of revealing objects as small as six inches. On this surveillance system's failures, see Cockburn 2015.

[47] See for example the 2010 special issue of the Journal of Law, Information & Science on 'Unmanned vehicles, legal, social and ethical issues' (including a commentary by Philip Alston), and the 2015 special issue of the International Journal of Human Rights on drone warfare.

[48] For example, Kevin Jon Heller evaluates the legality of 'signature strikes' under IHL and IHRL (Heller 2013); Mahmood Ahmad addresses the legality of drone use outside the combat zone (Ahmad 2014); Rebecca Sanders considers the extent to which international laws are able to constrain state practices of targeted killing (Sanders 2014).

[49] 'IHL applicability in NIACs is unconstrained geographically'; see Schmitt 2014, at 19.

[50] See the exchange between Kahn 2013 and Moyn 2013.

[51] Schmitt 2012, at 596. Schmitt argues that the means have little bearing upon the legal implications of the acts, which could be legally analogous if carried out through other forms of weaponry. Michael Boyle claims that the policies – such as anticipatory self-defense – are more relevant than the means; see Boyle 2015.

targeted killing and law.[52] Much commentary has observed the 'blurring' between the sub-fields of international law, as when the UN Special Rapporteur on extrajudicial, summary, or arbitrary executions characterises targeted killings as 'a highly problematic blurring and expansion of the boundaries of the applicable legal frameworks'.[53] Others have pointed out the blurring of lines between different parts of the armed forces and the CIA in the U.S. context. One commentator contends that a claim by the director of the National Counterterrorism Centre—that it matters little whether an operation is carried out by the armed forces, the CIA, or the Joint Special Operations Command (JSOC) as long as it is most legally advantageous—reveals how these indistinctions between actors and roles are becoming normalised.[54]

Some critics have claimed that the line between warfare and policing is also increasingly unsettled through drone warfare and targeted killing. Here the territorial implications are more clear: as political philosopher Mark Neocleous observes, 'what becomes possible with the drone is permanent police presence across the territory'.[55] Long noted in critical theory,[56] the view of contemporary warfare as a police operation has been made increasingly explicit by military actors. For example, the U.S. Army and Marine Corps manual was updated for the first time in a quarter of a century in 2006; it now states that 'warfighting and policing are dynamically linked'.[57] Other scholars have drawn upon Carl Schmitt's argument in *The Nomos of the Earth* concerning the technological imbalances of air power to illustrate how the use of drones transforms asymmetrical warfare into a 'policing action and the adversary becomes a criminal or a mere object of violent reprisal.'[58] Chamayou points out how targeted killing proponent Kenneth Anderson appears to subtly suggest a 'curious legal hybrid, somewhere between warfare and policing', moving away from the contested frame of self-defence, 'that could benefit from the liberalities of both regimes without being obliged to accept the constraints of either.'[59] Conceptualising targeted killing and drone warfare as policing suggests an immanent frame, where there is no territorial space beyond the 'everywhere war'. It also suggests an entrenched asymmetry, justified by the police mandate to enforce order within this frame while bearing the monopoly of force. In this sense it is far from the traditional understanding of warfare as a contest between enemies.

---

52 Leander 2013 and Krasmann 2012.

53 Alston P, Report of the Special Rapporteur on extrajudicial, summary, or arbitrary executions, Study on targeted killings, UN Doc. A/HRC/14/24/Add.6, 28 May 2010, para 3.

54 Leander 2013, at 819.

55 Neocleous 2013, at 590.

56 Hardt and Negri 2000, at 12: 'war is reduced to the status of police action', with the U.S. at the centre.

57 As noted in Neocleous 2011, at 146.

58 Hussain 2013. Chamayou makes a similar observation, drawing upon Schmitt: 'The verticalization of armed violence implies a tendency toward the absolute hostilization of the enemy, both politically and juridically. He is no longer positioned, in any sense of the term, on the same ground as oneself.' Chamayou 2015, at 166.

59 Chamayou 2015, at 172.

The 2011 assassination of Anwar al-Awlaki illustrates how drone warfare extends the battlespace beyond the territory of active conflict. Awlaki was a dual U.S.-Yemeni citizen whose targeting became the topic of extensive legal deliberations. As a consequence of his citizenship, he would be entitled to constitutional protections, which were outlined in a confidential memorandum from the U.S. Department of Justice.[60] Yet Awlaki was regarded as an enemy combatant fighting for Al Qaeda of the Arabian Peninsula in a continuing non-international armed conflict with the U.S.[61] This assumes a legal construction that builds upon the 2001 Authorization for Use of Military Force (AUMF), a temporally boundless assertion of force that has been interpreted to extend the conflict to foreign countries outside the area of active hostilities.[62] It also relies upon an interpretation of self-defence under international law that presumes an individual poses an 'imminent threat of violent attack'.[63] Awlaki was killed in Yemen in a 2011 drone strike conducted jointly by the CIA and the U.S. military's Joint Special Operations Command, an event foretold by his addition to the 'disposition matrix', colloquially known as the 'kill list'.

Although the operations were carried out with the consent of Yemen, and thus not formally in violation of its sovereignty, U.S. legal memoranda and official speeches indicate that it could have been conducted even without the state's consent. One military official observed that the Yemeni government 'could not effectively govern the entire state' and that, 'when faced with the dilemma of a U.S. ultimatum, Yemen sought to cooperate rather than resist'.[64] This claim that ineffective internal sovereignty may justify intervention forms part of a broader reconfiguration of the relationship between sovereignty and territory as imagined in

[60] The memorandum concludes that there are no constitutional barriers to taking lethal action because 'the U.S. citizen in question has gone overseas and become part of the forces of an enemy with which the United States is engaged in an armed conflict, that person is engaged in continual planning and direction of attacks upon U.S. persons from one of the enemy's overseas bases of operations; the U.S. government does not know when such attacks will occur; and a capture operation would be infeasible.' See U.S. Department of Justice Office of Legal Counsel, 'Memorandum for the Attorney General re: Applicability of Federal Criminal Laws and the Constitution to Contemplated Legal Operations Against Shaykh Anwar al-Aulaqi', 16 July 2010, at 39.

[61] Kevin Jon Heller asserts that there is no armed conflict in this instance because 'the "combat" is not even close to being sufficiently protracted or intense', and Awlaki was not connected to the non-international armed conflicts in Afghanistan or Pakistan. Heller 2011, at 183.

[62] The Authorization for Use of Military Force (AUMF) states that 'the President is authorized to use all necessary and appropriate force against those nations, organizations or persons he determines planned, authorized, committed or aided the terrorist attacks that occurred on September 11, 2001, or harbored such organizations or persons, in order to prevent any future acts of international terrorism against the United States by such nations, organizations, or persons.' 107th Congress Public Law 40, Joint Resolution, 18 September 2001.

[63] This is highly contested in international legal scholarship. For an effort to establish principles governing a state's right to self-defence against an imminent attack, see Bethlehem 2012.

[64] Hendrickson 2014, at 18. Hendrickson was a major in the U.S. Air Force at the time of writing.

U.S. political and legal discourse. A leaked 2011 Department of Justice white paper addressing the legality of Awlaki's targeting asserts that

> a lethal operation in a foreign nation would be consistent with international legal principles of sovereignty and neutrality if it were conducted, for example, with the consent of the host nation's government or after a determination that the host nation is unable or unwilling to suppress the threat posed by the individual targeted.[65]

This position was reiterated in a public speech by the U.S. Attorney General in 2012, who claimed that 'the use of force in foreign territory would be consistent with these international legal principles if conducted, for example, with the consent of the nation involved—or after a determination that the nation is unable or unwilling to deal effectively with a threat to the United States.'[66] The following year, then-President Obama himself explained that, despite a 'strong preference for the detention and prosecution of terrorists, sometimes this approach is foreclosed' in certain contexts. He gave the example that in parts of Somalia and Yemen, 'the state only has the most tenuous reach into that territory. In other cases, the state lacks the capacity or will to take action.'[67] With this focus on internal or positive sovereignty, the map of the world appears divided between 'effective states' that exercise control over their territories and those who do not. Some have even referred to the latter as 'fictitious states', in that they do not fulfil the underlying UN Charter-based assumption of a central authority projecting territorial control.[68]

Just as territorial control is regarded by 'unwilling or unable' proponents as a fiction undergirding the UN Charter system, one might make a similar claim about the notion of consent. Awlaki's assassination was carried out with state consent, as then-President Saleh had granted permission for the U.S. to conduct counterterrorism operations within the territory of Yemen.[69] Yet as has been publicly acknowledged, the U.S. would have acted—and indeed has acted—without securing consent, as it did with the 2011 killing of Osama bin Laden in the territory of Pakistan. President Obama expressly invoked the 'unwilling or unable' theory in relation to Pakistan in a 2008 presidential debate.[70] Whether a determination about

[65] United States Department of Justice 2011, at 1–2.

[66] Holder 2012.

[67] Obama 2013.

[68] 'These entities are not states that 'failed' but rather territories where the paradigm of traditional statehood is inapplicable.' Finucane 2012, at 35. The article's author went on to work as an attorney-adviser for the U.S. Department of State.

[69] This consent was documented in the most recent Report on the Legal and Policy Frameworks Guiding the United States' Use of Military Force and Related National Security Operations' of December 2016, at 22; available at https://www.justsecurity.org/wp-content/uploads/2016/12/framework.Report_Final.pdf, accessed 17 January 2017.

[70] Stated in a presidential debate on 28 September 2008, 'If Pakistan is unable or unwilling to act' against al-Qaida leaders, 'then we should take them out.' https://www.youtube.com/watch?v=LqOncFQUZsw, accessed 10 January 2017. As noted by Deeks 2012, at 485.

each state's willingness and ability was in fact carried out is unclear.[71] Even if it were, the nature of that analysis has not been established as a matter of international law, and the status of the 'unwilling or unable' theory as an international legal form is heavily disputed.

As a rhetorical tactic for justifying territorial incursions, the 'unwilling or unable' theory has been advanced in academic circles, by state actors, and before the United Nations. As critics have pointed out, the phrase has no status as international law.[72] Yet as J.L. Austin observed about how utterances gain force and conventions take hold: 'we even have the case of procedures which someone is initiating. Sometimes he may "get away with it" like, in football, the man who first picked up the ball and ran.'[73] The theory has gathered force through further iterations, suggesting that some of its proponents may 'get away' with casting it as a legal standard despite its tentative emergence at the intersection of scholarship and policy.[74] In an article that attempts to ground the 'unwilling and unable' argument in a history of state practice, for example, Deeks refers to it as a 'test', going so far as to assert that 'it is possible that the test has become customary international law'.[75] Even if the 'test' has no substantive content and gives no procedural guidance, as Deeks herself points out, referring to the 'unwilling and unable' argument in such a way already elevates it to something beyond mere political assertion.[76] Others have treated the international legality of the theory as a *fait accompli*. Describing what he claims is both the U.S. position as well as his own, Schmitt argues:

[71] Deeks presumes it can be inferred in the Pakistan example, but there is no evidence that it was carried out for Yemen. Deeks 2012, at 485 and 500.

[72] Corten 2016. See also Kevin Jon Heller's criticisms on *Opinio Juris* regarding the lack of supporting state practice and the scholarly (re)production of the concept: Heller KJ (2015) The Absence of Practice Supporting the "Unwilling or Unable" Test, http://opiniojuris.org/2015/02/17/unable-unwilling-test-unstoppable-scholarly-imagination, accessed 10 January 2017; and Heller KJ (2015) The Seemingly Inexorable March of "Unwilling or Unable" Through the Academy, http://opiniojuris.org/2015/03/06/the-seemingly-inexorable-march-of-unwilling-or-unable-through-the-academy, accessed 10 January 2017.

[73] Austin 1962, at 30.

[74] Corten traces its emergence back to the Chatham House 'Principles of International Law on the Use of Force by States in Self Defence' (2006) and the more recent Leiden Policy Recommendations on Counter-terrorism and International Law (2010). Corten 2016, at 778. The U.S. recently referred to 'unwilling or unable' as a 'legal standard'; see Report on the Legal and Policy Frameworks Guiding the United States' Use of Military Force and Related National Security Operations' of December 2016, at 10.

[75] Deeks 2012, at 503.

[76] Carsten Stahn also identified a 'trend', building upon the 'overall control' test adopted by the ICTY Appeals Chamber in the *Tadic* case. 'If it becomes evident that the host state is unable or unwilling to act, the injured may, as an *ultima ratio* measure, take military action to stop the persisting threat', noting that it is doctrinally based on conceptualizing sovereignty as responsibility, and the 'relative character of territorial integrity'. Stahn 2003, at 47.

> if the sanctuary State fails to remedy the situation because it is either unwilling to do so (perhaps out of sympathy for the attackers) or unable to do so (for instance, due to a lack of the necessary military equipment), the victim State, in realization of its right of self-defence, may cross into the sanctuary State's territory for the sole purpose of defending itself.[77]

Schmitt's example of inability relates to military capacity, hinting at another variable, the economic dimension of this assessment. If states assessing unwillingness or inability have some of the most developed military capacities in the world, and particularly in the absence of agreed standards, it would seem that the theory easily devolves into political opportunism. As with the broader contemporary discourse of 'asymmetric warfare' into which this argument fits, powerful states are presented as vulnerable victims, further justifying a militarist moral economy.[78]

The unwilling branch of the claim appears problematic as a matter of law, since the designation immediately opens the political question of whether a 'sanctuary' state may refuse to support the political objectives of the 'victim' state. The categories themselves can depend upon future wagers presented as present realities: for example, Awlaki is designated as the author of attacks that he *will have* accomplished through a future perfect grammatical construction that is reformulated as an 'imminent threat'. This temporal sleight of hand is one dimension of contemporary efforts to refigure the terms of intervention. Although 'unwilling' states are typically cast as illiberal, one can imagine a state that could refuse to accept the counterinsurgency action against Awlaki on their territory on the basis of liberal precepts, including the principle of legality, in resisting this future perfect logic of imminent threat.

In spite of its indeterminate nature, both in content and application, the 'unwilling and unable' theory has since been explicitly invoked in letters from the U. S., Canada, Australia, and Turkey to the United Nations as forming part of their justifications for intervening in Syrian territory to combat the Islamic State of Iraq and the Levant (ISIL).[79] These interventions took place in spite of Syrian objections that they constituted violations of the state's sovereignty. Furthermore, as Corten observes, they also appeared to tacitly weaken the UN Charter Article 2(4) restriction on the use of force by presuming that Syria had an objective responsibility to end ISIL's activities that was not met, thereby justifying intervention: 'Syria was not criticized for having instigated and acquiesced to ISIL activities, nor for tolerating them, but simply for having not *succeeded* in defeating this terrorist group.'[80] Sovereignty is figured as a responsibility to exert territorial control rather

---

[77] Schmitt 2013, at 86–87.

[78] Yves Winter has shown how the discourse of asymmetric warfare 'tends to moralize and depoliticize contemporary conflict constellations'; further, '[t]he asymmetric sleight of hand is that the actors rendered most vulnerable to asymmetric warfare are the most powerful states, those with the largest militaries and most sophisticated technologies and weapons systems.' Winter 2011, at 490 and 496.

[79] Corten 2016, at 780; Bannelier-Christakis 2016, at 767.

[80] Corten 2016, at 792.

than as a right to non-intervention; as Amitai Etzioni argues in a recent articulation of 'unwilling or unable', 'states should be expected to prevent terrorists from using their territories. If they do not or cannot live up to this responsibility, they give up the relevant part of their sovereignty claims.'[81] This argumentative structure follows the logic of the 'responsibility to protect', another form of contingent sovereignty that is conditioned upon a state's capacity to protect its own population. Just as a state's failure to protect permits a breach of its territorial integrity, so too with a failure to prevent terrorist threats emanating from its territory.[82]

A key distinction lies with the population perceived to be at risk. In the first (humanitarian) instance with the 'responsibility to protect', threats to the population of another state trigger a third-party state intervention. In the second (security) instance with the 'unwilling or unable' claim, the population of the *intervening* state is seen to be threatened by action on another state's territory. The trait of vulnerability moves from a population threatened proximately and internally to a population facing external threats, possibly from a great distance. This militarily privileged population is supported by a state that not only exercises effective control within its own territory but is also capable of intervening abroad to mitigate threats. Chamayou describes this as a general vitalist logic that moves swiftly to the particular: 'the humanitarian imperative is to save lives. And the drone does indeed save *our* lives.'[83] As a technology of territorial control, the opening of a kill box privileges the lives of remote populations over those more proximate to the threat that animates the intervention. The 'unwilling or unable' argument similarly moves from a general premise—the territorial obligations that sovereignty implies, such as the obligation to exercise effective control—to a particular conclusion, that the threats to *our* population are more consequential than the threats to the population subjected to and bearing the burden of an intervention.

Practices such as drone warfare and political discourses such as 'unwilling or unable' are consequential for the relationship between sovereignty and territory. Through drone warfare, states project power across territorial lines and over the populations contained within them, who are subjected to the *de facto* collective punishment of an intensified surveillance that structures daily life through unseen but audible threats from above.[84] Foucault's triangulation of 'security, territory,

---

[81] Etzioni 2016, at 17.

[82] The Obama administration claimed that acting in this instance 'entails assessing whether the territorial state is able and willing to mitigate the threat emanating from its territory'. Report on the Legal and Policy Frameworks Guiding the United States' Use of Military Force and Related National Security Operations' of December 2016, at 10.

[83] Chamayou 2015, at 136.

[84] Nasser Hussain observed that '[b]ecause drones are able to hover at or above 30 thousand feet, they are mostly invisible to the people below them. But they can be heard. Many people from the tribal areas of Pakistan (FATA) describe the sound as a low-grade, perpetual buzzing, a signal that a strike could occur at any time. The locals call the drones *machar*, mosquitos. Because the drone can surveil the area for hours at a time, and because each round of surveillance may or may not result in a strike, the fear and anxiety among civilians is diffuse and chronic.' Hussain 2013. See also the Stanford and NYU Law School study 'Living Under Drones'; Cavallaro et al. 2012.

population' reminds us that these terms should be thought together.[85] In international law, however, the third term tends to be overshadowed by the first two. Although the population is fundamental to the grant of sovereignty in political theory, it recedes in state-centric international legal conceptions of sovereignty, which are bound up with security as the sovereign's objective and territory as its spatial aspect. A state may consent or not to drone operations within its territory, but the lived reality is reserved for the populations inhabiting those locations where the state's capacity to project power is considered weak. As a rhetorical form, the 'unwilling or unable' theory is an argument for bringing remote power into proximity, allowing territorial control to be exercised from elsewhere. But as a temporary measure with a particular security agenda, it is premised upon the principle that some populations will endure these incursions for the benefit of others.

4.4 Conclusion: Cartographies of Contingent Sovereignty

> In the modern conception, state sovereignty is fully, flatly and evenly operative over each square centimetre of a legally demarcated territory. But in the older imagining, where states were defined by centres, borders were porous and indistinct, and sovereignties faded imperceptively into one another.[86]

Benedict Anderson described the distinction between modern and pre-modern approaches to sovereignty as if studying the making of a map. Through this optic, modern sovereignty's territorial dimension appears full and flat, whereas pre-modern sovereignty is represented as porous and overlapping. The cartographies of our political present appear to unsettle this historical distinction between pre-modern and modern statehood, along with the modern legal analogue of Westphalian sovereignty. As an articulation of contingent sovereignty, the 'unwilling or unable' theory divides the international order into states that can adequately handle threats of force and those who cannot, either due to a lack of will or capacity. The hinge on which this division turns is effective territorial control, itself a product of many historical, geopolitical, and economic factors. As a political claim masquerading as a legal standard, 'unwilling or unable' reorients the international legal imaginary. It shifts its starting premise from a field of uniformly sovereign states toward a relative orientation, where states appear in relation to one another according to their capacity to project territorial control and uphold shared security priorities. In many ways this logic marks a political realist appropriation of international legal forms. Perhaps more accurately, and as some critics have noted,

---

[85] Foucault 2007.

[86] Anderson 2006, at 19.

it represents a hierarchical thinking much like the 'standard of civilization' discourse that shaped earlier legal theory and practice.[87]

The cartographic representation of this reoriented world picture might begin as a sheet of porous tracing paper with existing territorial boundaries pencilled in. From a well of ink below, the paper would then gather colour that fills in the contours of the territory in relation to the state's ability to project control across it. Unfilled spaces become subject to the spreading ink from neighbouring states, and indeed, from states far across the map if their respective wells of ink are large enough. Yet this cartographic projection does not indicate what territorial control is and how it can be measured and assessed. It would seem that in the dominant framing, control is quickly conflated with the capacity to use force, as opposed to other ways that a state may project power—through administrative frameworks, for example, or governing movement across territory. Inability is then read in relation to policing and military capacity, with the former marked by the projection of ink across the territory and the latter by the ability to keep foreign ink from entering into the territory. Indeed, Deeks describes the most straightforward example of inability in terms of military and police: 'A state that has very limited military and police forces and no control over broad swaths of its territory almost certainly is "unable" to suppress a large and sophisticated set of nonstate actors acting in that ungoverned area.'[88] In this imagined map, 'broad swaths' of 'ungoverned' territory are open to security interventions from elsewhere, as is reflected in the Security Council's 2015 resolution calling on states to 'take all necessary measures…to redouble and coordinate their efforts to prevent and suppress terrorist acts' in Syrian territory.[89] As Elden claims, 'the complete or partial absence of sovereign power has been rescripted as a global danger, justifying intervention.'[90] Here it is evident how territory operates as a political technology, as the register in which effective

[87] Ntina Tzouvala (2016) persuasively draws upon James Lorimer's late-nineteenth century distinction between civilized, semi-civilized and uncivilized states to argue that 'the "unwilling or unable" doctrine replicates this hierarchy, directly adopting certain "civilization" criteria, such as the existence of a strong effective centralized state with a certain level and a certain mode of control over its territory. Mark Neocleous (2011) contends that the 'war on terror' has led to the return of 'civilization' as a category of international power. And according to anthropologist Hugh Gusterson, drones 'can be used only against countries that lack the technological sophistication to shoot down the slow-moving planes and whose internal affairs, conforming to Western stereotypes of "failed states", provide a pretext for incursion that is as persuasive to liberal interventionists today as the white man's burden was to their Victorian ancestors.' Gusterson 2016, at 148.

[88] Deeks 2012, at 505. Elsewhere she claims '[a]ssuming that most states have inherent incentives to avoid violations of their sovereignty, this might mean that a territorial state has stronger incentives to improve its ability to suppress nonstate threats by having adequate criminal laws on its books and strong, noncorrupt law enforcement and military forces' (509–510).

[89] UNSC Resolution 2249 on 20 November 2015. Here as well, much commentary addresses whether or not the Security Council was acting under Chapter VII powers in authorising the use of force without addressing the conception of territory the resolution presents, which casts a global landscape of ISIS activity (Sousse, Ankara, Sinai, Beirut, Paris) emanating from uncontrolled Syrian state territory to justify the use of force.

[90] Elden 2009, at 69.

statehood is measured. The uncoloured—and thus ungoverned—surfaces on the map then offer themselves to the military gaze.

This cartography draws upon a set of presumptions in the international legal imaginary that produce and re-produce a view of compromised or contingent sovereignty.[91] Here sovereignty appears measurable, open to evaluation on at least two registers. In the humanitarian register, it has been recast in terms of responsibility—the responsibility to protect the population.[92] In the security register considered here, it is tied to territorial control. These two dimensions appear to intersect in a remarkable but underexplored claim contained in the text of the 2011 U.S. Department of Justice white paper. The lawfulness of the operation against Awlaki, which the text argues could be undertaken with or without Yemen's consent, was derived in part from 'the President's constitutional responsibility to protect the nation'.[93] Here the sovereign responsibility to protect its population is detached from territorial considerations, and the ink from one state's well of territorial control floods the map entirely.

References

Aalberts T (2012) Constructing Sovereignty Between Politics and Law. Routledge, London

Aalberts T (2014) Rethinking the Principle of (Sovereign) Equality as a Standard of Civilization. Millenium: Journal of International Studies 42:767–789

Aalberts T, Werner W (2011) Mobilizing Uncertainties and the Making of Responsible Sovereigns. Review of International Studies 37:2183–2200

Agnew J (1994) The Territorial Trap: The Geographical Assumptions of International Relations Theory. Review of International Political Economy 1:53–80

Agnew J (2010) Still Trapped in Territory? Geopolitics 15:779–784

Ahmad M (2014) The Legality of Unmanned Aerial Vehicles Outside the Combat Zone: A Case Study of the Federally Administered Tribal Areas of Pakistan. Defense and Security Analysis 30:245–253

Anderson B (2006) Imagined Communities: Reflections on the Origin and Spread of Nationalism. Verso Books, London

Anghie A (2005) Imperialism, Sovereignty and the Making of International Law. Cambridge University Press, Cambridge

Austin J L (1962) How to Do Things with Words. Harvard University Press, Cambridge

Bannelier-Christakis K (2016) Military Interventions against ISIL in Iraq, Syria and Libya, and the Legal Basis of Consent. Leiden Journal of International Law 29:743–775

Bartelsen J (2014) Sovereignty as Symbolic Form. Routledge, New York

[91] Jens Bartelsen observes that 'sovereignty has been turned into something granted, contingent upon its responsible exercise in accordance with the norms of an imagined international community.' Bartelson 2014, at 97.

[92] On the implications of 'responsibility to protect' for territorial integrity, see Elden 2009, 151–165; more generally see Duffield 2007. On the nexus between responsibility to protect and interventionism, see Mamdani 2010.

[93] United States Department of Justice 2011, at 2.

Beck U (2002) The Terrorist Threat: World Risk Society Revisited. Theory, Culture and Society 19:39–55
Bethlehem D (2012) Self-Defense Against an Imminent or Actual Armed Attack by Nonstate Actors. American Journal of International Law 106:769–776
Boyle M (2015) The legal and ethical implications of drone warfare. International Journal of Human Rights 2:105–126
Brown W (2010) Walled States, Waning Sovereignty. Zone Books, Boston
Chamayou G (2015) Drone Theory. Penguin Books, London
Cavallaro J, Sonnenberg S, Knuckey S (2012) Living Under Drones: Death, Injury and Trauma to Civilians from US Drone Practices in Pakistan. International Human Rights and Conflict Resolution Clinic, Stanford Law School, Stanford; NYU School of Law, Global Justice Clinic, New York
Cockburn A (2015) Kill Chain: Drones and the Rise of High-Tech Assassins. Verso Books, London
Corten O (2016) The 'Unwilling or Unable' Test: Has it Been, and Could it Be, Accepted? Leiden Journal of International Law 29:777–799
Deeks A (2012) 'Unwilling or Unable': Toward a Normative Framework for Extraterritorial Self-Defense. Virginia Journal of International Law 52:483–550
Derrida J (1998) Archive Fever: A Freudian Impression. University of Chicago Press, Chicago
Desautels-Stein J (2015) Structuralist Legal Histories. Law and Contemporary Problems 78:37–59
Duffield M (2007) Development, Security and Unending War. Polity, Cambridge
Dreyfus H, Rabinow P (1982) Michel Foucault: Beyond Structuralism and Hermeneutics. University of Chicago Press, Chicago
Elden S (2006) Contingent Sovereignty, Territorial Integrity, and the Sanctity of Borders. SAIS Review 26:11–24
Elden S (2009) Terror and Territory: The Spatial Extent of Sovereignty. University of Minnesota Press, Minneapolis
Elden S (2010) Thinking Territory Historically. Geopolitics 15:757–761
Elden S (2013) The Birth of Territory. University of Chicago Press, Chicago
Etzioni A (2016) Defining Down Sovereignty: The Rights and Responsibilities of Nations. Ethics and International Affairs 30:5–20
Finucane B (2012) Fictitious States, Effective Control, and the Use of Force Against Non-State Actors. Berkeley Journal of International Law 30:35–93
Foucault M (1977) Discipline and Punish: The Birth of the Prison. Pantheon, New York
Foucault M (2007) Security, Territory, Population: Lectures at the Collège de France 1997–1978. Palgrave Macmillan, Basingstoke
Garland D (2014) What is a 'History of the Present'? On Foucault's Genealogies and Their Critical Preconditions. Punishment & Society 16:365–384
Gregory D (2004) The Colonial Present. Blackwell, Oxford
Gregory D (2011) The Everywhere War. The Geographical Journal. 177(3):238–250
Gregory D (2013) Dis/Ordering the Orient: Scopic Regimes and Modern War. In: Barkawi T, Stanski K (eds) Orientalism and War, Oxford University Press, Oxford, pp 151–176
Grovogui S (1996) Sovereigns, Quasi Sovereigns, and Africans: Race and Self-determination in International Law. University of Minnesota Press, Minneapolis
Gunneflo M (2016) Targeted Killing. Cambridge University Press, Cambridge
Gusterson H (2016) Drone: Remote Control Warfare. MIT University Press, Boston
Halblieb R, Earley M (1998) Transition to the Vertical Dimension: Advancing Airfighting Vehicles – The Army's Future Fighting Force. Carlisle Barracks, U.S. Army War College/ Harvard University, Cambridge
Handl G, Zekoll J, Zumbansen P (eds) (2012) Beyond Territoriality: Transnational Legal Authority in an Age of Globalization. Martinus Nijhoff, Leiden
Hardt M, Negri A (2000) Empire. Harvard University Press, Cambridge
Heller KJ (2011) Targeted Killing: The Case of Anwar Al-Aulaqi. University of Pennsylvania Law Review 159:175–201

Heller KJ (2013) 'One Hell of a Killing Machine': Signature Strikes and International Law. Journal of International Criminal Justice 11:89–119
Hendrickson E (2014) Just War Theory Applied to US Policy in Pakistan and Yemen. Unpublished monograph, School of Advanced Military Studies, United States Army and Command and General Staff College
Holder E (2012) Attorney General Eric Holder Speech at Northwest University Law School. https://www.justice.gov/opa/speech/attorney-general-eric-holder-speaks-northwestern-university-school-law. Accessed 10 August 2016
Hussain N (2013) The Sound of Terror: Phenomenology of a Drone Strike. Boston Review
Kahn P (2013) Imagining Warfare. European Journal of International Law 24:199–226
Kendall S (2016) On Academic Production and the Politics of Inclusion. Leiden Journal of International Law 29:617–624
Kennedy D (2006) Of War and Law. Princeton University Press, Princeton
Klabbers J (2009) The Bridge Crack'd: A Critical Look at Interdisciplinary Relations. International Relations 23:119–125
Koskenniemi M (2006) From Apology to Utopia. Cambridge University Press, Cambridge
Krasmann S (2012) Targeted Killing and its Law: On a Mutually Constitutive Relationship. Leiden Journal of International Law 25:665–682
Kratochwil F (2012) The Status of Law in World Society: Meditations on the Role and Rule of Law. Cambridge University Press, Cambridge
Kritsiotis D (2009) Introduction: Public International Law and its Territorial Imperative. Michigan Journal of International Law 30:547–566
Leander A (2013) Technological Agency in the Co-Constitution of Legal Expertise and the US Drone Program. Leiden Journal of International Law 26:811–831
Mamdani M (2010) Responsibility to Protect or Right to Punish? Journal of Intervention and Statebuilding 1:53–67
Mawani R (2012) Law's Archive. Annual Review of Law and Social Science 8:337–365
McConnell F (2010) The Fallacy and the Promise of the Territorial Trap: Sovereign Articulations of Geopolitical Anomalies. Geopolitics 15:762–768
Moyn S (2013) Drones and Imagination: A Response to Paul Kahn. European Journal of International Law 24:227–233
Munro C (2014) Mapping the Vertical Battlespace: Toward a Legal Cartography of Aerial Sovereignty. London Review of International Law 2:233–261
Neocleous M (2011) The Police of Civilization: the War on Terror as Civilizing Offensive. International Political Sociology 5:144–159
Neocleous M (2013) Air Power as Police Power. Environment and Planning D: Society and Space 31:578–593
Obama B (2013) Remarks by the President at the National Defense University. https://www.whitehouse.gov/the-press-office/2013/05/23/remarks-president-national-defense-university. Accessed 10 August 2016
Pahuja S (2011) Decolonizing International Law: Development, Economic Growth, and the Politics of Universality. Cambridge University Press, Cambridge
Patrick S (2004) The Role of the U.S. Government in Humanitarian Intervention. https://2001-2009.state.gov/s/p/rem/31299.htm. Accessed 6 January 2017
Rajah J (2016) Law as Record: the Death of Osama bin Laden. No Foundations: An Interdisciplinary Journal of Law and Justice 13:45–69
Sanders R (2014) Legal Frontiers: Targeted Killing at the Borders of War. Journal of Human Rights 13:512–536
Sassen S (2009) Bordering Capabilities versus Borders: Implications for National Borders. Michigan Journal of International Law 30:567–597
Scharf M (2003) Earned Sovereignty: Juridical Underpinnings. Denver Journal of International Law and Policy 31:373–387

Schmitt M (2012) Unmanned Combat Aircraft Systems and International Humanitarian Law: Simplifying the Oft Benighted Debate. Boston University International Law Journal 30:595–619

Schmitt M (2013) Extraterritorial Lethal Targeting: Deconstructing the Logic of International Law. Columbia Journal of Transnational Law 52:77–112

Schmitt M (2014) Charting the Legal Geography of Non-International Armed Conflict. International Law Studies 90:1–19

Shaw M (1982) Territory in International Law. Netherlands Yearbook of International Law 13:61–91

Stahn C (2003) Terrorist Acts as 'Armed Attack': The Right to Self-Defense, Article 51 (1/2) of the UN Charter, and International Terrorism. Fletcher Forum of World Affairs 27:35–54

Tzouvala N (2016) TWAIL and the 'Unwilling or Unable' Doctrine: Continuities and Ruptures. AJIL Unbound 109. https://www.asil.org/blogs/symposium-twail-perspectives-icl-ihl-and-intervention-twail-and-%E2%80%9Cunwilling-or-unable%E2%80%9D-doctrine. Accessed 15 August 2016

United States Department of Justice (2011) Lawfulness of a Lethal Operation Directed Against a U.S. Citizen Who is a Senior Operational Leader of Al-Qa'ida or an Associated Force. https://www.law.upenn.edu/live/files/1903-doj-white-paper. Accessed 10 August 2016

Werner W (2011) The Curious Career of Lawfare. Case Western Reserve Journal of International Law 43:61–72

Winter Y (2011) The Asymmetric War Discourse and its Moral Economies: A Critique. International Theory 3:488–514

Chapter 5
Data Territories: Changing Architectures of Association in International Law

Fleur Johns

Abstract Territoriality is a powerful architecture of association in international law, performing significant bounding, distributive and placement functions. Yet it has always interacted with other global legal architectures of affiliation and disaffiliation, among them informational geographies. So what becomes of territoriality amid the turn to data analytics—the automated analysis of massive, distributed data sets—as a basis for international legal and policy decision, action, thinking, and prediction? This chapter recounts processes and practices already underway on the global plane that are effecting, on one hand, the 'datafication' of territory (and the related rise of a logic of association) and, on the other, the 'territorialisation' of data (and the emergence or recurrence of 'data territories') in international legal order. Through these kinds of processes, and in its variable configurations, data might yet parallel physical territory (landed and maritime) as a primary medium for the conduct of juridical global life and conflict, a prospect that raises important questions for international law and lawyers.

Keywords Territory · International law · Data analytics · Law and technology

Contents

The author is indebted to Hans Lindahl for conversation about this piece, and to two anonymous reviewers for insightful and instructive comments. Thanks are also due to Dr. Pornsakol Dao Coorey for research assistance.

F. Johns (✉)
University of New South Wales, Sydney, Australia
e-mail: fleur.johns@unsw.edu.au

M. Kuijer and W. Werner (eds.), *Netherlands Yearbook of International Law 2016*, Netherlands Yearbook of International Law 47,
DOI 10.1007/978-94-6265-207-1_5

Writing of the inability of the ancient Greeks or Romans 'to establish, or even conceive of, any other social organization than the city', the nineteenth century French historian Fustel de Coulanges listed some of the near-unthinkable questions that this would have posed for the Ancients, among them: 'What would become of the inviolable limits which had from the beginning marked out the territory of the city, and which separated it forever from the rest of the earth's surface?'[1] It seems, at times, as if international lawyers are similarly challenged by the inconceivability of displacing territory and territorial sovereignty as the primary basis for marking out the earth's surface and organizing its inhabitants in law, even as many announce its declining salience.[2] Yet this is more or less the prospect that the editors of this volume have invited me, alongside others, to contemplate. If not territoriality's wholesale displacement, then we have been asked to consider the prospect of its reconfiguration in profound ways.

Territoriality remains a powerful—probably still the predominant—architecture of association in international legal practice and thinking. Yet it has always interacted with other global legal architectures of affiliation and disaffiliation with which it has often been in tension: the architecture of national and regional currencies, for instance, and of constitutional and international human rights regimes, among others. Premised on continuing interaction between the politico-legal technology of territoriality and other architectures of association on the global plane, this chapter examines shifts and challenges that may be identified with the deployment of technologies of automated data collection, representation and analysis in international law and policy.

The turn to data analytics—and to the analysis of massive, distributed data sets—as a basis for legal and policy decision, action, thinking, and prediction on the global plane is, to a significant extent, already underway, as well as being widely and keenly anticipated to a further degree. This is evidenced, for instance, by the United Nations' inauguration of the UN Global Pulse initiative aimed at harnessing big data for development and humanitarian action; by the championing of 'data for development' in influential settings such as the World Economic Forum; and by the proliferation of literature on so-called 'digital humanitarianism', the 'digitized battlefield' and on the automated assessment or remote detection of environmental

---

[1] Fustel de Coulanges 2006, at 202–203.

[2] See, e.g., Handl 2012, at 4: '[I]n a seemingly borderless world social, economic or environmental problems and their solutions tend to be transnational in nature, or "de-territorialised", thus calling into question territorial sovereignty as a fundamental organising principle of the global legal architecture'.

and health risks.[3] Additional examples of this 'turn' are given throughout this chapter. Among the ramifications of this shift in practice and aspiration are changes —incipient yet nonetheless discernible—in how those who work in and with international law visualize or map distributions of authority and resources, and configure relationships for juridical purposes: changes that amount, actually and prospectively, to a reconfiguration of territoriality in international law.

Contending with the prospect of a reconfiguration of territoriality in international law—and its implications for the field—demands some investigation of what work territoriality has been doing in the international legal field to date. This chapter will begin in Sect. 5.1 by elucidating three key effects that territoriality has had in this context, or three key ways in which territoriality has traditionally operated in international legal work. First, territoriality erects and maintains boundary marks and invests them with some hallowedness; second, territoriality effects a presumptive division of resources, including a distribution of lawful authority; and third, territoriality engenders a sense of relational placement and, in many instances, evokes fealty to that placement, or a sense of its relative obduracy. International legal work may, however, be becoming somewhat less dependent on or guided by territoriality for these purposes, or so this chapter contends. Sections 5.2 and 5.3 of this chapter put forward an argument to that effect. That is, conventional operations of territoriality in the international legal field now operate in parallel to, and may be in the course of being incipiently displaced by, processes that may be grasped, on one hand, in terms of the 'datafication' of territory (and the related rise of a logic of association) and, on the other hand, the 'territorialisation' of data (and the recurrence of patterns that might be thought of as assembling data territories). Sections 5.2 and 5.3 of this chapter describe these concurrent processes of transformation and explain how particular configurations and analyses of data may be transforming or replacing conventional understandings of territoriality as a medium for juridical boundary-marking, distribution, and placement on the global plane. Section 5.4 of this chapter identifies some questions raised for international law and lawyers by the prospect of data displacing or remaking territoriality in the ways described.

5.1 Territoriality in International Law

In his magisterial study of the emergence of the concept of territory in Western political thought, from ancient Greece to the seventeenth century, Stuart Elden reminds us of the following: 'Territory is a word, concept, and practice, and the complicated relation between these three terms can only be grasped with historical, geographical, and conceptual specificity'.[4] The same may be said, with equal cogency, of territoriality, a term denoting the condition or status of territory, as

---

[3] Johns 2013, 2016; Frater and Ryan 2001; Yam 2008; Meier 2015.

[4] Elden 2013, at 328.

much as a protective, proprietary or similar mode of conduct towards territory.[5] Far from positing a general ontology of territory in and for the field of international law, then, this section highlights three types of practice that both constitute territoriality for governmental, administrative and other juridical purposes on the global plane, and attest to its efficacy and significance for international law in particular. The first of these practices, as noted above, is that of bounding or boundary making.

5.1.1 Territoriality as a Practice of Bounding

To say that territoriality is significant as a boundary-making mechanism in international law evokes a large body of legal doctrine concerning the delimitation of land, maritime and aerial boundaries among states and the territorial determination of jurisdiction.[6] It also calls to mind a long history of such boundaries' disputation before international courts, tribunals, commissions and arbitrators and in legally informed diplomatic exchanges.[7] Legal delimitation of territorial boundaries and oversight of their modification and disputation have long been regarded as axiomatic to the maintenance of peace among states (or at least the maintenance of those global conditions commonly characterized as peaceful, ongoing violence notwithstanding). In 1758, the Swiss diplomat considered one of international law's progenitors, Emmerich (Emer) de Vattel, observed that '[t]o remove every subject of discord, every occasion for quarrel, one should mark with clarity and precision the limits of territories'.[8] Indeed for some, the modern international legal system is effectively founded on, and sustained by, a 'territorial covenant' ensuring the stability of state boundaries and discouraging their revision.[9]

Beyond its significance in delimiting states' respective politico-legal reach, and tempering (ideally, or perhaps inflaming) their propensities for over-reach, territoriality also bounds the disciplinary terrain of international law in other ways; it does so, for example, by conditioning particular entities' standing on the international legal plane. Territorial attachment and control feature as criteria for statehood according to the 1933 Montevideo Convention on Rights and Duties of States[10] and the customary law it is said to enshrine.[11] Accordingly, territoriality is a *precondition* for the assertion of sovereign authority (and associated rights and capacities) on the international legal plane, and a basis for *sidelining or disregarding* some

[5] Elden 2013, at 4; Oxford English Dictionary (OED) Online (2016), http://www.oed.com, accessed 6 June 2016.

[6] See generally Prescott and Triggs 2008; Ryngaert 2015.

[7] Prescott and Triggs 2008; Brunet-Jailly 2015.

[8] Vattel 1760, at 137.

[9] Jackson and Zacher 1997.

[10] 1933 Montevideo Convention on Rights and Duties of States, 165 LNTS 19.

[11] Grant 1999.

actors on that plane, as well as being an *outcome* of international legal rules on title to territory and boundary delimitation alluded to above. A want of territory or want of territorial control on the part of any would-be state may translate into a condition of relative impotence for that entity within the international legal order.

At a smaller scale, territorial locations of people and things similarly affect natural and legal persons' access to rights and exposure to liabilities under international law. On one side of a territorial boundary between states—the 'home' side—an individual might enjoy a range of international legal rights that the state in question owes its citizens, while on the other side of the same border she might possess the more tenuous international legal status of an immigrant, an alien or a refugee vis-à-vis the state in whose territory she is located. Territoriality thus serves as a basis for switching on a particular international legal status or switching it off, for non-state as well as state actors. The arrangement and operation of such territorial switches (that is, those territorial boundaries and distinctions by reference to which particular international legal status may be turned on and off) establish a litany of nested and intersecting boundaries in law.[12] Territoriality thus mediates international legal practices of inclusion and exclusion—or boundary making—in a wide range of ways. Material, symbolic, and psychic investments made in, or by reference to, boundaries that result from these practices help to explain the durability of territoriality as a mainstay of international legal order.

5.1.2 Territoriality as a Practice of Distribution

In addition to and through its boundary-making operations, territoriality also has important distributive effects in international law. For individuals and groups, territoriality introduces an organized randomness—and thereby, a valence of deservedness (and undeservedness)—to the lawful distribution of resources worldwide, conditioned as that distribution is by place of birth and resulting citizenship or immigration status.[13] In determining the life chances of any one individual or group, much is decided by the natural resources and economic, social and political infrastructure that happen to be located in their immediate territorial vicinity at crucial times; that this is the case—and that this is regarded, for the most part, as fitting—is in large part a consequence of international law having entrenched territorial understandings of vicinity, jurisdiction and politico-legal allegiance. In these ways, the territoriality of international law distributes agency and potential, along with resources.

Among the resources so territorially distributed are those of ready or legitimate access to, and cognisability by, one or more national legal system(s). Territoriality structures the distribution of lawful authority and amenability to its purview on the

---

[12] Kesby 2007.

[13] See, e.g., Moore et al. 2009; and Gagnon et al.2009.

global plane and thereby distributes entitlement (and disentitlement). Robert Wai's analysis of legal principles that permit or elicit territorial 'touchdown' by state and non-state actors makes apparent this distribution of regulatory capacity (as well as of regulatory-evasive capacity) in the international legal order.[14] By envisaging and analyzing agglomerations of beings, things and jurisdictions largely in territorial terms, those working with international law acquire a default rubric for judgment, or a way of ruling some interests and claims in and others out of consideration; Wai's work makes this clear.

From territoriality, international lawyers and others informed by international legal thought also draw a primary unit of analysis for purposes of drawing connections and assembling larger scale heuristics or aggregations of interest. In this sense, territoriality effects a global distribution of concern. Many of those arenas of international legal making that purport to lie between or above territorial nation states are nonetheless proprietary in conception, retaining or evoking key instincts of territoriality. Consider, for example, the notion of common heritage of mankind which, although it is conceived in opposition to territorial sovereignty, retains a sense of proprietary inheritance and defensiveness characteristic of territoriality.[15] Consider, also, as a more explicit example of territoriality's generalization on the global plane, instances of 'internationalized territory'.[16] Territoriality thus plays a critical role in shaping distributions of agency, entitlement and interest, as well as resources, on the global plane.

5.1.3 Territoriality as a Practice of Placement

Alongside its boundary-making and distributive effects in international law, a further role of territoriality in this context merits highlighting: namely its effect as a mode of placement in international legal order, that is, with regard to the fact or situation of being placed, arranged or positioned in relation to other elements of that order.[17] The operations of territorial bounding and distribution just described are, of course, practices of placement as well. Nonetheless, territoriality effects placement in and for international law in another sense as well: by making international law liveable and understandable under certain relational conditions.

Some subset of international legal norms—including those concerning the nature and structure of the international legal 'system' or 'order' (and the very idea that there is such a thing)—attract fealty through the investment of those norms with an infrastructural necessity; a sense that they are 'hard-wired' into the conditions of

[14] Wai 2002.
[15] Noyes 2011; Pahuja 2012.
[16] Wilde 2008.
[17] Oxford English Dictionary (OED) Online (2016), http://www.oed.com, accessed 6 June 2016.

global life. Territorial placement plays an important role in this investiture and, in turn, in the reproduction of territoriality as infrastructural necessity.

International law acquires and retains inevitability and compulsiveness in part by constituting places to inhabit and build careers, to flee or reform, and placing them in systemic relationship to one another, or binding them into a common order. The former places (for living and working), and the rituals and lives conducted there, become markers of what is pivotal to the international legal order. One might think of places such as the Peace Palace and the International Criminal Court in The Hague, the UN headquarters in New York, and the headquarters of the World Trade Organization in Geneva. Those who travel to such places from afar become embodiments of convergence; their traversal of territory and gathering at particular locales tend to be characterized in terms of normative growth, education, socialization or progress. The latter places (for leaving and changing), and the ways of life with which they are identified, become signposts for all that international law seeks to transcend or temper: deprivation, scarcity, violence, ignorance, fundamentalism. One might think of a village in Nabarangpur district in the Indian state of Orissa, or in the Sekong province of the Lao People's Democratic Republic, for instance.

The movement of those who work in and with international law to and from such central and peripheral places has been vital to international law's expansion and entrenchment and the prevalence of a sense that it comprises a system, and one yet to be completed. It is through such territorial placement and movement—and through related technologies of mapping and measurement, and narratives of distinction—that international law has become a *lingua franca* of global economic and political life.

The practices of territorial bounding, distribution and placement just described remain ongoing in and around the international legal order; there is no evidence of their diminishing prevalence. One could seek to diagnose this persistence of territoriality by reference to some other phenomenon: as a manifestation of ideology, for instance.[18] For purposes of this paper, however, territoriality is taken to describe a set of practices and investments that sustain themselves irreducibly as practices of international legal work (even as any such description reveals the insufficiency of those practices as underpinnings for territoriality's axiomatism). Territorial commitments are not taken here to be masks for, or symptoms of, something else; rather, they are studied on their own terms.

Nonetheless, there are indications that the normative purchase of international law—its hold on experience, knowledge and action—could yet become somewhat less contingent on or guided by these conventional territorial practices. Instead, particular configurations of data—flows, pathways, and assemblages in and of data—may yet come to do at least some of the work that territoriality was just recounted doing in and for the international legal order. And it remains to be seen whether this

[18] See generally, for example, Sugarman 1983; Zizek 1989.

reconfiguration will occasion a redoubling of the commitments of territoriality, or their calling into question. Perhaps the most obvious indication of this shift may be gleaned from the increasing 'datafication' of territory.

5.2 The Datafication of Territory and the Rise of Association

To say that territory has been or is being 'datafied' is to highlight the rendering of territory as information, as distinct from its sometime rendering as or in connection with landscape, spirit, resource, repository, national or common heritage or otherwise. The practice of rendering territory as information for international legal purposes is not a recent phenomenon. The division of a spherical world into evenly spaced meridians utilizing a lattice of latitude and longitude, for example, is of ancient provenance, although it was not until the eighteenth century that a reliable way of measuring longitude at sea and on land was devised.[19] Furthermore, it would take until the late nineteenth century, and an international conference, to establish one such meridian as a common, international point of reference for locational and time-keeping purposes, including for the lawful fixing of time.[20] With the universalization of this system of geographical information, a sense of one's placement north or south of the Equator, and east or west of the Prime Meridian, became at least potentially an experience common to all, as did the resulting capacity to measure, survey and describe parcels of territory with accuracy. 'Datafication' in this mode has long been vital to the projects and potency of international law, including to its territoriality.

The representation of territory in and as data has, however, intensified to a very significant degree with the advent of orbital satellites, the satellite-based radio navigation system known as the global positioning system (GPS), and technologies of automatic sensing, Google mapping and the like.[21] A profusion of sensor networks, and advances in their sophistication, have fostered aspirations to 'seed the planet' with continuously operating data-collection and data-generation nodes—to create a 'central nervous system for the Earth', in the words of Hewlett Packard's landmark CeNSE project, to serve as a basis for legal and policy decisions.[22] In regulating nuclear testing, for example, the Comprehensive Test-Ban-Treaty Organisation (CTBTO) is said to operate '170 seismic stations worldwide, 11 under hydroacoustic centres detecting sound waves in the oceans, 60 listening stations for atmospheric infrasound (low-frequency acoustic waves that can travel

---

[19] Evans 1998; Samama 2008.

[20] Perrin 1927; Higgitt and Dolan 2010.

[21] Leszczynski 2012.

[22] Hardy 2009; Hewlett Packard (2016), Products and solutions / Eco solutions: CeNSE, http://www8.hp.com/us/en/hp-information/environment/cense.html, accessed 6 June 2016.

long distances) and 96 labs and radionuclide-sampling facilities'.[23] The CTBTO is, moreover, committed to installing an even more comprehensive network of 337 seismic, hydroacoustic, infrasound and radionuclide detecting stations through which to determine when and where a nuclear device of any size is detonated and, thereafter, evaluate its lawfulness.[24]

Territory so 'datafied', and thereby made actionable for law and policy decisions, still performs bounding, distributive and placement functions for international legal purposes, but does so in quite a different mode to that earlier described. Territoriality becomes a matter of managing and maintaining a dynamic, vital, information-rich, would-be seamless 'planetary skin' available for navigation by those with access to the real time data of which it is comprised. (The term 'planetary skin' here references a program illustrative of the emergent territoriality in question: the ALERTS system is a decision support system for remote change evaluation, reporting and tracking, in near real-time, of global land use, land cover change, and land use disturbance released in 2010 by the Planetary Skin Institute: a non-profit organization co-founded by Cisco and NASA).[25] Territory so activated for analysis seems less predisposed to parceling and fencing, in the manner conventionally required to evidence and sustain property rights for example. Rather, it seems constituted more with a view to its curation (that is, sifting and organizing for presentation) and personalization (that is, being tailored to a particular audience's needs or preferences, however unreliably).[26] Amid such a diffuse and dynamic territoriality, the sense of security, wellbeing and agency that any one individual or group enjoys may depend less on their location within politico-legal boundaries, access to juridical infrastructure or proximity to natural resources than on their access *to* data concerning the conditions and risks that they must confront, on any number of concurrent scales, at any one moment, and their recording *in* datasets assembled for such purposes. Boundaries of international juridical concern in this context may just as likely be those of data access and technical proficiency than traditional territorial boundaries.

This 'datafication' of territory carries with it also changing expectations of what law can and should accomplish on the international plane. Projections of a globalism that waxes and wanes, pools and eddies with the flow, accumulation or blockage of data imply similarly altered understandings of international legality, as compared to legality premised on the territorial sovereignty of nation states. Accounts of a 'self-aware' globe imply that international legal norms and practices

[23] Economist (2015) Monitoring Nuclear Weapons: The Nuke Detectives, 5 September 2015, http://www.economist.com/topics/nuclear-weapons, accessed 6 June 2016.

[24] Oleson (2015) Beyond the Bomb: The World's Nuclear Watchdog Expands its Science, Earth Magazine, 27 April 2015, http://www.earthmagazine.org/article/beyond-bomb-worlds-nuclear-watchdog-expands-its-science, accessed 6 June 2016.

[25] Stanley and Liao 2011.

[26] On "corrupt" personalization, see C Sandvig (2014), Corrupt Personalization, Social Media Collective Research Blog, 26 June 2014, https://socialmediacollective.org/2014/06/26/corrupt-personalization/, accessed 6 June 2016.

will or should be capable of effecting 'interoperability' among the various combinations of legal rights, routes, liabilities and undertakings surrounding data, wherever those data may be located.[27] Expectations of laws' global 'interoperability'—and a presumptive antipathy to either data or laws' territorial sequestration—seem implicit in the piecemeal, endlessly fluid, information-oriented assemblages of global territory alluded to above. The collapse of the EU-US Safe Harbor Arrangement permitting transfer of EU citizens' data to the US, and its replacement with a conditionally permeable EU-US Privacy Shield, may be representative of the ongoing re-casting of the territorial in international legal order along these lines; law and policy thinking framed around harbors, islands and other territorial strongholds appears increasingly ill-attuned to the prevailing data 'ecosystem'.[28]

One way in which shifts in the modes of bounding, distribution and placement newly encouraged through the 'datafication' of territory might best be captured or explained is by reference to the growing prevalence of a logic of association in international law and policy work. Notions of international legality deemed fit for 'datafied' global territory evoke the ideal of a global 'information economy' regulated less through planning, mapping or strategic oversight than through a series of associations, inferences, and correlations.[29] And association rules are, indeed, one form of rule with which those engaged in the technicalities of data mining and data analytics—for global juridical and other purposes—are frequently concerned.[30] Such rules are features of a particular kind of automated data-mining technique; one way of mining large collections of data is to discover certain rules by which that data may be usefully represented. Such rules are not equivalent to legal rules, but they nonetheless play a role, in a range of contexts, in generating, delimiting, distributing and placing lawful authority, when that authority depends on certain events or conditions becoming discernible in data. Because of this role, and in order to present a sharpened sense of the shift in logic that they may encapsulate, this section will proceed from this point onwards *as if* association rules could be regarded as new formulations of international legal rule, without attempting any parsing of their lawful from their non-lawful force in particular instances.

An association rule is 'a simple probabilistic statement about the co-occurrence of certain events in a database'.[31] Association rules 'concern whether a group of variables [...] is more significantly associated than we would normally expect' and they look something like this: '$X \rightarrow Y$ with support A% and confidence B%, where X and Y are sets of items'.[32] Rules, in this context, are not understood to direct

[27] Hardy 2009 (on a self-aware globe); Johns 2013, at 12-14 and 34 (on legal interoperability).

[28] European Commission (2016), EU Commission and United States agree on new framework for transatlantic data flows: EU-US Privacy Shield, Press Release, 2 February 2016, http://europa.eu/rapid/press-release_IP-16-216_en.htm, accessed 6 June 2016; Boyd and Crawford 2012.

[29] Benkler 2003, 2006.

[30] Rauch 2005.

[31] Hand et al. 2001, at 158.

[32] Lee and Lee 2011, at 483 and 488. See generally Agrawal et al. 1993.

conduct. Rather, data analysis algorithms designed to find associations (statistical correlations meeting certain predetermined thresholds) between sets of items in a database proceed according to IF-THEN logic, without generating any causal explanations for those associations or any theorization of how they came about. The so-called democratic peace phenomenon—the theoretical 'rule' that democracies less frequently engage in armed conflict with other identified democracies than they do with non-democracies, or than non-democracies do with either democracies or non-democracies—is an example of an association rule generated from the mining of historical datasets.[33]

As a mechanism for generating, delimiting, distributing and placing lawful authority (such as the presumptive authority of democratic polities, with which the example above is concerned), the association rule exhibits a number of characteristics that distinguish it from other forms of rule with which international lawyers may be more familiar. First among these is association rules' embedded and often inscrutable origination. Association rules are not parameters or coordinates set for a certain inquiry, survey or task from the outset comparable to the earth's meridians; rather, they are the *outcomes* of automated, iterated inquiry. They emerge in ways that may not always be explicable even to those well versed in relevant data-mining techniques. This is especially the case when unsupervised or semi-supervised machine learning is employed in their generation. Unlike supervised learning (which starts with a training set of 'properly labeled' data and organises unlabelled data according to that signature), unsupervised learning commences without an initial model, hypothesis, or norm from which deviation must be sought. Its aim is to generate and explore regularities and anomalies or to locate 'densities' of probability within a dataset and then, independently and by recourse to other methods, determine which of those patterns may merit interest or further investigation.[34] Research in this area tends to make far more of search efficiencies realised than the features, components and criteria of different data-mining algorithms:

> In many papers, the descriptions of the model structure [that is, the high level way that a data set is represented], the score function [a way of numerically expressing the preferability of one model over another according to specified aims], and the search method [computational methods used for model- and pattern-fitting in data-mining algorithms] are abstrusely intertwined.[35]

For these and other reasons, it is often 'hard to explain how the system reached a decision' with respect to any one association revealed.[36] To the extent that the mining of data by recourse to association rules gives rise to certain placements or distributions within those data, it may not be possible to grasp the predicates for that placement or distribution from outside the process in question.

[33] Aragones et al. 2005.

[34] Hastie et al. 2009.

[35] Hand et al. 2001, at 163 and 235.

[36] Loh et al. 2003, at 358.

A second, related consideration, with regard to the boundary-making implications of association rules, is that the scope of what might be 'potentially useful' in this context need not be determined a priori; data mining itself frequently generates a sense of what merits interest.[37] This will depend upon measurements of 'interestingness' that 'will inevitably be application-dependent and subjective'. What may be deemed useful and usable from a mass of association rules will depend, to a significant degree, upon the happenstance of various design features' confluence and interaction with a data set or data sets.[38] Furthermore, the 'actionable decision' formulated on the basis of associations meeting such 'interestingness' or 'usefulness' thresholds may itself be realised through or by data handling in a way that serves to confirm the usefulness it was initially presumed to hold.[39] For instance, the action in question may entail the automated screening, selection and targeting of material in a way responsive to the probable association represented in the rule—thereby conditioning the target to demonstrate, and confirming the significance of, the association inferred from the dataset. In other words, by way of example, people may develop preferences based on the tailored material to which they are exposed in an online environment. Meanwhile, that tailoring is meant to have been premised on, and responsive to, the preferences that they were already supposed to hold as a matter of associational inference.[40] In both respects, the force of the expectation to which an association rule gives rise may, at least in part, result from the ongoing, iterative generation of the association and the taking of action on that basis.

A third feature of association rules—and the logic of association—noteworthy for international legal purposes is their tendency towards superfluity. In the course of mining data, there are often many meaningless association rules discovered.[41] Algorithms designed to generate association rules 'find all rules satisfying the frequency and accuracy thresholds' prescribed for them and only some portion of the 'mass of discovered rules' may turn out to be 'potentially interesting' or meaningful.[42] Accordingly, association rules are not designed to be 'right' or reliable at the outset; rather, there is an expectation that most of them will be discarded. The cartographic equivalent would be to define every territorial boundary using a litany of dotted lines in the hope that one or a small number of these would attract loyalists. This lessens the gravity and dispenses with the ceremony of rule-making, or boundary-setting, and subordinates the practice to an expectation of continual, ubiquitous tinkering.[43] Contrasted to other modes of international legal rule, this predisposition towards tinkering suggests prospects for

---

[37] Azzalini and Scarpa 2012, at 5.

[38] Hand et al. 2001, at 295 and 440–441.

[39] Wang et al. 2005; Hand et al. 2001, at 295.

[40] Wang et al. 2005.

[41] Li 2005.

[42] Hand et al. 2001, at 431.

[43] Ciborra 2002.

a different mode of claim-making and contestation surrounding territoriality. Perhaps in place of stability and durability as international law's driving concerns with respect to territory, more contingent assemblages of the territorial might be advanced in this mode, justified on particular grounds.

A further characteristic of association rules—and the associative logic they foster —is that patterns in data represented by such rules need not feature subjects, objects or places as such, nor stories of the relations among them. The unit of analysis with which an association rule is concerned may not be recognisable as a place, person, field, or thing that registers as familiar.[44] The democracy-peace association referred to above is atypical in this respect; association rules often do not work with or around anything as coherent as a territorial nation state. They are often formulated at a much lower, or cross-cutting level of analysis, on the basis of correlations between bits of data and piecemeal records drawn from widely dispersed and dissimilar sources, such that a change in the value or expected incidence of one datum is mathematically associated with a change in the value or expected incidence of other data. Consider, for example, the use of mobile phone call detail records to generate inferences about human mobility patterns and socioeconomic welfare and the use of satellite data to provide early warning of epidemics, uprisings and other crowd states.[45] In such cases, the data in question tends to be 'remarkably unwieldy', 'unstructured', and drawn from a wide range of sites and sources, and may not yield a compelling representation of any individual or group.[46]

Moreover, in order for such unstructured data to be made useful and actionable for legal or policy purposes—or potentially so—no legal jurisdiction as such need be configured. That is, there is no need, as part of such processes, to recruit some groups, entities or beings to experience themselves and others as legal persons, identified with a distinct territory, with all that that implies (usually, possession of a relatively stable identity and physical location). Similarly, there is no need for an actionable insight represented by an association rule to elicit concrete things, locations or objects. One might generate a prediction of crop yield based on a mathematical correlation 'found' in satellite imaging data indicative of vegetation density, and evaluate the risk of impending food insecurity on that basis, as some international organizations seek to do through data mining, without ever calling forth an image or understanding of a plant or a paddock as such, or determining the location or legal status of nearby territorial boundaries.[47]

The sorts of relationships and imperatives generated through association are, accordingly, founded in momentary, mathematically recorded co-occurrence between discernible properties or records, the significance and extent of which will often be unclear. An association rule along the lines of 'if X then Y' does not operate on the basis of presumptions of cause and effect, common purpose or

---

[44] Amoore 2009.

[45] Vaitla 2014.

[46] World Bank 2014, at 23.

[47] Quinn et al. 2010.

normative commitment, proximity in time or space, similarity of identity, or affective or communicative connection as between set X and set Y or the elements of those sets. The association of X and Y in the aforementioned rule is based only on analysis of a large data set having generated, for the time being, a greater probabilistic affinity of co-occurrence or overlap between set X and set Y, or particular subsets of the same, than between X and all other sets that may be assembled from the database at the relevant time. As additions and eliminations are made to and from the dataset(s) being analyzed, that association may diminish in importance as stronger correlations emerge. New association rules may yet be formulated that are capable of overcoming the relevant interestingness threshold. The association of X to Y is not, therefore, equivalent to an assumption that all persons properly attributable to territory W shall presumptively enjoy status Z for international legal purposes. Taking an example alluded to above, the observation that there is a strong correlation between a particular mobile phone use pattern and the principal phone user's state of economic development, for example, says nothing about what may have brought about the latter. It simply describes a probability that certain data will co-occur in relevant datasets.[48]

Because of their contingency upon endlessly revisable probabilistic calculations, placements in data of the kind that association rules bring about are, it seems, only fleetingly discernible and may often elude analysis altogether. This makes any abiding normative force on the part of international law, guided by such associations, difficult to sustain and subordinates that law to demands for 'usefulness' that may be generated largely from outside the discipline of law. It is, however, important not to overstate the fleetingness of data associations or their immunity to, or non-translatability for, normative influence. Many databases from which association rules are derived have historical content—'memories' as it were. A database's historical content might generate, for instance, a rule along the lines of the following: people who performed action A over the past three years were more likely to combine this with action B than they were likely to combine it with any other form of action represented in the dataset(s). The analysis of such historical content towards one or more association rule(s) is not concerned with charting historical patterns or broad historical narratives as such. Yet it is premised on the historic possibility of action A and B both being open for people to take—a possibility for which legal measures and institutions may quite plausibly be relevant. Even so, the relationship between action A and action B—and the respective places and conditions of their performance—in the aforementioned example will only hold for so long as no stronger association can be detected between some other combination of recorded actions, as noted above. Likewise, a database's historical content will only survive culling to the extent that it is capable of generating associations strong enough, according to specified criteria, to serve as a basis for action or prediction.

Associations of the sort just described are not, of course, wholly unknown to international law otherwise. One could, perhaps, read international human rights

[48] Eagle et al. 2010.

law instruments and efforts concerned with particular institutional features (or their absence) as operating with something like an association rule. A set of institutional characteristics that excludes certain stipulated features (that lacks, for instance, any mechanism designed to ensure that those who are arrested are promptly informed of the reasons for their arrest) is probabilistically associated, in international human rights law, with a particular set of human experiences (oppression, domination, vulnerability to abuse of power, lack of freedom, access to limited or no avenues of recourse or appeal, etc.).[49] Their relation could perhaps be imagined in terms of diverse data points drawn together in association—through the analysis of correlations—to produce an actionable forecast of events to come.[50]

It seems, however, a distortion to characterise the relationship between people who have experienced (or been responsible for) unexplained arrest, and those who have experienced (or been responsible for) officially sanctioned abuse or oppression, in terms of an association rule. The relationship seems more amenable to characterisation in terms of the narration and communication of histories, the active cultivation of political allegiances and the pursuit of strategies of reform or redress. International law worries about arrest practices because people in a range of jurisdictions have mobilised around the public regularisation of this and other aspects of criminal procedure, on the basis of a range of experiences and commitments, some of them shared and some not. To cite another, not entirely unrelated example (given the historical record of indigenous deaths in custody across a number of jurisdictions) international law addresses indigenous people globally as a group not on the basis of any association rule probabilistically aligning properties of indigeneity with which they are attributed. Rather, they are treated as a group because of their political mobilisation as such and because of the commonalities of experience and practice identified with colonialism.

The sorts of ephemeral, presentist associations and assemblages foregrounded in data-mining and analysis, including in the actual or prospective analysis of 'datafied' territories, and the relationships of place, people and things that they draw together, are not configurations to which conventional international legal thought and practice are well-attuned. International legal work continues to be conducted largely on the basis of global associations presumed much thicker, stickier and more durable than those instantiated in data by association rules: above all, those framed by territorial arrangements and allegiances. It is for this reason that the growing 'datafication' of territory, related reliance on data mining for juridical and policy decision-making, and the ensuing rise of a logic of association together signal such a momentous shift in and for international legal order. That shift is not, however, synonymous with the demise of territoriality all together. As the next section will show, the accretion, navigation, and deployment of data globally continue to follow certain juridical pathways, patterns and divisions; these give rise to what one might think of as data territories.

---

[49] 1966 International Covenant on Civil and Political Rights, 999 UNTS 171, Article 9(2).

[50] Amoore 2009.

5.3 The Territorialisation of Data and the Persistence of Juridical Patterns and Precincts

Global data flows may have fostered new architectures of association, as the preceding section has suggested, but these are not a-territorial. Global data flows remain guided by the acquisitive, distinctive, defensive and mimetic impulses characteristic of territoriality, and marked by pathways, patterns and arrangements in which territorial sovereigns continue to loom large. And data are so territorialized in part through the operations of international law.

International law has long been concerned with arranging the world into domains of visibility and invisibility, allegiance and non-allegiance, civilization and barbarism; data flow has always played a significant role in sustaining such global geographies.[51] The juridical map of global data sharing for intelligence purposes, established and maintained by treaty, is illustrative in this regard; it reveals an informational geography that is both territorial in its routings and routines, and designed to transcend or overlay territorial boundaries. One could point to a number of other examples of data's territorialisation: Linnet Taylor and Dennis Broeders have described, for instance, how low- and middle-income countries are increasingly shepherded, in their international legal, political and economic affairs, by 'data doubles' and 'shadow-maps': 'new forms of visibility separate from state mapping efforts'. These are generated as varying configurations of intergovernmental, non-governmental and corporate actors make use of new remote sensing and data analytics capabilities to produce 'alternative, dynamic and highly detailed account[s] of the spatial dynamics of even very remote places where accurate mapping has previously been limited or nonexistent'.[52] For the purposes of this short chapter, however, let us consider only one example of territoriality expressed in data through the operations of law—an example drawn from the domain of intelligence-gathering and-sharing.

The 1947 UKUSA Agreement between the US National Security Agency and the British Government Communications Headquarters, to which Canada, Australia and New Zealand became 'second parties' (with Norway, Denmark, West Germany and Turkey as 'third' parties), famously established the so-called '5 Eyes' arrangement for the sharing of signals intelligence and the division of associated labor among five governments and nation state territories.[53] That post-war arrangement has since been cross-cut by a range of international arrangements for which data access (and its denial) serve as pivot and fuel, even as longstanding

[51] Anghie 2007.

[52] Taylor and Broeders 2015, at 230–235.

[53] Reveron 2006, at 460; United States National Security Agency (NSA) (2010), Declassified UKUSA Signals Intelligence Agreement Documents Available, Press Release, 24 June 2015, https://www.nsa.gov/news-features/press-room/press-releases/2010/ukusa.shtml, accessed 6 June 2016.

international legal alliances such as UKUSA and NATO remain crucial.[54] These cross-cutting arrangements include those in place among the cohort of governments granted access to the US' Secret Internet Protocol Router Network (SIPRNet), for instance.[55] They include, too, a veritable thicket of international agreements, both formal and informal, providing for bilateral and regional cooperation around intelligence data.[56]

International legal norms operate as part of the engineering of these arrangements—and of the geographies that they produce—rather than just operating before-the-fact or after-the-fact of data assemblage. Regulations around the classification of intelligence data, for instance—around, say, deployment and interpretation of the classifiers 'NOFORN' (not releasable to foreign nationals) and 'ORCON' (originator controlled) when affixed to a document or datum—may have explicit provenance in US national law.[57] Yet the international agreements to which we have referred will have a direct bearing on the use and interpretation of classifiers such as 'NOFORN' and 'ORCON' along the length of global data circuits. Such classifiers will also be operationalised in view of a domain of intelligence 'tradecraft' or 'best practice' often perceived as global in scale, albeit not all-inclusively so. As was the case with respect to data mining association rules, categorizations such as the 'NOFORN' and 'ORCON' classifiers will be treated here *as if* they were legal categorizations (although they might plausibly be described otherwise), for purposes of sharpening focus on the territorialisation of data that they mark, and help to effect, for international law and policy purposes.

Law-data combinations such as the 'NOFORN' classifier produce quite concrete (albeit thin) geographies: the range of people, machines and places to which a datum classified 'NOFORN' may be distributed (both within and beyond US territory) are connected to one another by this mechanism, and may be distinguished from those to which 'NOFORN' data may not lawfully be distributed. Material marked 'NOFORN' 'may not be provided in any form to foreign governments (including coalition partners), international organizations, foreign nationals, or immigrant aliens without the originator's approval', even when those parties are located in US territory.[58] With the requisite security clearance, one could map those sites (tracking infrastructural as well as human storage or reception points) to and within which data classified 'NOFORN' might lawfully move; one might call this the 'territory' of NOFORN-classified data. Yet that territory will clearly not equate to US territory; what is treated as 'FORN' for 'NOFORN' purposes does not correspond to, nor does it demand explicit comparison to, territorial boundaries demarcated elsewhere or

[54] Rudner 2004, at 209–210; Lefebvre 2003, at 531–532.

[55] Reveron 2006, at 460; BBC (2010), Siprnet: Where the Leaked Cables Came From, 29 November 2010, http://www.bbc.co.uk/news/world-us-canada-11863618, accessed 6 June 2016.

[56] Svendsen 2008; Sepper 2010, at 154–159; Svendsen 2012.

[57] Church 2011–2012: Reveron 2006, at 457; Fenster 2011–2012, at 492, note 189; Department of Defense (DOD) 2012.

[58] Department of Defense (DOD) 2012, at 63.

otherwise. As such, there does not appear to be any institutionally mandated point of encounter between these geographic instantiations—between, say, the data territory lawfully unreachable by data marked 'NOFORN' for US legal purposes (and related treaty-governed distribution), and territory deemed to lie outside US jurisdiction for other, international legal purposes.

Data are, of course, not the only media for this virtual cross-hatching, carving and tunneling of global space, any more than public international law comprises the primary rubric or vehicle for data's movement or obstruction in this context. These configurations have institutional, embodied, and material dimensions as well as resting upon significant private law architecture (comprised of contract law, tort law —norms surrounding breach of confidence for instance—and intellectual property law). The FBI maintains personnel in fifty-eight countries through its legal attaché or 'legat' program; this program positions and provides for a set of bodies and employment relationships around the world through which data may be generated and transmitted.[59] The global distribution of language competence is important, as is apparent from the fact of the seers of the 5 Eyes all being Anglophone nations. The location and direction of infrastructure is also critical to these arrangements' maintenance and routing. Martin Rudner has highlighted, for instance, the importance of satellites' orbital position, targeting and control in intelligence operations[60] Surprisingly obtuse or thin attributions of group identity, allegiance or political motivation also play a significant role in the distribution of data. Recently, for example, two researchers, proposing a framework for detecting 'agro-terrorism intentions' using overt or public data sources, identified 'environmental activists' as one 'cluster' with 'a history of sabotage' on which global data search and analysis efforts should focus.[61]

Nevertheless, data are increasingly viewed—more or less independently of the loci of their storage or provenance—as the lifeblood of global intelligence-gathering and-sharing endeavours and of the domains of relative safety and danger that they demarcate. Global intelligence cooperation has conventionally taken government agencies—certain governments and certain agencies in particular—as its central switching points, with their interaction typically cloaked in secrecy.[62] In contrast, global intelligence cooperation is often now framed as a decentralised, collective, data-centric endeavour, in a way that corresponds to broader, contemporary preoccupations and framings in international legal thought (preoccupations with the power and potential of non-state actors, for instance). Robert Steele is among a range of intelligence specialists who have championed 'non-secret, non-governmental, and non-intelligence liaison and information sharing

---

[59] FBI website, https://www.fbi.gov/contact-us/legat, accessed 6 June 2016. See also Sepper 2010, at 159–166 (emphasizing the importance of professional community, professional reputation, professional 'ethos' and peer relationships in intelligence networks).

[60] Rudner 2004, at 200.

[61] Rohn and Erez 2013.

[62] Rudner 2004, at 222; Sepper 2010, at 156–157.

arrangements', and an orientation towards the 'smart' mining of publicly available information or 'Open Source Intelligence' (OSINT).[63] It is in this sense that data flows—intelligence data flows, as merely one example—are shaping the global landscape into a shifting yet durable arrangement of 'data territories'. These territories are 'open' to the extent that they are assembled, in part, from OSINT flows. Yet they cleave, nonetheless, very closely to the installations and allegiances of territorial sovereigns. Such data territories comprise one among a number of forms of re-territorialization currently underway on the global plane.[64]

5.4 The Challenge of Data Territories

The foregoing sections have recounted changing practices of bounding, distribution, and placement in international law associated with a turn to data analytics on the global plane. They have described an emergent logic of association within international legal order that diverges in significant ways from the conventional logic of territoriality, and the emergence of new 'territories', pathways and patterns constituted by the global movement (and non-movement) of data. These changes pose challenges to those 'inviolable limits which had from [international law's] beginning marked out the territory...of the earth's surface', to paraphrase Fustel de Coulanges, although they by no means dispense with those limits all together.[65]

Among those challenges is precisely the difficulty of conception, or re-conception, to which Fustel de Coulanges alluded in the quote with which this chapter opened. International legal thought, practice, and doctrine have seen so much invested in the conventional territorial organization of global affairs that it is extraordinarily difficult to think of arranging and governing the world otherwise. Absent territoriality, or in the face of its transformation, it is tempting to envision only chaos and cacophony, much as the International Court of Justice foresaw a descent into 'fratricidal struggles provoked by the challenging of frontiers' if it were to 'disregard the principle of *uti possidetis juris*, the application of which gives rise to [...] respect for intangibility of [territorial] frontiers'.[66]

Yet the territorial sovereign state—and an international legal order premised largely on the sanctity and 'intangibility' of its frontiers—are, it must be remembered, relatively recent innovations when viewed over the long term of social organization among humans. Recalling this, it cannot be the case that the only two options facing international lawyers are, on one hand, to reinstate, affirm, stabilize and defend those frontiers—and the modes of territoriality with which they come

[63] Steele 2007.

[64] See, e.g., Bach 2011.

[65] Fustel de Coulanges 2006, at 202–203.

[66] *Case Concerning the Frontier Dispute (Burkina Faso/Republic of Mali),* ICJ, Judgment, 22 December 1986, para 20.

loaded—wherever possible or, on the other hand, to relinquish any aspiration for non-violent, fair and equitable conduct being fostered through law on the global plane.

International law already accommodates and engenders a multiplicity of ways of associating. It configures a world of right-bearers and those accountable for their protection; a world of co-consumers and generators of energy; a world linked and delinked by narratives of progress and decline, community and faith; a world of story-tellers and listeners, the rulers and the ruled, the entitled and the disentitled, the human and the nonhuman, the gendered, the racialized and those who embody 'neutral' norms from which such differences are drawn, all arranged slightly differently in different substantive areas of international law. Territoriality is, as noted at the outset, but one of the global architectures of affiliation and disaffiliation in which international law trades, even if it sometimes seems the most important of these.

Data territories, and the architecture of association that accretes in and around them, put up new frontiers, while undermining others. Territoriality does not wash away in a 'world of flows' and big data as many have observed before me.[67] Indeed, a world of data flows is no more borderless than a world in which trade is relatively free and capital unfettered; just ask any migrant without economic means who has an Arabic-language surname. Yet it is equally the case that all is not continuously and necessarily reconcilable with what has come before when it comes to territoriality in international law. Contemporary data practices (practices, that is, of collection, dissemination and analysis) in international law and policy do encourage a logic of association in data that is distinguishable from that which prevailed before the burgeoning of these practices. It is by no means clear that we can and should try to fit that mode of association into one of the aforementioned international legal frames: to think of data practices, for example, through the lens of rights, natural resources, property, communication or community. Much is distorted, elided or missed in the course of so doing, as recent debates surrounding privacy rights make plain. To approach the global practices of bounding, distribution and placement associated with contemporary data flows equipped mainly with a discourse of privacy seems a bit like trying to grapple with global financial affairs by recourse to plant breeders' rights.[68] So too, it would likely prove paradoxical, if not impossible, to try to analyse the 'data territories' of this chapter's description using doctrinal rubrics and principles adapted from the traditional corpus of international law.

Far more difficult, yet potentially far more promising, it is to try to grasp the logic of association and the characteristics of data territories described here more or less on their own terms, both in their specifics and in the aggregate: to think, that is, of an international legal order made of and in data. How might such an order yet be crafted or envisioned? What are, or should be, its operative units for purposes of analysis and action? In what shapes, arrangements and patterns might we envision

---

[67] E.g., Paasi 1998.

[68] Johns 2013; Johns and Joyce 2014.

that order's elements co-placed, if not primarily in territorial terms? What would it take to try to make such an order just, fair, liveable? These are the kinds of questions that the 'datafication' of territory and the territorialisation of data on the global plane open up for international legal thought and argument, if international lawyers dare to take them on.

References

Agrawal R, Imielinski T, Swami A (1993) Mining Association Rules between Sets of Items in Large Databases. Proceedings, ACM SIG-MOD Conference on Management of Data. http://www.almaden.ibm.com/cs/quest/papers/sigmod93.pdf. Accessed 6 June 2016

Amoore L (2009) Lines of Sight: On the Visualization of Unknown Futures. Citizenship Studies 13:17–30

Anghie A (2007) Imperialism, Sovereignty and the Making of International Law. Cambridge University Press, Cambridge

Aragones E, Gilboa I, Postlewaite A, Schmeidler D (2005) Fact-Free Learning. American Economic Review 95:1355–1368

Azzalini A, Scarpa B (2012) Data Analysis and Data Mining: An Introduction. Oxford University Press, Oxford

Bach J (2011) Modernity and the Urban Imagination in Economic Zones. Theory, Culture & Society 28(5):98–122

Benkler Y (2003) Freedom in the Commons: Towards a Political Economy of Information. Duke Law Journal 52:1245–1276

Benkler Y (2006) The Wealth of Networks: How Social Production Transforms Markets and Freedom. Yale University Press, New Haven

Boyd D, Crawford K (2012) Critical Questions for Big Data. Information, Communication & Society 15:662–679

Brunet-Jailly E (2015) Border Disputes: A Global Encyclopedia. ABC-CLIO, Santa Barbara

Church KA (2011–2012) Espionage 2.0: Protecting Human Intelligence Sources in the Digital Age. South California Law Review 85:1183-1228

Ciborra C (2002) The Labyrinths of Information: Challenging the Wisdom of Systems. Oxford University Press, Oxford

Department of Defense (DoD) (2012) DoD Information Security Program: Marking of Classified Information. Department of Defense Manual No. 5200.01, Vol. 2. http://www.dtic.mil/whs/directives/corres/pdf/520001_vol2.pdf. Accessed 6 June 2016

Eagle N, Macy M, Claxton R (2010) Network Diversity and Economic Development. Science 328 (5981):1029–1031

Elden S (2013) The Birth of Territory. University of Chicago Press, Chicago/London

Evans J (1998) The History and Practice of Ancient Astronomy. Oxford University Press, Oxford

Fenster M (2011–2012) The Transparency Fix: Advocating Legal Rights and Their Alternatives in the Pursuit of a Visible State. University of Pittsburgh Law Review 73:443–503

Fustel de Coulanges ND (2006) The Ancient City: A Study of the Religion, Laws, and Institutions of Greece and Rome, tr. W Small [1874]. Dover Publications, New York

Frater MR, Ryan MJ (2001) Electronic Warfare for the Digitized Battlefield. Artech House, Boston

Gagnon AJ, Zimbeck M, Zeitlin J (2009) Migration to Western Industrialized Countries and Perinatal Health: A Systematic Review. Social Science & Medicine 69:934–946

Grant TD (1999) Defining Statehood: The Montevideo Convention and its Discontents. Columbia Journal of Transnational Law 37:403–458

Hand D, Mannila H, Smyth P (2001) Principles of Data Mining. MIT Press, Cambridge

Handl G (2012) Extraterritoriality and International Legal Authority. In: Handl G, Zekoll J, Zumbansen P (eds) Beyond Territoriality: Transnational Legal Authority in an Age of Globalization. Brill, Leiden, pp 3–12
Hardy Q (2009) The Self-Aware Earth. Forbes Asia 5(9):50–50
Hastie T, Tibshirani R, Friedman J (2009) The Elements of Statistical Learning. Springer, New York
Higgitt R, Dolan G (2010) Greenwich, Time and 'The Line'. Endeavour 34(1):35–39
Jackson RH, Zacher MW (1997) The Territorial Covenant: International Society and the Stabilization of Boundaries. Institute of International Relations, University of British Columbia Working Paper No. 15. http://www.ligi.ubc.ca/sites/liu/files/Publications/webwp15.pdf. Accessed 6 June 2016
Johns F (2016) Global Governance Through the Pairing of List and Algorithm. Environment and Planning D: Society and Space 33:126–149
Johns F, Joyce D (2014) Beyond Privacy. Is Prevailing Legal Debate too Analog for a Digital Age? Human Rights Defender 23(3):24–25
Johns F (2013) The Deluge. London Review of International Law 1:9–34
Kesby A (2007) The Shifting and Multiple Border and International Law. Oxford Journal of Legal Studies 27:101–119
Lee KC, Lee S (2011) Interpreting the Web-Mining Results by Cognitive Map and Association Rule Approach. Information Processing & Management 47:482–490
Lefebvre S (2003) The Difficulties and Dilemmas of International Intelligence Cooperation. International Journal of Intelligence and CounterIntelligence 16:527–542
Leszczynski A (2012) Situating the Geoweb in Political Economy. Progress in Human Geography 36(1):72–89
Li Y (2005) A User-Guided Association Rules Mining Method and its Application. Fifth International Conference on Computer and Information Technology, Shanghai, pp 150–156. http://ieeexplore.ieee.org/xpls/abs_all.jsp?arnumber=1562643. Accessed 6 June 2016
Loh S, Palazzo Moreira de Oliveira J, Gameiro MA (2003) Knowledge Discovery in Texts for Constructing Decision Support Systems. Applied Intelligence 18:357–366
Meier P (2015) Digital Humanitarians: How Big Data is Changing the Face of Humanitarian Response. CRC Press, Boca Raton
Moore AR, F Amey, Y Bessa (2009) Earnings Attainment of Immigrants in the USA: The Effects of Race, Gender, and Place of Birth. Equal Opportunities International 28(6):500–512
Noyes JE (2011) The Common Heritage of Mankind: Past, Present, and Future. Denver Journal of International Law and Policy 40:447–471
Paasi A (1998) Boundaries as Social Processes: Territoriality in a World of Flows. Geopolitics 3 (1):69–88
Pahuja S (2012) Conserving the World's Resources? In: Crawford J, Koskenniemi M (eds) The Cambridge Companion to International Law. Cambridge University Press, Cambridge, pp 398–420
Perrin WG (1927) The Prime Meridian. The Mariner's Mirror. 13(2):109–124
Prescott V, Triggs GD (2008) International Frontiers and Boundaries: Law, Politics and Geography. Martinus Nijhoff, Leiden
Quinn JA, Okori W, Gidudu A (2010) Increased-Specificity Famine Prediction Using Satellite Observation Data. Proceedings of the First ACM Symposium on Computing for Development. Article No. 18. http://dx.doi.org/10.1145/1926180.1926203. Accessed 6 June 2016
Rauch J (2005) Logic of Association Rules. Applied Intelligence 22:9–28
Reveron DS (2006) Old Allies, New Friends: Intelligence-Sharing in the War on Terror. Summer Orbis 50:453–468
Rohn E, Erez G (2013) A Framework for Agro-terrorism Intentions Detection Using Overt Data Sources. Technological Forecasting and Social Change 80(9):1877–1884
Rudner M (2004) Hunters and Gatherers: The Intelligence Coalition Against Islamic Terrorism. International Journal of Intelligence and CounterIntelligence 17:193–230
Ryngaert C (2015) Jurisdiction in International Law, 2nd edn. Oxford University Press, Oxford

Samama N (2008) Global Positioning: Technologies and Performance. Wiley, Hoboken
Sepper E (2010) Democracy, Human Rights, and Intelligence Sharing. Texas International Law Journal 46:151–208
Stanley J, Liao L (2011) Planetary Skin Institute ALERTS: Automated Land Change Evaluation, Reporting and Tracking System. Proceedings of the 2nd International Conference on Computing for Geospatial Research and Applications, Article No. 65. http://dl.acm.org/citation.cfm?doid=1999320.1999388. Accessed 6 June 2016
Steele RD (2007) Foreign Liaison and Intelligence Reform: Still in Denial. International Journal of Intelligence and Counterintelligence 20:167–174
Sugarman D (1983) Legality, Ideology, and the State. Academic Press, New York
Svendsen A (2008) The Globalization of Intelligence Since 9/11: Frameworks and Operational Parameters. Cambridge Review of International Affairs 21:129–144
Svendsen A (2012) Understanding the Globalization of Intelligence. Palgrave Macmillan, Basingstoke
Taylor L, Broeders D (2015) In the Name of Development: Power, Profit and the Datafication of the Global South. Geoforum 64:229–237
Vaitla B (2014) The Landscape of Big Data for Development. UN Foundation/Data2X. http://data2x.org/wp-content/uploads/2014/08/Data2X_LandscapeOfBigDataForDevelopment.pdf. Accessed 6 June 2016
Vattel E (1760) The Law of Nations or the Principles of International Law. Newbery et al, London
Wai R (2002) Transnational Liftoff and Juridical Touchdown: The Regulatory Function of Private International Law in an Era of Globalization 40:209–274
Wang K, Zhou S, Yang Q, Yeung JMS (2005) Mining Customer Value: From Association Rules to Direct Marketing. Data Mining and Knowledge Discovery 11:57–79
Wilde R (2008) International Territorial Administration: How Trusteeship and the Civilizing Mission Never Went Away. Oxford University Press, Oxford
World Bank (2014) Big Data in Action for Development. The World Bank. http://live.worldbank.org/sites/default/files/Big%20Data%20for%20Development%20Report_final%20version.pdf. Accessed 6 June 2016
Yam P (2008) Digital Humanitarianism. Scientific American 298(6):18–18
Zizek S (1989) The Sublime Object of Ideology. Verso Books, London/New York

Chapter 6
'Spoofed Presence Does not Suffice': On Territoriality in the Tallinn Manual

Lianne J.M. Boer

Abstract This chapter explores how the internet materializes in one of the most influential writings on cyberwar and international law, the Tallinn Manual on the International Law Applicable to Cyber Warfare. Based on the work of Molly Sauter, this chapter examines the metaphor used in the Manual to describe the internet, what effect this particular metaphor has, and at which points specific situations made possible by 'cyberspace' escape the confines of this particular metaphor.

Keywords Cyberspace · Metaphor · Tallinn Manual · Jurisdiction · Sovereignty

Contents

6.1 Introduction

In a 2015 article on wired.com, several 'maps' of the internet were shown. One map showed the globe as we know it, highlighting the frequency of internet use in its different parts; one displayed the location of cables transporting internet traffic;

Assistant Professor of Public International Law, Faculty of Law, Vrije Universiteit Amsterdam; Research Fellow, Centre for the Politics of Transnational Law; l.j.m.boer@vu.nl.

L.J.M. Boer (✉)
Vrije Universiteit Amsterdam, Amsterdam, The Netherlands
e-mail: l.j.m.boer@vu.nl

M. Kuijer and W. Werner (eds.), *Netherlands Yearbook of International Law 2016*, Netherlands Yearbook of International Law 47,
DOI 10.1007/978-94-6265-207-1_6

another 'plots the major Internet players and websites as stops on the Tokyo Metro system'.[1]

In the accompanying text, its author Betsy Mason explains how the internet

> is of course a physical architecture of cables, wires and switches that exists, but these material things are more like a backbone or a substrate that enables the Internet to exist. And while these tangible aspects of the Internet are hard enough to visualize, the conceptual part is a mind bender. People have assigned all sorts of physical descriptors to it, attempts to give it a shape [...] Perhaps the most ubiquitous nickname is also the least concrete: cyberspace. But even this amorphous moniker implies a geography, or at least a spatial aspect. And where there is a spatial aspect of any sort, even imagined, there will be maps.[2]

What the above quote shows, is how difficult it is to think of the internet in terms other than 'physical descriptors': the moment we talk about it we imagine a 'physical architecture', in an 'attempt to give shape' to something that is very difficult to grasp.

The importance for the application of law of something *physically* existing is obvious: after all, if something is 'physically there' it implies there is a location to it, which, in turn, implies jurisdiction.[3] In the words of John Agnew, 'space is represented as having effects' (something he refers to as 'spatiality').[4] This chapter enquires into the way the internet materializes in one of the most influential writings on cyber and international law: the Tallinn Manual on the International Law Applicable to Cyber Warfare.[5] This Manual was written by a group of international legal scholars and purports to be a handbook for, for example, State legal advisors. In 95 'rules', the Manual details how existing *jus ad bellum* and *jus in bello* apply to war waged in cyberspace. Here, I focus on the first two rules of the Manual: those on sovereignty and jurisdiction respectively. What I seek to point out is how the discussion in the Manual is limited to that which, in its own words, is 'actually physically present'[6] and what, as a result, is excluded in the same text. My argument builds on a 2015 article by Molly Sauter, in which she explains that the assumption underlying the Manual's discussion of sovereignty and jurisdiction is an

---

[1] B Mason (2015) Beautiful, Intriguing, and Illegal Ways to Map the Internet, Wired, https://www.wired.com/2015/06/mapping-the-internet/, map no. 13, accessed 24 October 2016; on these attempts at 'mapping' see also Cohen 2007, at 237–239.

[2] B Mason (2015) Beautiful, Intriguing, and Illegal Ways to Map the Internet, Wired, https://www.wired.com/2015/06/mapping-the-internet/, accessed 24 October 2016; for a critique of the view that the 'non-material' elements of the internet are legally relevant, see Zeno-Zencovich 2016, at 9, and the discussion outlined below.

[3] Sauter 2015, at 73; Post 2007, at 892; Franzese 2009, at 12; Byassee 1995, i.a. at 199. For a reflection on the relation between space and place, see Cohen 2007, at 230–232.

[4] Agnew 1994, at 55.

[5] Schmitt 2013; for the verb 'materializing' with regard to the internet, see Graham 2013, at 181. It should be noted that this chapter was finalized prior to the appearance of the 'sequel' to the Tallinn Manual (Schmitt 2017); this new edition may contain changes to the sections discussed in this chapter. This chapter, however, is based on the first Tallinn Manual.

[6] Schmitt 2013, at 19 (paraphrased).

idea of the internet as 'an online environment [...] organized at the levels of infrastructure.'[7] What this achieves, as Sauter points out, is the affirmation of the continuance of States' existing legal rights in a new context.[8] Picking up the argument where Sauter left it, I elaborate on what the Manual's choice of 'physical descriptors' results in, and how it manages to 'map' international law onto the internet; how it is understood as something territorial and how the Manual displays a need for it to 'stay there'; where we see glimpses of the internet emerging 'as a distinct place',[9] and the particular phraseology used when this happens.[10]

The chapter is organized as follows: Sect. 6.2 starts with the outline of an ongoing debate on the relation between jurisdiction and the internet, situating the Manual's approach in this debate and subsequently expanding the scope of the discussion to its rule on sovereignty. Section 6.3 presents Sauter's point, further elaborating on the kind of 'space-making'[11] done in the Tallinn Manual, what sort of law-application it results in, and where the particularities of the internet manifestly escape the territorial confines of the Manual's approach. Section 6.4 concludes the chapter.

Finally, a note on the text is in order: the words 'internet' and 'cyberspace' are used interchangeably here. Though according to some they are not the same, the use of the cyberspace metaphor is so ingrained in our normal language use that we hardly 'recognize' it as a metaphor anymore—but see Sect. 6.3 of this chapter—and it would therefore be bordering on the artificial to distinguish between the two.[12]

6.2 Sovereignty and Jurisdiction in the Tallinn Manual

By positing its rule on jurisdiction, the Tallinn Manual positions itself in a decades-old debate on what jurisdiction in cyberspace means exactly.[13] The basic issue here is whether the relation between the two—e.g. the exercise of jurisdiction

[7] Sauter 2015, at 73.

[8] Ibid., at 73.

[9] Johnson and Post 1995, at 1381.

[10] As elaborated on below, this is based on ideas developed by Benoliel and Cohen. On 'mapping' 'law space' onto cyberspace, see Cohen 2007, at 221; Johnson and Post 1995, at 1372 (who use the same phraseology).

[11] Lambach 2016, at 11.

[12] On the artificiality of this distinction, because of the inevitability of the use of metaphors in space-making, see Cohen 2007, at 229; see also 234–235; but see Franzese 2009, at 9, on the distinction between 'internet' and 'cyberspace' (maintaining a different view from the one held here). For a similar argument about the 'embedded[ness] into our daily lives' of the cyberspace metaphor, see Graham 2013, at 180.

[13] See also Tsagourias 2015, at 16–17. For an argument against this stark opposition, see Herrera 2005 and, for different reasons, Cohen 2007 (see, more elaborately, footnote 16).

over cyberattacks—is a problematic one, or whether existing law can continue to operate as it always has.[14] David Post labels the two camps in this debate as the 'exceptionalists' and the 'unexceptionalists': fairly self-explanatory terms, where the first denotes those scholars who hold that a distinct legal regime is necessary for the exercise of jurisdiction in cyberspace; the other camp claiming that existing law suffices.[15] What the opposition between 'exceptionalists' and 'unexceptionalists' demonstrates is different answers to the question 'what kind of space cyberspace "is"': whether cyberspace and 'real space' are fundamentally different, or whether the second can be 'mapped' onto the first.[16] For example, given the features of actions performed via digital infrastructures—the speed at which the data moves around, the unpredictability of the particular trajectory it will follow to get from A to B, etc.[17]—some scholars have argued that the 'space' of cyberspace is fundamentally different from the geographic space covered by existing law.[18] In the words of one commentator, under this view 'information itself has no physicality, and having none, has no borders.'[19] Others, however, maintain that existing law suffices to regulate these actions: after all, a hacker is always operating from or using devices or servers based on one State's particular territory, and the effects will always 'be felt and measured' in one State and/or the other.[20]

---

[14] See also Lambach 2016, at 2–3. For an IR perspective on the challenge posed by cyberspace to the state-system, see Steinberg and McDowell 2003.

[15] Post 2007, at 889 et seq; see also Cohen 2007, i.a. at 212. For an IR perspective on these positions, see McEvoy Manjikian 2010.

[16] Cohen 2007, at 212 and 213–214, 237–239, who similarly refers to these camps as 'exceptionalists' and 'unexceptionalists', with regard to their notion of cyberspace as distinct (or not) from 'real space'. See also Hollis 2015, at 136. Hollis similarly refers to Cohen here; the latter points out that both ideas of 'sameness' as well as 'difference' rest upon '[the] metaphoric construct of cyberspace as separate space' (at 215). In her piece, she reflects on critiques of the metaphor of cyberspace and rejects the question as to the 'real nature' of cyberspace – instead, she says, we have to enquire into 'what kind of space a world that includes cyberspace is and will become' (at 213). Benoliel similarly argues against the distinction between the unexceptionalists and the exceptionalists; see Benoliel 2005, at 150; Ryngaert 2014, at 18; see also Lambach 2016, at section 3.2. Herrera argues the 'gap' between 'cyberspace' and the state's territoriality is not as wide as commonly assumed. See Herrera 2005, e.g. at 2–3. Underlying his argument in part is his claim that the idea of technology having a fixed 'nature' is 'at odds' with the fact that technology is man-made; he states that 'technology is political' (Herrera 2005, at 9); see also Tsagourias 2015, at 14 and Cohen 2007, at 217, pointing out the 'essentialist' label applied to this view of the internet. On theories based on 'the technological malleability of cyberspace' see ibid., at 221 et seq. and 250 et seq. on STS. For the tripartite division in 'law space', 'real space' and cyberspace, see Benoliel 2005, at 146 et seq.; for the word 'law space' Benoliel refers to Johnson and Post 1995, at 1368.

[17] Herrera 2005, at 3 and 4–5.

[18] Johnson and Post 1995, i.a. at 1370 et seq.

[19] Herrera 2005, at 3; note that he is elaborating on a particular position here, he does not adhere to this view himself. See, for this view, Johnson and Post 1995, at 1370 et seq.

[20] Pirker 2013, at 193–194. This is a very brief summary of this position; for examples, see Stein 1998.

David Johnson and David Post—in the exceptionalist camp—describe cyberspace as follows:

> Because events on the Net occur everywhere but nowhere in particular, are engaged in by online personae who are both "real" ... and "intangible" (not necessarily or traceably tied to any particular person in the physical sense), and concern "things" (messages, databases, standing relationships) that are not necessarily separated from one another by any physical boundaries, no physical jurisdiction has a more compelling claim than any other to subject these events exclusively to its laws.[21]

What they portray here, is the internet as an almost 'ethereal'[22] realm, referring to the 'everywhere' and 'nowhere' of online events, the 'intangible' nature of 'online personae' and the absence of 'physical boundaries' in separating 'things'. The question, here, is not so much whether cyberspace affects States' existing legal rights: the more relevant one is whether these rights can still be exercised in a meaningful way.[23]

In contrast, consider the work of the unexceptionalists. For example, Alan Stein argues that statements such as the one quoted above are simply the result of a lack of understanding of technology: '[a]s we master and understand the technology', he says, 'we demystify it. We experience it as a medium, not as a place.'[24] He proceeds by stating that

> [t]he injuries inflicted over the Internet are inflicted by people on people. In this sense, the Internet is no different from the myriad of ways that people from one place injure people in other places [...] interstate activity no longer confounds the courts. There is a rich and complex body of law to test the legitimacy of sovereign claims to regulate and redress interstate claims.[25]

Though Stein does identify 'doctrinal challenges' resulting from exchanges online, these challenges are 'difficult, [but] not intractable', and 'to answer the challenge, we must consider the *existing* jurisdictional framework.'[26] The language used by Stein is markedly different from the language used by Johnson and Post: in his conviction that jurisdiction 'online' may be difficult but ultimately no different than jurisdiction in 'physical space', Stein's language becomes determined and clearly directed at those who argue the unicity of the internet.[27]

---

[21] Johnson and Post 1995, at 1376. For their proposal as to a distinct legal regime, see e.g. at 1401. For an account of this view, see also Herrera 2005, at 3–5.

[22] Graham 2013, at 179.

[23] Post 2007, at 891–893. In response, see MN Schmitt (2015) PILAC Lecture on Cyber Operations and IHL: Fault Lines and Vectors, 3 April 2015, https://www.youtube.com/watch?v=ZWwrVAMSOT4, accessed 11 May 2016, at 7.00. See, for a critique of exceptionalism, Cohen 2007, at 215–219.

[24] Stein 1998, at 1175.

[25] Ibid., at 1180.

[26] Ibid., at 1181 (emphasis added).

[27] For a critique of unexceptionalism, see Cohen 2007, at 219–221.

The very first pages of the Tallinn Manual tell us that it places itself squarely in the latter, the 'unexceptionalist' camp. It opens as follows:

> the International Group of Experts rejected any assertions that international law is silent on cyberspace in the sense that it is a new domain subject to regulation only on the basis of new treaty law. On the contrary, the Experts unanimously concluded that general principles of international law applied to cyberspace.[28]

Existing law applies, the experts state here, and there is no need to develop new laws just because a new phenomenon has appeared on stage. It is echoed in similar statements made by the project's director, Michael Schmitt: that international law can be applied in a 'logical and meaningful' way to cyberspace, and that legal scholars should '[a]pply the law that already exists.'[29] The Manual subsequently posits 95 rules, ranging in scope from sovereignty to the law of occupation as it applies (or does not—which I will return to, below) in cyberspace.[30] Headed by a number (e.g. 'Rule 32') these 'black-letter rules' are presented in bold, containing statements such as, for example, '[t]he civilian population [...] shall not be the object of cyber attack.'[31] The rule in question is then followed by a numbered 'Commentary', usually listing, first, an outline of the international legal norm underlying it, and second, its application to cyber.[32]

The first two rules of the Manual give us its perspective on how sovereignty and jurisdiction operate on the internet exactly: first, '[a] State may exercise control over cyber infrastructure and activities within its sovereign territories',[33] it states, and '[w]ithout prejudice to applicable international obligations, a State may exercise its jurisdiction: (a) over persons engaged in cyber activities on its territory; (b) over cyber infrastructure located on its territory; and (c) extraterritorially, in accordance with international law.'[34] At first glance, and taken together, these rules may be seen as stating the obvious: the State has the right to exercise control over what happens and over whoever acts on its territory. So far, we may think nothing really

---

[28] Schmitt 2013, at 13; see also Hollis 2015, at 146.

[29] MN Schmitt (2015) PILAC Lecture on Cyber Operations and IHL: Fault Lines and Vectors, 3 April 2015, https://www.youtube.com/watch?v=ZWwrVAMSOT4, accessed 11 May 2016, at 7.00; MN Schmitt (2012) ILD 2012 Panel Discussion: Cyber Conflict and the Law of Armed Conflict, 25–27 June 2012, https://www.youtube.com/watch?v=sglT605YIu4, accessed 13 May 2016, at 5.32.

[30] See Schmitt 2013, at 239 et seq; I will briefly return to 'occupation in cyberspace', below.

[31] Ibid., at 113.

[32] See also Werner and Boer 2017. In so doing, the Tallinn Manual places itself squarely in a tradition of international legal handbooks on the application of the laws of war to a new phenomenon—such as armed conflict at sea and air and missile warfare, aimed at 'examin[ing] how extant legal norms applied to [a specific kind] of warfare.' See Schmitt 2013, at 1; on this positioning, see Boer 2017, Chapter 5.

[33] Schmitt 2013, at 15. On the use of the 'infrastructure' metaphor in the Manual, see Sauter 2015, at 70–71, and Sect. 6.3 of this chapter.

[34] Schmitt 2013, at 18.

spectacular happens: this is 'merely restat[ing] the law' that is already out there.[35] In that sense, the experts may be said to have 'add[ed] ... the adjective "cyber"' to what we already know is the law:[36] 'a State may exercise control over its territory', it states, as well as jurisdiction over infrastructure, people and activities.

However, if we look a little closer at how this restatement is achieved, something emerges which may, if not spectacular, at least be noteworthy. Simply put, the territorial sovereignty of the State and its concomitant jurisdiction are applied to those elements of the internet that are 'physically present'.[37] What we find here is a world wide web consisting of physical attributes: sovereignty and jurisdiction over the internet extend to that which is physically possible to control. So, in the commentary accompanying its rule on sovereignty, the experts claim that

> although no State may claim sovereignty over cyberspace *per se*, States may exercise sovereign prerogatives over any cyber infrastructure located on their territory, as well as activities associated with that cyber infrastructure.[38]

The Manual explains that this means the State can exercise sovereignty over 'cyber infrastructure situated in the land territory, internal waters, territorial sea (including its bed and subsoil), archipelagic waters, or national airspace.'[39] Similar references to the 'physicality' of sovereignty in cyberspace can be found elsewhere in this first rule, e.g., '[a] coastal State's sovereignty over the seabed lying beneath its territorial sea allows that State full control over the placement of any submarine cables thereon.'[40] And, '[t]he fact that cyber infrastructure located in a given State's territory is linked to the global telecommunications network cannot be interpreted as a waiver of its sovereign rights over that infrastructure.'[41] Something similar happens in the Manual's 'Rule 2', on jurisdiction:

> It may be difficult to determine jurisdiction within cyberspace because cloud or grid distributed systems can span national borders, as can the replication and dynamic relocation of data and processing. This makes it challenging at any particular time to determine *where all of a user's data and processing reside* since such data can be *located* in multiple jurisdictions simultaneously. These technical challenges do not deprive a State of its legal right to exercise jurisdiction over persons and cyber infrastructure located on its territory.[42]

---

[35] Roscini 2014, at 41. 'Restating' the law in a new context, however, does have a creative force of its own. On this, see Werner 2017; Boer 2013.

[36] Roscini 2014, at 31; see also Werner and Boer 2017.

[37] As pointed out by Sauter 2015: see Sect. 6.3 for an elaboration on her work. The phrase 'physically present' is used in the Manual; see below.

[38] Schmitt 2013, at 16. This statement is echoed in Lambach's discussion of Mueller, who differentiates between 'sovereignty *in* cyberspace' and 'sovereignty *over* cyberspace'. See Lambach 2016, at 6. For Lambach's alternative, see 7–9.

[39] Schmitt 2013, at 16.

[40] Ibid., at 17; see also Finnemore and Hollis 2016, 460.

[41] Schmitt 2013, at 17.

[42] Ibid., at 19 (emphases added).

Here, the Manual talks explicitly of data 'residing' in a jurisdiction. It is not a problem that we do not know where the data is, the experts claim, as it is always at least 'geographically *somewhere*'.[43] In other words, assessing the location of 'data and processing' may be technically difficult, but at heart it is a *jurisdictional* problem. Thus, its diagnosis of 'technical challenges' existing with regard to assessing jurisdiction, is immediately followed by the comforting claim that, whatever the outcome may be, States' 'legal rights' continue to exist: they can still 'exercise jurisdiction' over their own territory. Again, what we find here is the equation of the internet with something that is physical, i.e. *located*; and with location comes sovereignty and jurisdiction.[44]

In the next section, I will elaborate on this link between cyberspace, physical space and jurisdiction,[45] first, by considering the work of Molly Sauter on the use of metaphors in the Tallinn Manual, and, second, by looking more closely at what the use of this particular phraseology reveals.

6.3 The Use of Metaphor in the Tallinn Manual

Roughly speaking, jurisdiction of the State is exercised over that which is physical, be it territory, people, or, stretching the relation somewhat more, effects.[46] This raises the question of what place there is for jurisdiction in a 'virtual', i.e. by implication, 'non-physical universe'?[47] The conclusion drawn in the Manual as to the continued application of existing law becomes inevitable, once one considers that it is simply the result of understanding jurisdiction online as pertaining to that which is 'actually physically present'.

In a 2015 article, Molly Sauter claims (in reference to Johnson and Lakoff's work on metaphors[48]) that the use of metaphors to describe the internet[49] does the trick: how the Manual's legal analysis follows from the metaphor it uses.[50] She doesn't argue against the use of metaphors *as such*—they might simply be tools

[43] Johnson and Post 1995, at 1378 (emphasis added); similarly, Cohen 2007, at 244. See also the references to and elaboration of Sauter's work, below—specifically with regard to the verb 'reside'.

[44] A similar phraseology is used by Lambach 2016, at 4; see also the references in footnotes 3 and 4.

[45] As stated, this threefold distinction is based on Benoliel 2005, at 146–151.

[46] Byassee 1995, at 199; see also Schmitt 2013, at 18.

[47] Based on Byassee 1995, at 198; see also Finnemore and Hollis 2016, 459 (with reference to Cohen 2007).

[48] Lakoff and Johnson 1980.

[49] Sauter 2015; see also Olson 2005, who also refers to the 'cyberspace as place metaphor' (at 10). For her discussion of other metaphors, see at 14–17; for further references to works on cyberspace and metaphors, see Lambach 2016, at 9–10. On the impact of metaphors on policy choices, see footnote 52, below, and the conclusion of this chapter.

[50] Sauter 2015. For a different critique of the Tallinn Manual's reasoning, see Hollis 2015, at 143–145.

necessary to reduce the technical complexities of the internet to something that can be made sense of by, in this case, lawyers.[51] She *does* argue, however (as others have done before her), that the use of a particular metaphor determines the policy choices that follow from it.[52] For example, the metaphor of the internet as a 'global commons' drives the policy maker in a different direction than the metaphor of 'cyberspace'.[53] Sauter points out how particularly the idea of the internet as 'ha[ving] real world geography'[54] facilitates

> an understanding of the internet as being easily and intuitively divided according to the geographic and political divisions that constitute nation-state borders in the physical world. It assumes that attributing a given code action to a space within the *digital* borders of a nation-state would be simple [...].[55]

So, the idea of the internet as susceptible to geographic breakdowns implies a specific location, and thus a specific *physical* space where we can say the internet 'happens'—at least for legal purposes. Something similar emerged from the quote used in the introduction of this chapter, pertaining to maps of the internet: the use of 'cyberspace' as a 'physical descriptor', the article was quoted as saying, 'implies geography'—which, in turn, immediately flags something physically existing *somewhere*. Sauter explains how this idea of the internet as geographic space is precisely the metaphor found in the Manual's sections on sovereignty and jurisdiction.[56] For example, the Manual explicitly refers to data 'residing' in a jurisdiction—which makes it possible to reduce the issue of jurisdiction to who gets to exercise it.[57] The verb 'reside', moreover, is precisely the one used by Sauter to explain the implications of this particular metaphor of the internet as 'having real world geography': it facilitates a view on 'nation-states as having special power and control over those aspects of the internet', she writes, 'that "reside" within their geographic and political borders.'[58] By reducing the internet to its physical components it becomes possible to think of the internet in 'jurisdictional terms'.[59] After all, the globe is divided in territories, so anything that physically exists always

---

[51] Ibid., at 64–66; for the inevitability of this move, see also Cohen 2007, at 229.

[52] Sauter 2015, at 77; see also Cohen 2007, at 211 and Graham 2013, at 177. Lambach similarly talks of 'attempt[s] at space-making', see Lambach 2016, at 11 (emphasis removed).

[53] Sauter 2015, at 64, 67, 68 and 77. For a discussion and critique of cyberspace as a commons, see Brunnée and Meshel 2015 at 22–25; Tsagourias 2015, at 24–28; and Franzese 2009, at 14–18.

[54] Sauter 2015, at 72 et seq.

[55] Ibid., at 73 (emphasis in original).

[56] Ibid., at 73.

[57] Schmitt 2013, at 19; for Sauter's argument about the relation between data and the 'internet has a real-world geography', see Sauter 2015, at 73. She discusses the 'data as an object' metaphor separately, but also suggests this metaphor and the one described in this section support each other. See ibid., at 72.

[58] Sauter 2015, at 73, see also 74; see also Hollis 2015, at 138.

[59] See also Lambach 2016, at 2; see also the references to Herrera 2005; Cohen 2007 and Benoliel 2005, above.

exists somewhere, i.e. within a particular State's jurisdiction.[60] So, as Sauter explains, a view of the internet as possessing 'real world geography'

> allow[s] the rules and guidelines laid out in the [Tallinn] manual to rely on traditional ideas of accountability and attribution [...] the idea of accountability and attribution relies on a physically-based understanding of activities as occurring in a distinct geographic place.[61]

This idea stands in sharp contrast to the ideas of Johnson and Post, elaborated on above, that 'events on the Net occur everywhere but nowhere in particular'. The legal experts involved in the Manual would vehemently disagree with this qualification: there is most certainly a 'particularity' to the location of 'events on the Net', they would argue, and this is what facilitates the exercise of jurisdiction by the State.

The point Sauter makes is that this is made possible by means of the use of a particular metaphor. To the Tallinn Manual scholars, however, the internet is a very physical thing, and *does*—to quote Sauter against herself—'[possess] real-world geography'.[62] The wired.com article quoted in the introduction to this chapter described it as 'this weird combination of physical and conceptual things', very difficult to grasp in its entirety perhaps, but there is no doubting the existence of 'cables, wires and switches'.[63] At the very least, for the international legal scholars such as the ones participating in the Tallinn Manual project, to say that these 'cables, wires and switches' are subject to a State's jurisdiction does not follow from the use of a particular metaphor, but from the materiality of the thing itself.[64] However, whether that is the whole story and whether as a result of this, jurisdiction can be meaningfully exercised, is precisely the point of contention laid out in the previous section between the 'exceptionalists' and the 'unexceptionalists'.

To understand this point of contention better, it is useful to turn to the work of Daniel Benoliel. He defines the discussion between the exceptionalist and the unexceptionalist camp as revolving around the relation between 'law space', 'physical' or 'real space' and 'cyberspace'.[65] What happens in international legal thinking, as we can see from John Agnew's argument, is a mapping of 'law space' onto 'physical space'.[66] In other words, and as cited above, to the international legal mind, 'space is represented as having effects', i.e., jurisdiction and sovereignty. There is no place, Benoliel explains, that is free from the exercise of sovereignty (and thus, jurisdiction): 'the physical world is presently subject to a default rule of a

[60] Sauter 2015, at 73; Agnew 1994, i.a. at 55–56; Franzese 2009, at 12; Benoliel 2005, at 155; 171; Byassee 1995, at 199.

[61] Sauter 2015, at 73.

[62] Ibid., at 72; similarly, Cohen 2007, at 211 and 217–218 (reflecting on the physical presence of cyberspace users). Thanks to Sofia Stolk for a discussion on this point.

[63] B Mason (2015) Beautiful, Intriguing, and Illegal Ways to Map the Internet, Wired, https://www.wired.com/2015/06/mapping-the-internet/, accessed 24 October 2016.

[64] See also Lambach 2016, at 4.

[65] Benoliel 2005, at 146–148; see also footnote 16, above.

[66] Ibid., at 146.

continuous public sphere.'[67] The question is whether cyberspace, as a 'third', can be neatly mapped onto those first two, or whether there are elements that escape 'this strict comparison between cyberspace and the physical world'.[68] Another way to explain this, is by—as another author does—distinguishing between 'cyber territory' and 'cyberspace'. The first denotes 'the particular notion that a state may own part of cyberspace through claiming it as territory'; the second, in the author's understanding, 'that events and agreements are taking place in cyberspace or virtual space rather than in real space'.[69] What we see happening in the Tallinn Manual, however, is an equation of 'cyber territory' with 'cyberspace', or, in the words of Benoliel, the equation of 'law space', 'real space', and 'cyberspace'.

The internet, however, may occasionally escape these confines of physical space —or at least, the law and its territorial connotations may only get one so far when considering other kinds of events or activities. These limits manifest themselves at several points in the Manual. For example, in its section on jurisdiction, the experts discuss the possibility that the location of the computer used to perpetrate harm is manipulated by the attacker, something known as 'spoofing'. This corrupts the information as to the actual location of the computer, making the person doing the locating think the computer is located somewhere, while in fact it is located somewhere *else*. At this point in the text, the Manual issues a warning: '[a]ctual physical presence', it states, 'is required, and sufficient, for jurisdiction based on territoriality.'[70] 'Spoofed coordinates', it states, will not do as a basis for jurisdiction, as here, nothing is 'actually physically present' on the State's territory. In these cases, the Manual states, jurisdiction cannot be exercised on the basis of territoriality: 'spoofed presence', it says, 'does not suffice.'[71] We might add that 'spoofed presence does not suffice' for the purposes of territorial jurisdiction as understood by the legal experts—when nothing is 'actually physically present'. In other words, false location is no location for the purposes of jurisdiction.[72] This phrase from the Manual thus also serves as the title of this chapter: it points out precisely where the equation of law space, with physical space, with cyberspace fails.

Another example of those points where 'law space', 'physical space' and 'cyberspace' fail to overlap in the Manual, is that of the law of occupation: traditionally, in international humanitarian law a 'territory is "occupied" once it is actually placed under the authority of [a] hostile army.'[73] It basically means that another State controls the territory of the State it has just conquered and 'exercise[s]

---

[67] Ibid., at 155.

[68] Ibid., at 147.

[69] Manjikian 2015, at 65.

[70] Schmitt 2013, at 19.

[71] Ibid., at 19.

[72] Note that the possibility of spoofing is one of the reasons Johnson and Post argue against the idea of an analogy between physical (territorial) space and the internet. See Johnson and Post 1995, at 1374.

[73] Schmitt 2013, at 239.

… military authority' on that particular territory.[74] Applied to cyberspace, however, this notion of occupation becomes completely moot—and this much is stated in the Manual itself: 'There is no legal notion of occupation of cyberspace', it says.[75] Being one of the last rules in the Manual, it echoes the very first: 'no State may claim sovereignty over cyberspace *per se*'. Here, the Manual's reduction of cyberspace to a physical place fails, and the gap between 'physical space' and 'cyberspace' widens.[76] The assumption that we could 'map' the real world onto cyberspace—that '[it] is politically organized in an identical way to the real world'[77]—as attempted in those maps displayed in the wired.com article, fails here.

What Sauter's work brings to the fore, is that to say that the internet has an 'infrastructure' has a particular effect on how the law is applied. Here, we find 'container notions of the territorial state […] something static that other things happen in.'[78] The territorial space occupied by the State is something that, in the view of the legal experts, cyberspace 'happens in', thereby subjecting cyberspace to the control of the State. In one of his presentations on the Manual, the group's director, Michael Schmitt, reveals—perhaps unwittingly—the force of this idea. Here, he discusses how the legal scholars involved in the Manual were accompanied by technical experts, as part of the drafting process. The importance of their participation is described by Schmitt as follows:

> I spent the first year thinking 'the cloud' was like really up there […] I didn't think it was a cloud floating [along] […] but I did think there were like these waves, like radios and then you just reach up and you grab them out of the sky and then about a year into it finally one of the techies who spoke some language that was incomprehensible to me, finally got through to me and I went 'oh!' and it makes a huge difference. Huge difference obviously in law because of the principle of sovereignty.[79]

The 'huge difference' referred to here by Schmitt follows from the idea that 'the cloud' is located somewhere. This means, quite simply, that the law can be applied: again, location in law equals territory, equals sovereignty, equals jurisdiction.[80] In sum, what we find in the Tallinn Manual is an idea of 'cyberspace … [as] tightly enmeshed in the logic of physical space.'[81] From this perspective, it certainly makes sense to consider that which is 'actually physically present' as subject to the State's sovereignty and thus, territorial jurisdiction.

---

[74] Ibid., at 239.

[75] Ibid., at 239.

[76] For a reflection, see Cohen 2007, at 212–213; and Benoliel 2005, at 149–151.

[77] Sauter 2015, at 73; see also Lambach 2016, at 2.

[78] Lambach 2016, at 10 (single quotation marks omitted); see also Agnew 1994, at 68–71 on the 'container notion of the state'; Steinberg and McDowell 2003, at 204.

[79] MN Schmitt (2012) CyCon 2012 Tallinn Manual Part I, 4th Annual International Conference on Cyber Conflict (CyCon), 5–8 June 2012, Tallinn, https://www.youtube.com/watch?v=wY3uEo-Itso, accessed 26 April 2016, at 8.08.

[80] See also Lambach 2016, at 4; Benoliel 2005, at 171, and generally, Agnew 1994.

[81] Lambach 2016, at 2 (emphasis omitted).

The conclusion of this chapter briefly elaborates on the function of the metaphor used in the Tallinn Manual, as described above.

6.4 Conclusion

This chapter has enquired into the way the Tallinn Manual understands the relation between cyberspace and law; it has positioned that claim in an ongoing debate about this particular relation, and finally it has brought to the fore how this position is facilitated by the use of a particular metaphor—and where it visibly fails to do its work.

According to Molly Sauter, the importance of the metaphor used by the Tallinn Manual lies in that it is in NATO's interest that similar borders apply in cyberspace as well as in 'real space'.[82] As pointed out by one commentator, '[s]pace-making is an exercise of power [...] claiming control is [...] a powerful act.'[83] Though I agree with Sauter's and others' claim that the metaphor used has a particular (policy, or legal) effect, I would emphasize that here, the interested party is primarily the group of experts, not NATO itself.[84] The metaphor, I would argue, serves the political project of the Tallinn process: to ensure that the Manual is used by States. I do not claim that the reduction of the internet to its 'physical' manifestations was 'consciously chosen'[85] by the legal experts—it may or may not be. But, however it came to be used, it ensures—as the Manual itself explicitly points out—the continuance of States' existing legal rights in cyberspace. In the words of Daniel Lambach, the legal experts are engaged in 'territorialization': 'the process by which "empty space" is brought under control of some actor.'[86] This is precisely what happens by means of the metaphor employed by the experts. If 'space-making' is, indeed, an 'exercise of power', this is the power exercised here: what the Manual does, is fulfill its own purpose of being used by, for example, State legal advisors.[87] The 'users' or 'customers' of the Manual, as phrased by the director himself, are

---

[82] Sauter 2015, at 73.

[83] Lambach 2016, at 3. This doesn't mean we can do without; see Cohen 2007, at 234–235 ('[o]ne cannot simply refuse to talk about cyberspace as space, and to do so is to abandon powerful tools.').

[84] It should be noted that any link between a formal doctrine on cyberwar as adhered to by NATO, and the work of the Tallinn Manual experts has been vehemently denied time and again by the experts and their director themselves. See, for example, Schmitt 2013, at 11; and MN Schmitt (2012) CyCon 2012 Tallinn Manual Part I, 4th Annual International Conference on Cyber Conflict (CyCon), Tallinn, 5–8 June 2012, https://www.youtube.com/watch?v=wY3uEo-Itso, accessed 26 April 2016, at 1.48.

[85] On '[(un)]consciously chosen' metaphors, see Cohen 2007, at 229.

[86] Lambach 2016, at 12.

[87] MN Schmitt (2015) PILAC Lecture on Cyber Operations and IHL: Fault Lines and Vectors, 3 April 2015, https://www.youtube.com/watch?v=ZWwrVAMSOT4, accessed 11 May 2016, at 52. 31.

primarily States.[88] Confirming that cyberspace is to a very large extent no different from what they already know, means, to continue the market analogy, that States might just 'buy' (into) the Manual and its legal claims.[89] The function of the Manual may not just be the application of law, but a place for the Manual on State legal advisors' bookshelves.[90]

References

Agnew J (1994) The Territorial Trap: The Geographical Assumptions of International Relations Theory. Review of International Political Economy 1:53–80

Benoliel D (2005) Law, Geography and Cyberspace: The Case of On-Line Territorial Privacy. Cardozo Arts & Entertainment Law Journal 23(1):125–196

Boer LJM (2013) Restating the Law 'As It Is': On the Tallinn Manual and the Use of Force in Cyberspace. Amsterdam Law Forum 5(3):4–18

Boer LJM (2017) International law as we know it: Cyberwar discourse and the construction of knowledge in international legal scholarship. Dissertation Vrije Universiteit Amsterdam

Brunnée J, Tamar M (2015) Teaching an Old Law New Tricks: International Environmental Law Lessons for Cyberspace Governance. In: Odendahl K, Matz-Lück N, von Arnauld A (eds) German Yearbook of International Law, Vol 58. Duncker & Humblot, Berlin, pp 129–168

Byassee WS (1995) Jurisdiction of Cyberspace: Applying Real World Precedent to the Virtual Community. Wake Forest Law Review 30:197–220

Cohen JE (2007) Cyberspace as/and Space. Columbia Law Review 107:210–256

Finnemore M, Hollis D (2016) Constructing Norms for Global Cybersecurity. American Journal of International Law 110: 425–479

Franzese PW (2009) Sovereignty in Cyberspace: Can it Exist? Air Force Law Review 64:-1–42

Graham M (2013) *Commentary* Geography/internet: Ethereal alternate dimensions of cyberspace or grounded augmented realities? The Geographical Journal 179: 177–182

Herrera GL (2005) Cyberspace and Sovereignty: Thoughts on Physical Space and Digital Space. First International CISS/ETH Conference on The Information Revolution and the Changing Face of International Relations and Security, Lucerne, Switzerland

Hollis D (2015) Re-Thinking the Boundaries of Law in Cyberspace: A Duty to Hack? In: Ohlin JD, Govern K, Finkelstein C (eds) Cyber War: Law and Ethics for Virtual Conflicts. Oxford University Press, Oxford, pp 129–174

Johnson DR, Post D (1995) Law and Borders: The Rise of Law in Cyberspace. Stanford Law Review 48:1367–1402

Lakoff G, Johnson M (1980) Metaphors we Live By. The University of Chicago Press, Chicago/London

Lambach D (2016) The Territorialization of Cyberspace. Conference Paper. https://www.researchgate.net/publication/308720083_The_Territorialization_of_Cyberspace. Accessed 16 February 2017

[88] Schmitt 2013, at 6, 7; MN Schmitt (2012) CyCon 2012 Tallinn Manual Part I, 4th Annual International Conference on Cyber Conflict (CyCon), Tallinn, 5–8 June 2012, https://www.youtube.com/watch?v=wY3uEo-Itso, accessed 26 April 2016, at 11.17; MN Schmitt (2015) PILAC Lecture on Cyber Operations and IHL: Fault Lines and Vectors, 3 April 2015, https://www.youtube.com/watch?v=ZWwrVAMSOT4, accessed 11 May 2016, at 52.59.

[89] Sauter suggests this might happen, see Sauter 2015, at 70.

[90] For a similar point, see Ryngaert 2014, at 1.

Manjikian M (2015) Confidence-building in Cyberspace: A Comparison of Territorial and Weapons-based Regimes. Strategic Studies Institute and United States Army War College Press, Carlisle Barracks

McEvoy Manjikian M (2010) From Global Village to Virtual Battlespace: The Colonizing of the Internet and the Extension of Realpolitik. International Studies Quarterly 54: 381–401

Olson KK (2005) Cyberspace as Place and the Limits of Metaphor Convergence: The International Journal of Research into New Media Technologies 11(1):10–18

Pirker B (2013) Territorial Sovereignty and Integrity and the Challenges of Cyberspace. In: Ziolkowski K (ed) Peacetime Regime for State Activities in Cyberspace: International Law, International Relations and Diplomacy. NATO Cooperative Cyber Defence Centre of Excellence (CCD COE) Publications, Tallinn, pp 189–216

Post DG (2007) Governing Cyberspace: Law Symposium Review. Santa Clara High Technology Law Journal 24:883–913

Roscini M (2014) Cyber Operations and the Use of Force in International Law. Oxford University Press, Oxford

Ryngaert CMJ (2014) The End of Territory? The Re-Emergence of Community as a Principle of Jurisdictional Order in the Internet Era. https://papers.ssrn.com/sol3/papers.cfm?abstract_id=2523354. Accessed 6 December 2016

Sauter M (2015) Show Me On the Map Where They Hacked You: Cyberwar and the Geospatial Internet Doctrine. Case Western Reserve Journal of International Law 47:63–77

Schmitt MN (2012) ILD 2012 Panel Discussion: Cyber Conflict and the Law of Armed Conflict, 25–27 June 2012, https://www.youtube.com/watch?v=sglT605YIu4, accessed 13 May 2016

Schmitt MN (2012) CyCon 2012 Tallinn Manual Part I, 4th Annual International Conference on Cyber Conflict (CyCon), 5–8 June 2012, Tallinn, https://www.youtube.com/watch?v=wY3uEo-Itso, accessed 26 April 2016

Schmitt MN (ed) (2013) Tallinn Manual on the International Law Applicable to Cyber Warfare. Cambridge University Press, Cambridge

Schmitt MN (2015) PILAC Lecture on Cyber Operations and IHL: Fault Lines and Vectors, 3 April 2015, https://www.youtube.com/watch?v=ZWwrVAMSOT4, accessed 11 May 2016

Schmitt MN (ed) (2017) Tallinn Manual 2.0 on the International Law Applicable to Cyber Operations. Cambridge University Press, Cambridge

Stein AR (1998) The Unexceptional Problem of Jurisdiction in Cyberspace. The International Lawyer 32:1167–1194

Steinberg P, McDowell S (2003) Global Communication and the Post-Statism of Cyberspace: A Spatial Constructivist View. Review of International Political Economy 10:196–221

Tsagourias N (2015) The Legal Status of Cyberspace. In: Tsagourias N, Russel B (eds) Research Handbook on International Law and Cyberspace. Edward Elgar Publishing, Cheltenham/Northampton, pp 13–29

Werner WG (2017) The Law at Hand: What Does it Mean to Restate International Humanitarian Law in the Form of a Manual? In: Krieger H (ed) Legitimacy in International Humanitarian Law. Forthcoming

Werner WG, Boer LJM (2017) It Could Probably Just as Well Be Otherwise: Imageries of Cyberwar. In: Ambrus M, Rayfuse R, Werner W (eds) Risk and the Regulation of Uncertainty in International Law. Oxford University Press, Oxford, pp 39–55

Zeno-Zencovich V (2016) Around the CJEU Schrems Decision: Digital Sovereignty and International Governance of Telecommunication Networks. https://papers.ssrn.com/sol3/papers2.cfm?abstract_id=2788789. Accessed 27 November 2016

Chapter 7
Cybercrime, Evidence and Territoriality: Issues and Options

Jan Kleijssen and Pierluigi Perri

Abstract This chapter aims to explore policy proposals to deal with one of the most complicated problems posed by the Internet, namely that of jurisdiction. While cybercrime is a phenomenon without borders, the effective prosecution of such a crime is seriously hampered by conflicts of territoriality and jurisdiction. These problems are exacerbated by the evolution of information technology, in particular cloud computing which creates 'loss of location' problems for collecting the electronic evidence indispensable for prosecuting crime. The Cloud Evidence Group—a Working Group established by decision of the Cybercrime Convention Committee (T-CY) of the Council of Europe—has proposed, within the limits of agreed legal principles of territoriality and jurisdiction, a series of measures which, together with proper implementation of the Convention, would enable fast and effective access to electronic evidence, while respecting human rights and the rule of law.

Keywords Council of Europe · Cloud computing · Territoriality · Budapest Convention on Cybercrime · Location of data · Jurisdiction

---

Jan Kleijssen is Director of Information Society and Action against Crime at the Council of Europe. Pierluigi Perri is Associate Research Professor at University of Milan, and Advisor on Cybercrime at the Council of Europe. The views and opinions expressed in this contribution are those of the authors and do not necessarily reflect the official position of the Council of Europe.

J. Kleijssen (✉)
Information Society and Action Against Crime, Council of Europe, Strasbourg, France
e-mail: jan.kleijssen@coe.int

P. Perri
University of Milan, Milan, Italy
e-mail: pierluigi.perri@unimi.it

M. Kuijer and W. Werner (eds.), *Netherlands Yearbook of International Law 2016*, Netherlands Yearbook of International Law 47,
DOI 10.1007/978-94-6265-207-1_7

Contents

7.1 Introduction

Millions of attacks against computers and data are recorded each day worldwide. At the same time, only a very small fraction of computer-related crime or cybercrime,[1] that is offences against and by means of computers, is actually prosecuted and adjudicated.

The difference with other forms of crime, for example 'ordinary' crimes or transnational crimes, may be found in the specifics of cybercrime, which can be performed from a distance, using different methods to hide IP addresses[2] or electronic traces,[3] and may not be detected for a long time.[4] Moreover, the general understanding of 'crime' as such is different in many ways.

There are five elements that characterise cybercrime that should be recalled. First is the change of the *scena criminis*, which becomes intangible; second, the emergence of completely new types of crime (i.e. phishing);[5] third, the impact on law

[1] Defined here as offences against and by means of computer data and systems in the sense of Articles 2 to 11 of the Budapest Convention on Cybercrime, ETS No 185, 23 November 2001.

[2] The IP address is a unique address represented by a number, which identifies the device over the Internet. It is important to underline, with regard to criminal investigations, that an IP address identifies only the device and not the user behind it.

[3] One of the best known tools with which to achieve a good anonymization is TOR (The Onion Router), which is a network of computers (nodes) that distributes the transactions over several places on the Internet, so that it is almost impossible from one single node to trace the user.

[4] Consider, for example, the recent case of hacking of the SWIFT global banking system that affected at least twelve central banks like the Bank of Bangladesh, the Bank of Vietnam, the Bank of Philippines, the Bank of Ecuador and the Ukrainian Bank, with a loss of hundreds of million dollars.

[5] Phishing is one of the most widespread cybercrimes that consists of computer fraud to obtain sensitive information of the victim, such as credit card numbers, usernames and passwords for internet banking platforms, personal data of the victim, etc. According to the draft version of the Comprehensive Study on Cybercrime of UNODC (United Nations Office on Drug and Crime), '[i]ndividual cybercrime victimization is significantly higher than for "conventional" crime forms. Victimization rates for online credit card fraud, identify theft, responding to a phishing attempt, and experiencing unauthorized access to an email account, vary between 1 and 17% of the online population'. UNODC 2013, at 25.

enforcement procedures, requiring international co-operation between law enforcement agencies and a multi-stakeholder approach;[6] fourth, the decentralisation of the control over digital networks, which has major consequences for the identification of the country, company or place where the evidence is transmitted or stored; fifth, the openness and interdependence of the Internet, which creates shared vulnerabilities affecting all people accessing a specific digital network.[7]

Other types of crime may not always be sufficiently prosecuted, for lack of resources in case of ordinary crime or for lack of specific provisions in case of transnational crimes. However, cybercrimes are hardly ever prosecuted due to the difficulties connected with the very nature of the network and of the electronic evidence, which requires immediate access to the data as well as cooperation between the law enforcement agencies and the providers.[8]

Moreover, nowadays evidence in relation to any crime is increasingly available only in electronic form on computer systems or storage devices and needs to be preserved for criminal proceedings.[9] Criminal investigations not relying on electronic evidence are becoming the exception, not only for cybercrime but also for 'ordinary' crime, because virtually every investigation now involves digital evidence.[10] Access to electronic evidence—in relation to cybercrime and any other type of crime—is thus essential for criminal justice authorities as well as for ensuring the rule of law in general, which requires that there can be no overall impunity for criminals.

[6] Some provisions of the Budapest Convention on Cybercrime are focused on the cooperation between the Parties (see Articles 23 and 25).

[7] Balkin et al. 2007.

[8] There are different definitions of 'provider', according to the service that they deliver to their customers. In fact, under the general category of the Internet Service Provider (ISP), we can identify for example access providers, hosting providers, cloud providers, VoIP providers and content providers.

[9] For example, the recent disputes over the encryption of iPhones were not related to cybercrime but to cases of terrorism and drug trafficking. D Chmielewski (2016) Apple-FBI Encryption Battle Shifts to New York, 8 April 2016, http://www.recode.net/2016/4/8/11585978/apple-fbi-encryption-battle-shifts-to-new-york, accessed 20 January 2017.

[10] Kerr 2015. Already in this paper of eleven years ago, the Author argues how the law of criminal procedure must be changed as a result of the increasing number of cases based largely on digital evidence. The rise of the number of mobile and personal devices that store not only our personal information (i.e. e-mail, instant messaging contents, bank account movements) but also other information automatically (i.e. location, heart rate, circadian rhythm) combined with the spreading of this information on social network platforms, is creating a large amount of data related to the person under investigation that must be taken into account.

However, the matter is complex. A major problem is that electronic evidence is often not located in the territory of the investigating criminal justice authority. Data is increasingly stored on, mirrored on, or fragmented or moving between servers 'somewhere in the cloud', in possibly multiple or unknown jurisdictions, while criminal justice authorities are normally limited by the principle of territoriality.[11] Even if data is stored in the territory of an investigating authority and a server or device could be lawfully searched and seized, this will not be sufficient if the natural or legal person in possession or control of the data—that is, the person with the 'keys' to the data—is elsewhere.[12] The question, therefore, is how electronic evidence can be secured lawfully and effectively for criminal justice purposes while meeting human rights and rule of law requirements and respecting the principles of State sovereignty.

To address this question, in December 2014 the Cybercrime Convention Committee (T-CY)–the entity representing the Parties to the Council of Europe's Budapest Convention on Cybercrime–established a Cloud Evidence Working Group (CEG) which was tasked with identifying solutions by the end of 2016.[13] This contribution is based on the findings and recommendations of this Group.

---

[11] Usually, the starting point of this endless debate is identified in the paper by Johnson and Post published in 1996 in the Stanford Law Review 'Law and Borders—The Rise of Law in Cyberspace', in which the Authors argued that 'The rise of the global computer network is destroying the link between geographical location and: (1) the power of local governments to assert control over online behavior; (2) the effects of online behavior on individuals or things; (3) the legitimacy of a local sovereign's effort to regulate global phenomena; and (4) the ability of physical location to give notice of which sets of rules apply' (see Johnson and Post 1996, at 1370). But the debate is still open and many scholars focus their research on the new challenges for the principle of territoriality in cyberspace, for example Goldsmith 1998; Reidenberg 2005; Bach and Newman 2006; Kulesza 2008; Schultz 2008; de Hert and Kopcheva 2011; Daskal 2015; Osula 2015; Svantesson and Gerry 2015; Svantesson and van Zwieten 2016; Zoetekouw 2016.

[12] The 'un-territoriality' of data in the cloud is, in fact, one of the most challenging problems for government authorities to search and seize digital evidence: firstly due to the difficulties of determining where the data is stored, so as to identify the applicable jurisdiction, and secondly due to the clash of different judicial systems. See Daskal 2015.

[13] The Cloud Evidence Group (CEG) was a Working Group established by decision of the Cybercrime Convention Committee (T-CY) in December 2014. The aim of this Group is to explore solutions on criminal justice access to evidence stored on servers in the cloud and in foreign jurisdictions, including through mutual legal assistance. The members of CEG are the members of the T-CY Bureau plus up to five extra additional members. The objective of the Cloud Evidence Group was to prepare a report on criminal justice access to data in the cloud. During its activity, the Cloud Evidence Group issued several reports, including the Guidance Note on Article 18 of the Budapest Convention (production order) and the final report "Criminal justice access to data in the cloud: recommendations for considerations by the T-CY", that are all published on http://www.coe.int/en/web/cybercrime/ceg (accessed 18 July 2017). During the last Plenary of 7-9 June 2017, the T-CY decided to follow one of the recommendations included in the final report and approved the Terms of Reference for an Additional Protocol to the Budapest Convention in order to help law enforcement to secure evidence on servers in foreign, multiple or unknown jurisdictions. This will be the second Additional Protocol to the Budapest Convention after the Additional Protocol concerning the criminalisation of acts of a racist and xenophobic nature committed through computer systems.

7.2 Challenges

7.2.1 Cybercrime and Electronic Evidence: The Globalization of Threats

Reportedly, trillions of security incidents are noted on networks each year[14] and millions of attacks against computer systems and data are recorded every day.[15] The amount of daily news on ongoing threats is hard to follow.[16]

As pointed out by the members of the Cloud Evidence Group, cybercrime is not simply a matter of attacks against machines. A review of the current scale, scope and challenges related to cybercrime and electronic evidence (that is, evidence in the form of data generated by or stored on a computer system) suggests that cybercrime has become a serious threat to the fundamental rights of individuals, to the rule of law and to democratic societies.[17]

The theft and misuse of personal data processed and stored in electronic form (i.e. email account data, credit card details, address books, patient records, etc.) affect the right to private life (including the protection of personal data) of hundreds of millions of individuals. Recent examples of huge personal data breaches[18] include the theft of personal details of 37 million users—combined with extortion—from the website Ashley Madison,[19] of 15 million users from T-Mobile US, or of 150,000 customers of TalkTalk UK.[20] In May 2016, it was reported that the

[14] See Symantec Internet Security Threat Report, Volume 21, April 2016, http://www.symantec.com/deepsight-products, accessed 20 October 2016.

[15] See for example the Overview of current cyberattacks on Deutsche Telekom sensors, http://www.sicherheitstacho.eu/?lang=en, accessed 30 October 2016.

[16] To give an example, see the web page on the ongoing threats managed and constantly updated by the CERT-EU (Computer Emergency Response Team for the EU institutions, bodies and agencies): http://cert.europa.eu/cert/filteredition/en/CERT-LatestNews.html, accessed 30 October 2016.

[17] See T-CY 2015b, at 4.

[18] A personal data breach is defined by Article 4 of the EU General Data Protection Regulation (Regulation EU 2016/679) as 'a breach of security leading to the accidental or unlawful destruction, loss, alteration, unauthorized disclosure of, or access to, personal data transmitted, stored or otherwise processed'.

[19] It is necessary to point out that the theft of subscribers' data from the Ashley Madison website is more sensitive if compared to other websites, considering that it is an online dating service and social networking service marketed to people who are married or in committed relationships. An unfortunate end of this story, among others, was the suicide committed by a pastor outed by the publication of Ashley Madison's account. Recently, the website settled the customer class action for 11.2 million dollars.

[20] See Talbot 2016.

passwords and sexual preferences of 40 million users[21] were up for sale on the dark web.[22]

Cybercrime thus represents an attack against the dignity and integrity of individuals, in particular children.[23] The Internet Watch Foundation, a UK independent organisation established in 1996 by the UK internet industry, recently reported a four-fold increase in child abuse imagery over the past two years[24] because new technologies reportedly help offenders groom and procure children for abuse and are 'fuelling a global boom in child sex tourism'.[25]

Other types of cyberattacks, such as distributed denial of service (DDOS) attacks,[26] website defacement[27] and others attacks aimed to compromise the availability of resources on the web, which can be used against media, civil society organisations, individuals or public institutions, also affect freedom of expression.

Consequently, cybercrime, even if carried out by ordinary criminals or terrorists, poses a grave threat to democracy and to our security. Governments, parliaments

---

[21] For more information, see J Murdock (2016) Fling.com Breach: Passwords and Sexual Preferences of 40 Million Users Up For Sale on Dark Web, IBTimes, 6 May 2016, http://www.ibtimes.co.uk/fling-com-breach-passwords-sexual-preferences-40-million-users-sale-dark-web-1558711, accessed 20 October 2016.

[22] Experts use the expression 'dark web' to identify websites that host illegal content and that are not indexed by normal search engines like Google, Yahoo!, Bing, etc. (the indexed web is called 'surface web'). The dark web is intentionally hidden, to some extent anonymous, and is inaccessible with the standard configuration of web browsers, requiring other tools to join in these websites and get the contents.

[23] *K.U. v Finland*, ECtHR, No. 2872/02, 2 March 2009.

[24] See Internet Watch Foundation (2015) Annual Report, https://www.iwf.org.uk/report/2015-annual-report, accessed 20 October 2016.

[25] See ECPAT (2016) Global Study on Sexual Exploitation of Children in Travel and Tourism, http://cf.cdn.unwto.org/sites/all/files/docpdf/global-report-offenders-move-final.pdf, accessed 21 October 2016.

[26] A distributed denial of service (DDOS) attack is an attack where multiple compromised servers are used to target a single system flooding it with many fake requests, with the result that the server becomes inaccessible for the legitimate users and the service is taken down.

[27] A defacement is an attack aimed to change the content of a webpage without the consent of the owner of the webpage. This type of attack is often used to cause reputational damages to companies or to spread political or other propaganda. For example, following the Charlie Hebdo attack of 7 January 2015, more than 20,000 websites in France were under attack, rendering websites inaccessible either by defacing them or by sending multiple requests to a server to render its services inaccessible. Another example are the attacks against the French channel TV5 that targeted their Facebook and Twitter accounts, Internet website as well as the broadcasting programme, shutting down the network for several hours. See J Campbell (2015) French TV network TV5Monde 'hacked by cyber caliphate in unprecedented attack' that revealed personal details of French soldiers, The Independent, http://www.independent.co.uk/news/world/europe/french-tv-network-tv5monde-hijacked-by-isis-hackers-in-unprecedented-attack-that-revealed-personal-10164285.html, accessed 21 October 2016.

and other public institutions as well as critical infrastructure[28] are faced with attacks every day that require specific competences and tools to investigate and contain possible damages. Last year, for example, the German Parliament was the victim of a cyberattack that infected 20,000 machines forcing the entire network to shutdown and set up a new system,[29] and recently ransomware[30] paralyzed a hydroelectric power plant in the United States by infecting its computer systems.[31]

In this scenario, where cybercrime is a direct threat to our societies, and information and communication technologies can be used to foster radicalisation and spread terrorist propaganda, the Internet serves as an echo chamber, and facilitates the process of radicalization,[32] criminal justice authorities are facing the problem that evidence in relation to almost any crime is now often stored in electronic form on computer systems placed abroad. In fact, the findings of a survey conducted by the Cybercrime Convention Committee (T-CY), involving 42 States that are Parties to the Convention, show that most international requests for data are related to fraud and financial crime, followed by violent and serious crimes. These may include murder, assault, smuggling of persons, trafficking in human beings, drug trafficking, money laundering, terrorism and the financing of terrorism, extortion and, in particular, child pornography and other forms of sexual exploitation and abuse of children.[33]

If we look at what could happen in the near future, with the Internet of Everything,[34] the widespread adoption of cloud services and the new forms of mobile payment, cybercrime can be expected to grow significantly.

At the same time, cybercrime is largely underreported. Among the offences reported and recorded by law enforcement authorities, only an infinitesimal part is

[28] 'Critical infrastructure' is defined by Article 2(a) of the Directive 2008/114/EC as 'an asset, system or part thereof located in Member States which is essential for the maintenance of vital societal functions, health, safety, security, economic or social well-being of people, and the disruption or destruction of which would have a significant impact in a Member State as a result of the failure to maintain those functions'.

[29] See C Von Ulrich (2015) Cyber-Angriff auf Kanzleramt und Bundestag, 7 January 2015, http://www.welt.de/politik/deutschland/article136114277/Cyber-Angriff-auf-Kanzleramt-und-Bundestag.html, accessed 21 October 2016.

[30] Ransomware is software able to restrict the access to a computer system and its content until a ransom is paid. Usually the ransomware encrypts the whole disk drive of the computer and show a message containing the procedure to pay the ransom and obtain the decrypting key.

[31] Lacy and Reed 2016.

[32] von Behr et al. 2013.

[33] T-CY 2013b, at 5.

[34] The Internet of Everything (IoE) is an evolution of the Internet of Things (IoT) and refers to a possible near future, in which everything will be connected: people, process, data, and things, intended as devices and consumer products. This 'hyperconnection' will improve the possibility to deliver services, but will also imply an incredible exposure of data that need to be protected. For more information please visit http://ioeassessment.cisco.com, accessed 30 October 2016.

eventually investigated. Of these only a very small fraction is prosecuted and of these, again, only a few are adjudicated.[35]

The *de facto* impunity of the perpetrators and the massive violations of the rights of victims of cybercrime are compelling reasons why it is urgent to provide concrete solutions to criminal justice authorities regarding the question of access to data in the cloud. One of the key messages at the occasion of the Octopus Conference organized by the Council of Europe in 2015 was that

> [t]he protection of victims and their rights should be put at the forefront in order to ensure the effectiveness of the criminal justice system. The impact of victims is often underestimated. More co-operation amongst law enforcement, private sector and victim services is needed.[36]

As stated by the Cloud Evidence Group:

> If only a minuscule fraction of offences involving computer data and systems can be prosecuted, victims have a very limited expectation of justice. This raises questions regarding the rule of law in cyberspace.[37]

7.2.2 Cloud Computing, Territoriality and Jurisdiction

The nature of cybercrime calls for an effective access to electronic evidence in investigations. The problem of these investigations, however, can be summarized as follows:

- The resources available to criminal justice authorities cannot keep pace with the increasing number of devices, services, users and victims of cybercrime.
- A range of technical challenges render investigations complex, including peer-to-peer networks, The Onion Router (TOR) and other anonymisers, the widespread use of encryption,[38] Voice over Internet Protocol (VOIP) or Carrier-grade Network Addressing Translators (CGN).[39]

---

[35] See Brown 2015. On this topic see also: Office of the Police and Crime Commissioner for Surrey (2015/16) South East Cybercrime Survey, https://www.cybersafesurrey.org/surveyresults, accessed 22 October 2016.

[36] See Octopus Conference 2015, Cooperation against Cybercrime, Key messages, http://rm.coe.int/CoERMPublicCommonSearchServices/DisplayDCTMContent?documentId=0900001680319026, accessed 22 October 2016.

[37] See T-CY 2015b.

[38] See C Metz (2016) Forget Apple vs the FBI: WhatsApp Just Switched on Encryption for a Billion People, 5 April 2016, http://www.wired.com/2016/04/forget-apple-vs-fbi-whatsapp-just-switched-encryption-billion-people/, accessed 22 October 2016.

[39] See Huston 2013.

To complicate this scenario even more, cloud computing[40] and related questions about applicable law and jurisdiction add another layer of challenges that criminal justice authorities are confronted with.[41]

'Cloud computing' means that data—and thus also electronic evidence—is less held on a specific device or in closed networks but is distributed over different services, providers, locations and often jurisdictions. While in traditional computer forensics procedures, due to the centralized nature of the information technology system, investigators can have full control over the forensic artefacts (router, process logs, hard disks), in the cloud ecosystem, due to the distributed nature of the information technology systems, control over the functional layers varies among cloud actors, depending on the service model. Therefore, investigators have reduced visibility of and control over the forensic artefacts.[42]

Within this context, how can a State exercise its powers to investigate and prosecute? Is the principle of territoriality, firmly established in international law, still applicable?

The academic literature often considers the principle on territorial jurisdiction emerging from the famous *Lotus* case[43] as a general departure point for the study of public international law on conflict of jurisdiction between States.

In this case, on the one hand, the Permanent Court of International Justice (PCIJ) of 1927 determined that:

> the first and foremost restriction imposed by international law upon a State is that – failing the existence of a permissive rule to the contrary – it may not exercise its power in any form in the territory of another State. In this sense jurisdiction is certainly territorial; it cannot be exercised by a State outside its territory except by virtue of a permissive rule derived from international custom or from a convention.[44]

This principle means that a State cannot exercise its jurisdiction outside its territory, unless an international treaty or other laws permit to do so.

On the other hand, the PCIJ established as second principle that, within its territory, a State may exercise its jurisdiction on any matter even if there is no specific rule of international law permitting it to do so. With this principle, States have a wide measure of discretion in exercising their jurisdiction, unless it is expressly limited by some rules of international law.

---

[40] The definition of 'cloud computing' provided by NIST, a branch of the US Department of Commerce responsible for developing standards and guidelines, including minimum requirements, for providing adequate information security for all agency operations and assets, is: 'a model for enabling ubiquitous, convenient, on-demand network access to a shared pool of configurable computing resources (e.g., networks, servers, storage, applications, and services) that can be rapidly provisioned and released with minimal management effort or service provider interaction.' See Mell and Grance 2011.

[41] See Narayanan 2012.

[42] See NIST 2014.

[43] *Case of the S.S. 'Lotus' (France v Turkey)*, PCIJ Series A, No 10, 7 September 1927 ('*Lotus*').

[44] Ibid., at 18–19.

The case, and the related issues about jurisdiction, was summarized by the Court as follow:

> The French Government contends that the Turkish Courts, in order to have jurisdiction, should be able to point to some title to jurisdiction recognized by international law in favour of Turkey. On the other hand, the Turkish Government takes the view that Article 15 allows Turkey jurisdiction whenever such jurisdiction does not come into conflict with a principle of international law.[45]

Within this framework, the Court issued its famous *dictum* about the nature of international law as permissive or prohibitive, stating that:

> International law governs relations between independent States. The rules of law binding upon States therefore emanate from their own free will as expressed in conventions or by usages generally accepted as expressing principles of law and established in order to regulate the relations between these co-existing independent communities or with a view to the achievement of common aims. Restriction upon the independence of States cannot therefore be presumed.[46]

There are three possible interpretations of the *Lotus* principle about jurisdiction: the first is that the principle must be used as residual: when there are no other governing principles or rules of international law, States are free to act as they please; the second is that the *Lotus* principle could be intended as a residual principle with a presumption attached that, when it is not clear which international rule can be applied to a situation, it is possible to presume that there are no rules and that the States are free to act; the third possible interpretation, finally, is that the *dictum* of the PCIJ means that States are presumed to be unrestrained by international law, unless there are some rules providing such restraint.[47]

The *Lotus* principles, however, have been subjected to criticism by legal doctrine[48] and jurisprudence,[49] but despite their 'vagueness and generality'[50] are still

---

[45] Ibid., at 18.

[46] Ibid.

[47] This reflect the dissenting opinion posed by Judge Loder who commented that '[...] every door is open unless it is closed by treaty or by established custom' (*Lotus* case, Dissenting Opinion by M. Loder, at 34).

[48] Handeyside 2007.

[49] In the *Kosovo* Advisory Opinion, Judge Simma disagreed with the methodology used by the Court for deciding the case, which derive from the *Lotus* principles. In particular, he criticized the principle, declaring that 'by upholding the *Lotus* principle, the Court fails to seize a chance to move beyond this anachronistic, extremely consensualist vision of international law. The Court could have considered the scope of the question from an approach which does not, in a formalistic fashion, equate the absence of a prohibition with the existence of a permissive rule; it could also have considered the possibility that international law can be neutral or deliberately silent on the international lawfulness of certain acts.' *Accordance with international law of the unilateral declaration of independence in respect of Kosovo*, Advisory Opinion of 22 July 2010, Declaration of Judge Simma, para 3.

[50] Brownlie 2003, at 301.

considered valid in judgements concerning jurisdictional conflicts,[51] even if these principles were rarely used by the International Court of Justice.

Concerning cyberspace and the relevance of the *Lotus* case to address the problems posed by the new technologies, it may be useful to recall the general principle stated by PCIJ in the *Lotus* case about jurisdiction:

> Though it is true that in all systems of law the principle of the territorial character of criminal law is fundamental, it is equally true that all or nearly all these systems of law extend their action to offences committed outside the territory of the State which adopts them, and they do so in ways which vary from State to State. The territoriality of criminal law, therefore, is not an absolute principle of international law and by no means coincides with territorial sovereignty.[52]

The implications of this principle applied to cloud computing are highly relevant, if the bottom line is that States are not limited to their territorial boundaries in applying their laws,[53] but of course it is clear that other boundaries need to be identified to guarantee respect for the rule of law.

The problem of jurisdiction in cyberspace is still an issue before international courts, and it was recently addressed by the European Court of Justice in Case C-618/15, where the Advocate General Wathelet noted that '[t]he issue of crime committed on the internet ("cybercrime") is not a straightforward one inasmuch as, since the internet is a network which is by definition universal, the location of such crime, be it the causal event or the loss sustained, is particularly difficult to determine.'[54]

---

[51] Ireland-Piper 2014.

[52] *Lotus* case, at 20.

[53] Some suggestions could come from other sources, like the Restatement of the Law (Third) of the Foreign Relations Law of the United States, that provides the following rules: '(2) Whether exercise of jurisdiction over a person or activity is unreasonable is determined by evaluating all relevant factors, including, where appropriate: (a) the link of the activity to the territory of the regulating state, i.e., the extent to which the activity takes place within the territory, or has substantial, direct, and foreseeable effect upon or in the territory; (b) the connections, such as nationality, residence, or economic activity, between the regulating state and the person principally responsible for the activity to be regulated, or between that state and those whom the regulation is designed to protect; (c) the character of the activity to be regulated, the importance of regulation to the regulating state, the extent to which other states regulate such activities, and the degree to which the desirability of such regulation is generally accepted; (d) the existence of justified expectations that might be protected or hurt by the regulation; (e) the importance of the regulation to the international political, legal, or economic system; (f) the extent to which the regulation is consistent with the traditions of the international system; (g) the extent to which another state may have an interest in regulating the activity; and (h) the likelihood of conflict with regulation by another state'. See Hixson 1988; and Swanson 2011.

[54] Opinion of Advocate General Wathelet delivered on 9 November 2016, *Concurrence SARL v Samsung Electronics France SAS and Amazon Service Europe Sàrl*, ECJ, Case C-618/15, ECLI: EU:C:2016:843, para 2. This case is just one of the newest discussed in front of a superior Court, but cases regarding the jurisdiction in cyberspace are quite numerous. We can cite, for example: *LICRA v Yahoo! & Yahoo France*, Tribunal de Grande Instance de Paris, 22 May 2000; *R v Töben*, BGH, 12 December 2000; *R v Perrin*, EWHC Criminal Division, 22 March 2002; *Arzneimittelwerbung im Internet*, BGH, 30 March 2006; *Persönlichkeitsverletzungen durch ausländische Internetveröffentlichungen*, BGH, 2 March 2010; *Vidal-Hall & Ors v Google Inc*,

This is why some have therefore called for a 'paradigm shift' and to abandon traditional concepts of jurisdiction corresponding to territorial sovereignty.[55] However, such a 'shift', if at all possible, will take a very considerable time. Meanwhile, therefore, the best and likely the only way forward would appear to be finding innovative solutions compatible with the *Lotus* principles of State jurisdiction.

Against this backdrop, a number of challenges have been identified for criminal justice in combating cybercrime, particularly with regard to the applicable law and the jurisdiction to enforce.[56]

The first challenge is about location of data to set the applicable law. Unfortunately, location is of limited relevance in cloud computing. A service provider may have its headquarters in one jurisdiction and apply the legal regime of a second jurisdiction while the data is stored in a third jurisdiction. Data may be mirrored in several, or move between, jurisdictions. It is unclear which legal regime applies and it is far from clear which rules apply for lawful access by criminal justice authorities.[57] If the location of data determines the jurisdiction, it is conceivable that a cloud service provider systematically moves data to prevent criminal justice access.

Moreover, a service provider may be under different layers of jurisdictions for various legal aspects related to its services at the same time. The sharing and pooling of resources is a key characteristic of cloud computing. Cloud services may entail a combination of service models (Cloud Software as a Service (SaaS), Cloud

---

(Footnote 54 continued)

EWHC, 16 January 2014; *Google Spain SL, Google Inc v Agencia Española de Protección de Datos*, ECJ Grand Chamber, 13 May 2014; *Yahoo! v Belgium*, Court of Cassation, P.13.2082.N, 1 December 2015.

[55] Svantesson 2015, at 79, proposes to focus on the following 'core principles':

'In the absence of an obligation under international law to exercise Jurisdiction, a State may only exercise jurisdiction where:

(1) there is a substantial connection between the matter and the State seeking to exercise jurisdiction

(2) the State seeking to exercise jurisdiction has a legitimate interest in the matter and

(3) the exercise of jurisdiction is reasonable given the balance between the State's legitimate interests and other interests.'

[56] See T-CY 2015b.

[57] This topic was recently discussed in front of the Second Circuit Court of Appeal in the case *Microsoft v United States*, USCA II Circuit, 14-2985, 14 July 2016, where the Court stated that the government cannot compel Microsoft, or other companies, to turn over customer emails stored on servers outside the United States. The main question presented was whether the Section 2703(a) of the Stored Communications Act (SCA)–the provision under which the government sought and received a search warrant for the email account–applies extraterritorially. The government argued that when the SCA used the word 'warrant', the statute was actually referring not to a traditional warrant, but to legal process or 'compelled disclosure' more akin to a subpoena. A warrant, according to the Second Circuit, and conceded by the government, has domestic boundaries. This important decision complicates even more an already uncertain framework. See Svantesson and Gerry 2015.

Platform as a Service (PaaS), Cloud Infrastructure as a Service (IaaS)) and it is often unclear which service provider—when providing one or more types of services—is in possession or control of which type of data (subscriber information, traffic data, content data) so as to be served a production order.

Cloud services also make unclear whether data is stored or in transit and thus whether production orders, search and seizure orders, interception or real-time collection orders are to be served.

The non-localised nature of cloud computing causes problems for live forensics (online forensics) and searches because of the architecture of the cloud (multi tenancy, distribution and segregation of data) as well as legal challenges related to the integrity and validity of the data collection, evidence control, ownership of the data or jurisdiction.[58]

In short, the Cloud Evidence Group identified these questions:

> What governs jurisdiction to enforce for criminal justice purposes: Location of data? Nationality of owner of data? Location of owner of data? Nationality of data owner? Location of data controller? Headquarters of a cloud service provider? Subsidiary of a cloud service provider? Territory where a cloud provider is offering its services? Laws of the territory where the data owner has subscribed to a service? The territory of the criminal justice authority?[59]

The crucial question to address is therefore which options are available to permit effective and lawful access to electronic evidence for criminal justice purposes? This question gives rise to a number of issues and options that will be briefly described in the next section of this chapter.

7.3 Issues and Recommendations for a Jurisdiction 'in the Cloud'

7.3.1 Issues

As stated in the introduction, the analysis of the issues and recommendations is based on the findings of the Cloud Evidence Group (CEG) of the Cybercrime Convention Committee (T-CY). The CEG consulted external experts from academia and private consultants. In light of the challenges posed by cloud computing to the territoriality principle, the Cloud Evidence Group identified the following specific issues.[60]

---

[58] See NIST 2014.

[59] See T-CY 2015b, at 15.

[60] See T-CY 2016a.

7.3.1.1 Types of Data Required

The first question that the CEG tried to address was: which type of data are necessary for investigating a computer-related crime? This topic is important because it involves data protection regulation[61] and is open to different regional approaches even in the EU, at least until the EU General Data Protection Regulation will be in force.

The CEG finds that criminal justice authorities typically need three types of data to investigate, that is:

- subscriber information[62] indicating the user of a service (such as a webmail account) and which may also include the login Internet Protocol (IP) address;
- traffic data;[63]
- content data.

The type of data most often needed in criminal investigations is 'subscriber information', that is less privacy-sensitive than traffic and in particular content data. Obtaining subscriber information therefore represents a lesser interference with the rights of individuals than obtaining other types of data.[64] However, this is not always reflected in domestic laws on access to evidence. In some States, the requirements for criminal justice access to subscriber information in specific investigations are rather low, while in others court orders may be required. This

[61] See Sect. 7.3.1.7.

[62] Defined in Article 18 of the Budapest Convention as follows:

'[...] the term "subscriber information" means any information contained in the form of computer data or any other form that is held by a service provider, relating to subscribers of its services other than traffic or content data and by which can be established:

(a) the type of communication service used, the technical provisions taken thereto and the period of service;

(b) the subscriber's identity, postal or geographic address, telephone and other access number, billing and payment information, available on the basis of the service agreement or arrangement;

c) any other information on the site of the installation of communication equipment, available on the basis of the service agreement or arrangement.'

[63] Defined in Article 1 of the Budapest Convention as follows: '[...] "traffic data" means any computer data relating to a communication by means of a computer system, generated by a computer system that formed a part in the chain of communication, indicating the communication's origin, destination, route, time, date, size, duration, or type of underlying service.'

[64] The same conclusions are reported in the Conference Report of the Presidency Conference 'Crossing Borders: Jurisdiction in Cyberspace' held in Amsterdam on 7–8 March 2016 (7323/16). On this specific issue, the conclusions of the policy experts and practitioners participating in the Conference are summarized as follows: 'Subscriber data is the most often requested type of data for the purposes of criminal proceedings, followed by traffic data and finally content data. It was acknowledged by participants that the interference with the rights of the investigated person is lower in the case of subscriber data compared to traffic data and content data and therefore a lighter regime for obtaining such data could be reasonably envisaged. It was concluded that this distinction should be systematically reflected in the current legal frameworks (both national and international) and that such a solution could substantially release pressure from the existing system for international cooperation for obtaining e-evidence.' (at 6).

affects domestic investigations and hampers international co-operation. In this sense, further harmonisation of rules for access to subscriber information is needed.[65]

In this context, it is also worth pointing out that subscriber information is normally held by private sector service providers and is typically obtained through production orders[66] that usually represent a lesser interference with the rights of individuals and the interests of third parties than the search and seizure of computer systems or the interception of communications.[67]

7.3.1.2 Mutual Legal Assistance to Obtain Data Required for Investigation

Connected with the problems of the data that are required for investigation is the issue of obtaining these data when stored outside of the country. Here the issues of territoriality and jurisdiction in the cloud come into play. As the jurisdiction to enforce is normally limited to the territory of the criminal justice authority, mutual legal assistance (MLA) is and is likely to remain the primary mean to obtain evidence located in foreign jurisdictions.

The Council of Europe has developed a large number of treaties on international co-operation in criminal matters, including in particular the European Convention on Mutual Assistance in Criminal Matters[68] and its Additional Protocols.[69] The application of these treaties is monitored by the Council of Europe Committee of Experts on the Operation of European Conventions on Co-operation in Criminal Matters (PC-OC). In order to facilitate the use by practitioners of the MLA treaties, the PC-OC developed guidelines on practical measures to improve co-operation in respect of transfer of proceedings[70] and a model request form for mutual assistance in criminal matters.[71] In addition, subject-matter specific treaties contain provisions

---

[65] See T-CY 2014.

[66] See Article 18 of the Budapest Convention.

[67] The production order aims to get some information in possession of a person—typically an Internet Service Provider or a telecommunication company—under request. This means that the amount of data is by itself less intrusive than in a search and seizure of computer systems or in an interception of communications, which can allow data dragnet. In fact, the production order must identify precisely the scope and the extension of the request.

[68] 1959 European Convention on Mutual Assistance in Criminal Matters, ETS No 030.

[69] 1978 Additional Protocol to the European Convention on Mutual Assistance in Criminal Matters, ETS No 099, 2001 Second Additional Protocol to the European Convention on Mutual Assistance in Criminal Matters, ETS 182.

[70] See PC-OC 2012.

[71] See PC-OC 2014.

on mutual legal assistance[72] such as the Convention on the Protection of Children against Sexual Exploitation and Sexual Abuse,[73] the Convention on Laundering, Search, Seizure and Confiscation of the Proceeds from Crime[74] and the Convention on the Prevention of Terrorism.[75]

However, it seems that the feasibility of mutual legal procedures is limited with regard to electronic evidence in a cloud context. In 2013 and 2014, the Cybercrime Convention Committee (T-CY) carried out a detailed assessment of the functioning of the mutual legal assistance provisions of the Budapest Convention and concluded that 'mutual legal assistance procedures are considered too complex, lengthy and resource intensive, and thus too inefficient'[76] to permit effective measures against cybercrime and other offences involving electronic evidence, given the transnational and volatile nature of electronic evidence.[77] Therefore, the MLA process needs to be made more efficient in view of the scale of requests concerning electronic evidence and the volatility of such evidence.

7.3.1.3 'Loss of Location'

Apart from its shortcomings, situations also arise where mutual legal assistance is not a feasible option at all. For specific situations, such as where the origin of an attack is unknown, where servers in multiple jurisdictions are involved, or other 'loss of location' situations[78] where the principle of territoriality is not applicable, solutions need to be found, including transborder access to data in specific criminal investigations.

However, the current Article 32b of the Budapest Convention on transborder access to data is too limited because it requires knowledge on where the data are located. In fact, as noted by the T-CY, Article 32b would not cover situations where the data are not stored in another Party or where it is uncertain where the data are located, and a Party may not use Article 32b to obtain disclosure of data that is stored domestically.[79]

As pointed out by the Cloud Evidence Group, 'in the absence of international solutions, governments increasingly pursue unilateral solutions. This creates risks

[72] See PC-OC 2015.

[73] 2007 Council of Europe Convention on the Protection of Children against Sexual Exploitation and Sexual Abuse, CETS No 201.

[74] 1990 Council of Europe Convention on Laundering, Search, Seizure and Confiscation of the Proceeds from Crime, ETS No 141.

[75] 2005 Council of Europe Convention on the Prevention of Terrorism, CETS No 196.

[76] See T-CY 2013b.

[77] The same conclusions are drawn by some scholars. See Svantesson and van Zwieten 2016, at 673; Walden 2011, at 11.

[78] For example, in cloud computing it could happen that the provider does not know where the data are exactly located. On this issue see Vaciago 2011, at 7.

[79] See T-CY 2013a.

for State to State relations and the rights of individuals. A common international solution is required to provide a framework for lawful transborder access to data.'[80]

While Article 19.2 of the Budapest Convention requires Parties to authorise competent authorities to extend searches from an initial computer system to a connected system 'in its territory', this territorial limitation has been dropped in a number of States, including in Europe and in the United States. For example, a change of the US Federal Rule 41 of Criminal Procedure will allow remote searches if the origin of an attack 'has been concealed through technological means', with inevitable concerns from the civil rights associations.[81] Similarly in Europe the recent UK Investigatory Powers Act 2016 expressly allows the use of bulk equipment interference to obtain overseas-related communications, information or data.[82]

Thus, a clearer, generally accepted framework that includes conditions and safeguards for transborder searches is urgently required.

7.3.1.4 'Offering a Service in the Territory' of a State

Another problem typically posed by the ubiquitous nature of internet services is that a service provider or other natural or physical person located in the territory of a State, which is subject to the laws of that State, may have possession or control of data stored in another jurisdiction and may also be coerced to retrieve and produce such data.

A more complicated situation arises when a service provider is offering a service in the territory of a State without being present in the State. Examples are webmail, social media or cloud storage services. In this sense, some clarifications are needed as to when a service provider is indeed present or 'offering a service in the territory' of a State and is thus subject to a domestic production order or other type of coercive order. This would help clarify the applicable law and which jurisdiction has the power to enforce.

Moreover, if subscriber information can be obtained lawfully through domestic orders, the need for international co-operation and thus the pressure on the mutual legal assistance system would be reduced considerably.

7.3.1.5 'Voluntary Co-Operation' by Providers

Some providers—in particular US-based service providers—may respond directly to lawful requests for subscriber information by criminal justice authorities in other jurisdictions where they are offering a service. Voluntary disclosure of 'customer

---

80 T-CY 2016a, at 2.

81 See on this topic the action taken by the Electronic Frontier Foundation at the following URL: https://act.eff.org/action/stop-the-changes-to-rule-41, accessed 30 October 2016.

82 For this Act also some civil rights associations have filled a complaint addressing the ECtHR for alleged violations of fundamental rights, especially Articles 8, 10 and 14 of ECHR.

records'—and of contents in emergency situations—is possible under US law, that is, the Electronic Communications Privacy Act.[83] Parties to the Budapest Convention—other than the US—send every year more than 100,000 such requests to Apple, Facebook, Google, Microsoft, Twitter and Yahoo. According to the result of a survey conducted between the Parties to the Budapest Convention, these companies disclose data in about 60% of all cases.[84]

While the voluntary disclosure of data by US providers is highly useful for criminal justice authorities worldwide, it raises a number of concerns. For example, providers tend to notify customers of such requests and this compromises investigations. Providers also frequently change their policies and procedures for data request, which makes co-operation volatile and unpredictable. It must be considered also that, in some States, data obtained in this way is not admissible as evidence in court.

Furthermore, such voluntary disclosure raises concerns regarding data protection and confidentiality requirements.[85] Therefore, European providers already do not disclose data directly to criminal justice authorities in foreign jurisdictions, and this protection could be enforced under the forthcoming EU General Data Protection Regulation. Again, to address this issue, a clearer and more stable framework is required.

7.3.1.6 Emergency Procedures

In certain circumstances, to prevent imminent danger to life and public security, emergency procedures would be needed to obtain electronic evidence stored in foreign jurisdictions through mutual legal assistance but also via direct co-operation with a service provider in a foreign jurisdiction. While such procedures are in place in the US and while US service providers may also disclose content in emergency situations, in most other Parties to the Budapest Convention this is not the case, as a recent survey conducted by the Cloud Evidence Group shows.[86]

7.3.1.7 Data Protection

The processing of personal data requires a legal basis. In principle, criminal justice authorities can access, collect, share or otherwise process data if provided for by law. The international sharing of a personal data would be lawful if it is based on bilateral or multilateral co-operation agreements. The mutual legal assistance process is designed to ensure that rule of law requirements are met and that the rights of

---

[83] 18 U.S. Code §2702.

[84] See T-CY 2016b.

[85] See Sect. 7.3.1.7.

[86] See T-CY 2016c.

individuals are protected, in particular if the data sought are to be used as evidence in criminal proceedings.

At present, out of 49 Parties to the Budapest Convention,[87] 40 are Parties to the Council of Europe Convention for the Protection of Individuals with regard to Automatic Processing of Personal Data,[88] and 25 are member States of the European Union and thus subject to European data protection rules.[89]At the Council of Europe level, the negotiation of an Amending Protocol[90] to modernise the Convention for the Protection of Individuals with regard to Automatic Processing of Personal Data is ongoing. However, the question of transborder disclosure of data from a private sector entity in one Party to the criminal justice authority of another Party, that is the asymmetric transfer of data, is not specifically addressed at present.

7.3.2 Recommendations

Several approaches are proposed in the academic literature[91] trying to provide a solution to the issues described above, and the Council of Europe's Cloud Evidence Group suggested to pursue several specific options that combine immediate and practical measures with the negotiation of an Additional Protocol to the Budapest Convention on Cybercrime. The analysis of these options is valuable because they must take into account the suggestions and the complexities coming from the Parties of the Budapest Convention.

---

[87] See the Chart of signatures and ratifications of the Budapest Convention, Council of Europe Treaty Office, http://www.coe.int/en/web/conventions/full-list/-/conventions/treaty/185/signatures?p_auth=EIwx3ZYf, accessed 30 October 2016.

[88] 1981 Council of Europe Convention for the Protection of Individuals with regard to Automatic Processing of Personal Data, ETS No 108. See Chart of signatures and ratification of Convention 108, Council of Europe Treaty Office, http://www.coe.int/en/web/conventions/full-list/-/conventions/treaty/108/signatures?p_auth=etR46XGN, accessed 30 October 2016.

[89] The main data protection instruments referred to are the following: 1981 Council of Europe Convention for the Protection of Individuals with regard to Automatic Processing of Personal Data, ETS No 108; Council of Europe Recommendation R(87)15 Regulating the Use of Personal Data in the Police Sector; European Union Directive 95/46/EC on the Protection of Individuals with Regard to the Processing of Personal Data and on the Free Movement of Such Data; Framework Decision 2008/977/JHA of the European Union on the Protection of Personal Data Processed in the Framework of Police and Judicial Co-Operation in Criminal Matters. At the European Union level, a new comprehensive data protection framework, the so-called new 'data protection package' was adopted in April 2016 and include the EU General Data Protection Regulation, which, among other things, will replace Directive 95/46/EC and which will be directly applicable in EU member States, and a Directive on data protection in the criminal justice sector.

[90] On this negotiation please see http://www.coe.int/t/dghl/standardsetting/dataprotection/Cahdata_en.asp and http://www.coe.int/t/dghl/standardsetting/dataprotection/TPD_documents/CAHDat.%203_Report_CM(2015)40_En.pdf, accessed 30 October 2016.

[91] See Daskal 2015; Svantesson and van Zwieten 2016.

7.3.2.1 Rendering Mutual Legal Assistance More Efficient

Mutual legal assistance remains the accepted and primary tool to obtain evidence in foreign jurisdictions. In December 2014, the Cybercrime Convention Committee adopted a report with 24 recommendations.[92] The first fifteen of them fall under the responsibility of domestic authorities and do not necessarily require a new international legal instrument. Their implementation is primarily a question of resources, skills and streamlining procedures. States should also fully implement the provisions of the Budapest Convention, in particular Article 18 on domestic production orders and Articles 16, 17, 29 and 30 on expedited preservation.[93]

In particular, Recommendation 8 concerns emergency procedures: 'Parties are encouraged to establish emergency procedures for requests related to risks of life and similar exigent circumstances. The T-CY should document practices by Parties and providers.' Emergency procedures seem particularly important but are not available in most Parties.[94] If necessary, provisions for emergency procedures may need to be made available in the forthcoming second Additional Protocol to the Budapest Convention.

7.3.2.2 Domestic Production Orders (Article 18 Budapest Convention)

Article 18 of the Budapest Convention covers production orders with respect to two distinct situations. It would seem that this provision has not been fully understood and implemented by all Parties to the Budapest Convention. The Cloud Evidence Group has, therefore, drafted a Guidance Note for consideration by the Cybercrime Convention Committee,[95] which suggests the following:

- Under Article 18.1.a, competent authorities are to compel any natural or legal person to produce subscriber information in its possession or control irrespective of where the data are actually stored.[96]
- Under Article 18.1.b, competent authorities of a Party are to compel a service provider 'offering a service on its territory'[97] to produce subscriber information when:

---

[92] See T-CY 2013b.

[93] These provisions have not been fully implemented by all Parties as shown in assessments carried out by the Committee: http://www.coe.int/en/web/cybercrime/assessments, accessed 30 October 2016.

[94] See T-CY 2016c.

[95] T-CY 2015a.

[96] In fact, Article 18.1.a covers any type of data. However, the draft Guidance Note is focusing on subscriber information only.

[97] As reported into the final version of the Article 18 Guidance Note approved by the T-CY by written procedure last 20th of February 2017, Parties could consider that a service provider is 'offering a service in the territory of a Party' when the service provider enables persons in the territory of the Party to subscribe to its services and the service provider has established a real and

- the service provider enables persons in the territory of the Party to subscribe to its services;
- orients its activities at subscribers, or makes use of the subscriber information in the course of its activities, or interacts with subscribers in the Party;
- the subscriber information to be produced is relating to services of a provider offered in the territory of the Party.

If accepted, this interpretation of Article 18 could make a major difference at least with respect to subscriber information and offer a legal basis for the disclosure of such data by service providers in one State to the criminal justice authorities of a State where they are offering a service. As this is a domestic measure, it would considerably reduce the pressure on the mutual legal assistance system.

7.3.2.3 Practical Measures to Facilitate Co-Operation with Providers

Pending domestic legal measures and the negotiation of international legally binding instruments—namely the second Additional Protocol to the Budapest Convention—a number of practical measures may help improve consistency in the co-operation between US service providers and Parties to the Budapest Convention.

The Cloud Evidence Group held meetings with providers on 30 November 2015[98] and—in a less formal setting—on 25 April 2016. Proposals include: regular meetings of the Cybercrime Convention Committee with service providers; the establishment of an online tool with up-to-date provider policies and procedures as well as information on relevant legislation and criminal justice authorities responsible in the Parties; and common templates for requests for subscriber information.

Such increased co-operation with the private sector is also one of the expected results of the Internet Governance Strategy for 2016–2019 recently adopted by the Council of Europe Committee of Ministers,[99] that is to establish 'a platform between governments and major Internet companies and representative associations on their respect for human rights online, including on measures (such as model contractual arrangements for the terms of service of Internet platform, and principles of accountability and transparency to the multi-stakeholder community regarding the collection, storage, and analysis of personal data) to protect, respect

(Footnote 97 continued)

substantial connection to a Party. To identify this connection some factors could be the following: providing local advertising or advertising in the language of the territory of the Party, make use of the subscriber information in the course of its activities or interact with subscribers in the Party.

[98] For a general overview of the policies adopted by the providers, please see http://www.coe.int/en/web/cybercrime/hearing.

[99] See Council of Europe (2016) Internet Governance—Council of Europe Strategy 2016–2019, CM(2016)10-final, https://search.coe.int/cm/Pages/result_details.aspx?ObjectId=09000016805c1b60, accessed 30 October 2016.

and remedy challenges and violations to them'. Several practical measures are expected due to this strategy in the future and, among these, there is also '[d]eveloping solutions regarding the access by law enforcement officers to data on cloud servers and related issues of jurisdiction. Solutions may include a Protocol to the Budapest Convention.'

Following this suggestion, the expected results of the second Additional Protocol to the Budapest Convention are the following:

- Provisions for more effective mutual legal assistance;

  i) a simplified regime for mutual legal assistance requests for subscriber information;
  ii) international production orders;
  iii) direct cooperation between judicial authorities in mutual legal assistance requests;
  iv) joint investigations and joint investigation teams;
  v) requests in English language;
  vi) audio/video hearing of witnesses, victims and experts;
  vii) emergency MLA procedures.

- Provisions allowing for direct cooperation with service providers in other jurisdictions with regard to requests for subscriber information, preservation requests, and emergency requests.
- Clearer framework and stronger safeguards for existing practices of transborder access to data.
- Safeguards, including data protection requirements.

The second Additional Protocol is expected to be finalised by December 2019, but the drafting of such a new legally binding text is still in the early stages and much intense and substantive negotiation between the Parties to the Budapest Convention is to be expected. Certain Governments consider that, in view of the global nature of the issue, the United Nations should be the framework for a new binding instrument, but solutions at the level of the United Nations are unlikely to be found for several reasons, mainly related to the difficult process in achieving an international consensus at UN level. In fact, there is no consensus between UN member States whether a UN treaty or other instrument is needed and what it would be all about, while the Budapest Convention is at present the recognized international reference to combat cybercrime and other computer-related crimes. In addition to this, a global instrument probably might set a lower standard while two-thirds of States already make use of the Budapest Convention. The proponents of a new treaty seem to want to exercise stronger control of contents. This may adversely affect free speech and other fundamental rights.

An important number of problems encountered are operational in nature and these should be addressed through improved information exchange and capacity building. There is global consensus on capacity building as an effective mean for immediate progress.

7.4 Conclusions

As argued in this chapter, cybercrime is a serious threat to the core values of societies, that is, human rights, democracy and the rule of law, which—without doubt—will become more serious every day. One only needs to consider the particular threat of cyberterrorism, for instance against nuclear facilities or other critical infrastructures, to understand the potentially disastrous consequences on our way of life.[100] Moreover, the ubiquitous use of cloud services poses various challenges in combating cybercrime and other computer-related crime. One of these challenges is the principle of territoriality and consequently the applicable jurisdiction.

The increasing threats posed by the switch of almost every human activity into a digital form require new ways to address the problem of territoriality and to distinguish between what is 'here' and 'there' in an electronic form.

The approach followed by the academic literature is often focused on specific requirements of domestic law,[101] but trying to draw a solution demands a more comprehensive approach that fully takes into account the transnational nature of the online world. Here, the basic principles of territoriality established under international law do not provide for clear solutions.[102] However, as States will not wish to

---

[100] Terrorism and the Internet is one of the priority areas for the biennium 2016–2017 of the Council of Europe Committee of Experts on Terrorism (CODEXTER), http://www.coe.int/t/dlapil/codexter/about_en.asp?expandable=0, accessed 30 October 2016.

[101] For example, the academic literature of US scholars is mainly focused on the Fourth Amendment issues posed by online investigations. See Kerr 2015; Daskal 2015; Daskal and Woods 2015.

[102] For a summary of different decisions in applying territoriality principles in cyberspace, see Daskal 2015, at 334–365. From an EU perspective, an important decision, already referred to in footnote 55 is *Yahoo! v Belgium*, where the Belgian Court of Cassation in December 2015 found that, unlike Yahoo!'s opinion, there was no issue of extraterritorial jurisdiction because the request for disclosure to an operator of an electronic communication network or an electronic communications service provider who is active in Belgium does not imply any intervention outside the territory of Belgium. Also, notwithstanding the place of location of such an operator or provider, its refusal to comply with such request constitutes an offence that takes place in Belgium. The Court of Cassation then concluded that Yahoo! 'voluntarily' submits itself to the Belgian law due to some peculiarities, like for example using the domain name.be or by displaying ads referred to Belgian users (see *Yahoo! v Belgium*, Court of Cassation, P.13.2082.N, 1 December 2015). The European Court of Justice dealt with the problem of territoriality in the *Weltimmo* case where, among other questions related to data protection law and the Directive 94/46/EC, the ECJ discussed the meaning of 'establishment' to decide the applicable law. On this specific issue the Court broadly follows the approach of the Advocate General, especially points 28 and 32 to 34 of his Opinion, agreeing upon a flexible definition of the concept of 'establishment', 'which departs from a formalistic approach whereby undertakings are established solely in the place where they are registered. Accordingly, in order to establish whether a company, the data controller, has an establishment, within the meaning of Directive 95/46, in a Member State other than the Member State or third country where it is registered, both the degree of stability of the arrangements and the effective exercise of activities in that other Member State must be interpreted in the light of the specific nature of the economic activities and the provision of services concerned. This is

move away from these principles, solutions are required which, if not found within these agreed principles, should at least be compatible with them.

To start the discussion about such an approach to the problem, in June 2015, at the Council of Europe's Octopus Conference on Cybercrime, cybercrime experts from all over the world were asked about the rule of law online. Survey results showed they did not consider that 'cyberspace is basically safe, that crime and violation of rights are the exception and that offenders are brought to justice.' The ability of governments to protect society against crime and the right of individuals in cyberspace was considered to be limited.[103]

Solutions need to be identified and agreed upon that permit effective access to electronic evidence. In this respect, it is fundamental that these solutions meet human rights and rule of law requirements at the same time. The Cybercrime Convention Committee—based on proposals of its Cloud Evidence Group—is now considering a set of measures:

- rendering mutual legal assistance more efficient;
- differentiating between types of data to be secured, with a lighter regime for the production of subscriber information;
- ensuring proper implementation of Article 18 of the Budapest Convention based on the Guidance Note on the production or subscriber information;
- facilitating direct public/private transborder co-operation;
- establishing a framework with safeguards for transborder access to data in specific circumstances.

Similar efforts are now also underway within the European Union and have been promoted in particular by the Netherlands Presidency.[104] Common solutions, however, cannot be limited to the European Union[105] nor to the Council of Europe, but will need to be of a global nature as outlined before.

Therefore, the Council of Europe's Budapest Convention on Cybercrime with its currently 48 Parties[106] from all over the world, and including the US where much of the Internet infrastructure is based, remains at present the best framework to provide

(Footnote 102 continued)

particularly true for undertakings offering services exclusively over the Internet.' (see *Weltimmo s. r.o. v. Nemzeti Adatvédelmi és Információszabadság Hatóság*, ECJ, ECLI:EU:C:2015:639, 1 October 2015, para 29).

[103] See Octopus Conference 2015, Cooperation against Cybercrime, Key messages, http://rm.coe.int/CoERMPublicCommonSearchServices/DisplayDCTMContent?documentId=0900001680319026, accessed 22 October 2016.

[104] See http://english.eu2016.nl/events/2016/03/07/crossing-borders-jurisdiction-in-cyberspace, accessed 30 October 2016.

[105] See EU Directive 2013/40/EU on Attacks Against Information Systems, http://eur-lex.europa.eu/LexUriServ/LexUriServ.do?uri=OJ:L:2013:218:0008:0014:EN:PDF, accessed 30 October 2016.

[106] Another 18 States are signatories or have been invited to accede the Convention. This number is constantly increasing.

the urgently needed solutions on securing cloud evidence for criminal justice purposes while respecting human rights and the established principles of State jurisdiction.

References

Bach D, Newman AL (2006) Local Power, Global Reach: The Domestic Institutional Roots of Internet Governance. http://www18.georgetown.edu/data/people/aln24/publication-25786.pdf. Accessed 20 October 2016

Balkin J, Grimmelmann J, Katz E, Kozlovski N, Wagman S, Zarsky T (2007) Cybercrime: Digital Cops in a Networked Environment. NYU Press, New York

Brown CSD (2015) Investigating and Prosecuting Cyber Crime: Forensics Dependencies and Barriers to Justice. International Journal of Cyber Criminology 9:55–119

Brownlie I (2003) Principles of Public International Law, 6th edn. Oxford University Press, Oxford

Daskal J (2015) The Un-Territoriality of Data. Yale Law Journal 125:326–398

Daskal J, Woods AK (2015) Cross-Border Data Requests: A Proposed Framework. https://lawfareblog.com/cross-border-data-requests-proposed-framework. Accessed 30 October 2016

Goldsmith J (1998) The Internet and the Abiding Significance of Territorial Sovereignty. Indiana Journal of Global Legal Studies 5:475–491

Handeyside H (2007) The *Lotus* Principle in ICJ Jurisprudence: Was the Ship Ever Afloat? Michigan Journal of International Law 29(1):71–94

de Hert P, Kopcheva M (2011) International Mutual Legal Assistance in Criminal Law Made Redundant: A Comment on the Belgian Yahoo! Case. Computer Law & Security Review 27:291–297

Hixson K (1988) Extraterritorial Jurisdiction Under the Third Restatement of Foreign Relations Law of the United States. Fordham International Law Journal 12(1):127–152

Huston G (2013) IP Addresses and Traceback. APNIC Labs. https://labs.apnic.net/?p=433. Accessed 22 October 2016

Ireland-Piper D (2014) The Enrica Lexie and St Antony: A Voyage into Jurisdictional Conflict. QUT Law Review 14(2):74–89

Johnson DR, Post DG (1996) Law and Borders: The Rise of Law in Cyberspace. Stanford Law Review 48(5):1367–1402

Kerr OS (2015) Search and Seizure in a Digital World. Harvard Law Review 119:531–585

Kulesza J (2008) Internet Governance and the Jurisdiction of State: Justification of the Need for an International Regulation of Cyberspace. https://www.researchgate.net/profile/Joanna_Kulesza3/publication/228228013_Internet_Governance_and_the_Jurisdiction_of_States_Justification_of_the_Need_for_an_International_Regulation_of_Cyberspace/links/564e522108ae4988a7a62701.pdf. Accessed 20 October 2016

Lacy E, Reed SR (2016) BWL cyberattack bills reach nearly $2M. http://www.lansingstatejournal.com/story/news/local/2016/09/22/bwl-ransomware-attack-costly-details-emerging/90826176/. Accessed 22 October 2016

Mell P, Grance T (2011) The NIST Definition of Cloud Computing: Recommendations of the National Institute of Standards and Technology. NIST Special Publication 800–145. http://faculty.winthrop.edu/domanm/csci411/Handouts/NIST.pdf. Accessed 23 October 2016

Narayanan V (2012) Harnessing the Cloud: International Law Implications of Cloud-Computing. Chicago Journal of International Law 12(2):783–809

NIST (2014) Cloud Computing Forensic Science Challenges. Draft NISTIR 8006. http://csrc.nist.gov/publications/drafts/nistir-8006/draft_nistir_8006.pdf. Accessed 25 October 2016

Osula A-M (2015) Transborder Access and Territorial Sovereignty. Computer Law & Security Review 31:719–735

PC-OC (2012) Guidelines on Practical Measures to Improve Co-Operation in Respect of Transfer of Proceedings, Including a Model Request Form. PC-OC INF 78. http://www.coe.int/t/dghl/standardsetting/pc-oc/Source/PC_OC_INF_78%20Guidelines%20and%20model%20request%20form%20on%20transfer%20of%20proceedings.doc. Accessed 25 October 2016

PC-OC (2014) Model Request Form for Mutual Assistance in Criminal Matters. PC-OC Mod (2014) 10rev.6. http://www.coe.int/t/dghl/standardsetting/pc-oc/PCOC_documents/Documents%202015/PC-OC%20Mod%20(2014)10rev6%20Model%20request%20form%20for%20MLA.pdf. Accessed 25 October 2016

PC-OC (2015) Mutual Legal Assistance in the Treaties of the Council of Europe: Note for Practitioners. PC-OC(2015)03. http://www.coe.int/t/dghl/standardsetting/pc-oc/PCOC_documents/Documents%202015/PC-OC%20(2015)03%20Note%20for%20practitioners%20on%20mutual%20legal%20assistance.pdf. Accessed 25 October 2016

Reidenberg JN (2005) Technology and Internet Jurisdiction. University of Pennsylvania Law Review 153:1951–1974

Schultz T (2008) Carving up the Internet: Jurisdiction, Legal Orders, and the Private/Public International Law Interface. European Journal of International Law 19(4):799–839

Svantesson D (2015) A New Jurisprudential Framework for Jurisdiction: Beyond the Harvard Draft. AJIL Unbound 109:69–74

Svantesson D, Gerry F (2015) Access to Extraterritorial Evidence: The Microsoft Cloud Case and Beyond. Computer Law & Security Review 31:478–489

Svantesson D, van Zwieten L (2016) Law Enforcement Access to Evidence Via Direct Contact With Cloud Providers – Identifying the Contours of a Solution. Computer Law & Security Review 32:671–687

Swanson SR (2011) Google Sets Sail: Ocean-Based Server Farms and International Law. Connecticut Law Review 43(3):709–751

Talbot D (2016) Cybersecurity: The Age of the Megabreach. MIT Technology Review. https://www.technologyreview.com/s/545616/cybersecurity-the-age-of-the-megabreach/. Accessed 30 October 2016

T-CY (2013a) Guidance Note#3: Transborder Access to Data (Article 32). http://rm.coe.int/CoERMPublicCommonSearchServices/DisplayDCTMContent?documentId=09000016802e726a. Accessed 27 October 2016

T-CY (2013b) Assessment Report: The Mutual Legal Assistance Provisions of the Budapest Convention on Cybercrime. http://rm.coe.int/CoERMPublicCommonSearchServices/DisplayDCTMContent?documentId=09000016802e726c. Accessed 23 October 2016

T-CY (2014) Rules on Obtaining Subscriber Information. Report. https://rm.coe.int/CoERMPublicCommonSearchServices/DisplayDCTMContent?documentId=09000016802e7ad1. Accessed 25 October 2016

T-CY (2015a) Guidance Note#10 (Draft): Production Orders for Subscriber Information (Article 18 Budapest Convention). https://rm.coe.int/CoERMPublicCommonSearchServices/DisplayDCTMContent?documentId=090000168064b77c. Accessed 28 October 2016

T-CY (2015b) Criminal Justice Access to Data in the Cloud: Challenges. Discussion Paper. https://rm.coe.int/CoERMPublicCommonSearchServices/DisplayDCTMContent?documentId=0900001680304b59. Accessed 22 October 2016

T-CY (2016a) Criminal Justice Access to Electronic Evidence in the Cloud - Informal Summary of Issues and Options Under Consideration by the Cloud Evidence Group. https://rm.coe.int/CoERMPublicCommonSearchServices/DisplayDCTMContent?documentId=09000016805a53c8. Accessed 25 October 2016

T-CY (2016b) Criminal Justice Access to Data in the Cloud: Co-Operation with 'Foreign' Service Providers. Background Paper. https://rm.coe.int/CoERMPublicCommonSearchServices/DisplayDCTMContent?documentId=090000168064b77d. Accessed 27 October 2016

T-CY (2016c) Emergency Requests for The Immediate Disclosure of Data Stored in Another Jurisdiction Through Mutual Legal Assistance Channels or Through Direct Requests to Service

Providers: Compilation of Replies to the Questionnaire. http://rm.coe.int/CoERMPublicCommonSearchServices/DisplayDCTMContent?documentId=0900001680644318. Accessed 27 October 2016

UNODC (2013) Comprehensive Study on Cybercrime. https://www.unodc.org/documents/organized-crime/UNODC_CCPCJ_EG.4_2013/CYBERCRIME_STUDY_210213.pdf. Accessed 20 October 2016

Vaciago G (2011) Cloud Computing and Data Jurisdiction: A New Challenge for Digital Forensics. CYBERLAWS 2012: The Third International Conference on Technical and Legal Aspects of the e-Society

von Behr I, Reding A, Edwards C, Gribbon L (2013) Radicalisation in the Digital Era. The Use of the Internet in 15 Cases of Terrorism and Extremism. http://www.rand.org/pubs/research_reports/RR453.html. Accessed 22 October 2016

Walden I (2011) Accessing Data in the Cloud: The Long Arm of the Law Enforcement Agent. Queen Mary School of Law Legal Studies Research Paper No 74/2011. https://ssrn.com/abstract=1781067. Accessed 27 October 2016

Zoetekouw M (2016) Ignorantia Terrae Non Excusat. https://english.eu2016.nl/binaries/eu2016-en/documents/publications/2016/03/7/c-mzoetekouw—ignorantia-terrae-non-excusat—discussion-paper-for-the-crossing-borders—jurisdiction-in-cyberspace-conference-march-2016—final/c-mzoetekouw-ignorantia-terrae-non-excusat-discussion-paper-for-the-crossing-borders-jurisdiction-in-cyberspace-conference-march-2016-final.pdf. Accessed 20 October 2016

Chapter 8
Reconfiguring Territoriality in International Economic Law

Alessandra Arcuri and Federica Violi

Abstract Recent scholarship in international law has studied the phenomenon of deterritorialization and, in this context, has framed territoriality and functionality as competing modes of organizing the global political order. In this chapter, we challenge this vision by exploring the hypothesis that territoriality and functionality, rather than mere substitutes or competitors, impart meaning to each other. To test this hypothesis, we identify different modes by which functionality and territoriality interact in the reconfiguration of the international legal space, and in particular in the trade and investment regimes. In the context of international trade law, we show how territoriality is multiplied, and how it gives meaning to functionality, in particular at the intersection of the trade regime and regimes for the protection of health and environment. We further develop the idea of the emergence of techno-territoriality, where norms allegedly promoting global technocracy are being shaped by territoriality. The analysis of the international investment regime engages with the threats that contractual clauses exert on territoriality in the context of investment operations, the significance of the territorial nexus requirement in the definition of investment, when intangible financial instruments are involved, as well as the 'international-territoriality' mode conveyed by the activities of sovereign investors abroad. We conclude by arguing that territoriality is not subsumed by functionality, but is rather undergoing a process of transformation into 'non-modern' territoriality: the reassertion of territori-

The authors wish to thank Pedro Alejandro Villarreal Lizárraga, Marjolein Schaap and two anonymous referees for their insightful comments. The usual disclaimer applies. This chapter is the result of the joint work of the authors and reflects their shared views. For the purposes of evaluation of our work by Italian academic institutions, we declare that Sects. 8.1, 8.2 and 8.5 were jointly drafted, Sect. 8.3 was drafted by Alessandra Arcuri and Sect. 8.4 was drafted by Federica Violi.

A. Arcuri (✉) · F. Violi
Erasmus School of Law (ESL), Erasmus University Rotterdam,
Rotterdam, The Netherlands
e-mail: arcuri@law.eur.nl

F. Violi
e-mail: violi@law.eur.nl

M. Kuijer and W. Werner (eds.), *Netherlands Yearbook of International Law 2016*, Netherlands Yearbook of International Law 47,
DOI 10.1007/978-94-6265-207-1_8

ality in investment and trade regimes, albeit in different forms, should be looked at as a positive development to keep alive the 'public' core of international law.

Keywords Territoriality · Functionality · WTO law · International investment law · Techno-territoriality · Extraterritoriality · Stabilization clauses · Sovereign investors

Contents

8.1 Introduction

Economic and political tenets of modernity are embedded in the principle of territoriality. Globalization processes, however, are eroding its role as an organizing category, affecting both territorial sovereignty and the democratic principle intrinsic in political territoriality.[1] The inability of States to cope with trans-boundary phenomena has produced disentanglement between authority and the State, thus loosening the imperative of the territorial nexus. Regulatory processes are now shaped beyond traditional structures, through the recourse to deformalized instruments and networks. As a matter of fact, social and economic complexity has boosted the detachment between the juridical and political sphere, thus magnifying pluralism. Observing these phenomena, a wide scholarship in international law and

[1] Di Martino 2010, at 270. The observation can be traced back to the work of Carl Schmitt on the relation between *Ordnung* and *Ortung*, Schmitt 1950.

in socio-legal theories has argued that territorial borders have been gradually substituted by functional 'borders' as criteria of differentiation.[2]

Functional boundaries contribute to redefine and delimit different spheres of activities. Interestingly enough, while advancing the 'Gesellschaftswelt',[3] functional boundaries still maintain the binary mechanism that is typical to borders: exclusion from and inclusion in. Hence, functionality produces a compartmentalization of regimes and systems, which is 'issue-specific', rather than territorial.[4] The phenomenon of self-contained regimes, and the fragmentation that comes with it, proves exemplary in this regard.

The redistribution of powers beyond the State and the empowerment of 'non-State actors' has led several authors to talk of deterritorialization of international law, a term commonly used to refer to the disconnection between authority and a specific territory.[5] The emphasis on deterritorialization has shifted the attention of scholars on functionality as an alternative analytical grid to better understand the dynamics of global law.[6] This new focus has sparked important analyses on the fragmentation of the legal system, which reflects the idea of 'islands of law in a sea of regulation.'[7]

In this context, several authors have emphasized problems related to such a decentralized, fragmented and rapidly changing legal (dis-)order. In a system dominated by functional regimes, some have pointed at the problematic asymmetry between the far-developed trade and investment systems vis-à-vis the relatively fragmented and less powerful international environmental and human rights regimes. More generally, while guaranteeing a certain level of flexibility, the informal character of the normativity of global governance tools, casts a shadow on the very basis of its legitimacy, given their detachment from a norm-validity process, which was traditionally embedded in the principle of territoriality. The exercise of power in the global space hampers accountability and control mechanisms.

We do not challenge the by-now common wisdom that a shift towards functionality is occurring and we concur with the (normative) studies asserting the need of making these regimes compatible, legitimate and (more) accountable. Our claim, however, is that the schism territoriality—functionality may obscure some facets of the transformation of the way in which authority is exercised in the contemporary system of international economic law. This chapter contributes to the existing debate by exploring the hypothesis that territoriality and functionality, rather than

[2] Ruggie 1993, at 165; Paulus 2004, at 59; Fischer-Lescano and Teubner 2004, at 1008–1009 et seq; Luhmann 1982 at 235, Kahn 2012, at 225.

[3] Di Martino 2010, at 285; Krasner 1982, at 497.

[4] On the impact of fragmentation on legal pluralism, see Teubner and Korth 2010, at 23.

[5] This definition draws on Brölmann 2007, at 86.

[6] Paulus 2004.

[7] On the predominance of a fragmented functional logic governed by technocrats over the pursuit of integrated public policy, see Mégret 2012, at 86.

mere substitutes or competitors, *impart meaning* to each other. To test this hypothesis, we identify different modes by which functionality and territoriality interact in the reconfiguration of the international legal space, and in particular in the trade and investment regimes.

We start in Sect. 8.2 by presenting a brief recollection of the notion of territoriality in international law and the emergence of theories emphasizing the shift to functionality as substitute criterion to allocate power. We then explain why territoriality, as a criterion for the organization of the (global) political space is still meaningful. In Sect. 8.3, we describe how territoriality is variously transformed in the international trade regime. Rather than deterritorialization, we observe that, in this context, territoriality is being multiplied and employed to impart meaning to the functional-trade regime. Section 8.4 focuses on the investment regime, a field where deterritorialization is particularly salient, as host States' regulatory power is somewhat limited compared to the latitude granted to investors, both within and beyond territorial borders. Paradoxically, this process of deterritorialization is intimately bound-up with territoriality, as investments are in the first place protected by virtue of territory (e.g. the rules in Bilateral Investment Treaties which define investments are extremely territorial, as well as the rhetoric justifying current regimes of international investment law). Conclusions are drawn in Sect. 8.5.

8.2 The Transformation of Territoriality in International Law

Territoriality refers to the exercise of authority by a certain entity over a given territory. At a more general level of abstraction, territoriality is a legal construct,[8] loading territory with normativity.[9] While the State continues to play a central role in territorial regimes, territoriality is conceivable beyond the static terms of *modern* territoriality and it encompasses more than one way of linking authority to territory.[10] In this chapter, we will mainly focus on this legal construct within the international economic order. In focusing on ways in which territoriality is reconfigured, we want to shed light on how the relationship between authority and territory is changing.

---

[8] Buxbaum 2009, at 635.

[9] The conceptualization of territorial sovereignty as 'functional sovereignty' understands territory neither as an object, nor as an element of the State, but rather 'as one of the (spatial) ambits in which sovereignty displays its functions and it is hence protected by international law. This presupposes the attribution of a normative meaning to territory, which is inseparable from the *effective* exercise of sovereign powers (and clearly, obligations, i.e. functions) of States over that particular spatial sphere. See on this Milano 2015, at 63, referring to Quadri's seminal work: Quadri 1968, at 633.

[10] See the distinction between territory and territoriality, as elaborated by Sassen 2013.

8.2.1 From Modern Territoriality to Functionality

In his 1993 landmark article, Ruggie identified different ways to organize the political space in relation to territoriality, ranging from absence of territoriality to modern territoriality. To begin with, territoriality is not a necessary condition to organize the political space, as evidenced by primitive societies, which were organized 'on the basis of kinship.' Further, territoriality can be non-fixed (e.g. nomadic property rights) and non-exclusive.[11] The classical example of non-exclusive territoriality is medieval Europe, with 'crisscrossing jurisdictions' where claims to authority were contextually emanating from different sources, such as the empire, the church and feudal jurisdictions.[12]

The advent of modern territoriality is characterized by a shift towards unity and mutual exclusivity. Modern territoriality implies that authority cannot be exercised beyond its own territory. According to Ruggie, the chief characteristic of modern territoriality is the *differentiation* between the internal and the external and between the private and the public.[13] Modern territoriality shapes also the 'divide' between national and international: '[t]he state's territorial boundary delimitates its political and legal power and vice versa, and constitutes its border with international law.'[14]

At this point, it is worth emphasizing how modern territoriality has been strongly 'racialized' and the evolution of positive international law has been based on the distinction between the civilized and the uncivilized.[15] As put by one international scholar in 1866: 'Is there a uniform law of nations? There certainly is not the same one for all the nations and states of the world. The public law, with slight exceptions, has always been, and still is, limited to the *civilized and Christian people of Europe* or to those of European origin.'[16] Likewise, in the eighteenth and nineteenth centuries, the distinction between the private and the public was affirmed and at the same time blurred as companies, like the East Indian Company, were de facto exercising sovereign powers in the non-European territories.[17] Modern territoriality is, accordingly, a relational construct where its main tenet, mutual exclusivity, is valid only among equals, i.e. the civilized European states, and where the public/private divide has not always been sharp. Or should we rather ask: has territoriality ever been modern? But here we follow Nietzsche, who said that 'the big problems were like cold baths: you have to get out as fast as you got in.'[18]

---

[11] Ruggie 1993, at 149.

[12] Sassen 2006, at 32–33.

[13] Ibid., at 151.

[14] Brölmann 2007, at 85.

[15] For a comprehensive analysis see Anghie 1999. In her analysis, Sassen well illustrates how the emergence of territorial authority was bound up with imperial geography, see Sassen 2006, at 74–96.

[16] Weathon, quoted in Anghie 1999, at 21.

[17] Anghie 1999, at 33. The East Indian Company was abolished in 1857, see Sassen 2006, at 94.

[18] The quote is borrowed from Latour 1993.

Ruggie concludes his analysis hinting at processes by which territoriality is unbundled: 'in the modern international polity an institutional negation of exclusive territoriality serves as a means of situating and dealing with those dimensions of collective existence that territorial rulers recognise to be irreducibly transterritorial in character.'[19] Ruggie's analysis has been followed by several studies, which have all emphasized patterns of deterritorialization.[20]

Fischer-Lescano and Teubner have argued that territoriality has lost salience vis-à-vis 'functionality', which is now considered one of the most distinguishing traits of the global order.[21] Under functionality, authority is exercised on the basis of regimes specifically set up to attain certain goals, from trade liberalization, the promotion of foreign direct investment, to the protection of human rights and the harmonization of technical standards. In this context, Brölmann has characterized functionality as 'the most prominent *substitute* for territoriality as an organizing principle for regulatory authority.'[22]

8.2.2 Back to the Future: Non-Modern Territoriality

While it is unquestionable that functionality plays an important role in contemporary legal systems, the global legal order is still significantly shaped along territorial lines.[23] The rhetoric of the dissolution of States' traditional space does encounter at least three objections. The first one relates to the prosaic observation that most treaties still take State territory as the spatial application, hence scope and delimitation, of the norms they include. In those cases where this reference is not spelled out, the presumption is still towards territoriality.[24]

On a second note, effective territorial control allows international law to function.[25] The absence of a centralized international authority, which guarantees the application and the enforcement of international norms, sheds light on the

[19] Ruggie 1993, at 165.

[20] Fischer-Lescano and Teubner 2004; Paulus 2004; Brölmann 2007; Ryngaert 2014. For a critique of the ways in which the modern territorial state, as an analytical construct, has constrained the conventional thinking in international relations theory, see Agnew 1994; the author refers to this problem as to a 'territorial trap'.

[21] As put by Fischer-Lescano and Teubner 2004, '[t]he traditional differentiation in line with the political principle of territoriality into relatively autonomous national legal orders is thus overlain by a sectoral differentiation principle: the differentiation of global law into transnational legal regimes, which define the external reach of their jurisdiction along issue-specific rather than territorial lines, and which claim a global validity for themselves'; Fischer-Lescano and Teubner 2004, at 1009. The authors draw on the seminal work by Luhmann 1995.

[22] Brölmann 2007, at 87 (emphasis added).

[23] Sassen 2006.

[24] Kamminga 2013, at 2.

[25] See on this Tancredi 2015, at 49, referring to the seminal work of Schmitt 1950.

functional character of territoriality. In fact, compliance and implementation of rules are left to the decentralized system of States or other (novel) territorial units, such as custom unions. If the latter were not effectively able to control their territory, this would, at the same time, jeopardize both the respect and protection of subjective rights and the fulfilment of international obligations that are due *erga omnes*, but still require the commitment of the State *ratione loci* for their implementation. Hence, 'territoriality hugely contribute[s] to the *functioning* of international law.'[26]

This is also reflected at the level of responsibility. If sovereignty is conceived as the power over a certain territory, this implies, at the same time, corresponding duties and accountability, to avoid the *horror vacui* of not having any entity responding for infringements. As a matter of fact, although the shift of traditional decision-making powers of the State to other international actors has helped to establish a system of multilevel governance, this was not accompanied by either (1) the creation of a corresponding apparatus, capable of performing the traditional economic and social duties of the States,[27] or (2) by a system of global protection, which safeguards individuals in the event that the decisions taken by these international actors directly or indirectly affect their legal sphere.

Finally, while legal pluralist, transnational and functionalist theories have been able to identify and describe the shift away from territoriality as the main organizing principle within the international legal order, the legitimacy conundrum of a deterritorialized international legal order is still not fully solved. In this sense, it has been rightly noted that even the most interconnected regulatory systems (e.g. the EU), still need to relate to territory and application *ratione loci* in order to be effective and consolidating.[28]

It is clear, therefore, that States cannot 'dissolve' and their territorial endeavour is still prominent in this new inter-spatial dialectic, especially in the attainment of general interests, which tend to be particularized in pure issue-specific regimes. The State territory becomes, then, the spatial ambit where the State fulfils its functions. As these functions change over time, the type of authority exercised also transforms (some would say is eroded). Hence, far from the absolute sovereignty tenet of modern international law, territoriality is to be conceived as an instrument in the effective functioning of international law.

This certainly does not mean denying that the global socio-economic context poses a number of external pressures on the State: accepting that sovereignty is a dynamic concept, means acknowledging its evolution towards a functional[29] and

[26] Ibid., 2015, at 52 (emphasis added).

[27] Bassiouni 2012, at 1.

[28] Milano 2015, at 69, the author clarifies that the relation between Ordnung and Ortung as instrumental rather than dissociative.

[29] Dupuy 2002, at 102.

less absolute approach, the former understood as an exclusive exercise of the *public* functions of the State for the pursuit of general objectives. It is not, therefore, the existence of the State which has to be questioned,[30] but rather the difficulty of adapting and re-reading the concept of sovereignty in the light of the new socio-economic scenario. In this sense, modern territoriality transforms into new forms of non-modern territorialities, where territory and authority remain linked in different ways.

The renewed interest in the principle of subsidiarity, as a principle that allocates powers between multiple levels of governance at the global level,[31] lends support to the idea that territoriality is not passé. One reason why functionality seems still tightly bound to territoriality is that the realm of politics is far from being emancipated from the (State) territory. To the extent that politics remains territorial, it appears difficult for functionality to articulate in a complete way the organization of the political space. From this perspective, the demise of territoriality as a criterion to understand the transformation of contemporary legal orders may be premature. The great attention paid to functionality and the legal techniques that can be employed to address the problems of fragmentation and proliferation of legal orders, has left the question of how territoriality is reconfigured in the postmodern era underexplored.

In the following analysis, we study the transformation of territoriality and the interaction between territoriality and functionality. By focusing on two salient fields of international economic law—the international trade and the international investment regimes—we further analyse how territoriality is being put under pressure and how territoriality and functionality impart meaning to each other.

8.3 Territoriality and the International Trade Regime

At first glance, the system of international economic law appears as a clear manifestation of the phenomenon of deterritorialization, in which authority is removed from specific territories (most notably, State territories). By joining the General Agreement on Tariffs and Trade (GATT)[32] first, and the World Trade Organization (WTO) later, States relinquished part of their sovereignty in trade-related legal fields. The debate on sovereignty and the system of international economic law is rich and, while certainly contiguous to the theme of this chapter, is not our main

[30] On this extensively Pikalo 2007, at 17; Wolf 2001, at 178; Weiss 2000, at 1.

[31] See the most recent issue (2016) of Law and Contemporary Problems dedicated to Subsidiarity in Global Governance. For an earlier analysis see Howse and Nicolaïdis 2003.

[32] 1947 General Agreement on Tariffs and Trade, 55 UNTS 187 (GATT).

focus.[33] Instead, we aim at coming to a better understanding of 'legal spatiality' in international economic law.[34] In this context, we posit that the thesis that deterritorialization is occurring within the system of international trade law may be unable to capture the ongoing reconfiguration of territoriality. At a closer look, the international trade regime has been built and continues to be shaped along territorial lines.

First of all, the GATT has a strong territorial component. For example, Article I:1 GATT reads:

> With respect to customs duties and charges of any kind imposed on or in connection with importation or exportation [...] any advantage, favour, privilege or immunity granted by any contracting party to any product originating in or destined for any other country shall be accorded immediately and unconditionally to the like product originating in or destined for the *territories* of all other contracting parties. (emphasis added)

Likewise the formulation of Article III:2 GATT places territory central in the architecture of the national treatment principle and reference to territory/territories features in many GATT provisions. The multiple references to territories reflect the fact that the obligations and rights established by the international trade regime are to be operationalized in relation to territory. The point here is that in the unquestionable move towards transnationalism, territoriality still plays a role.[35] Granted, territoriality is configured in ways that go beyond modern territoriality.

8.3.1 Multiplication of Territoriality

An example of the reconfiguration of modern territoriality is the multiplication of territoriality. By this term we mean the multiplication of *territorial* units that count as legally relevant within the international trade regime. Next to the nation-state, customs unions and free trade areas have gained a unique legal status within the international trade regime. Customs territories possessing 'full autonomy in the conduct of [their] external commercial relations and of the other matters provided

[33] The literature on sovereignty and international economic law is burgeoning. Jackson 1997, 2003 and 2006; Petersmann 2008; Raustiala 2003. The latter argues that sovereignty ought to be conceptualized as the capacity to revoke the delegation of powers and the availability of exit and that eventually international economic institutions are sovereignty-enhancing. Notably, Raustiala argues that 'embedded liberalism' is a key factor in strengthening sovereignty with the WTO law system. The loss of sovereignty has been often used as an argument to oppose the WTO project. Cf. Shaefer 2002, at 342–343.

[34] The term legal spatiality has been used by Raustiala to refer to the 'supposition that law and legal remedies are connected to, or limited by, territorial location.' Raustiala 2005, at 2503.

[35] This point resonates with Gregory Shaffer's analysis and critique of post-nationalism as an insufficiently accurate descriptor of the contemporary legal order. Shaffer argues: 'The legal ordering that we see is transnational because it implicates multiple states and constituencies within them, but it is not post-national in that *states remain central* to the creation, implementation, and contestation of transnational legal ordering.' Shaffer 2012, at 579 (emphasis added).

for in this Agreement', were/are eligible to become Contracting Parties/Members under GATT 1947 and the WTO Agreement.[36] While Chinese Taipei (or Taiwan)[37] is the only separate customs territory to have started its accession procedure under Article XXXIII GATT 1947, the existence of this provision (as further reflected in Article XII of the Marrakesh Agreement) attests to the formal recognition of customs unions as equal to States.[38] Accepting customs territories as WTO (and previously GATT) Members is an interesting manifestation of the encounter between functionality and territoriality.[39] The criterion to multiply the legally relevant territorial units is manifestly functional: what is required to become a WTO Member is the full autonomy in the conduct of external commercial relations. Yet, the criterion remains bitingly territorial: the customs *territory* is the unit to be eligible.

Another instance of the multiplication of territoriality is the 'dual' membership to the WTO of the European Union (EU, formerly the European Communities) and of *all* the EU Member States. After having being treated as a de facto contracting party under GATT,[40] the European Communities (EC) became one of the founding Members of the WTO, by virtue of Article XI of the WTO Agreement.[41] While all EU Member States have full WTO membership, it is common that at most meetings, only the European Commission speaks. It is also normal that, in settling disputes, the European Union (and not its Member States) acts as disputant,

---

[36] Cf. Article XXXIII GATT 1947; and Article XII of the 1994 Marrakesh Agreement Establishing the World Trade Organization, 1867 UNTS 14 (WTO Agreement; or Marrakesh Agreement).

[37] We use the nomenclature 'Taiwan', even though it is politically controversial, as discussed in Charnovitz 2006, at 403. As noted by this author, in the WTO Taiwan is named inconsistently, since in the Accession Documents it is called Separate Customs Territory of Taiwan, Penghu, Kinmen and Matsu and abbreviated as Chinese Taipei and, at the same time, on the website it is listed under the letter 'T'.

[38] Cf. WTO, Report of The Working Party on the Accession of The Separate Customs Territory of Taiwan, Penghu, Kinmen and Matsu, WT/MIN(01)/4, 11 November 2001. Note that Chinese Taipei started its accession process under Article XXXIII GATT 1947 and, when the WTO was established the accession process was under Article XII of Marrakech Agreement. For an analysis of the implications of the accession by Chinese Taipei, see Charnovitz 2006.

[39] Note that the customs territories of Hong Kong and Macau were GATT contracting parties from 1986 and 1991 respectively.

[40] For a detailed description of the history the European Community in GATT, see Antoniadis 2004. Interestingly GATT preceded the European Economic Community; in this respect Antoniadis notes that the original legal architecture of the EEC has been shaped by Article XXIV GATT 1947.

[41] The WTO website names the European Union as a WTO Member, see https://www.wto.org/english/thewto_e/countries_e/european_communities_e.htm, accessed 27 July 2016. As of 1 December 2009, the European Union has replaced the European Community; see van den Bossche and Zdouc 2013 at 106–107, in particular note 167, where the authors explain how, on 29 November 2009, the Council of the European Union and the Commission sent a Verbal Note to the WTO stating that the European Union 'replaces and succeeds the European Community' (WTO, Verbal Note from the Council of the European Union and the Commission of the European Communities, WT/L/779, 30 November 2009).

independently from the origin of the policy measures contested and from the interests at stake.[42] In spite of the prominent role played by the European Union, it is worth emphasizing that the EU Member States maintain their full status of WTO Members, retaining voice and power. The world trade system, by recognizing the parallel existence of these territorial units, contributes to the normalization of the coexistence of multiple territories. In this particular instance of multiplication of territoriality, functionality remains vital. Territoriality is apparent because the European Union, as a political entity, is encased in a precise geography and authority is exercised only within these boundaries; yet, territoriality is meaningful vis-à-vis functionality, as the European Union participates in the world trade system because of its exclusive competence in the area of common commercial policy. The inscription of functionality into territoriality is well captured by the following passage of the Appellate Body: 'However, the European Communities constitutes a customs union, and as such, once goods are imported into any Member State, they circulate freely within the *territory of the entire customs union*. The export market, therefore, is the European Communities, not an individual Member State.'[43]

Last but not least, the multiplication of territoriality is also apparent from the important carve out for Regional Trade Agreements (RTAs) provided for by Article XXIV GATT 1994, Article V GATS[44] and para 2(c) of the Enabling Clause. These rules allow WTO Members to establish regional trade areas (in the form of free-trade areas or customs unions), provided that certain conditions are respected.[45] RTAs have proliferated at an exponential rate since the adoption of GATT, reaching the impressive number of 267 physical RTAs.[46] Some of these Agreements are geographically constrained by the proximities of the States involved (e.g. NAFTA,[47] MERCOSUR,[48] ASEAN).[49] Others are cross-regional, such as the agreements being negotiated at the time of writing, commonly labelled as mega-regionals, for their broad coverage (e.g. the Comprehensive Economic and

[42] See Antoniadis 2004. While this tends to be the norm, there are cases in which the EU and certain Member States act together as respondents (e.g. WTO Appellate Body Report, European Communities and Certain Member States—Measures Affecting Trade in Large Civil Aircraft, WT/DS316/AB/R, 18 May 2011) or cases where a WTO dispute has been brought by a Member State against the EU (e.g. WTO, European Union—Measures on Atlanto-Scandian Herring, Request for consultations by Denmark in respect of the Faroe Islands, WT/DS469/1, 7 November 2013).

[43] EC—Customs Classification, Appellate Body Report, at para 96, as quoted in Antoniadis 2004.

[44] 1994 General Agreement on Trade in Services, 1869 UNTS 183 (GATS).

[45] Cf. Article XXIV:5 and XXIV:8 GATT 1994. For a detailed analysis of these conditions, see Lockhart and Mitchell 2005.

[46] Data taken from the Summarizing Table prepared by the WTO, http://rtais.wto.org/UI/publicsummarytable.aspx, accessed 27 July 2016.

[47] 1992 North American Free Trade Agreement, 32 I.L.M. 289 (NAFTA).

[48] 1991 Treaty for the establishment of a Common Market (Asunción Treaty) between the Argentine Republic, the Federative Republic of Brazil, the Republic of Paraguay and the Eastern Republic of Uruguay, 2140 UNTS 257 (MERCOSUR).

[49] 2007 Charter of the Association of Southeast Asian Nations, 2624 UNTS 223 (ASEAN).

Trade Agreement with Canada (CETA)[50] and the the Transatlantic Trade & Investment Partnership (TTIP)).

Some considerations are in order here. The multilateral trading system, since its origins, has been designed in recognition of the parallel existence of States, RTAs and the international realm. Article XXIV GATT 1994 could be seen as an attempt to regulate the co-existence of these different orders. Article XXIV, however, has remained largely inoperative and in practice the WTO compatibility of RTAs is at best uncertain.[51] On the one hand, the conditions established by Article XXIV are fraught with ambiguous formulations, and thus it may be difficult to assess in concrete the WTO compatibility of a given RTA;[52] on the other hand, WTO Members lack incentives to initiate disputes on this question and accordingly the WTO adjudicatory bodies have had little occasion to clarify this body of law.[53]

The international trade regime, with its rules on regionalism, sets few constraints on the freedom of States to engage in RTAs. While the State operates and is constrained by multiple structures, it remains the main actor to create this new (geo-)political order. At the same time, once a regional area is established, the State's authority is eroded, or better transformed. The multiplication of territorial units can be read as a shift away from *modern* territoriality, towards an organization of legal spatiality, where authority is exercised at different levels.[54] The degree and forms of this redistribution of authority depends on the specific RTA: some include only basic rules about liberalization of trade (e.g. removal of tariffs within the area); some have established their own dispute settlement mechanism; others have included rules that go beyond the obligations already assumed under the WTO regime (e.g. TRIPS-plus regimes).[55]

This reconfiguration of territoriality may have an impact on the international legal order as well. The proliferation of regionalism has led several scholars and practitioners to advocate for the adoption of a 'variable geometry' in the international trade regime; that is the move away from multilateralism and the single undertaking towards plurilateralism along issue-specific areas. In other words, the movement from modern territoriality to multiple territorialities, unfolding within

---

[50] European Commission, Proposal for a Council Decision on the conclusion of the Comprehensive Economic and Trade Agreement between Canada of the one part, and the European Union and its Member States, of the other part, COM(2016) 443 final, 5 July 2016 (CETA).

[51] Lockhart and Mitchell 2005. According to Fabbricotti 2008, the fact that Article XXIV GATT 1994 has been largely inoperative, could be read as the emergence of a 'customary 'regional exception'.

[52] See World Trade Organization, Synopsis of 'Systemic' Issues Related to Regional Trade Agreements, WT/REG/W/37, 2 March 2000; World Trade Organization, Compendium of Issues Related to Regional Trade Agreements, WTO Doc TN/RL/W/8/Rev.1, 1 August 2002.

[53] Few cases have dealt with the exceptions in Article XXIV GATT 1994; WTO Appellate Body Report, Turkey—Restrictions on Imports of Textile and Clothing Products, WT/DS34/AB/R, 22 October 1999.

[54] This argument echoes John Jackson's idea that sovereignty mainly refers to 'questions about the allocation of power'. Jackson 2003, at 790.

[55] Mercurio 2006.

international trade law, is likely to affect the very nature of this body of law. Interestingly, the metaphor 'variable geometry' evokes the *spatiality* of the multiplication and crisscrossing of different sources of authority.

8.3.2 The Territorial Boundaries of Functionality

As briefly mentioned in the previous section, one of the main challenges of the shift to functionality is 'regime collisions'.[56] To illustrate these collisions, Fisher-Lescano and Teubner provide several examples pertaining to WTO law, and more particularly to the 'trade and …' debate. An important argument developed by the authors is that these collisions may be read as conflicts 'between competing rationalities.'[57] In this context, they use the example of the US challenging a Brazilian law, which allows the granting of compulsory licensing for medicines, if the patented medicine is not manufactured in Brazil (local working requirements).[58] After the establishment of a Panel, the dispute was resolved by a mutually agreed solution reached by the parties and notified to the WTO Dispute Settlement Body (DSB).[59] Fischer-Lescano and Teubner maintain that this episode can be read as a conflict unfolding at three different levels: (1) between national law and patent owners; (2) between international organizations, in particular the WTO and the World Health Organization (WHO); and (3) between different rationalities (in this example, the protection of economic interests vs. the protection of health).[60] In their view, the latter conflict is the most salient to understand the transformation of global law.

The WTO regime regulates the conflict between competing rationalities (in this case, the protection of patents—economic rationality—and the protection of health) with the exceptional regime established by Articles 30 and 31 of the Agreement on Trade-Related Aspects of Intellectual Property (TRIPS Agreement).[61] According to the joint reading of these two Articles, WTO Members are granted certain

[56] Fisher-Lescano and Teubner 2004.

[57] Ibid., at 1028.

[58] WTO Dispute Settlement Body, Brazil—Measures Affecting Patent Protection, Request for the Establishment of a Panel by the United States, WT/DS199/3, 9 January 2001.

[59] WTO Dispute Settlement Body, Brazil—Measures Affecting Patent Protection, Notification of Mutually Agreed Solution, WT/DS199/4, 19 July 2001. The gist of the proposed solution is that Brazil should 'hold prior talks with the United States with sufficient advance notice to permit constructive discussions in the context of a special session of the US—Brazil Consultative Mechanism, should Brazil deem it necessary to apply Article 68 to grant a compulsory license on patents held by U.S. companies.'

[60] Fischer Lescano and Teubner 2004, at 1024–1032.

[61] WTO Agreement, Annex 1 C—Agreement on Trade-Related Aspects of Intellectual Property Rights, as amended on 23 January 2017 (TRIPS Agreement) (Final Act Embodying the Results of the Uruguay Round of Multilateral Trade Negotiations).

flexibilities in the application of the TRIPS Agreement, and in particular the right of granting compulsory licencing in case of national emergencies. Moreover, the TRIPS Agreement has been amended by the Decision of the General Council of 6 December 2005 on an Amendment of the TRIPS Agreement,[62] which implements the 2001 Doha Declaration on the TRIPS agreement and public health.[63]

Fisher-Lescano and Teubner read in these provisions the emergence of a 'compatibilization technique': '[i]n our reading, the economically oriented WTO regime has created an internal limitation on its own logic through the reformulation of a principle of health protection.'[64] While we share much of this analysis, our aim is to show that, at the intersection of the trade regime with other areas, functionality is *co-determined* by territoriality. The point is that the shaping of a principle of health protection occurs through the mediation of States, which are able to represent concrete and local interests. A principle of health protection remains abstract and does not tell whether 'any disease' can be considered a national emergency or to what extent it is desirable to limit the criteria of patentability for medicines in order to facilitate health protection. The practical ways in which these questions are answered reveals how territoriality imparts meaning to functionality.

In the illustrative example chosen by Fischer-Lescano and Teubner, territoriality has played a role in managing the conflict between different rationalities. First of all, the conflict was triggered by the US decision to challenge the Brazilian domestic law. In a regime, like the one established by the TRIPS Agreement, there is always a margin of discretion on how to interpret and implement certain rules. The conflict of rationalities is accordingly not static, but dynamic—the way in which the rules are interpreted is crucial to strike the balance between different rationalities (e.g. economic rationalities vs the protection of human health). Even if ultimately it is the WTO adjudicatory bodies that interpret the treaty text, in practice in the game of articulating conflicts of rationalities, States remain central: it is States that perceive a certain law as in violation of WTO law and decide that it should be challenged (in this case the US), it is States that implement global law (in this case, Brazil), it is States that will be arguing for or against certain interpretations and it is States that can mutually agree on how to eventually manage a specific conflict (in this case through the institutionalization of transnational dialogue).

To further clarify this point, think of another case relating to the same conflict of rationalities. In 2005, India (the most important producer of generic drugs until then) adopted a new law, to implement the TRIPS Agreement.[65] The Indian Patents (Amendment) Act includes provisions that make it more difficult to obtain patents

[62] See Decision of the General Council: WTO General Council, Amendment of the TRIPS Agreement, WT/L/641, 6 December 2005, http://www.wto.org/english/tratop_E/trips_e/wtl641_e.htm, accessed 20 January 2017.

[63] WTO, Declaration on the TRIPS agreement and public health, DOHA WTO Ministerial 2001, WT/MIN(01)/DEC/2, 14 November 2001 (Doha Declaration).

[64] Fisher-Lescano and Teubner 2004, at 1030.

[65] India was granted a transitional period until 2005 in order to comply with the TRIPS Agreement. For a detailed analysis of this case, see Arcuri and Castro 2008.

on medicines than in many other countries. As the law entered into force, Novartis AC tried unsuccessfully to obtain a patent for Gleevec (imatinib mesylate), its well-known drug used mainly to treat blood cancer. Simplifying somewhat, Novartis AC argued that the patent system, as established by the reformed Indian Patents Act, was in violation of Article 27 TRIPS, because the conditions for granting patents were not sufficiently stringent.[66] A WTO challenge of the Indian law would have been (politically sensitive but) legally plausible. It should be noted that Gleevec received patent protection in nearly 40 countries. Moreover, the formulation of the Indian Patent Act is rather unique, establishing criteria that are to be found in no other domestic legal system. In spite of the plausible arguments of Novartis against the Indian law on the basis of its WTO-incompatibility, no WTO Member initiated a dispute against India before the WTO adjudicatory bodies. As a result, the question of whether Article 27 of the TRIPS Agreement should be interpreted so as to demand a highly homogenous patent system among WTO Members remains open.[67]

Given the high interests at stake and the plausibility of the WTO-incompatibility of the measure, it is remarkable that no dispute has been initiated on this question. Arguably, there was no interest to clarify the issue, in this particular delicate context. In our view, this is a clear illustration of how the system of global trade rules is still partly realized through the behaviour, interests and needs of individual States. In practice, States remain critical actors in determining how the rules of the international trade system are applied, interpreted and ultimately shaped.

This becomes even more evident at a closer scrutiny of the negotiations on the Doha Declaration on TRIPS and Public Health, which today constitutes a central pillar of the 'compatibilization techniques' between the protection of patents and the protection of health. The negotiations that led to the Doha Declaration (and the subsequent Decision of the General Council to amend the TRIPS) have been strongly influenced by the US and Brazil. The story told is that the initial position of the US was supportive of a rather restrictive text, strictly circumscribed to the AIDS/HIV pandemic. However, in the immediate aftermath of 9/11, in October 2001, US government buildings received mails with anthrax powder. Under the fear of a bioterrorist attack, the US threatened to issue a compulsory license for the patent on ciprofloxacin, an antibiotic patented by Bayer.[68] This sequence of events

[66] For a detailed analysis of this case, see Arcuri and Castro 2008. The major concern was that Section 3(d) of the Patents Act that did set very stringent rules for the granting of patents for medicines. Section 3(d) identifies not patentable inventions, listing among them: 'the mere discovery of a new form of a known substance which does not result in the enhancement of the known efficacy of that substance [...]' On the basis of this provision, in 2005, Gleevec (imatinib mesylate), a drug widely patented Novartis throughout the world, was denied patent protection by the Chennai patent office. The fact that Gleevec has been patented virtually everywhere but in India, bear witness to the unique features of the Indian Patent Act.

[67] Arcuri and Castro 2008 have argued that the rule should be interpreted in the sense of allowing heterogeneous patent systems, at 7–12.

[68] Abbott 2002, at 486–487.

has allegedly softened the US position and favoured the adoption of a more developing countries-friendly Doha Declaration. In referring to public health, the Doha Declaration acknowledges the interests of developing and least-developed countries affected by pandemics, such as the HIV/AIDS pandemics, tuberculosis and malaria and eventually it is open-ended, so as to allow potentially any disease to be considered as national emergency.[69] The text leaves the freedom to States to determine what constitutes a national emergency.[70]

The rules established by the TRIPS Agreement in relation to the protection of health can then be read as placeholders, to be filled by the national needs and interests, as articulated by States in different legal contexts and in a dynamic way.[71] The question of how global patent law is and should be framed in order to accommodate the protection of health is moulded by very local concerns, and not decided in the abstract. Against this background, territoriality and functionality, rather than substitute appear as co-evolving criteria to organize the global political space.

8.3.3 Reconfiguration of Territoriality in the Shadow of the Law

The linkage between trade and environment is another site, where the role of territoriality as a legal construct plays an important role. As is well known, Article XX GATT is the central provision to mediate the trade-environment conflict. Our main argument is that the interpretation of Article XX is bound up with how territoriality is conceptualized and at the same time is a process by which territoriality is reconfigured.

In the first *Tuna—Dolphin* dispute, Mexico challenged US measures limiting the imports of tuna harvested with fishing techniques endangering the life of dolphins. The GATT Panel considered the US measure to be in violation of Article XX, 'on

[69] Cf. Doha Declaration, para 2.

[70] Paragraph 4(c) of the Doha Declaration provides that: 'Each *member* has the right to determine what constitutes a national emergency or other circumstances of extreme urgency, it being understood that public health crises, including those relating to HIV/AIDS, tuberculosis, malaria and other epidemics, can represent a national emergency or other circumstances of extreme urgency.' This is not to say that the issue is uncontroversial and settled globally. There is an ongoing debate about to what extent a country can declare an emergency in order to justify its use. For example, there has been a controversy between the Colombian Minister of Health Gaviria and Novartis precisely on this point. In February 2016, a Colombian government committee proposed to issue a compulsory license for cancer-treating drug Gleevec. Novartis considered that there was no national emergency, whereas the Minister of Health did. We are thankful to Pedro Alejandro Villarreal Lizárraga for this observation.

[71] Clearly, the acknowledgement of these interests by a global organization, such as the WHO or the UN, contributes to the identification of what a legitimate interest is.

the notion of inherent *territorial* limits on the environmental exceptions.'[72] In practice, the conceptualization of extraterritoriality submitted by Mexico was accepted: 'To accept that one contracting party might impose trade restrictions to conserve the resources of another contracting party would have the consequence of introducing the concept of *extraterritoriality* into the GATT.'[73] Extraterritoriality in this case was used by a party and by the Panel to impart meaning to the operation of the norm that should mediate the trade-environment conflict. From the perspective of the US, a counterclaim on the basis of territoriality was made: 'The United States replied that the [Mammal Protection Act] specified the requirements for tuna imported into the United States. It did not subordinate the jurisdiction of one contracting party to the legislation of another contracting party.'[74]

In this context, it may be recalled that 'territoriality' and 'extraterritoriality' have been conceptualized as 'claims of authority, or of resistance to authority, that are made by particular actors with particular substantive interests to promote.'[75] The point here is that territoriality can be appropriated as a criterion to facilitate a given rationality over another (in this case the economic rationality over the environmental rationality). Framing a unilateral environmental measure affecting another jurisdiction (because of the trade nexus) as extraterritorial is not a neutral exercise. When can we talk of extraterritoriality, in an interconnected world, where a wide variety of regulatory measures are likely to affect a different jurisdiction? Without the international trade regime, it would have been implausible to postulate such extraterritoriality. In this sense, functionality imparts meaning to territoriality.

Under WTO law, in the famous *Shrimp—Turtle* case, the Appellate Body seems to have rejected the strict territorial criterion embraced by the Panel in *Tuna—Dolphin*.[76] Yet, territoriality, with some ambiguities, retains its place in the unfolding relation between trade and environment. The major source of ambiguity flows from this passage of the Appellate Body Report: 'We do not pass upon the question of whether there is an implied jurisdictional limitation in Article XX(g), and if so, the nature or extent of that limitation. We note only that in the specific circumstances of the case before us, there is a sufficient nexus between the migratory and endangered marine populations involved and the United States for

[72] Howse 2002, at 500 (emphasis added).

[73] GATT Dispute Panel, United States—Restrictions on Import of Tuna (Report of the Panel), DS/29/R, 16 June 1994 (*Tuna—Dolphin I*), para 3.31 (emphasis added).

[74] Ibid., para 3.32.

[75] Buxbaum 2009, at 635.

[76] The Appellate Body Report reads: 'It appears to us, however, that conditioning access to a Member's domestic market on whether exporting Members comply with, or adopt, a policy or policies unilaterally prescribed by the importing Member may, to some degree, be a common aspect of measures falling within the scope of one or another of the exceptions (a) to (j) of Article X8.' WTO Appellate Body Report, United States—Import Prohibition of Certain Shrimp and Shrimp Products, WT/DS58/AB/R, 14 December 1998 (*Shrimp—Turtle*), para 121.

purposes of Article XX(g).'[77] From this, it could be derived that, if a territorial limitation is to be read in Article XX, this would be reduced to the existence of a *nexus* between the environmental good protected and the territorial unit imposing the measure. In other words, a WTO Member should be able to prove that the environmental good protected is *related to its territory*. Territoriality is further re-configured where the Appellate Body, in interpreting the Chapeau of Article XX, requires Members wanting to adopt environmental measures to engage in good-faith negotiations for the conclusions of bilateral/multilateral agreements.[78] Moreover, Members in designing their environmental measures should take into account the conditions prevailing in the countries that would be affected by such measures and should abide by criteria of transparency.[79]

From the above, we can conclude that rather than instigating a process of deterritorialization, international trade rules related to the environmental exception as interpreted across time, are redesigning territoriality and creating new *transnational regulatory dialectics*. The criteria devised by the Appellate Body put pressure on the regulatory State to be more outward-oriented. In practice, States' environmental regulatory authority has been reconfigured as a 'relational' and 'other-regarding' authority over the environment. The application of Article XX illustrates how territoriality, rather than supplanted by functionality, is being reconfigured in the shadow of international trade law.

8.3.4 Techno-Territoriality

With the establishment of the WTO, the international trade regime has witnessed an important shift towards positive harmonization and global technocracy. The Sanitary and Phytosanitary (SPS) Agreement is a relevant example of this trend.[80] The SPS Agreement, dealing with issues such as food safety, promotes harmonization of safety standards in at least two ways: (1) by conferring legal normativity to the standards established by international standardization bodies, such as the Codex Alimentarius Commission and (2) by introducing parameters of legality that are informed by an allegedly neutral scientific rationality, which is realized through

[77] Ibid., para 133.

[78] Ibid., paras 166 et seq.

[79] Ibid., paras 177–182. This line of reasoning has been followed by the Appellate Body in subsequent case law; most recently Cf. WTO Appellate Body Report, European Communities—Measures Prohibiting the Importation and Marketing of Seal Products (EC—Seal Products), WT/DS400/AB/R and WT/DS401/AB/R, 22 May 2014.

[80] WTO Agreement, Annex 1A—Multilateral Agreement on Trade in Goods, Agreement on the Application of Sanitary and Phytosanitary Measures (SPS Agreement) (Final Act Embodying the Results of the Uruguay Round of Multilateral Trade Negotiations). Other important examples are the WTO Agreement, Annex 1 A—Multilateral Agreement on Trade in Goods, Technical Barrier to Trade (TBT Agreement) and the TRIPS Agreement.

the risk analysis paradigm.[81] In both cases, scientific rationality—as operationalized by certain scientific elites[82]—takes centre stage to determine the legality of domestic safety measures. In practice, this Agreement is a tool of global governance through which power is delegated to international standardization bodies (e.g. the Codex Commission)[83] and, more generally, to those with the 'powers to know.'[84] The freedom of WTO Members to introduce new sanitary and phytosanitary standards is constrained by the decisions adopted by the Codex Commission and/or by the risk assessment conducted by domestic and transnational scientific bodies. In this sense the SPS Agreement could be considered the vanguard of global technocracy.[85]

In terms of territoriality, the legal architecture established by this Agreement has at least two implications. On the one hand, by spreading globally the regulatory model according to which risk regulation should be informed by risk assessment, the legal architecture established by the SPS Agreement can be seen as a manifestation of what Sassen calls 'Americanization.'[86] The risk analysis paradigm, with its risk assessment/risk management dualism originates in the US.[87] While it became the dominant paradigm (possibly thanks to the SPS Agreement), it is by no means the only way to conceive of risk regulation.[88] On the other hand, the delegation of authority to international scientific elites (such as those operating in Codex) could be read as deterritorialization. Yet, even when the legal architecture appears as a straightforward instance of deterritorialization, its implementation tells a far less linear story.

In interpreting the text of the SPS Agreement, the adjudicatory organs of WTO have displayed different approaches.[89] What is interesting for the purposes of this chapter is that a number of findings of the Appellate Body destabilize an idealized global technocratic regime. Most notably, the Appellate Body has offered interpretations of the notion of risk assessment that may be conceptualized as the re-territorialization of an apparently a-territorial practice. In *EC—Hormones* the Appellate Body started to 'localize' risk assessment by stating that 'the risk that is to be evaluated in a risk assessment […] is not only risk ascertainable in a science laboratory operating under strictly controlled conditions, but also risk in human

[81] Gruszczynski 2010; Winickoff and Bushey 2010; Arcuri 2015.

[82] Demortain 2008, 2011.

[83] Buthe 2008.

[84] Winickoff and Bushey 2010.

[85] For an early analysis of the problematique of the technocratic dimensions of the SPS Agreement, see Howse 1998.

[86] Sassen 2006, at 266.

[87] Demortain 2011.

[88] For a discussion of alternatives see, for instance, Heyvaert 2011.

[89] Arcuri 2011 argued that the adjudicatory bodies of the WTO are juggling between different logics when interpreting the SPS Agreement.

societies as they actually exist, [...] in the real world where people live and work and die.'[90] In *US-Continued Suspension* the Appellate Body has strengthened this vision, by endorsing a more sophisticated understanding of risk assessment, as a practice intimately related to the political autonomy of the Member: 'the appropriate level of protection chosen by a Member affects the scope or method of the risk assessment.'[91] Under this vision, risk assessment is conceptualized as a scientific practice embedded in territorial preferences. It is plausible to read in this line of jurisprudence an attempt to link risk assessment to legal spatiality; risk assessment is made contingent on the preferences of people as represented in law-embedded scientific processes.[92] This reading of the SPS Agreement shows how a pure technocratic regime, avulse from territory, may be re-configured as a regime in which the *technê* is blended with territoriality. We call this techno-territoriality.

8.4 International Investment Law and Territoriality

The world economy has reached a significant level of integration and interconnectedness, which is reflected in the steady expansion of the 'global' regulatory regime[93] and a constantly more emphasized hybridization of the public/private divide. International investment law makes no exception in this regard.

The fundamental functionalist logic of international investment law is inspired by the need of enabling a favourable environment for the investment flow in the global market, which materializes in the protection of investments—and investors—within and beyond territorial boundaries. This tenet has highly contributed to the well-known debate on fragmentation and the rise of so-called self-contained regimes.[94] There is, however, a subsequent interesting aspect that flows from the

[90] WTO Appellate Body Report, European Communities—Measures Concerning Meat and Meat Products (Hormones), WT/DS26/AB/R, WT/DS48/AB/R, 16 January 1998 (*EC—Hormones*), para 187.

[91] WTO Appellate Body Report, United States—Continued Suspension of Obligations in the EC —Hormones Dispute, WT/DS320/AB/R, 16 October 2008 (*US- Continued Suspension*), para 534.

[92] The argument that the Appellate Body in *EC—Hormones* also recognized that 'borrowed' risk assessments (i.e. conducted by a different country or international organization) may validly be used to justify an SPS measure does not detract from our argument. The point is that a WTO Member may well consider a certain risk assessment conducted by the scientific body of an international organization as adequate; yet, it does not have to do so. A Member retains the discretion to conduct a risk assessment, and there is no transnational norm of scientific unity, which could be seen as a mechanism of deterritorialization.

[93] Ortino and Ortino 2008, at 89.

[94] Another interesting aspect is raised by Vadi 2016, at 108, on the functional comparative approach which, mainly driven by the idea of international constitutionalism, seeks transmigration of other legal systems into concept of international investment law, regardless of the risk of depriving law of its systemic meaning and the policy choices at its basis.

functionalist approach to international investment law, which our contribution aims to identify.

In particular, functionalism tends to allocate 'authority'[95] to actors, independently of their formal position, following the function that actors perform within the international (or, rather, global) community. In the case of investors, this is usually connected to the ability of companies to bring claims against host States before an arbitral tribunal and the impact of their significant political and economic influence. While much attention has been devoted to international investment arbitration and the consequent 'internationalization' of investment disputes to the alleged detriment of host States, this part addresses three different phenomena, where those elements intrinsic to the disarticulation of territoriality are particularly prominent, namely the detachment of host States' regulatory power from the investment operation via contractual clauses (Sect. 8.4.1); the volatile nature of financial products and their characterization as 'investments' (Sect. 8.4.2) and the 'extraterritorial' activity of sovereign investors (Sect. 8.4.3).

The following section identifies the legal tools that materialize investors' (private and public) interests to see their investment fully protected, and how they might affect the principle of territoriality.

8.4.1 The Removal of States' Regulatory Power over Foreign Direct Investment Activities

The protection of investments well exemplifies the hybridization intrinsic in the private/public conundrum, signature to globalization mechanisms. This is evident, in particular, on two levels: the nature of the norms regulating foreign investments and the interests involved in the deals. State contracts incorporate both aspects. While being usually integrated within the framework of a Bilateral Investment Treaty (BIT), the regulation of the single investment deal is left to the provisions included in the contract between the investor and the host State.

What is interesting is that, on the one hand, via State contracts sovereign prerogatives are subject to a private agreement; on the other hand, investors might recur to the protection granted by public international law at the treaty or customary law level. Hence, while States' interests into development find their way through a (formally) private tool, umbrella and stabilization clauses (respectively included in BITs and State contracts) 'internationalize' investors' private interests and allow companies to claim their rights before an arbitral tribunal.

---

[95] Many identify 'authority' in the idea of international legal personality of non-state actors, see on this Kulick 2012, at 64.

This section is limited to the analysis of the removal of States' regulatory power from investment activities taking place in host States' territories. Our reasoning focuses on the intriguing observation that private tools, substantiated into contractual clauses,[96] are able to significantly impact on the (notably) public concept of territoriality and contribute to the phenomenon of deterritorialization.

8.4.1.1 Choice of Law Clauses

The contractual provisions contributing most significantly to the phenomenon of deterritorialization are choice of law and stabilization clauses included in State contracts. Because of their characteristics, State contracts can be considered a hybrid instrument: the dual role played by the State as contracting party and sovereign legislator[97] has made the regulation of such contracts particularly controversial.[98]

The coexistence of conflicting interests (of the investor on one side, and of the host State, on the other) has raised the issue of the identification of the 'most appropriate' law applicable to such contracts. The determination of the regulatory system to govern the contract is considered a particularly sensitive issue: on the one hand the State, in its dual role, might want to preserve its regulatory power; the investor, on the other hand, tends towards choosing a regulatory regime that protects its interests and a stable and predictable legal environment, removed from the territorial power of the host State.

In the attempt to circumvent the supremacy of the State in the regulation of the contract, scholars and arbitrators have made numerous efforts to justify the subjugation of these agreements to a different legal order than the territorial one, which have been identified in either international law, general principles of law or transnational law (mostly identified in *lex mercatoria*). Accordingly, these contracts would be subject to a phenomenon of *internationalization*,[99] specifically conceived

---

[96] Umbrella clauses within BIT also greatly contribute to the phenomenon of internationalization. However, our analysis is only related to contractual clauses. More in general on the processes by which sovereignty becomes subject to private law, see extensively Muir Watt 2011.

[97] Shan 2010, at 448.

[98] See Sornarajah 2000, at 86.

[99] On the origin of the phenomenon, see among others Sornarajah 2010, at 223 and 281. In the international case law see the *Case Concerning the Payment of Various Serbian Loans issued in France (The Government of the French Republic v The Government of the Kingdom of the Serbs, Croats and Slovenes)*, PCIJ, Judgment, 12 July 1929, where the PCIJ underlines that '[t]out contrat qui n'est pas un contrat entre des États en tant que sujets du droit international a son fondement dans une loi nationale'. The arbitration practice which is usually considered to have given birth to the theory of internationalization can be traced back to three cases related to the exploitation of oil resources, *Saudi Arabia v Arabian American Oil Company (Aramco)*, Arbitration Award, 27 ILR 117, 23 August 1958; *Petroleum Development Ltd v Sheikh of Abu Dhabi*, Arbitral Award, 18 ILR 144, September 1951; and *Ruler of Qatar v International Maritime Oil Company, Ltd.*, Arbitral Award, 20 ILR 534, June 1953.

to remove the contractual relationship from the domestic law of the host State and neutralize the latter's territorial authority, in order to avoid crippling the expectations of the investor.

Theories at the basis of the concept of internationalization traditionally distinguish between *direct* and *indirect* internationalization of State contracts, respectively, by virtue of either the immediate application of an external regulatory system[100]—in which the contract is to be legally grounded—or in the presence of a choice of law clause. Our analysis relates to indirect internationalization.

Indirect internationalization, much more common in most recent investment contracts, is essentially based on the typical private international law mechanism for the identification of a law applicable to contractual relationships. Such an approach appears, *prima facie,* fully legitimate: in conformity with the principle of party autonomy, the *lex contractus* identified through the conflict of laws rule may be different from the domestic law of the host State and include a foreign domestic law, or any other 'rules of law',[101] general principles of law, *lex mercatoria,*[102] or international law.[103]

The key criterion at the basis of the theories of *indirect* internationalization is the principle of party autonomy.[104] The *ratio* for the choice of law freedom is associated with the need of the parties to be able to meet their economic needs in accordance with a regulatory system that suits them.[105]

The question remains how far party autonomy might go, both in the elaboration of substantive clauses—which might override the public interest inherent to

[100] The first set of theories is based on the assumption that State contracts can be considered similar to treaties by virtue of their almost international nature which would require the estrangement of the contractual relationship from a specific domestic regulatory system and the applicability, *proprio vigore*, of international law, see Böckstiegel 1974, at 159; Verdross 1964, at 230. See Voss 2010 for an in-depth analysis of direct and indirect internationalization theories. On the almost international nature of the State contracts, see among others *Texaco Overseas Petroleum Company And California Asiatic Oil Company v The Government of the Libyan Arab Republic*, Arbitral Award, 53 ILR 389, 19 January 1977; *In the Matter of Revere Copper and Brass, Inc. v Overseas Private Investment Corporation,* Arbitral Award, 56 ILR 258, 24 August 1878; and *Sapphire International Petroleum Ltd v National Iranian Oil Company*, Arbitral Award, 35 ILR 136, 15 March 1963.

[101] 1965 Convention on the Settlement of Investment Disputes Between States and Nationals of Other States, 575 UNTS 159 (ICSID Convention), Article 42(1).

[102] On the identification, rationale and definition of *lex mercatoria* see, extensively, Boschiero 2005, at 83; Schill 2012. Similarly, some authors believe the general principles of law to be applicable to these transactions. See Mann 1959, at 34; Lalive 1965 at 987.

[103] See Crespi Reghizzi 2009, at 31.

[104] UNGA, Arbitration Rules of the United Nations Commission on International Trade Law, UN Doc A/31/98, 15 December 1976 (UNCITRAL Arbitration Rules), Article 33.1; International Chamber of Commerce (ICC), Rules of Arbitration of the International Chamber of Commerce, https://iccwbo.org/dispute-resolution-services/arbitration/rules-of-arbitration/, accessed 28 February 2017, Article 17.1; ICSID Convention, Article 42.

[105] Several developing countries' private international law systems exclude the principle of party autonomy for those contracts regulating the exploitation of natural resources.

investment activities—and the selection of an applicable law, which is not territorially based or is devoid of any links with the territorial State. The detachment from the territorial legal system is particularly relevant in case of investment activities related to natural resources or other developmental needs of States, which present a significantly tight connection with the territory of host countries.

Consider, for example, the Contrat d'Exclusivité pour l'Utilisation de Terre entre AgroAfrica (Norvège) et Kounkane, Sénégal.[106] This contract, stipulated between a Norwegian company and the Communauté Rurale de Kounkane, grants to the investor an exclusive right of use over 10,000 ha of land located in Senegal and has an (initial) duration of 99 years. Article 5 of this agreement selects French Law as the law applicable to the contract and the International Chamber of Commerce (ICC), Paris, as the dispute settlement *forum.*[107]

While the territorial element of the investment is particularly visible, both in terms of the characteristics of the activity and the salient public interests involved in the management of natural resources, the selected law is deprived of any nexus with the spatial ambit of the contract. Therefore, the question is whether the application of the territorial legal system, in the pursuit of the host State's interests, is excluded *tout court* in the presence of such choice of law clauses.[108]

8.4.1.2 Stabilization Clauses

Even if the host State's law is designated as the law applicable to the contract, the presence of stabilization clauses, also known as 'petrification clauses' (often included in investment contracts) might still convey a deterritorializing effect. These clauses typically provide either a compensation or an exemption mechanism in favour of the investor, in the event that the legislative and economic framework governing the investment activities covered by the contract is amended by the host State.[109]

---

[106] Farmlandgrab.org, Contrat D'Exclusivité pour l'Utilisation de Terre entre AgroAfrica (Norvège) et Koukane, Sénégal, 7 Mars 2008, http://www.farmlandgrab.org/post/view/14253-contrat-d-exclusivite-pour-i-utilisation-de-terre-entre-agroafrica-norvege-et-kounkane-senegal, accessed 30 July 2016.

[107] See also *Autopista Concesionada de Venezuela, C.A. v Bolivarian Republic of Venezuela*, ICSID, Arbitral Award, Case No. ARB/00/5, 23 September 2003, where the arbitral tribunal held that the reference to mere specific instruments of the domestic law do not necessarily amount to a general choice of that law. Other 'rules of law' become equally applicable to questions beyond the scope of application of the specific domestic legal instruments referred to.

[108] This will be further addressed in Sect. 8.4.1.3.

[109] As indicated by the Report conducted by the International Finance Corporation of the World Bank and by the UN Special Representative to the Secretary-General on Business and Human Rights, stabilization clauses can be classified into three categories: a) freezing clauses, which de facto freeze the law applicable to the contract at the moment of its conclusion, and limited freezing clauses, that cover only some of the regulatory activities of the host State; b) economic equilibrium clauses, which require the investor to comply with the new rules introduced by the host State, but

As in the case of choice of law clauses, the purpose of petrification clauses is to protect investors against the risk that host States' (legislative or administrative) actions could interfere with the investment activities. Such provisions raise the level of protection granted to investors, while lowering the threshold required in order to obtain compensation for governmental actions. These provisions are able to place serious constraints on the effective enforcement of domestic law and the regulatory power of the host State, thus putting a high risk on the pursuit of the public interest. Hence, the inclusion of stabilization clauses within State contracts may lead to a kind of regulatory chill.[110] In other words, host States prefer to settle on regulatory protection levels that are much lower than those actually conforming to public purposes, in order to avoid the risk of having to pay compensation to the investor.[111]

When stabilization clauses take the form of an exemption (or 'freezing') clause, investors are discharged from complying with the new legislative or administrative measure introduced by the host State. The consequence is an alteration of the regulatory framework applicable to the activities of the investor. This implies that stabilization clauses have often the effect of creating a 'legal enclave' for the investors, whereby the domestic legal system is replaced with a *corpus* of norms, consisting of a crystallized system of rules that have no autonomous legal value and are not necessarily in force at the time of the dispute.

The effect of these clauses on the principle of territoriality is clear. While Foreign Direct Investments (FDIs) do need territory in order to be implemented, the contractual discipline is conceived in a way as to detach completely the regulation of the economic activity from the territorial legal system and power of control of the host State, thus producing an asymmetry between the normative significance of

(Footnote 109 continued)

allow him to claim compensation for the costs of compliance; c) hybrid clauses, which could be described as a sort of prescriptive requirement for the *restitutio in integrum*, or take the form of opt-outs from the application of the new rules introduced in the host country. Even more serious is the situation in which stabilization clauses enjoy coverage of BIT umbrella clauses, resulting in further reinforcement of the legal effect thereof (International Finance Corporation—World Bank Group 2009). See for example Convention between Republic of Cameroon and SG Sustainable Oils Cameroon PLC, 17 September 2009, http://www.farmlandgrab.org/post/print/21028, accessed 1 March 2017, Section 20.4: Change of Law: '(a) If any Change of Law has the effect of impairing, conflicting or interfering with the implementation of Investor Activities, or limiting abridging or adversely affecting the value of the Production Area or any of the rights [...] (i) take all actions available to it to reverse the effect of such Change of Law upon Investor Activities [...] The foregoing obligation shall include the obligation to take all appropriate measures to resolve promptly by whatever means may be necessary, including by way of exemption, legislation, decree and/or other authoritative acts, any conflict or anomaly between this Convention or any Project Agreement and Law; or (ii) compensate Investor for the present and the future Costs incurred by Investor as a result of the Change of Law [...]'.

[110] See in the international investment context, Simma 2011, at 576.

[111] See on this, Cotula 2006, at 111; Stern 2011; Leader 2006, at 658; Bertoli and Crespi Reghizzi, 2014, at 43.

territory and the implementation of the investment, which, in fact, needs to be localized.

The disarticulation from the domestic legal system transforms territory into land for grabs on the global market at disposal of those investors, who might take advantage of party autonomy. This might lead to depriving territory of its legal meaning and transforming it de facto into an enclave.[112] However, as we will see in the section below, some safeguards may counterbalance this trend.

8.4.1.3 The Resistance of Territoriality

While playing a predominant role, the exercise of party autonomy does not automatically translate into a mere self-governing contractual reception of the law selected by the parties. In practice, while arbitrators do not derive their jurisdiction from a *lex fori*,[113] it is possible to observe that in the arbitral case law there is a growing tendency to take the *lois de police*[114] and the public needs of host States into account, via the recourse to mandatory rules and the public policy clause of the host State. These tools might be useful in trying to contain the detachment from territoriality, potentially conveyed by party autonomy in investment contracts.

In this context, it might be useful to distinguish between applicable law—which governs the interpretation, execution and consequences of a breach of contract—and regulatory measures.[115] The latter category is part of the (host State's) territorial legal environment where the contract is implemented, and covers fiscal provisions, environmental issues or working conditions. These regulatory measures function as mandatory rules, which apply to the investment operation. They either *prevail* over the law selected by the parties, if it is different from the domestic law of the host State, or apply as part of *lex contractus*, if the applicable law is the host country's legal system.[116] In other words, 'arbitrary choices (*of the parties*) may not have the effect of avoiding the application of those host State's rules which are required to be applied in any event.'[117]

The identification and application of mandatory rules and public policy norms are particularly challenging and, at the same time, extremely significant to our debate, since they convey the dual role of the State as party to the investment transaction and vehicle of public interests. To this extent, regulatory measures guarantee that relevant public interests of host States are not subject to a detriment, because of the exercise of party autonomy.

---

[112] Violi 2015, at 36.

[113] Carbone 2007, at 205.

[114] Radicati di Brozolo 2005, at 269.

[115] Bertoli and Crespi Reghizzi 2014, at 35.

[116] See on that, Blessing 1997, at 13; Croff 1982, at 613.

[117] These norms clearly influence the execution of contractual obligations on the part of the host State, see Giardina 1982, at 682.

By contrast, as for stabilization clauses, arbitral practice tends to be more deferential. For example, both in *Revere Copper and Brass* and *Parkerings-Compagniet v Lithuania* the validity of stabilization clauses has not been questioned.[118] Even in cases widely considered as progressively interpreting BITs, such as *Methanex*, arbitrators concluded that State measures cannot be considered expropriatory 'unless *specific commitments* had been given by the regulating government to the then putative foreign investor contemplating investment that the government would refrain from such regulation.'[119]

Scholars have questioned whether 'petrification' clauses can be considered fully legal. According to some authors, stabilization clauses would be in stark contrast with the principle of permanent sovereignty of States over natural resources.[120] An opposite trend tends to recognize the exercise rather than the waiver of permanent sovereignty in such provisions, since the host State is free to determine the conditions of use and managing of natural resources. In fact, as mentioned, arbitrators tend to assign particular importance to cases where the State has bound itself in terms of stability of its legislation.[121]

Different mechanisms might be put in place, in order to give relief to the above-mentioned dual role of the territorial State. The background logic is that the State is a unitary entity. Investment activities should not clash with those obligations to which the host State is bound as a sovereign entity of a public nature, towards, for example its population or the environment. A recent theory tries to re-read stabilization clauses in the light of the respect of human rights, making use of what is called the *civic approach towards investment contracts.*[122] The effect of 'petrification' clauses should be limited to those matters that do not affect human rights enjoyed by the people in the territory of the host country. The latter, in particular, should be categorized as *third parties* to the contractual relationship between the State and the investor and, as such, holders of rights that cannot be infringed on by the negotiating activity of the State.

The argument does not a priori question the validity of stabilization clauses, but rather their legitimate scope. In other words, this approach introduces a human rights exception, thus circumscribing the effects of petrification provisions, so that they cannot be *extended* to the point of jeopardizing the realization of the human rights involved.[123]

---

[118] Cf. *Parkerings-Compagniet AS v Lithuania*, ICSID, Arbitral Award, 11 September 2007, Case No. ARB/05/8, paras 332–333.

[119] *Methanex Corporation v United States*, UNCITRAL/NAFTA, Final Award of the Tribunal on Jurisdiction and Merit, 3 August 2005, para 7.

[120] Sornarajah 1981, at 187.

[121] See, in particular, *Revere Copper and Brass.*

[122] Leader 2006, at 628.

[123] See, in this context, the The Baku-Tbilisi-Ceyhan Pipeline Company (2003) BTC Human Rights Undertaking, 22 September 2003, http://subsites.bp.com/caspian/Human%20Rights%20Undertaking.pdf, accessed 1 March 2017, which involves a (binding) unilateral commitment

In the same vein, the demise of host States' right to regulate and, hence, of States' functions as territorial sovereigns, might be considered an 'impossible' object in a private contract, and, therefore, not likely to be transacted. A stabilization clause might then well be considered valid—resorting to the *effet utile* doctrine—until the point where it realizes a definitive divestiture of host States' police powers.

8.4.2 Investments 'in the Territory' of the Host State

The dynamics and evolution of investment flows have raised a number of questions as to the persisting viability of the territorial nexus with the host State.[124] The need of a 'physical' connection becomes particularly complex in relation to portfolio investments and other financial products, such as credit default swaps or derivatives, in light of their peculiar nature. These intangible instruments have gained considerable position within the international financial system.[125] However, the volatile and dispersed characteristics of these financial flows have spurred quite some controversy[126] as to their inclusion under protected investments pursuant both Article 25 of the ICSID Convention[127] and the BITs concluded between States. Be that as it may, the integration of financial markets has stimulated increased recourse to this kind of investments, a circumstance that cannot be overlooked.

As mentioned, there has been a rich discussion among academics and practitioners[128] on the 'informal presumption' that these financially negotiable products disqualify automatically *per se* as protected investments, because of their substantial difference from the FDI model. However, both arbitral practice and investment treaty clauses do consider financial instruments as being included under the notion of investment, hence the presumption does not seem to be justified. While this discussion is extremely interesting in light of contemporary capital movements, it is beyond the scope of this section to give a final word on this very issue.

(Footnote 123 continued)

of the BTC consortium not to interpret the contractual stabilization clauses in a way as to prevent the pursuit of environmental protection and human rights.

[124] *Fedax N.V. v Republic of Venezuela*, ICSID, Arbitral Award, Case No. ARB/96/3, 9 March 1998 (*Fedax v Venezuela*).

[125] Dekastros 2013, at 288.

[126] Schreuer 2009, at 122, they would cause negative impacts on the economy of the host States.

[127] 1965 Convention on the Settlement of Investment Disputes Between States and Nationals of Other States, 575 UNTS 159 (ICSID Convention).

[128] Dolzer 2005, at 269; Sornarajah 2010, at 227; Sacerdoti 1997, at 307; *Abaclat and Others v The Argentine Republic*, ICSID, Decision on Jurisdiction and Admissibility, Case No. ARB/07/5, 4 August 2011 (*Abaclat*), Dissenting Opinion of Professor Georges Abi Saab of 28 October 2011.

For the purpose of this study, the point of departure for the analysis is that portfolio and other financial negotiable products are not excluded *per se* from the protection granted at the international investment law level. However, even if contained within the enumeration of 'investments' under a BIT, this does not mean that the inclusion of financial transactions operates automatically; it will be necessary to assess it against other substantive protection criteria, depending on the specific language of the overarching Bilateral Investment Treaty. This is precisely where the territorial nexus still finds its way through.

While Article 25 ICSID is silent as to the content of the notion of investment, the definition of many BITs and other multilateral investment treaties explicitly requires the investment to be made 'in the territory' of the host State. Therefore, even if financial products are enlisted under valid investment instruments, it will be necessary to assess whether the single legal transaction has determined a physical transfer of funds, if so required under the relevant BIT. In other words, the territorial link crystallized in the language of treaties cannot be overthrown, merely on the basis of the different features of financial instruments.

Nevertheless, recently, arbitrators in the *Abaclat*[129] award have provided a purely 'functional' interpretation of the territorial nexus requirement, clearly oriented towards extending investment protection to the financial products at stake. The dispute was related to a mass claims action against Argentina for the non-payment of security entitlements purchased on the secondary market (from the underwriters of the bonds previously issued by Argentina). According to the majority, the security entitlements could be considered as being 'made in Argentina,' since

> [w]ith regard to investments of a purely financial nature, the relevant criteria should be where and/or for the benefit of whom the funds are ultimately used, and not the place where the funds were paid out or transferred. Thus, the relevant question is where the invested funds ultimately made available to the Host State (*sic*) and did they support the latter's economic development [...] it was used by Argentina to manage its finances, and as such must be considered to have contributed to Argentina's economic development and thus to have been made in Argentina.[130]

Openly, the presumption goes that if the funds are utilized by the host country as the beneficiary, this would automatically satisfy the territorial dimension of the investment. However, this clearly goes against the ordinary meaning of the words included in the treaty.[131] In fact, the emphasis is where the investment has been implemented and not 'to the benefit' of whom.[132] Nevertheless, no explanation is provided by the tribunal as to the logical step allowing such a conclusion.

---

[129] *Abaclat.*

[130] *Abaclat*, para 373 and 378.

[131] 1990 Bilateral Investment Treaty between Argentina and Italy (BIT Argentina-Italy) (entered into force on 14 October 1993).

[132] *Abaclat,* Dissenting Opinion of Professor Georges Abi Saab of 28 October 2011; see also *SGS Société Générale de Surveillance S.A. v Republic of Philippines*, ICSID, Decision on Jurisdiction, Case No. ARB/02/6, 29 January 2004, para 99 where the arbitrators held that '[i]n accordance with

Apparently, this reasoning is based on the nature of financial transactions, 'which are significantly different from business operations and/or involving manpower and property.' While this might be true, Article 1(1) of the BIT between Argentina and Italy applicable to the dispute requires all investments to be made in the territory of the host State. Hence, the nature of the instrument cannot arbitrarily be considered apt to overrule the language of the treaty:[133] neither can it influence the determination of the place (i.e. the *situs*) of the investment.

The problem related to the inclusion of financial transaction in the notion of 'investment' is not a matter of the characteristics of these instruments; it is rather related to the remoteness of these products from the economic activity, project or enterprises that materialize the investment within the territory of the host State. In the same direction, many investment treaties, including NAFTA,[134] specify that loans and other credits[135] have to be connected to an enterprise or activity in the territory of one of the Party to be protected as investment under the relevant provision and considered qualified in comparison to ordinary commercial transactions. The *ratio* of including financial products, notwithstanding their distance to the activities materializing the investment, is that they still finance economic projects taking place over the territory of the host State. In the case of *Abaclat*,[136] the security entitlements had allegedly no connection to the issuance of the bonds in the primary markets. While the tribunal had considered them to be part of a unique economic operation, the issuance of bonds on the secondary market was both economically and legally independent from the issuance on the primary market. Hence, the *situs* of the bonds was completely severed from the territory of Argentina, both in relation to the regulation of the underlying contracts—disciplined under a foreign law—and the material elements of the performance and intermediation. Therefore, it was not possible to trace back or anchor the alleged investment to any economic activity in Argentina.

(Footnote 132 continued)

normal principles of treaty interpretation, investments made outside the territory of the Respondent State, however beneficial to it, would not be covered by the BIT'.

[133] *Abaclat*, Dissenting Opinion of Professor Georges Abi Saab of 28 October 2011, interesting at 97–98 on the unified economic category of investment under ICSID and the remoteness of the financial products.

[134] See e.g. NAFTA, Article 1139.

[135] Also the BIT between Argentina and Italy specifies that a credit must be directly connected to an investment. BIT Argentina-Italy, Article 1(1)(d).

[136] Arbitrators have based their reasoning on *Fedax v Venezuela*, where the tribunal held a similar opinion as to the non-necessity of the physical transfer of funds in case of financial products. This award has also been significantly criticized because of its very broad definition of territorial nexus. Furthermore, the case was different as to the instruments involved in the dispute. In *Fedax*, the controversy was related to promissory notes given in exchange for services in Venezuela. The question, therefore, was whether the endorsement of these promissory notes outside Venezuela would severe the link with the underlying transaction, to which they were connected.

The presumption of benefit to the development of the country could not be used as a sufficient tool to avoid demonstrating the territorial nexus required under the relevant BIT. This is all the more valid if one considers two recent awards related to commercial transactions, *Bayview v Mexico*[137] and *Canadian Cattlemen,*[138] issued under Chapter 11 of NAFTA where the Tribunals have rejected jurisdiction, because claimants had not made investment 'in the territory' of the respondent State.

As suggested in the literature,[139] arbitral tribunals have become more restrictive in their interpretation of the notion of both investment and investor. This is also true for the territoriality requirement. In both cases, the tribunals have focused their attention on the need for the investment to be made in *another* State party, different from the national State of the investor, since NAFTA has been interpreted as covering only foreign and not domestic investments.

In both cases, claimants complained about measures adopted by the respondent States, allegedly affecting their rights. However, in order to be protected under Chapter 11, the investment has to have a 'legally significant connection' with the respondent State. The fact that an enterprise, located and operating fully within its home country, has been affected by a measure taken by another NAFTA Party is not sufficient to this purpose. According to the Tribunal in *Bayview v Mexico*:

> in order to be an "investor" under Article 1139 one must make an investment in the territory of another NAFTA State, not in one's own. [...] the economic dependence of an enterprise upon supplies of goods - in this case, water - from another State is not sufficient to make the dependent enterprise an investor in that other State.[140]

In *Canadian Cattlemen*, the Tribunal similarly stated that

> These exclusions establish that mere cross border trade interests are not sufficient to trigger Chapter 11 - something more permanent - such as a commitment of capital or other resources in the territory of a Party to economic activity in such territory - is necessary for a contractual claim for money based on cross-border trade to rise to the level of an investment[141]

---

[137] *Bayview Irrigation District and others v United Mexican States*, ICSID, Arbitral Award, Case No. ARB(AF)/05/1, 19 June 2007 (*Bayview v Mexico*).

[138] *The Canadian Cattlemen for Fair Trade v United States of America*, UNCITRAL/NAFTA Ad Hoc Tribunal, Award on Jurisdiction, IIC 316 (2008), 28 January 2008.

[139] Knahr 2009, at 53.

[140] *Bayview v Mexico*, paras 102 and 104.

[141] *Canadian Cattlemen*, para 144.

What emerges from these awards is that, while the level of integration, especially signature to systems such as NAFTA, is becoming steadily more prominent, the requirement of territoriality still performs its organizational task.[142]

The fact that, on one side, economic activities in the globalized and interconnected world are affected by spill-over effects of measures endorsed beyond national borders and, on the other, companies are able to export without duties, does not automatically allow economic operators to qualify as investors. In the words of the Tribunal in *Canadian Cattlemen* 'the fact that NAFTA indisputably seeks to promote economic integration among industries in the three State Parties, does not mean that the border has been eliminated for purposes of investor protection, no matter how similar or integrated the industries on each side of the border may be.'[143]

8.4.3 The 'Extraterritorial' Element in Sovereign Investing

Sovereign investors, by which we include both Sovereign Wealth Funds (SWFs) and State-owned enterprises (SOEs), have reached a significant position in the globalized market.[144] While many doubts still remain as to the highly diversified nature of these entities, their activities seem worth investigating, especially in a context of globalization and integration. The participation of States in economic mechanisms traditionally estranged from the public realm raises a number of questions about risks and potential of sovereign investing.

While the ultimate goal of sovereign investors[145] is advancing public revenue, the very nature of the legal transactions they make recourse to, for their investment activities, significantly resembles those of private companies.[146] The traditional public/private divide seems completely blurred, thus raising a series of doubts as to the legal treatment of these entities. As a matter of fact, if considered as a means to pursue public policy objectives, sovereign investors might be subject to a less constrained host State's regulation.[147] On the other hand, if the emphasis is on the sole interest of maximizing profit, thus approximating to private entities, host States' regulatory system might fully apply.

---

[142] In the same direction, Chapter Thirteen of CETA on Financial Services refers to the definition of investment provided in Chapter Eight, Article 8.1, which explicitly requires the investment to be made in the territory of the other Party.

[143] *Canadian Cattlemen*, para 169.

[144] UNCTAD 2011.

[145] Or of their parent State, if they have distinct personality. On sovereign investing, see Catà Backer 2010; Bassan 2011, 2015.

[146] Many BITs expressly refer to sovereign investors as protected under the notion of investor, see e.g. BITs concluded by Kuwait.

[147] On the immunity from regulation, see Gaukrodger 2010; Catà Backer 2010, at 13.

This ambiguity spurs quite some confusion and appears even more dangerous in light of the possibility that sovereign investors might claim immunity from jurisdiction and enforcement for the activities implemented on the territory of the host country, thus critically restraining judicial protection.[148]

The main fear for host States is that these entities might project and advance the sovereign power of the national State, thus allowing home countries to exercise sovereignty beyond their territorial borders. Hence, the hybrid nature of sovereign investors stimulates a first consideration on the 'extraterritorial' element intrinsic to their activity.

The notion of 'extraterritoriality', in the case at hand, might be further unfolded into three sub-articulations. The first one is merely descriptive and acknowledges the already mentioned fact that sovereign investors act beyond the boundaries of the national State.

Depending on circumstances, this factor might trigger a second meaning, which is compliant to the idea of extraterritoriality under human rights law. An extensive elaboration on the reason justifying extraterritorial jurisdiction are beyond the scope of this paper, suffice it to recall that if an agent of a State is exercising effective control over a portion of territory of another State, this might activate the responsibility of the former to respect human rights over the territory of the latter[149] (functional jurisdiction).[150] However, this certainly represents an extreme hypothesis in our case.

The final, and probably most interesting aspect is related to the ontological circumscribing function of jurisdiction under international law. While this is usually connected to its territorial dimension, jurisdiction as ground to regulate conducts might extend beyond State's borders and address the activity of nationals operating elsewhere, within the limit of the non-intervention principle. Traditionally, this has always been considered a prerogative of States, rather than an obligation and has been usually linked to the mere possibility of regulating private enterprise activities, which could prove detrimental for host States. While it is true that under international law States have no obligation in this regard, this argument might prove less compelling for SWFs and SOEs—depending on the participation of the State in the companies—considering the sovereign element signatory to these entities.

As interestingly pointed out, the possibility for sovereign investors to 'use the logic of globalization, and its markets,'[151] might serve the purpose of letting the State regain a central role within the globalized market. In fact, while sovereign

---

[148] See ext. Adinolfi 2015, at 223.

[149] Ext. De Schutter 2014.

[150] Milano 2015, at 64.

[151] Catà Backer 2013, at 19.

investors utilize a private tool, which operates within the territories of a different number of States, they still remain 'very much instruments of the state and tightly bound up in the formal structures of the state and legal systems grounded in respect for territorial borders.'[152]

While this circumstance is the product of a diversification of governance and authorities between private and public,[153] the regulation of sovereign investors might offer a framework of harmonization instead of fragmentation. Considering also the flaws in the prescriptive nature of corporate social responsibility, according to Catà Backer, the Norwegian Sovereign Wealth Fund[154] offers a remarkable example of harmonization. Instead of abandoning the idea of territoriality *tout court*, this entity has elaborated mechanisms that operate on three different levels: the territorial-based State, the extraterritorial corporate governance and international governance, thus pursuing an 'intersystemic governance project.'[155] In short, the Fund is advancing Norwegian public interests. However, these are not based on the projection of country parochial self-interest. Rather, the extraterritorial application of both law and corporate governance mechanisms[156] have first gone through a domestic incorporation of internationally recognized standards, especially those related to human rights via a set of Ethical Guidelines, based on international law and Norwegian law, enforced through an Ethics Council. Responsible investing is thus advanced in the global market via the twofold role of the State as market participant and regulator, thus allowing the State to act as mediator in the forces of globalization. Hence, it is possible to observe a shift in the extraterritorial application of 'domestic' law as a 'new form through which states conceive of themselves as equally bound to apply international law and norms to all activities within their control.'[157]

While conveying international norms, rather than domestic law *per se*, this second generation extraterritoriality still functions through the projection of States' reception of international law and the projection of 'internationalized' domestic law beyond their territory. This circumstance further highlights the fact that, while the territoriality principle might have lost its prerogative as unique organizing principle of the international regulatory level, it still fulfils a fundamental role and

---

[152] Catà Backer 2013, at 108, referring to SWFs.

[153] On collision, see Fischer-Lescano and Teubner 2004, at 1005–1006.

[154] This definition collectively refers to the entities Government Pension Fund Global and Government Pension Fund Norway.

[155] Catà Backer 2013, at 7.

[156] Active ownership and exclusion of 'non-complying' companies being an example.

[157] Catà Backer 2013, at 90; ext. Seck 2011.

demonstrates a chameleonic attitude in reigniting public policy and advancing general interests via private tools, allowing the State a central role in the regulation of market forces.[158]

8.5 Conclusions

In the contemporary global order of overlapping and crisscrossing *loci* of authority, the widespread emphasis on deterritorialization and functionality of recent literature may have missed the mark that territoriality, albeit in new forms, continues to play a critical role. These approaches overlook the fact that fragmentation and functionalism are taking place *also* within the system of international law, and via its very mechanisms and institutions. Disregarding the role that territoriality plays within globalization provides a partial and diverted understanding of the phenomenon.

The regimes of international trade and investment law contribute to reconfigure territoriality in different ways. In the context of international trade law, we have identified several ways in which territoriality rather than being erased is *reconfigured*. Firstly, by granting legal status to new territorial units (e.g. customs unions), the international trade regime contributes to *multiply* territoriality and to stimulate the new constellation of regionalism, which in turn is a force arguably putting pressures on the multilateral paradigm. Secondly, States (and other territorial units) are central in imparting meaning to the way in which conflicts are managed between different functional regimes. The 'trade and…' conundrum is to be understood as a site of tensions where territoriality and functionality impart meaning to each other and establish new norms for transnational regulatory dialectics. Finally, even in areas where it is plausible to expect the most extreme forms of deterritorialization, such as the new legal universe established by the SPS Agreement favouring technocratic global governance, territoriality is discernible. In this context, we have coined the term 'techno-territoriality', to refer to the reconfiguration of a pure technocratic regime avulse from territory into a regime in which the *technê* is (or at least can be) encased into territorial interests.

The international investment regime, by contrast, displays a stronger tendency towards deterritorialization. Besides the most obvious instance of deterritorialization, realized through the Investor State Dispute Settlement system, this chapter has

---

[158] Catà Backer 2013. See also Oddenino 2015, at 128, on the need of territoriality in advancing *erga omnes* rules.

shown that there are several other mechanisms (e.g. choice of law and stabilization clauses) contributing to detach the State's authority from its territory. In this context, we argued that the disarticulation from the domestic legal system transforms territory into land for grabs on the global market. At the same time, we have also identified a resistance to this trend, by which territoriality is reasserted (e.g. by declaring void petrification clauses) and highly vibrant in the requirements of investment treaties, as recent interpretations of the notion of investment clearly show. In this field, an interesting case of reconfiguration of territoriality is the way in which sovereign investors (could) assert a form of 'international-territoriality', by which States' reception of international law is projected extraterritorially, while maintaining territorial-based mechanisms and institutions.

The patterns identified in this chapter show that the regimes of international trade and investment law still engage with territoriality, albeit rather differently. The system of investment law remains most problematic in so far as the removal of authority from States corresponds to the empowerment of actors that by definition pursue only their private interests. The risk here is that the overthrow of the State system is conducive to a market-oriented pluralism, which does not take into account the pursuit of general, properly integrated interests. In this sense, resistance of territoriality in investment regimes and the ways in which territoriality continues to impart meaning to functionality in the trade regime should be looked at as positive examples or avenues to keep alive the 'public' core of international law.

References

Abbott FM (2002) The Doha Declaration on the Trips Agreement and Public Health: Lighting a Dark Corner at the WTO. Journal of International Economic Law 5:469–505

Adinolfi G (2015) SWFs and State Immunity: Overcoming the Contradiction. In: Bassan F (ed) Research Handbook on Sovereign Wealth Funds and International Investment Law. Edward Elgar Publishing, Cheltenham, pp 223–272

Agnew J (1994) The Territorial Trap: The Geographical Assumptions of International Relations Theory. Review of International Political Economy 1:53–80

Anghie A (1999) Finding the Peripheries: Sovereignty and Colonialism in Nineteenth-Century International Law. Harvard International Law Journal 40:1–71

Antoniadis A (2004) The Participation of the European Community in the World Trade Organisation: An External Look at European Union Constitution-Building. In: Tridimas T, Nebbia P (eds) European Union Law for the 21st Century: Rethinking the New Legal Order. Hart Publishing, Oxford, pp 321–344

Arcuri A (2011) Food Safety at the WTO after 'Continued Suspension': A Paradigm Shift? In: Antoniadis A, Schütze R, Spaventa E (eds) The European Union and Global Emergencies: A Law and Policy Analysis. Hart Publishing, Oxford, pp 205–224

Arcuri A (2015) Global Food Safety Standards: The Evolving Regulatory Epistemology at the Intersection of the SPS Agreement and the Codex Alimentarius Commission. In: Delimatsis P (ed) The Law, Economics and Politics of International Standardisation. Cambridge University Press, Cambridge, pp 79–103

Arcuri A, Castro R (2008) How Innovative is Innovative Enough? Reflections on the Interpretation of Article 27 TRIPS from Novartis v. Union of India. Society of International Economic Law (SIEL) Inaugural Conference 2008 Paper. https://papers.ssrn.com/sol3/papers2.cfm?abstract_id=1159821. Accessed 27 February 2017

Bassan F (2011) The Law of Sovereign Wealth Funds. Edward Elgar Publishing, Cheltenham

Bassan F (ed) (2015) Research Handbook on Sovereign Wealth Funds and International Investment Law. Edward Elgar Publishing, Cheltenham

Bassiouni MC (2012) The Future of Human Rights in the Age of Globalization. Denver Journal of International Law and Policy 40:22–43

Buxbaum HL (2009) Territory, Territoriality and the Resolution of the Jurisdictional Conflict. The American Journal of International Law 57:631–76

Bertoli P, Crespi Reghizzi Z (2014) Regulatory Measures, Standards of Treatment and the Law Applicable to Investment Disputes. In: Treves T, Seatzu F, Trevisanut S (eds) Foreign Investment, International Law and Common Concerns. Routledge, London, pp 26–49

Blessing M (1997) Mandatory Rules of Law Versus Autonomy in International Law. Journal of International Law Arbitration 14:23–40

Böckstiegel KH (1974) Der Staat als Vertragspartner Auslaendischer Privatunternehmen. Athenäum, Frankfurt

Boschiero N (2005) La Lex Mercatoria nell'Era della Globalizzazione, Considerazioni di Diritto Internazionale Pubblico e Privato. Sociologia del Diritto 2/3: 83–155

Brölmann C (2007) Deterritorializing International Law: Moving Away from the Divide Between National and International Law. In: Nollkaemper A, Nijman J (eds) New Perspectives on the Divide Between National and International Law. Oxford University Press, Oxford, pp 84–109

Buthe T (2008) The Globalization of Health and Safety Standards: Delegation of Regulatory Authority in the SPS Agreement of the 1994 Agreement Establishing the World Trade Organisation. Law and Contemporary Problems 71:219–255

Carbone SM (2007) L'autonomia Privata nei Rapporti Economici Internazionali e i Suoi Limiti. Rivista di Diritto Internazionale Privato e Processuale 43(4):891–920

Catà Backer LC (2010) Sovereign Investing in Times of Crisis: Global Regulation of Sovereign Wealth Funds, State Owned Enterprises and the Chinese Experience. Transnational Law & Contemporary Problems 19:3–144

Catà Backer LC (2013) Sovereign Investing and Markets-Based Transnational Rule of Law Building: The Norwegian Sovereign Wealth Fund in Global Markets. American University International Law Review 29:1–122

Charnovitz S (2006) Taiwan's WTO Membership and its International Implications. Asian Journal of WTO & International Health Law and Policy 1:401–432

Cotula L (2006) Stabilization Clauses and the Evolution of Environmental Standards in Foreign Investment Contracts. Yearbook of International Economic Law 17:111–138

Crespi Reghizzi Z (2009) Diritto Internazionale e Diritto Interno nelle Controversie Sottoposte ad Arbitrato ICSID. Rivista di Diritto Internazionale 45:9–44

Croff C (1982) The Applicable Law in an International Commercial Arbitration: Is it Still a Conflict of Laws Problem? The International Lawyer 16:613–645

De Schutter O (2014) International Human Rights Law, Cases, Materials, Commentary. Cambridge University Press, Cambridge

Dekastros M (2013) Portfolio Investments: Reconceptualizing the Notion of Investments Under the ICSID Convention. The Journal of World Investment and Trade 14:286–319

Demortain D (2008) Standardising Through Concepts: The Power of Scientific Experts in International Standard-Setting. Science and Public Policy 35:391–402

Demortain D (2011) Scientists and the Regulation of Risk: Standardising Control. Edward Elgar Publishing, Cheltenham

Di Martino A (2010) Il territorio dallo Stato-nazione alla Globalizzazione: Sfide e Prospettive. Giuffrè Editore, Milan
Dolzer R (2005) The Notion of Investment in Recent Practice. In: Charmovitz S, Steger DP, van den Bossche P (eds) Law in the Service of Human Dignity: Essays in Honour of Florentino Feliciano. Cambridge University Press, Cambridge, pp 261–275
Dupuy P (2002) L'unité de l'Ordre Juridique International: Cours Général de Droit International Public. In: Académie de Droit International de La Haye (ed) Recueil des Cours, Vol. 297. Brill Nijhoff, Leiden/Boston
Fabbricotti A (2008) The Interplay Between the WTO and RTAs: Is It a Question of Interrelation Between Different Sources of International Law? Society of International Economic Law (SIEL) Inaugural Conference 2008 Paper. http://ssrn.com/abstract=1151386. Accessed 3 August 2016
Fischer-Lescano A, Teubner G (2004) Regime-Collisions: The Vain Search for Legal Unity in the Fragmentation of Global Law. Michigan Journal of International Law 25:999–1046
Gaukrodger D (2010) Foreign State Immunity and Foreign Government Controlled Investors. OECD Working Papers on International Investment No. 2010/02. http://dx.doi.org/10.1787/5km91p0ksqs7-en. Accessed 3 August 2016
Giardina A (1982) Le Legge Regolatrice dei Contratti d'Investimento nel Sistema ICSID. Rivista Italiana di Diritto Internazionale Privato e Processuale 4:677–692
Gruszczynski L (2010) Regulating Health and Environmental Risks under WTO Law: A Critical Analysis of the SPS Agreement. Oxford University Press, Oxford
Heyvaert V (2011) Governing Climate Change: Towards a New Paradigm for Risk Regulation. The Modern Law Review 74:817–844
Howse R (1998) Science, Democracy and Free Trade: Risk Regulation on Trial at the World Trade Organization. Michigan Law Review 98:2329–2357
Howse R (2002) The Appellate Body Rulings in the Shrimp/Turtle Case: A New Legal Baseline for the Trade and Environment Debate. Columbia Journal of Environmental Law 27:489–519
Howse R, Nicolaïdis K (2003) Enhancing WTO Legitimacy: Constitutionalization or Global Subsidiarity? Governance 16:73–94
International Finance Corporation – World Bank Group (2009) Stabilization Clauses and Human Rights. A Research Project Conducted for IFC and the United Nations Special Representative of the Secretary-General on Business and Human Rights. http://www.ifc.org/wps/wcm/connect/9feb5b00488555eab8c4fa6a6515bb18/Stabilization%2BPaper.pdf?MOD=AJPERES. Accessed 1 March 2017
Jackson JH (1997) The Great 1994 Sovereignty Debate: United States Acceptance and Implementation of the Uruguay Round Results. Columbia Journal of International Law 36:137–88
Jackson JH (2003) Sovereignty-Modern: A New Approach to an Outdated Concept. American Journal of International Law 97:782–802
Jackson JH (2006) Sovereignty, the WTO, and Changing Fundamentals of International Law. Cambridge University Press, Cambridge
Kamminga MT (2013) Extraterritoriality. Max Planck Encyclopedia of Public International Law. http://opil.ouplaw.com/view/10.1093/law:epil/9780199231690/law-9780199231690-e1040. Accessed 24 February 2017
Khan D (2012) Territory and Boundaries. In: Fassbender B, Peters A (eds) The Oxford Handbook of the History of International Law. Oxford University Press, Oxford, pp 225–249
Knahr C (2009) Investments 'In The Territory' of The Host State. In: Binder C, Kriebaum U, Reinisch A, Wittich S (eds) International Investment Law for the 21st Century: Essays in Honour of Christoph Schreuer. Oxford University Press, Oxford, pp 42–53
Krasner SD (1982) Regimes and the Limits of Realism: Regimes as Autonomous Variables. International Organization 36:497–510

Kulick A (2012) Global Public Interest in International Investment Law. Cambridge University Press, Cambridge
Lalive JF (1965) Contracts Between a State or a State Agency and a Foreign Company. International and Comparative Law Quarterly 13:987–1021
Latour B (1993) We Have Never Been Modern. Harvard University Press, Cambridge
Leader S (2006) Human Rights, Risks and New Strategies for Global Investment. Journal of International Economic Law 9:657–705
Lockhart N, Mitchell AD (2005) Regional Trade Agreements under GATT 1994: An Exception and its Limits. In: Mitchell AD (ed) Challenges and Prospects for the WTO. Cameron May Ltd, London, pp 217–252
Luhmann N (1982) Territorial Borders as System Boundaries. In: Strassoldo R, Dello Zotti G (eds) Cooperation and Conflict in Border Areas. Franco Angeli Editore, Milan, pp 235–244
Luhmann N (1995) Das Recht der Gesellschaft. Suhrkamp Verlag, Frankfurt
Mann FA (1959) The Proper Law of Contracts Concluded by International Persons. British Yearbook of International Law 35:34–57
Mégret F (2012) International Law as Law. In: Crawford J, Koskenniemi M (eds) The Cambridge Companion to International Law. Cambridge University Press, Cambridge, pp 64–92
Mercurio BC (2006) TRIPS-Plus Provisions in FTAs: Recent Trends. In: Bartels L, Ortino F (eds) Regional Trade Agreements and the WTO Legal System. Oxford University Press, Oxford, pp 215–237
Milano E (2015) The Deterritorialization of International Law: Setting the Context. In: Di Stefano A (ed) A Lackland Law? Territory, Effectiveness and Jurisdiction in International and European Law. G. Giappichelli Editore, Turin, pp 53–69
Muir Watt M (2011) Private International Law: Beyond the Schism. Transnational Legal Theory 2:347–428
Oddenino A (2015) Law and Territory Happily Ever After: Some Reflections on Globalization and International Law. In: Di Stefano A (ed) A Lackland Law? Territory, Effectiveness and Jurisdiction in International and European Law. G. Giappichelli Editore, Turin, pp 115–138
Ortino M, Ortino F (2008) Law of the Global Economy: In Need of a New Methodological Approach? In: Arner W, Bunn ID, Picker CB (eds) International Economic Law – The State and Future of the Discipline. Hart Publishing, Portland, pp 89–106
Paulus A (2004) From Territoriality to Functionality? Towards a Legal Methodology of Globalization. In: Dekker IF, Werner WG (eds) Governance and International Legal Theory. Martinus Nijhoff Publishers, Leiden/Boston, pp 59–95
Petersmann EU (2008) State Sovereignty, Popular Sovereignty and Individual Sovereignty: From Constitutional Nationalism to Multilevel Constitutionalism in International Economic Law? In: Shan W, Simons P, Singh D (eds) Redefining Sovereignty in International Economic Law. Hart Publishing, Oxford/Portland, pp 27–60
Pikalo J (2007) Economic Globalisation, Globalist Stories of the State, and Human Rights. In: Benedek W, De Feyter K, Marrella F (eds) Economic Globalisation and Human Rights. Cambridge University Press, Cambridge/New York, pp 17–38
Quadri R (1968) Diritto Internazionale Pubblico, 5th edn. Liguori, Naples
Radicati di Brozolo LG (2005) Arbitrage Commercial International et Lois de Police: Considerations sur les Conflicts de Jurisdiction dans le Commerce International. In: Académie de Droit International de La Haye (ed) Recueil des Cours, Vol. 315. Brill Nijhoff, Leiden/Boston
Raustiala K (2003) Rethinking the Sovereignty Debate in International Economic Law. Journal of International Economic Law 6(4):841–78
Raustiala K (2005) The Geography of Justice. Fordham Law Review 73:2501–2560
Ryngaert C (2014) Whither Territoriality? The European Union's Use of Territoriality to Set Norms with Universal Effects. http://ssrn.com/abstract=2523157. Accessed 24 February 2017

Ruggie JG (1993) Territoriality and beyond: Problematizing Modernity in International Relations. International Organization 47:139–174
Sacerdoti G (1997) Bilateral Treaties and Multilateral Instruments on Investment Protection. In: Académie de Droit International de La Haye (ed) Recueil des Cours, Vol. 269. Brill Nijhoff, Leiden/Boston
Sassen S (2006) Territory, Authority, Rights: From Medieval to Global Assemblages. Princeton University Press, Princeton
Sassen S (2013) When Territory Deborders Territoriality. Territory, Politics, Governance 1:21–45
Schill S (2012) Lex Mercatoria. In: Wolfrum R (ed) Max Planck Encyclopedia of Public International Law. Oxford University Press, Oxford, vol. VI, pp 823–830
Schmitt C (1950) Der Nomos der Erde im Völkerrecht des Jus Publicum Europaeum. Duncker & Humblot, Berlin
Schreuer C (2009) The ICSID Convention: A Commentary, 2nd edn. Cambridge University Press, Cambridge
Seck SL (2011) Conceptualizing the Home State Duty to Protect Human Rights. In: Buhmann K, Morsing M, Roseberry L (eds) Corporate Social and Human Rights Responsibilities: Global, Legal and Management Perspectives. Palgrave Macmillan, Hampshire, pp 25–51
Shaefer M (2002) Sovereignty, Influence, Realpolitik and the World Trade Organization. Hastings International and Comparative Law Review 25:341–369
Shaffer G (2012) A Transnational Take on Krisch's Pluralist Postnational Law. The European Journal of International Law 23:565–582
Shan W (2010) Towards a Balanced Liberal Investment Regime: General Report on the Protection of Foreign Investment. XVIII International Congress of Comparative Law Washington 2010. ICSID Review Foreign Investment Law Journal 25:421–497
Simma B (2011) Foreign Investment Arbitration, A Place for Human Rights? International and Comparative Law Quarterly 60:573–596
Sornarajah M (1981) The Myth of International Contract Law. Journal of World Trade 15(3):187–217
Sornarajah M (2000) The Settlement of Foreign Investment Disputes. Kluwer Law International, The Hague
Sornarajah M (2010) The International Law on Foreign Investment, 2nd edn. Cambridge University Press, Cambridge
Stern B (2011) The Future of International Investment Law: A Balance between the Protection of Investors and the States' Capacity to Regulate. In: Alvarez JE, Sauvant KP (eds) The Evolving International Investment Regime: Expectations Realities, Options. Oxford University Press, Oxford
Tancredi A (2015) Some Thoughts on Deterritorialization and Effectiveness in International Law. In: Di Stefano A (ed) A Lackland Law? Territory, Effectiveness and Jurisdiction in International and European Law. G. Giappichelli Editore, Turin, pp 47–52
Teubner G, Korth P (2010) Two Kinds of Legal Pluralism: Collision of Transnational Regimes in the Double Fragmentation of World Society. In: Young MA (ed) Regime Interaction in International Law: Facing Fragmentation. Cambridge University Press, Cambridge, pp 23–54
UNCTAD (2011) World Investment Report – Non-Equity Modes of International Production and Development. United Nations Publications, New York/Geneva
Vadi V (2016) Analogies in International Investment Law and Arbitration. Cambridge University Press, Cambridge
van den Bossche P, Zdouc W (2013) The Law and Policy of World Trade Organization. Cambridge University Press, Cambridge
Verdross A (1964) Quasi-International Agreements and International Economic Transaction. Yearbook of World Affairs 18:230–247

Violi F (2015) The Practice of Land Grabbing and Its Compatibility with the Exercise of Territorial Sovereignty. In: Romanin Jacur F, Bonfanti A, Seatzu F (eds) Natural Resources Grabbing. An International Law Perspective. Brill Nijhoff, Leiden/Boston, pp 17–37
Voss JO (2010) The Impact of Investment Treaties on Contracts between Host States and Foreign Investors. Martinus Nijhoff Publishers, Leiden
Weiss L (2000) Globalization and State Power. Development and Society 29:1–15
Winickoff DE, Bushey D (2010) Science and Power in Global Food Regulation: The Rise of the Codex Alimentarius. Science, Technology & Human Values 35:356–381
Wolf M (2001) Will the Nation-State Survive Globalization? Foreign Affairs 80:178–190

Chapter 9
Extraterritorial Obligations and the Obligation to Protect

Sigrun Skogly

Abstract Since the late 1970s, what we today label 'globalisation' has altered many aspects of international law, not least international human rights law. This has been reflected *inter alia* in increased calls for universal respect for human rights beyond a state's territorial border. The challenges to territoriality in this regard does not only relate to the actions of states abroad, but also with respect to their regulation of the conduct of business enterprises over which they exert significant influence. The chapter analyses the European Court of Human Rights' jurisprudence and practice of the UN human rights bodies, and argues that extraterritorial human rights obligations have become an integral part of international human rights law. It is held that what has been seen as 'exceptional' now represent 'common practice'. This conclusion is then applied to the discussion of the new treaty on human rights as currently being drafted.

Keywords Extraterritorial human rights obligations · Business and human rights · Obligation to protect · Jurisdiction · Transnational corporations · Treaty on business and human rights

Contents

Professor of Human Rights Law, Centre for International Law and Human Rights, Lancaster University Law School, UK

S. Skogly (✉)
Human Rights Law, Centre for International Law and Human Rights, Lancaster University Law School, Lancaster, UK
e-mail: s.skogly@lancaster.ac.uk

M. Kuijer and W. Werner (eds.), *Netherlands Yearbook of International Law 2016*, Netherlands Yearbook of International Law 47,
DOI 10.1007/978-94-6265-207-1_9

9.1 Introduction

The significant shift that occurred in international relations and particularly in international financial relations from the late 1970s onwards, commonly labelled 'globalisation', has had a profound impact on international human rights law. This part of international law has in the last few decades had to respond to realities in a world that is very different to the one in which the drafters of the Charter of the United Nations, and subsequent international human rights treaties found themselves. Some of the new challenges relate directly to concepts of territoriality. The post-Second World War environment was characterised by the domination of nation states, with emerging intergovernmental organisations aimed at solving international problems 'in economic, social, cultural, educational, health, and related fields'[1] under the leadership of states. The last 30 years have seen a reduction in the role of the state in international relations, and the rapid growth of other actors on the international arena, including the increasingly powerful transnational corporations (TNCs).

The challenge and shift in terms of territoriality relate to states' human rights obligations. While the rights contained in international human rights law (as proclaimed particularly in the Universal Declaration on Human Rights) are supposed to be *universal* in their enjoyment, traditionally states were considered to be under obligations to secure these rights for the citizens and residents within their physical territory only.

In the twenty-first century, where individuals' lives are commonly impacted by the actions of foreign actors (whether another state, international organisations, or TNCs), this territoriality of human rights obligations has been challenged. It has been questioned whether suffering from human rights breaches committed by actors other than an individual's own government, is not covered by human rights law due to its territorial constraints. In her important contribution to the human rights obligations discourse, Margot Salomon argues that 'the proper regulation of non-state actors, notably transnational corporations (TNCs), [...] requires revisiting international standards and mechanisms to ensure that their activities are consistent with human rights',[2] and that doing so is necessary 'if human rights law is to remain relevant'.[3]

[1] 1945 Charter of the United Nations, 1 UNTS XVI (UN Charter), Article 57.

[2] Salomon 2007, at 11.

[3] Ibid., at 12.

In this chapter, I ask the question as to whether the interpretation of international human rights law through the practice of international human rights courts and committees now considers extraterritorial reach of state obligations to be an integral part of human rights law, and, if so, what this means for states' obligations to regulate the conduct of business enterprises over which they exert control when they operate outside the territory of the state. I will first discuss the meaning of extraterritoriality in international human rights law from a theoretical perspective, and how such extraterritoriality relates to the obligation to protect individuals against human rights violations committed by private entities (Sect. 9.2), before addressing how the concept of extraterritoriality has evolved in human rights practice (Sect. 9.3). Much of the opposition to extraterritorial human rights obligations are based on the view that jurisdiction is territorial, and due to the wording of human rights treaties, obligations stemming from them are only relevant if a state acts within its jurisdiction. Therefore, much of this section will focus on how the European Court of Human Rights (ECtHR) has interpreted the concept of jurisdiction, and also how this relates to the attribution of acts to states. The section will also address the views of various UN human rights bodies on the obligation of states to protect against human rights abuses by third parties. The final section (Sect. 9.4) will address what the consequences of these findings will be for states' obligations related to the regulation of activities of TNCs and other business enterprises, and how this may impact upon the work currently undertaken to draft a treaty on business and human rights.[4]

9.2 The Concept of Extraterritorial Obligations in Human Rights Law and the Obligation to Protect

In international human rights law, the term extraterritorial obligations is now used to describe obligations related to the 'acts and omissions of a State, within or beyond its territory, that have effects on the enjoyment of human rights outside of that State's territory'.[5] Obligations pertaining to such acts and omissions have been recognised for a considerable amount of time both within international human rights law, and also other areas of international law, such as international humanitarian law,[6] and international environmental law.[7]

---

[4] UN Human Rights Council, Elaboration of an international legally binding instrument on transnational corporations and other business enterprises with respect to human rights, UN Doc A/HRC/26/L.22/Rev.1, 25 June 2014.

[5] Maastricht Principles on States' Extraterritorial Obligations in the area of Economic, Social and Cultural Rights, adopted by a group of experts in Maastricht in September 2011, http://www.etoconsortium.org/nc/en/main-navigation/library/maastricht-principles/?tx_drblob_pi1%5BdownloadUid%5D=23, accessed 27 January 2017, Principle 8.

[6] International humanitarian law is in its origin extraterritorial in that it consists of legal regulation of conduct when a state is engaged in military conflict abroad.

[7] Knox 2010, at 82.

While the principles underlying extraterritorial human rights obligations have been recognised, the question as to what to call such acts and omissions of states beyond their territory has received significant attention and been subject to discussion for a number of years.[8] Some authors have used the term 'transnational obligations'; others 'international obligations', 'shared obligations', or 'global obligations'.[9]

The term extraterritorial obligations has been criticised from a number of different perspectives: First, some commentators hold that 'extraterritorial' implies that the obligations go just beyond a state border, rather than encompassing all the various locations where a state's acts or omissions may have an impact.[10] Others will argue that the use of 'extraterritorial' places too much emphasis on territory and gives the impression that obligations are considered to be largely confined to the physical territory of the state, rather than where a state has influence over the acts or omissions that result in human rights violations even beyond its territory.[11] Furthermore, the use of the term extraterritorial has also been criticised as it has connotations to rather narrow use in US anti-trust law,[12] or criminal law,[13] and it is therefore not a concept that US lawyers readily associate with human rights law.

The term 'international obligations' has been preferred by several UN bodies, including the Committee on Economic, Social and Cultural Rights. For instance, the Committee holds, in its General Comment No. 14 on the right to the highest attainable standard of health, that:

> To comply with their *international obligations* in relation to article 12, States parties have to respect the enjoyment of the right to health in other countries, and to prevent third parties from violating the right in other countries, if they are able to influence these third parties by way of legal or political means, in accordance with the Charter of the United Nations and applicable international law.[14]

However, to use international obligations as a term has been criticised as it may be confused with the regular horizontal obligations between states in international law, where treaty obligations are reciprocal and owed to the other states that have ratified a treaty. What extraterritorial obligations imply is rather that obligations relate to individuals within another state and whose human rights are being affected

[8] Gibney 2013.

[9] For a thorough discussion on the terminology used to describe the phenomenon often referred to as 'extraterritorial human rights obligations', see Gibney 2013.

[10] UN Committee on Economic, Social and Cultural Rights, General Comment No. 14, The right to the highest attainable standard of health (Article 12 of the International Covenant on Economic, Social and Cultural Rights) UN Doc E/C.12/2000/4, 11 August 2000, para 39.

[11] Gibney 2013, at 40.

[12] See, for instance, Beckler and Kirtland 2003, at 11.

[13] Gibney 2013, at 41.

[14] UN Committee on Economic, Social and Cultural Rights (2000), General Comment No. 14, The right to the highest attainable standard of health (Article 12 of the International Covenant on Economic, Social and Cultural Rights), UN Doc E/C.12/2000/4, 11 August 2000, para 39 (emphasis added).

by acts or omissions by the foreign state. This relationship therefore depicts a different obligations' relationship as the link between the right-holder and the obligation-holder transcends a territorial border, and therefore produces what can be called a 'diagonal relationship'.[15] Or in other words, *international obligations* could refer to the obligations one ratifying state has vis-à-vis the other states parties to the same human rights treaty, rather than to the population within those other states. Similarly, the use of 'transnational' obligations have by some been considered to indicate too much of a state-to-state relationship, rather than (again) the link to individuals in another state. Finally, the term 'global obligations' is used, but the reference here is usually applied to describe obligations of the international community as a whole and relates to structures in this community which may hinder or assist in human rights enjoyment worldwide.[16]

While not necessarily an ideal term, 'extraterritorial human rights obligations' is now increasingly used by academics and practitioners. It also reflects the changing approach to territoriality and will therefore be the chosen term in this chapter.

The next question to be addressed is how these extraterritorial obligations relate to the conduct of TNCs. Obligations pertaining to human rights are both of a negative and positive nature. This means that states need to refrain from interfering in rights' enjoyment by individuals, as well as taking positive steps to ensure that human rights may be enjoyed by individuals. These negative and positive obligations have been further conceptualised into three main categories of obligations: the obligation to respect; the obligation to protect; and the obligation to fulfil. The Maastricht Guidelines on Violations of Economic, Social and Cultural Rights provides this explanation of the categories:

> Like civil and political rights, economic, social and cultural rights impose three different types of obligations on States: the obligations to respect, protect and fulfil. Failure to perform any one of these three obligations constitutes a violation of such rights. The obligation to respect requires States to refrain from interfering with the enjoyment of economic, social and cultural rights. [...] The obligation to protect requires States to prevent violations of such rights by third parties. [...] The obligation to fulfil requires States to take appropriate legislative, administrative, budgetary, judicial and other measures towards the full realization of such rights.[17]

---

[15] Knox 2010, at 83.

[16] Margot E. Salomon holds that '[t]he collective obligations of the international community of states [...] pertain to obligations to ensure arrangements that are just, and thereby conducive to the fulfilment of the socio-economic rights of all people'. Salomon 2007, at 182.

[17] Maastricht Guidelines on Violations of Economic, Social and Cultural Rights, adopted by a group of international experts in Maastricht, 22–26 January 1997,

http://hrlibrary.umn.edu/instree/Maastrichtguidelines_.html, accessed 22 August 2016, para 6. This categorisation is commonly used by international human rights bodies. For instance, in the General Comment on the Right to Adequate Food, the UN Committee on Economic, Social and Cultural Rights confirms that: '[t]he right to adequate food, like any other human right, imposes three types or levels of obligations on States parties: the obligations to respect, to protect and to fulfil. [...] The obligation to respect existing access to adequate food requires States parties not to take any measures that result in preventing such access. The obligation to protect requires measures by the State to ensure that enterprises or individuals do not deprive individuals of their access

While this tripartite classification of obligations was first articulated in relationship to economic, social and cultural rights, it is now generally accepted that all human rights carry both positive and negative obligations, and the classification is being applied to all categories of human rights. Thus, the question raised about states' obligations to ensure that TNCs do not infringe upon an individual's enjoyment of human rights relates in particular to the second category of obligations, namely the obligation to *protect*. This category of obligations concerns the state's duty to regulate the conduct of private parties, whether individuals or other entities. The UN Human Rights Committee has confirmed that this category of obligations is also relevant for the International Covenant on Civil and Political Rights (ICCPR):[18]

> [T]he positive obligations on States Parties to ensure Covenant rights will only be fully discharged if individuals are protected by the State, not just against violations of Covenant rights by its agents, but also against acts committed by private persons or entities that would impair the enjoyment of Covenant rights in so far as they are amenable to application between private persons or entities.[19]

An essential part of this obligation is to ensure that business enterprises do not breach human rights in their operations. In the UN Guiding Principles on Business and Human Rights (UNGP),[20] this has been framed in the recognition that '[s]tates must protect against human rights abuse within their territory and/or jurisdiction by third parties, including business enterprises. This requires taking appropriate steps to prevent, investigate, punish and redress such abuse through effective policies, legislation, regulations and adjudication.'[21]

To comply with the obligation to protect, states need to legislate and regulate the conduct of private individuals and entities, including businesses. This can be considered a requirement to carry out due diligence. Due diligence is a concept that is often used in business circles, and has, in the framework of the UNGP been defined as:

(Footnote 17 continued)

to adequate food. The obligation to fulfil (facilitate) means the State must proactively engage in activities intended to strengthen people's access to and utilization of resources and means to ensure their livelihood, including food security. Finally, whenever an individual or group is unable, for reasons beyond their control, to enjoy the right to adequate food by the means at their disposal, States have the obligation to fulfil (provide) that right directly. This obligation also applies for persons who are victims of natural or other disasters.' UN Committee on Economic, Social and Cultural Rights (CESCR), General Comment No. 12, The right to adequate food (Article 11), UN Doc E/C.12/1999/5, 12 May 1999, para 15.

[18] 1966 International Covenant on Civil and Political Rights, 999 UNTS 171 (ICCPR).

[19] UN Human Rights Committee (HRC), General Comment No. 31 [80], The Nature of the General Legal Obligation Imposed on States Parties to the Covenant, CCPR/C/21/Rev.1/Add.13, 26 May 2004, para 8.

[20] UN Guiding Principles on Business and Human Rights, Implementing the United Nations 'Protect, Respect and Remedy' Framework, HR/PUB/11/04, 2011.

[21] Ibid, at 3.

> An ongoing risk management process that a reasonable and prudent company needs to follow in order to identify, prevent, mitigate and account for how it addresses its adverse human rights impacts. It includes four key steps: assessing actual and potential human rights impacts; integrating and acting on the findings; tracking responses; and communicating about how impacts are addressed.[22]

However, due diligence is not only relevant for the conduct of businesses themselves. States' obligation to protect requires legislation and regulation of the conduct of businesses to ensure that they do not threaten or breach human rights of individuals by applying a due diligence process. The importance of due diligence is that it focuses on the process of ascertaining what can reasonably be predicted as human rights consequences of certain actions or omissions. A legal definition of due diligence includes the proviso of 'measure of prudence, activity, or assiduity, as is properly to be expected from, and ordinarily exercised [...] under the particular circumstances; not measured by any absolute standard, but depending on the relative facts of the special case'.[23] In human rights terms, this can be considered as a *normative* function, rather than the *de facto* degree of control.[24] Legislation requiring businesses to carry out such due diligence considerations regarding potential human rights effects of their operations should create accountability on part of these enterprises for potential failure to comply with such provisions. This would be one way for states to comply with their obligation to protect.

The link between a state's obligation to protect and extraterritorial human rights obligations concerns the question whether the content of this level of obligation goes beyond the territorial limitations of the state. In the commentary to the UNGP it is held that '[a]t present States are not generally required under international human rights law to regulate the extraterritorial activities of businesses domiciled in their territory and/or jurisdiction. Nor are they generally prohibited from doing so, provided there is a recognized jurisdictional basis.'[25] In the following, I will consider the practice of the ECtHR and UN Human Rights bodies to ascertain whether such an interpretation of the relevant human rights treaties is as straightforward as the commentary to the UNGP imply or whether human rights obligations are now considered to extend extraterritorially to include a duty to regulate the conduct of entities other than the state (including TNCs) when they operate beyond that state's territory.

---

[22] UN Guiding Principles Reporting Framework, Glossary, Human Rights Due Diligence, http://www.ungpreporting.org/resources/glossary/, accessed 22 August 2016.

[23] Black's Law Dictionary Online, What is Due Diligence, http://thelawdictionary.org/due-diligence/, accessed 23 August 2016.

[24] De Schutter 2016, at 54.

[25] UNGP, at 3–4.

9.3 Interpretation of Human Rights Treaties by International Human Rights Bodies

9.3.1 Background

Article 31 of the Vienna Convention on the Law of Treaties is the starting point for any treaty interpretation. This provision gives the general rules of interpretation, namely that '[a] treaty shall be interpreted in good faith in accordance with the ordinary meaning to be given to the terms of the treaty in their context and in the light of its object and purpose.'[26] Thus, this provision establishes three general principles for treaty interpretation: the textual ('ordinary meaning'); the treaty's 'context'; and the teleological ('object and purpose'). While practitioners and academics have debated whether this listing in Article 31 is an expression of a hierarchy of interpretation principles,[27] there seems to be a relative consensus that while all three principles should be applied in any treaty interpretation, the relative weight may vary dependent upon the character of the treaty, and the material content of it.[28] Having said this, the view among scholars and international judges have been that the contextual or teleological principles cannot be applied in a manner that ignores the 'ordinary meaning' of the text.[29] In addition, Article 32 provides for supplementary means of interpretation, which include the preparatory work of the treaty and the circumstances of its conclusion.[30]

It therefore becomes essential to address the relevant provisions in the various treaties to ascertain whether they contain text whose interpretation in accordance with the VCLT principles may confirm extraterritorial obligations. The most relevant provisions to be addressed are the general obligations provisions in each of the main human rights treaties.

9.3.2 Obligations Terminology in Human Rights Treaties

The first multilateral treaty to codify human rights law on a universal level was the UN Charter in 1945.[31] The Charter clearly states general, yet fundamental, principles of human rights as being one of the purposes of the collective of nations joining together under the auspices of the new organisation. Even so, the Charter does not address in much specificity what the concrete obligations of the member

[26] 1969 Vienna Convention on the Law of Treaties, 1155 UNTS 331 (VCLT), Article 31.

[27] Çali 2014, at 528.

[28] Ibid., at 533.

[29] Jonas and Saunders 2010, at 581.

[30] VCLT, Article 32.

[31] See in particular Articles 1(3), 55 and 56 of the UN Charter.

states of the UN are. The most precise reference to the content of such obligations is found in Articles 55 and 56 read together, where the members of the United Nations 'pledge themselves to take joint and separate action in co-operation with the Organization'[32] to achieve 'universal respect for, and observance of, human rights and fundamental freedoms for all without distinction as to race, sex, language, or religion'.[33] The reading of these provisions shows that the drafters envisaged more than domestic concern for human rights realisation, as 'joint' necessarily will involve efforts beyond at least one state's border.[34]

9.3.2.1 Universal Human Rights Treaties

Article 2 in both of the International Covenants on Human Rights from 1966[35] contain their general obligations provisions. However, the content of the two vary considerably. Article 2(1) of the International Covenant on Economic, Social and Cultural Rights (ICESCR) provides that the states parties to the covenant shall 'take steps, individually and through international assistance and cooperation [...] to achieve progressively the full realization of the rights' recognized in the Covenant. On the other hand, Article 2(1) of the International Covenant on Civil and Political Rights (ICCPR) contains a rather different wording: 'Each State Party to the present Covenant undertakes to respect and to ensure to all individuals within its territory and subject to its jurisdiction [...]' the rights recognised in the Covenant. It is important to note here that the ICCPR refers to both 'territory' and 'jurisdiction', while the ICESCR refers to neither of these terms, but includes a specific reference to international assistance and cooperation.

The International Convention on the Elimination of All Forms of Racial Discrimination (ICERD)[36] does not contain any references to territory or jurisdiction in its general obligations provision (Article 2), but refers to negative and positive obligations for 'public authorities and public institutions, national and local',[37] who are under obligations to act in accordance with the provisions of the treaty. Similarly, Article 2 of the International Convention on the Elimination of All Forms of Discrimination against Women (CEDAW)[38] does not refer to any specific activity of an international character, focusing on obligations to take legislative

---

32 UN Charter, Article 56.

33 UN Charter, Article 55.

34 For further elaboration of the importance of these passages in an extraterritorial context, see Skogly 2010.

35 1966 International Covenant on Economic, Social and Cultural Rights, 993 UNTS 3 (ICESCR); and ICCPR.

36 1965 International Convention on the Elimination of All Forms of Racial Discrimination, 660 UNTS 195 (ICERD).

37 ICERD, Article 2(1)(a).

38 1979 Convention on the Elimination of All Forms of Discrimination Against Women, 1249 UNTS 13 (CEDAW).

measures on constitutional and other levels to prohibit discrimination against women.[39] Other sections of Article 2 include obligations to take measures to prevent *de facto* discrimination against women, and are non-specific as to the locality for such measures.[40]

In contrast to the previous two conventions mentioned, the International Convention against Torture, or Other Cruel, Inhuman or Degrading Treatment or Punishment (CAT), is more explicitly restrictive in its wording:

> Each State Party shall take effective legislative, administrative, judicial or other measures to prevent acts of torture in any territory under its jurisdiction.[41]

Thus, the text of this treaty specifies both territory and jurisdiction in its provisions detailing state parties' obligations. By contrast, the Convention on the Rights of the Child (CRC)[42] is explicit on obligations beyond the national setting. Article 4 of this Convention starts by stating that the '[s]tates Parties shall undertake all appropriate legislative, administrative, and other measures for the implementation of the rights recognized in the present Convention'. This is non-specific in terms of territorial or jurisdictional application. The provision continues to provide that '[w]ith regard to economic, social and cultural rights, States Parties shall undertake such measures to the maximum extent of their available resources and, where needed, within the framework of international co-operation'. 'Such measures' here refers to 'all appropriate legislative, administrative, and other measures', and there is therefore no territorial or jurisdictional limitation specified for the obligations of states with regards to the rights in the convention, and it is additionally provided that for economic, social and cultural rights, these shall be implemented within the framework of international co-operation.

The most recent comprehensive UN Convention—the Convention on Rights of Persons with Disabilities (CRPD),[43] has a very detailed general obligations provision in its Article 4. The first part of the article does not contain any territorial or jurisdictional limitations. Additionally, similar to Article 4 CRC, Article 4(2) CRPD states that:

> With regard to economic, social and cultural rights, each State Party undertakes to take measures to the maximum of its available resources and, where needed, within the framework of international cooperation, with a view to achieving progressively the full realization of these rights [...].

Furthermore, this treaty is unique in terms of universal human rights treaties as it contains a separate article confirming the importance and necessity of international

[39] CEDAW, Article 2(a).

[40] See in particular Article 2(d) and (e) of CEDAW.

[41] 1984 Convention Against Torture and Other Cruel, Inhuman or Degrading Treatment or Punishment, 1465 UNTS 85 (CAT), Article 2(1).

[42] 1989 Convention on the Rights of the Child, 1577 UNTS 3 (CRC).

[43] 2006 Convention on the Rights of Persons with Disabilities, 2515 UNTS 3 (CRPD).

cooperation for the protection of rights of persons with disabilities.[44] This article details what state parties are supposed to do in terms of international cooperation to that end.

As a preliminary observation going through the various treaties adopted under the auspices of the United Nations over the past 70 years, several treaties contain language that is open-ended in terms of the reach of obligations, and some also include specific provisions requiring international co-operation.

9.3.2.2 Regional Human Rights Treaties

On the regional level, the four main conventions again differ with respect to the general obligations' provisions. The first of these, the European Convention on Human Rights and Fundamental Freedoms (ECHR),[45] provides in its Article 1 that '[t]he High Contracting Parties shall secure to everyone within their jurisdiction the rights and freedoms defined in Section I of this Convention.' The American Convention on Human Rights (ACHR)[46] has a similar provision in its Article 1, which reads: '[t]he States Parties to this Convention undertake to respect the rights and freedoms recognized herein and to ensure to all persons subject to their jurisdiction the free and full exercise of those rights and freedoms'. Thus, these two conventions include specific references to the ratifying state's jurisdiction, but there is no mention of territory. The later regional treaty, the African Charter on Human and Peoples' Rights (ACHPR) of 1981[47] has a general obligation provision that does not refer to jurisdiction or territory: '[t]he Member States of the Organisation of African Unity, parties to the present Charter shall recognise the rights, duties and freedoms enshrined in the Charter and shall undertake to adopt legislative or other measures to give effect to them.'[48] Finally, the Arab Charter on Human Rights (ArCHR) of 2004[49] returns to a very similar wording to that of the American Convention by stating in its Article 3 that '[e]ach State party to the present Charter undertakes to ensure to all individuals subject to its jurisdiction the right to enjoy the rights and freedoms set forth herein.'

From this brief overview, it is interesting to note that only two conventions, namely the ICCPR and the CAT, specifically refer to territory when it comes to the ratifying states' obligations to respect and protect the rights contained in the treaties.

---

[44] CRPD, Article 32.

[45] 1950 European Convention for the Protection of Human Rights and Fundamental Freedoms, as amended, ETS 5 (ECHR).

[46] 1969 American Convention on Human Rights 1144 UNTS 123 (ACHR).

[47] 1981 African Charter on Human and Peoples' Rights, 1520 UNTS 217 (ACHRP).

[48] ACHPR, Article 1.

[49] League of Arab States, Arab Charter on Human Rights (ArCHR) translation by Dr. Mohammed Amin Al-Midani and Mathilde Cabanettes, revised by Professor Susan M. Akram, 2004, http://www.eods.eu/library/LAS_Arab%20Charter%20on%20Human%20Rights_2004_EN.pdf, accessed 27 January 2017 (ArCHR).

Three treaties (ICESCR, CRC and CRPD) include a specific mention of international assistance and cooperation for economic, social, and cultural rights; while five treaties (ICCPR, CAT, ECHR, ACHR and ArCHR) refer to jurisdiction in their obligations provisions. Finally, three treaties (CERD, CEDAW and ACHPR) do not make any mention of territory, jurisdiction or international assistance and cooperation in the text providing the general obligations for ratifying states. Thus, the common interpretation that obligations stemming from human rights treaties are limited to the territory of the ratifying state cannot stem from a textual interpretation of the treaty texts. In fact, the ICCPR and CAT would be seen as the only two treaties that have a text to provide for such interpretation. The textual justification for claiming that human rights obligations are (primarily) territorial must lie elsewhere, and this may be in a textual understanding of 'jurisdiction' as implying territorial limitations. This will be addressed in the section below analysing relevant case law.

The work of the various international human rights bodies differ dependent on their mandate. The regional human rights courts deal with specific complaints, while few (apart from the UN Human Rights Committee) of the UN human rights bodies have a similar body of considerable case law to refer to. This does not mean that the work of the UN bodies is less significant, but rather that the focus of the work is different and consequently, so is the nature of their interpretation.

9.3.3 The Evolution of Extraterritoriality in International Human Rights Practice

The most important issue in much of the case law that has developed regarding extraterritorial obligations of states relates to the question of jurisdiction. In spite of the fact that only some of the treaties have jurisdictional limitations, the question of jurisdiction (of the state and the international supervisory organ) is seen as essential to enable the relevant court or committee to address alleged violations of human rights abroad.

The first cases to be heard relating to situations involving what we would now consider an extraterritorial application of obligations emerged from the ECtHR and the UN Human Rights Committee in the 1980s. As early as 1981, the UN Human Rights Committee heard the case of *Sergio Euben Lopez Burgos v Uruguay*.[50] In this case, Mr. Lopez Burgos, who was a political refugee in Argentina after being persecuted by the Uruguayan government for his trade union involvement, was abducted by Uruguayan security forces and forcibly taken back to Uruguay. He was subjected to treatment that amounted to torture. The UN Human Rights Committee found that Uruguay was in violation of its obligations under the ICCPR even

[50] *Sergio Euben Lopez Burgos v Uruguay*, UN Human Rights Committee, Communication, UN. Doc CCPR/C/13/D/52/1979, 29 July 1981 (*Lopez Burgos*), at 176.

though the activities had taken place outside Uruguayan territory. In this case, the Committee held that:

> [t]he reference in article 1 of the Optional Protocol to 'individuals subject to its jurisdiction' [...] is not to the place where the violation occurred, but rather to the relationship between the individual and the State in relation to a violation of any of the rights set forth in the Covenant, wherever they occurred.[51]

It further held that:

> Article 2 (1) of the Covenant places an obligation upon a State party to respect and to ensure rights 'to all individuals within its territory and subject to its jurisdiction', but this does not imply that the State party concerned cannot be held accountable for violations of rights under the Covenant which its agents commit upon the territory of another State, whether with the acquiescence of the Government of that State or in opposition to it.[52]

In this early case, the UN Human Rights Committee thus confirmed that it is the relationship between the State and the human rights violation taking place, rather than the location of the act, which is of importance to ascertain whether a state obligation has been breached.

A few years later, in 1989, the ECtHR heard the case of *Soering v United Kingdom*.[53] In this case, the United States requested extradition of Mr. Soering—a German national—to be tried for alleged murder. He had left the United States after the alleged crime and gone to the United Kingdom. Mr. Soering held that he was likely to be given the death penalty in the state of Virginia if extradited and found guilty, and that the conditions surrounding such sentencing would breach his rights under Article 3 ECHR.[54] The UK held that this article 'should not be interpreted so as to impose responsibility on a Contracting State for acts which occur outside its jurisdiction'.[55] The Court held that:

> the Convention does not govern the actions of States not Parties to it, nor does it purport to be a means of requiring the Contracting States to impose Convention standards on other States. Article 1 (art. 1) cannot be read as justifying a general principle to the effect that, notwithstanding its extradition obligations, a Contracting State may not surrender an individual unless satisfied that the conditions awaiting him in the country of destination are in full accord with each of the safeguards of the Convention.[56]

However, the Court continued to say that '[t]hese considerations cannot [...] absolve the Contracting Parties from responsibility under Article 3 (art. 3) for all and any foreseeable consequences of extradition suffered outside their

[51] Ibid., para 12.2.

[52] Ibid., para 12.3.

[53] *Soering v the United Kingdom*, ECtHR Plenary, Judgment, No. 14038/88, 7 July 1989 (*Soering*).

[54] Article 3 ECHR provides the right to be free from torture, inhuman and degrading treatment or punishment.

[55] *Soering*, para 83.

[56] Ibid., para 86.

jurisdiction.'[57] In its reasoning, the Court referred to the special character of the ECHR as a treaty for the 'collective enforcement of human rights and fundamental freedoms', the 'object and purpose of the Convention' and that the interpretation of it should be consistent with 'the general spirit' of the Convention.[58] On this basis, the Court found that the circumstances of the *Soering* case would 'give rise to a breach of Article 3(3)' if the applicant was extradited.[59] The Court confirmed that while Contracting States are not responsible for human rights violations committed by non-parties to the Convention, there are circumstances when a state can foresee that their actions may have negative consequences on an individual's human rights' enjoyment, and that carrying out such actions will trigger responsibility of the state. This is particularly so when the right in question is one of the non-derogable rights according to the Convention.[60]

These two early cases set the scene for treaty interpretation regarding the extraterritorial reach of human rights obligations of states. They represent the start of a process of consideration of the content of jurisdiction, how it relates to territory, and how it can extend beyond the physical boundaries of the ratifying state. These cases (some of which will be analysed below) raise questions of control over people and territory, and how acts and omissions of the authorities of a state may produce effects outside a state's territory which may cause human rights abuses and be the responsibility of the state.

It would lead too far in this chapter to carry out a comprehensive analysis of all the relevant cases. Therefore, the chapter concentrates on some of the key cases before the ECtHR and how they have developed the understanding of 'jurisdiction', and also how the concept of attribution is relevant.

9.3.3.1 Jurisdiction

Following the *Soering* case, the next major case before the ECtHR receiving significant attention for establishing that the obligations of the convention may reach beyond the territorial borders of the ratifying state is the *Loizidou v Turkey* case from 1995.[61] In this case, the complainant argued that Turkey had breached her rights according to Article 1 of Protocol 1[62] guaranteeing peaceful enjoyment of property. The occupation by Turkey of the Northern part of Cyprus resulted in Ms. Loizidou not being able to access her home and possessions. The government of

---

[57] Ibid.

[58] Ibid., para 87.

[59] Ibid., para 111.

[60] Ibid, para 88.

[61] *Loizidou v Turkey*, ECtHR Grand Chamber, Judgment, No. 15318/89, 18 December 1996 (*Loizidou*).

[62] 1952 Protocol 1 to the European Convention for the Protection of Human Rights and Fundamental Freedoms, ETS 9.

Turkey argued that the Court did not have jurisdiction to hear the case as the alleged violations had taken place outside the territory of Turkey and therefore outside its jurisdiction.[63] The Court, however, did not accept this argument, as the large number of Turkish troops in Northern Cyprus clearly indicated Turkish control over the area.[64] It consequently found that Turkey had breached the Convention, and held that:

> in conformity with the relevant principles of international law governing State responsibility, [...] the responsibility of a Contracting Party could also arise when as a consequence of military action - whether lawful or unlawful - it exercises effective control of an area outside its national territory. The obligation to secure, in such an area, the rights and freedoms set out in the Convention, derives from the fact of such control whether it be exercised directly, through its armed forces, or through a subordinate local administration.[65]

Hence, the Court here established that effective control of an area outside its territory will extend the reach of jurisdiction within the meaning of Article 1 ECHR. Furthermore, such effective control can result from military occupation.

Building on this case, the Court, sitting in Grand Chamber, heard the case of *Banković and others v Belgium and others* and delivered its judgement in 2001.[66] This case was brought by survivors and relatives of deceased individuals of the NATO bombing of the television tower in Belgrade in 1999. The applicants held that the bombing and the resulting deaths represented violations of the right to life, as guaranteed by Article 2 ECHR, as well as violations of Articles 10 and 13.[67] The respondent governments contested the admissibility of the case on the basis that the alleged victims were not within the jurisdiction of the high contracting parties in the meaning of Article 1 ECHR.[68] After significant deliberations, the Court found that it did not have jurisdiction to hear the case on the basis that the actions taken by the European NATO member states happened outside the territory covered by the Convention, namely in the former Yugoslavia, and it was therefore outside the jurisdiction of the Court as understood by reference to Article 1. The case was consequently found inadmissible.[69] This conclusion was different from that of the *Loizidou* case as Cyprus is a high contracting state, just like Turkey, and hence both states involved were parties to the treaty. The Court, thus, made a distinction between the area covered by the treaty, and territory outside this geographic area. It also determined in *Banković* that individuals in such external geographic areas were

---

[63] Ibid., para 51.

[64] Ibid., para 56.

[65] Ibid., para 52.

[66] *Banković and Others v Belgium and Others*, ECtHR Grand Chamber, Admissibility, Decision, No. 52207/99, 12 December 2001 (*Banković*).

[67] Ibid., para 28; Article 10 guarantees the freedom of expression, Article 13 the right to an effective remedy.

[68] Ibid., para 31.

[69] Ibid., para 85.

not under effective control of the respondent governments when they carried out aerial attacks resulting in death and serious injury.

However, in spite of its conclusions in the *Banković* case, the Court confirmed that in exceptional circumstances the convention could have reach beyond the geographic territory of the members of the Council of Europe.[70]

Since Bankovic, there have been a number of other cases where the Court has found that such exceptional circumstances exist and that the Convention therefore applies. Most notably, in the cases of *Issa v Turkey*[71] and *Al-Skeini v UK*[72] the Court found that a state's jurisdiction within the meaning of Article 1 ECHR could be triggered in situations of control both over territory and over persons within another state not party to the ECHR.[73] Similarly, in cases brought against Russia and Moldova,[74] the Court found that there were shared obligations for both Russia and Moldova for human rights violations that had taken place in Transdniestria—a region in Moldova where Russia has significant control. In all of these cases, the Court has confirmed that states may be under an obligation to respect the rights in the Convention in times of occupation or other military control over territory in another state.

In a more recent case involving military activity, the Court dealt with the question of whether a state other than the formal occupying power may be considered to exercise jurisdiction. In *Jaloud v the Netherlands*,[75] relatives of Mr. Jaloud brought the case after he was shot and killed by Dutch troops in Iraq in 2004. In this case, the Netherlands held that they could not be considered to be operating within their jurisdiction within the meaning of Article 1 ECHR, as they were not an occupying power, and their troops were deployed to Iraq on the basis of a UN Security Council Resolution. After careful consideration of the intricate structure of the international Stabilization Force in Iraq (SFIR) the Court found that:

> Although Netherlands troops were stationed in an area in south- eastern Iraq where SFIR forces were under the command of an officer from the United Kingdom, the Netherlands assumed responsibility for providing security in that area, to the exclusion of other participating States, and retained full command over its contingent there.[76] [...] [Therefore] the

[70] Ibid., para 67.

[71] *Issa v Turkey*, ECtHR Second Section, Judgement, No. 31821/96, 16 November 2004.

[72] *Al-Skeini and Others v The United Kingdom*, ECtHR Grand Chamber, Judgement, No. 55721/07, 7 July 2011 (*Al-Skeini*).

[73] Ibid., para 133.

[74] *Ilaşcu and Others v Moldova and Russia*, ECtHR Grand Chamber, Judgment, No. 48787/99, 8th July 2004 (*Ilaşcu*); *Ivantoc and Others v Moldova and Russia*, ECtHR Fourth Section, Judgment, No. 23687/05, 15th November 2011; *Catan and Others v The Republic of Moldova and Russia,* ECtHR Grand Chamber, Judgment, No. 43370/04, 18454/06 and 8252/05, 19 October 2012; and *Mozer v The Republic of Moldova and Russia,* ECtHR Grand Chamber, Judgment, No. 11138/10, 23 February 2016.

[75] *Jaloud v the Netherlands,* ECtHR Grand Chamber, Merits and Just Satisfaction, Judgment, No. 47708/08, 20 November 2014 (*Jaloud).*

[76] Ibid., para 149.

> Court cannot find that the Netherlands troops were placed 'at the disposal' of any foreign power, whether it be Iraq or the United Kingdom or any other power, or that they were 'under the exclusive direction or control' of any other State.[77]

Consequently, the Court found that the Netherlands 'exercised its "jurisdiction"' within the limits of its SFIR mission and for the purpose of asserting authority and control over persons passing through the checkpoint.'[78]

In this case it can be argued that the Court showed an approach to the question of jurisdiction which is less formalistic in terms of formal power and more aimed at assessing the *de facto* situation on the ground.

On the basis of these and other cases that involve the military, the police or security personnel's activities in another state's territory, there is now a strong recognition that the Convention has extraterritorial reach. In fact, in situations of occupation or custodial or other control over individuals by a state party acting extraterritorially, the Court has found that the Convention regularly applies outside the territory of the ratifying state. However, the question becomes whether the jurisdictional reach is only applicable in situations where a state's military or law-enforcement personnel are involved. If this was the case, the question of extraterritorial obligation to protect, through the regulation of private business entities' operations abroad, would be largely responded to in the negative. Therefore, it is necessary to consider if other forms of states' international interactions will be covered by extraterritorial jurisdiction as well.

Staying with the ECHR, there are a number of other cases that have been heard by the (previous) Commission and Court that deal with complaints stemming from different forms of states' international interaction or cooperation. These have not received the same amount of attention from media and academic commentators, but they are still of interest to ascertain whether it is now commonly accepted that extraterritorial obligations go beyond the military/security spheres.

Referring to its own case law, the ECtHR has held that extraterritorial jurisdiction is exceptional, but may exist when 'the respondent State, through the effective control of the relevant territory and its inhabitants abroad as a consequence of military occupation or *through the consent, invitation, acquiescence of the Government of that territory, exercises all or some of the public powers normally to be exercised by the Government*'.[79] This position is confirmed in *Al-Skeini*, and in this case the Court added that:

> where, in accordance with custom, treaty or other agreement, authorities of the Contracting State carry out executive or judicial functions on the territory of another State, the Contracting State may be responsible for breaches of the Convention thereby incurred, as long as the acts in question are attributable to it rather than to the territorial State.[80]

---

[77] Ibid., para 151.

[78] Ibid., para 152.

[79] *Banković*, para 71 (emphasis added).

[80] *Al-Skeini*, para 135.

Thus, the Court itself recognises that it is not only in cases of military occupation that the extraterritorial obligations of the ratifying states may be engaged. For example, in *Drozd and Janosek v France and Spain*,[81] which considered whether France and Spain exercised jurisdiction in Andorra as a result of French and Spanish judges practicing in that country, the Court held that France and Spain could not be considered to exercise extraterritorial jurisdiction in this context, as the judges were not 'subject to supervision by the authorities of France and Spain'.[82] However, the Court accepted that if such supervision had been carried out, then France and Spain could have been responsible 'because of acts of their authorities producing effects outside their own territory'.[83] Furthermore, in *X and Y v Switzerland*,[84] concerning a treaty incorporating Lichtenstein into Switzerland's customs area, and where the question was whether decisions by the Swiss authorities had an effect outside Swiss territory, the then European Commission on Human Rights held that '[a]cts by Swiss authorities with effect in Liechtenstein bring all those to whom they apply under Swiss jurisdiction within the meaning of Article 1 of the Convention.'[85]

Similarly, the *Manoilescu and Dobrescu v Romania and Russia*[86] case concerned the restitution of property to two Romanian nationals. Their property had been transferred to the Romanian State after the Second World War, and was later subject to a property exchange with the Soviet Union (ultimately transferred to the Russian Federation). It was confirmed in 1994 that the property would be used by the Russian Embassy in Romania. The court found the complaint inadmissible, and the applicants had not been able to show that they were within the jurisdiction of the Russian Federation in this case. Nevertheless, the Court in its deliberations held that:

> [e]ven in the absence of effective control of a territory outside its borders, the State still has a positive obligation under Article 1 of the Convention to take the diplomatic, economic, judicial or other measures that it is in its power to take and are in accordance with international law to secure to the applicants the rights guaranteed by the Convention.[87]

Indeed, in this case, the Court said that the principle quoted above was a broadening of its earlier position that the exceptional circumstances only referred to situations of effective control through 'military occupation or through the consent, invitation or acquiescence of the government of that territory'.[88]

---

[81] *Drozd and Janousek v France and Spain*, ECtHR Plenary, Judgment, No. 12747/87, 26 June 1992.

[82] Ibid., para 96.

[83] Ibid., para 91.

[84] *X and Y v Switzerland*, European Commission of Human Rights, Plenary, Admissibility, No. 7289/75 and 7349/76, 14 July 1977.

[85] Ibid., at 73.

[86] *Manoilescu and Dobrescu v Romania and Russia*, ECtHR Third Section, Decision, No. 60861/00, 3 March 2005.

[87] Ibid., para 101.

[88] Ibid.

9.3.3.2 Attribution of Acts to the State

While it may be concluded that the Court has accepted that jurisdiction may extend beyond the territorial borders of a ratifying state, the above discussion has not dealt with one of the main conditions brought forward by the ECtHR, namely that of attribution. As quoted in the *Al-Skeini* case, the Court held that 'the Contracting State may be responsible for breaches of the Convention thereby incurred, as long as the acts in question are attributable to it rather than to the territorial State'.[89] When acts are carried out by the military or the police, the question of attribution to the state is relatively straightforward. However, if acts are done by private entities, the question becomes more complex. For the purpose of the present chapter, the question becomes whether the requirement of attribution to the state may be satisfied in situations of transnational corporations' behaviour abroad.

In the commentary to the International Law Commission's Articles on Responsibility of States for Internationally Wrongful Acts from 2001,[90] it is held that 'the general rule is that the only conduct attributed to the State at the international level is that of its organs of government, or of others who have acted under the direction, instigation or control of those organs, i.e. as agents of the State',[91] and '[a]s a corollary, the conduct of private persons is not as such attributable to the State'.[92] Thus, the regular understanding of acts or omissions attributable to the state would not be those engaged in by private parties, including private business enterprises, and it could be concluded that this understanding of attribution would prevent responsibility for a state related to the acts of private enterprises. However, the distinction between the actions of private parties and the state is not necessarily that firm. Notwithstanding the clear definition of attribution as quoted above, the commentary to the Articles also confirms that 'a State may be responsible for the effects of the conduct of private parties, if it failed to take necessary measures to prevent those effects',[93] and that the question of attribution relates both to actions and omissions.[94]

Attribution in the context of extraterritorial obligations should be seen in light of two concepts already mentioned: 'acts producing effects abroad' and 'due diligence'. In several cases, including the *Jaloud* case, the Court has held that 'a Contracting State's jurisdiction under Article 1 may extend to acts of its authorities which produce effects outside its own territory'.[95]

[89] *Al-Skeini*, para 135.

[90] International Law Commission, Draft articles on Responsibility of States for Internationally Wrongful Acts, with commentaries, UN Doc. A/56/10, 2001.

[91] Ibid., at 38.

[92] Ibid.

[93] Ibid.

[94] Ibid., at 35.

[95] *Jaloud*, para 133.

While it is rare that negative acts by TNCs can be directly attributed to the home state, their acts should be seen in the context of potential failure 'to take necessary measures to prevent those effects'.[96] If a state is in a position to regulate the conduct of a company's actions abroad, but fails to do so, and this omission results in human rights abuses, the question of responsibility upon the state may be raised. This is the approach taken by the UNGP where, in the commentary to the Principles, it is held that:

> [s]tates are not per se responsible for human rights abuse by private actors. However, States may breach their international human rights law obligations where such abuse can be attributed to them, *or where they fail to take appropriate steps to prevent, investigate, punish and redress private actors' abuse.*[97]

On the basis of the brief consideration of the case law above, some general observations can be made. First, the ECtHR has confirmed that while jurisdiction is primarily territorial, there are exceptional circumstances whereby the jurisdictional reach goes beyond the territory of the ratifying state, and indeed also the territory covered by the total membership of the Council of Europe. Second, these exceptional circumstances do not only cover situations of occupation or other forms of effective control over territory. Control over persons is also included, and so are actions of states that produce human rights effects outside their territory. Third, the Court has confirmed that contracting parties have a positive duty to take 'the diplomatic, economic, judicial or other measures that is in its power to take [...] to secure [...] the rights guaranteed by the Convention'.[98] Finally, attribution of actions may be made to states even if they have been carried out by private parties. The significance of these developments in case law for the question of obligations of states to regulate the conduct of TNCs will be further addressed in Sect. 9.4 below.

9.3.4 The United Nations Bodies

Most of the work of UN bodies in this area comes in the form of Concluding Observations to state reports, General Comments from UN Committees, or reports from Special Rapporteurs. While not considered legally binding decisions, such statements are considered to represent authoritative interpretations of the various treaties. There is a growing trend among the UN bodies to address extraterritorial obligations of states in these documents, including those related to states' regulation of the conduct of private parties. The Global Initiative for Economic, Social and Cultural Rights monitors UN pronouncements on extraterritorial human rights

---

[96] International Law Commission, Draft articles on Responsibility of States for Internationally Wrongful Acts, with commentaries, UN Doc. A/56/10, 2001 (see Commentary on Article 2, at 35).

[97] UNGP, at 3 (emphasis added).

[98] *Ilaşcu*, para 331.

obligations, and has in its latest collection documented 41 references to such obligations since 2010.[99] These pronouncements come from a large variety of UN human rights bodies, including: the Committee on Economic, Social and Cultural Rights, The Human Rights Committee; the Committee on Elimination of Discrimination against Women; the Committee on Elimination of Racial Discrimination; the Committee on the Rights of the Child; several special rapporteurs (both on civil and political and on economic, social and cultural rights) through the Special Procedures, and the Universal Periodic Review.

As noted in Sect. 9.3.2 above, only the ICCPR and the CAT refer to both 'jurisdiction' and 'territory' in their general obligations provisions. The question raised in the interpretation of these provisions is whether this wording implies that the two concepts should always be considered in conjunction with each other, or whether they are considered separate: 'jurisdiction' on the one hand and 'territory' on the other. If that were to be the case, one could expect that the wording used in the treaties would have been 'jurisdiction *or* territory' rather than 'jurisdiction *and* territory', as stated in the ICCPR. However, in General Comment No. 31, the UN Human Rights Committee does not take this view. Quite the contrary, they hold that:

> States Parties are required by article 2, paragraph 1, to respect and to ensure the Covenant rights to all persons who may be within their territory and to all persons subject to their jurisdiction. This means that a State party must respect and ensure the rights laid down in the Covenant to anyone within the power or effective control of that State Party, even if not situated within the territory of the State Party.[100]

This view confirms the position taken in the *Lopez Burgos* case, as discussed above.[101]

The UN Committee against Torture has also addressed the meaning of 'jurisdiction' and 'territory' in its General Comment on Article 2 of the Convention. They have not quite taken the same specific view on the separation of the two concepts as the UN Human Rights Committee has done. However, they clearly do not interpret these two concepts in a narrow or restrictive manner. The General Comment provides that:

> [t]he Committee [...] understands that the concept of 'any territory under its jurisdiction,' linked as it is with the principle of non-derogability, includes any territory or facilities and must be applied to protect any person, citizen or non-citizen without discrimination *subject to the de jure or de facto control* of a State party.[102]

---

99 The Global Initiative for Economic, Social and Cultural Rights 2015.

100 UN Human Rights Committee, General Comment No. 31, The Nature of the General Legal Obligations Imposed on State Parties to the Covenant, UN Doc CCPR/C/21/Rev.1/Add. 13, 26 May 2004, para 10.

101 See the *Lopez Burgos* case.

102 UN Committee Against Torture, General Comment No. 2, Implementation of Article 2 by States Parties, UN Doc CAT/C/GC/2, 24 January 2008, para 7 (emphasis added).

Furthermore, the General Comment goes on to state that:

> Article 2, paragraph 1, requires that each State party shall take effective measures to prevent acts of torture not only in its sovereign territory but also 'in any territory under its jurisdiction.' The Committee has recognized that 'any territory' includes *all areas where the State party exercises, directly or indirectly, in whole or in part, de jure or de facto effective control*, in accordance with international law. The reference to 'any territory' in article 2 [...], refers to prohibited acts committed not only on board a ship or aircraft registered by a State party, but also during military occupation or peacekeeping operations and in such places as embassies, military bases, detention facilities, or other areas over which a State exercises factual or effective control. The Committee notes that this interpretation reinforces article 5, paragraph 1 (b), which requires that a State party must take measures to exercise jurisdiction 'when the alleged offender is a national of the State.' The Committee considers that the scope of 'territory' under article 2 must also include situations where a State party exercises, directly or indirectly, *de facto* or de jure control over persons in detention.[103]

As is evident from these two quotes, the Committee against Torture does not see the references to 'territory' and 'jurisdiction' in the Convention in any way to signify a strict adherence to the physical territorial boundaries of the ratifying state. They understand these terms with reference to both *de jure* and *de facto* control not only over territory, but indeed also over persons—and these persons may be in areas far away from the actual territory of the state, including in foreign states' territory in terms of peace keeping or detention during occupation. It is also emphasised that this control can be either direct or indirect.

These two committees monitor the implementation of treaties that have more restrictive language on territorial jurisdiction than the other treaties, including the ECHR as discussed above. Yet, they have accepted a broader interpretation of situations that may involve the jurisdiction of the state party in question. The way in which this may impact on the role of the state regarding the regulation of private parties, was also confirmed by the UN Human Rights Committee in paragraph 8 of General Comment No. 31.[104]

Beyond the question of jurisdiction, many of the UN human rights bodies have given attention to situations where states should take measures to protect individuals from negative effects of acts taken by private parties over which the state has control or significant influence. It is not possible to give a full account of the statements by these bodies in this chapter, but a few should be mentioned for illustration.

For instance, in its concluding observations from 2016 on the report from the United Kingdom, the CRC expressed its concern about the effect of the UK's development cooperation, where they contribute to 'for-profit schools', and that the

---

[103] Ibid., para 16 (emphasis added).

[104] UN Human Rights Committee, General Comment No. 31, The Nature of the General Legal Obligations Imposed on State Parties to the Covenant, UN Doc. CCPR/C/21/Rev.1/Add. 13, 26 May 2004.

right to education may be in jeopardy.[105] The UN Human Rights Committee in its concluding observations on the report by the United States in 2006, held that it 'notes with concern the restrictive interpretation made by the State party of its obligations under the Covenant, as a result in particular of [...] its position that the Covenant does not apply with respect to individuals under its jurisdiction but outside its territory'.[106]

The Special Rapporteur on the rights of peaceful assembly and of association held that states shall:

> (c) Take appropriate measures to meet extraterritorial obligations, particularly by providing access to remedy for victims of violations of the rights to freedom of peaceful assembly and of association; measures should include but are not limited to: [...]
>
> (ii) Enacting, implementing and enforcing laws that prohibit and provide penalties for conduct by corporations that violates human rights abroad;
>
> (iii) Ensuring that trade and other agreements on investment in natural resource exploitation activities, whether concluded bilaterally or multilaterally, recognize and protect the exercise of peaceful assembly and association rights for affected individuals and groups[.][107]

The UN Committee on Economic, Social and Cultural Rights held in a statement from 2011 that '[s]tates parties should [...] take steps to prevent human rights contraventions abroad by corporations which have their main offices under their jurisdiction, without infringing the sovereignty or diminishing the obligations of the host States under the Covenant.'[108] And in recent concluding observations on the report from Canada, the same Committee, held that:

> The Committee is concerned that the conduct of corporations registered or domiciled in the State party and operating abroad are, on occasions, negatively impacting on the enjoyment of Covenant rights by local populations. [...] The Committee recommends that the State party strengthen its legislation governing the conduct of corporations registered or

[105] The Committee holds that: '[i]n the context of international development cooperation the Committee is concerned about the State party's funding of low-fee, private and informal schools run by for-profit business enterprises in recipient States. Rapid increase in the number of such schools may contribute to sub-standard education, less investment in free and quality public schools, and deepened inequalities in the recipient countries, leaving behind children who cannot afford even low-fee schools.' (para 17) and that '[t]he Committee recommends that the State party ensure that its international development cooperation supports the recipient States in guaranteeing the right to free compulsory primary education for all, by prioritizing free and quality primary education in public schools, refraining from funding for-profit private schools, and facilitating registration and regulation of private schools.' (para 18), UN Committee on the Rights of the Child, Concluding observations on the fifth periodic report of the United Kingdom of Great Britain and Northern Ireland, CRC/C/GBR/CO/5, 12 July 2016.

[106] UN Human Rights Committee, Concluding Observations, United States of America, UN Doc CCPR/C/USA/CO/3, 18 December 2006, para 10.

[107] Maina Kiai, Special Rapporteur, Report on the rights to freedom of peaceful assembly and of association, UN Doc A/HRC/29/25, 28 April 2015, para 72.

[108] UN Committee on Economic, Social and Cultural Rights, Statement on the Obligations of States Parties regarding the corporate sector and economic social and cultural rights, UN Doc E/C.12/2011/1, 12 July 2011, para 5.

> domiciled in the State party in their activities abroad, including by requiring these corporations to conduct human rights impact assessments prior to making investment decisions. It also recommends that the State party introduce effective mechanisms to investigate complaints filed against these corporations, and adopt the necessary legislative measures so as to facilitate access to justice before domestic courts by victims of these corporations' conduct.[109]

In its Concluding Observations regarding China, the Committee expressed its concern 'about the lack of adequate and effective measures adopted by the State party to ensure that Chinese companies, both State-owned and private, respect economic, social and cultural rights, including when operating abroad' and recommended that China establish a regulatory framework for Chinese companies to 'ensure that their activities promote and do not negatively affect the enjoyment of economic, social and cultural human rights'; and that the country should '[a]dopt appropriate legislative and administrative measures to ensure the legal liability of companies and their subsidiaries operating in or managed from the State party's territory regarding violations of economic, social and cultural rights in the context of their projects abroad'.[110]

The UN Human Rights Committee has expressed its satisfaction that Germany has established the opportunity for remedies against German companies acting abroad when they are in contravention of relevant human rights standards. However, the Committee has noted that the standards may not always be sufficient. Therefore, the State party was asked to set out clearly the expectation that all business enterprises 'domiciled in its territory and/or its jurisdiction respect human rights standards in accordance with the Covenant throughout their operations. It is also encouraged to take appropriate measures to strengthen the remedies provided to protect people who have been victims of activities of such business enterprises operating abroad.'[111]

From the discussions above it is shown that the ECtHR has the most extensive case law when considering extraterritorial reach of jurisdiction, while the UN bodies have addressed specifically the question of jurisdiction for those treaties that have jurisdictional limitation, and have found that jurisdiction is not limited to territory. In addition to considering the specific issue of jurisdiction, other monitoring bodies in the UN have clearly taken the position that the obligation to protect includes states' obligations to ensure regulation of the conduct of private parties over which they exercise control or influence. This conclusion is in accordance with the approach taken by the drafters of the Maastricht Principles of Extraterritorial Obligations in the area of Economic, Social and Cultural Rights, which in its

[109] UN Committee on Economic, Social and Cultural Rights, Concluding observations on the sixth periodic report of Canada, UN Doc E/C.12/CAN/CO/6, 23 March 2016, paras 15–16.

[110] UN Committee on Economic, Social and Cultural Rights, Concluding observations on the second periodic report of China, including Hong Kong, China, and Macao, China, UN Doc E/C.12/CHN/CO/2, 13 June 2014, para 13.

[111] UN Human Rights Committee, Concluding Observations on the sixth periodic report of Germany, UN Doc CCPR/C/DEU/CO/6, 12 November 2012, para16.

preamble states that 'the Maastricht Principles do not purport to establish new elements of human rights law. Rather, the Maastricht Principles clarify extraterritorial obligations of States on the basis of standing international law.'[112]

The final section of the chapter will consider how these findings may impact upon the new initiative to draft a treaty on business and human rights, which is currently being undertaken.

9.4 Impact on the New Treaty on Business and Human Rights

In order to link the question of jurisdiction and the obligation to protect, there are a number of different issues that need to be connected. The ECtHR has confirmed that jurisdiction is not uniquely territorial, and this is indeed in line with the common understanding of jurisdiction in international law, which accepts that prescriptive jurisdiction does not have territorial limitations, as long as it is exercised in accordance with international law.[113] Thus, states are free to legislate or otherwise regulate for the conduct of TNCs when operating abroad. It is the right of states to include whatever they want in the legislation regulating the establishment or incorporation of businesses within their national legislative setting. This right to regulate was also confirmed in the commentary to the UNGP, as referred to above.[114] However, the right to regulate does not necessarily imply an obligation to regulate. Therefore, the understanding of jurisdiction as not preventing regulation is important, but not sufficient to generate an obligation. The source of such obligation is found in the tripartite classification of human rights obligations combined with the interpretation of the reach of the rights guaranteed in the various human rights treaties. As has been demonstrated above, the ECtHR and the UN human rights bodies are increasingly accepting that the obligation to protect includes obligations that go beyond the national physical borders of a ratifying state.

De Schutter argues that the human rights obligation to protect includes the obligation for states to ensure that TNCs do not breach human rights of individuals when they operate in a country other than their home state.[115] He criticises the weak formulation of the UNGP in this regard, and holds that a new legally binding

[112] Maastricht Principles on States' Extraterritorial Obligations in the area of Economic, Social and Cultural Rights, adopted by a group of experts in Maastricht in September 2011, http://www.etoconsortium.org/nc/en/main-navigation/library/maastricht-principles/?tx_drblob_pi1%5BdownloadUid%5D=23, accessed 27 January 2017, Preamble; See also De Schutter et al. 2012.

[113] According to Dixon and McCorquodale: '[a]s a general rule, a State's prescriptive jurisdiction is unlimited and a State may legislate for any matter irrespective of where it occurs (even if in the territory of another State) or the nationality of persons involved. [...] Enforcement jurisdiction is, on the other hand, generally considered to be territorial' (Dixon and McCorquodale 2000, at 281).

[114] UNGP, at 3–4.

[115] De Schutter 2016, at 45.

instrument could clarify and be explicit on the extraterritorial reach of the obligation to protect.[116] If included, the new treaty will confirm existing obligations and make them explicit, rather than breaking new ground in human rights obligations.

Explicit recognition will normalise extraterritorial obligations even further than what they are now. There is still much state opposition to accepting these obligations, and making them explicit will demystify them and bring them into mainstream human rights discourse. The distinction between prescriptive and enforcement jurisdiction in relationship to regulation of TNCs will be useful in explaining what is expected of states in this context. To prescribe regulation of conduct for TNCs over which a state exercises authority no matter where these businesses operate is clearly within the jurisdiction of the home state. To enforce such regulation in situations where the host state fails to do so is also within the jurisdiction of the home state.

Furthermore, an inclusion of the obligation to protect (domestically as well as extraterritorially) will provide for the state's central role in ensuring that TNCs and other businesses do not violate human rights. One of the dangers with the proposed new treaty could be that the role of the state is taken out of the equation, and that the TNCs are given direct obligations based on the treaty only. In this respect, states may feel that they have done what they need to do to protect individuals from human rights violations carried out by the TNCs just by ratifying the treaty, and then leave it up to the TNCs and whatever implementation structures will be provided for in the treaty to deal with violations of human rights by TNCs. Thus, by including the state and its obligations to regulate the conduct of the TNCs over which they exercise home-state jurisdiction explicitly, the treaty will ensure that states may be held accountable if they fail to regulate the conduct of TNCs and to hold these TNCs to such standards. This does not mean that TNCs may not be held directly accountable under the terms of the treaty; a combination of direct and indirect accountability of TNCs could be possible within one treaty in the same sense of subsidiarity as is employed in the Statute of the International Criminal Court.[117]

As has been argued throughout this chapter, the acceptance of extraterritorial obligations as part of already exciting human rights treaties is now commonly the case of the bodies implementing and supervising international human rights treaties. By making this explicit in the text of the new treaty it will not revolutionise human rights law, but it will bring universal protection forward. The fact that states may initially oppose this concept explicitly in a treaty does not mean that it is not already recognised in international law. After all, international human rights law aims to regulate the conduct of states, and has traditionally been altering the practice of states in how they treat individuals. The obligations that this legal regime carry will by necessity curtail the freedom of manoeuvre of states. It is therefore to be expected that they oppose what at times is perceived to be adding more obligations

---

[116] Ibid.

[117] 1998 Rome Statute of the International Criminal Court, 2187 UNTS 3, Article 17.

upon them. Consequently, it is necessary to emphasise that these are obligations that come from the object and purpose of the treaties they have already ratified. The globalization that has taken place over the past few decades makes a strengthening of the protection of individuals from human rights abuses committed both by states and non-state actors imperative. By including such obligations explicitly in the new treaty, the drafters can ensure that it remains relevant for the lives people lead in the twenty-first century.

9.5 Conclusions

International human rights law is dynamic and needs to respond to changing societal realities. Human rights treaties have been recognised as living instruments by courts and academics.[118] The recognition that human rights obligations may be extended to individuals other than those within the territorial boundaries of a state, has been developing over the past few decades. The work of the UN human rights bodies demonstrates that the extraterritorial application of the universal human rights treaties is now an integral part of their operations.

However, by emphasising that extraterritorial obligations are only relevant in exceptional circumstances, the ECtHR gives the impression that applying such obligations does not represent 'business as usual', but rather that it is only on rare occasions that states need to consider the effect of their decisions or actions, or omissions, on the human rights enjoyment of individuals beyond their borders. While the content of obligations may be of an extraterritorial nature, the use of such terminology by the Court may in fact underscore an exceptionalism that is not a reality in law. As has been demonstrated, the ECtHR and other international bodies now find, in a large variety of situations, that states can be held accountable for conduct beyond their borders, and the 'exceptional' seems to have become 'common practice'. This reality should be reflected in the new treaty on business and human rights.

References

Beckler RW, Kirtland MH (2003) Extraterritorial Application of U.S. Antitrust Law: What Is a 'Direct, Substantial, and Reasonably Foreseeable Effect' Under the Foreign Trade Antitrust Improvements Act? Texas International Law Journal 38:11–25

Çali B (2014) Specialized Rules of Treaty Interpretation: Human Rights. In: Hollis DB (ed) The Oxford Guide to Treaties. Oxford University Press, Oxford, pp 525–547

De Schutter O (2016) Towards a New Treaty on Business and Human Rights. Business and Human Rights Journal 1(1):41–67

[118] Moeckli and White 2016.

De Schutter O, Eide A, Khalfan A, Orellana M, Salomon ME, Seiderman I (2012) Commentary to the Maastricht Principles on Extraterritorial Obligations of States in the Area of Economic, Social and Cultural Rights. Human Rights Quarterly 34(4):1084–1169

Dixon M, McCorquodale R (2000) Cases and Materials on International Law, 3rd edn. Blackstone Press, Oxford

Gibney M (2013) On Terminology: Extraterritorial Obligations. In: Langford M, Vandenhole W, Martin S, van Genugten W (eds) Global Justice, State Duties: The Extra-Territorial Scope of Economic, Social and Cultural Rights in International Law. Cambridge University Press, Cambridge, pp 32–47

Jonas DS, Saunders TM (2010) The Object and Purpose of a Treaty: Three Interpretive Methods. Vanderbilt Journal of Transnational Law 43, 3:565–608

Knox JH (2010) Diagonal Environmental Rights. In: Gibney M, Skogly S (eds) Universal Human Rights and Extraterritorial Obligations. University of Pennsylvania Press, Philadelphia, pp 82–103

Moeckli D, White ND (2016) Treaties as 'Living Instruments'. In: Bowman M, Kritsiotis D (eds) Conceptual and Contextual Perspectives on the Modern Law of Treaties. Cambridge University Press, Cambridge. Forthcoming

Salomon ME (2007) Global Responsibility for Human Rights: World Poverty and the Development of International Law. Oxford University Press, Oxford

Skogly S (2010) Extraterritoriality: Universal Human Rights Without Universal Obligations. In: Joseph S, Adam M (eds) Research Handbook on International Human Rights Law. Edward Elgar, Cheltenham/Northampton, pp 71–96

The Global Initiative for Economic, Social and Cultural Rights (2015) Human Rights Law Sources: UN Pronouncements on Extra-Territorial Obligations. Concluding Observations, General Comments and Recommendations, Special Procedures, UPR Recommendations. Working Paper. http://globalinitiative-escr.org/wp-content/uploads/2015/11/151027-Human-Rights-Law-Sources-ETOs.pdf. Accessed 23 January 2017

Chapter 10
Citizenship at Home and Across Borders

Ernst M.H. Hirsch Ballin

Abstract This chapter focuses on citizenship as an increasingly important aspect of the relationship between international law and the delineation of territories. Traditionally, nation-states are tilted towards an identification of their established population with its nationality. In times of rapidly growing migration and border-crossing relations, this identification is under pressure and requires additional—often contested—rules about acquisition and loss of citizenship. At first sight, increasing hyper-connectivity on a global scale would seem to diminish the importance of territoriality for citizenship. However, a re-assessment of the importance of citizenship for the realization of fundamental rights supports paradoxically a connection of citizenship with the territoriality of a democratic society. The notion of citizenship has to be reconnected to that of territory, but in a different manner than in the past. The territorial state provides the constitutional setting for citizenship free from ethnic privileges and prejudices. This means that the state should constitute the democratic home for people who participate in its social, economic and cultural life.

Keywords Citizenship · Territoriality · Nationality · Human rights · Democracy · Migration

Contents

Distinguished University Professor (Tilburg University), President of the Asser Institute for International and European Law, and Professor of Human Rights Law (University of Amsterdam).

E.M.H. Hirsch Ballin (✉)
Asser Institute, The Hague, The Netherlands
e-mail: E.HirschBallin@asser.nl

M. Kuijer and W. Werner (eds.), *Netherlands Yearbook of International Law 2016*, Netherlands Yearbook of International Law 47,
DOI 10.1007/978-94-6265-207-1_10

10.1 Introduction

The present chapter focuses on citizenship as an increasingly important aspect of the relationship between international law and the delineation of territories. This relationship is much less simple than the 'political' geography of atlas maps, where each state is identified as a delineated territory, apparently the sole determinant of the extension of 'domestic' legal systems. But that is not really new. Application of foreign law on the basis of international private law or trade agreements, the former so-called concessions, and extraterritorial powers have always interfered with the notion of exclusive jurisdiction of a state within the borders of its 'own' territory. Supranational powers of international organizations have made more inroads on the supposedly exclusive jurisdiction of sovereign states. That does not mean that territory is unimportant. In the end, states reserve the legitimate power to use force within their territory for themselves, including the power to enforce—or not to enforce—decisions legitimately given by foreign authorities concerning actions on their territory.

According to general theories of the state as well as international law theories of recognition, the state can be defined as the political structure holding effective power in a defined territory over a permanent population.[1] These theories assume—mostly tacitly—that the population coincides mainly with the people who are the subjects or nationals of this state. Citizenship is the default legal status of individuals who belong to the nation of any 'nation-state'. Non-citizens or aliens are viewed as persons who are only temporarily subjected to the authority of the state where they are residing or on visit, or maybe illegally staying (until either having been admitted or obliged to leave). Aliens, although temporarily under the authority

[1] According to Article 1 of the 1933 Montevideo Convention on the Rights and Duties of States, 165 LNTS 19, signed 26 December 1933, '[t]he state as a person of international law should possess the following qualifications: (a) a permanent population; (b) a defined territory; (c) government; and (d) capacity to enter into relations with the other states'.

of that state, maintain a subsistent legal bond with the state of their nationality—unless they are stateless—, which entitles them when necessary to consular and diplomatic, and in the past also military (see the pretexts for several nineteenth century wars) protection.

This chapter deals with the dynamic relation between citizenship and territoriality. Traditionally, nation-states are tilted towards an identification of their established population with its nationality. In times of rapidly growing migration (including temporary migration) and border-crossing relations, this identification is under pressure and requires additional—often contested—rules about acquirement and loss of citizenship. At first sight, growing hyper-connectivity on a global scale would diminish the importance of territoriality for citizenship. However, a re-assessment of the importance of citizenship for the realization of fundamental rights supports paradoxically a connection of citizenship with the territoriality of a democratic society.

In this chapter, the expressions 'nationals' and 'citizens' will be used as legally synonymous, but with different connotations about the meaning of the relation between person and state. Following the comparative law study by Rubenstein and Lenagh-Maguire[2] the term 'citizenship' is preferred here because of its explicit relation with fundamental rights, but other legal scholars prefer to use 'nationality' to denote a legal status. 'Nationality' evokes associations with a 'nation-state' that decides on this status by virtue of its 'sovereignty', whereas 'citizenship' refers to the legal status of a citizen of a polity.[3]

This is more than a mere question of terminology. In this chapter, the view will be developed that a human rights approach to citizenship will have to be grounded in an understanding of what it effectively means to be members of a specific commonwealth, sharing a territory as their place to live. It is in this territory where they create and accept rules governing their societies and the use of resources. Therefore, the notion of citizenship has to be reconnected to that of territory, but in a different manner than in the past: not anymore in the sense that boundaries delineate the powers of the rulers, but in the sense that they circumscribe the primary field within which citizens share rights and responsibilities.

10.2 From Subjects to Citizens

Notwithstanding the shift in international law to a more open concept of actorship (including persons in their own right,[4] 'either in terms of "belonging" [...] or as a desire for autonomy and freedom')[5] states continue to be its foremost authors and

[2] Rubenstein and Lenagh-Maguire 2011.

[3] Hirsch Ballin 2014, at 71.

[4] Hirsch Ballin 1995.

[5] Koskenniemi 2012, at 58.

actors. In the words of MacCormick, '[t]he state is primarily a political entity, characterized by territoriality and stability in government. That is, a state has territory, and exercises effective government in that territory over the population, all or most of whom are citizens of the state.'[6] States exercise external and internal sovereignty.[7] The relation between these two aspects of sovereignty is the basis of the international legal doctrines on jurisdiction. From the external viewpoint of scholars of international law, 'the law of jurisdiction is dominantly an inter-state matter—individuals and corporations being treated as "objects" rather than right-holders.'[8] From the internal viewpoint of constitutional scholars, 'difficulties of coordinating multiple jurisdictions' within one state or even 'within the component units of governance' arise.[9] These are two sides of the same coin, i.e. of the concept that specifies the *extension* of legitimate normative decisions in a legal order.

The territoriality principle is the backbone of contemporary jurisdiction theories. 'As a rule, a state has jurisdiction over everything materialising in its territory.'[10] Territory is the spatial extension of jurisdiction of a state.[11] The international legal doctrine of 'territorial' jurisdiction is complemented by three other principles: two principles of specific jurisdiction, i.e. the personality or nationality principle and the protection principle, and the universality principle. Simma and Müller remind us of the historical fact that 'the jurisdiction of sovereigns over "their people" [is] older than over their territory, as personal jurisdiction dates back to the time before the emergence of the modern territorial state.'[12] In the old times, individuals were the 'subjects' of their sovereign and remained subordinated to them wherever they might go, of wherever the sovereign might order them to go, following his commands, for example on war.

The younger territoriality principle has gained precedence over the other principles. That was the result of the ability, developed in the late Middle Ages, to delineate and organize territories, at first as feudal states, followed by dynastic states, and since the 18th century territorial (including dynastical-territorial) states.[13] This historical process was decisively stimulated by the growing importance, since the late Middle Ages, of towns and cities, which 'broke free from the world of feudalism' and its 'network of personal relations'.[14] Since then public powers have been depersonalized. Allegiance of the subjects to the ruler—often the

---

[6] MacCormick 1999, at 17.

[7] Troper 2012.

[8] Crawford and Koskenniemi 2012, at 9.

[9] Halberstam 2012, at 589 and 591.

[10] Simma and Müller 2012.

[11] Koja 1993, at 17.

[12] Simma and Müller 2012, at 141–142.

[13] Lesaffer 2009, at 382.

[14] Ibid., at 233. Serfs who sheltered for a year and a day in a medieval city became free citizens ('Stadtluft macht frei'); see Hirsch Ballin 2014, at 4.

hereditary prince of their tribe or nation—was step by step replaced by an allegiance to an abstract entity: the state, in ceremonies and oath taking often represented by (but no longer identified with) the head of state. Being the subject of the tribe's or nation's ruler was transformed into being the national of a state, whilst the 'state was identified with its territory.'[15]

This transformation also entailed a juridification of the bond: the 'natural' relation within a tribe or nation through 'bloodlines' and specific tribal traditions gave way to a legal bond between the state and its subjects or nationals. Since the nineteenth century, in the course of emancipation and democratization, this was followed by a transformation from *nationality* in subordination to the state, to *citizenship* endowed with voice in public affairs and reciprocal rights. This transformation was certainly not an easy-going transition, but a struggle of ideas and power that in many parts of the world has not yet come to an end. In this chapter, I will focus on the latter transformation, which is at present supported but also complicated by a differentiated time-space identification of people in our times.

In contemporary democratic theory, the legitimacy of a state depends on the voice and rights of its citizens. Citizenship is, however, definitely not despotism upside down. In a democracy governed by the rule of law, the idea of citizenship is that of a *reciprocal* bond between persons and society, with rights and responsibilities as characteristic elements resulting in freedom and solidarity. Citizenship is the membership of a commonwealth, governed on their behalf on the conditions and according to the procedures enshrined in the constitution. The ethnic origins of bonds between rulers and rules may be superseded by this idea of citizenship, but transformed into a sort of inherited cultural identity expressed in habits and traditions, they are still alive as a source of emotional allegiance. Recent and contemporary history has evidenced how politicians can play the ethnical card against minorities and immigrants.

10.3 The Relation Between Territory and Citizenship

In the life of nomadic peoples, bloodlines were the only reliable criterion for allegiance and inclusion. The territorially delineated state (see above, para 2) was the effect of the historical transformation that induced tribes or peoples, after having become sedentary, to accept geographical borders between the territories of the rulers who emerged from the successes of their armies. These borders increasingly included a mixture of peoples that—at least initially—had been subjugated by the most powerful people.

The borders between these in many cases multi-ethnic states have often been redrawn after wars and peace negotiations, but became gradually more permanent. The borders in Africa were drawn arbitrarily at the Berlin Conference of 1884–1885

[15] Ibid., at 383.

by the colonial power and were mainly left unchanged when the *uti possidetis* principle was applied to the decolonization process, i.e. the principle to respect previously accepted borders. Likewise, the present state borders in the Middle East are mainly the result of the infamous Sykes-Picot agreement of 1916.[16] The Declaration adopted at the Conference on Security and Co-operation in Europe in 1975 confirmed the principle of territorial integrity with respect to the post-war borders in Europe. Since the twentieth century, all over the world borders are more stable than ever before.

This shift from tribal to territorial states came with the ability to measure time and space.[17] Territorial states were organized with written rules and instructions, hierarchies and boundaries.[18] Only gradually, the territorial state began to identify itself with a more or less congruent nation, at first by adopting a distinctive official language, but since the nineteenth century—in Germany especially under the influence of romanticism—also in an ethnical sense.[19] This identification as a nation was often a mixture of pre-existing socio-cultural realities and deliberate construction for political purposes and power games.[20] '[T]he state sovereignty of today's international system is […] defined by a particular collection of ideas and practices of political authority: specifically, territorial demarcation and mutual exclusion.'[21]

This transformation entailed a change in the understanding of what it means to be a 'nation'. Its original meaning referred to a shared ethnic identity, whereas the actual meaning refers to a shared fate within a constitutional structure based on recognized power within a certain territory. The osmosis between the two is apparent in the nowadays widely used expression 'nation-state', which was first used less than a century ago.[22] It was at that time when 'the recently consolidated territorial state was transformed into the territorial *nation*-state'.[23] In the English language, 'nation' means both a people and a state. Although other languages like French, German and Spanish might also use the word *nation*, *Nation*, *nación* in both senses, preferably different expressions are used, e.g. or *peuple* and *état*, *Volk* and *Staat*, *pueblo* and *estado*. Since the bond between state and people can no longer be determined by 'natural' criteria of belonging to a tribe,[24] nationality had to be redefined as a legal status that is subject to the sovereign power of a specific state, with a cultural—and therefore developing—connotation, replacing the former natural connotation. According to MacCormick, 'nations in the "civic" sense are

[16] McMeekin 2013.

[17] Crosby 1997; Branch 2014.

[18] Glenn 2013, at 63.

[19] Ibid., at 93.

[20] Judson and Rozenbilt 2005.

[21] Branch 2014, at 19.

[22] According to the Oxford English Dictionary (see Glenn 2013, at 92) for the first time in 1918.

[23] Branch 2014, at 96.

[24] Leerssen 2010; Leerssen 2011.

communities of a certain kind [...]. They are cultural, but not necessarily ethnic, communities of persons conscious of their attachment to a country (a geographical space) and its civic institutions and culture as historically evolved parts of human social reality.'[25]

Nationality laws specify the criteria for acquirement of this status.[26] The supposedly 'normal' situation and most common criterion for recognition as a national of the state, is birth on the territory of the state as the child of a parent who is a national of the same state. The introduction of the concept of 'autochthon' inhabitants of the Netherlands—at first for statistical purposes, but subsequently included in a growingly xenophobic public discourse—reflects the prejudice that people born on Dutch territory from parents who were themselves also born on Dutch territory meet conditions of normalcy; everybody else is an 'allochthon', a sort of second-hand Dutchman.[27]

Supplemental criteria extend nationality—either *ex jure* or based on an individual decision—also to persons who have been born abroad from parents who are nationals of that state (sometimes with additional requirements), to persons who have been born on the state's territory from foreign parents, and/or to persons who marry a national living with him/her on the territory of the state. Acquirement of the nationality by a separate decision is usually based on factual integration of legally residing foreigners in the society of the state concerned, sometimes under the condition that they give up their existing nationality. Traditionally, states that welcome immigrants prioritize in their legislation and policies the place where someone usually lives, whereas emigrant nations usually prioritize descendancy ('blood lines') because they want to keep a legal bond with the departed sons and daughters of their nation. Latin expressions summarize the first approach as nationality law based on the *ius soli* ('law of the soil'), and the latter as based on the *ius sanguinis* ('law of the blood').[28]

In these laws, states manifest their sovereignty as the power to decide which (classes of) persons will be recognized as nationals and which not, a view that originated from a naturalistic or authoritarian view on the relation between state authority and its subjects. This view was expressed in the famous *Nottebohm* case: '[...] nationality is a legal bond having as its basis a social fact of attachment, a genuine connection of existence, interests and sentiments, together with the existence of reciprocal rights and duties.'[29]

One problematic aspect of the *Nottebohm* doctrine is the implicit view that a state is almost free to decide who it will include in its nationals; Liechtenstein overstepped this freedom because of the absence of a real bond between this state and Mr. Nottebohm. Another blind spot in the judgement in this case was that

[25] MacCormick 1999, at 182.

[26] de Groot 1989.

[27] de Jong 2010.

[28] See the overview in Bauböck et al. 2006.

[29] *Nottebohm (Liechtenstein v Guatemala)*, ICJ, Second Phase, Judgement, 6 April 1955, at 4.

Mr. Nottebohm—being a man who had lived outside Germany most of his life—was at risk to be disenfranchised and even detained as an 'enemy subject' because of the German warfare against the allied forces.

Ten years before the Nottebohm judgement was pronounced, the Universal Declaration of Human Rights (UDHR)[30] had already recognized the right to a nationality in Article 15:

(1) Everyone has the right to a nationality.
(2) No one shall be arbitrarily deprived of his nationality nor denied the right to change his nationality.

However, without any criterion as to *which* state has to fulfil this obligation, this 'right' offers little protection, even if it were included in the International Covenant on Civil and Political Rights (ICCPR) (*quod non*): it merely protects against de-nationalization. The ICCPR does, however, include the right to acquire a nationality for every child[31] and the right not to be arbitrarily deprived of the right to enter one's own country.[32] Specific treaties also offer protection against unwilling loss of citizenship, for example Articles 5–9 of the 1961 Convention on the Reduction of Statelessness (1961 Convention),[33] as well as Article 8(2) of the Convention on the Rights of the Child (CRC).[34] At the regional level for example the American Convention on Human Rights (ACHR)[35] ensures the right to a nationality and protects against arbitrary deprivation thereof.[36] Furthermore, the European Convention on Nationality (ECN) provides for rules on the loss of nationality *ex lege* or at the initiative of a State Party.[37] In its judgement in the *Rottmann* case,[38] the European Court of Justice accepted that under domestic law of the Member

[30] 1948 Universal Declaration of Human Rights, UNGA Resolution 217 A (III), UN Doc A/810 91 (UDHR).

[31] 1966 International Covenant on Civil and Political Rights, 999 UNTS 171 (ICCPR), Article 23 (4).

[32] Article 12(4) ICCPR, which relates to nationality, as this is a right that is generally associated with this status. This right recognizes the special relationship of a person to that country, see also UN Human Rights Committee, General Comment No. 27, Article 12 (Freedom of Movement), UN Doc CCPR/C/21/Rev.1/Add.9, 2 November 1999.

[33] 1961 Convention on the Reduction of Statelessness 1989 UNTS 175.

[34] 1989 Convention on the Rights of the Child, 1577 UNTS 3.

[35] 1969 American Convention on Human Rights, 1144 UNTS 123.

[36] To some extent, one can see similar developments in the context of the 1950 European Convention for the Protection of Human Rights and Fundamental Freedoms, ETS 5 (ECHR) when looking at the case law of the European Court of Human Rights regarding Article 8 ECHR (cf. *Karassev v Finland*, ECtHR, Decision on Admissibility, No 31414/96, 12 January 1999, and ensuing case law).

[37] 1997 European Convention on Nationality, ETS 166 (ECN), Article 7.

[38] *Case C-135/08 (Janko Rottmann v Freistaat Bayern)* ECJ Grand chamber, Judgement, ECLI: EU:C:2010:104, 2 March 2010.

States, decisions about denationalization would have to meet the requirement of proportionality with a view of the possible consequences for European citizenship.

This means that the 'birthright lottery'[39] produces privileges for those persons who have been born in the territory of the state where they later on still prefer to live. If however love, career, war or other facts of life necessitate migration to a different country, they will have to meet additional criteria. Their 'original' citizenship may even be a burden, instead of a benefit. Under recently proposed Dutch legislation (already adopted by the Second Chamber of Parliament, the Dutch House of Representatives),[40] Dutch fighters in terrorist organisations like Da'esh, as far as they carry with them a second citizenship (in the case of some nationalities, including that of Morocco, even without the possibility to renounce it) can be confronted with denaturalization. This amounts to an additional punishment that single-nationality Dutch fighters will not have to fear. Similar initiatives were taken in several other western countries.[41] These proposals have rightly been criticized because of the ensuing unequal treatment of 'dual-citizens' compared to 'mono-citizens'.[42]

Taken together, all the legally binding norms about nationality point in the same direction: the law as it stands favours the *status quo* of citizenship as a result of intergenerational domiciliation within the territory of the state above an adaptation to changed circumstances.

10.4 Three Major Trends in the Understanding of Citizenship

Three major trends point in the direction that the implicit preference for nationality on the basis of intergenerational domiciliation needs to be supplemented or even replaced by a different anchor point. The need to do so is the more obvious since technical and social advancement on the one hand, and extreme situations of poverty, violence and need on the other hand have created a situation of ongoing migration, especially to the cities and urbanized parts of the world.[43]

---

[39] Shachar 2009.

[40] The Dutch Senate [Eerste Kamer] is currently considering this proposal, see Kamerstuk, Wijziging van de Rijkswet op het Nederlanderschap in verband met het intrekken van het Nederlanderschap in het belang van de nationale veiligheid. *Kamerstukken I* 2015-16 34356-(R2064) No. A.

[41] van Waas 2016.

[42] Ibid., at 481–482.

[43] See also Soysal 1994.

10.4.1 From Nationality to Citizenship

In the first place, democratic development has transformed the nature of nationality. Instead of being the subjects of their sovereign, present-day citizens co-decide on the laws that bind them. The origins of this transformation go back to the time of the French Revolution, when in 1789 the rights of the citizen were juxtaposed to the rights of man: the *Déclaration des Droits de l'Homme et du Citoyen* (Declaration of the Rights of Man and of the Citizen) passed by France's National Constituent Assembly in August 1789. At that time women and slaves were still excluded, but a lengthy and often painful process of democratization had started. The result, after many more years of struggle, was an inversion of the relation between state and nationals. Instead of subjects (German *Untertanen*, Dutch *onderdanen*, i.e. subordinated persons), citizens have as a result of the human rights revolution become the 'owners' of authority and the collective source of legitimacy. Citizenship is a constitutional institution which—through political rights—transfers the decisive role from inherited 'sovereigns' and ruling classes to the people: 'We the people' in the preamble of the Constitution of the United States has become a shibboleth for a democratic constitution—or constitutions which falsely pretend to be democratic. Several human rights treaties now protect the right of citizens to vote and to be elected (see the right to free elections in Article 3 of Protocol 1 ECHR,[44] Article 25 ICCPR, Article 7 of the Convention on the Elimination of All Forms of Discrimination against Women (CEDAW),[45] etc.) The missing link is, however, the entitlement to be a citizen with these fundamental rights.

10.4.2 Rising Importance of Extraterritorial Citizenship

In the second place, emigration has resulted in the continued presence of nationals who live in a different state but nevertheless wish to maintain a bond with the state where they come from, where their families may live and to which they in some cases—possibly dependent on life events—want to be able to return. Therefore they do not want to be deprived from their original citizenship. Many states accept the continuation of their original citizenship, even if they are naturalized by their new state of residence. Especially well-established democracies extend the rights to vote and to be elected to their diaspora,[46] either limited to a certain period of time after their emigration, or, like the United States and since 1986 the Netherlands, indefinitely. This extends the practical significance of extraterritorial citizenship. In

[44] 1952 Protocol 1 to the European Convention for the Protection of Human Rights and Fundamental Freedoms, ETS 9.

[45] 1979 Convention on the Elimination of All Forms of Discrimination Against Women, 1249 UNTS 13.

[46] Pildes 2012.

general, the acceptance by the receiving states that immigrants might wish (and have good reasons) to keep their original citizenship next to the acquired citizenship of their new home, has increased. Aleinikoff and Klusmeyer see 'an emerging international consensus that the goal is no longer to reduce plural nationality as an end in itself, but to manage it as an inevitable feature of an increasingly interconnected and mobile world.'[47] In recent years, however, anti-immigrant feelings have resulted in a political wish to require renouncing the existing citizenship before being accepted as a citizen in the new home country. Dutch politics has struggled with this subject since 25 years.[48]

The recognition of emigrants as (still) citizens, therefore often called 'expatriates',[49] was in several countries a reason to extend voting rights to them. Italy has as a result of an amendment in 2000 to Article 48 of the Constitution a separate electoral 'district' for Italians abroad.[50] This apparent reinforcement of the democratic voice for citizens is, however, not unproblematic from the viewpoint of legislation as collective autonomy of the citizens: expatriates have an interest with respect to public services and taxation that is different from that of the people who reside in the country where the elected representatives will decide on laws and policies.

Extension of extraterritorial citizenship like that to Slovaks and Romanians of Hungarian language and descent is also problematic.[51] It could serve as the first step in an expansionist or revisionist policy toward neighbour countries. The United States were right when they sought to fight tax evasion by their citizens with banking accounts abroad, but the extension of taxation in the Foreign Account Tax Compliance Act (2010) to people who legally and really live abroad was a step too far. This extension of tax jurisdiction exceeds the necessities of a division of work between states according to generally accepted standards for extraterritorial jurisdiction,[52] which preferably should be regulated through bilateral or multilateral treaties.

Jurisdiction, liability and democratic voice should preferably follow the same pattern, primarily on a territorial basis. Recognizing that retaining the citizenship of someone's country of origin is legitimate (and with respect to travelling to visit family and property in that country even almost necessary), the extension of citizens' rights to decisions on legislation might be detrimental to a balanced outcome of the democratic process.

---

[47] Aleinikoff and Klusmeyer 2001 at 87.

[48] Hirsch Ballin 2014; Adviescommissie voor Vreemdelingenzaken (Advisory Committee on Migration Affairs, ACVZ) (2008), Nederlanderschap in een Onbegrensde Wereld. Advies over het Nederlandse Beleid Inzake Meervoudige Nationaliteit (Dutch Citizenship in a Borderless World. Opinion on the Dutch Policy on Multiple Nationality), https://acvz.org/wp-content/uploads/2015/06/Advies-ACVZ-NR27-2008.pdf, accessed 10 February 2017.

[49] Cf. the use of this expression by Orr 2008.

[50] Malfatti et al. 2011, at 101–112.

[51] Hirsch Ballin 2014, at 68.

[52] Avi-Yonah 2002.

10.4.3 Necessity to Avoid Intraterritorial Non-Citizenship

In the third place, immigration—which has to be distinguished from visits of tourists, tradesmen and others for a short period—has created the presence of a sometimes large number of non-citizens who find and make themselves a new home in their state of residence. Refugees and other immigrants coming from a different state have the nationality of their state of origin or no nationality at all. In some cases these immigrants share the situation of non-citizenship with other—maybe already over generations—resident people belonging to deprived population groups, possibly in the unfortunate condition of statelessness. This intraterritorial non-citizenship is often detrimental to equal treatment with respect to social and economic rights. These adverse effects are mitigated by the tendency that—according to Glenn—'[t]he actual legal use of citizenship as a criterion for benefits or entitlements has [...] declined in most states, while more cosmopolitan notions of domicile or residence (requiring no grant of conferment by a state) have become more frequent in application.'[53] For this reason naturalization procedures and the meaning of the human right to have a nationality have to be reviewed (i.e. Article 15 UDHR).

Xenophobic political movements are well aware of the integrative power of citizenship. They reverse the game with the introduction of additional barriers for the acquisition of citizenship, adding sometimes even unreasonable criteria. Their scenario is that of creating legal separation walls between the 'autochthonous' insiders and immigrants. Such a negative instrumentalisation gives citizenship a Janus head.[54]

10.5 A Human Rights Approach to Citizenship

Because of the unjust disadvantages for people who—as immigrants and children of immigrants—have become effectively participating *de facto* citizens, I propose to convert Article 15 UDHR into a really effective and enforceable human right. That requires the identification of the state that has to accept the person concerned as a citizen. Criteria like descent or place of birth are insufficient in an era where many people have a biography that brings them to various places in different episodes of their life.[55] These traditional criteria for the acquisition of nationality—known as *ius sanguinis* and *ius soli*—are both related to facts in the past. Human rights, however, are related to the actual living conditions and the perspectives for a life in dignity. Relating citizenship more closely to the chosen domicile[56] and the effective bonds

[53] Ibid., at 199.

[54] Cf. the Janus-faced nature of citizenship as noted by Butenschøn 2003, at 556.

[55] Weidenhaus 2015.

[56] Cf. Domingo 2010, at 106–107.

with a community appears to be much more appropriate: citizenship based on *ius nexus*, i.e. the presence of a genuine bond.[57] The right to vote and other citizens' rights should reflect their effective relations within a society. An effective step forward could be the inclusion in the human rights framework of the right—under reasonable conditions such as the ability to communicate in the common language—to become a citizen of the state where someone is 'at home', i.e. participates in social and economic life, deploys his activities, lives with his or her family and/or assumes responsibilities like paying taxes and assisting the people near to him or her.

This argument goes beyond the widely accepted insight, developed by Arendt, that without citizenship, an effective protection of human rights is impossible. She has called this the 'right to have rights': 'The fundamental deprivation of human rights is manifested first and above all in the deprivation of a place in the world which makes opinions significant and actions effective.'[58] For that reason, the right to be a citizen is certainly required, but the democratic dimension brings the idea one step further. The notion that citizenship has the dimension of being a participant in the democratic process has already found a partial recognition with the attribution of active and passive voting rights for European citizens in the Member State where they are residing for municipal elections and elections for the European Parliament.[59] A recent proposal by a parliamentary group in Curaçao to restrict voting rights for non-born or recently immigrated inhabitants with the same citizenship[60] clearly infringes upon the fundamental rights of these citizens and amounts to discrimination on the basis of race or origin.[61]

10.6 Reconsideration and Recommendations

These major developments require a reconsideration of the constitutional and legal model of citizenship.

Extraterritorial citizenship (the second development) creates inconsistencies that mirror those of internal non-citizenship. In the first place with respect to the

[57] Shachar 2011, at 115; Hirsch Ballin 2014, at 83.

[58] Arendt 2000, at 37.

[59] 2012 Treaty on the European Union (Consolidated version), C 326/13 (TEU), Articles 9 and 10, which establish EU citizenship and democratic representation, as well as 2012 Treaty on the Functioning of the European Union (Consolidated version), C 326/47 (TFEU), Article 20 regarding the rights and duties of EU citizens, and specifically Article 22 TFEU which arranges the voting rights mentioned above.

[60] See an interview with D. Boersma in the newspaper Amigoe, 18 February 2016, http://www.amigoe.com/curacao/222843-beperking-kiesrecht-europese-nederlanders-in-strijd-met-staatsregeling-en-statuut?format=pdf.

[61] The Kingdom of the Netherlands consists of four autonomous countries in Europe and the Caribbean with a common single nationality and a mainly federalist constitutional structure. Equal rights are also under attack in the Netherlands, where—so far unsuccessful—attempts were made to limit the right of access of citizens from the Caribbean to the European territory of the state.

defective reciprocity of their entitlements and burdens; in the second place with respect to their voice in public affairs, i.e. the right to participate in decision-making on public affairs. As long as all this is with indifference accepted as a consequence of the sovereign right of a state to decide who will be included as citizens, and who not, the legal story would end here. However, since the human story—a story of recognition versus deprivation—does *not* stop here, we have to ask ourselves whether additional legal considerations are required.

The rule that the state's authority over people is limited to its territory and the territorial principle of international jurisdiction is less convincing then before. Increasingly people are connected with others in long distance relations, either as a result of increased possibilities to travel and aspirations to migrate (possibly temporarily), or in a pattern of online connectivity. These developments, according to Branch,

> suggest the theoretical possibility of forms of community that are utterly non-territorial and non-spatial, instead being based on person-to-person ties. Yet the persistent strength of socialization by the 'schoolroom map' – [...] also afterwards in the media and elsewhere – may leave little room for complex, non-cartographic forms of identity, community, and authority to take hold.[62]

Disparities between the extension of citizenship and the reciprocity of entitlements and obligations create tensions and frustrations. Is it just to give a right to co-decide on the composition of the legislature to people who will neither 'suffer' under taxes nor need the state for whose legislature they vote, for protection against, for example, unemployment or violence? And is it fair to make other people dependent on the good will of an electorate of which they are not part, although they are paying taxes like any other inhabitant? We see here over-inclusion at one side, and under-inclusion on the other side.

I suggest therefore a renewal of the conceptual relation between citizenship and territoriality. Ill-judged answers may induce deprivation of emigrants from their (original) citizenship. Life in our times has its episodes, people may be connected to different places at the same time and may have reasons to remigrate at some point of their life.[63] But it would be justified to limit the right to vote to those nationals who at present or in the near future will be the addressees of the legislation on which they co-decide through their vote. Also false, however, is the long-time exclusion from citizens' rights of people who are in that society at home, contribute to the common good, and are able and willing to take up the responsibilities of being a citizen. The full realization of fundamental rights requires a realistic reappraisal of the states through which the law has to be established.

[62] Branch 2014, at 184.

[63] Cf. Weidenhaus 2015.

10.7 Evaluation and Conclusion

The transformations in the understanding of nationality transpire in a shift of terminology. The expression 'citizenship' emphasizes much more than 'nationality' that, in a democratic context under the rule of law, this legal status is not characterized by subjugation (the 'subjects' of the state in an older terminology). On the contrary, a citizen has 'voice' and 'rights' in the constitutional structure of her or his state. This transition is in many parts of the world yet an unaccomplished process with steps forward but also setbacks, here in the Netherlands and elsewhere. Uneasiness about the complex relation between territory and real-life relations in an intensively connected world explains the historical and actual attempts to make territorial, legal and cultural borders coincide. The proponents of this counter-movement seek to diminish situations in which individuals have legal bonds with more than one state and to create culturally homogeneous nations within the territory of their state.

A human rights perspective on the requirements for acquisition and loss of citizenship and on the rights and obligations following from citizenship should accept, in the first place the equal dignity of people whose biography is continuously located at and around a stable centre, and people whose life encompasses different episodes, possibly at different places, in evolving networks, by choice or by necessity. Democratic voice and rights are related to each other. Therefore, a paramount requirement is that disparities between the citizens' right to vote and to be elected and the field of application of laws decided by them or their representatives should have, as much as possible, the same territorial extension.

Secondly, the equality between aliens and citizens with respect to their obligations within one society should be maximized. Persons with a double nationality might be confronted with double obligations for military service or legal systems that overstep the rationale of citizenship for jurisdiction over expatriates. For this reason, extraterritorial personal jurisdiction of a state over its expatriate nationals should be avoided, both with respect to obligations like military service and with respect to limitations on their political freedoms and freedom of expression. International private law should be complemented with law on conflicts of public law. A priority rule for the exercise of jurisdiction should protect expatriates against situations in which they are torn between different legal systems. Paradoxically, the growing interconnectedness of lives across borders requires a prioritization of the territoriality jurisdiction principle for expatriate citizens.

Migration is the most compelling reason to rethink the relation between territoriality and citizenship. In a century where migration is an ongoing process, people who moved to a country, and have effectively become members of their new home country, should not be discriminated against. Citizenship programs and citizenship tests are supposed to encourage integration, with the acquirement of the legal status of citizen as its coronation. Nevertheless, naturalisation is also—the other way around—a gateway to the full realisation of the idea behind citizenship.

> Citizenship is not just a formal legal status, with accompanying rights and obligations. It is also a social role that encompasses a wide variety of everyday activities, ranging from joining neighborhood associations and conservation groups to protesting against government policies that treat some of your fellow citizens (or indeed foreigners) unfairly.[64]

Time has come to recognize a human right to be (i.e. to remain or to become) a citizen in the country where someone is at home.[65]

The state has to accept the voice of its inhabitants, when they have proceeded to being citizens, and the citizens have to accept the decisions that were taken on their behalf within the constitutional framework of the commonwealth that connects them. It is therefore an essential feature of citizenship to belong to a commonwealth organized on a geographically delineated territory, known as a state. That does not exclude the relevance of citizenship or—depending on someone's personal story—a second citizenship as a legally recognized relation with another state. There are no compelling reasons to fight the possibility of extraterritorial citizenship, possibly including dual citizenship; it is, on the contrary, a suitable expression of facts of life. Paradoxically yet, in an era of growing migration and trans-border connectivity, the democratic meaning of citizenship finds its fulfilment within the territoriality of states. The territorial state provides the constitutional setting for citizenship free from ethnic privileges and prejudices. This means that the state should constitute the democratic home for the people who participate in its social, economic and cultural life.

References

Aleinikoff TA, Klusmeyer D (2001) Plural Nationality. Facing the Future in a Migratory World. In: Aleinikoff TA, Klusmeyer D (eds) Citizenship Today. Global Perspectives and Practices. Carnegie Endowment for International Peace, Washington D.C., pp 63–88

Arendt H (2000) The Perplexities of the Rights of Man (from 'The Origins of Totalitarianism', 1951). In: Baehr P (ed) The Portable Hannah Arendt. Penguin Books, New York, pp 31–48

Avi-Yonah RS (2002) National Regulation of Multinational Enterprises: An Essay on Comity, Extraterritoriality, and Harmonization. University of Michigan Public Law Research Paper No. 15. http://ssrn.com/abstract=323224. Accessed 10 February 2017

Bauböck R, Ersbøll E, Groenendijk K, Waldrauch H (eds) (2006) Acquisition and Loss of Nationality: Policies and Trends in 15 European States, vol. I: Comparative Analyses. Amsterdam University Press, Amsterdam

Branch J (2014) The Cartographic State: Maps, Territory, and the Origins of Sovereignty. Cambridge University Press, Cambridge

Butenschøn N (2003) Citizenship and Human Rights. Some Thoughts on a Complex Relationship. In: Bergsmo M (ed) Human Rights and Criminal Justice for the Downtrodden. Essays in Honor of Asbjørn Eide. Martinus Nijhoff Publishers, Leiden, pp 555–570

[64] Miller 2016, at 141.

[65] Hirsch Ballin 2014, Chap. 4.

Crawford J, Koskenniemi M (2012) Introduction. In: Crawford J, Koskenniemi M (eds) The Cambridge Companion to International Law. Cambridge University Press, Oxford, pp 1–21
Crosby AW (1997) The Measure of Reality: Quantification and Western Society, 1250–1600. Cambridge University Press, Cambridge
de Groot GR (1989) Staatsangehörigkeitsrecht im Wandel: Eine Rechtsvergleichende Studie über Erwerbs – und Verlustgründe der Staatsangehörigkeit. Heymanns, Cologne
de Jong L (2010) Being Dutch, More or Less. Rozenberg Publishers, Amsterdam
Domingo R (2010) The New Global Law. Cambridge University Press, Cambridge
Glenn HP (2013) The Cosmopolitan State. Oxford University Press, Oxford
Halberstam D (2012) Federalism: Theory, Policy, Law. In: Rosenfeld M, Sajó A (eds) The Oxford Handbook of Comparative Constitutional Law. Oxford University Press, Oxford, pp 576–608
Hirsch Ballin EMH (1995) Wereldburgers – Personen in het Internationale Recht. W.E.J. Tjeenk Willink, Zwolle
Hirsch Ballin EMH (2014) Citizens' Rights and the Right to Be a Citizen. (Developments in International Law, vol 66). Brill Nijhoff, Leiden
Judson PM, Rozenbilt ML (2005) (eds) Constructing Nationalities in East Central Europe (Austrian and Habsburg Studies). Berghahn, New York/Oxford
Koja F (1993) Allgemeine Staatslehre. Manz, Vienna
Koskenniemi M (2012) International Law in the World of Ideas. In: Crawford J, Koskenniemi M (eds) The Cambridge Companion to International Law. Cambridge University Press, Cambridge, pp 47–63
Leerssen J (2010) National Thought in Europe: A Cultural History. Amsterdam University Press, Amsterdam
Leerssen J (2011) De Bronnen van het Vaderland: Taal, Literatuur en de Afbakening van Nederland 1806–1890. Vantilt, Nijmegen
Lesaffer R (2009) European Legal History: A Cultural and Political Perspective. Cambridge University Press, Cambridge
MacCormick N (1999) Questioning Sovereignty – Law, State, and Nation in the European Commonwealth. Oxford University Press, Oxford
Malfatti E, Pertice A, Rossi E (2011) Manuale di Diritto Costituzionale Italiano ed Europeo, vol. II. Giappichelli Editore, Turin
McMeekin S (2013) The Russian Origins of the First World War. Belknap Press of Harvard University Press, Cambridge/London
Miller D (2016) Strangers in Our Midst: The Political Philosophy of Immigration. Harvard University Press, Harvard
Orr GD (2008) Citizenship, Interests, Community and Expression: Expatriate Voting Rights in Australian Elections. University of Queensland TC Beirne School of Law Research Paper No. 10-04. http://ssrn.com/abstract=1211662. Accessed 10 February 2017
Pildes P (2012) Elections. In: Rosenfeld M, Sajó A (eds) The Oxford Handbook of Comparative Constitutional Law. Oxford University Press, Oxford, pp 528–544
Rubenstein K, Lenagh-Maguire N (2011) Citizenship and the Boundaries of the Constitution. In: Ginsburg T, Dixon R (eds) Comparative Constitutional Law. Edward Elgar, Cheltenham/Northampton, pp 143–169
Shachar A (2009) The Birthright Lottery: Citizenship and Global Inequality. Harvard University Press, Harvard
Shachar A (2011) Earned Citizenship. Property Lesson of Immigration Reform. Yale Journal of Law & the Humanities 23:110–158
Simma B, Müller AT (2012) Exercise and the Limits of Jurisdiction. In: Crawford J, Koskenniemi M (eds) The Cambridge Companion to International Law. Cambridge University Press, Cambridge, pp 134–157
Soysal YN (1994) Limits of Citizenship: Migrants and Postnational Membership in Europe. The University of Chicago Press, Chicago

Troper M (2012) Sovereignty. In: Rosenfeld M, Sajó A (eds) The Oxford Handbook of Comparative Constitutional Law. Oxford University Press, Oxford, pp 350–369

van Waas L (2016) Foreign Fighters and the Deprivation of Nationality. In: de Guttry A, Capone F, Paulussen C (eds) Foreign Fighters under International Law and Beyond. TMC Asser Press, The Hague, pp 469–487

Weidenhaus G (2015) Soziale Raumzeit. Suhrkamp Verlag, Berlin

Chapter 11
Territoriality and Asylum Law: The Use of Territorial Jurisdiction to Circumvent Legal Obligations and Human Rights Law Responses

Hemme Battjes

Abstract The framework for refugee protection established around 1950 seemed to be essentially territorial. In this chapter, the ways in which states redefined entry into territory and indeed territory itself in order to accommodate schemes for migration control and to limit refugee law obligations is explored, as well how states, drawing on the notion that refugee law applies within the territory, set up border controls away from their borders. Furthermore, the responses of human rights treaty monitoring bodies are analysed - both as regards the redefinitions of borders and territory, as well as regards extraterritorial acts. The picture is mixed: on the one hand human rights law did develop constraints on state actions, on the other hand the notion of territoriality limits alternative human rights law approaches to define state responsibility.

Keywords Refugee · Territory · Human rights · Jurisdiction · Extraterritorial · Non-refoulement

Contents

H. Battjes (✉)
Faculty of Law, VU Amsterdam, Amsterdam, The Netherlands
e-mail: h.battjes@vu.nl

M. Kuijer and W. Werner (eds.), *Netherlands Yearbook of International Law 2016*, Netherlands Yearbook of International Law 47,
DOI 10.1007/978-94-6265-207-1_11

11.1 Introduction

When shortly after World War II the foundations for the international refugee protection system were laid, the link between asylum and territory seemed obvious. In the 1950 *Asylum* case, the International Court of Justice succinctly addressed the notion of territorial (as opposed to diplomatic) asylum:

> In the case of extradition, the refugee is within the territory of the State of refuge. A decision with regard to extradition implies only the normal exercise of the territorial sovereignty. The refugee is outside the territory of the State where the offence was committed, and a decision to grant him asylum in no way derogates from the sovereignty of that State.[1]

The basis for granting asylum is territorial sovereignty. A corollary of this right is, in the words of the European Court of Human Rights, the states' 'right, as a matter of well-established international law and subject to their treaty obligations [...], to control the entry, residence and expulsion of aliens'.[2] Thus, as sovereign a state has the right and the ability to offer the alien protection on its territory, and to refuse it. An *obligation* to grant protection is an exception to this main rule of state discretion.

One such exception is the Convention Relating to Status of Refugees (RC), adopted 28 July 1951.[3] It lists a catalogue of rights refugees shall enjoy within the territory of the state of refuge. In the preamble the right of states to grant asylum is mentioned, but the instrument does not codify a right to seek and receive asylum.[4] The provision coming closest to it is Article 33:

> No Contracting State shall expel or return ('refouler') a refugee in any manner whatsoever to the frontiers of territories where his life or freedom would be threatened on account of his race [...].

At face value, Article 33 seems to mean that once a refugee reached the territory of a Contracting state he cannot be sent back to territories where he fears persecution. But the link with territory is ambiguous in two respects.

First, Article 33 distinguishes between 'to expel' and 'to return' (*refouler*). Expulsion was (and is) usually assumed to mean 'removal of persons from the

[1] *Asylum case (Colombia/Peru)*, ICJ, Judgment, 20 November 1950, at 274.

[2] *Vilvarajah and others v UK*, ECtHR, Ser. A 215, 30 October 1991; and repeated in about every case since regarding claims to Article 3 ECHR against expulsion. The principle was mentioned well before the *Vilvarajah* judgment—see for the origins of this unwritten rule McKeown 2008.

[3] 1951 Convention Relating to Status of Refugees, UNTS 189, 137 (RC).

[4] Preamble RC: 'considering that the grant of asylum may place unduly heavy burdens on certain countries, and that a satisfactory solution of a problem of which the United Nations has recognized the international scope and nature cannot therefore be achieved without international co-operation'.

territory',[5] and return to mean 'to repulse', 'an act of resistance at the border'.[6] Thus, the provision introduces a distinction between persons 'within the territory' and those 'at the border' of a Contracting state, who might or might not be 'within' the territory. Second, 'return to the frontiers of territories' focuses on the destination of the measure rather than the whereabouts of the refugee, which opens up the possibility that the provision might apply extraterritorially. That extraterritorial obligations as regards asylum were conceivable, was shown by the Resolution adopted by the *Institut du Droit International*, adopted a year before the text of the Refugee Convention was finalized, in its 1950 Bath Session:

> [L]e terme 'asile' désigne la protection qu'un Etat accorde sur son territoire ou dans un autre endroit relevant de certains de ses organes à un individu qui est venu la rechercher.[7]

The 'autres endroits' mentioned were defined in the resolution as embassies, consulates, military ships and airplanes and 'places abroad where the state exercises authority'.[8]

Thus, the *Asylum* case rooted the notion of asylum firmly in territorial sovereignty, yet the Bath definition suggests that obligations as regards asylum may extend to other instances where a state exerts control. Article 33 RC reflects this ambiguity: it links protection to presence on the territory, yet is unclear as to when a person is on the territory for the purposes of protection from refoulement, and leaves open the possibility of extraterritorial application. States have exploited both ambiguities for the purpose of controlling migration. They have in several ways redefined the border, the demarcation line between who is in and who is not in the territory, and attached special control regimes. And they have established control schemes outside the territory, on the assumption that the Refugee Convention and other relevant treaty law does not apply. From the perspective of the Refugee Convention and human rights law, these schemes can be seen as attempts to escape international law obligations. Below, I will discuss these schemes, and how human rights law has at times opposed or reshaped these policies. The chapter does not pretend to give an exhaustive overview of state practices concerning territoriality and refugee law. Rather, examples have been picked that are particularly illustrative for the issue under discussion.

The set-up is as follows. In Sect. 11.2, I discuss various legal practices employed on the state territory, that is migration rules that exploit the notion of the border and

---

[5] Grahl-Madsen 1963, Commentary to Article 33, para (2).

[6] *Sale v Haitian Centers Council*, Supreme Court, 509 U.S. 155 (1993), para 182; cf. Grahl-Madsen 1963, Commentary to Article 33, para (2).

[7] Institut de Droit International (1950) L'asile en droit international public (à l'exclusion de l'asile neutre), Session de Bath, http://justitiaetpace.org/resolutions_chrono.php?start=1947&end=1952, accessed 16 January 2017. This definition is invoked here because a definition in an international treaty is as yet non-existent. A similar link to territory can be found in Article 1(1) of the Draft Convention on Territorial Asylum (ExCom Reports 1974, A/AC.96/508/Add.1), and in Article I of the 1954 Convention on Territorial Asylum (OAS, TS 19).

[8] Article 3(1).

presence in situations that are located within the geographical territory for all or most other purposes than migration law, and how human rights law has responded. In Sect. 11.3, I discuss practices abroad. I address how human rights law developed alternative bases for state responsibility in such situations, and in how far territoriality sets limits on such alternatives (11.3.1). The distinction between acts on territory and abroad is intersected by another one: situations where sea crossings are relevant (Sects. 11.2.2 and 11.3.2) and where they are not (Sects. 11.2.1 and 11.3.3). Sea crossings obviously matter on the high seas and at sea borders, but also in certain cases of overseas territories where the refugee protection regimes apply only partially, or not at all.

11.2 On the Territory

11.2.1 At the Border

11.2.1.1 Rejection

A contested issue, especially in the first decades after the adoption of the Refugee Convention, were obligations at the border, the frontier between the own and the neighbouring state. There were some reasons to assume that rejection was allowed for. The drafters had been unwilling to include an article on admission.[9] Furthermore, during the drafting process, the Dutch and Swiss delegates had let it put on record that the provision applied only to people who had entered the territory;[10] as later commentators have emphasized, they stated so as regards situations of mass influxes[11]—hence a precautionary proviso for emergency situations. The leading expert on refugee law in the 1960s, Grahl-Madsen, addressed the matter in some detail in his 1963 Commentary. Basing himself on the drafting history as well as state practice, he held that states 'may refuse admission'.[12] So refugees who had managed to elude the border guard were protected by the provision, and those who were caught, not. And if the control post was located at a certain distance from the 'actual frontier' ('a yard, a hundred meters'), a person who had passed the border and approached the guard might be stopped there, but not be sent back. Grahl-Madsen found a justification for these distinctions in public opinion that was more 'apt' to concern itself about people who had entered the country than to persons 'who had not yet materialized as human beings'; 'it is much easier to shed

[9] France had proposed it (E/AC.32/L.3, Articles 1 and 2). Instead, a reference to asylum was included in the Preamble (E/AC.32/SR. 26, at 10–11).

[10] UN Doc A/CONF.2/SR.16 (1951), at 6 and 10.

[11] Goodwin-Gill and McAdam 2007, at 206.

[12] Grahl-Madsen 1963, Commentary to Article 33, para (3).

responsibility for a mass of unknown people than for the individual whose fate one has to decide'.[13]

In the course of time, the reading according to which rejection at the border is also prohibited by Article 33 RC prevailed. According to the 1967 UNGA Resolution on Territorial Asylum, persons entitled to asylum should not 'be subjected to measures such as rejection at the frontier or, if he has already entered the territory in which he seeks asylum, expulsion or compulsory return to any State where he may be subjected to persecution.'[14] Still, the resolution made exception for situations of mass influx.[15] According to most authors, state practice as well as expressions of their views in international declarations and jurisprudence of treaty monitoring bodies has established that the prohibition of refoulement applies to the border, also in cases of mass influx.[16] Accordingly, European Union asylum law applies to applications 'at the border and international zones',[17] no exceptions being made for mass influxes.[18] And yet, in times of mass influxes, it does happen that states close their borders—as Coleman has demonstrated, during the Yugoslav refugee crisis in the 1990s, without being criticized for that.[19] Recently Austria adopted a law that places a cap of 3.200 asylum seekers that will be allowed to enter proceedings, implying that others will be rejected at the border.[20] Although this measure is openly defiant of the Asylum Procedures Directive (APD), the European Commission did not (yet) start infringement proceedings against Austria.[21] How treaty monitoring bodies will respond has to be seen.

[13] Ibid.

[14] UN General Assembly, Declaration on Territorial Asylum, 14 December 1967, A/RES/2312 (XXII).

[15] Article 3(2): 'Exception may be made to the foregoing principle only for overriding reasons of national security or in order to safeguard the population, as in the case of a mass influx of persons'.

[16] See for an extensive overview with ample references to instruments and authors Goodwin-Gill and McAdam 2007, at 208–244; Lauterpacht and Bethlehem 2003, at 113–115 and 119–121.

[17] Article 3(1) Asylum Procedures Directive (APD), Directive 2013/32/EU of the European Parliament and of the Council of 26 June 2013 on common procedures for granting and withdrawing international protection.

[18] Temporary protection as defined in the Temporary Protection Directive serves to alleviate the burden mass influxes may bring to asylum procedures (cf. Article 2(a)), not to extend or diminish the personal scope of protection for the purposes of non-refoulement.

[19] Coleman 2003, at 31–33 and 38–40.

[20] UN High Commissioner for Refugees (2016) UNHCR Concerned by build up along borders and additional hardships for refugees and asylum seekers, 23 February 2016, http://www.unhcr.org/news/press/2016/2/56cc521c6/unhcr-concerned-build-along-borders-additional-hardships-refugees-asylum.html, accessed 16 January 2017.

[21] Situation on 5 May 2016.

11.2.1.2 Detention

Grahl-Madsen stated that a person who passed the actual frontier before being stopped by a border guard should not be expelled, but could be stopped there. This border regime was for him geographically closely connected to the state border line. Since, states have developed the notion of border regimes in a way that the link to the geographical border has been far stretched.

Union Law

Union migration law is a case in point. Pursuant to Article 3(1) APD,[22] directives on asylum law, including rules on detention, apply to applications for asylum 'made in the territory, including at the border, in the territorial waters or in the transit zones of the Member States'. The provision thus prohibits member states to define the border or the international zone out of their territories. At the same time, the provision also singles out applications made at the border or in transit zones. These applicants have an ambiguous position as regards their presence.

On the one hand, a person who has applied for asylum has the right to stay 'in the member state' for the purpose of the procedure.[23] 'In the member state' means 'to remain in the territory, including at the border or in transit zones'.[24] This presence is lawful.[25] These applicants thus seem to be in a position not different from that of other lawfully present persons. But Member States may process applications in 'border procedures', that is 'at the border or transit zones'.[26] Importantly, asylum seekers may be held in detention 'in order to decide, in the context of a procedure, on the applicant's right to enter the territory',[27] in fact whether they satisfy all conditions for 'entering' the state (or rather, the Schengen zone) stated in the Schengen Border Code.[28] So although lawfully present, the asylum seeker can be detained 'at the border' (hence 'in the territory') in order to decide on his application and his right to 'enter' the territory he is in already.

---

[22] Directive 2013/32/EU of the European Parliament and of the Council of 26 June 2013 on common procedures for granting and withdrawing international protection (Asylum Procedures Directive, APD).

[23] Article 9(1) APD. The provision mentions two exceptions that do not concern us here (to wit, repeated applications and extradition).

[24] Article 2(p) APD.

[25] Case 357/09 PPU, *Kadzoev* [2009] ECR I-11189, para 41.

[26] Article 43(1) APD.

[27] Article 8(3)(c) APD.

[28] Regulation (EC) No 562/2006 of the European Parliament and of the Council of 15 March 2006 establishing a Community Code on the rules governing the movement of persons across borders (Schengen Borders Code), OJ [2006] L 105, 1, Article 13.

Where is this border located? The Asylum Procedures Directive does not define 'border' or 'transit zone' but indicates that the geographical location is flexible. When the influx is such that applications cannot be processed 'at the border or transit zones' (again an emergency situation), border procedures may be applied too 'where and for as long as these third-country nationals or stateless persons are accommodated normally at locations in proximity to the border or transit zone'.[29] So depending on the circumstances, being near the border, hence well into territory, counts also as being 'at' the border.

Interestingly, the provision implies that under normal circumstances (thus if there is no mass in influx), the border procedure takes place not 'in the proximity to the border or transit zone', but 'at' the border. Where else than 'in the proximity to the border' could the detention and processing center be located? In fact, the location where the asylum seeker is being held 'at' the border or 'in' the international zone has no necessary link with a specific geographical spot. In the Netherlands, for example, there is only one detention centre where applications are being processed in a border procedure, and it is located near Schiphol. This centre is placed well outside the international zone.[30] The authorities entitled to carry out checks at 'external border crossing points', apart from Schiphol Airport also the Rotterdam harbour, will bring over asylum seekers who do not fulfil requirements for entry to this centre.[31] People who enter over the land borders (or did enter via Schiphol and applied for asylum later) cannot be detained on the same basis. Thus, in the context of the border procedure, the processing of a claim 'at the border' here means bringing over a person from the sea border far into the territory—and hence does not refer to processing on some specific geographic location. Rather, 'border' indicates a special processing and detention regime for persons who applied for asylum at certain external border crossing points.

The European Convention on Human Rights

And even this link with applications made at the border is quite flexible, as the case of *Saadi v UK* shows.[32] It concerned an Iraqi who applied for asylum upon arrival at Heathrow airport. As there was no place in a processing centre, he was granted 'temporary admission' and allowed to stay in a hotel of his choice in London. Saadi reported daily as required and after four days, he was detained at Oakington for seven days. According to the Strasbourg Court, the UK was fully justified to detain this perfectly cooperative asylum seeker with a view to 'prevent' his 'unauthorised entry into the country' as meant in Article 5(1)(f) ECHR:

---

[29] Article 43(3) APD.

[30] See https://www.dji.nl/Organisatie/Locaties/Detentiecentra/Detentiecentrum-Noord-Holland/#paragraph3.

[31] See Aliens Circular A1/7.1 and 7.3, Stcrt. 2015, 20854.

[32] *Saadi v United Kingdom*, ECtHR Grand Chamber, No. 13229/03, 29 January 2008.

> To interpret the first limb of Article 5 Para 1(f) as permitting detention only of a person who is shown to be trying to evade entry restrictions would be to place too narrow a construction on the terms of the provision and on the power of the State to exercise its undeniable right of control.[33]

The right of states to control migration hence justifies detention with a view to preventing unauthorized entry of a person who had already been lawfully admitted, at a place far from 'the actual frontier', even if no attempt to unauthorized entry had been made. In fact, references to unauthorized entry merely serve to justify detention for purely logistical reasons—'in suitable conditions to enable his claim to asylum to be processed speedily', in the words of the Court.[34]

An extreme albeit somewhat odd variant is the case of Mr. Chui. He had entered the Netherlands in 2008 on the request of the ICC; Dutch border authorities did not perform entry controls and, in accordance with the Headquarters Agreement between the Netherlands and the Court, transported him on the request of the ICC to its premises where he was held in custody under jurisdiction of the ICC, not of the Netherlands.[35] After his acquittal in 2012 Dutch authorities brought him, again on the request of the ICC in accordance with the Agreement, to Schiphol airport. There, Chui requested for asylum. According to the Dutch judiciary, this request amounted to 'leave to enter the Netherlands, outside the scene of the Agreement', and therefore Dutch authorities could deny 'access' and place the man in border detention as he did not possess a valid visa.[36] Thus, after a stay of over four years on what is otherwise perceived as Dutch soil that was perfectly legal on the basis of the Headquarters Agreement his request to enter rendered it possible to detain him in order to preclude unauthorized entry.

11.2.1.3 Redefined Territory

By redefining border, 'being at the border' is possible anywhere on the territory, in the sense the relevant legal regime does not apply (or is not necessarily restricted to) a specific geographical area. Singling out parts of territory from the general legal regime and submitting it to special regimes in order to control entry and presence, has also been employed to the same effect. Indeed, before the emergence of Union migration law on the matter, certain European states maintained that the international zone was outside their jurisdiction for the purposes of protection standards. Thus, France stated so in the case of *Amuur*.[37] It concerned Somali asylum seekers who arrived at Orly airport on a flight from Syria. Their applications were turned

---

[33] *Saadi*, para 65.

[34] *Saadi*, para 80.

[35] 2007 Headquarters Agreement between the International Criminal Court and the Host State, ICC-BD/04-01-08, Article 44.

[36] Judicial Division Council of State, ECLI:NL:RVS:2013:2050, 23 November 2013.

[37] *Amuur v France*, ECtHR, No. 19776/92, 25 June 1996.

down. They were apparently in France for the purposes of the Refugee Convention, but French law on detention, including guarantees such as appeal to a court, did not apply at the airport—although they did apply elsewhere on French territory. Eventually, the European Court rejected the argument that the international zone was extraterritorial: 'holding them in the international zone of Paris-Orly Airport made them subject to French law. Despite its name, the international zone does not have extraterritorial status'.[38]

However, in other cases, human rights law proved quite able to accommodate such special status, as the European Court of Human Rights did in the case of *Longa*.[39] It concerned a DRC national who had been brought over to The Hague in order to stand witness before the International Criminal Court. He and several other witnesses remained on the premises of the ICC.[40] Having delivered testimony, Longa and some other witnesses applied for asylum with the Netherlands. The Dutch government initially stated that only the Refugee Convention applied, not domestic law—a standpoint reminiscent of the legal regime defined by Australia for its excised territories—but a Dutch court ruled that their applications should be processed in accordance with all Dutch national and international rules.[41] While the processing of the applications continued, the witnesses asked for leave to enter Dutch territory and stated refusal would violate the prohibition on arbitrary detention of Article 5 ECHR. The ICC ruled it could not end the detention—it was bound by an agreement to send them back to the DRC (where they were charged with serious crimes), but also bound to respect the refoulement obligations of the Netherlands.

The European Court of Human Rights declared the complaint under Article 5 inadmissible. It stated that the rule of territorial jurisdiction could be subject to exceptions, inter alia pursuant to agreements establishing international organizations.[42] That the custody happened to take place on Dutch soil was insufficient to bring the detention within Dutch jurisdiction in the sense of Article 1 ECHR. The European Court saw no legal vacuum, as Article 93 of the Statute provided for a legal basis,[43] even though the International Criminal Court did not.[44] Thus, Longa and other witnesses were in the Netherlands for the purposes of the prohibition of refoulement, but not for the purposes of habitas corpus, although Dutch authorities clearly controlled the situation. The ECHR also allows for tailoring jurisdiction.

---

[38] *Amuur*, para 52.

[39] *Djokaba Lambi Longa v The Netherlands*, ECtHR, No. 33917/12, 9 October 2012.

[40] 1998 Rome Statute of the International Criminal Court, 2187 UNTS 90.

[41] District Court The Hague, ECLI:NL:RBSGR:2011:BU9492, 28 December 2011, para 9.1.

[42] *Longa*, para 69.

[43] *Longa*, para 75.

[44] *The Prosecutor v Germain Katanga and Mathieu Ngudjolo Chui*, Trial Chamber, Decision on an Amicus Curiae application, Case ICC-01/04-01/07-3003, 9 June 2011, para 85.

11.2.2 *Redefined Jurisdiction*

An approach not unlike the one under discussion in *Amuur* but on a much grander scale has been adopted by the US and Australia. Below the schemes adopted by the US in Guantanamo Bay and by Australia in its excised territories will be discussed first, and human rights law responses subsequently.

11.2.2.1 Guantanamo Bay

Guantanamo Bay was taken into use as an immigration screening centre in 1991 in response to large numbers of Haitian boat migrants, and again in 1994 for Cubans.[45] After that, the centre remained in use for smaller numbers of boat migrants intercepted at sea until 2005. At Guantanamo Bay, US officials would screen the migrants and either send them to the country of origin when the migrants were found not to be in need of protection or in the case of Haiti, when unrest had eased, or to a third country. Refugees and others in need of protection were not allowed to enter mainland United States.

The Guantanamo Bay scheme was based on the status of the territory as a lease from Cuba. According to this lease, the US had 'control and jurisdiction', but 'sovereignty' remained with Cuba.[46] In *Sale*, the Supreme Court had ruled that not only the Refugee Convention but also domestic immigration law did not apply there —an explicit legal provision would be required.[47]

Thus, the regime was set up as an emergency measure in response to a mass influx. The US made use of the possibility to take control over migrants on the high seas and so deflect their routes to Guantanamo Bay, precluding these migrants could make contact with the mainland territory and invoke the Refugee Convention and other guarantees.

11.2.2.2 Australia's Excised Territories

Since 2001, overseas Australian territories, such as islands in the Pacific and Indian Ocean, have been 'excised' from the 'Australia Migration zone'.[48] People arriving there without authorization by boat, are not entitled to an entry visa for mainland Australia, and Australia's domestic migration law does not apply—which means that no recourse to the judiciary against expulsion or other acts is possible. The

[45] See for elaborate descriptions and discussions of the Guantanamo Bay regime, Legomsky 2006 and Den Heijer 2011, at 277–279 with further references.

[46] Legomsky 2006.

[47] *Sale v Haitian Centers Council*, Supreme Court, 509 U.S. 155 (1993), para 177. The reasoning as regards the territorial scope of Article 33 will be discussed in Sect. 11.3.1.

[48] See for a discussion McAdam 2013, Den Heijer 2011.

corollary of the scheme was the intent to move these asylum seekers to a third country where their applications would be processed and from where they, eventually, could be resettled to enjoy asylum in Australia or elsewhere. Agreements to that end were operative between 2001 and 2007 (with Nauru) and from 2013 till 2016 (with Papua New Guinea). In 2008, a centre was set up on St Christmas Island (an excised territory) where migrants were held in mandatory detention, some for years, and applications were tested to the Refugee Convention (not to domestic migration law). Persons qualifying for refugee status were usually allowed entry to mainland Australia.[49]

When implementing the excised territories policy, Australia like the United States, made use of the geographical possibility to intercept boat migrants in order to preclude contact with mainland Australia. Different from the Guantanamo Bay scheme, the excision of Australian territories is not a temporary measure in answer to a mass influx, but intended as a permanent solution. Also different from the Guantanamo Bay scheme, Australia works on the assumption that the Refugee Convention does apply to its territorial waters and territory, also the excised parts. Where the United States were consistent in denying applicability of the Refugee Convention and human rights treaties and domestic law that serves to implement it, Australia has held the position that it abides with its international obligations while denying basic safeguards such as access to courts.[50] And as mentioned above, it did allow qualified refugees into its mainland, albeit after sometimes lengthy detention or after expelling them first to a third country where their status was determined.

11.2.2.3 Human Rights Responses

Litigation aimed at invoking human rights at Guantanamo Bay proved not to be successful. In 1995, the 11th Circuit Court rejected requests by Haitian and Cuban asylum seekers on Guantanamo Bay who sought to invoke the Refugee Convention, US immigration legislation and the US Constitution.[51] It overturned the District Court ruling that the asylum seekers in Guantanamo Bay could rely on Constitutional rights as the US had 'control and jurisdiction' over the area.[52] Years after Guantanamo Bay fell into disuse for migrants, the Supreme Court ruled that persons held detained there could file claims with US Courts and rely on Constitutional rights.[53] In 2014, the US government acknowledged that the

[49] Wood and McAdam 2012.

[50] See McAdam 2013 and Den Heijer 2011 at 280–287 for an argument why that position is untenable.

[51] *Cuban American Bar Association, Inc. v Christopher*, 43 F.3d 1412, *Haitian Refugee Center, Inc. v Christopher*, 43 F.3d 1431, US Court of Appeals, 11th Circuit, 18 January 1995.

[52] This line of argument is not dissimilar to the way treaty monitoring bodies construe the scope of application of human rights treaties—see Sect. 11.3.2 below.

[53] *Boumediene v Bush*, Supreme Court, 553 U.S. 723 (2008).

Convention Against Torture applies,[54] but maintained its position that the Covenant did not apply, as Article 2(a) requires presence within jurisdiction and territory[55]—a standpoint at odds with the reading of the Human Rights Committee itself and of the International Court of Justice.[56] It remains to be seen how the US will interpret its refugee law obligations if Guantanamo Bay would be taken into use again for retaining boat migrants.

As to the Australian refugee policy, both the HRC and the Committee Against Torture have repeatedly concluded that Australia breached its treaty obligations for the lengthy detention of boat migrants on the excised territories,[57] which did not result in change of policy however.

11.2.3 Concluding Remarks

Among the various cases discussed, the position of people in the Guantanamo Bay scheme is relatively straightforward—they are outside, because migration law does not apply. Most ambiguous is the position of the asylum seeker in pre-entry detention under Union and Strasbourg law. The asylum seeker is both in *and* not in the territory; this presence is lawful although his unauthorized entry may still be prevented; border detention may mean bringing a person far into the territory.

These qualifications only make sense when the asylum seeker is being seen from two opposed perspectives. For the purpose of migration control, a person who does not possess a visa or does not fulfil other requirements for lawful entry is an illegally present person, and the request for asylum merely suspends this illegality —if the request will be turned down, the government must start (or continue) return proceedings. Therefore, his unauthorized entry must be precluded; he is out and must stay at the other side of the border. From the perspective of refugee law, the asylum seeker must be treated as if he were eligible for asylum, because that is also a possible outcome. As a refugee or person otherwise eligible for asylum, he has the right to enter (even without valid passport or visa) and stay legally in the country. The notion of 'border' here serves to conciliate these two opposites. At the border, the asylum seeker is and is not in the country, is lawfully present but not

[54] Concluding observations on the third to fifth periodic reports of United States of America, CAT/C/USA/CO/3-5, 20 November 2014, para 10.

[55] Concluding observations on the fourth periodic report of the United States of America, CCPR/C/USA/CO/4, 23 April 2014; and One-Year Follow-up Response of the United States of America to Priority Recommendations of the Human Rights Committee on its Fourth Periodic Report on Implementation of the International Covenant on Civil and Political Rights, https://www.state.gov/documents/organization/242228.pdf, accessed 16 January 2017, para 24.

[56] This matter will be discussed in Sect. 11.3.2.1 below.

[57] *P.A.C. v Australia*, CAT, No. 211/2002, 5 September 2005; *F.K.A.G.* et al., HRC, No. 2094/2011, 23 October 2013.

yet allowed to enter. Indeed, a link to a specific geographical place is quite unnecessary for it to fulfil its function.

The other cases are somewhere in between the Guantanamo Bay scheme and pre-entry detention. Persons in the international zone, on ICC premises or on excised territories are in for the purposes of the Refugee Convention. But they are out in so far they are not (yet) allowed to enter and even rely on *habeas corpus* guarantees. Compared to the Union law scheme addressed above, they seem to be placed in a geographically fixed, temporarily extended pre-entry detention.[58]

11.3 Beyond the Border

The Guantanamo Bay scheme was no isolated instant, in the sense that states have increasingly resorted to acting extraterritorially in order to control and deflect migrants from their borders. Deflection of ships carrying migrants at the high seas has been a fairly common practice.[59] Control may also take place on the territories of other states; in particular the EU has sought to establish a whole system of pre-border controls. The common visa policy has listed states whose nationals must possess visas in order to enter the EU legally.[60] States producing significant numbers of asylum seekers are invariably on that list.[61] European and Northern-American states further introduced carrier sanctions, an obligation for carriers to check whether passengers possess the required visas and fines for carriers that bring in passengers who do not meet the entry conditions.[62] International liaison officers, member states officials stationed at airports where illegal migrants might come from, serve to assist carriers or foreign border officials in identifying who should be allowed to leave the country and board. Although these measures do not preclude states from allowing refugees in by waiving visa requirements and so on, these measures do not require so and hence leave open the possibility that refugees are refused access this way.

Hence, the presumption underlying these schemes is that obligations under the Refugee Convention and other relevant treaties do not apply extraterritorially. Indeed, the link between asylum and territory established in the *Asylum* case could be taken to be exclusive. But we also saw that the *Institut de Droit International* suggested that asylum could be issued as well on vessels and embassies. In line with this, treaty monitoring bodies and the International Court of Justice have held

---

[58] The temporal aspect of these variants of pre-border detention schemes cannot be further exploited here. See on the issue of time and migration regulation Stronks 2017.

[59] See for thorough discussions Goodwin-Gill and McAdam 2007, at 270–284; and Den Heijer 2011, at 221–272.

[60] Cf. Article 3 Regulation (EC) No 810/2009 of the European Parliament and of the Council of 13 July 2009 establishing a Community Code on Visas (Visa Code), OJ [2009] L 243, 1.

[61] See for this response to the Syrian civil war Battjes et al. 2016, para 2.

[62] Feller 1989; Scholten 2014.

that various human rights provisions do apply when states exert jurisdiction or control extraterritorially. What this means for invoking non-refoulement abroad is not yet fully clear, as only few cases addressed the issue.

Below, I will first discuss the scope of application of the treaties relevant for non-refoulement (11.3.1). Particular provisions, in our case those on non-refoulement, may have a narrower scope. I will address the implications of the relevant provisions for invoking refoulement on the high seas (11.3.2) and on foreign soil (11.3.3), on the basis of both cases on non-refoulement as well as deduction from the general scope. The purpose of the discussion is partially to map in how far states can elope treaty obligations by acting extraterritorially. Furthermore, where jurisdiction and control may serve as an alternative basis to territoriality for state responsibility, the analysis serves to find out how territoriality still informs those alternative bases.

11.3.1 Human Rights Treaties and Extraterritorial Jurisdiction

11.3.1.1 The International Covenant on Civil and Political Rights

Article 2(1) ICCPR states that the Covenant binds a state as regards 'all individuals within its territory and subject to its jurisdiction'.[63] The Human Rights Committee has consistently held that 'States Parties are required by Article 2, Para 1, to respect and to ensure the Covenant rights to [...] anyone within the power or effective control of that State Party, even if not situated within the territory of the State Party',[64] that is 'within the jurisdiction' of the state.[65] Thus, the HRC in effect established next to jurisdiction on a state's territory jurisdiction resulting from control over a person, and being affected by an act state seems enough to assume such jurisdiction. This approach has been endorsed by the International Court of Justice in *Legal Consequences of the Construction of a Wall in the Occupied Palestinian Territory*, where it stated that the Covenant 'is applicable in respect of acts done by a State in the exercise of its jurisdiction outside its own territory'.[66] In

---

[63] 1966 International Covenant on Civil and Political Rights, 999 UNTS 171 (ICCPR).

[64] HRC, General Comment 31, Nature of the General Legal Obligation on States Parties to the Covenant, U.N. Doc. CCPR/C/21/Rev.1/Add.13, adopted on 29 March 2004, para 10. The HRC had stated that the Covenant may apply extraterritorially since *Lilian Celiberti de Casariego v Uruguay*, HRC Communication No. 56/1979, 29 July 1981, U.N. Doc. CCPR/C/OP/1 at 92 (1984).

[65] *Vidal Martins v Uruguay*, HRC, No. 57/1979, 23 March 1982, para 7; see Den Heijer 2011, at 43–44 for more examples.

[66] *Legal Consequences of the Construction of a Wall in the Occupied Palestinian Territory*, ICJ, Advisory Opinion, 9 July 2004, para 111; it found the reading of the HRC in accordance with object and purpose of the treaty as well as the preparatory works, see paras 108–110.

Armed Activities on the Territory of the Congo the ICJ broadened this conclusion to human rights law in general: 'international human rights instruments are applicable "in respect of acts done by a State in the exercise of its jurisdiction outside its own territory", particularly in occupied territories'.[67] In *Application of the International Convention on the Elimination of All Forms of Racial Discrimination*, the ICJ addressed the applicability of the Convention on the Elimination of All Forms of Racial Discrimination (CERD)[68] to acts by Russian authorities in Georgia before and during the war with that state. It observed that 'that there is no restriction of a general nature in CERD relating to its territorial application in particular,' that 'neither Article 2 nor Article 5 of CERD, alleged violations of which are invoked by Georgia, contain a specific territorial limitation' so that 'these provisions of CERD generally appear to apply, like other provisions of instruments of that nature, to the actions of a State party when it acts beyond its territory'.[69] Den Heijer concludes that the ICJ seems to presume that human rights treaties apply unless a provision states a territorial limitation, that this approach applies to human right treaties in general, and that the ICJ focuses on actions of states and leaves issues as control aside.[70] While the first two conclusions seem fully justified, it is, arguably, not clear from these cases whether the ICJ would accept that human rights treaties apply to rather incidental extraterritorial actions such as the refusal to issue a new passport. All ICJ cases mentioned concern acts during or connected with occupation of foreign territory, and in the *Armed Activities* case quoted above the ICJ restated its findings on applicability of human rights treaties to occupied territories 'particularly'.

11.3.1.2 The Convention Against Torture

The Committee Against Torture applied an approach similar to that of the HRC. The Convention Against Torture (CAT)[71] does not contain a general provision on its territorial scope, but some provisions limit application to 'any territory under [the Contracting state's] jurisdiction'. In a General Comment, the Committee has stated that 'any territory' includes any area where the state exerts *de jure* or *de facto* effective control, such as on board of ships,[72] and applies to 'all persons' under the effective control.[73]

---

[67] *Armed Activities on the Territory of the Congo (Democratic Republic of the Congo v Uganda)*, ICJ, Judgment 19 December 2005, para 216.

[68] 1965 International Convention on the Elimination of All Forms of Racial Discrimination, UNGA Resolution 2106 (XX) of 21 December 1965 (CERD).

[69] *Application of the International Convention on the Elimination of All Forms of Racial Discrimination (Georgia v Russian Federation)*, ICJ, Order 15 October 2008, para 109.

[70] Den Heijer 2011, at 57.

[71] 1984 Convention against Torture and Other Cruel, Inhuman or Degrading Treatment or Punishment, UNGA Resolution 39/46, 10 December 1984 (CAT).

[72] CAT/C/GC/2, 24 January 2008, para 16.

[73] CAT/C/USA/CO/2, 25 July 2006, para 15.

11.3.1.3 The European Convention of Human Rights

Article 1 ECHR states that Contracting states 'shall secure to everyone within their jurisdiction'[74] the rights defined in the Convention. According to well-established Strasbourg case law, 'jurisdiction' is 'primarily' territorial, but it may have 'incidental' extraterritorial effects.[75] In the case law of the European Court of Human Rights two strands can be distinguished.[76] First, jurisdiction due to effective overall control over a certain area, that is, after military occupation.[77] Second, 'as an exception to the principle of territoriality, a Contracting State's jurisdiction under Article 1 may extend to acts of its authorities which produce effects outside its own territory'.[78] When exactly such jurisdiction is established abroad is uncertain. In *Bankovic*, the Court stated on the threshold criterion of 'effective control' that the obligation to secure Convention rights for people within a state's jurisdiction cannot 'be divided and tailored in accordance with the particular circumstances of the extra-territorial act in question',[79] which seemed to imply that the authority over a person abroad should have a certain duration and overall repercussions on that person.[80] But the Court seems to have distanced itself somewhat from *Bankovic* in what now seems to be the leading case of *Al-Skeini*. It identified three instances of 'state agent authority and control' abroad. First, 'the acts of diplomatic and consular agents, who are present on foreign territory in accordance with provisions of international law, may amount to an exercise of jurisdiction when these agents exert authority and control over others'; second, a state that exercises public powers on foreign territory with the consent of the government of that territory and third, due to 'the use of force by the State's agents'.[81] The Court added that

> whenever the State, through its agents, exercises control and authority over an individual, and thus jurisdiction, the State is under an obligation under Article 1 to secure to that individual the rights and freedoms under Section I of the Convention that are relevant to the situation of that individual. In this sense, therefore, the Convention rights can be "divided and tailored".[82]

It seems to follow from *Al-Skeini* that when states act on the high seas or on foreign territory, they exercise jurisdiction in the sense of Article 1 ECHR if they

---

[74] 1950 Convention for the Protection of Human Rights and Fundamental Freedoms, 213 UNTS 222, 312 ETS 5 (ECHR).

[75] *Al-Skeini and others v United Kingdom*, ECtHR (GC) No. 55721/07, 7 July 2011, para 131 with references to earlier case law.

[76] Milanovic 2012.

[77] *Al-Skeini*, paras 138–140.

[78] *Al-Skeini*, para 133, referring to earlier case law.

[79] *Bankovic and Others v Belgium and 16 Other States*, ECtHR (GC), No. 52207/99, 12 December 2001, para 75.

[80] Den Heijer 2011, at 46.

[81] *Al-Skeini*, paras 133–136.

[82] *Al-Skeini*, para 137.

act in accordance with international law or consent of the host state.[83] Examples are cases where states held individuals on foreign soil in custody at military bases or in detention centres.[84] Furthermore, jurisdiction has been accepted over persons in cases of kidnapping or arresting persons on foreign soil.[85]

11.3.2 The High Seas

11.3.2.1 The Convention Against Torture

Article 3(1) CAT prohibits states to 'expel, return ("refouler") or extradite a person to another State where there are substantial grounds for believing that he would be in danger of being subjected to torture.' The extraterritorial application of the prohibition was addressed by the Committee in the case of *J.H.A. v Spain*.[86] It concerned migrants on board of a vessel that was in distress in international waters and rescued by a Spanish military vessel that towed the ship to Mauretania. In cooperation with local authorities, Spanish officials sorted out who was to be brought to Spain in order to lodge asylum claims, and who was to be repatriated to India and Pakistan. For a considerable time, the complainant had been held in (*de facto*) detention. On the Spanish argument that the case fell outside Spanish jurisdiction for the purposes of the Convention, the Committee referred to its General Comment and stated that

> jurisdiction must also include situations where a State party exercises, directly or indirectly, de facto or de jure control over persons in detention. This interpretation of the concept of jurisdiction is applicable in respect not only of article 2, but of all provisions of the Convention.[87]

The complaint under Article 3 CAT eventually failed, as the Spanish authorities had correctly processed the asylum applications, but what matters here is that the Committee found that the prohibition can apply to extraterritorial acts—a conclusion that is, if compared to *Sale*, the more striking as the language of the provision is similar to that of Article 33 Refugee Convention.

11.3.2.2 The European Convention on Human Rights

Likewise, the European Court of Human Rights has ruled that acts on the high seas can amount to a breach of the prohibition of refoulement under Article 3 ECHR, in

---

[83] Gammeltoft-Hansen 2014, at 125.

[84] E.g. *Al-Skeini*; and *Al -Saadoon and Mufdhi v UK*, ECtHR, No. 61498/08, 2 March 2010.

[85] E.g. *Oculun v Turkey*, ECtHR (GC), No. 46221/99, 12 May 2005.

[86] *J.H.A. v Spain*, CAT, No. 323/2007, 21 November 2008.

[87] *J.H.A. v Spain*, para 8.2.

Hirsi Jamaa.[88] The case concerned a ship with Somalian and Ethiopian nationals on its way from Libya in an attempt to reach Italy. On the high seas, the ship was intercepted by Italian military ships. The passengers were brought over to the Italian ships that brought them back to Libya, without any form of processing asylum claims. They had been 'under the continuous and exclusive *de jure and de facto* control of the Italian authorities'.[89] The Court proceeded to assess whether Italy had acted at odds with the obligation flowing from Article 3 ECHR 'not to remove' persons to a country where they run the risk of being ill-treated. It concluded that all illegal immigrants run such a risk in Libya.

It follows that obligations as regards refugee law do apply outside the territory where control on the high seas is concerned. It is not certain however what follows from these cases for other types of actions at the high seas. Both *J.H.A.* and *Hirsi Jamaa* concern cases where state authorities took over full control over ships and passengers, and actually removed them to another state. Thus, the degree of control did not differ that much from control within the territory. Whether jurisdiction would have been established if e.g. a coast guard vessel just shouted directions towards a vessel, or just pushed a vessel into another direction than the territorial waters cannot be deduced from these cases. The case of *Xhavara* suggests that full control is not required.[90] The case concerned an Albanian ship that Italian authorities tried to stop, but did not board. The ship sank, and Italy was obliged to perform an investigation into the deaths pursuant to Article 2.

11.3.3 Foreign Territory

Apart from the cases discussed in the previous section, there is as yet no jurisprudence of treaty monitoring bodies on instances of migration control performed by a Contracting state on foreign soil. Yet the jurisprudence on jurisdiction in general does allow for a number of conclusions about responsibility under human rights treaties for refusing entry visas and the acts of liaison officers.

As we saw it is well-established that jurisdiction for the purposes of human rights treaties is exerted if there is 'effective overall control' over an area of a foreign state.[91] Gammeltoft-Hansen suggests that the UK juxtaposed control scheme at Calais and other French ports and at Eurostar train stations where the UK border agency has exclusive control to enforce UK immigration laws could amount

---

[88] *Hirsi Jamaa and others v Italy*, ECtHR (GC), No. 27765/09, 28 February 2012.

[89] *Hirsi Jamaa*, para 81.

[90] *Xhavara and fifteen others v Italy*, No. 39473/98, 11 January 2001.

[91] See, apart from the examples mentioned in Sect. 11.3.3, *Issa and others v Turkey*, ECtHR, No. 31821/96, 16 November 2004, para 74.

to such extraterritorial jurisdiction.[92] But in most instances, if extraterritorial jurisdiction is being exerted, it would be on account of authority over individuals.

We saw that acts by consular authorities were explicitly recognized as examples of extraterritorial jurisdiction by the ICCPR and the ECHR. The same holds true for cases where states were held responsible for effects of legislation felt outside their territory.[93] We also saw it is uncertain whether the ICJ accepts that human rights treaties apply to such incidental extraterritorial actions (see Sect. 11.3.2.1). Still, it seems safe to conclude that at least some of the mentioned forms of migration control may fall within the jurisdiction of the contracting states for the purposes of the ICCPR and the ECHR as read by the HRC and ECtHR. It does not follow, however, that the prohibitions of *refoulement* do apply in those situations. In fact, territoriality affects extraterritorial jurisdiction over persons in three ways.

11.3.3.1 The Jurisdiction of the Territorial State

The International Court of Justice ruled in the *Asylum case* that asylum can be granted on foreign soil only if there is a legal basis for it such as an international agreement; otherwise, the territorial state would not have to tolerate it as a breach of its sovereignty.[94] Obviously, many instances of extraterritorial migration control would be perfectly acceptable to the territorial state. The territorial state may consent with the acts of a liaison officer or border guard of another state on its territory; Mauretania's consent in *J.H.A. v Spain* is an example. This may apply when the territorial state is another state than the one where the asylum seeker fears persecution, or even when it is the state where persecution is feared and that state is willing but unable to grant protection.

Still, the situation may occur that a state faces a conflict between, on the one hand, responsibility due to extraterritorial jurisdiction and on the other hand, the duty to respect the territorial sovereignty of the host state. Den Heijer suggests two possible solutions.[95] First, in such a case extraterritorial jurisdiction should be assumed not to exist. It is the territorial state that exerts authority and control, so extraterritorial jurisdiction does not exist *de jure* in such a case. Second, jurisdiction in human rights law has a meaning independent from jurisdiction in international law, and does not serve to delimit jurisdiction *vis-à-vis* another state. If there is a legal or other link with a person on foreign territory, that person may fall within the extraterritorial jurisdiction, regardless of whether the territorial state exerts jurisdiction. We should note that in *Al-Skeini*, the European Court of Human Rights stated that acts by consular authorities and others exerting public powers counted as jurisdiction, 'in accordance with provisions of international law' and 'the consent of

[92] Gammeltoft-Hansen 2014, at 120.

[93] See Den Heijer 2011, at 41–51 for cases and discussion.

[94] *Asylum case (Colombia/Peru)*, ICJ, Judgment, 20 November 1950, at 275.

[95] Den Heijer 2011, at 167–172.

the government' of the host state (see Sect. 11.3.1.3 above). And in *Hirsi Jamaa*, it explicitly remarked that the Contracting state had 'de jure' as well as 'de facto' control over the persons concerned.[96] Thus, the territorial jurisdiction of the host state seems to remain relevant for determining extraterritorial jurisdiction.

11.3.3.2 Territorial Restrictions Implied by the Wording

Furthermore, Article 33 RC and Article 3 CAT imply a territorial restriction. Above we saw that the Supreme Court of the United States concluded that Article 33 RC applies only on the territory. If the territorial scope of Article 33 is defined in the same way as the scope of human rights provisions, it may be wider.[97] An extraterritorial act could amount to 'return' the refugee—push backs on the high seas for example. But the provision speaks of expel or return 'to the territories' where persecution is feared. And according to Article 1 of the Refugee Convention, a person cannot qualify as refugee if he still is in his country of origin. The House of Lords ruled in 2005 that the provision did therefore not apply to applications for asylum made by persons still in their country of origin.[98] The case concerned Czech Roma, whom British immigration officials refused leave to enter the UK at Prague airport; no air carrier therefore wished to carry them. Thus, if Article 33 RC has extraterritorial application it is limited to the high seas and to other states than the one of origin. A similar limitation may apply to Article 3 CAT, which prohibits expulsion 'to another State where' the person would be in danger of being tortured.[99]

11.3.3.3 Control and Responsibility

The restrictions to Articles 33 RC and 3 CAT just discussed do not or not necessarily apply to the prohibitions of refoulement under the ICCPR and ECHR. These prohibitions have been derived from Articles 7 ICCPR and 3 ECHR, and are hence not constrained by a specific wording. The Strasbourg Court usually speaks of an obligation not to 'extradite',[100] 'expel',[101] or 'remove'[102] a person, all terms that suggest forced physical removal from a territory, which would hardly apply to

[96] *Hirsi Jamaa*, para 81.

[97] Den Heijer 2011, at 141; Lauterpacht and Bethlehem 2003, at 114; Gammeltoft-Hansen 2014, at 116.

[98] *Regina v Immigration Officer at Prague Airport and Another, Ex parte European Roma Rights Centre and Others*, UKHL, [2004] UKHL 55, 9 December 2004.

[99] Den Heijer 2011, at 142–144.

[100] *Soering*, ECtHR, No. 14038/88, 7 July 1989, para 91.

[101] *Chahal*, ECtHR, No. 22414/93, 15 November 1996, para 74.

[102] *Chahal*, para 80.

refusal to issue a visa or leave to enter on a foreign airport. But then again, these cases all concerned (decisions to start) physical removal which might have prompted these wordings. In *Soering*, the case where the Court considered in some length why Article 3 ECHR prohibits refoulement, it stated that 'in so far as a measure of extradition has consequences adversely affecting the enjoyment of a Convention right, it may, assuming that the consequences are not too remote, attract the obligations of a Contracting State under the relevant Convention guarantee';[103] and

> In so far as any liability under the Convention is or may be incurred, it is liability incurred by the extraditing Contracting State by reason of its having taken action which has as a direct consequence the exposure of an individual to proscribed ill-treatment.[104]

This implies that other measures than forced physical removal could also attract the protection of Article 3 ECHR. Den Heijer concludes that this amounts to an obligation on the state to take measures to prevent risk of ill-treatment from materializing.[105]

If this is true, the scope of obligations in situations of extraterritorial jurisdiction over persons remains uncertain. In general, the degree of control over a person informs that scope. Obligations of a socioeconomic nature, such as providing for housing or food, may serve as an example. Standards as regards treatment of prisoners within the Contracting state are very strict in this regard—even 'a shortage of toilet paper may raise an issue under Article 3'.[106] Towards other persons within the territory, such obligations may arise only in exceptional circumstances. And very bad detention conditions abroad are insufficient to conclude that the risk of ill-treatment is real.[107]

Likewise, where the control is limited to denying or allowing entry, it can be doubted whether Article 3 ECHR imposes a duty to allow entry safe for exceptional situations. As noted above, the Court stated in *Soering* that measures adversely affecting the enjoyment of Convention rights might attract responsibility under the Convention, 'assuming that the consequences are not too remote'. A person applying for a visa or requesting leave to enter from a liaison officer may, as a consequence of refusal, suffer ill-treatment. But that consequence is dependent upon many circumstances, such as the willingness of other states to allow for entry. When a person asks permission to enter a plane while being followed by persecutors, the link between refusal and ill-treatment may be sufficiently close. But in just that type of situation allowing boarding is likely to contravene the territorial jurisdiction of the state where the asylum seeker and liaison officer are present.

---

[103] *Soering*, para 85.
[104] *Soering*, para 91.
[105] Den Heijer 2011, at 149.
[106] Slingenberg 2012.
[107] Alpes et al. 2016, paras 5 and 6.

11.3.4 Conclusion

The scope of application of the various conventions discussed above have been defined and interpreted in such a way that control or jurisdiction can and do serve as a basis for state responsibility, complementary to territoriality. The application of relevant provisions to situations at the high seas proved to be unproblematic—towing ships to another jurisdiction quite resembles the territorial act of removal, and there is no competing jurisdiction compromising control. Such findings have already been made as to Article 3 CAT and Article 3 ECHR. There is no reason to hold otherwise for Articles 7 ICCPR or 33 RC. But as to acts on foreign soil, there is a number of limitations to construing such acts as measures resulting in refoulement that all derive in one way or the other from the notion of territoriality. First, establishing jurisdiction over persons abroad is abridged by the territorial jurisdiction of the state where the agent of another state is approached by the asylum seeker. Second, the wording of Article 3 CAT and 33 RC seems to exclude their application on the territory of the state where a person fears persecution or is in danger of being tortured. Third, it perspires from the case law of the European Court of Human Rights that the scope of obligations under Article 3 ECHR depends on the scope of control a Contracting state exerts. As jurisdiction over persons abroad asking entry in order to escape ill-treatment is limited, the obligations incumbent on the Contracting state may be limited as well.

11.4 Concluding Remarks

The link between territory and asylum that laid at the basis of the refugee protection system established 65 years ago has substantially eroded. Various schemes of migration control could be imposed within the territory by redefining borders and territories. The link also eroded in the sense that it is not exclusive anymore. Control or jurisdiction now serves as an alternative basis for state responsibility. Yet these developments do not allow for the conclusion that territoriality is becoming irrelevant. It still is in many ways decisive for who receives protection and who does not. Furthermore, as we saw human rights law did put some checks on evasive policies (*Amuur, Hirsi Jamaa*), though not on other ones (*Saadi, Longa*). And it turned out that territoriality informs the delimitation of extraterritorial jurisdiction or control.

The degree of erosion caused by the various control schemes varies too. Maybe the severest are the denial of presence –in the Guantanamo Bay scheme, but also in the acceptance of rejection at the border: openly up to the UNGA resolution of 1967, tacitly during the mass influx of the 1990s in Balkan states and nowadays, *vis à vis* the closed border policies of various European states. Far more subtle are the various border detention regimes discussed above that do not refuse presence on territory, but deny entry in order to justify detention. Another subtle way of eroding the relevance of presence came along only sideways, the Australia agreement with first Nauru and later Papua New Guinea to bring over applicants for asylum from its excised territories, in order to have their applications be examined over there. Removing a person to another state can be in accordance with the prohibition of refoulement Article 33 RC as it is generally taken to mean that expulsion to another, third, country than the one where persecution is feared is allowed for, provided certain guarantees are provided for. If all asylum seekers are being treated as if they were refugees, hence if for all of them it is established that the third country is safe, the obligations under the prohibitions of refoulement are deemed to be met.[108] The European Court of Human Rights held that Libya was unsafe for *Hirsi Jamaa* because of the threat of refoulement to Ethiopia and Somalia.[109] So again, human rights law can and does set restraints on this devise of migration control. But if a country is deemed safe for all asylum seekers, or if only very summary examinations of the safety of a country take place, as seems to be the case with asylum seekers who entered Greece from Turkey since the EU-Turkey deal, a refugee's contact with the territory of a state loses much of its relevance for the purposes of refugee protection.[110]

References

Alpes J, Battjes H, Tentere D, Ramdani L, Rodrigues K (2016) Illegal at Home: Return Risks and the Criminalisation of Emigration in Cameroon. Forthcoming

Battjes H, Brouwer E, Slingenberg L, Spijkerboer T (2016) The Crisis of European Refugee Law. Lessons from Lake Success. Vrije Universiteit, Amsterdam. http://christenjuristen.nl/wp-content/uploads/2016/05/H.-Battjes-E.-Brouwer-L.-Slingenberg-T.-Spijkerboer-The-Crisis-of-European-Refugee-Law.pdf. Accessed 16 January 2017

Coleman N (2003) Non-Refoulement Revisited. Renewed Review of the Status of the Principle. European Journal of Migration and Law 5:23–68

Den Heijer M (2011) Europe and Extraterritorial Asylum. Leiden University, Leiden (dissertation). https://openaccess.leidenuniv.nl/bitstream/handle/1887/16699/000-Heijer-07-03-2011.pdf. Accessed 16 January 2017

Feller E (1989) Carrier Sanctions and International Law. International Journal of Refugee Law 1:48–66

Gammeltoft-Hansen T (2014) Extraterritorial Migration Control and the Reach of Human Rights. In: Chetail V, Bauloz C (eds) Research Handbook on International Law and Migration. Edward Elgar Publishing, Cheltenham, pp 113–131

Goodwin-Gill G, McAdam J (2007) The Refugee in International Law. Oxford University Press, Oxford

Grahl-Madsen A (1963) Commentary of the Refugee Convention 1951 (Articles 2–11, 13-37), October 1997, Commentary to Article 33. www.unhcr.org/3d4ab5fb9.html. Accessed 16 January 2017

[108] E.g. Goodwin-Gill and McAdam 2007, at 390–407.

[109] *Hirsi Jamaa*, para 156.

[110] See for a critical analysis of the EU-Turkey Deal Battjes, Brouwer, Slingenberg and Spijkerboer 2016, para 3.3.5.

Lauterpacht E, Bethlehem D (2003) The Scope and Content of the Principle of Non-Refoulement: Opinion. In: Feller E, Türk V, Nicholson F (eds) Refugee Protection in International Law: UNHCR's Global Consultations on International Protection. Cambridge University Press, Cambridge, pp 89–177

Legomsky S (2006) The USA and the Caribbean Interdiction Program. International Journal of Refugee Law 18:677–695

McAdam J (2013) Australia and Asylum Seekers. International Journal of Refugee Law 25:(I) 435–48

McKeown A (2008) Melancholy Order: Asian Migration and the Globalization of Borders. Columbia Studies in International and Global History. Columbia University Press, New York

Milanovic M (2012) Al-Skeini and Al-Jedda in Strasbourg. European Journal of International Law 23:121–137

Scholten S (2014) The Privatisation of Immigration Control Through Carrier Sanctions. Brill, Leiden

Slingenberg L (2012) Between Sovereignty and Equality. The Reception of Asylum Seekers under International Law. Vrije Universiteit, Amsterdam

Stronks MC (2017) Grasping Slippery Time. A Legal and Philosophical Analysis of the Notion of Time in European Migration Law. Vrije Universiteit, Amsterdam (dissertation). Forthcoming

Wood T, McAdam J (2012) Australian Asylum Policy All at Sea: Shifting Boats, Rights and Responsibility. International & Comparative Law Quarterly 61:274–300

Chapter 12
Schrödinger's Cake? Territorial Truths for Post-Brexit Britain

Ciarán Burke, Ólafur Ísberg Hannesson and Kristin Bangsund

Abstract Any post-Brexit accord between the UK and the EU will redefine who exercises jurisdiction—and sovereign control—over the UK's territory. Every engagement in an international agreement by a State may be viewed as entailing a loss of sovereignty, and in certain circumstances, an alienation of its power to regulate its territory. However, it may also be construed as an exercise of sovereignty. States enter such agreements precisely because they have the power to do so. A corollary thereof is the power to regain control over their own affairs. However, in an era when interdependence has superseded independence as the norm, we may question whether defining states based on territorial sovereignty is even appropriate anymore. Securing investment and trade requires international oversight, once integration surpasses a certain threshold. In such circumstances, a state's territory becomes the subject of overlapping jurisdiction. Brexit will not come without a cost, and mitigating this may ironically involve further alienation of sovereignty, via parasitic attachment to the EU, whereby the UK may find itself forced to accept European norms without having a role in their elaboration. The alternative is a future involving an unambiguous reassertion of control, but with a virtual certainty of less prosperity. One may view the equation facing the UK as a balancing act between exclusive territorial control and economic prosperity.

Ciarán Burke, Professor of International Law, Friedrich Schiller University of Jena, Germany, ciaran.burke@eui.eu; Ólafur Ísberg Hannesson, Officer at the EFTA Surveillance Authority, olafur.hannesson@eui.eu; Kristin Bangsund, Officer at the EFTA Surveillance Authority, kristin. bangsund@gmail.com. The views expressed in this contribution are strictly personal, and cannot in any way be attributed to the EFTA Surveillance Authority.

C. Burke (✉)
Friedrich Schiller University of Jena, Jena, Germany
e-mail: ciaran.burke@eui.eu

Ó.Í. Hannesson · K. Bangsund
EFTA Surveillance Authority, Brussels, Belgium
e-mail: olafur.hannesson@eui.eu

K. Bangsund
e-mail: kristin.bangsund@gmail.com

M. Kuijer and W. Werner (eds.), *Netherlands Yearbook of International Law 2016*, Netherlands Yearbook of International Law 47,
DOI 10.1007/978-94-6265-207-1_12

Keywords Brexit · Territoriality · Jurisdiction · Interdependence · Sovereignty · EEA

Contents

12.1 Introduction

The development of international law in the latter half of the twentieth century represented an unprecedented challenge to the traditional notion of statehood, and more particularly, to the conception of territoriality as a component of the international system. Classical accounts of the constitutive theory of the state posit that mandatory requirements for statehood include a permanent population, a government, and a defined territory.[1] The logic of the territorial component is simple to explain. Although states may vary considerably in terms of their ethnic, cultural, and social composition, and also in terms of the governmental *modus operandi* applicable thereto, bounding the notion, the power, and in most cases, the jurisdiction of the state requires a delimitation in terms of spatial reach.[2] While debates concerning subjects as diverse as sinking islands in the Pacific Ocean and *de facto* autonomy of the Kurdish people provide interesting fodder for modern academic discourse, Oppenheim's classic dictum that 'a State without a territory is not possible'[3] still rings true, with Shaw noting that there must be 'some piece of land […] before one can accept the establishment of a state'.[4]

---

[1] Jellinek 1963, at 21; Jellinek's requirements (and the additional requirement of the capacity to enter into international agreements) are now prescribed in Article 1 of the 1933 Montevideo Convention on the Rights and Duties of States, 165 LNTS 19.

[2] Jellinek 1963, at 21.

[3] Oppenheim 1955, at 451.

[4] Shaw 1982; similarly: Crawford 2011, para 15.

Despite the above, the territorial notion of statehood has come under increasing pressure in recent decades. Much of this has to do with the transformation of the international legal regime, which has fundamentally altered international relations. Historically, international law was chiefly customary, 'a general, uniformly applicable law between States [...] abstract or rudimentary [in nature], by virtue of which States have the power to create specific obligations.'[5] These features resulted in obligations that were often vague and ill-defined, allowing for a certain degree of normative contestation. This allowed for a flexible international legal system, capable of evolution to take account of changing circumstances, providing a good degree of freedom of action to states, in accordance with the notion of sovereignty, but often failing to attain the desideratum of legal certainty, or indeed deep institutional co-operation.[6] The sovereign remained, incontestably, *rex in regno suo*. The twentieth century witnessed a significant alteration of this tradition. A plethora of problems may be associated with customary law. Not only are many such standards often ambiguous, but establishing hierarchies between them, as well as determining the very existence of a customary rule, represent notoriously complicated questions.[7] Clearly, such concerns served to undermine both the normativity and the effectiveness of international law. However, the relentless march of new technology, allied to the logic of global markets, as well as new interests such as human rights, necessitated a more stable means of conducting international affairs, with legal certainty supplanting sovereign flexibility as the pre-eminent interest. The model chosen in this regard was a proliferation of treaty law, based upon a transposition of contract theory and private law doctrines to the international legal arena. While this development is often termed as the 'codification' of international law, such a label is a misnomer. The development of international law was piecemeal rather than systematic. In particular, it consisted of advent of so-called 'self-contained regimes',[8] comprising rules relating to a particular domain, topic, or sub-species of law. Such regimes were implemented to further particular interests held as common between groups of states, and in many cases included institutional apparatus. This apparatus occasionally included an authoritative norm interpreter, usually a court, removing space for contestation between competing interested actors, and furthering legal certainty. The certainty thereby generated represented fertile ground upon which to ground trade relations in particular.

---

[5] Koskenniemi 2005, at 390.

[6] See Fuller 1969, at 79–81.

[7] Verdross proposes six separate categories of rules which may be classed as constituting customary international norms: (1) norms which constitute the law's structural basis (e.g. *pacta sunt servanda*); (2) norms which guarantee inter-State communication (e.g. diplomatic immunity); (3) norms which are based on the *opinio juris* (e.g. space law); (4) consensus norms, arising from claims and their acceptance; (5) norms arising from conflict-resolution; and (6) norms upheld by an informal consensus. See Verdross 1969, at 642ff.

[8] The nomenclature is that of the ICJ in the *Case Concerning the United States Diplomatic and Consular Staff in Tehran (United States of America v Iran)*, ICJ, Merits, Judgment, 24 May 1980, para 86. See also Simma 1985.

However, authoritative norm interpretation exercised by a judicial authority independent from state governments poses a problem to traditional notions of sovereignty, including the ability of states to control their own territory. This also applies to institutions created via international treaties endowed with power to make decisions from states. Both interpretation of pre-existing norms and the creation of new instruments with normative force have the power to challenge notions of the state as the master of his own house. While domestic analogies have shaped international law, the egalitarian logic of contractual theory borrowed from domestic private law sits uneasily with the concept of dominium, with the former relegating previously unfettered sovereigns to the status of mere contracting parties. This anomaly was discussed at length by the ICJ in the *Right of Passage* case.[9] Here, the notion of an easement, widely recognised by a great number of legal systems, was not upheld by the Court as a general principle of law (*qua* Article 38 (1)c of the ICJ Statute)[10] due to the distinction between territorial control of a landowner *in foro domestico,* being necessarily fettered by state regulation and the unfettered sovereign control of a state over its own territory. Such a conclusion effectively entailed that the very nature of international law was such as to imply the very narrowest construction of any dilution of sovereign competence, even in cases where cross-border co-operation was necessary. As the ICJ had noted in the *Lotus* case, 'restrictions upon the independence of States cannot [...] be presumed'.[11]

Exacerbating the tension between domestic dominium and the necessities of international intercourse, certain special regimes provided for the direct enforceability of rights prescribed by international treaties by individuals or legal persons in the domestic courts of states parties, a novel *lex specialis* reversing the principle that treaties could only create relations between sovereigns.[12] This had the effect of elevating individuals and economic entities to the extent that they could challenge the actions of sovereign states with regard to domestic governance measures that clashed with international obligations. It also relegated the domestic lawmaker to playing second fiddle to international treaties, even in domestic fora. The secondary rules employed by self-contained regimes also restricted freedom of action on the part of states parties, to the extent that they often provided less room for normative contestation than would have applied under general international law, particularly where based upon chiefly open-textured custom. Where the substantive content of rules covered trans-boundary trade, rules and restrictions upon the exploitation of

[9] *Right of Passage Over Indian Territory (Portugal v India)*, ICJ, Merits, Judgment, 12 April 1960.

[10] 1945 Statute of the International Court of Justice, 33 UNTS 993.

[11] *Case of the SS Lotus (France v Turkey)* PCIJ, Judgment, 27 September 1927.

[12] The earliest example in this regard is most probably the PCIJ's *Danzig Courts* Advisory Opinion concerning the Beamtenabkommen Agreement. Here, the court held that 'it cannot be disputed that the very object of an international agreement, according to the intention of the contracting Parties, may be the adoption by the Parties of some definite rules creating individual rights and enforceable by the national courts.' *Jurisdiction of the Courts of Danzig (Pecuniary Claims of Danzig Railway Officials who have Passed into the Polish Service, against the Polish Railways Administration)*, PCIJ, Advisory Opinion, 3 March 1928.

sovereign resources, and the provision of special privileges—such as the right to enter and work on one's territory—to alien citizens, the relentless momentum towards a more concrete, more restrictive, and less flexible model of international law implied a progressive restriction upon the exclusive jurisdictional competence of state governments over their own territory. The fact that international courts—rather than governments themselves—might have the final say over the scope of the rules also allows for evolution of norms beyond the extent to which states themselves feel they agreed, as demonstrated by the 2009 *Dispute regarding Navigational and Related Rights on the San Juan River* case.[13]

The example *par excellence* of regional development of international law fettering the domestic jurisdiction of member states is the European Economic Community (now the European Union). Based, from its inception in the 1950s, upon the concept of pooling resources and fostering trade, the *raison d'être* of the Community challenged certain core competences associated with the existence of state frontiers, eliminating border posts, customs inspections, and even passport controls. The success of the organisation, and its goal of 'an ever closer union', predicated upon the logic of economic integration, necessitated a progressive transfer of competences from individual member states to the central authorities in order to accommodate successive deepening of market integration. This included jurisdictional competences, with the logic of integration demanding that everyone play by the same rules, and its corollary demanding that those rules be policed by an overarching authority with power to compel state governments to comply, even within their own territorial jurisdiction. However, for the member states, the transfer of powers was not an unambiguous good. Questions of sovereignty, self-determination and economic independence began to permeate domestic political discourses on the question of 'Europe' from the 1980s onwards, particularly in Britain. This so-called Euroscepticism culminated in the United Kingdom's decision to leave the EU on 23 June 2016. While the precise nature of the UK's future relationship with the EU remains to be decided, the vote would seem, on the face of it at least, to represent a reassertion of the UK's territorial sovereignty on the part of the UK electorate, a desire to once again be master of one's own house. This chapter aims to discuss the implications of Brexit from a territorial perspective, offering an assessment of how and whether the UK authorities will re-establish control over core prerogatives associated with sovereignty, in particular exclusivity of territorial jurisdiction, or whether post-Brexit developments are likely to result in mere rebalancing, since complete isolation seems unlikely, as well as the *modi operandi* through which this may be achieved, and the difficulties that may arise *en route*.

[13] *Dispute regarding Navigational and Related Rights (Costa Rica v Nicaragua)*, ICJ, Judgment, 13 July 2009, para 213; see M Milanovic (2009) The ICJ and Evolutionary Treaty Interpretation, *EJIL: Talk!*, 14 July 2009, http://www.ejiltalk.org/the-icj-and-evolutionary-treaty-interpretation/, accessed 6 February 2017.

12.2 Brexit—The Solution to a Very British Problem

When discussing core issues of inter-state international law (such as withdrawal from international agreements), international lawyers are often guilty of replicating the sins of international relations theorists, namely a formalist viewpoint that perceives states as unitary actors with individual interests. However, in democratic states, such an analysis occasionally fails to grasp the subtleties underpinning core decisions. So it is with the Brexit vote, carried by a 52/48% majority, and ultimately representing the denouement of an uncomfortable—yet mutually beneficial—relationship between the UK and its continental cousins. In this regard, a few words on domestic UK law are warranted. The history of the UK's engagement with the European Union has been described elsewhere as 'the story of how Parliament's legislative omnipotence came to be lost.'[14] It has transformed the British constitutional system, with the latter evolving from 'a constitution firmly based on politics to one increasingly based on law.'[15] This has led to the transformation of the UK Parliament from a sovereign legislature to one of limited competence, and has empowered the courts far beyond what could previously have been considered possible. The UK is the only EU member state without a written constitution. This system entailed that 'for some three hundred years the courts chose to adopt an essentially subordinate role vis-à-vis Parliament. They did so by adhering to the doctrine of parliamentary sovereignty as the constitution's dominant principle.'[16] The role of the courts was to enforce each and every statute, and not to question the validity of Acts of Parliament by reference to any other standard.[17] This deferential model, placing Parliament at the apex of the organs of government, firmly rejects Montesquieu's separation of powers, or indeed Jefferson's checks and balances. Rather than a *legal* constitution based upon a fettering of each governmental organ's exercise of power by the control of another organ, with the limits of the latter determined by law, the UK model hands supreme power to the politicians, and is a *political* constitution.

Such domestic legal idiosyncrasies led to a unique conception of territoriality in the collective British consciousness. Britain's history as an island nation rendered the demarcation between its territory and that of its neighbours primarily a geographical, rather than a legal matter, a distinction acknowledged from the outside as early as Roman times. Tacitus' *Agricola(Tacitus)* presents an early example in this regard, wherein Tacitus favorably contrasts the liberty of the native Britons to the

---

[14] Nicol 2001, at 1.

[15] Ibid.

[16] Ibid.

[17] *Cheney v Conn*, England, High Court of Justice, Chancery Division, [1968] 1 All ER 779, 3 July 1967; *British Railways Board v Pickin*, England, House of Lords, [1974] AC 765, 30 January 1974. From these cases, Munro notes that 'any notion that doctrines of morality or the rules of international law could prevail against acts of Parliament found no support in case law.' (Munro 1999, at 133).

corruption and tyranny of the Empire, despite legal subjugation of the former to the latter.[18] Later, while all the states of Europe subscribed to the post-Westphalian conception of sovereignty as primarily territorial,[19] Britain's control over its own land was doubly guaranteed.[20] The island remained unconquered throughout the post-Westphalian era, and participation in continental conflicts was generally viewed as a choice, rather than an imperative. The combination of legal and geographical demarcation of its territory obviated the necessity to depend entirely on a legal regime for its protection. Indeed, it is germane to note that some scholars argue that the idea that the territorial state is a unified, bounded, homogeneous and naturally occurring entity, in a world of equivalent but unique entities is itself cartographic—a *mise à jour* of the representation of islands on sixteenth-century portolan charts, suggestive of a historical link between the Renaissance-era imagination of islands and the modern imagination of states. Per such a construction, Britain itself is a 'natural' manifestation of a state, whereas other states require artificial legal boundaries as an *Ersatz* for a maritime moat.[21]

A legal system conferring all power to the sovereign—first the monarch, later the Parliament—married with a geographical position providing both security and certainty of borders made Britain an ambivalent partner in international institutionalism. Its attitude to the independent normativity of international law was consistently dismissive, with the mid-twentieth century courts holding that '[e]ven if a treaty is signed, it is elementary that [UK] courts take no notice of treaties as such. We take no notice of treaties until they are embodied in laws enacted by Parliament, and then only to the extent that Parliament tells us.'[22] The message was clear: unless the Westminster Parliament incorporated international legal acts into domestic law, those acts, like so many enemies, would fail to traverse the English Channel and make roots in British soil.

However, the aggregation of all power to the sovereign Parliament came under pressure from the moment that the United Kingdom joined the European Economic Community (EEC) on 1 January 1973. This was above all due to the twin doctrines of supremacy and direct effect devised by the European Court of Justice to give effect to EU law in domestic fora.[23] Applied in tandem, these innovative formulae distinguished the EU legal order from that of general international law in a number

[18] See Tacitus 2010; see also Clarke 2001.

[19] See Ohmae 1990; Held et al. 1999; Sassen 2000.

[20] Gross 1948.

[21] Steinberg 2005.

[22] Lord Denning, in *Blackburn v Attorney-General*, England, Court of Appeal, Civil Division, [1971] 2 All ER 1380, 10 May 1971, at 1382. This position was confirmed by *Attorney General (McWhirter) v Independent Broadcasting Authority*, England, Court of Appeal, [1973] 1 ALL ER 689.

[23] See, in particular, *Case 26/62 (N. V. Algemene Transport- en Expeditie Onderneming van Gend & Loos v Nederlandse administratie der belastingen (Netherlands Inland Revenue Administration))*, ECJ, Judgment, ECR 1, 5 February 1963; and *Case 6/64 (Flaminio Costa v ENEL)*, ECJ, Judgment, ECR 585, 15 July 1964.

of manners. From the UK perspective, most importantly, they entailed the obligation to apply European norms even in the face of contrary subsequent legislative enactments by Parliament, with the UK courts co-opted for the purpose. These obligations became readily apparent in the aftermath of the *Equal Opportunities Commission* case decided in the early 1990s.[24] While Lord Bridge's famous statement in the earlier *Factortame* case, that 'whatever limitation of its sovereignty Parliament accepted when it enacted the [1972 European Communities Act, the basis for UK membership of the EU] was entirely voluntary' provided a neat justification for the new reality, it was clear that the world of EU law never sat easily with British legal doctrine.[25] The fetters placed upon Parliament's ability to control British territory and appurtenant maritime zones were particularly exposed in *Factortame*, where the House of Lords was ultimately obliged to give effect to the right of freedom of establishment, enshrined in EU primary law, which allowed Spanish fishermen to own British-registered vessels, despite the fact that Parliament had enacted the 1988 Merchant Shipping Act, seeking to restrict registration of UK seafaring vessels to companies with a majority of British shareholders. Not only was the UK Parliament restricted in making the law of the land, but Britannia ruled the waves no more, it seemed. This conclusion came on foot of a ruling by the European Court of Justice, an organ with its seat in the Grand Duchy of Luxembourg, empowered by EU law to issue *Diktats* to Britain's highest court. The disconnection between the domestic lawmaker and its territory could hardly be more apparent.

Discombobulated by this rupture with embedded tradition, the British people demanded opt-outs from further transfers of power to the EU from the early 1990s onwards. The 2016 Brexit referendum decision represented the culmination of a campaign promising to 'take back control' from Europe. Indeed, many issues of contention during the referendum campaign represented erstwhile traditional state competences that had come within the EU's remit over time, including control over migration, fisheries and maritime zones, compulsory judicial surrender of those subject to European Arrest Warrants (replacing the executive-led extradition process) and, of course, subjection to an arcane array of supranational regulations, as devised by a cabal of Brussels bureaucrats and authoritatively interpreted by a French-speaking *tribunal de dernière instance* in Luxembourg. In all of these matters, the Parliament had been free to legislate as it wished in the past, whereas its hands were now tied by European rules, which the UK courts would follow in the event of divergences between national and supranational law. Escaping from these strictures was intended to repatriate powers to British soil, restore parliamentary

[24] *R v Secretary of State for Employment, ex parte Equal Opportunities Commission and another*, England, House of Lords, [1995] 1 AC 1, 3 March 1994.

[25] Lord Bridge, in *R v Secretary of State for Transport, ex parte Factortame Ltd. (No.2)*, England, House of Lords, [1991] AC 603, 11 October 1990, at 658.

supremacy, and ensure that the traditional territorial conception of *dominium* would be restored.[26]

12.3 A Twist in the Tale? Brexit and the Dynamics of Economic Interdependence

The revanchist esprit of the Brexit movement is perhaps unsurprising in the context of British history. Reactions to legal and constitutional novelties elsewhere have long been viewed with conservatism.[27] The UK's engagement with the EU is typified by a wish to harvest the fruits of free trade without bearing the perceived burdens of the associated accoutrements such as Union Citizenship and the Common Foreign and Security Policy. As Timothy Meyer has noted, state engagement in treaty regimes, and the benefits they perceive as deriving from them, are 'limited by the realities of the way states behave when making legal rules.'[28] States will be uninterested in enhancing collaborative regimes unless they manage thereby 'to increase their individual share of the benefits of cooperation.'[29] Securing opt-outs or derogations from areas such as Schengen, the Area of Freedom Security and Justice, the Single European Currency, the Charter of Fundamental Rights of the European Union, and the Common Foreign and Security Policy is indicative of the fact that the UK has long felt ambivalent about the depths of 'ever-closer union'.

From a jurisdictional perspective, the EU is something of a novelty. Essentially entailing a pooling of competences, the Union's organs are vested with certain—but certainly not all—powers traditionally held within the purview of individual sovereign states. The overlap between sovereignty, territory and jurisdiction is clear, and has been described in detail elsewhere.[30] Statehood is defined by reference to a particular slice of territory; jurisdiction, in the sense of a sovereign's authority over persons or events, is defined by reference to their location within that territory. The idea of overarching norms that transcend territorial boundaries, and that, in the event of conflict, supersede domestic law, poses significant challenges to territorial jurisdiction thus defined, particularly when the organs of territorial jurisdiction—specifically courts—are co-opted so as to apply norms that call this jurisdiction into question.

---

[26] These rationales are explained in detail in many official Brexit campaign materials. See, for example, Campaign for an Independent Britain, 7 Reasons Why We Should Leave the EU, http://campaignforanindependentbritain.org.uk/the-economy/, accessed 6 February 2017.

[27] See Burke 1790.

[28] Meyer 2012, at 1003.

[29] Ibid.

[30] Mann 1964, at 30.

On the basis of the above, the EU approximates a federal quasi-state, insofar as it exercises decisive jurisdiction over a defined territory, namely that of its member states. However, the jurisdictional authority possessed by the EU organs relates solely to those competences covered by EU law. Any and all other matters remain within the remit of domestic law. As such, the UK's territory, including its maritime zones, is subject to two overlapping and occasionally conflicting jurisdictional bases, one superior to the other, which restricts and constrains the sovereign UK government on both the domestic and international plains. Perhaps ironically, nowhere is this more apparent than the procedure to leave the European Union. Article 50 TEU[31] provides a specific *modus operandi* in this regard, separate and distinct from general international law. In particular, it prescribes a time limit of two years subsequent to notification by a state of its intent to exit the Union for the exiting state and the remaining member states to negotiate a new framework for the regulation of trade and related issues. In default of such an agreement, after two years, Union law shall cease to apply to the exiting state and the state's membership of the EU will lapse. The interpretation of Article 50 is thus crucial in this regard. It is worthwhile noting that the Court of Justice of the EU (ECJ) has consistently held that EU law is distinct from international law, and that alternative rules of interpretation are applicable thereto.[32] The standard rules of customary international law and the 1969 Vienna Convention on the Law of Treaties[33] are therefore not applicable. Rather, the ECJ interprets European Union law based upon (1) the text (2) the context and (3) the *teleos* of the rule.[34] This approach has significant consequences. The context and *teleos* of Article 50 strongly suggest that the latter was devised so as to ensure that the Union was placed into a strong position vis-à-vis the leaving state, in order to avoid the EU being unduly inconvenienced thereby, as well as to discourage would-be leavers. Moreover, the rejection of the Vienna Convention rules entails that there will be minimal—if any—consideration afforded to extraneous norms applicable in the relations between the parties. (This has extended as far as effectively rejecting consideration of the United Nations Charter in applying EU law, despite the 'supremacy clause' contained in Article 103 of the former.[35]) The implication of this construction would seem to be that the right to withdraw a notification to leave an international organization—normally applicable in international law—is not available to the UK. As such, the two-year time limit represents a fixed deadline, unless the remaining 27 member states agree unanimously to an extension. If the negotiating parties fail to reach an agreement within

[31] 2012 Treaty on the European Union (Consolidated version), C 326/13 (TEU).

[32] *Van Gend & Loos*, at 12.

[33] 1969 Vienna Convention on the Law of Treaties, 1155 UNTS 331.

[34] *Case 53/81 (Levin v Staatssecretaris van Justitie)*, ECJ, Judgment, ECR 1035, 23 March 1982, para 9.

[35] See *Joined Cases C–402/05 P and C–415/05 (P. Kadi and Al Barakaat International Foundation v Council of the European Union and Commission of the European Communities)*, ECJ Grand Chamber, Judgment, ECR I–6351, 3 September 2008.

the two-year timeframe, the UK will leave the Union without a subsequent arrangement. The upshot of the above is that while the UK government might wish to simply leave the EU, in the manner prescribed by general international law, it is restricted by the continuing supremacy of EU law in its choice of exit.

Thereafter, however, things would seem considerably simpler. On the face of it, once Britain achieves an exit from the EU, by hook or by crook, as it were, the concurrence of jurisdiction between EU law and domestic law will cease. The UK will reassert unfettered sovereignty over its territory. UK courts would have the final say over all matters within domestic jurisdiction, and would apply only those norms enacted by the Westminster Parliament. However, the dynamics of a UK exit entail that a 'clean break' will be complicated from both a domestic legal perspective and from an international one, with legacy issues arising from engagement with the EU and the broader international community meaning that asserting exclusive jurisdiction over its territory may be more difficult to achieve than it appears at first glance.

The UK courts have utilized an array of techniques to reconcile the supremacy of EU law with parliamentary sovereignty over the past decades. The courts have, *inter alia*: a) applied *special meanings* and *special interpretations* to certain domestic statutes, which would not otherwise apply, in order to 'read them' harmoniously with EU law; b) *directly applied* provisions of EU law in order to *confer rights on individuals*, even in the absence of implementing legislation; and c) *disapplied* properly enacted *domestic statutes* for failure to comply with EU law. Repeal of the 1972 European Communities Act would entail, in accordance with UK constitutional law doctrines, that: (a) the special meanings and special interpretations would be called into question, since there would be no need to read such statutes harmoniously with EU law; (b) the rights conferred upon individuals would be lost; and (c) the statutes in question—since they no longer contradict EU law—would apply in full.[36] The result of the above would cause severe complications at a domestic level, and could have unfortunate repercussions elsewhere, certainly destabilizing the UK economy as an array of rights and obligations were expunged and repurposed from one day to the next.

From an international viewpoint, the consequences of the clean break scenario are if anything, even more significant. The rights and obligations associated with EU membership are myriad, with rights in particular accruing both for EU citizens and economic operators in the United Kingdom, and for UK citizens and economic operators based elsewhere in the EU, with a softening of borders and a flexible notion of shared territory throughout the member states. The legal basis for residence and citizenship rights (Directive 2004/38)[37] as well as the vast array of

[36] For more detailed discussion on this point, see Burke et al. 2016.

[37] Directive 2004/38/EC of the European Parliament and of the Council of 29 April 2004 on the right of citizens of the Union and their family members to move and reside freely within the territory of the Member States, amending Regulation (EEC) No 1612/68 and repealing Directives 64/221/EEC, 68/360/EEC, 72/194/EEC, 73/148/EEC, 75/34/EEC, 75/35/EEC, 90/364/EEC, 90/365/EEC and 93/96/EEC.

secondary law guaranteeing market access for UK companies would cease, as would the freedom of establishment, and the continued ability of the UK to trade with the European Union would thenceforth be governed by the Covered Agreements of the World Trade Organisation (WTO), entailing an array of tariffs and no guarantee of freedom of establishment for companies or freedom of movement for individuals, with restrictions on goods, services and capital also being applicable. The UK financial services sector would lose its ‘passport’ to clear transactions denominated in euro, and the basis for the City of London as a financial hub would be severely undermined.

In such a scenario, it is germane to note that, since the UK’s trade relations would thenceforth be governed by the WTO regime, the UK would still be obliged to implement the WTO Covered Agreements’ provisions on rules of origin, national treatment and scientific standards, while respecting the maximum tariff levels applicable under the regime. Failure to do so would result in resort to compulsory dispute settlement under the Dispute Settlement Understanding mechanism. While the reports of the Panels and Appellate Body are technically not binding in and of themselves, in reality, they are adopted as a matter of course by the Dispute Settlement Body (composed of the WTO Members). Thus, escape from the EU does not necessarily free the UK of the obligation to abide by legal rules, for example on the marketing and taxing of goods on its own territory. While the courts might return to their pre-1972 position that international law is not binding on British territory *per se*, unless Parliament has acted so as to transpose it, the chances are that Parliament would feel compelled to do so with regard to WTO norms, otherwise risking censure, fines, and potentially sanctions from fellow WTO members, thus crippling the economy. Subjection to jurisdictional supremacy under the EU regime will be substituted for subjection to economic hegemony under the WTO rules.

However, the solution proposed is quite possibly the least restrictive model for those who wish to see the UK reassert its exclusive territorial sovereignty. Any alternative to the above entails that the UK will seek to negotiate a subsequent agreement with the EU, in order to avoid the pitfalls that a clean break with the Union might entail. Indeed, the narrow victory for leave in the 2016 referendum appears indicative of an ambivalence on the part of the British electorate, wishing to re-assert sovereign control of their borders, laws, immigration and fisheries, but fearful that such an outcome might amount to sacrificing economic prosperity. The ideal outcome, it would seem, is one that manages to achieve the former without the latter. It remains to be seen whether the UK’s negotiating team are sufficiently adept to square that particular circle, and what concessions the EU are prepared to offer, given the implications for other potential wantaway states if the UK secures some order of ‘sweetheart deal’. However, one can nonetheless furnish some tentative comments on how such an agreement might function and what it may mean for the UK and its territorial sovereignty.

12.4 A Leap into the ... Known?

Any attempt to sketch the nuances of a Brexit deal between the UK and the EU before the fact is necessarily speculative. There is no precedent in this regard, with the closest thing to a negotiated 'exit plus bilateral' outcome being Greenland in 1985, hardly a useful comparator, though certainly a good example of a loss of a large portion of territory for the then EEC. It is also germane to note that the Greenland Treaty took 30 months to negotiate, somewhat more than the 24 month allowed by the TEU for a post-Brexit deal, while it also provided for a multilateral governance regime concerning access to Greenland's abundant maritime zones for the purposes of commercial fishing; hardly a clean break, given that fisheries are Greenland's most obvious and abundant sovereign resource. That the details of a deal concerning an island of sixty thousand people took longer than the time allotted for a country of over sixty million is revealing. Even in the 1980s, EU law constituted a complicated apparatus. Negotiating extrication from the vastly more intricate structure applicable in the 2010s is likely to require more, rather than less time, even before one considers the relative size and complexity of the respective economies. Such a conclusion suggests that any deal for the UK is likely to borrow heavily from the modalities of existing EU deals with third states in order to obviate the necessity to start negotiations with a blank sheet. Two models are instructive in this regard, and have been pointed to by commentators as representing the likely models upon which any post-Brexit arrangement will be based.[38] The first is the complex system of bilateral agreements governing trade relations between the EU and Switzerland, while the second is the European Economic Area (EEA) model, providing for an expanded Single Market—albeit with less pronounced integration—encompassing the EU, Iceland, Norway and Liechtenstein. The latter would seem significantly more likely than the former, as a cursory look at the recent history of the EU's relations with Switzerland shows an increasing scepticism towards the model on the part of the EU.[39]

In any event, the challenges the UK's negotiators will face are formidable. Although based on identical rules, an international agreement exporting *acquis* to a third country and the EU remain different arrangements, based on different treaties,

[38] See for example the various models proposed in Buckle et al. 2015. Most borrow much from one of the two proposed options.

[39] The EU Council has been advocating an EEA-style framework agreement with Switzerland to supplant the current model—seen as unsustainable in the medium-term—incorporating a 'mechanism for [...] homogeneous interpretation of the rules,' cf. Council of the European Union, Draft Council conclusions on EU relations with EFTA countries, Council Doc. 1665/1/08 Rev I, 5 December 2008, paras 29 and 32.

implying that even identical provisions of the constituent treaties may have to be interpreted differently, depending on the context of the provision and the object and purpose of the treaties.[40] Textual parallelism between certain provisions of an international agreement and those of the EU Treaties is not necessarily sufficient to ensure an identical interpretation if these provisions are invoked under the international agreement. As such, the UK achieving internal market access will require something more than a mere undertaking to continue extending protection to foreign operators via domestic law.

In this respect, the *Polydor* case is instructive.[41] The question was whether the (now-defunct) Free Trade Agreement (FTA) between Portugal and the EU—which contained almost literally identical provisions on the elimination of restrictions on trade and quantitative restrictions to those in the EU treaties—should be interpreted in the same way as EU law. Here, the ECJ concluded that this 'similarity of terms' constituted an insufficient reason to extend its treaty-based case law to the EEC-Portugal Agreement. The Court highlighted the institutional disparities between the two systems. It held that the FTA did not have the same objective as the EU, i.e. creating 'a single market reproducing as closely as possible the conditions of a domestic market'. The ECJ went on to argue that this conclusion was supported by instruments which the Community had at its disposal in order to achieve the uniform application of its law, which would clearly not be replicated in a looser free trade arrangement denuded of such institutions.[42] This question of the context in which norms would be interpreted, influencing the content of those norms in the UK courts on the one hand, and the EU courts on the other, could create a lop-sided trading platform, something that the EU is plainly keen to avoid.

The ECJ has confirmed that the *Polydor* doctrine applies to the EU-Switzerland bilateral agreements, a model that has also been proposed as providing a post-Brexit template for EU-UK relations.[43] This case law led the President of the European Free Trade Association (EFTA) Court to note that '[c]ertain discriminations are [...] possible under [the Swiss] agreement which would be unlawful under the TFEU and under the EEA Agreement'.[44] Furthermore, and importantly, a cursory look at the recent history of the EU's relations with Switzerland shows a strong and

[40] Such a differentiated interpretation of the treaties is also supported by the normal canons of treaty interpretation, see Article 31 of the 1969 Vienna Convention on the Law of Treaties, which have been rejected by the ECJ for the purposes of interpreting the *sui generis* EU legal order, but which remain relevant for most international agreements.

[41] *Case 270/80 (Polydor v Harlequin Record Shops)*, ECJ, Judgment, ECR 329, 9 February 1982. See also *Case C-312/91 (Metalsa)*, ECJ, Judgment, ECR 1-3751, 1 July 1993, para 12.

[42] *Polydor*, para 19.

[43] *Case C-351/08 (Chistian Grimme v Deutsche Angestellten-Krankenkasse)*, ECJ, Judgment, ECR I-10777, 12 November 2009; *Case C-541/08 (Fokus Invest v Finanzierungsberatung-Immobilientreuhand und Anlageberatung GmbH (FIAG))*, ECJ, Judgment, ECR I-1025, 11 February 2010, para 28; *Case C-70/09 (Alexander Hengartner and Rudolf v Landesregierung Vorarlberg)*, ECJ, Judgment, ECR I-7233, 15 July 2010, para 42; see discussion in Öberg 2016.

[44] Baudenbacher 2012.

increasing scepticism towards the model on the part of the EU.[45] This is perhaps unsurprising, as it is deeply questionable whether reciprocal enforcement can be ensured from both sides. The EU has signalled, in unusually frank terms, that the Swiss *à la carte* bilateral approach to EU market access is exhausted, and is very unlikely to countenance a similar arrangement with the UK.[46]

Clearly, therefore, a lack of institutional structure does not come without consequence. It is likely to cause legal fragmentation with respect to any prospective FTA's application. While such an agreement could allow the UK to self-police, permitting British courts to act as authoritative norm interpreters as to the meaning of internationally negotiated norms on British soil, the courts would in such circumstances have two options. Either they would slavishly adhere to the interpretations followed by the ECJ, thereby preserving the cogency of the internal market, or they would exercise their own judicial discretion. In the latter case, maintaining the EU-UK internal market would quickly become unworkable, as different rules (or rather different authoritative interpretations of the same rules) would apply in different jurisdictions. In the former, the object of jurisdictional independence would be defeated by the knowledge that judges were obliged in any event to follow the ECJ, lest their diverging opinions upset the proverbial apple cart.

It appears clear, therefore, that in order for the UK to access the internal market, a legal framework designed to support an extended internal market must be to the UK, based on the freedoms of the internal market, along with instruments for a certain uniformity of application of those freedoms. What this entails in concrete terms is that a supranational apparatus must exercise effective competing, concurrent, or overarching jurisdiction over the domestic territory in areas concerning the internal market in order for the latter to function effectively.

12.5 The EEA Alternative

The Court in *Polydor* provides some guidance on the conditions that need to be met for similarly worded provisions to be interpreted in a similar manner (thus permitting effective market access), pointing to institutional bases and pooled jurisdiction as being the *sine qua non* of such an arrangement. It appears clear that in order for the UK to access the internal market, the UK must be party to a legal framework designed to support an extended internal market based on the freedoms

[45] Ibid.

[46] It is an open secret that the EU hopes the Swiss—overburdened with individual European regulatory measures, and under-represented with regard to the content of the latter—will soon join the EEA. Indeed, it is relevant to note that the Swiss referendum, held on 6 December 1992 only rejected EEA membership by 50.3% to 49.7%. See MA Miscrez (2012) Switzerland poised to keep EU at arm's length, SwissInfo, 2 December 2012, http://www.swissinfo.ch/eng/20-years-on_switzerland-poised-to-keep-eu-at-arm-s-length/34083578, accessed 6 February 2017.

of that market, with instruments ensuring uniformity of application of those freedoms.[47] However, given that a supranational jurisdictional apparatus, capable of directly enacting, enforcing and authoritatively interpreting rules with independent normative force on UK territory, was exactly the arrangement from which the UK wished to extricate itself, any such construction would be difficult to square with a meaningful repatriation of previously alienated tenets of national sovereignty.

Similar qualms were relevant in the drafting of the EEA Agreement in the early 1990s. The latter provides for a novel institutional apparatus, which aims to bring the EFTA States (except Switzerland) under the internal market umbrella.[48] However, the EEA does not share the same commitment to a new political community as the EU. The EFTA States firmly stated that they did not want to join the EU. Nor did they wish to create a superior legal order that would impose obligations upon them, grant rights to their citizens without their consent, and strip them of sovereign control of their territories. Thus, the doctrines of direct effect and supremacy are absent.[49] What this entails in concrete terms is that EEA law, in and of itself, has no independent normative force in Norway, Iceland and Liechtenstein, until such time as it is implemented in the respective domestic legal orders. The compulsive force of law comes from an act of the domestic legislator (incorporation); the domestic territoriality of jurisdiction remains unfractured. Furthermore, since the EFTA States have not transferred legislative powers (and thereby sovereignty),[50] there is no single authoritative mechanism for enforcing EEA law. Rather, the EEA Agreement is accompanied by a so-called 'two-pillar institutional structure',[51] entailing that the EEA Agreement is administered, monitored and adjudicated in two independent pillars (one for the 28 EU member states, and one

---

[47] Per Baudenbacher, the Court, in *Polydor*, has set a normative standard that ought to be met before to guarantee that the interpretation given to EU provision apply to other treaties. Thus, 'substantive homogeneity, which is secured by institutions, is a precondition for the non-application of Polydor.' See Baudenbacher 2013.

[48] The CFI stated in *Case C-452/01 (Proceedings brought by Margarethe Ospelt and Schlössle Weissenberg Familienstiftung)*, ECJ, Judgment, ECR I-9743, 23 September 2003, para 29, that 'one of the principal aims of the [EEA] Agreement is to provide for the fullest possible realisation of the free movement of goods, persons, services and capital within the whole [EEA], so that the internal market established within the European Union is extended to the EFTA States'.

[49] See *Case E-1/07 (Criminal proceedings against A)*, EFTA Court, Judgement, EFTA Ct. Rep. 246, 3 October 2007, para 40–41. This holding was confirmed in *Cases E-9/07 and E-10/07 (L'Oreal Norge AS v Aarskog Per AS and Others and Smart Club Norge)*, EFTA Court, Judgment, EFTA Ct. Rep. 259, 8 July 2008. See also the ECJ's Opinion 1/91, *Opinion pursuant to the second subparagraph of Article 228 of the EEC Treaty*, ECJ, ECR I-6079, 14 December 1991, later confirmed in Opinion 1/92, *Opinion of the Court pursuant to the second subparagraph of Article 228(1) of the EEC Treaty*, ECJ, ECR I-2821, 10 April 1992.

[50] The preamble to 1994 Protocol 35 on the Implementation of EEA Rules, OJ L 001 explicitly proclaims that no legislative powers have been transferred to supranational institutions.

[51] This structure is outlined more specifically in the 1994 Agreement Between the EFTA States on the Establishment of a Surveillance Authority and a Court of Justice, (Surveillance and Court Agreement), OJ L 344/1 (SCA).

for the 3 EFTA States), with the EFTA States having their own Court and Surveillance Authority, separate from the ECJ and the Commission.[52]

In the EEA, it is the very goal of establishing and operating a *shared internal market* with strong institutions, which led the ECJ, in September 2013, to define the Agreement as 'a close association between the European Union and the EFTA States based on special, privileged links between the parties concerned',[53] in comparison to other international agreements. This system of parallel enforcement and development of EEA law has allowed the EFTA States to maintain the shared internal market—and in this sense, the Agreement differentiates itself both from standard international agreements and from EU law, representing something of a middle way. The existing apparatus in place for the EFTA EEA States could, in principle, be easily expanded to accommodate the United Kingdom. Preserving single market access would also ensure a soft landing for the UK economy post-Brexit, though questions remain as to the concessions necessary to ensure UK accession to the EFTA pillar.[54]

The EEA system has been in place for almost a quarter of a century. However, from the perspective of taking back control over governance of its territory, questions about the feasibility of such a model necessarily remain. While EEA law seems a valiant attempt to 'have one's cake and eat it too', namely to escape the doctrines of direct effect and supremacy of EU law—thus allowing the UK to return to its pre-1972 conception of international law—while preserving the clear economic benefits brought about by internal market membership, it is worth reminding one's self that having the best of both worlds is rarely as straightforward as it sounds. The fact is that EEA rules are continuously updated via the addition of new EEA-relevant EU legislation. This essentially entails that EFTA EEA member states are obliged to update their domestic law in accordance with secondary rules (*acquis*) decided by the EU member states, while the EFTA EEA States are without a formal vote on the matter. Such an arrangement led former Prime Minister David Cameron to discount the EEA option, as the UK would have no say over the rules applicable in its territory, whereas as a member state of the EU, at least it could cast a vote in the Council.[55] While as a future EFTA/EEA member, the UK would not be legally bound to implement the rules of the EU supranational order *in foro domestico* due to the lack of direct effect, failure to do so could result in the suspension of particular chapters of the EEA Agreement and a loss of market

[52] On the two-pillar structure, see Baudenbacher and Bull 2007.

[53] *Case C-431/11 (United Kingdom of Great Britain and Northern Ireland v Council of the European Union)*, ECJ, Judgment, ECLI:EU:C:2013:589, 26 September 2013, para 49.

[54] See P Wintour (2016) Norway may block UK return to European Free Trade Association, The Guardian, 9 August 2016, https://www.theguardian.com/world/2016/aug/09/norway-may-block-uk-return-to-european-free-trade-association, accessed 9 February 2017.

[55] J Jónsdóttir (2013) It would be difficult for the UK to follow the 'Swiss' or 'Norwegian' models as an alternative to EU membership, London School of Economics, European Politics and Policy Blog, 28 January 2013, http://blogs.lse.ac.uk/europpblog/2013/01/28/uk-eu-euroscepticism-norway-model-swiss-model-efta/, accessed 5 January 5 2015.

access. As such, much like in the case of the WTO, and indeed the Swiss model, the line between legal compulsion and politico-economic compulsion seems a thin one.

12.6 Territorial Implications

It would seem likely from the above that the UK is faced with one of two possible scenarios post-Brexit. Either it will face the financial turmoil involved in a clean break from the EU, or it will submit itself to a looser multilateral arrangement on a basis akin to the existing EEA model. As discussed, subjection either to the WTO regime or that of the EFTA/EEA model will involve complying with the judgments of what are, *de facto*, international courts. Either scenario will also entail implementing rules about which it has no meaningful say, either the existing rules of the WTO Covered Agreements, or many of the very norms of EU law from which it wished to escape, reproduced verbatim via the EEA Agreement. While the substantive scope and legal enforcement powers of both the WTO and the EEA system fall far short of those provided for by the EU system, the economic imperatives underlying the three are essentially equal—fostering trade and interdependence through reciprocal obligations. Equally, while *de lege lata*, the UK courts may be empowered to read subsequent domestic legislation in light of the 1972 European Communities Act, thus undermining the exclusivity of domestic jurisdiction over the national territory, the logic of economic integration suggests that the compulsion to toe the line in order to harvest the fruits of the EEA or WTO models would not weigh less heavily, and that a largely compliant attitude from the organs of state is to be expected.

In light of the above we may ask ourselves whether a return to truly exclusive territorial sovereignty is ever possible. The answer, clearly, is no. In the twenty-first century, fundamental rules such as the preservation of human rights and international peace and security are ensured by reference to international institutional arrangements that involve vesting rights to act—essentially jurisdiction to do so—in actors beyond the sovereign state. The vesting of such powers in international institutions is a matter of *ius cogens*. No act of a state can extricate itself from such commitments. In the specific domain of trade, splendid, or perfect isolationism might be feasible for some states, but surely not for a small, densely populated island such as Britain, without inducing significant economic difficulties.

Either of the two feasible post-Brexit scenarios involves effective—if not legal—subjugation of the British territory to norms devised elsewhere in order to maintain an ability to trade, to a greater or lesser degree, with the rest of the world. In terms of substantive law, each way forward has specific territorial implications, which limit, alter, or loosen the *status quo ante*. An exhaustive discussion is beyond the scope of a composition such as the present one. However, in order to furnish an illustration, two areas will be discussed, namely the law of the sea and the free movement of persons.

12.6.1 Law of the Sea

It may seem rather counter-intuitive to include a discussion of rights to maritime zones in an analysis focusing on territory. However, the development of the law of the sea has been overwhelmingly based on the notion of appurtenance to land territory, to the extent that the modern legal regime, governed by the United Nations Convention on the Law of the Sea (1982) and customary law, defines a number of adjacent zones, such as the internal waters,[56] the territorial sea and the contiguous zone,[57] conferring rights exclusively to the coastal state—subject only to innocent passage of foreign states' ships.[58] In the context of the European Union legal order, however, the most important measurement is that of the Exclusive Economic Zone (EEZ), prescribing a 200 nautical mile limit, measured from the base line of the coastal state's land coastline, in which states possess the exclusive right to regulate fisheries under international law. In the EU context, the Common Fisheries Policy (CFP) mandates a pooling of the collective EEZs of the member states, entailing that fishing rights are redistributed according to a formula determined by the European Commission.[59] The UK, as a maritime state and traditional fishing power, is perceived to have suffered as a result of the CFP, while UK fishermen feel that they have been treated unfairly.[60] EU law prescribes strict quotas on fishing for each member state according to national quotas, and also prescribes restrictions on fishing as such, for example conservation measures concerning certain species, in order to ensure that only the permitted quantities of fish are landed.[61] Fisheries are an exclusive competence of the European Union, and this also entails that the UK's fishing rights in other areas—for example in the Arctic—are also regulated by the

[56] 1982 United Nations Convention on the Law of the Sea, 1833 UNTS 3 (UNCLOS), Article 8.

[57] Ibid., Part II.

[58] This stands in contradistinction to the High Seas, and the deep sea bed, where a loosely regulated regime predicated upon the notion of a 'common heritage of mankind', with shared rights for all states, is applicable.

[59] Regulation (EU) No. 1380/2013 of the European Parliament and of the Council of 11 December 2013 on the Common Fisheries Policy amending Council Regulations (EC) No 1954/2003 and (EC) No 1224/2009 and repealing Council Regulations (EC) No 2371/2002 and (EC) No 639/2004 and Council Decision 2004/585/EC, OJ L 354/22, Article 5(1).

[60] See e.g. interview with Mike Walker by the New York Times: K. De Breytas-Tamura (2016) In Brexit Debate, English Fishermen Eye Waters Free of E.U., The New York Times, 14 April 2016, http://www.nytimes.com/2016/04/15/business/international/many-in-british-fishing-port-want-eu-out-of-their-waters.html?_r=1, accessed 12 July 2016.

[61] For this purpose a Community control system was established: Council Regulation (EC) No. 1224/2009 of 20 November 2009 establishing a Community control system for ensuring compliance with the rules of the common fisheries policy, amending Regulations (EC) No 847/96, (EC) No 2371/2002, (EC) No 811/2004, (EC) No 768/2005, (EC) No 2115/2005, (EC) No 2166/2005, (EC) No 388/2006, (EC) No 509/2007, (EC) No 676/2007, (EC) No 1098/2007, (EC) No 1300/2008, (EC) No 1342/2008 and repealing Regulations (EEC) No 2847/93, (EC) No 1627/94 and (EC) No 1966/2006, OJ L 343/1.

CFP, despite the fact that the zones in question lie neither in EU nor UK waters.[62] Finally, one should mention the *Factortame* line of cases, which concerned a rule enacted by the UK Parliament (the 1988 Merchant Shipping Act) prescribing that to register a vessel as British, its owners must to be British nationals and residents. This legislation was aimed at preventing Spanish-owned companies from registering vessels in the UK and fishing within the UK quota, further reducing UK fishermen's share of the catch in the UK's waters. Here, the ECJ found that the UK had acted inconsistently with EU law, and that EU entrepreneurs must be allowed to register vessels in the UK, further eroding the UK's access to the fruits of its seas.[63] Britannia ruled the waves no more, it seems.

A 'clean break' after Brexit would represent outright repatriation of a territorial competence surrendered in its entirety to Brussels. Retaking full control of the regulation of its EEZ—the largest in the EU in terms of squared kilometre area—would garner the UK and its fishermen a far larger potential catch than that allotted to them under EU secondary law. However, a caveat should be appended to this conclusion. The vast majority of fish landed in UK waters is consumed within the EU. Tariffs on produce, especially if it is unfrozen, and therefore quickly perishable, may severely diminish, or indeed entirely reverse, any gains made through the UK liberating itself from the strictures of the CFP. Additionally, WTO rules are considerably more permissive in terms of allowing health inspections, technical controls, and other equivalent measures, which may serve to impede the flow of fish products from the UK to EU member states, even if trade is allowed. If demand for British fish is decreased as a result of such measures, the additional catches by British fishermen will not be of much use.

The EEA excludes fisheries, meaning the UK would, in that scenario, also reassert some jurisdictional competence over the EEZ. However, questions have arisen as to whether EEA law may apply to other maritime zones, including the continental shelf. The territorial scope of the EEA Agreement is clearly defined by Article 126(1) EEA. It provides that the EEA Agreement 'shall apply to the territories to which the Treaty establishing the European Economic Community is applied and under the conditions laid down in that Treaty and to the territories of Iceland, the Principality of Liechtenstein and the Kingdom of Norway'. However, whereas Article 126 EEA employs the word 'territory', the equivalent provision of EU law, namely Article 52 TFEU[64] simply lists the EU member states. This has led Norway to claim that the EEA Agreement does not apply to the continental shelf.[65]

---

[62] For additional discussion in this regard, see Wolf 2013.

[63] *Joined cases C-46/93 and C-48/93 (Brasserie du Pêcheur SA v Bundesrepublik Deutschland and The Queen v Secretary of State for Transport, ex parte: Factortame Ltd and others)*, ECJ, Judgment, ECR I-01029, 5 March 1996.

[64] 2012 Treaty on the Functioning of the European Union (Consolidated version), C 326/47 (TFEU).

[65] See excerpt from the Norwegian Ministry of Foreign Affairs' report to the Norwegian Parliament: Norwegian Ministry of Foreign Affairs (2012), The EEA Agreement and Norway's other Agreements with the EU, Meld. St. 5 (2012–2013) Report to the Storting (White Paper),

In the EU context, the ECJ has held that EU law does apply to the continental shelf, most notably in the *Salemink* case,[66] in which the Court stated that since a member state has a sort of functional, limited sovereignty over the continental shelf adjacent to it, works carried out on fixed or floating installations positioned on the continental shelf, in the context of exploitation of natural resources or similar activities, are to be regarded as works carried out in the territory of that state for the purposes of applying EU law (in that case, Regulation No 1408/71).[67]

In light of the above, the EEA Agreement offers distinct advantages, insofar as it specifically excludes the CFP, while allowing market access as a platform for the sale of fish products in Europe. However, the question as to whether foreign economic operators may exercise their freedom of establishment and engage in fishing and other economic activities in UK maritime zones—the point in dispute in *Factortame*—remains an open question. As such, while a clean break with the EU offers complete regulatory autonomy (and severely impeded market access to the EEA's internal market), securing access to EU consumers via the Single Market would seem to require at least some contemplation of restrictions upon maritime sovereignty and the ability to exercise jurisdiction. Neither *mare liberum* nor *mare clausum* provide optimal outcomes.

12.6.2 Free Movement of Persons

One of the main bones of contention during the Brexit referendum debate was the issue of non-UK EU nationals living in the United Kingdom. The 'four freedoms' of EU law have long included the free movement of workers, later expanded to the free movement of EU citizens in general (that is, for economic and non-economic motives) in the years since the Maastricht Treaty.[68] EU law removes the complete and exclusive command over territory from states, as well as the right to distinguish between one's nationals and aliens in many contexts, as individuals from all member states enjoy the guarantee of free movement and the possibility to work anywhere they choose. In this area, the discontinuation of EU law post-Brexit will entail the cessation of privileges that EU citizens enjoy in the UK.[69] The

(Footnote 65 continued)

Recommendations of the Ministry of Foreign Affairs of 12 October 2012. https://www.regjeringen.no/globalassets/upload/ud/vedlegg/europa/nou/meldst5_ud_eng.pdf, accessed 6 February 2017, at 13.

[66] *Case C-347/10 (Salemink v Raad van bestuur van het Uitvoeringsinstituut werknemersverzekeringen)*, ECJ Grand Chamber, Judgment, ECLI:EU:C:2012:17, 17 January 2012.

[67] *Salemink*, para 35.

[68] 1992 Treaty of Maastricht on European Union, OJ C 191.

[69] Directive 2014/54/EU of the European Parliament and of the Council of 16 April 2014 on measures facilitating the exercise of rights conferred on workers in the context of freedom of movement for workers, OJ L 128/8, para 1.

consequences are myriad, but one may highlight Article 1(2) of Regulation (EU) No. 492/2011,[70] which states that any national of a member state has the right to take up employment in the territory of another member state, while Directive 2004/38 provides an array of guarantees related to the rights of EU citizens to move to and reside in other member states, even when they are not engaged in economic activity. These provisions will no longer be applicable post-Brexit, in any scenario in which the WTO rules are applicable. Entry to UK territory will thenceforth be entirely dependent upon UK migration law. The UK will thus be exclusively entitled to enact stricter legislation in this regard and deny entry—and continuance of stay—to EU nationals. It will also reassert full control over criminal law, freeing itself from the strictures of the European Arrest Warrant. However, it is worth wondering whether the UK government will wish to contemplate unilateral renunciation of the rights and obligations incumbent by virtue of EU law in relation to free movement, as such a scenario could have undesirable knock-on effects. The 761,000 UK nationals in Spain, for example could find themselves subject to retaliatory discrimination,[71] while excluding economic operators from other EU member states who have established businesses that provide jobs in the UK would seem, on the face of it, to make little sense.

The rights of free movement of persons in the EEA differ from those of the EU in two ways. Firstly, the EEA Agreement was not concluded in the context of developing a common immigration policy.[72] Since the EEA Agreement is explicitly restricted to nationals of the EU and EFTA States, secondary EU immigration law is also excluded, thus excluding any legislation on third country nationals.[73] As noted elsewhere,

> [t]he EFTA States party to the EEA Agreement have thereby avoided direct exposure to the EU's emerging and assimilative policies on these fronts, and its drive to secure a wider range of rights for economically inactive EU citizens and third country nationals and a more equal protection to that afforded to all EEA nationals under the rules governing the free movement of workers.[74]

[70] Regulation (EU) No 492/2011 of the European Parliament and of the Council of 5 April 2011 on freedom of movement for workers within the Union, OJ L 141/1.

[71] Sriskandarajah and Drew 2006. This is, of course, merely the tip of the proverbial iceberg. The Spanish example is instructive in this regard. As well as trade and employment disputes, the position of Gibraltar and the many businesses run by UK nationals in Spain could be seriously affected by any Brexit that is not agreeable to Spanish interests.

[72] Article 79 TFEU.

[73] Only family members within the meaning of Directive 2004/38, having third country nationality, would enjoy certain derived rights when entering or moving to the host country. However, these rights are acquired through their status as family members of the EU/EEA national concerned. Accordingly, these dependent rights do not limit the EEA EFTA Member States' autonomy regarding third country policies. See the Joint Declaration by the Contracting Parties to decision No 158/2007 incorporating Directive 2004/38/EC of the European Parliament and of the Council into the Agreement, OJ L 124/23.

[74] Fredriksen and Franklin 2015, at 639–640.

Secondly, since the EEA Agreement has not evolved in tandem with the EU treaty changes over the past two decades, the EEA Agreement, which entered into force on 1 January 1994, does not include the concept of EU Citizenship, introduced to the EU via the Maastricht Treaty. In this respect, it should be emphasized that new policy areas, which were not present when the Agreement was drafted, cannot affect its scope or interpretation, even if they affect the functioning of the internal market.[75] It is obvious that the gap between the two pillars, which has emerged since 1992, has widened over the years. As noted by the EFTA Court, this development has created certain discrepancies at the level of primary law, which, depending on the circumstances, may have an impact on the interpretation of the EEA Agreement.[76]

Nuancing the above picture somewhat is the fact that, although the EEA Agreement does not include the concept of EU Citizenship, Directive 2004/38, geared to bolster the right of Union citizens to move to and reside in any member state, is not restricted in its application to EU nationals alone. As it built upon the provisions of previous directives, which also formed part of the EEA Agreement, it was transposed into the Agreement almost unchanged, thus extending its scope to nationals of the EEA/EFTA States.[77]Agreement, OJ L 124/20. Decision 158/2007 of the Joint Committee and the declaration annexed thereto state that the concept of Union citizenship does not apply within the EEA legal order, and that the case law of the Court of Justice of the European Union (ECJ) relating to this concept is of no relevance within the EEA. Thus, the divergent legal contexts within which the Directive is situated in EU and EEA law—in addition to the fact that it was never really designed to operate in the EEA context—entails that the legal situation in which it operates is particularly complex in nature.[78] However, it is important to bear in mind that the scope of Directive 2004/38 is quite narrow by comparison to Articles 20 and 21 TFEU. The EEA relevance of cases such as *Zambrano*, where the ECJ based its decision solely on rights flowing from Article 20 TFEU and where free movement rights had not been exercised, would therefore seem doubtful.[79]

What the EEA Brexit model would achieve in concrete terms is that while cross-border activity flowing from the Single Market (free movement of goods, services, capital, and workers) must be permitted in the UK, it would have the

---

[75] See, for example, the *Case E-1/01 (Hörður Einarsson v The Icelandic State)*, EFTA Court, Judgment, EFTA Ct. Rep. 1, 22 February 2002, para 45, where the EFTA Court refused to countenance arguments based on provision of the EC Treaty introduced by the Treaty of Amsterdam.

[76] *Case E-28/15 (Yankuba Jabbi v The Norwegian Government, represented by the Immigration Appeals Board)*, EFTA, Judgment, 26 July 2016, para 62.

[77] The Directive was incorporated into Annex V to the EEA Agreement at point 1 and Annex VIII at point 3 by Decision of the EEA Joint Committee No 158/2007 of 7 December 2007 amending Annex V (Free movement of workers) and Annex VIII (Right of establishment) to the EEA.

[78] Fredriksen and Franklin 2015, at 640.

[79] See discussion in Fredriksen and Franklin 2015, at 641–642.

possibility to exclude the more recent, more *avant garde* interpretative advances in deepening the market, both in cases where they have been achieved solely through the introduction of the notion of citizenship and where they have arrived as a result of 'citizenship reading' of workers' rights under EU law.[80] However, with regard to economic cross-border activity, subjection to supranational—or at least international—governance and jurisdiction would—*de facto*—subsist.

12.7 Conclusion

The United Kingdom faces an uncertain future. Its immediate destiny may well hinge on how it negotiates its post-Brexit relationship with the EU. Any arrangement reached between the parties will have fundamental implications for the question of which powers exercise jurisdiction—and thereby sovereign control over the UK's territory. The power to determine Britain's future is in the hands of Theresa May's government. It remains to be seen how it will utilize this power. Every engagement in an international agreement by a state may be viewed as entailing a loss of sovereignty, a loss of control, and in certain circumstances, an alienation of its power to regulate its territory, a fundamental component of statehood. However, an alternative way of viewing such relationships is in terms of an *exercise* of sovereignty. States enter international agreements and attribute powers to organizations precisely because they have the *power* to do so. A corollary of this power is the power to regain control of their own affairs when the activities and mandate of the organization to which they are a party cease to concord with their own objectives. However, in an era where interdependence has superseded independence as the 'normal' condition of statehood, we may pose the question as to whether the tripartite test for statehood usually described in the constitutive theory is even fit for purpose anymore. The truth is that while states continue to possess a population and a territory, governance thereof is, in many cases, no longer achieved solely by an omnipotent national government. Securing investments from overseas and meaningful engagement with international actors requires international oversight, once integration surpasses a certain threshold. In such circumstances, a state's territory becomes the subject of overlapping jurisdiction and overlapping forms of government.

In the case of the UK, the choices are stark. The lessons described above in relation to fisheries and freedom of movement could well be transposed to other areas of the law. What is certain is that Brexit will not come without a cost, and mitigating this cost may ironically involve a not insignificant further alienation of sovereignty, ostensibly by a parasitic attachment to the EU, where the UK may find itself forced to accept many European norms without having a great deal of say in their elaboration—hardly the realisation of full control proposed by proponents of a

[80] Ibid., at 640–641.

UK exit. Participation in international decision-making may *céder place* to rule by effective *Diktat* from Brussels, without a British seat at the table, hardly a reassertion of exclusive control by Westminster.

The alternative to the above is a future involving an unambiguous reassertion of control, but with a virtual certainty of less prosperity, a land of abundant fish that is impossible to export, where companies struggle to attract foreign investment and skilled workers, but equally where the tripartite test of the Montevideo Convention is clearly satisfied. One may view the equation facing the UK as a balancing act between exclusive territorial control and economic prosperity. The inconvenient truth is that there is no likely way to achieve both at once.

References

Baudenbacher C (2012) Some Thoughts on the EFTA Court's Phases of Life. In: EFTA Court (ed) Judicial Protection in the European Economic Area. German Law Publishers, Stuttgart, pp 2–28

Baudenbacher C (2013) The EFTA Court and Court of Justice of the European Union: Coming in Parts But Winning Together. In: Court of Justice of the European Union, The Court of Justice and the Construction of Europe: Analyses and Perspectives on Sixty Years of Case-law - La Cour de Justice et la Construction de l'Europe: Analyses et Perspectives de Soixante Ans de Jurisprudence. TMC Asser Press, The Hague, pp 183–203

Baudenbacher C, Bull H (2007) European Integration Through Interaction of Legal Regimes. Universitetsforlaget, Oslo

Buckle R, Hewish T, Hulsman JC, Mansfield I, Oulds R (2015) Brexit: Directions for Britain Outside the EU. Institute of Economic Affairs, London

Burke C, Hannesson OÍ, Bangsund K (2016) Life on the Edge: EFTA and the EEA as a Future for the UK in Europe. European Public Law 22(1):69–96

Burke E (1790) Reflections on the Revolution in France and on the Proceedings in Certain Societies in London Relative to that Event. Dodsley, London

Clarke K (2001) An Island Nation: Re-Reading Tacitus' Agricola. Journal of Roman Studies 91:94–112

Crawford JR (2011) State. Max Planck Encyclopedia of Public International Law. http://opil.ouplaw.com/view/10.1093/law:epil/9780199231690/law-9780199231690-e1473?rskey=V7vSXZ&result=1&prd=EPIL. Accessed 6 February 2017

Fredriksen HH, Franklin CNK (2015) Of Pragmatism and Principles: The EEA Agreement more than 20 Years On. Common Market Law Review 52(3):629–284

Fuller LL (1969) The Morality of Law, 2nd edn. Yale University Press, New Haven

Gross L (1948) The Peace of Westphalia. American Journal of International Law 42(1):20–41

Held D, McGrew A, Goldblatt D, Perraton J (1999) Global Transformations. Stanford University Press, Stanford

Jellinek G (1963) System der Subjektiven Öffentlichen Rechte (System of Subjective Public Rights), reprinted edn. Wissenschaftliche Buchgesellschaft, Darmstadt

Koskenniemi M (2005) From Apology to Utopia, The Structure of International Legal Argument, Reissue with a new Epilogue. Cambridge University Press, Cambridge

Mann FA (1964) The Doctrine of Jurisdiction in International Law. Recueil des Cours 111:1–162

Meyer T (2012) Codifying Custom. University of Pennsylvania Law Review 160: 995–1069

Munro CR (1999) Studies in Constitutional Law. Butterworths, London

Nicol D (2001) EC Membership and the Judicialization of British Politics. Oxford University Press, Oxford

Öberg ML (2016) From EU Citizens to Third Country Nationals: The Legacy of Polydor. European Public Law 22(1):97–114
Ohmae K (1990) The Borderless World: Power and Strategy in the Interlinked Economy. Harper Business, New York
Oppenheim L (1955) International Law: A Treatise. Vol. I – Peace, 8th edn (edited by Lauterpacht H). Longman, London
Sassen S (2000) Territory and Territoriality in the Global Economy. International Sociology 15 (2):372–393
Shaw MN (1982) Territory in International Law. Netherlands Yearbook of International Law 13:61–91
Simma B (1985) Self-Contained Regimes. Netherlands Yearbook of International Law 16:111–136
Sriskandarajah D, Drew C (2006) Brits Abroad: Mapping the Scale and Nature of British Emigration. Institute for Public Policy Research (IPPR) Report. http://www.ippr.org/publications/brits-abroad-mapping-the-scale-and-nature-of-british-emigration. Accessed 6 February 2017
Steinberg PE (2005) Insularity, Sovereignty and Statehood: The Representation of Islands on Portolan Charts and the Construction of the Territorial State. Geografiska Annaler Series B Human Geography (Swedish Society for Anthropology and Geography) 87(4):253–265
Tacitus C (2010) Agricola and Germania (transl. by Mattingly H, edited by Rives J). Penguin Classics, London
Verdross A (1969) Entstehungsweisen und Geltungsgrund des Universellen Völkerrechtlichen Gewohnheitsrechts (Modes of Origin and Validity of the Universal Customary Law of International Law). ZaöRV (Journal of International Public Law and International Law) 29:636–653
Wolf S (2013) Svalbard's Maritime Zones, Their Status under International Law and Current and Future Disputes Scenarios. German Institute for International and Security Affairs Working Paper. https://www.swp-berlin.org/fileadmin/contents/products/arbeitspapiere/WP_Wolf_2_2013.pdf. Accessed 3 February 2017

Part II
Dutch Practice in International Law

Chapter 13
The Dutch Contribution to the Armed Coalition Against ISIS

Gelijn Molier and Martijn Hekkenberg

Abstract The central topic of this chapter is Dutch state practice with regard to the international armed fight against ISIS in Iraq and Syria. This state practice manifested itself as a Dutch contribution to aerial bombardments in Iraq from October 2014 onwards, and in Syria from January 2016 onwards. In order to uncover its details, the authors primarily examined the various parliamentarian debates held on the international legal aspects of contribution to this armed struggle. What is striking about these debates is that international law played a particularly important role in answering the question of whether the Netherlands should contribute militarily to the fight against ISIS. Remarkably, the Dutch government changed its legal position on the legality of bombarding ISIS in Syria within a period of nine months. The fact that the Dutch government and an increasing number of Western states have started to give a more extensive interpretation of the right of collective self-defence with regard to the fight against ISIS in Syria, has everything to do with the current global disorder, in which failed states and militant non-state actors are commonplace. Public international law adapts to this new 'world disorder' by incorporating that state practice which allows for more lenient interpretations of the rules regarding the use of force.

Dr. G. Molier LL.M. (g.molier@LAW.leidenuniv.nl) is associate professor at the Department of Jurisprudence, Leiden University. He wrote his dissertation on the legality of humanitarian intervention. His main field of research pertains to the law of peace and security, in particular to questions relating to the (legitimacy of the) use of force in international relations and the protection of human rights. M. Hekkenberg (m.g.hekkenberg@umail.leidenuniv.nl) holds an LL.M. in Public International Law as well as an LL.M. in Jurisprudence and Philosophy of Law from Leiden University. He currently has a teaching position at its Department of Jurisprudence.

G. Molier (✉) · M. Hekkenberg
Department of Jurisprudence, Leiden University, Leiden, The Netherlands
e-mail: g.molier@LAW.leidenuniv.nl

M. Hekkenberg
e-mail: m.g.hekkenberg@umail.leidenuniv.nl

M. Kuijer and W. Werner (eds.), *Netherlands Yearbook of International Law 2016*, Netherlands Yearbook of International Law 47,
DOI 10.1007/978-94-6265-207-1_13

Keywords International armed coalition against ISIS · Use of force · Right of (collective) self-defence · Humanitarian intervention · Responsibility to protect · Syria · Iraq · Non-state actors · Failed states · State practice · Customary international law · The Netherlands · Parliamentary debates

Contents

13.1 Introduction

The Netherlands has been part of a United States-led international armed coalition against ISIS since October 2014. Initially, the Dutch military contribution was limited to the armed fight against ISIS in Iraq, but the Dutch expanded their aerial bombardments to ISIS' territory in Eastern Syria from January 2016 onwards. The central theme of this chapter is Dutch state practice with regard to this international armed fight against ISIS in Iraq and Syria.

From the moment that military intervention in Syria was initially contemplated, a fierce debate pertaining to its legality was waged in the Dutch parliament. When the debate first arose in October 2014, there were several parties in parliament that believed that there was a legal basis for armed intervention.

The Dutch government however, initially adhered resolutely to the course charted since the Davids Committee (2010), which entailed that there needed to be an *adequate* international legal mandate, not just for participation in a military intervention, but for supporting one as well.[1] This mandate existed for Iraq, as Iraq had granted permission for military operations against ISIS to be staged within its borders. With respect to Syria however, no permission from the government was granted (or requested), nor would the conditions for invoking the right to (collective) self-defence be met, nor was there a Security Council Resolution providing the go-ahead for the use of force. Thus initially, there was but one feasible conclusion: there was no adequate international legal mandate with regard to contributing to the armed fight against ISIS in Syria, and therefore the Dutch contribution needed to be limited to Iraq.

There were however political parties which resisted this relatively restrictive interpretation of the international rules governing the use of force. According to them, either the humanitarian intervention doctrine, the principle of necessity,[2] or the right to collective self-defence could legally justify armed action against ISIS in Syria. Remarkably, the Dutch government later revised its position in June 2015, shifting to the opinion that there was in fact a legal basis for aerial bombardments against ISIS in Syria. Subsequently, the Dutch government commenced the bombardment of ISIS positions in Syria in January 2016. The Dutch military mission ended and was transferred to the Belgian military on 28 June 2016.[3]

In this chapter, we discuss the debates that took place in the Dutch parliament from October 2014 until January 2016 between the government and the *Tweede Kamer* (the lower house of parliament) on the legal aspects of a Dutch contribution to the international armed coalition against ISIS in Iraq and Syria. What is striking about these debates is that international law played a particularly exceedingly

---

[1] The 'Independent Research Committee Decision-Making Iraq' (Davids Committee) investigated the preparation and decision-making regarding Dutch political support for the invasion of Iraq in the summer 2002 to summer 2003 period. The Committee—which was enacted in January 2009—presented the results of its research on 12 January 2010. The report is available at: https://www.rijksoverheid.nl/documenten/rapporten/2010/01/12/rapport-commissie-davids. Incidentally, the demand for an 'adequate international legal mandate' was first mentioned in the coalition-agreement of the fourth cabinet under Prime Minister Balkenende. Under point 4 of this agreement's first pillar, entitled 'an active international and European role', we read: 'Participation in missions which require the effort of Dutch military personnel requires an adequate international legal mandate'. This is clarified further in the governmental Note "Legal basis and mandate of missions with a contribution of Dutch military units" at page 3: 'The demand for a legal basis must be separated from the mission's *mandate*. The "mandate" refers to the provision of an assignment whereby the political and military goals, and more specifically the task description, are detailed. Both aspects—an international legal basis and clear mandate—are crucial factors in the decision-making process regarding the *commitment of Dutch military units*. While political support is of a different order than participation in a military mission, it also requires the existence of an international legal basis; a mandate however is not necessary in that case.' Mandates always stem from the United Nations, principally in the form of a Security Council resolution. Such resolutions can be adopted without reference to Chapter VII of the Charter. The point is that the legal basis and mandate for contributing to the armed coalition against ISIS in Iraq and Syria were muddled together within the different discussions detailed in this article. *Kamerstukken II*, 2006/07, 29521, nr. 41, at 3–6.

[2] E.g. Article 25 ILC Articles on Responsibility of States for Internationally Wrongful Acts.

[3] *Kamerstukken II* 2014/15, 27925, nr. 598, at 2.

important role in answering the question of whether the Netherlands should contribute militarily to the fight against ISIS. Both the government as well as the different factions in parliament attached great importance to compliance with the body of international law governing the use of force. In addition, the advice of Professor Nollkaemper, acting as the external advisor on international law, weighed heavily in their decision-making processes.[4]

Furthermore, these debates serve as an illustration of the position underlying this chapter, i.e., that the advent of non-state actors such as ISIS is making the classic system of public international law, which primarily governs the relations between states, crack at the seams. Given this new global security situation, it is unsurprising that an increasing number of states is starting to wield a more extensive interpretation of the rules governing the use of force with regard to the fight against ISIS. The concluding paragraph will further scrutinise this development, as well as indicate whether or not it is to be seen as a positive advancement.

13.2 The October 2014 Parliamentary Debate

13.2.1 Article 100 Letter of 24 September 2014

13.2.1.1 Introduction

On 24 September 2014, the government sent a letter to the Tweede Kamer in which it informed it—in accordance with Article 100 of the Dutch Constitution—about the decision to join the fight against ISIS.[5] In addition, the letter was a reaction to the Tweede Kamer's request to be informed about the air offensive against ISIS in Syria.[6] In the letter, the government claimed to have decided to provide, in addition to political and humanitarian support, a military contribution to the fight against ISIS in Iraq, in cooperation with the United States and other countries. The government indicated that it would provide six operational F-16 fighter jets for up to a

[4] In 2011, Professor Nollkaemper was appointed the external advisor on international law by the Minister of Foreign Affairs. With this measure, the Minister heeded the advice of the Davids Committee, which had recommended safeguarding the Ministry of Foreign Affairs' decision-making process with the addition of international legal advice. See https://www.rijksoverheid.nl/actueel/nieuws/2011/05/25/andre-nollkaemper-benoemd-tot-externe-volkenrechtelijk-adviseur.

[5] Article 100 was added to the Dutch Constitution in 2000 with the purpose of explicitly arranging the participation of parliament in deciding to supply Dutch military personnel to international peace- or crisis-management operations. It states: '1. The Government shall inform the States General in advance if the armed forces are to be deployed or made available to maintain or promote the international legal order. This shall include the provision of humanitarian aid in the event of armed conflict.' Such informational memos sent by the government to parliament are referred to as 'Article 100 letters'.

[6] *Kamerstukken II* 2014/15, 27925, nr. 506, at 1.

year. Additionally, in order to aid the fight with ISIS on the ground, the Dutch would provide Iraqi and Kurdish forces with advice and military training during this same period.[7]

The government provided three reasons for participating in the international coalition against ISIS. Firstly, the Dutch contribution was directed at de-escalating the conflict in the region, with the primary purpose of restoring regional security. Secondly, 'preventing and ending serious breaches of fundamental human rights by ISIS in Iraq and Syria' was another explicitly mentioned aim.[8] The government stated that it is highly likely that ISIS had committed crimes against humanity as well as genocide,[9] and that the government wished to contribute to stopping these horrors.[10] It can therefore be said that the Dutch contribution was also aimed at protecting the civilian population. Lastly, the government noted that the Dutch effort is directed at the threat to Dutch national security emanating from jihadists in Iraq and Syria. ISIS needed to be weakened in order to limit this threat.

Translating these three reasons to the parlance of international law, we recognise the 'responsibility to protect' and humanitarian intervention doctrine on the one hand, and the right to collective and individual self-defence on the other. How did the Dutch government initially argue for supporting the bombing of ISIS in Iraq (but not in Syria) and what were the reactions of the different parties in parliament to the government's position?

13.2.1.2 Legal Justification for the Dutch Military Contribution

Under the heading 'mandate', the government established the legal basis for Dutch participation in the fight against ISIS. The point of departure was the Iraqi authorities' request for military support in a letter of 25 June 2014 to the Security Council, which was later repeated on 20 September the same year.[11] A legal basis for the Dutch military effort in Iraq was thus found in the request for support by its legitimate government. Regarding the question of whether or not there was also a legal mandate for intervention in Syria, the government noted that at the time there was no international consensus. It was noted that in practice there are no more borders between Iraq and Syria, and there was a risk that ISIS could form a direct threat to Iraq from within Syria. Additionally, were ISIS to be combated exclusively from within Iraq, the terrorists might simply move to Syria and other countries in the region. Nonetheless, the Dutch commitment was to be limited to Iraq, as it was questionable whether collective self-defence might be invoked as the international

[7] Ibid., at 2.

[8] Ibid.

[9] Ibid.

[10] Ibid.

[11] Ibid., at 4. For the Iraqi letter of 25 June 2014, see S/2014/440, 25 June 2014; for the Iraqi letter of 20 September 2014, see S/2014/691, 22 September 2014.

legal basis for military action.[12] At the same time however, the government recognised that the United States did in fact find that the aforementioned letters from Iraq to the Security Council provided a basis for the right to collective self-defence to be invoked and thus for intervention within Syrian borders.[13] While the Dutch government did not directly support the aerial offensive above Syria, it did—in accordance with the course charted since the Davids Committee report—'understand' the American effort.[14]

13.2.2 Parliamentary Reactions

On 2 October 2014, the parliamentarian committees on Foreign Affairs, Defence, Foreign Trade and Development Cooperation, and Security and Justice, held a deliberation on the aforementioned Article 100 letter of 24 September 2014 with the Ministers of Foreign Affairs, Defence, and Foreign Trade and Development Cooperation. During this meeting, a letter from the external advisor on international law regarding the legal basis for aerial strikes against ISIS targets in Iraq and Syria was also discussed, as well as a letter from the Minister of Foreign Affairs on various aspects of international law pertaining to such aerial strikes.[15]

All political parties but two—the Socialist Party (SP) and the Party for the Animals (PvdD)—expressed their support for the Dutch mission in Iraq. The debate was therefore focused primarily on whether bombardments in Syria would also be warranted and if there was an international legal mandate for such military action. The governmental parties: the People's Party for Freedom and Democracy (VVD) and the Labour Party (PvdA), again stuck to the Davids Committee course, i.e., that Dutch military contributions to international operations require an adequate international legal mandate. According to the VVD and the PvdA, such a mandate was lacking with regard to Syria. To the VVD however, an adequate legal mandate does not form a *sine qua non* regarding military contributions. The VVD spokesperson named vital interests, international and humanitarian considerations, genocide, the threat of ethnic cleansing, mass murder or the use of chemical, nuclear or biological weapons as examples which obviate the need for an international legal mandate.[16] In cases such as ethnic cleansing, mass murder or

---

[12] Ibid., at 5.

[13] Ibid. For the letter by the United States Representative to the United Nations Samantha Power, see http://justsecurity.org/15436/war-powers-resolution-article-51-letters-force-syria-isil-khorasan-group.

[14] Ibid.

[15] *Kamerstukken II* 2014/15, 27925, nr. 925, nr. 523, at 1.

[16] *Kamerstukken II* 2014/15, 27925, nr. 523, at 7.

genocide, military intervention as an *ultimum remedium* should not be precluded by a (Russian or Chinese) veto in the Security Council.[17]

To the PvdA, an adequate or 'clear'—in the words of its spokesperson—international mandate *did* form a necessary condition for action within Syria. However, this party also recognised that legal justifications for the use of force were further taking shape. The spokesperson mentioned the US' arguments for collective self-defence, quotes from the Syrian Foreign Minister (which appeared to establish implicit consent for bombardments on Syrian territory),[18] and the developments in Kobani (which indicated an impending mass killing by ISIS). These factors seemed to indicate, respectively: collective self-defence, (implied) consent, and humanitarian intervention as three possible justifications for the use of force. At the time however, no 'clear' international legal mandate could be established.[19] The Socialist Party was simply against the Dutch military mission because it did not believe that Western interference and an increase in violence could lead to an improvement of the situation in Iraq and Syria.

The Christian Democratic Appeal (CDA) was of the opinion that intervention in Syria could be justified. This justification could be found in the right to collective self-defence (in line with the United States' argumentation) on the one hand,[20] and in the 'responsibility to protect', humanitarian intervention doctrine or principle of necessity on the other.[21] These last concepts were used somewhat interchangeably by the CDA spokesperson. A precise reading shows that the CDA found that, in addition to the right to collective self-defence, the principle of necessity could provide a legal justification for armed intervention in Syria.[22] Given this justification, there would also be an adequate international legal mandate with regard to the situation in Syria. Since the government left open the option to act in Syria at a later point in time, the Christian Union inquired whether acting in Syria would also be possible without an international legal mandate. The coalition agreement between the VVD and PvdA after all stated that: 'A contribution to international operations of crisis-management requires an international legal mandate, or a situation of humanitarian emergency'.[23] The Christian Union indicated to have no

[17] Ibid.

[18] Statement by H.E Walid Al-Moualem, Deputy Prime Minister, Minister of Foreign Affairs and Expatriates Of The Syrian Arab Republic at The General Debate of the 69th Session of the UNGA, UN Doc. A/64/PV.11 [GA/10865], 29 September 2014.

[19] *Kamerstukken II* 2014/15, 27925, nr. 523, at 11.

[20] Ibid., at 19.

[21] Ibid., at 19, 20, 23.

[22] Ibid., at 21. Referring to Article 25 ILC Articles on Responsibility of States for Internationally Wrongful Acts. For the legal argumentation that necessity can provide a justification for the use of force to end systematic and severe violations of fundamental human rights, see Molier 2006, at 52–60.

[23] See: VVD and PvdA (2012) Bruggen slaan. Regeerakkoord VVD—PvdA. [Building bridges. Coalition agreement VVD—PvdA.]. 2012, at 16. http://www.rijksoverheid.nl/documenten-en-publicaties/rapporten/2012/10/29/regeerakkoord.html. Accessed 6 October 2016.

problem with a contribution to the fight in Syria in the context of a humanitarian emergency, even without a clear legal mandate.[24] The Reformed Political Party (SGP)—another small Christian party—agreed with the CDA in that there were also sufficient legal grounds for intervention against ISIS in Syria. The collective self-defence in protection of Iraq, legally actuated by its request for aid to the United Nations, would provide a sufficient mandate for acting against the threat of ISIS from Syria.[25] The SGP spokesperson subtly pointed to the fact that the PvdA spokesperson used the term 'clear' international legal mandate, while the Davids Committee report expressly spoke of an adequate or sufficient mandate.[26] Finally, the two-man splinter group Bontes/van Klaveren was also in favour of acting against ISIS in Syria, but did not indicate what kind of legal grounds would support such action, nor if any grounds for action had been met.

In light of all the issues raised by the different parties, the government—represented by the Minister of Foreign Affairs—noted the following. According to the Minister, all parties, with the exception of the VVD and SGP, supported the findings of the report of the Davids Committee. These stated that even merely providing political support for an international military mission, let alone joining one, required an adequate international legal mandate. The Minister found that there is no doubt such a mandate exists with regard to Iraq. With regard to Syria however, it is impossible to determinedly establish whether there is a mandate or not. For this reason the government did not pronounce direct support for the United States' actions in Syria, but merely conveyed 'understanding' these actions.[27] The Minister did express his hope that, given the possible risks of a 'waterbed effect', there will come a moment when an international legal mandate for Syria can also be established. The Minister stated, in answer to the CDA spokesperson, that the 'responsibility to protect' could not provide for a mandate to end a situation of humanitarian emergency through armed intervention without a Security Council resolution.[28] He did note that the international community should discuss the possibility of somehow limiting the power of veto in cases of humanitarian need, in order to provide the 'responsibility to protect' with more significance.[29] He finally noted that the Tweede Kamer should perhaps reconsider the Davids Committee's conclusions in light of recent developments.[30]

[24] *Kamerstukken II* 2014/15, 27925, nr. 523, at 31.

[25] Ibid., at 35.

[26] Ibid.

[27] *Kamerstukken II* 2014/15, 27925, nr. 523, at 41.

[28] Ibid., at 43.

[29] Ibid.

[30] Ibid.

13.2.3 The Advice of the External Advisor on International Law of 24 September 2014[31]

On 24 September, the Minister of Foreign affairs asked the external advisor on international law for advice on the airstrikes performed by the US-led coalition on ISIS targets in Iraq since 8 August 2014, and in Syria since the 23 August. More specifically, the advisor was asked to answer the following three questions:

(1) Is there a legal basis for third states to attack ISIS targets in Iraq?
(2) Could (collective) self-defence successfully be invoked with regard to the use of force against ISIS in Syria? What about the criteria applicable in the present case, such as the condition of an armed attack, and the 'ability and willingness' of relevant authorities to act against independent armed groups within their own territory?
(3) Are there any other legal bases for the use of force against ISIS in Syria?

With regard to the first question, the advisor on international law simply noted that although the Iraqi government did not exercise effective control over the entirety of its territory, it should be regarded as the legitimate representative of the state of Iraq. Therefore, a request from Iraqi authorities could be seen as a sufficient legal basis for third state attacks on targets within Iraq.[32]

To the second question, the advisor replied that military actions against ISIS in Syria could in principle be justified by invoking the collective self-defence of Iraq. This would require first of all, that Iraq had been the victim of an armed attack stemming from Syria. Secondly, Iraq must in fact have requested for third country military support. Thirdly, the use of force would have to meet the conditions of necessity and proportionality. Assuming that the second condition had been met, the advisor on international law focused on the first condition. He noted first of all that it is questionable whether the ISIS leaders and combatants stationed within Syria had a sufficient connection to ISIS' military actions in Iraq to be able to speak of an armed attack (stemming from Syria) in the sense of Article 51 UN Charter. A continuous supply of armaments and combatants from Syria to Iraq would be enough to fulfil the demands of Article 51. On the basis of the information available to the advisor at that time, he found it likely that this first condition can be met. An additional question would be whether an attack by a non-state actor such as ISIS could qualify as an armed attack in the first place. The advisor noted that since the events of 9/11, the customary international law on this subject has been developing such that this might also be possible. He emphasised however that this legal basis remained in development.[33]

[31] *Kamerstukken II* 2014/15, 27925, nr. 507, blg-384833.

[32] Ibid., at 2.

[33] Ibid., at 3.

In order to prevent abuse of the right, self-defence against non-state actors does have to meet substantial demands. According to the advisor, self-defence against a non-state actor, without prior approval by the state on whose territory it resides, would be allowed only in two cases. The first case occurs when the state on whose territory the non-state actor resides is unwilling to effectively deal, or even actively colludes, with said non-state actor. In the second case, the state harbouring the non-state actor does not have the means to effectively deal with it, leaving the defending state with no viable alternative by which to react to attacks other than the use of force. The advisor here seems to refer to the unwilling/unable criteria as conditions for the exercise of collective self-defence against non-state actors.[34] The advisor on international law found that with regard to the situation in Syria, whether it met these criteria was still unclear and required further factual analysis. What the advisor also found legally relevant, was the fact that the US and several other states had not asked for Syrian authorisation because they no longer recognised Assad's regime to be Syria's legitimate representative. However, he doubted whether this political reality, concocted by the US and its allies themselves, would provide a sufficient legal basis for the use of force.[35]

As to the remaining grounds for the use of force in Syria, the advisor noted that the 'principle of humanitarian intervention' offered the only other basis possibly applicable to the situation at hand. However, he found that state practice on this subject was still insufficient to be able to speak of a true legal justification.[36]

13.2.4 The Parliamentary Debate Regarding the Situation in Kobani

An emergency debate was held in the Tweede Kamer on 7 October 2014 concerning the worsening conditions in Kobani. At that time, this Syrian town situated on the border with Turkey was under attack by ISIS, creating the threat of crimes against humanity and war crimes being committed upon the thousands of civilians still trapped inside the town.[37] Its main subject was whether this state of humanitarian emergency could now provide the international legal mandate for humanitarian intervention in Syria.

---

[34] For an elaboration on this academic discussion regarding the "unable and unwilling test", see our concluding paragraph and the relevant literature mentioned in footnotes 95 and 96.

[35] Ibid., at 4.

[36] Ibid., at 5.

[37] See for the stance of Adama Dieng, Special Adviser of the Secretary-General on the Prevention of Genocide, and Jennifer Welsh, Special Adviser of the Secretary-General on the Responsibility to Protect, on the situation in Kobane, Syria http://www.un.org/en/preventgenocide/adviser/pdf/10.10.14%20Statement%20of%20the%20Special%20Advisers%20on%20the%20situation%20in%20Kobane.pdf.

In a letter to the Tweede Kamer, the government explicitly stated that, in case of a humanitarian emergency situation and a lack of Security Council unanimity, humanitarian intervention is an option—albeit as an *ultimum remedium*—but that this would ultimately be a political decision. When bypassing the Security Council, the humanitarian intervention doctrine would not provide a legal basis for the use of force.[38] Were the international community to act under these exceptional circumstances, it would have to act in as much unison as possible. At the time however, no consolidated international view on how to react to the Kobani situation had emerged.[39]

Despite the letter's relative clarity, several parties in parliament were not entirely clear on the government's position. They therefore asked the Minister of Foreign Affairs whether a state of humanitarian emergency really could not supply a legal justification for alleviating said emergency through the use of force. Both coalition parties, the People's Party for Freedom and Democracy (VVD) and the Labour Party (PvdA), supported the government's position as stated in the letter. According to them, there was no sufficient legal mandate, nor could humanitarian emergency supply such a mandate.[40] The VVD, Socialist Party (SP), Christian Democratic Appeal (CDA) and Reformed Political Party (SGP) however found that, in case of an emergency situation such as that of Kobani, a sufficient legal mandate was no longer a *sine qua non* for the use of force.[41] The Christian Union interpreted the letter as saying that humanitarian intervention in case of emergency could provide a legal basis.[42] The SGP called upon the principle that necessity trumps legal requirements and raised the question whether a Dutch contribution to the fight in Syria should be reconsidered, given the possible threat of genocide in Kobani: 'Of course we understand the objections regarding the lack of an international legal mandate. Sometimes however, necessity knows no law, especially when so many human lives are at risk.'[43]

The Minister of Foreign Affairs responded to the other parties' questions as follows. Once more the Davids Committee position was repeated: any use of force, or support thereof, requires an international legal mandate. A situation of humanitarian emergency would at most provide a political reason for deviating from this position, but not a legal justification for the use of force.[44] Nor could such a justification be found in the sole fact that the criteria for humanitarian intervention may have been met.[45] In answer to the question raised by the Christian Union, the Minister noted that a legal humanitarian intervention always requires a Security

[38] *Kamerstukken II* 2014/15, 27925, nr. 521, at 2.

[39] Ibid.

[40] *Kamerstukken II* 2014/15, 27925, nr. 524, at 4–5.

[41] Ibid., at 4 (VVD), at 7 (SP), at 9 (CDA), at 19 (SGP).

[42] Ibid., at 16.

[43] Ibid., at 19.

[44] Ibid., at 22.

[45] Ibid., at 22.

Council resolution, even in case of an emergency situation.[46] Ultimately, a humanitarian intervention without Security Council approval would be illegal. Even if all other requirements had been met, they could only serve as a political reason for action, despite its illegality.[47] While the Davids Committee concluded that in such a case one should refrain from the use of force, the Minister's words seemed to imply that this course of (in)action should not necessarily be maintained.

13.3 The June 2015 Parliamentary Debate

13.3.1 Article 100 Letter of 19 June 2015

13.3.1.1 Introduction

On 19 June 2015, the government sent again an Article 100 letter to the Tweede Kamer. The reason for this letter was the government's decision to prolong the Dutch military contribution to the fight against ISIS until October 2016. In it, the government indicated that it would provide, from October 2015 onwards, four operational F-16 fighter jets with approximately 200 military personnel and 130 trainers to support Iraqi and Kurdish forces.[48] After this extra year, Belgium would relieve the Dutch mission. The reasons for participation had remained unchanged from those contained in the Article 100 letter of September 2014.

13.3.1.2 Legal Justification for the Dutch Military Contribution

It is interesting to look again at the legal grounds provided by the Dutch government. When discussing the mandate for the use of force, the government still distinguished between Iraq and Syria. As said, the legal basis for participation in Iraq remained the Iraqi government's request for military support to the UN.[49] Remarkably, while nine months earlier the Dutch government was still of the opinion that there was no international legal mandate for intervention in Syria, it now did find such a mandate. This remarkable shift in legal opinion appears to have been informed by a renewed analysis of the facts:

> It has now been factually established that there have been continuous assaults upon Iraq stemming from Syria. These attacks were overseen by the ISIS-headquarters in Syria. It has become apparent that the government in Syria is incapable of stopping ISIS' armed attacks upon Iraq. Additionally, it has become apparent that the government is unable to stop the

---

[46] Ibid., at 24.

[47] Ibid., at 25.

[48] *Kamerstukken II* 2014/15, 27925, nr. 539, at 1.

[49] Ibid., at 6.

> continuous flow of combatants and armaments from Syria to Iraq, which are being used to support the armed fight in Iraq. The legal affairs departments of the Ministries of Foreign Affairs and Defence conclude on these grounds that there is now a legal basis for the use of force against ISIS in Syria. This legal basis is established through the right to collective self-defence defined in Article 51 of the UN Charter, for the purpose of Iraq's defence.[50,51]

The government however added to this that a legal basis is in itself insufficient reason to decide on Dutch military action above Syria. That decision would additionally require a widely supported political strategy for solving the Syrian conflict, which had at the time not been established. Finally, the government noted that were it nevertheless to decide upon military action in Syria, it would inform the Tweede Kamer in a timely fashion.[52]

13.3.2 The Advice of the External Advisor on International Law of 23 June 2015[53]

On 26 June 2015, the government presented the Tweede Kamer with the external legal advisor's further advice regarding the use of force against ISIS in Syria, as well as its own appraisal of said advice.[54] As might be expected, the external advisor also—in defiance of his own letter of 24 September 2014—was now of the opinion that the demands for invoking the right to collective self-defence had been met. The reasons for this were that there was still a legitimate request for assistance from the Iraqi government, that the right to self-defence also extended to actions by non-state actors, and that the Syrian government was both unable and unwilling to itself effectively act against ISIS.[55] As the Syrian government had not been unequivocal in its consent to the use of force against ISIS on Syrian territory, requesting said consent was no longer required. The use of force against ISIS in Syria did have to actually contribute to the defence of Iraq, and needed therefore to be restricted to combating ISIS' military branch. It could not extend to support for opposition groups attempting to overthrow Assad's regime, so long as those groups did not form a direct threat to Iraq (conform the principle of necessity). The clearest difference with the advisor's letter of 24 September 2014 lay in him no longer being of the opinion that the pursuit of military actions would be problematic, so long as the approval of the Syrian government had not been sought or received.[56]

---

[50] Ibid.

[51] Please note that all quotations stemming from government or political party statements were translated by the authors from the original Dutch.

[52] *Kamerstukken II* 2014/15, 27925, nr. 539, at 6.

[53] *Kamerstukken II* 2014/15, 27925, nr. 543, blg-539390.

[54] *Kamerstukken II* 2014/15, 27925, nr. 543.

[55] *Kamerstukken II* 2014/15, 27925, nr. 543, blg-539390, at 1.

[56] *Kamerstukken II* 2014/15, 27925, nr. 543, blg-539390, at 2.

The cabinet agreed with this new advice, and repeated that: 'it can now be concluded with satisfactory certainty that there is an international legal basis for the use of force against ISIS in Syria'.[57] As said, this basis was founded in the right to collective self-defence of Iraq. The difference with the situation of September 2014 is that the cabinet had now found sufficient factual evidence for continuous armed assaults against Iraq stemming from Syria and dispatched by the ISIS-headquarters in Raqqa.[58] For now, however, the Dutch contribution in Syria was to be limited to supporting the UN special envoy to Syria, Staffan de Mistura, as well as moderate opposition groups within Syria. The reason for this was the lack of a widely supported political strategy with regard to solving the Syrian conflict.[59]

13.3.3 Parliamentary Reactions

On 30 June 2015 the parliamentarian committees concerned again held a deliberation on the new Article 100 letter of 19 June 2015 with the Ministers of Foreign Affairs, Defence, and Foreign Trade and Development Cooperation.[60]

The People's Party for Freedom and Democracy (VVD) spokesperson indicated that his party had in the past already emphasised the need for operating within Syria. He now asserted, without direct reference to the principle of collective self-defence, that there was no longer any legal objection to such action.[61] The other coalition-party, the Labour Party (PvdA), indicated to be satisfied with collective self-defence as the legal basis and mandate for acting in Syria. The party also supported the government's position that a mandate for Syria was a necessary, but not sufficient prerequisite for bombardments in Syria.[62] Democrats 66 (D66) established that the government was of the opinion that there was an international legal mandate, and asked the Minister to indicate which other European countries shared this interpretation. GreenLeft recognised the mandate for Syria rooted in collective self-defence, but posited that this mandate was limited to acting on behalf of Iraq's defence and therefore that it could not justify general assistance to the Syrian population; indeed it might actually strengthen Assad's position (by weakening or destroying ISIS in Syria). For this reason, GreenLeft opposed expanding the mission to Syria.[63] The Christian Democratic Appeal (CDA) spokesperson pointed out that his party had already recognised a mandate for acting in Syria a year ago, founded on both collective self-defence, as well as the 'responsibility to protect',

---

[57] *Kamerstukken II* 2014/15, 27925, nr. 543, at 1.

[58] Ibid.

[59] Ibid., at 2.

[60] *Kamerstukken II* 2014/15, 27925, nr. 560, at 1.

[61] Ibid., at 7.

[62] Ibid., at 16.

[63] Ibid., at 23.

which the CDA believed could provide a legal justification even without a Security Council mandate. This was rooted in the presumption that ISIS had committed genocide.[64] The CDA did not blame the government for failing to ascertain a legal basis in collective self-defence earlier, but did lament its decision not to commence bombing until a widely supported or common European strategy could be devised.[65] Geert Wilders' Party for Freedom (PVV) shared this opinion.[66] The Reformed Political Party (SGP) was glad to see an end to the scrutiny over an international legal mandate for Syria, but echoed the CDA's doubts regarding the government placing additional conditions on expanding the mission.[67] The Christian Union took things a step further, positing that in so far as there was still no clear mandate for Syria, in the case of humanitarian intervention they saw no reason not to provide air-support even without a Security Council resolution.[68]

In response, the Minister of Foreign Affairs first of all repeated that the international legal mandate for Syria stems from the right to collective self-defence. He disagreed with several parties' critiques of the government's supposed 'flip-flop'. According to the Minister, based on the facts available per September 2014, the government simply could not conclusively establish the presence of a legal mandate. Recently however, the fact that the ISIS-headquarters in Raqqa was mounting continuous assaults from Syria into Iraq had become more apparent.[69] In short, the key to then accepting the legal basis had been changes in the factual situation.

The Minister again pointed out that the government had not taken the demands of international law lightly: extensive legal advice from both the Ministries of Foreign Affairs and Defence, as well as the advisor on international law, had preceded this conclusion. In addition, the Minister stated that, at the request of the CDA, the government would now express political support for the American and Canadian assaults on ISIS' positions in Syria.[70] With regard to the stances of other countries, the Minister noted that other than the US, Canada and the UK, Germany had also found a legal justification for acting against ISIS in Syria in the principle of collective self-defence as defined by Article 51 of the UN Charter. However, Germany found this basis to be insufficient to serve as a national mandate for action. Italy also recognised a legal basis for military action in Syria, but did not take part in either the bombardments in Syria, nor those in Iraq.[71] Finally, the Minister repeated that the legal mandate for Syria was a necessary, but not sufficient, condition for military involvement. He nonetheless did not exclude a Dutch contribution, but did not indicate the changes in the political situation required for

[64] Ibid., at 24.
[65] Ibid.
[66] Ibid., at 4.
[67] Ibid., at 28.
[68] Ibid., at 29.
[69] Ibid., at 43.
[70] Ibid., at 45.
[71] Ibid., at 46.

this to occur. In her responses to the questions raised by opposition parties, the Minister of Defence actually offered quite a succinct synopsis of the government's position: 'The presence of a mandate does not mean we will bombard. The absence of a political strategy does not mean we will never be able to act militarily.'[72]

13.4 The February 2016 Parliamentary Debate

13.4.1 Article 100 Letter of January 2016

On 23 November 2015, France—as a reaction to the ISIS-claimed terrorist attacks of 13 November 2015—implored EU member-states for assistance in the fight against ISIS in Iraq and Syria, on the basis of Article 42(7) of the 1992 Treaty on European Union (TEU).[73] On 2 December, the US asked the Netherlands to intensify their contribution to the fight against ISIS.[74] The government sent a letter to the Tweede Kamer on 11 December, informing them that they were contemplating these requests, and ensuring that the Kamer would be informed further on any measures that might follow. On 29 January 2016, the government indicated to the Tweede Kamer that much had changed with regard to the political process in Syria; for the first time in five years the Security Council agreed on a plan for political transition, entrenched in UN Security Council Resolution 2254 of 18 December 2015.[75] In reaction to the terrorist attacks in Paris, the Security Council had also adopted Resolution 2249 on 20 November, calling upon all member states—including the Netherlands—to contribute to an intensification of the fight against ISIS, and in particular, to eradicate ISIS' safe havens in Iraq and Syria.[76] The Resolution however did not authorise use of force on the basis of Chapter VII of the UN Charter, nor mentioned other legal bases (such as collective self-defence) as providing such authorisation.[77] The Dutch government, accepting the Security Council resolution as political legitimisation, again emphasised to have already recognised the existence of

---

[72] Ibid., at 56.

[73] *Kamerstukken II* 2015/16, 27925, nr. 570, at 1. - Article 42(7) TEU reads: 'If a Member State is the victim of armed aggression on its territory, the other Member States shall have towards it an obligation of aid and assistance by all the means in their power, in accordance with Article 51 of the United Nations Charter'.

[74] *Kamerstukken II* 2015/16, 27925, nr. 570, at 1.

[75] UNSC Res 2254, 18 December 2015, particularly para 4.

[76] UNSC Res 2249, 20 November 2015, para 5.

[77] Although in para 5 of Resolution 2249 the Council 'calls upon Member States that have the capacity to do so to *take all necessary measures*, in compliance with international law, in particular with the United Nations Charter …', para 5 could not be interpreted as Security Council authorisation for the use of force because the Council did not use the terms 'acting under Chapter VII', nor the term 'decides'. See, e.g., O'Connor 2016, at 76; and http://www.ejiltalk.org/the-constructive-ambiguity-of-the-security-councils-isis-resolution/.

an international legal mandate for acting against ISIS in Syria, namely the right of collective self-defence.[78]

All these developments led the government to reconsider its position. It ultimately chose an integrated approach to the fight against ISIS in both Iraq as well as in Syria. Militarily, this meant that Dutch F-16 s would, until July 2016, also bomb strategic targets in eastern Syria that were part of ISIS' supply lines from Syria to Iraq.[79] With this new approach, the Dutch government answered the calls of the French, Americans and the Security Council.[80] The government conceded that by bombing ISIS in Syria, the chance of a terror attack in the Netherlands would increase. Most of the Dutch who had joined ISIS after all resided in Syria, and ISIS would use these combatants to plot terror attacks in the Netherlands. On the other hand, the government also surmised that by dealing with ISIS in Syria, this threat would diminish. The decision of the Netherlands to finally also use force in Syria thus seemed to be informed by three factors: the terror attacks of 13 November in Paris and the subsequent French request for EU Member States to intensify the fight against ISIS in Iraq and Syria, the similar request from the US, as well as the Security Council seemingly reaching a consensus on a solution to the Syrian conflict.

13.4.2 Parliamentary Reactions

On 10 February 2016, the different parliamentarian sub-committees once more conferred with the Ministers of Foreign Affairs, Defence, and Foreign Trade and Development, this time about the Article 100 letter of 29 January.[81] Few political parties explicitly discussed the extension of the Dutch mission to Syria in relation to its previously established international legal mandate. The People's Party for Freedom and Democracy (VVD) applauded the extension to Syria and remarked that it had pleaded for the government to do so ever since the mission started.[82] The Labour Party (PvdA) did note with regard to the legal mandate that the government had leaned rather heavily on the advice imparted by the advisor on international.[83] The Freedom Party (PVV) spokesperson stated that the mandate had already existed one-and-a-half years ago and therefore the situation had remained the same.[84] The Christian Democratic Appeal (CDA) spokesperson similarly emphasised that his party had already established that there was a mandate for armed action in Syria

[78] *Kamerstukken II* 2015/16, 27925, nr. 570, at 3.
[79] Ibid., at 5.
[80] Ibid., at 2.
[81] *Kamerstukken II* 2015/16, 27925, nr. 587, at 1.
[82] Ibid., at 3.
[83] Ibid., at 8.
[84] Ibid., at 9, 18.

back in October 2014, and that the Netherlands should have acted earlier.[85] The one-man splinter faction Klein was the only one to doubt collective self-defence as a legal basis for the use of force.[86] GreenLeft was also against the decision to act against ISIS in Syria, not on legal grounds, but rather because the party did not envisage how the bombardments could contribute to a betterment of the situation, given that they did not seem rooted in a political process.[87]

All other parties supported the government's decision to start bombing ISIS in Syria as well, though some regarded it as 'too little too late', given that it concerned merely four F-16 s to be deployed for only four months. Some parties emphasised that Assad and the Russians presented a bigger problem than ISIS and that bombing ISIS would not suffice in reaching a political solution for Syria. Some parties thus found that a clearer stance should be taken with respect to Russia. During the closing debate, the Minister of Foreign Affairs again emphasised that there was a consensus, not just between the ministry's lawyers, but within the international community as a whole, on the right to self-defence providing a basis for action against ISIS in Syria.[88] Because many parties had pointed out the terrible crimes the Assad regime had wrought with Russian and Iranian support, the Minister of Defence stressed that however gladly some parties might want to also act against Assad, there was no international legal mandate to support such action.[89] On the same day as this debate, the Netherlands sent a letter to the Security Council, in accordance with Article 51 of the UN Charter, reporting that 'the Kingdom of the Netherlands is taking necessary and proportionate measures against the so-called Islamic State in Iraq and the Levant (ISIL, also known as Da'esh) in Syria in the exercise of the inherent right of collective self-defence of Iraq.'[90]

13.5 Conclusion and Outlook: Towards a More Extensive Interpretation of the Rules on the Use of Force?

Central to this chapter has been Dutch state practice with regard to the international armed fight against ISIS in Iraq and Syria. This state practice manifested itself as a Dutch contribution to aerial bombardments in Iraq from October 2014 onwards, and in Syria from January 2016 onwards. In order to uncover its details, we have primarily examined the various parliamentarian debates held on the international legal aspects of contribution to this armed struggle.

---

[85] Ibid., at 13.
[86] Ibid., at 29.
[87] Ibid., at 26.
[88] Ibid., at 43.
[89] Ibid., at 45.
[90] S/2016/132, 10 February 2016.

The question of whether these military actions were in compliance with international law was painstakingly discussed in these debates between the government and parliament. In these debates, the government took three different stances within the span of a year and a half. In its Article 100 letter of 24 September 2014, the government's position was that there was a legal mandate for acting in Iraq, but not for acting in Syria. Therefore, the Dutch mission was to be limited to Iraq. In the letter of 19 June 2015, the government was of the opinion that there was now also a mandate for the use of force against ISIS in Syria, based on the right to collective self-defence. In the absence of a shared political strategy for Syria however, it did not want to revert to military action yet. Then, finally, in its letter of 29 January 2016, it found the Syrian political situation to have changed in such a way that it decided to now also fly bombing missions on ISIS in Syria.

Notably, many parliamentarian parties generally supported the government's legal line of reasoning. Only a few political parties found that Syria should have been bombarded from the beginning, and that there was a legal basis for doing so, be it in the form of the right to collective self-defence (CDA, SGP, PVV), or be it in the form of the principle of necessity or humanitarian intervention (CDA, CU). The largest governmental party, the VVD, found that in some cases military action does not require a legal mandate. It shared this perception with the SGP and CU.

By basing its actions against ISIS in Syria on the right to collective self-defence, the government attempted to keep with the course exacted since the Davids Committee report, namely that the Netherlands supports or takes part in international military missions only when they are based on an adequate international legal mandate. In doing so however, it ultimately interpreted this right so extensively that it is still questionable whether there really was a legal mandate in this case.

For its interpretation and application of the conditions for collective self-defence, the government leaned almost exclusively on the argumentation of its external advisor on international law. A further examination of this advice tells us that the expansion of the right to collective self-defence to allow for third states to use force against non-state actors without attribution of the non-state actor's conduct to the territorial state, is still in active development. On this, the external legal advisor stated in his advice of 24 September 2014:

> Although it has traditionally been accepted that the right to self-defence only applies to armed attacks by other *states*, customary law on this topic has been developing ever since the US' exertion of the right to self-defence following September 11, 2001. What we have is a *developing* legal basis that, in exceptional circumstances, provides states with the right to use force against non-state actors residing within another state. ... This legal basis is not yet supported by extensive state practice. I do deem further development of this legal basis to be desirable.[91]

Then in his advice of 23 June 2015, the external legal advisor states:

> While Article 51 UN Charter's text limits the right to self-defence to an armed attack by another state, *it can now be assumed that*, in exceptional circumstances, *states have the*

[91] *Kamerstukken II* 2014/15, 27925, nr. 507, blg-384833, at 3.

right to use force against non-state actors based in another state on the basis of (collective) self-defence.[92]

This can at the very least be called a remarkable shift. It appears that within a year's time, a 'developing legal basis' was transformed into a *right*, albeit under exceptional circumstances.

This sounds almost too good to be true. Could the fact that the United States, together with some other states, cited the right of collective self-defence, particularly based on the unable/unwilling criteria, as a legal basis for military operations in Syria, and (some of them) in fact resorted to the use of force, have led to this development in customary law?[93] The fact that, from June 2015 onwards, the Dutch government suddenly did deem the right to collective self-defence to constitute a legal basis was justified primarily on factual grounds; it now had better insight into the factual situation on the ground, which exposed a direct line running from ISIS in Syria to ISIS in Iraq. The existence of a right to collective self-defence against non-state actors *as such*, however, was not open to discussion for the government. The point nevertheless remains, that *de jure* it cannot yet be said without question that the right to collective self-defence also justifies the use of force by third states against non-state actors, without any sort of connection having been established between this non-state actor and the state on whose territory it operates.[94]

When applied to the Davids Committee course—so carefully maintained by the Dutch government—this means the following: yes, the right to collective

---

[92] *Kamerstukken II* 2014/15, 27925, nr. 543, blg-539390, at 4.

[93] For a thorough discussion on this matter, see O'Connor 2016. Notably, at 88 she notes that all states that provided a legal basis for the use of force claimed to be acting in collective self-defence. However, merely 'four of the nine states also referred to Syria being unwilling or unable to prevent the attacks'. Ultimately, on the basis of an analysis of state practice she concludes at 96: 'International law may be moving towards the "unwilling or unable" standard, but the evidence does not yet support this.'For another critical stance with regard to the claim that the unable/unwilling criteria have been crystallized as the standard for applying collective self-defence against non-state actors, see Arimatsu and Schmitt 2014 at 24 and 29.

[94] See, e.g., O'Connor 2016, at 88: '[…] these invocations have not been at the level required for the ["unwilling or unable" standard] to be established under customary international law. The "unwilling or unable" standard in itself is problematic due to the lack of definition and that a simple inability by a state could excuse a violation of its sovereignty. The fact that four states referred to the "unwilling and unable" standard could be interpreted as evidence of growing support for it, but one must equally keep in mind that the other states did not reference this standard.'; O'Connell 2013, at 384: '[…] states have not accepted such a right [to resort to force against states "unable or unwilling" to control terrorism on their territory] and are unlikely to ever accept a rule this flexible on intervention.'; Arimatsu and Schmitt 2015, at 23, 24, 29; Tams 2009, at 385–386; Becker 2006, at 334, 354–355; Kammerhofer 2007, para 3.1.3; Molier 2011, at 331; and Ruys and Verhoeven 2005, at 312, 317, 319. Contrary: Wettberg 2007, at 209, 228; Van Steenberghe 2010, at 199, 207.

self-defence may indeed generally provide an adequate mandate under international law. However, the question certainly remains whether this is also true for the case at hand, of a non-state actor which has no ties to the state on whose territory it operates. For this reason, the government was to our mind actually on much shakier legal ground that it professed to.

It seems then that the reason why an international legal mandate was ultimately 'found' has much more to do with the current global disorder, in which failed states and militant non-state actors are commonplace. Public international law adapts to this new 'world disorder' by incorporating that state practice which allows for more lenient interpretations of the rules regarding the use of force. We were able to witness this within the Dutch debates on participation in the armed struggle against ISIS. This is not necessarily a bad thing. After all, only an international law that is rooted in reality, rather than in a socially desirable construction thereof, maintains its relevance as a system able to regulate state behaviour: *Ex factis jus oritur*. Such has it always been, and such shall it remain. To end with the words of the Minister of Foreign Affairs, while debating parliament on participating in the armed coalition against ISIS:

> International law is, like all kinds of law, alive. In this case it is, perhaps more so than other kinds of law, also dynamic. The legal system is usually a step behind on practice and the challenges it raises. We are witnessing that right now.[95]

References

Arimatsu L, Schmitt MN (2015) Attacking 'Islamic State' and the Khorasan Group: Surveying the International Law Landscape. Columbia Journal of Transnational Law Bulletin 53:1–29

Becker T (2006) Terrorism and the State – Rethinking the Rules of State Responsibility. Hart Publishing, Oxford

Kammerhofer J (2007) The Armed Activities Case and Non-State Actors in Self-Defence Law. Leiden Journal of International Law 20:89–113

Molier G (2006) Humanitarian Intervention and The Responsibility to Protect After 9/11. Netherlands International Law Review 53:37–62

Molier G (2011) The War on Terror and Self-Defence against Non-State Actors. In: Ellian A, Molier G, Suurland D (eds) Terrorism: Ideology, Law and Policy. Republic of Letters Publishing, Dordrecht, pp 305–336

O'Connell ME (2013) Dangerous Departures. The American Journal of International Law 107:380–386

O'Connor L (2016) Legality of the use of force in Syria against Islamic State and the Khorasan Group. Journal on the Use of Force and International Law 3:70–96

Ruys T, Verhoeven S (2005) Attacks by Private Actors and the Right of Self-Defence. Journal of Conflict and Security Law 10:289–320

Tams CJ (2009) The Use of Force against Terrorists. The European Journal of International Law 20:359–397

[95] *Kamerstukken II* 2014/15, 27925, nr. 523, at 43.

Van Steenberghe R (2010) Current Legal Developments – Self-Defence in Response to Attacks by Non-State Actors in the Light of Recent State Practice: A Step Forward? Leiden Journal of International Law 22:209–240
Wettberg G (2007) The International Legality of Self-Defence against Non-State Actors. State Practice from the U.N. Charter to the Present. Peter Lang, Berlin

Chapter 14
The Dutch Referendum on the EU-Ukraine Association Agreement: Legal Implications and Solutions

Guillaume Van der Loo

Abstract This chapter will analyse the legal consequences of the outcome of the Dutch referendum of 6 April 2016 concerning the EU-Ukraine Association Agreement. The result of the referendum raised the question whether a single Member State can 'veto' the entry into force of a bilateral association agreement. Due to the unprecedented nature of this situation and the fact that the EU Treaties do no give a clear answer to this question, many issues related to the non-ratification of mixed agreements remain unclear. Therefore, after briefly analysing the 'mixed' nature of the EU-Ukraine Association Agreement and its current legal status, the legal consequences of the Dutch '*tegen*' (against) are explored, focussing on the provisional application of the agreement. Finally, the solution of the Dutch government to deal with the outcome of the referendum, and some alternatives, are discussed.

Keywords EU · Ukraine · Association Agreement · Referendum · Provisional application · Mixed agreements · Ratification

Contents

FWO postdoctoral researcher at the Ghent European Law Institute, and researcher at the Centre for European Policy Studies (CEPS).

G. Van der Loo (✉)
Ghent European Law Institute, Ghent University, Ghent, Belgium
e-mail: guillaume.vanderloo@ugent.be

G. Van der Loo
Centre for European Policy Studies (CEPS), Brussels, Belgium

M. Kuijer and W. Werner (eds.), *Netherlands Yearbook of International Law 2016*, Netherlands Yearbook of International Law 47,
DOI 10.1007/978-94-6265-207-1_14

14.1 Introduction

On 6 April 2016 the EU-Ukraine Association Agreement was rejected in the Netherlands in an advisory referendum, which was organised pursuant to the Dutch Advisory Referendum Act (DRA), with 61.1% of the votes. The fact that this advisory referendum, which had a low turnout of 32%, could complicate the ratification procedure of a landmark international agreement for the entire European Union raises several legal and political questions. It is actually the first time that a single Member State is (potentially) unable to ratify a bilateral EU mixed agreement (i.e. an international agreement that is concluded by the EU and its Member States on the one hand, and a third State on the other).[1] Because the political character of this referendum and the content and geopolitical implications of the Association Agreement have already been discussed elsewhere,[2] this chapter will mainly focus on the legal implications of this referendum for the EU-Ukraine Association Agreement. After briefly analysing the 'mixed' nature of the EU-Ukraine Association Agreement and its current legal status, the legal consequences of the Dutch '*tegen*' (against) are explored. Finally, the solution of the Dutch government to deal with the outcome of the referendum, and some alternatives, are discussed.

14.2 Mixed (Association) Agreements

The EU-Ukraine Association agreement is concluded as a mixed agreement. These are agreements concluded by third parties, on the one hand, and the EU and its Member States, on the other, because these agreements cover elements of both EU and Member State competence. The procedural consequence of 'mixity' is that the 28 Member States have to ratify the agreement alongside the EU, each according to their own 'constitutional' ratification procedures. Mixed agreements are a common feature in the EU's external relations. The fact that the expression 'mixed

[1] For a detailed analysis of mixed agreements, see Heliskoski 2001. For examples of exceptionally long ratification procedures, see Rosas 2014.

[2] For a comprehensive overview of the EU-Ukraine Association Agreement, see Van der Loo 2016a.

agreements' was absent from the original EEC Treaty did not prevent one of the first bilateral agreements concluded by the Community, the Association Agreement with Greece of 1961, from being mixed.[3] Also, the most recent agreement signed by the EU, the EU-Canada Comprehensive Economic and Trade Agreement (CETA), was categorized as a mixed agreement.

Traditionally, association agreements are concluded as mixed agreements for a number of reasons. First, they are typically comprehensive in nature providing a general framework for cooperation involving areas belonging to EU and Member State competences. Second, mixity is often a pragmatic solution to avoid internal competence battles among EU institutions and Member States. Third, the political importance of association agreements explains why Member States prefer to be a contracting party in their own right, in addition to the EU. It not only endows them with additional bargaining power during the negotiations and in the ratification process but also upholds their visibility vis-à-vis third countries.[4] The mixed nature of association agreements creates an *additional* reinforced unanimity as the procedural legal basis of such agreements is, *inter alia,* Article 218(8) TFEU,[5] which already requires unanimity in the Council for the conclusion of association agreements.

However, from a strict legal point of view, there is no requirement for association agreements to be mixed. As Rosas notes,

> generally speaking, [association agreements] do not need to be mixed, as the Treaty of Lisbon has widened the scope of the common commercial policy and has introduced a fairly wide formulation of supervening exclusivity in Article 3(2) TFEU and what seems to ban an even wider formulation of treaty-making powers in general in Article 216(1) TFEU as well as a more integrated CFSP competence also covered by Article 216 TFEU on Union treaty-making powers.[6]

Moreover, since the Lisbon Treaty[7] abolished the pillar structure and created a single legal personality for the EU, the inclusion of Common Foreign and Security Policy (CFSP) provisions in a broader framework agreement such as the EU-Ukraine Association Agreement does not automatically require mixity. In order to render mixity legally more defendable, clauses perceived to fall under Member States competences have been inserted into association agreements or bilateral agreements of a general nature, such as provisions on political dialogue or cultural cooperation.

Hence, the choice for mixity 'is not necessarily a result of legal orthodoxy but frequently the consequence of crude political interests on behalf of the Member

[3] Maresceau 2010.

[4] Ibid.

[5] 2012 Treaty on the Functioning of the European Union (Consolidated version), C 326/47 (TFEU).

[6] Rosas 2014, at 24.

[7] 2007 Treaty of Lisbon amending the Treaty on European Union and the Treaty establishing the European Community, 2702 UNTS 3.

States'.[8] This was recently illustrated during the process of the conclusion of the Stabilisation and Association Agreement with Kosovo. Because not all Member States recognise Kosovo as an independent State, the EU-Kosovo Association Agreement was concluded as an 'EU-only' agreement.[9] This option prevents that the EU Member States (including those who do not recognise Kosovo) need to ratify the agreement, which would entail a *de facto* recognition of Kosovo.

14.3 The Current Legal Status of the EU-Ukraine Association Agreement

After the Maidan revolution, which was sparked in November 2013 by the unexpected last-minute decision of the previous Ukrainian government not to sign the agreement, the EU-Ukraine Association Agreement was finally signed in March and June 2014. However, several procedural steps were—and still are—required before the agreement can fully enter into force. For example, the European Parliament needs to give its consent for association agreements,[10] which occurred for the EU-Ukraine Association Agreement simultaneously with the Ukrainian *Verkhovna Rada* on 16 September 2014.

As noted above, mixed agreements also require the ratification of all 28 Member States. Such a ratification procedure usually takes 3–4 years. However, in order to circumvent this long ratification process, most mixed agreements provide for the possibility of provisional application. Article 486 of the EU-Ukraine Association Agreement indeed States that the parties 'agree to provisionally apply this Agreement in part, as specified by the Union, [...] and in accordance with their respective internal procedures and legislation as applicable'.[11] A legal basis for the provisional application of international agreements concluded by the EU was included in the Amsterdam Treaty[12] (now Article 218(5) TFEU). It reflects Article 25 of the Vienna Convention on the Law of Treaties (VCLT),[13] according to which a treaty may provide for such provisional application or the negotiating States may agree to it. Another option which was used by the EU to alleviate the negative effect of mixity is to sign and conclude formally a separate agreement (often called an 'Interim Agreement') incorporating only those parts of the main agreement that fall squarely within the Union (before the Lisbon Treaty: 'Community') competences.[14]

[8] Van Elsuwege 2017.

[9] Ibid.

[10] Article 218(6)(a)(i) TFEU.

[11] Article 486(3) EU-Ukraine Association Agreement.

[12] 1997 Treaty of Amsterdam Amending the Treaty on European Union, 2700 UNTS 161.

[13] 1969 Vienna Convention on the Law of Treaties, 1155 UNTS 331 (VCLT).

[14] On such 'Interim Agreements', see Flaesch-Mougin and Bosse-Platière 2014.

Given the political significance of the Agreement, the Council agreed on an exceptional wide scope of provisional application of the EU-Ukraine Association Agreement. Usually, the provisional application or 'Interim Agreements' of association agreements or other framework agreements only cover the trade(-related) elements of the agreement. But in the EU-Ukraine Association Agreement, the scope of the provisional application goes beyond the trade part of the agreement (i.e. the deep and comprehensive free trade area (DCFTA)) and also includes the entire titles on General Principles, Financial Cooperation and General and Final Provisions and provisions regarding political dialogue, rule of law and movement of persons and economic and sector cooperation.[15] It has to be noted that the Commission even proposed a broader scope for provisional application, including, *inter alia*, the entire title on Political Dialogue and Reform, Political Association, Cooperation and Convergence in the field of Foreign and Security Policy.[16] However, the Member States, in particular the UK, triggered objections against the proposed scope of provisional application and agreed on a more limited—but still extensive—scope of provisional application.[17]

This broad scope raised questions on the potential provisional application of 'mixed' elements of the agreement. Evidently, only the provisions falling under EU competences (exclusive or shared) can be applied provisionally by the Council Decision for signature and provisional application. This problem is partially circumvented by the fact that the provisions responsible for the mixity of an agreement are never specifically indicated in the relevant Council Decision (or another document), mainly because the Commission and the Council would find it very difficult to agree on such a clear delineation of competences. The provisional application of mixed elements is also addressed in the Council Decisions on the signing and provisional application of the EU-Ukraine Association Agreement as they state that the listed provisions for provisional application shall be applied provisionally 'only to the extent that they cover matters falling within the Union's competence,

[15] Combined reading of the Council Decision of 17 March 2014 on the signing, on behalf of the European Union, and provisional application of the Association Agreement between the European Union and the European Atomic Energy Community and their Member States, of the one part, and Ukraine, of the other part, as regards the Preamble, Article 1, and Titles I, II and VII thereof, 2014/295/EU (Council Decision 2014/295/EU) and Council Decision of 23 June 2014 on the signing, on behalf of the European Union, and provisional application of the Association Agreement between the European Union and the European Atomic Energy Community and their Member States, of the one part, and Ukraine, of the other part, as regards Title III (with the exception of the provisions relating to the treatment of third-country nationals legally employed as workers in the territory of the other Party) and Titles IV, V, VI and VII thereof, as well as the related Annexes and Protocols, 2014/668/EU (Council Decision 2014/668/EU).

[16] European Commission, Proposal for a Council Decision on the signing, on behalf of the European Union, and provisional application of the Association Agreement between the European Union and its Member States, of the one part, and Ukraine, of the other part, COM(2013) 289 final, 15 May 2013.

[17] European Commission, 'Note à l'attention des membres du GRI', 6 June 2014 (not public, on file with the author).

including matters falling within the Union's competence to define and implement a common foreign and security policy'.[18] Their preambles also indicate that 'the provisional application of parts of the Agreement does not prejudge the allocation of competences between the Union and its Member States in accordance with the Treaties.'

The initiation of the provisional application of a mixed agreement requires at the EU's side the adoption of a Council Decision. Because the provisional application covers in this case an association agreement, unanimity is required in the Council for the adoption of this Decision.[19] Moreover, a practice has been developed by the Commission and the Council to only initiate the provisional application of mixed agreements that require the consent of the European Parliament after having received such a consent.[20] The provisional application of the EU-Ukraine Association Agreement started on 1 November 2014, however, the provisional application of the DCFTA was postponed until 1 January 2016 in response to political pressure from Russia.[21]

14.4 Legal Consequences of the Referendum

Meanwhile, all the EU Member States have ratified the EU-Ukraine Association Agreement, with one notable exception. In the Netherlands, the Approval Act for the ratification of the agreement was adopted by the House of Representatives (Second Chamber) on 7 April 2015 and the Senate (First Chamber) on 7 July 2015.[22] However, the entry into force of this Approval Act (and thus the Netherland's ratification) was suspended due to the start of the referendum procedure under the DRA.

It is now claimed that the Dutch voters have rejected the Association Agreement in the referendum, but the reality is more complex. The subject of the referendum was actually not the EU-Ukraine Association Agreement as such, but the Approval

[18] See for example Article 4 of Council Decision 2014/295/EU and Article 4 of Council Decision 2014/668/EU.

[19] The Council Decisions for the signature and provisional application of the EU-Ukraine Association Agreement (*ibid*) have as a legal basis, *inter alia*, subparagraph 2 of Article 218(8) TFEU, which requires unanimity for the conclusion of association agreements.

[20] In a Resolution adopted on 23 October 2013, the European Parliament called for the provisional application of the EU-Ukraine Association Agreement immediately upon signature, clearing the way for provisional application of the agreement. Moreover, the European Parliament gave its consent already on 16 September 2014, before the provisional application of the EU-Ukraine Association Agreement was (partially) initiated on 1 November 2014.

[21] For an overview of this process, see Van der Loo 2016a.

[22] Staatsblad van het Koninkrijk der Nederlanden, Wet van 8 juli 2015, houdende goedkeuring van de op 27 juni 2014 te Brussel tot stand gekomen Associatieovereenkomst tussen de Europese Unie en de Europese Gemeenschap voor Atoomenergie en haar lidstaten, enerzijds, en Oekraïne, anderzijds, (2015) Nr. 315, 28 July 2015.

Act that ratified the agreement. This law was the legal instrument by which the Kingdom of the Netherlands ratified the Member States' elements of the 'mixed' EU-Ukraine Association Agreement. Most likely, few Dutch voters were aware of this subtle technicality when they voted on 6 April. In fact, the situation is even more abstract as nowhere in the agreement or in the Council Decisions for signature of the agreement is it indicated which provisions of the agreement fall under exclusive Member State (and thus Dutch) competences. As noted above, such a delineation is traditionally avoided to prevent competence conflicts between the European Commission and the European Parliament on the one hand, and the Council and the Member States on the other. The scope of the provisional application of the agreement already gives an indication of which elements are not considered as Member States' competences, as only provisions falling under the EU competences can be provisionally applied. However, this does not give a complete and exact overview.

According to the DRA, the Dutch government now has to decide whether it will propose a law that repeals the Approval Act, or a law that confirms it. In either scenario, approval by the Parliament is required, but this 'repealing' or 'confirming' law cannot again be the subject of a new referendum.

In any case, the immediate legal consequences of the no-vote are limited. As long as the Netherlands does not ratify the Association Agreement, it cannot fully enter into force. The agreement can only enter into force if all the contracting Parties (thus the EU, the 28 Member States and Ukraine) have ratified it.[23] Because the Union only ratifies a mixed agreement after all the Member States have done so, also the EU still needs to conclude the agreement.[24] However, this has no impact on the provisional application of the agreement, which theoretically can continue indefinitely because there is no 'deadline' for the provisional application. The Dutch Foreign Minister has replied to a parliamentary question that it would not make sense to continue with the provisional application of the Association Agreement in the event it is not ratified.[25] It would indeed be paradoxical to indefinitely provisionally apply an agreement that it is not ratified, especially considering that the aim of provisional application is to bridge the temporal gap between signature and ratification of an agreement. However, the Council Decisions on the signing of the agreement do not specify an expiry date for the provisional application. Moreover, Member States cannot terminate the Union's provisional application of the agreement. The provision in the

[23] Article 486 EU-Ukraine Association Agreement.

[24] However, there are numerous examples of multilateral mixed agreements concluded by the EU, but not by all Member States. On this practice, see Heliskoski 2001.

[25] Tweede Kamer der Staten Generaal, Vragen van het lid Omtzigt (CDA), Verhoeven (D66) en Voordewind (ChristenUnie) aan de Minister van Buitenlandse Zaken over de voorlopige inwerkingtreding van het associatieverdrag tussen de EU en Oekraïne (ingezonden 5 januari 2016) —Antwoord van Minister Koenders (Buitenlandse Zaken) (ontvangen 5 februari 2016) (Minister of Foreign Affairs Bert Koenders, Answers to Members Omtzigt, Verhoeven, Voordewind on the provisional application of the EU-Ukraine Association Agreement), (2015–2016) Nr. 1401, 5 February 2016.

Association Agreement on provisional application (Article 486) states that either party may terminate the provisional application of the agreement. However, only the EU provisionally applies a part of the agreement (i.e. a large part of the provisions falling under Union competences), and not the Member States. As recognised by the Court of Justice of the European Union (CJEU), the decision authorising the Union's provisional application is adopted by the Council, 'and no competence is granted to the Member States for the adoption of such a decision'.[26] The termination of the Union's provisional application by a Member State would be clearly in breach with the principle of autonomy of the EU institutions and would be at odds with the duty of sincere cooperation, enshrined in Article 4(3) TEU.[27] Because Article 218 TFEU does not provide clear rules on how to terminate the provisional application of an agreement, the same procedure to initiate the provisional application should be followed. For association agreements (such as the EU-Ukraine Association Agreement) this would require at the EU's side a unanimous Decision of the Council. Therefore, this 'reversed unanimity' would imply that no single EU Member State (e.g. the Netherlands) can halt the provisional application of the agreement.

The situation where one Member State would be unable to ratify a mixed agreement is unprecedented. However, in the context of the signature of (EU-Canada) CETA some relevant statements and declarations were adopted by EU institutions and Member States with regard to the agreement's provisional application.[28] The signature of the mixed CETA Agreement was in October 2016 in limbo for almost two weeks because the Belgian region of Wallonia refused to give its consent to the federal Belgian government to sign the deal. In order to get the Walloon government on board, numerous statements and declarations have been adopted, mainly to accommodate the concerns of the Walloon government.[29] The Council adopted also the following statement relating to the provisional application of CETA:

> If the ratification of CETA fails permanently and definitively because of a ruling of a constitutional court, or following the completion of other constitutional processes and formal notification by the government of the concerned state, provisional application *must be and will be terminated*. The necessary steps will be taken in accordance with EU procedures.[30]

---

[26] *Case C-28-12 (European Commission v Council)*, ECJ (Grand Chamber), Judgment, ECLI:EU:C:2015:282, 28 April 2015.

[27] Ibid.

[28] These statements and declarations are published on the website of the Council: European Council—Council of the European Union (2016) EU-Canada trade agreement: Council adopts decision to sign CETA, 28 October 2016, http://www.consilium.europa.eu/en/press/press-releases/2016/10/28-eu-canada-trade-agreement/?utm_source=dsms-auto&utm_medium=email&utm_campaign=EU-Canada+trade+agreement%3a+Council+adopts+decision+to+sign+CETA, accessed 9 March 2017.

[29] For an analysis of these different statements and declarations, see Van der Loo 2016b.

[30] Council of the European Union (2016) Comprehensive Economic and Trade Agreement (CETA) between Canada, of the one part, and the European Union and its Member States, of the other part—Statements to the Council minutes, 13463/1/16 REV 1, http://data.consilium.europa.eu/doc/document/ST-13463-2016-REV-1/en/pdf, accessed 13 January 2017, at 14 (emphasis added).

Moreover, statements by Germany, Poland, Belgium and Austria declare that these countries can exercise their right to terminate the provisional application as provided in CETA.[31] This means that if one Member State refuses to ratify CETA, the provisional application will need to be terminated. This is remarkable because this implies that a Member State can block issues falling under exclusive EU competences. However, as argued above, this termination will not happen 'automatically', but would require the adoption of a Council Decision.

14.5 The Way Out

14.5.1 The Decision of the Heads of State or Government, Meeting Within the European Council

Although the referendum is not binding, Prime Minister Rutte stated that the ratification 'could not go ahead unhindered'. The Dutch government is now in the awkward position that it cannot ignore the outcome of the referendum, which would be a risky domestic move with general elections scheduled for March 2017, but it also would not want to block the conclusion of this landmark agreement. After months of informal negotiations and discussions in the Hague and Brussels, the Dutch government suggested in a letter on 31 October to the Dutch Parliament the option to ratify the agreement while accommodating the main concerns of the no-voters in a 'a legally binding solution'.[32] This would be a 'Decision of the Heads of State or Government, meeting within the European Council'. This Decision would need to accommodate the concerns that were raised during the referendum by specifying that:

(i) The Association Agreement is not a stepping-stone to EU Accession
(ii) The Association Agreement does not include a 'collective security guarantee' and does not impose military cooperation on the Member States
(iii) The Association Agreement does not give Ukrainian employers access to the EU labour market
(iv) The Association Agreement does not include an obligation for financial support to Ukraine
(v) Strengthening of the rule of law and anti-corruption policies are key elements of the Association Agreement.

---

[31] CETA's provision on provisional application (i.e. Article 30.7(3)) is similar to the one in the EU Ukraine Association Agreement, described above.

[32] Minister President M. Rutte and Minister of Foreign Affairs B. Koenders, Kamerbrief over referendum over het Associatieovereenkomst met Oekraïne, Ministerie van Buitenlandse Zaken, Nr. 2016Z19902, 31 October 2016.

Such a 'Decision of the Heads of State or Government, meeting within the European Council' was finally adopted on 15 December 2016 and annexed to the European Council conclusions that were adopted that day.[33] This Decision includes the five aforementioned points and states that it is 'in full conformity with the EU-Ukraine Association Agreement and the EU treaties'. It will take effect once the Netherlands has ratified the agreement and the Union has concluded it.

This option deserves some comments. First of all, it needs to be analysed to what extent it is actually 'a legally binding solution', as argued by the Dutch government. A 'Decision of Heads of State or Government, meeting within the European Council' is not something new. For example, a similar Decision was recently drafted in February 2016 in the context of adopting a 'new settlement for the United Kingdom with the European Union'.[34] As rightfully noted in a an Opinion of the legal counsel of the European Council, such a Decision is

> of an intergovernmental nature, not a decision of the European Council as an institution of the European Union under Article 15 TEU, within the meaning of the fourth paragraph of Article 288 TFEU, which would require to be based on a specific legal basis in the Treaties.[35]

Nevertheless, this draft Decision (which became defunct after the outcome of the Brexit referendum) was considered binding under international law because it constitutes 'an instrument of international law by which the 28 Member States agree on a joint interpretation of certain provisions of the EU Treaties and on principles and arrangements for action in related circumstances'.[36] This argument is essentially based on Article 11 VCLT which states that the consent of a State to be bound by an agreement may be expressed by any means agreed by the parties and Article 31(3)(a) VCLT which mentions that a subsequent agreement between the

---

[33] European Council and Council of the European Union (2016) European Council Conclusions on Ukraine, 15 December 2016, http://www.consilium.europa.eu/en/press/press-releases/2016/12/15-euco-conclusions-ukraine/, accessed 9 March 2017 (European Council Conclusions on Ukraine, 15 December 2016).

[34] European Council, Annex II to the Conclusions of the European Council meeting, Statement on Section A of the Decision of the Heads of State or Government, meeting within the European Council, concerning a new settlement for the United Kingdom within the European Union, EUCO 1/16, 19 February 2016. This draft Decision followed previous practice in comparable situations such as the Decision of the Heads of State and Government, meeting within the European Council, concerning certain problems raised by Denmark on the Treaty on European Union, which was adopted by the Heads of State or Government at Edinburgh, in the context of the European Council of 11 and 12 December 1992 or the Decision of the Heads of State or Government of the 27 Member States of the EU, meeting within the European Council, on the concerns of the Irish people on the Treaty of Lisbon, which was adopted in the context of the European Council of 18 and 19 June 2009.

[35] European Council, Opinion of the Legal Counsel, Draft Decision of the Heads of State or Government, meeting within the European Council, concerning a new settlement for the United Kingdom within the European Union (doc. EUCO 4/16) - Form, legal nature, legal effects and conformity with the EU Treaties, EUCO 15/16, 8 February 2016.

[36] Ibid.

parties on the interpretation of a previous treaty is part of the context to be taken into account for interpreting that treaty.

The Opinion of the legal counsel with regard to the Decision on the EU-Ukraine Association adds that that the Decision needs to be regarded 'as an instrument of international law, by which the EU Member States agree on how they understand and will apply, within their competences, certain provisions of an act by which they are otherwise all bound'.[37] It is therefore argued that this Decision is nothing less than an international agreement,[38] especially considering that the European Council noted in its conclusions that the Decision 'is legally binding on the 28 Member States of the European Union, and may be amended or repealed only by common accord of their Heads of State or Government.'[39]

However, the key difference between the Decision drafted in the 'UK context' and the one adopted with regard to the Ukraine Association Agreement is that the former was an instrument agreed upon by *all* the Member States on the interpretation of the EU Treaties, whereas the latter would be a *unilateral* interpretation of an international agreement with a third country (i.e. the EU-Ukraine Association-Agreement). As mentioned in Article 31(2) and (3) VCLT, a (subsequent) instrument can only constitute a legally binding interpretation of an international agreement when it is accepted by the other parties. Thus, as recognised in the Opinion of the legal counsel, the Decision would only be a legally binding instrument under international law, and bind the other parties, if it would be adopted jointly with, or formally accepted by, those other contracting parties. This would therefore not only require the consent of the Ukrainian government, but also of the EU. Noteworthy, in the context of the signature of CETA, the EU and Canada adopted a 'Joint Interpretative Instrument', which is a document that specifies how certain provisions of CETA need to be interpreted.[40] Because both parties agreed to this Joint Interpretative Instrument, it is a legally binding instrument as foreseen in Article 31 VCLT.[41] Whether Ukraine would agree with all the five points raised by the Dutch government is uncertain. Especially the membership-issue would be difficult for Ukraine to accept, even if the Association Agreement does not include an explicit membership perspective.

Thus, this Decision is binding in the sense that it imposes an interpretation of the Association Agreement on the Member States. Member States are legally bound by

[37] European Council, Opinion of the Legal Counsel, Draft Decision of the Heads of State or Government, meeting within the European Council, on the association agreement between the European Union and the European Atomic Energy Community and their Member States, of the one part, and Ukraine, of the other part, EUCO 37/16, 12 December 2016.

[38] Wessel 2016.

[39] European Council Conclusions on Ukraine, 15 December 2016.

[40] Council of the European Union, Joint Interpretative Instrument on the Comprehensive Economic and Trade Agreement (CETA) between Canada and the European Union and its Member States, 13541/16, 27 October 2016.

[41] This is explicitly recognised in the preamble of this document.

it as concerns the way they understand the Association Agreement and the way they will apply it.[42]

It is also crucial to note that the Decision does not contradict or change any of the provisions of the Association Agreement. As noted by Advocate-General Saggio: 'a unilateral interpretation of the agreement made in the context of an internal adoption procedure cannot—outside the system of reservations—limit the effects of the agreement itself'.[43] The five points in the Decision are indeed in conformity with the text of the agreement as they merely repeat what is or is not in the Association Agreement. Therefore, the Decision stresses that it is 'in full conformity with the EU-Ukraine Association Agreement'.[44]

14.5.2 Alternative Options

It appears that the two Dutch Chambers of Parliament will find this Decision a sufficient response to the outcome of the referendum. However, a swift approval should not be taken for granted at this point since the ruling coalition of Prime Minister Rutte has no majority in the Dutch Senate. Therefore, it is useful to map-out some alternative options for the Dutch Government.

In the worst-case scenario that the Dutch Parliament would reject the Decision of the Heads of State or Government as a response to the referendum and decide not to ratify the agreement, the Dutch government cannot only refuse to ratify the agreement for the Netherlands, it can also veto the EU's ratification of the agreement. As mentioned above, before the agreement can be concluded it must also be ratified by the EU on the basis of a unanimous Council Decision for the conclusion of the agreement. However, such a move would be difficult to reconcile with the principle of sincere cooperation, laid down in Article 4(3) TEU, which includes a mutual legal obligation for the EU and the Member States 'to assist each other in carrying out the tasks which flow from the Treaties'.

Another option would be that the EU, the Member States and Ukraine would adopt a kind of an 'adjusting protocol', which would delete the Netherlands as one of the contracting parties to the agreement. Such a strategy was adopted when Switzerland was not in a position to ratify the Agreement on the European Economic Area (EEA) in the early 1990s. This would mean that the Netherlands would not adopt the Approval Act (thus following the outcome of the referendum),

---

[42] The Opinion of the Legal Counsel even argues that the CJEU can use the Decision when interpreting the agreement in its reasoning to assess the intention of the Member States as to the scope of the commitments undertaken when becoming parties.

[43] Opinion of Advocate General Saggio, *Case C-149/96 (Portugal v Council)*, ECJ, ECR I-08395, 25 February 1999. On this point, see also the judgment of the International Court of Justice, *Case Concerning the Territorial Dispute (Libyan Arab Jamahiriya v Chad)*, ICJ, Judgment, 3 February 1994.

[44] This is also recognised in the Opinion of the Legal Counsel.

but would still ratify the agreement at EU level in the Council. As a EU Member State, the Netherlands would still be bound by the non-mixed elements of the agreement (which covers the most important parts of the agreement). However, such an option could create legal uncertainty because, as mentioned above, it is not entirely clear which elements of the agreement fall under Member States' competences. Moreover, it would be very difficult to put a clear delineation of competences on paper, especially considering the broad scope of the agreement. Such an adjusting protocol would also require the formal approval (e.g. ratification) of the Ukrainian authorities, the EU and the EU Member States.

There are also some non-binding solutions possible. For example the Dutch government can adopt a unilateral statement, in which is specifies its 5 points, to be entered in the Council minutes. Such statements, which are for example also adopted by EU Member States in the context of CETA's signature, are not binding EU acts but form an integral part of the context in which the Council adopts the decision to conclude an agreement.

A last scenario would be the combination of several of the options described above.

14.6 Conclusion

The Decision of the Heads of State and Government is the easiest solution to solve the ratification deadlock of this landmark agreement. While being compatible with the Association Agreement and EU and international law, it addresses the main concerns that were raised during the referendum and binds the Member States (but not the Union and Ukraine). Unfortunately, a repetition of this Dutch non-ratification saga cannot be excluded. Although the Lisbon Treaty reduced the need for mixed agreements, it appears that mixity is here to stay. More than 30 mixed agreements have been concluded in the post-Lisbon era and if the CJEU will follow the recent Opinion of Advocate General Sharpston on the EU-Singapore Free Trade Agreement, who argued that this this trade agreement is mixed,[45] the future for non-mixed EU trade agreements does not look bright. Considering the Eurosceptic climate in several Member States, it is almost bound to happen that a Member State will (threaten to) veto the conclusion of a mixed agreement in the future, for example in order to obtain some last-minute concessions. Whereas the creative legal solutions to these problems will provide interesting food for thought for scholars, they will further complicate the EU's treaty-making procedures and harm its role as a unified international actor.

[45] Opinion of Advocate General Sharpston: CJEU, Advocate General's Opinion in Opinion procedure 2/15, Press Release No 147/16, 21 December 2016.

References

Flaesch-Mougin C, Bosse-Platière I (2014) L'application Provisoire des Accords de L'Union Européenne. In: Govaere I, Lannon E, van Elsuwege P, Adam S (eds) The European Union in the World. Essays in Honour of Marc Maresceau. Martinus Nijhoff Publishers, Leiden/Boston

Heliskoski J (2001) Mixed Agreements as a Technique for Organizing the International Relations of the European Community and its Member States. Martinus Nijhoff Publishers, Leiden/Boston

Maresceau M (2010) A Typology of Mixed Bilateral Agreements. In: Hillion C, Koutrakos P (eds) Mixed Agreements Revisited. The EU and its Member States in the World. Hart Publishing, Oxford/Portland

Rosas A (2014) Exclusive, Shared and National Competence in the Context of EU External Relations: Do Such Distinctions Matter? In: Govaere I, Lannon E, Elsuwege P, Adam S (eds) The European Union in the World. Essays in Honour of Marc Maresceau. Martinus Nijhoff Publishers, Leiden/Boston

Van Elsuwege P (2017) The Stabilisation and Association Agreement between the EU and Kosovo: An Example of Legal Creativity. Forthcoming

Van der Loo G (2016a) The EU-Ukraine Association Agreement. A New Legal Instrument for EU Integration without Membership? Brill Nijhoff, Leiden/Boston

Van der Loo G (2016b) CETA's Signature: 38 Statements, A Joint Interpretative Instrument and an Uncertain Future. CEPS Commentary. https://www.ceps.eu/publications/ceta's-signature-38-statements-joint-interpretative-instrument-and-uncertain-future. Accessed 11 November 2016

Wessel R (2016) The EU Solution to Deal with the Dutch Referendum Result on the EU-Ukraine Association Agreement. European Papers. http://www.europeanpapers.eu/en/europeanforum/eu-solution-deal-dutch-referendum-result-on-the-eu-ukraine-association-agreement. Accessed 7 March 2017

Chapter 15
The Netherlands: A Tax Haven?

Eric C.C.M. Kemmeren

Abstract The taxation of multinational enterprises is currently subject to intensive international and national debates. In these debates the Netherlands has sometimes been labelled as a 'tax haven'. This term has a strong negative connotation. In any case, a country's reputation is at stake if it is qualified as a tax haven. The main research question of this chapter is: Is the Netherlands a tax haven? In this context, it will be discussed whether the following features make the Netherlands a tax haven: (1) The Dutch participation exemption (2) The non-existence of withholding taxes on outbound interest and royalties (3) The Dutch tax treaty network (4) The Dutch advanced tax ruling and advance pricing agreement practice (5) The Dutch exchange of information rules and practice.The chapter starts with the question of whether tax havens are a problem. Subsequently, it discusses a number of definitions of the term tax haven. Based on one of them, the Netherlands' position will be tested and the research question will be answered. At the end, the author sums up his main conclusions and suggestions for improvement of the Dutch tax system, inter alia in respect of letterbox companies.

Keywords Tax haven · Tax treaties · Multinational enterprises · Base erosion · Profit shifting · Letter box companies

---

Professor of international tax law and international taxation at the Fiscal Institute Tilburg (FIT) of Tilburg University, The Netherlands. Prof. Dr. Eric C.C.M. Kemmeren is also a member of the board of the European Tax College, deputy justice of the Arnhem Court of Appeals (Tax Division), and of counsel to Ernst & Young Belastingadviseurs LLP, Rotterdam, The Netherlands. The author can be contacted by e-mail: Kemmeren@uvt.nl.

E.C.C.M. Kemmeren (✉)
Tilburg University, Tilburg, The Netherlands
e-mail: Kemmeren@uvt.nl

M. Kuijer and W. Werner (eds.), *Netherlands Yearbook of International Law 2016*, Netherlands Yearbook of International Law 47,
DOI 10.1007/978-94-6265-207-1_15

Contents

15.1 Introduction

The taxation of multinational enterprises (MNEs) is currently subject to intensive international and national debates.[1] These debates are not restricted to only tax experts. The global debates have been fuelled, inter alia, by non-governmental organizations (NGOs).[2] The main international and national press have also picked up this debate and closely follow the developments.[3] Part of these debates concerns the position of the Netherlands as a potential 'tax haven'.[4]

The term 'tax haven' has a strong negative connotation. In any case, a country's reputation is at stake if it is qualified as a tax haven. Other countries may be reluctant to enter into tax treaties with such a country or may require to include (very) strict rules in such treaties. Furthermore, MNEs may be reluctant to invest in such a country or may be inclined to withdraw investments from the country in order to avoid potential reputational damage for the MNE concerned, which may arise if it is made public that the MNE invests in a country that is qualified as a tax haven.

In order to answer the question of whether the Netherlands could be considered a 'tax haven', a number of sub-questions will have to be answered. Firstly, the question will be raised: Why are tax havens a problem? Subsequently, an attempt will be made to answer the question: What is a tax haven? Does consensus exist on

[1] See, e.g., Resolution of member of parliament Van Vliet, *Kamerstukken* II 2012/13, 25087 no. 35; European Commission 2015; and OECD 2015a.

[2] See, e.g., Henry 2012; Oxfam Novib 2016; and Oxfam 2016.

[3] S. Alonso (2015) Hoe lang is Nederland nog een belastingparadijs?, NRC, 30 March 2015; C Giles and V Houlder (2016) G20 Threatens Tax Havens Over Standards, Financial Times, 15 April 2016.

[4] See, e.g., VPRO Tegenlicht (2013) The Tax Free Tour, 4 May 2013, https://www.youtube.com/watch?v=tvlLO_pTmeY, accessed 23 January 2017; Konrad and Stolper 2015; Oxfam Novib 2016; Castro 2016; and Oxfam 2016, at 6, 12–14, 16, and 25.

the definition of the term 'tax haven'? After discussing this term, a number of main features of the Dutch tax system, which are frequently addressed in the discussion on the position of the Netherlands in the international tax arena, will be discussed. An exhaustive discussion is beyond the scope of this chapter, and therefore, a selection had to be made. In this context it will be discussed whether the following features make the Netherlands a tax haven:

1. The Dutch participation exemption
2. The non-existence of withholding taxes on outbound interest and royalties
3. The Dutch tax treaty network
4. The Dutch advanced tax ruling (ATR) and advance pricing agreement (APA) practice
5. The Dutch exchange of information (EoI) rules and practice.

It is also beyond the scope of this chapter to discuss these main features in too much detail. On the basis of these main features, this contribution tests whether the Netherlands satisfies the definition(s) of the term tax haven. The final section of this chapter draws the main conclusions.

15.2 Why Are Tax Havens a Problem?

As indicated by the Organization for Economic Co-operation and Development (OECD) in 1998, tax havens may create problems. In particular, they may create a global welfare loss and undermine the confidence of taxpayers in the integrity of tax systems.[5]

Tax havens can affect tax competition between states. Tax competition may be defined as the reduction of the tax burden by sovereign countries (objective aspect) in order to improve their economy by increasing the competitiveness of domestic business and/or attracting foreign investment (subjective aspect).[6] The main beneficial effects of tax competition may be a decrease of countries' tax burdens coupled with an improved efficiency in the public administration and a reduction of its size. The main harmful consequences of tax competition may be an erosion of countries' corporate taxable bases, an increase of taxation on more immobile bases such as labour, which may cause a rise in unemployment, and an economic misallocation of resources.[7] In order to distinguish between desirable and harmful tax competition, the main criterion based on the subjective aspect should be a country's goal to improve its (unhealthy) economic situation, favour employment and development (in remote areas), or compensate for its smaller economic size (i.e., to *create* economic activity and investment), versus the goal to attract passive

[5] OECD 1998, at 8.

[6] See, e.g., Pinto 2003, at 52.

[7] See also, e.g., Bratton and McCahery 2001; and Kiekebeld 2004, at 3–34.

mobile income mainly at the expense of other countries (i.e., to merely *shift* economic activity and investment already undertaken).[8]

The impact of tax havens has been explained in the context of harmful tax competition.[9] They can affect the location of financial and other service activities, erode the tax bases of other countries, distort trade and investment patterns, and undermine the fairness, neutrality and broad social acceptance of tax systems generally. Governments and residents of tax havens can also be 'free riders' of general public goods created by non-haven countries. Therefore, on the spending side, there are potential negative spillover effects as well. To conclude, to the extent that tax havens contribute to harmful tax competition, the author believes that they are a problem.

15.3 What Is a Tax Haven?

The term 'tax haven' is not merely used in expert academic literature,[10] tax policy documents,[11] and case law,[12] but also in the regular press.[13] However, the term remains frequently undefined,[14] as is the case in the current global debate on the taxation of MNEs. Countries may be qualified as tax haven, with all reputational consequences, without there being established clear objective criteria for this qualification. In such a case, the qualifications seem to be based on a gut feeling or subjective appreciation by the authors or reporters. For a sound academic and

---

[8] See, e.g., Pinto 2003, at 1–52, and references; and Kemmeren 2005, at 2.

[9] See, e.g., OECD 1998, at 8, 14–16; Council of The European Union (1998) Resolution of the Council and the Representatives of the Governments of the Member States, Meeting within the Council of 1 December 1997 on a Code of Conduct for Business Taxation, OJ C 2, 06/01/1998, at 2; Platform for Tax Good Governance 2013, at 3–9; OECD 2015b, at 15–16; and Oxfam 2016, at 9.

[10] See, e.g., Ngoy 2001; Pinto 2003, at 13, 15, 254, 271–272, 287–288; Evers et al. 2011, at 60–65; Konrad and Stolper 2015; and Castro 2016.

[11] See, e.g., OECD 1998, at 19–21; and OECD 2000, at 2. Remarkable is the resolution of the Dutch Member of Parliament Van Vliet, which calls upon the Dutch government to decline the term and to insist in debates not to use this term (Resolution of member of parliament Van Vliet, *Kamerstukken* II 2012/13, 25087 no. 35).

[12] See, e.g., *X BV and TBG Limited v Staatssecretaris van Financiën*, CJEU, Judgment, Joined Cases C-24/12 (*X BV*) and C-27/12 (*TBG Limited*), ECLI:EU:C:2014:1385, 5 June 2014, paras 37, 51 and 53, which used the term in the context of (preventing) tax avoidance.

[13] See, e.g., K Scannell and V Houlder (2016) US Tax Havens: The New Switzerland, Financial Times, 8 May 2016.

[14] See, e.g, Henry 2012; *Felixstowe Dock and Railway Company Ltd, and others v The Commissioners for Her Majesty's Revenue & Customs*, CJEU, Judgment, Case C-80/12, ECLI:EU:C:2014:200, 1 April 2014 ('*Felixstowe*'), para 32; European Commission (2016) Communication from the Commission to the European Parliament and the Council on an External Strategy for Effective Taxation, Brussels, 28 January 2016, COM(2016) final 24, at 2. See for a similar observation, e.g., Evers et al. 2011, Sect. 2.

societal debate, it is necessary to provide an explicit description of the term 'tax haven', on the basis of which it can be assessed whether a country or a territory is rightfully qualified as a tax haven.

The context of this chapter does not allow us to exhaustively discuss the term tax haven. Therefore, below, only two illustrative examples of descriptions and definitions are critically addressed in order to shed more light on this sensitive issue and to be able to answer the research question of this chapter. They are diverse in respect of the authors' background and the more objective or more subjective nature of the descriptions and definitions.

15.3.1 OECD and Tax Havens

15.3.1.1 OECD's Position

The 1998 OECD Report on harmful tax competition distinguishes three broad categories of situations in which the tax levied in one country on income from geographically mobile activities, such as financial and other service activities, is lower than the tax that would be levied on the same income in another country. The *first* country:

1. Is a *tax haven* and, as such, generally imposes no or only nominal tax on that income;
2. Collects significant revenues from tax imposed on income at the corporate level but its tax system has preferential features that allow the relevant income to be subject to low or no taxation;
3. Collects significant revenues from tax imposed on income at the corporate level but the effective tax rate that is generally applicable at that level in that country is lower than that levied in the second country.[15]

The last category of countries is out of the scope of harmful tax competition and, therefore, these countries do not qualify as tax havens. The report acknowledges that a number of countries are able to finance their public services with no or nominal income taxes. However, it is also noted that some of them offer themselves as places to be used by non-residents to escape tax in their country of residence. Furthermore, it also acknowledges that the term tax haven does not have a precise technical meaning.

According to the OECD, four objective key factors assist in identifying harmful preferential tax regimes:

1. The regime imposes a low or zero effective tax rate on the relevant income;
2. The regime is ring-fenced, i.e., the regime is restricted to non-residents or it is otherwise isolated from the domestic economy;

[15] OECD 1998, at 19–20.

3. The operation of the regime is non-transparent;
4. The country operating the regime does not effectively exchange information with other countries.[16]

The report distinguishes tax havens from other countries with preferential regimes, *inter alia*, for the following reasons.[17] A tax haven does not have any interest in trying to curb the 'race to the bottom' with respect to income tax, since it does not impose an income tax or only a nominal one. Furthermore, it is actively contributing to the erosion of income tax revenues in other countries. In contrast, other countries which impose a significant corporate income tax, but whose systems include preferential regimes may have a significant amount of revenues that are at risk from the spread of harmful tax competition. Taking into account the scope of this chapter, it will subsequently focus solely on how to identify a tax haven according to the OECD report.

In order to qualify a jurisdiction as a 'tax haven', the report distinguishes two constitutive key factors and three key factors that confirm the qualification as a tax haven:[18]

1. Constitutive key factors
   a. No or only nominal taxation on the relevant income (generally or in special circumstances)[19]
   b. The fact that a country offers itself as a place, or is perceived to be a place, to be used by non-residents to escape tax in their country of residence.
2. Confirming key factors
   a. Laws or administrative practices (strict secrecy rules and other protections against scrutiny by tax authorities) which prevent the effective exchange of relevant information with other governments on taxpayers benefiting from the low or no tax jurisdiction[20]
   b. Lack of transparency in the operation of the legislative, legal or administrative provisions
   c. The absence of a requirement that the activity be substantial, since it would suggest that a jurisdiction may be attempting to attract investment or transactions that are purely tax driven.[21]

[16] OECD 1998, at 22–23.

[17] OECD 1998, at 20.

[18] OECD 1998, at 21–23.

[19] Even if the tax haven does impose tax, the definition of domestic source income may be so restricted as to result in very little income being taxed. See OECD 1998, at 23.

[20] It limits the access by tax authorities to the information required for the correct and timely application of their tax laws. See OECD 1998, at 24.

[21] Transactions may be booked there without the requirement of adding value so that there is little real activity, i.e. these jurisdictions are essentially 'booking centres'. It can be difficult to determine when and whether an activity is substantial. For example, financial and management services may

It should be noted that over the years the OECD became more reluctant to use the term 'tax haven'.[22] It increasingly replaced it by the term 'uncooperative tax haven',[23] which is used for jurisdictions that are not sufficiently transparent. However, the term tax haven has been referred to again in the base erosion and profit shifting (BEPS) discussion on the taxation of MNEs.[24]

In line with the OECD, Advocate General (AG) to the Court of Justice of the European Union (CJEU) Jääskinen describes the term tax haven as follows:

> A large number of fiscally sovereign territories and of States use tax and non-tax incentives to attract financial activities and other services. Those territories generally offer foreign investors an environment in which zero or minimal taxation is frequently accompanied by a relaxation of regulatory or administrative constraints. Those jurisdictions are generally classified as tax havens and are one of the crucial aspects of the concept of harmful tax rules.[25]

15.3.1.2 Criticism on OECD's Position on Tax Havens

The OECD's approach, although based on objective criteria, did not remain uncriticized.[26] One of the main points was the unjustified intrusion of the OECD in the internal affairs of sovereign countries, which were not allowed to build their own tax systems as they wished. The OECD project would be inconsistent with the basic principles of international law and international tax law. Indeed, sovereign states have the right to build their own tax system as they wish. Furthermore, it was also upheld that the OECD project, including the countermeasures against tax havens, served predominantly the interests of the OECD Member States in their capacity of states of residence of capital exporters. The author sympathizes with these points of criticism. They may also explain for a part why the OECD has become more reluctant to use the term tax haven, and that the OECD focusses in the context of uncooperative tax havens more on transparency and exchange of information conditions than on whether (certain items of) income are not or lowly taxed or whether substantial activities are carried out in a jurisdiction. The underlying idea of this approach is that with the obtained information, on the one hand, the OECD Member States as states of residence of capital exporters can take

(Footnote 21 continued)

in certain circumstances involve substantial activities. However, certain services provided by 'paper companies' may be readily found to lack substance. See OECD 1998, at 22 and 24.

[22] See also, e.g., Evers et al. 2011, Sect. 2.

[23] See, e.g., OECD (2004) The OECD's Project on Harmful Tax Practices: The 2004 Progress Report, OECD, Paris, 4 February 2004, at 14–15.

[24] See, e.g., OECD 2015b, at 15–16.

[25] *European Commission and Kingdom of Spain v Government of Gibraltar and United Kingdom*, AG Jääskinen, Opinion, Joined Cases C 106/09 P and C 107/09 P, ECLI:EU:C:2011:215, 7 April 2011, para 123 (references omitted). The AG refers to OECD 1998, para 47.

[26] See for an overview, e.g., Pinto 2003, at 279–286.

compensatory tax measures in order to neutralize the tax benefits obtained by their residents through the use of tax havens. For example, they can apply what is known as controlled foreign corporation (CFC) legislation. Under such a regime, profits allocated to a subsidiary in a tax haven can be included in the taxable base of the parent company and taxed at the higher effective tax rate in the parent's state of residence. On the other hand, the information obtained can also be used by OECD Member States to refuse a reduction of source state taxation, including withholding taxes, if the income is paid to a tax haven.

15.3.2 Broader Concepts of the Term 'Tax Haven'

By contrast, the OECD has also been criticized on the ground that its approach did not go far enough and that a broader approach is necessary.

15.3.2.1 Subjective Definition

For example, Ngoy deploys a very wide subjective and not at all objective tax haven concept:

> A tax haven is a real haven only as far as it brings satisfaction to the taxpayer (wherever he is from) who tries to use it to shield income from a determined tax treatment in the country that imposes the liability. Obviously, no matter how severe and well-conceived a tax law is, a taxpayer, by means of ingenious tax planning, will always try to get around it. Whenever a taxpayer succeeds in hiding income in a foreign territory without incurring taxation there, or incurring taxation lower than he would have had if he had left the income in his country of tax liability, he will have used a tax haven.[27]

Under this concept, unlike the OECD's definition of a tax haven, it is of no importance that a country qualifies as a tax haven because the tax authorities or the legislators designate it as such. The focus is only on the position of the taxpayer concerned (the relevant subject). If the taxpayer's purpose is just to avoid income tax in his state of residence or in his state of source, and a country allows that taxpayer to enjoy income tax free, this country will be a tax haven. The tax haven is a consequence of the taxpayer's behaviour. Therefore, any jurisdiction that taxes at a lower level than the taxpayer's state of residence or the taxpayer's state of source, respectively, qualifies as a tax haven. Such a taxation does not focus on taxation where real, genuine economic activities are carried out, which is the main goal of the BEPS project, at least, as expressed by the OECD.[28] The latter approach is also in line with an allocation of tax jurisdiction based on the principle of origin as

---

[27] Ngoy 2001, at 1.

[28] See, e.g., OECD 2015a, at 4–5, 9, 15–16.

advocated by the author.[29] That is to say, income should be taxed only in the state where that income has been generated. This is because the public facilities provided by that state have contributed to the carrying out of the income-producing activities (direct benefit principle). In substance, the direct benefit principle is part of the ability-to-pay principle. The state where the income has been created contributes to a person's wealth, which gives that person the capacity to pay taxes. Therefore, an origin-based allocation of tax jurisdiction is in line with the ability-to-pay principle. The author believes that only individuals can create income, and that things – in themselves – cannot. The intellectual element is the key component for the production of income. Through the action of an individual, with or without using a device (i.e. a capital component), value may be added to things. An origin-based taxation justifies taxation of income by a state if the income is created within the territory of that state, i.e. the cause of the income is within the territory of that state. A residence-based taxation is not in line with the starting-point that income should be taxed where the value is added. Therefore, the author also thinks that the criticism on the OECD meaning of the term tax havens is even more strongly relevant to the subjective approach as, *inter alia*, advocated by Ngoy. It does not in any way acknowledge a country's sovereignty. Furthermore, it would only strengthen more the position of OECD Member States as states of residence of capital exporters. Under this subjective approach, without doubt, the Netherlands would qualify as a tax haven, even if only one taxpayer succeeds in designing and implementing a plan to use the Netherlands in reducing his tax liability in his state of residence or state of source, respectively. Any country in a similar position would qualify as a tax haven. The author concludes that such a subjective approach lacks distinguishing character and, therefore, cannot be a useful instrument to counter harmful tax competition.

15.3.2.2 Oxfam (Novib)'s Concept

Another example of a broad tax haven concept can be found in a report from Oxfam Novib (the Dutch affiliate of Oxfam) published in May 2016.[30] This report refers to the 'Taxation Paper' on aggressive tax planning[31] to substantiate its position that the Netherlands is a tax haven.[32] Although the authors of the paper state that '[t]he views expressed in the Taxation Papers are solely those of the authors and do not necessarily reflect the views of the European Commission',[33] Oxfam Novib refers to the Taxation Paper as if its findings were the ones of the European Commission.[34]

[29] See, e.g., Kemmeren 2001, at 18–55.

[30] Oxfam Novib 2016, at 5–10 and 15–16.

[31] Meldgaard et al. 2015.

[32] Oxfam Novib 2016, at 5–6 and 15–16.

[33] Meldgaard et al. 2015, cover sheet.

[34] See, e.g., Oxfam Novib 2016, at 5.

Furthermore, the Taxation Paper is a study on aggressive tax planning (ATP), which has been defined as follows:

> Aggressive tax planning consists of taking advantage of the technicalities of a tax system or of mismatches between two or more tax systems for the purpose of reducing tax liability. Aggressive tax planning can take a multitude of forms. Its consequences include double deductions (e.g. the same loss is deducted both in the state of source and residence) and double non-taxation (e.g. income which is not taxed in the source state is exempt in the state of residence).[35]

The assessment methodology applies both objective and subjective criteria in determining whether or not given ATP indicators are problematic for a particular Member State.[36] ATP indicators are generally defined as generic characteristics of a tax system that can facilitate ATP.[37] The Taxation Paper lists 17 ATP indicators for the Netherlands.[38] In the context of ATP, it also uses the term tax haven without defining it.[39] It must be noted that the paper does not qualify the Netherlands as a tax haven. This qualification has autonomously been produced by Oxfam Novib based on the 17 ATP indicators listed in the Taxation Paper. However, the author of this chapter states that the ATP concept is not the same as the tax haven concept. The ATP concept indicates whether a country's legislation is vulnerable to ATP structures,[40] but it does not qualify a country as a tax haven as done by, e.g., the OECD and Ngoy. The Taxation Paper explicitly states:

> It should be understood that no value judgement is intended by the nomenclature used in this study. It is perfectly possible that Member State tax rules found to be ATP indicators for the purpose of this study may well pursue valid tax policy objectives.[41]

Therefore, the author believes that the underpinning of Oxfam Novib's qualification of the Netherlands as a tax haven, at least, be can be challenged.

Late December 2016, Oxfam published another report,[42] which may to a certain extent be considered as a follow-up to the Oxfam Novib report published earlier in 2016.[43] This latest report includes a definition of the term tax haven:[44]

---

[35] European Commission (2012) Recommendation on aggressive tax planning, 6 December 2012, C(2012) 8806 final, para 2. See also Meldgaard et al. 2015, at 15–16 and 23.

[36] Meldgaard et al. 2015, at 68. See for an overview of the 33 ATP indicators, Meldgaard et al. 2015, at 51–67. The scope of this chapter does not allow us to discuss them.

[37] Meldgaard et al. 2015, at 51.

[38] Meldgaard et al. 2015, at 120–123.

[39] Meldgaard et al. 2015, at 47–49, 57–58, 66, 74, 136 and 163.

[40] Meldgaard et al. 2015, at 15–16 and 18.

[41] Meldgaard et al. 2015, at 8.

[42] Oxfam 2016.

[43] Oxfam Novib 2016.

[44] Oxfam 2016, at 11.

Tax havens are jurisdictions or territories that have intentionally adopted fiscal and legal frameworks allowing non-residents (physical persons or legal entities) to minimize the amount of taxes they pay where they undertake substantial economic activity.

According to Oxfam, tax havens usually fulfil several of the following criteria:

- They grant fiscal advantages to non-resident individuals or legal entities only, without requiring that substantial economic activity be undertaken in the country or dependency.
- They provide a significantly lower effective level of taxation, including zero taxation for natural or legal persons.
- They have adopted laws or administrative practices that prevent the automatic exchange of information for tax purposes with other governments.
- They have adopted legislative, legal or administrative provisions that allow the non-disclosure of the corporate structure of legal entities (including trusts, charities, foundations, etc.), or the ownership of assets or rights.[45]

In any case, this follow-up report is much more precise in its terminology than the Oxfam Novib report, because it includes a definition of the term tax haven. Oxfam has also developed a set of indicators to identify countries that play, according to Oxfam, the greatest role as corporate tax havens.[46] Three key elements are taken into account to qualify a jurisdiction as a tax haven: corporate tax rates; tax incentives offered; and lack of cooperation with international efforts against tax avoidance. The Netherlands has been ranked third of the world's worst corporate tax havens based on the following elements: tax incentives; 0% withholding taxes; and evidence of large-scale profit shifting. As the author will partly discuss below, he does not think that these elements justify the qualification of the Netherlands as a tax haven. Here, the author emphasizes that the tax incentive referred to by Oxfam is the innovation box.[47] Under this regime, benefits from self-developed intangible assets are taxed at a rate of 5% instead of a rate of (at the most) 25%. The intangible assets must have been produced in the Netherlands or the European Union. The tax incentive is meant to promote research and development (R&D) activities. The incentive is available for both residents and non-residents, whether they operate internationally or merely domestically. Acquired intangibles are not facilitated. Therefore, the proceeds are taxed where the value has been added, although at a lower rate than the regular one. This policy is in line with the EU policy to boost R&D activities in the EU, also by means of tax instruments.[48] Furthermore, as from 1 January 2017, the innovation box has been aligned with the OECD proposals on

---

[45] Ibid.

[46] Oxfam 2016, at 12–13. It is beyond the scope of this chapter to discuss in detail Oxfam's methodology.

[47] Article 12b Corporate Income Tax Act 1969 (*Wet op de Vennootschapsbelasting 1969*; CITA 1969).

[48] See, e.g., Framework for State Aid for Research and Development and Innovation, OJ C 198, 27.6.2014, p. 20.

R&D tax incentives as laid down in OECD BEPS Action 5.[49] Oxfam argues that the innovation box is an element which makes the Netherlands a tax haven because the budget involved increased from € 361 million in 2010 to € 1.2 billion (estimation) in 2016, and because this box may not be the most effective way to stimulate R&D activities. However, the author believes that Oxfam's arguments do not contribute to the conclusion that the Netherlands qualifies as a tax haven according to its own definition of the term. The innovation box has not intentionally been adopted to allow non-resident legal entities to minimize the amount of taxes they pay where they undertake substantial economic activity. On the contrary!

Oxfam also refers to the Starbucks EU State aid case as evidence that the Netherlands qualifies as a tax haven.[50] However, it must be noted that in this case the European Commission does not use the term tax haven at all.[51] Furthermore, the European Commission also emphasizes that the Dutch advanced pricing agreement (APA) practice is sound, but that it questions in the Starbucks case only an individual APA.[52] It noted that the Netherlands seemed to generally proceed with a thorough assessment based on comprehensive information required from the taxpayer. The Commission therefore does not expect to encounter systematic irregularities in tax rulings. Therefore, the author believes that the Starbucks case cannot either be taken as evidence for the qualification of the Netherlands as a tax haven.

15.4 Is the Netherlands a Tax Haven?

It follows from the above that the term tax haven is not so easy to define.[53] There is no consensus.[54] Yet, the term has a strong negative connotation, and a country's reputation is at stake if it is qualified as a tax haven. It is obvious that the author believes that a subjective approach should not be used to define the term tax haven. Although the author did also criticize the 1998-OECD approach of the term, he nevertheless believes that it may be useful to apply this approach in the context of the global BEPS discussion, because the aim of that discussion is to allocate tax jurisdiction on income to the state where the value is added and because that

---

[49] OECD 2015b, at 24–36; and Articles 12b-12bg CITA 1969.

[50] Oxfam 2016, at 13 and 19.

[51] European Commission (2015) Commission Decision of 21 October 2015 on State aid SA.38374 (2014/C ex 2014/NN) implemented by the Netherlands to Starbucks, C(2015) 7143 final. Both the Netherlands (Case T-760/15 (*The Netherlands v Commission*)) and Starbucks (Case T-636/16 (*Starbucks and Starbucks Manufacturing EMEA v Commission*)) appealed the decision. For a more detailed discussion of these pending cases, see Kemmeren 2017.

[52] European Commission (2014) State aid: Commission investigates transfer pricing arrangements on corporate taxation of Apple (Ireland), Starbucks (Netherlands) and Fiat Finance and Trade (Luxembourg), Press Release, 11 June 2014, IP/14/663.

[53] See also, e.g., Evers et al. 2011, paras 2 and 5.

[54] See also, e.g., Oxfam 2016, at 10–11.

discussion is led by the OECD. Therefore, the 1998-OECD approach and factors will be applied to the Netherlands, at least to a number of main features of the Dutch tax system that are frequently addressed in the discussion on the position of the Netherlands in the international tax arena. Do they make the Netherlands a tax haven?

15.4.1 Participation Exemption

In respect of qualifying participations,[55] the Netherlands applies a participation exemption both on dividends and capital gains on shares.[56] This means that these items of income are not taxed in the Netherlands. As one of the constitutive key factors for the qualification as a tax haven is that no or only nominal taxation on the relevant income is imposed (generally or in special circumstances), the Netherlands qualifies prima facie as a tax haven. This qualification seems to be emphasized by the second constitutive key factor, i.e., the fact that a country offers itself as a place, or is perceived to be a place, to be used by non-residents to escape tax in their country of residence. The Netherlands itself emphasizes that the participation exemption is one of the crown jewels of its fiscal investment climate.[57]

However, the author strongly believes that the qualification of tax haven on the basis of the participation exemption is based on a misconception. The participation exemption is based on the economic policy of capital and labour import neutrality (CLIN).[58] This means that labour and capital funds originating in various states should compete on equal terms in the labour and capital markets of a state, irrespective of the place of residence of the worker or investor.[59] The participation exemption actually realizes that profits are taxed in the state where the business activity is carried out, and that is not necessarily the state of residence of the shareholder. The participation exemption enables businesses to compete with businesses and not owners with owners. It contributes to a level playing field for entrepreneurial activities. The participation exemption does not only contribute to an efficient allocation of the production factors capital and labour, but also to international neutrality which implies that the relation between taxes (burdens) and public goods (benefits) should not be disturbed to the disadvantage of transnational investment.

---

[55] In order to qualify, one of the conditions is that a taxpayer must hold at least a participation of 5% of the nominal paid-up capital of another company of which the capital is wholly or partly divided into stocks.

[56] Article 13 CITA 1969.

[57] See, e.g., Letter of State Secretary of Finance to Second Chamber of the Dutch Parliament of 20 June 2015, IZV/2015-314 U, at 1.

[58] See, e.g., Ministerie van Financiën, Notitie Fiscaal Verdragsbeleid 2011, 11 February 2011, at 39.

[59] See for more details, e.g., Kemmeren 2001, at 71–83.

Furthermore, the participation exemption is not applied unrestrictedly. With regard to lowly taxed passive investment participations, dividends and capital gains are taxed.[60] The foreign tax levied in connection with these items of income may be deducted from the corporate income tax due in the Netherlands. If a Dutch resident company holds an interest of 25% or more in such a company, the taxpayer must value the interest yearly on the market value, so that taxation cannot be deferred until realization.[61] The latter taxation comes close to CFC legislation. The participation exemption is not applied either to remuneration from a hybrid instrument to the extent that remuneration is deductible for the paying participation.[62] These limitations of the participation exemption are based on another economic policy: capital and labour export neutrality (CLEN) which is defined as follows: an income recipient should pay the same total (domestic plus foreign) tax, irrespective of whether that recipient derives a given amount of labour or investment income from foreign or domestic sources. The aim of this policy is to tax residents equally.

To sum up, the author does not believe that generally speaking the participation exemption is too generous, as is sometimes argued.[63] The participation exemption contributes to the realization of the allocation of tax jurisdiction to the states where the value is added, which is the main aim of the OECD in the BEPS discussion. It also realizes allocation of taxing power in line with the principle of origin, the direct benefit principle, the ability to pay principle, international neutrality and CLIN. Therefore, the author believes that the participation exemption cannot be used to qualify the Netherlands as a tax haven.

15.4.2 Non-Existence of Withholding Taxes on Interest and Royalties

The Netherlands does not levy a withholding tax (WHT) on interest and royalties. With regard to these items of income, it applies the economic policy of CLEN. This means that the Netherlands believes that the exclusive taxing power must be allocated to the state of residence of the recipient of the interest or royalty.[64] In this context, a WHT on interest or royalties does not fit. Again, taken into account two of the constitutive key factors for the qualification as a tax haven, the Netherlands qualifies prima facie as a tax haven.

---

[60] Article 13 in conjunction with Articles 13aa and 23c CITA 1969. See also, e.g., Letter of State Secretary of Finance to Second Chamber of the Dutch Parliament of 2 November 2016, no. 2016-0000163149, at 3.

[61] Article 13a CITA 1969.

[62] Article 13(17) CITA 1969.

[63] See, e.g., Meldgaard et al. 2015, at 120–121, and 123; and Oxfam Novib 2016, at 16.

[64] See, e.g., Ministerie van Financiën, Notitie Fiscaal Verdragsbeleid 2011, 11 February 2011, at 47, and Letter of State Secretary of Finance to Second Chamber of the Dutch Parliament of 20 June 2015, IZV/2015-314 U, p. 2.

However, the author thinks that the choice for an economic policy based on CLEN and building a tax system on this choice, *inter alia*, by choosing not to levy a WHT on interest and royalties, cannot be an indicator for the qualification of a country as a tax haven. With regard to royalties, it is even a long-standing OECD policy to confer exclusive taxing power to the state of residence of the recipient of the royalty.[65] The author also believes that not levying a WHT on royalties is in line with the OECD's starting-point in the BEPS discussion, i.e., that the income must be taxed where the value is added. Furthermore, he thinks that refraining from a WHT on royalties is also to a large extent consistent with the principle of origin, the direct benefit principle, the ability to pay principle, international neutrality and CLIN.[66] The state in which the intangible property was produced (not the state in which it is used) should be entitled to tax the income therefrom, namely lump-sum or periodic payments (royalties). This means that most of a royalty income must be allocated to the substantial activity state of the lessor. Only the interest component included in the royalty should be allocated to the substantial activity state of the lessee. The reason for this is, according to the author, that the current allocation of taxing power on interest income to the residence state of the creditor is not in line with the starting point that the income must be taxed where the value is added. This allocation is also inconsistent with the principle of origin, the direct benefit principle, the ability to pay principle, international neutrality and CLIN.[67] The interest income is not produced by the creditor, but by the income producing activities of the debtor, e.g., his business activities. Therefore, the state in which the debtor produces the interest income must be awarded unlimited tax jurisdiction with respect to interest. For the same reasons, capital gains on debt claims should be allocated to the same state. The expenses incurred for purposes of the interest income or capital gains (such as a bank's spread) should be deductible. A simple WHT on gross interest payments is, in itself, not a sufficient tool to satisfy an origin-based taxation. Nevertheless, a WHT could be a good starting point from an administrative perspective. However, the creditor must also have the opportunity to be taxed on a net basis. Developing countries would especially benefit from such a change in the system, as those countries seem to be more vulnerable to debt financing structures.[68]

In conclusion, although the author believes that the current system of the allocation of taxing power on interest income should be changed, the fact that the Netherlands does not currently levy a WHT on interest and royalties, does not make the Netherlands a tax haven.

---

[65] See, e.g., Article 12 of the OECD Model Tax Convention on Income and Capital (OECD Model); and the Commentary to this provision since the 1963 version until the most recent updated version of 2014.

[66] See for more details, e.g., Kemmeren 2016, at 163–173 and 177–183.

[67] See for more details, e.g., Kemmeren 2016, at 163–177.

[68] See, e.g., International Monetary Fund 2014; and UNCTAD 2015, at 172–212.

15.4.3 Dutch Tax Treaty Network

As a rule, tax treaties can only be invoked by residents of the contracting states.[69] This means that only residents can benefit from tax treaty provisions, such as the reduction of source state taxation, like a WHT on interest. In order to qualify as a resident for tax treaty purposes, which qualification is essential for getting access to tax treaties and its benefits, a person must qualify as a tax resident under the domestic laws of one of the contracting states. In respect of companies, in a number of countries, such as the Netherlands and the United States, it is sufficient that a company has been incorporated under the company laws of a state in order to qualify as a resident of that state for corporate income tax purposes.[70] Resident taxpayers are normally taxed on their worldwide income at a regular rate. This is also true for the Netherlands. Resident companies are taxed on their worldwide income at a rate of 25%, leaving aside a step-up rate of 20% for the first € 200,000 (year 2017).

As a consequence, in general, it is rather easy to get access to tax treaties of countries that also apply the incorporation principle for corporate income tax purposes. The mere fact that a company has been incorporated under Dutch company law makes the company a resident of the Netherlands. Consequently, such a company has also access to the Dutch tax treaties and to the benefits provided by them, unless specific provisions or general anti-abuse rules (GAARs) prevent this.[71] It means that non-resident persons can create rather easy access to the Dutch tax treaty network by incorporating a letterbox company without any substantial economic activity in the Netherlands. A number of reports show that the Netherlands is used for routing large amounts of investments from one country to another through what is known as a special purpose entity (SPE).[72] The taxable base of an SPE may

---

[69] See Article 1 in conjunction with Article 4 OECD Model. In general, the actual tax treaties include the same or similar provisions.

[70] See, for the Netherlands, Article 2(4) CITA 1969, and for the United States, IRC § 7701(a)(3), (4), and (30).

[71] See, e.g., limitation on benefits (LOB) rules, such as included Article 26 of the Convention between the Kingdom of the Netherlands and the United States of America for the Avoidance of Double Taxation and the Prevention of Fiscal Evasion with Respect to Taxes on Income (18 December 1992, effective as of 1 January 1994), the beneficial owner condition as included in Article 10–12 OECD Model, and the application of (domestic) GAARs in a tax treaty context, sometimes explicitly allowed by tax treaties, as done in Art. 23 of the Convention between the Federal Republic of Germany and the Kingdom of the Netherlands for the Avoidance of Double Taxation and the Prevention of Fiscal Evasion with Respect to Taxes on Income (12 April 2012, effective as of 1 January 2016).

[72] See, e.g., International Monetary Fund 2014, at 6 and 16. The report (at 17) makes the following observation in respect of the term tax haven: 'The otherwise unhelpful and ill-defined term 'tax haven' is used in this paper only to refer to specific lists of jurisdictions used in the literature cited.' See further: UNCTAD 2015, at 5, 8, 26, 41, 63, 68, 71, 73, 86, 93, 112, 115, 188–189, 192–193, and 198. It should be noted that this report (at 189) defines the term tax haven even without an element of tax in it: 'Small jurisdictions whose economy is entirely, or almost entirely, dedicated to

be rather small. For example, as a rule, interest or royalties payable are deductible from the interest or royalties received, respectively.[73] Although this taxable base will be taxed at the regular rate of 20–25%, the benefit of the reduction of the source state taxation claimed under the Dutch tax treaty network may be a multiple of the tax costs in the Netherlands.

These examples show that, on balance, the tax costs in the Netherlands on the flow of interest or royalties, respectively, may not be very high compared to the tax saved elsewhere, especially in source states. As one of the constitutive key factors for the qualification as a tax haven is no or only nominal taxation on the relevant income (generally or in special circumstances), the Netherlands seems to qualify *prima facie* as tax haven, also in this case. This qualification seems to be emphasized by the second constitutive key factor, i.e., the fact that a country offers itself as a place, or is perceived as a place, to be used by non-residents to escape tax in their country of residence.[74]

However, the author thinks that it is hard to uphold that interest and royalties are nominally taxed in the Netherlands. SPEs are subject to the regular rules for the calculation of the tax base and to the regular tax rate as applied to all Dutch tax resident companies. The benefit of these kind of structures is created by the reduction of taxes in other countries than the Netherlands. This reduction outweighs the (additional) tax costs by interposing a Dutch resident letterbox company that is taxed on a regular basis. Therefore, the author concludes that the Netherlands in this case does not meet the first constitutive key factor either. However, it does meet one of the confirming key factors, i.e., the absence of a requirement that the activity be substantial, which may suggest that a jurisdiction may be attempting to attract investment or transactions that are purely tax-driven. Technically, this factor is only relevant if both constitutive key factors are satisfied.

Nevertheless, the author believes that this situation is undesirable. Letterbox companies do not contribute to allocation of tax jurisdiction to states where the value is added. Therefore, the interposition of such SPEs does not meet the aim of the OECD in the BEPS discussion. Granting tax treaty benefits to such letterbox companies is also inconsistent with the principle of origin, the direct benefit principle, the ability to pay principle, international neutrality and CLIN.[75] Actually, the interposition of letterbox companies create additional transaction costs and,

(Footnote 72 continued)

the provision of offshore financial services.' At the same page it defines other offshore hubs as '[j]urisdictions (not identified as tax havens) offering SPEs or other entities that facilitate transit investment. Larger jurisdictions with substantial real economic activity that act as major global investment hubs for MNEs due to their favourable tax and investment conditions.' The Netherlands is included in this category.

[73] It should be noted that the CITA 1969 also includes a number of provisions which limit the deduction of interest. See, e.g., Articles 10a, 10b, 13 l and 15ad CITA 1969.

[74] See, e.g., International Monetary Fund 2014 and UNCTAD 2015, which perceive the Netherlands to be used by non-residents to escape taxes.

[75] See for further details Kemmeren 2001, at 257–301.

therefore, a welfare loss. Although it is true that (some) treaty partners, as the case may be, could deny tax treaty benefits to letterbox companies based on limitation on benefits rules, the beneficial owner condition, and (domestic) GAARs, the author believes that the Netherlands itself can contribute to end this undesirable situation by repealing the deemed residence provision of Article 2(4) CITA 1969 and replacing this provision by an origin-based residence provision. Such a provision could be framed as follows:

> A non-individual will be considered as resident of the Netherlands if:
>
> (1) It pursues or has pursued a substantial income-producing economic activity within the territory of the Netherlands *and*
> (2) The income or capital concerned has to be attributed to that activity on the basis of a functional analysis.
>
> A functional connection exists if the property concerned is used for pursuing that economic activity, i.e., this property is managed, and its operations are directed and controlled from within the Netherlands. This condition will prevent a fry shop, e.g., from being used to re-route millions of loans through the Netherlands.

As a result, a letterbox company would no longer qualify as a Dutch tax resident for corporate income tax purposes and, consequently, neither as tax treaty resident under the Dutch tax treaties. This means that such an SPE can no longer invoke the benefits of the Dutch tax treaties. In order to give start-ups a fair chance to develop substantial income-producing economic activities within the Netherlands, a company could be given the opportunity to demonstrate with objective evidence that it has the intention of becoming substantially active in the Netherlands. Such an approach is also in line with the freedom of establishment under EU law.[76] It could even be contemplated to give a company a certain period of time to build up such activities, e.g., three or five years. The Netherlands can realize this result unilaterally by amending its domestic tax laws. For this change, it is not necessary to amend the Dutch tax treaties. However, in November 2016, the Dutch State Secretary declined again to amend Article 2(4) CITA 1969, because he feared new forms of tax avoidance if this provision would be replaced by a residence provision based on a substance criteria.[77] He believed that the deemed residence rule prevents that companies are neither residents of the Netherlands nor of any other country. The author does not share this point of view. First of all, under the rule suggested by the author, a company which receives income, but which does not carry out a substantial income-producing economic activity within the territory of the Netherlands, must carry out such activities in another territory and will be a resident of that territory if that territory applies the same or similar rules as the Netherlands

---

[76] Compare, e.g., *The Queen v Secretary of State for Transport, ex parte Factortame*, CJEU, Judgment, Case C-221/89, ECLI:EU:C:1991:320, 25 July 1991 (*Factortame II*), para 21. See for further details, e.g., Kemmeren 2001, at 177–188.

[77] See, e.g., Letter of State Secretary of Finance to Second Chamber of the Dutch Parliament of 4 November 2016, no. 2016-0000194729, at 5.

would do.[78] A company, which is a legal fiction in itself, can only operate through human activities. Income does not come out of the blue, but is created by human activities. Secondly, in respect of income received by a company which is not functionally connected with a substantial income-producing economic activity of that company, it must be linked with a substantial income-producing economic activity of another person and be taxed in relation to that person. Again, income does not come out of the blue and income production requires human activity.

In the context of tax treaties, it must be noted that the Netherlands has offered to 23 developing countries to include an LOB provision in their tax treaties with the Netherlands in order to prevent undesirable use of these treaties by interposed Dutch resident companies that lack substantial activities in the Netherlands.[79] A number of them have already accepted this offer.

To conclude, although the author believes that the current system of determining residents for Dutch corporate income tax purposes should be changed, the fact that the current system gives access to the benefits provided by tax treaties by virtue of the deemed residence rule of Article 2(4) CITA 1969 does not make the Netherlands a tax haven.

15.4.4 Dutch ATR and APA Practice

The Netherlands has a long-standing tradition in respect of advanced tax rulings (ATR) and advanced pricing agreements (APA).[80] ATRs are settlement agreements that provide both the taxpayer and the Dutch Tax Administration with certainty in advance on the application of, e.g., the participation exemption in a specific case. APAs are also settlement agreements, but they provide certainty in advance to both the taxpayer and the Dutch Tax Administration on an arm's length compensation for a specific transaction or a methodology to establish such an arm's length compensation for specific transactions between associated enterprises or on an arm's length allocation of profits to a permanent establishment of entities. This practice fits in the general service-minded approach of Dutch administrative bodies. In principle, ATRs and APAs can be concluded by any taxpayer, irrespective of whether it concerns SMEs, large MNEs, domestic situations or cross-border

[78] Otherwise a classical disparity may arise. However, in such a case, it is not because of the Dutch tax system that income may not be taxed in the territory where value is added, where the origin of the income is. International coordination, one of the essential elements in the BEPS actions, can prevent such a disparity.

[79] See, e.g., Letter of Minister of Foreign Trade and Development Cooperation and State Secretary of Finance to Second Chamber of the Dutch Parliament of 18 June 2015, MINBUZA-2015.232574, at 2–3.

[80] See, e.g., Meussen and Velthuizen 2002, at 4–10.

situations.[81] The conclusion of ATRs and APAs with an international impact has been concentrated with one tax office in Rotterdam in order to better guarantee equal treatment and coherence,[82] *inter alia*, to prevent tax inspector shopping. Other ATRs and APAs are concluded between the taxpayer and his local tax office.

The conclusion of ATRs and APAs is subject to strict rules.[83] In general, ATRs and APAs are concluded for a period of four or five years. They may only be concluded in consistence with the law, case law and policy. This also means that group transactions must be consistent with the arm's length principle, i.e., conditions made or imposed between group companies in their commercial or financial relations may not differ from those that would be made between independent enterprises.[84] As follows from the Decrees, no advanced certainty will be granted in case:

- Of exploration of the tax boundaries by a taxpayer
- Of suspicion of inconsistency with the principle of good faith required in relation to treaty partners and/or in an international context
- The tax inspector is of the opinion that the contemplated (legal) acts
  - Have the sole or predominant purpose to avoid taxes
  - Do not have a real practical meaning for the taxpayer beyond the intended tax benefit, and
  - The object and purpose of the law or treaty would be disregarded if the application of the law claimed by the taxpayer would followed
- Of intermediate or top-holding companies in international structures
  - If the requesting company does not fulfil all conditions of real presence in the Netherlands, unless this is consistent with the character of the provision in respect of which certainty is asked for, e.g., certainty that a company has no permanent establishment in the Netherlands, or
  - The group of which the requesting company is a part of does not carry out operational activities in the Netherlands and does not have concrete plans to do so
- Of contemplated transactions by a financial service company[85]

---

[81] See, e.g., Letter of State Secretary of Finance to Second Chamber of the Dutch Parliament of 2 November 2016, no. 2016-0000163149, p. 4.

[82] See Decree of 3 June 2014, DGB 2014/296, Stcrt. 2014, 15954, V-N 2014/32.2, para 3.2.

[83] See Decrees of 3 June 2014, DGB 2014/3098, Stcrt. 2014, 15955, V-N 2014/32.3; 3 June 2014, DGB 2014/3099, Stcrt. 2014, 15956, V-N 2014/32.4; 3 June 2014, DGB 2014/3101, Stcrt. 2014, 15957, V-N 2014/32.5; and 3 June 2014, DGB 2014/3102, Stcrt. 2014, 15958, V-N 2014/32.6.

[84] See, e.g., Hoge Raad (Dutch Supreme Court), Judgment, no. 18 230, 31 May 1978, Beslissingen in belastingzaken Nederlandse Belastingrechtspraak (BNB) 1978/252; Article 8b CITA 1969; and Decree of 3 June 2014, DGB 2014/3098, Stcrt. 2014, 15955, V-N 2014/32.3.

[85] A financial service company is a resident taxpayer whose activities in a year are predominantly as a matter of law or of fact the direct or indirect reception and payment of interest, royalties, rent

- If the company does not satisfy one or more of the listed minimum conditions of real presence (substance) in the Netherlands, or
- If the functions carried out by the company in connection with its transactions, on balance, do not entail real risks

- Of intermediate or top holding companies in international structures which do not satisfy one or more of the listed minimum conditions of real presence (substance) in the Netherlands.

According to the author, the above demonstrates that the Dutch ATR and APA practice does not result in 'no or only nominal taxation on the relevant income (generally or in special circumstances)'. Taxes are levied consistently with the law, case law and policy, including the arm's length principle. Furthermore, the list of cases in which ATRs and APAs are not concluded shows that it cannot be upheld that the Netherlands, by means of its ATR and APA practice, offers itself as a place to be used by non-residents to escape tax in their country of residence. Therefore, the constitutive key factors of the tax haven description are not satisfied. The conditions for obtaining an ATR or an APA have been made public. Therefore, it cannot be upheld either that there is a lack of transparency in the operation of the provisions. Besides this, ATRs and APAs are not concluded if a list of minimum conditions of real presence (substance) in the Netherlands is not satisfied. Consequently, it cannot be said either that the confirming key factor of absence of a requirement that the activity be substantial is met. Therefore, the author thinks that the Dutch ATR and ATA practice does not make the Netherlands a tax haven. The author believes that this position is supported by the following statement of the European Commission:

> In particular, the Commission notes that The Netherlands seem to generally proceed with a thorough assessment based on comprehensive information required from the taxpayer. The Commission therefore does not expect to encounter systematic irregularities in tax rulings.[86]

Incidents of harmful tax competition may happen. According to the European Commission, it is the case in the Starbucks case, in which the Commission took the position that this particular APA constituted State aid under European law.[87] This decision has been appealed.[88] It is beyond the scope of this chapter to discuss this case into further detail.[89]

(Footnote 85 continued)

or lease instalments, under whatever name and in whatever form, from and to non-resident group companies.

[86] See European Commission Press Release of 14 June 2014, IP/14/663, at 2.

[87] See Commission Decision of 21 October 2015 on State aid SA.38374 (2014/C ex 2014/NN).

[88] See pending cases T-760/15 (*Netherlands v Commission*) and T-636/16 (*Starbucks and Starbucks Manufacturing EMEA v Commission*).

[89] See for further details, e.g., Kemmeren 2017.

To wrap up, the Dutch ATR an APA practice does not make the Netherlands a tax haven.

15.4.5 Dutch Exchange of Information Rules and Practice

Exchange of information between tax administrations is a key factor in the Dutch tax treaty policy.[90] The Netherlands takes the view that the OECD standards are only minimum standards. For instance, its aim is to increase the possibilities of spontaneously and automatically exchanging information. This policy is supported by extensive domestic legislation to enable the fulfilment of (tax) treaty obligations and obligations under EU law.[91] The Dutch system includes rules on country-by-country reporting[92] and exchange of information on ATRs and ATAs.[93] The Netherlands already spontaneously exchanges information on APAs if a group does not carry out more activities within the Netherlands than activities required by the minimum substance conditions for a financial service company in order to obtain certainty in advance, nor has concrete plans to extend its substance in the Netherlands.[94] In such a case, the exception of not supplying information that would disclose any commercial, industrial or professional secret is not applied. Similarly, in respect of financial service companies that do not ask for certainty in advance, obligations have been put in place which oblige them to report that they do not fulfil the substance conditions if they have invoked or can invoke Dutch tax treaties or the European Interest and Royalty Directive.[95]

As demonstrated above, the Netherlands is actively involved in exchanging information. Therefore, the author thinks that it cannot be argued that the Netherlands' exchange of information rules and practice contribute to 'no or only nominal taxation on the relevant income'. He believes that it cannot be upheld either that the Netherlands by virtue of its exchange of information rules and practice offers itself as a place, or is perceived as a place, to be used by

[90] See, e.g, Ministerie van Financiën, Notitie Fiscaal Verdragsbeleid 2011, 11 February 2011, at 63–64; and Letter of State Secretary of Finance to Second Chamber of the Dutch Parliament of 4 November 2016, at 2–4.

[91] See, e.g., *Wet internationale bijstandsverlening heffing belastingen* 1986 (Act on International Administrative Assistance Concerning Levying of Taxes 1986; AIAA 1986).

[92] Articles 29b-29 h CITA 1969.

[93] See also legislative proposal *Wet uitwisseling inlichtingen over rulings* (Act on exchanging information on rulings), which implements Council Directive (EU) 2015/2376 of 8 December 2015 amending Directive 2011/16/EU as regards mandatory automatic exchange of information in the field of taxation.

[94] See Decrees of 3 June 2014 V-N 2014/32.5 and V-N 2014/32.6.

[95] See Article 8(5) AIAA 1986 in conjunction with Article 3a *Uitvoeringsbesluit internationale bijstandsverlening heffing belastingen 2011* (Implementation decree act on international administrative assistance concerning levying of taxes 2011).

non-residents to escape tax in their country of residence. Again, the key factors for identifying a tax haven have not been satisfied. The author also believes the confirming key factors are not met. The Dutch laws or administrative practices do not prevent the effective exchange of relevant information with other governments. The above also shows that it cannot be argued that the Dutch system suffers from a lack of transparency in the operation of the legislative, legal or administrative provisions.

As a result, the author concludes that the Dutch rules and practice on exchange of information do not make the Netherlands a tax haven.

15.5 Conclusions

On the basis of the previous analysis, the author draws the following main conclusions:

1. The term tax haven has a strong negative connotation. A country's reputation is at stake if it is qualified as a tax haven.
2. To the extent that tax havens contribute to harmful tax competition, they are a problem.
3. There is no consensus on the description or definition of the term tax haven.
4. The subjective approach to the term tax haven lacks distinguishing character and, as a consequence, cannot be a useful instrument to counter harmful tax competition. Under this approach, the Netherlands would qualify as a tax haven even if only one taxpayer succeeds in designing and implementing a plan to use the Netherlands in reducing his tax liability in his state of residence or state of source, respectively. Any country in a similar position would qualify as a tax haven.
5. Although the 1998-OECD understanding of the term tax haven can be criticized as well, it may be useful to apply it in the context of the global BEPS discussion led by the OECD and which aims at allocating tax jurisdiction on income to the state where the value is added.
6. Oxfam Novib's and Oxfam's arguments do not contribute to the conclusion that the Netherlands qualifies as tax haven according to its own definition of a tax haven. Their qualification of the Netherlands as a tax haven has not been based on well-founded arguments and must be rejected.
7. The application of the 1998-OECD understanding of the term tax haven to some of the main features of the Dutch tax system leads to the conclusion that the Netherlands cannot be qualified as tax haven:

    a. The participation exemption contributes to the realization of allocation of tax jurisdiction to the states where the value is added. Generally speaking, the participation exemption is not too generous. It also satisfies allocation of taxing power consistent with the principle of origin, the direct benefit principle, the ability to pay principle, international neutrality, and CLIN.

b. The lack of Dutch WHT on interest and royalties is based on the economic policy of CLEN as far as it concerns interest, and on CLIN as far as it concerns royalties. Exclusive taxing power must be allocated to the state of residence of the recipient of the interest or royalty. In this context, a WHT on interest or royalties does not fit. Nevertheless, the current system of allocation of taxing power on interest income should be changed.
c. The fact that the current system gives access to Dutch tax treaties by virtue of the deemed residence rule of Article 2(4) CITA 1969 does not make the Netherlands a tax haven. However, this provision should be repealed and replaced by an origin-based residence provision: a non-individual should qualify as a resident of the Netherlands if:

   (1) It pursues or has pursued a substantial income-producing economic activity within the territory of the Netherlands *and*
   (2) The income or capital concerned is attributed to that activity on the basis of a functional analysis.
   A functional connection exists if the property concerned is used for pursuing that economic activity, i.e., this property is managed, and its operations are directed and controlled from within the Netherlands. As a result, a letterbox company would no longer qualify as a Dutch tax resident for corporate income tax purposes and, consequently, neither as a tax treaty resident under the Dutch tax treaties.

d. The conclusion of ATRs and APAs is bound by strict rules. ATRs and APAs may only be concluded in line with the law, case law and policy. This also means that group transactions must be consistent with the arm's length principle.
e. The Dutch system does not suffer from a lack of transparency in the operation of the legislative, legal or administrative provisions. The Netherlands is actively involved in exchange of information.

References

Bratton WW, McCahery JA (2001) Tax Coordination and Tax Competition in the European Union: Evaluating the Code of Conduct on Business Taxation. Common Market Law Review 38(3):677–718

Castro LFM (2016) Brazil/Netherlands: Dutch Holding Companies Included in Brazilian Grey List: Controlled Foreign Company, Thin Capitalization and Consolidation Rules Not Applicable for 2015. Bulletin for International Taxation 70(11)

European Commission (2015) A Fair and Efficient Corporate Tax System in the European Union: 5 Key Areas for Action, COM(2015) 302 final

Evers M, De Graaf ACGAC, Stevens AJA (2011) Zembla-uitzending 'Nederland belastingparadijs' nader beschouwd. Maandblad Belastingbeschouwingen 2011(2):60–65

Henry JS (2012) The Price of Offshore Revisited, New Estimates for Missing Global Private Wealth, Income, Inequality, and Lost Taxes. Tax Justice Network

International Monetary Fund (2014) Spillovers in International Corporate Taxation. IMF Policy Paper

Kemmeren ECCM (2001) Principle of Origin in Tax Conventions: A Rethinking of Models. Dissertation, Tilburg University. http://webwijs.uvt.nl/publications/304239_ext.pdf. Accessed 24 January 2017

Kemmeren ECCM (2005) Tax Competition and Compatibility with EU (State Aid) Rules: Balancing On What is Allowed and What is Not. Conference paper, Conference on International Markets and Corporate Governance, Washington DC, October 2005, pp 1–29

Kemmeren ECCM (2016) Legitimacy of Tax Claims of Developing Countries on Interest and Royalties of MNEs. In: Jochum H, Essers P, Lang M, Winkeljohann N, Wiman B (eds) Practical Problems in European and International Tax Law, Essays in Honour of Manfred Mössner. IBFD, Amsterdam

Kemmeren ECCM (2017) The Netherlands: Fiscal unity, Groupe Steria's per-element approach and currency losses relating to a non-resident subsidiary (C-399/16(X NV)); Starbucks and State aid (T-760/15 and T-636/16) In: Lang M et al (eds) CJEU - Recent Developments in Direct Taxation 2016. Series on International Tax Law, Linde Publishers Vienna, Austria:148–167

Kiekebeld BJ (2004) Harmful Tax Competition in the European Union, Code of Conduct, Countermeasures and EU Law. Europese Fiscale Studies. Kluwer, Deventer

Konrad KA, Stolper T (2015) Coordination and the Fight Against Tax Havens. CEPR Discussion Paper No. DP10519. http://ssrn.com/abstract=2588422. Accessed 23 January 2017

Meldgaard H, Bundgaard J, Weber KD, Floristean A (2015) Study on Structures of Aggressive Tax Planning and Indicators, Final Report. Taxation Papers, European Commission's Directorate-General for Taxation and Customs Union, Working Paper N. 61 – 2015, European Commission, Brussels

Meussen G, Velthuizen E (2002) APAs and ATRs: The New Dutch Regime in a European Perspective. EC Tax Review 2002/1

Ngoy JM (2001) The Paradox of Tax Havens: Consequences of the Subjective Approach. Journal of International Taxation 12:34, January 2001

OECD (1998) Harmful Tax Competition: An Emerging Global Issue. OECD

OECD (2000) The Application of the Permanent Establishment Definition in the Context of Electronic Commerce: Proposed Clarification of the Commentary on Article 5 of the OECD Model Tax Convention, Revised Draft for Comments. OECD

OECD (2015a) Explanatory Statement. OECD/G20 Base Erosion and Profit Shifting Project. OECD

OECD (2015b) Countering Harmful Tax Practices More Effectively, Taking into Account Transparency and Substance, Action 5 – 2015 Final Report. OECD/G20 Base Erosion and Profit Shifting Project. OECD Publishing, Paris

Oxfam (2016) Tax Battles, The Dangerous Global Race to the Bottom on Corporate Tax. Oxfam GB for Oxfam International, 12 December 2016

Oxfam Novib (2016) The Netherlands: A Tax Haven, Continuing its Contribution to the Corporate Tax Race to the Bottom. Policy Report

Pinto C (2003) Tax Competition and EU Law. EUCOTAX Series on European Taxation, vol 7. Kluwer Law International, The Hague

Platform for Tax Good Governance (2013) Draft Discussion Paper on the 'Tax Havens' Recommendation. European Commission, Brussels, 30 September 2013. Taxud/D1/JT, DOC: Platform/003/2013/EN

UNCTAD (2015) World Investment Report. United Nations Publication, United Nations, Geneva

Chapter 16
Recent Developments Regarding the Direct and Indirect Application of Treaties by Dutch Courts: Fresh Approaches to Self-Executing, Non-Self-Executing and Non-Binding International Law

Joseph Fleuren

Abstract In 2014, the Supreme Court of the Netherlands switched from a binary to a contextual approach to the question whether a treaty provision has direct effect. In this contribution, the new approach is discussed in a historical perspective and linked with some other developments in Dutch case law that further enhance the possibilities for the national courts to enforce treaties: the interpretation of treaty provisions by means of non-binding but authoritative decisions of international supervisory bodies and the treaty-consistent interpretation and application of domestic law.

Keywords Treaty enforcement by national courts · Direct effect · Consistent interpretation · International soft law

Contents

Associate Professor of Jurisprudence at Radboud University Nijmegen and Deputy Judge of the District Court Gelderland, The Netherlands, email: j.fleuren@jur.ru.nl.

J. Fleuren (✉)
Radboud University Nijmegen, Nijmegen, The Netherlands
e-mail: j.fleuren@jur.ru.nl

M. Kuijer and W. Werner (eds.), *Netherlands Yearbook of International Law 2016*, Netherlands Yearbook of International Law 47,
DOI 10.1007/978-94-6265-207-1_16

16.1 Introduction

A remarkable feature of human beings is that they introduce concepts and then have endless debates about the precise meaning of the concepts that were created by themselves. The concept of a self-executing treaty or treaty provision[1] is an illustrative example of a notion that all over the world has provoked a vast amount of literature and case law discussing its meaning and the criteria for its application.[2] In the Netherlands, the courts used to observe and apply treaties in an uncomplicated way until the concept of a self-executing provision was defined in the Constitution in 1956. Ever since, the notion played a pivotal role in the way the courts deal with treaties, but also constitutes one of the most difficult concepts in Dutch constitutional law. In recent years, however, there have been some rather spectacular developments in Dutch case law that made the concept more flexible and less dominant. In this contribution three of these developments are discussed: the rise of a contextual approach to the question of whether a treaty provision has direct effect (Sect. 16.2), the increasing importance of non-binding instruments of supervisory bodies for the interpretation and application of human rights treaties (Sect. 16.3), and the indirect application of treaties by means of treaty-consistent interpretation and application of domestic law (Sect. 16.4). The contribution concludes with a note on the prospect of holding the State liable for the non-compliance with treaty provisions that lack direct effect (Sect. 16.5).[3]

16.2 (Previous) History and Development of the Concept of Direct Effect in Dutch Constitutional Law

16.2.1 Origin of the Concept

Dutch courts have always been well aware of the distinction between treaty provisions that contain a legal rule or principle that may be applied by the courts on the one hand, and treaty provisions that oblige the state parties to enact domestic legislation on the other.[4] Until the concept of a self-executing treaty

[1] In this contribution the term 'treaty provision' equally applies to provisions of binding decisions by international organisations adopted in pursuance of a treaty.

[2] See, e.g., Sloss 2009; Shelton 2011.

[3] There are several introductions into the relationship between international law and Dutch law available in English: Brouwer 2005; Nollkaemper 2009; Alkema 2011. The present contribution draws upon, and provides an update to, the introductions by Fleuren 2010 and Gerards and Fleuren 2014, at 217–233.

[4] Fleuren 2004.

provision[5] was introduced in the Constitution of the Kingdom of the Netherlands in 1956, this distinction was not regarded as problematic, since it paralleled the difference between, for instance, a constitutional provision that was addressed to the legislature, and a constitutional provision that contained a legal rule or principle which could be enforced by the courts. Courts used to apply treaties in the same manner as they applied legal provisions of domestic origin. The fact that treaties may contain clauses that explicitly or implicitly require the enactment of domestic legislation was not considered to be a reason to treat the applicability of treaty provisions as a preliminary matter. Whether a treaty provision could be applied in a pending lawsuit depended on the question of whether it was invoked on good grounds, given the content of the provision and of the relevant domestic legislation, and given the facts and circumstances of the case. For example, it was self-evident that a treaty provision that obliged the State Parties to define in their national legislation a specified act or omission as a criminal offence did not itself constitute a penal provision.[6] Yet, the circumstance that a treaty provision was addressed to the legislature did not necessarily stop the courts from reviewing domestic legislation against such a provision.[7] For the courts, the application of treaty provisions did not fundamentally differ from the application of domestic law provisions. The distinction between provisions that contain legal rules and provisions that oblige or empower public bodies to make legal rules, was seen as a (generally not problematic) feature of national as well as international law.

Up to the midst of the twentieth century, the distinction was now and then touched upon in the legal literature about the relationship between Dutch and international law, but never seen as a key issue. Rather it was another topic that called for attention, namely the question whether the courts were empowered to test all Acts of Parliament (*wetten in formele zin*) and even the Constitution against treaties to which the Kingdom of the Netherlands had become a party, or whether this power of review was limited to Acts of Parliament which were enacted before the Kingdom of the Netherlands had entered into the treaty under consideration (last-in-time rule). For decades the Supreme Court (*Hoge Raad*) managed to avoid a ruling on this question. When an Act of Parliament seemed to be at variance with an earlier treaty, it construed the Act in such a way that the apparent inconsistency

[5] In this contribution the notions of self-executingness, direct effect and direct applicability are used interchangeably.

[6] *Openbaar Ministerie v J.P.Ph. B.*, Kantongerecht 's-Gravenhage (Subdistrict Court The Hague), Judgment, Nederlandse Jurisprudentie (NJ) 1934, p. 1398 (for an English translation see Annual Digest and Reports of Public International Law Cases (AD) 1933–1934, No. 220), 30 June 1934.

[7] E.g. *NV Gloeilampenfabriek "Radium" v Octrooihoudster*, Octrooiraad Centrale Afdeling (Patent Council, Central Division), Judgment, 7 Bijblad bij de Industriële Eigendom (1939), p. 19, 10 November 1938.

disappeared.[8] The Supreme Court used this technique of treaty-consistent interpretation even if it meant that a recently adopted Act of Parliament was in fact for a large part rendered inoperative.[9]

The controversy on the scope of the power of review was resolved in 1953. That year, the constitutional clauses on foreign relations were revised and expanded with articles that dealt explicitly with the domestic effect of treaties and of decisions of international organisations. The amended Constitution stated that treaties as well as decisions of international organisations were binding on everyone (i.e. private persons and legal persons) as far as they had been published. Furthermore, it stated that legal provisions in force within the Kingdom did not apply if their application would be inconsistent with treaties or decisions of international organisations that had been published either before or after these provisions were adopted.[10] I will refer to the latter clause—both in its 1953 version and its subsequent versions—as the 'supremacy clause'. The 'supremacy clause' extends to all provisions of domestic law, including the Constitution itself, Acts of Parliament and subordinate legislation.

Only three years later, in 1956, the constitutional sections on foreign relations were revised again in order to correct technical flaws in the 1953 amendment. On this occasion, the concept of a self-executing treaty provision was introduced into the Constitution. During the parliamentary debates on the bills that resulted in the 1953 amendment, the Government had now and then claimed that the proposed articles on the binding effect and supremacy of treaties and decisions of international organizations only pertained to treaties and decisions that were self-executing. Thus, the Governmental Committee that prepared the 1956 revisions inferred from the legal history of the 1953 amendment that it had always been the intention that the articles on the domestic effect of treaties and decisions of international organisations pertained only to self-executing provisions of treaties and decisions. Especially with regard to the 'supremacy clause' the Governmental Committee referred to the separation of powers as a rationale for introducing the concept of a self-executing treaty provision in the Constitution. It pointed out that, according to the present wording of the 'supremacy clause', the courts could feel obliged to disapply legislation for inconsistency with international treaties and decisions, even in cases where the treaty or decision in question did not entail a legal rule which the courts may apply instead. This might create legal gaps, which the courts could only fill by developing the law themselves and thus making policy

---

[8] E.g. *J.B.A. T. v Openbaar Ministerie*, Hoge Raad, Judgment, NJ 1919, p. 371, 3 March 1919 ('*Grenstractaat Aken*'); *Staat der Nederlanden v Joh. Boon and Société Anonyme Chantiers Navals du Rupel*, Hoge Raad, Judgment, NJ 1952, No. 125 (English translation: International Law Reports 1952, No. 34), 25 January 1952 ('*Stop te Lobith*').

[9] *Openbaar Ministerie v H.J. C.*, Hoge Raad, Judgment, NJ 1935, p. 5, 17 December 1934; *J. v.d. P. v Openbaar Ministerie*, Hoge Raad, NJ 1935, p. 11 (English translation: AD 1933–1934, No. 4), 17 December 1934.

[10] Articles 65–67 Const. (1953).

choices that should be left to the legislature.[11] As a result of these considerations, the Constitution states since 1956 that provisions of treaties and decisions of international organisations, which according to their content may be binding on everyone, have binding force on everyone after they have been published. Such provisions preclude the application of domestic law if its application would be inconsistent with them, regardless of whether the treaty or decision predates or outdates the domestic law in question. In 1983, when the Constitution underwent a general modernisation, these clauses have been refined, but this did not affect their meaning and scope. Since 1983, the clauses are laid down in the Articles 93 and 93.[12]

From the legal history of the 1956 and 1983 amendments of the Constitution it is clear that the phrase 'provisions of treaties and of decisions by international organisations which may be binding on everyone by virtue of their contents' is intended to make sure that only self-executing provisions of treaties and decisions have force of law towards (private and legal) persons and may preclude the application of national law.[13] Furthermore, it is well-established in case law that the 'supremacy clause' can also be read *a contrario*: it is not allowed to disapply provisions of domestic law for incompatibility with non-self-executing provisions of treaties and decisions or even with customary international law[14] (although in the Kingdom of the Netherlands customary international law is, just as treaties and decisions of international organisations, part of the law of the land).[15] Thus, the notion of direct effect or direct applicability plays a vital role in Dutch constitutional

[11] Kamerstukken II (Parliamentary documents of the Lower House) 1955/56, 4133 (R 19), No. 4, at 13–14.

[12] These Articles read as follows (my translation):

Article 93: 'Provisions of treaties and of decisions by international organisations which may be binding on everyone by virtue of their contents shall become binding [i.e. binding on everyone, JF] after they have been published.'

Article 94: 'Legal provisions in force within the Kingdom shall not be applicable if such application is in conflict with provisions of treaties or of decisions by international organisations that are binding on everyone'.

[13] Kamerstukken II 1955/56, 4133 (R 19), No. 4, pp. 13–15; Kamerstukken II 1979/80, 15 049 (R 1100), No. 7, p. 15.

[14] *Société Anonyme Maritime et Commerciale v Staat der Nederlanden*, Hoge Raad, NJ 1962 No. 2 (English translation: 10 NILR (1963) p. 82), 6 March 1959 ('*Nyugat II*'); *Criminal proceedings against Desi Bouterse*, Hoge Raad, Judgment, No. 00749/01 (CW 2323), ECLI:NL:HR:2001:AB1471 (English translation: 32 NYIL (2001) p. 282), 18 September 2001; *Criminal proceedings against X*, Hoge Raad, Judgment, No. 07/10063, ECLI:NL:HR:2008:BC7418 (Dutch) and ECLI:NL:HR:2008:BG1476 (English translation), 8 July 2008, para 6.4.

[15] In the Kingdom of the Netherlands domestic law and international law (treaties, decisions of international organisations and customary international law) are regarded as complementary: together they constitute the body of law which has to be respected by both public authorities and individuals, insofar as its norms concern them (monist tradition). However, treaties and decisions of international organisations can only create rights and duties for (private and legal) persons to the extent that they contain provisions that have direct effect, and only these provisions can override domestic law.

law, all the more since it is prohibited for the courts to review the constitutionality of Acts of Parliament.[16] A provision of an Act of Parliament can only be disapplied or be declared non-binding or unlawful by the courts if the provision or its application is found to be incompatible with a self-executing provision of a treaty or a decision by an international organisation.[17]

16.2.2 Approaches to the Question of Direct Effect

Although it can hardly be disputed that from 1956 onwards the wording of the Constitution suggests that the question whether a treaty provision may according to its content be binding on everyone (i.e. self-executing) is a preliminary question which has to be answered in the affirmative before the provision can have force of law towards private and legal persons and may prevent the application of domestic legislation, the legal history of the 1956 amendment points to another direction. During the parliamentary debates on the proposal to insert a description of the concept of a self-executing treaty provision into the Constitution, it was stressed that the description only served as a guideline. It was for the courts to decide whether a provision at hand was self-executing or not. The Minister of Foreign Affairs, who defended the proposal in these debates on behalf of the Government, pointed out that in answering this question the courts should not only take the intention of the state parties to the treaty into account, but also domestic legislation on the subject of the treaty. In this view the answer is, at least in part, determined by the interaction between international law and domestic law.[18]

From the legal history of the 1956 amendments, one might therefore conclude that the courts could have continued to apply treaties in the same non-complicated way as they had done in the past, if necessary overriding earlier or later acts of parliament. But the case law took a different turn. From the moment the 1956 amendments entered into force, the courts tended to consider a treaty provision as either having direct effect or not.[19] Whether or not a treaty provision was self-executing had to be established on the basis of an interpretation of the treaty at hand. Many legal scholars were of the opinion that the decisive question that should be answered by this interpretation was whether the contracting parties had intended the provision to be self-executing, while others did not attach overriding importance

[16] Article 120 Const.

[17] *Staat der Nederlanden v X*, Hoge Raad, Judgment, No. 14/00191, ECLI:NL:HR:2015:2723, 18 September 2015.

[18] Handelingen (Parliamentary Proceedings) II 1955/56, p. 800.

[19] *N.V. tot voortzetting van de Koninklijke Hollandsche Lloyd v Dampskibsselskabet Torm A.S.*, Hof 's-Gravenhage (Appeal Court The Hague), NJ 1957, No. 576 (English translation: 6 NILR (1959) p. 87), 27 March 1957.

to the intention of the parties. During the 1970s, the latter view became the prevailing one.[20] The diminishing importance of the parties' intention for determining whether a treaty provision has direct effect reached a climax in a landmark ruling on the direct effect of the right to strike defined in Article 6(4) of the European Social Charter (ESC), which was delivered by the Supreme Court on 30 May 1986.[21] On the occasion of the parliamentary approval of the ESC, the Government had pointed out that, according to the *travaux préparatoires*, the contracting parties had not intended the provisions of the Charter to have direct effect. The Supreme Court ruled that this was irrelevant:

> Whether or not the contracting parties intended Article 6(4) of the ESC to have direct effect is not relevant since it cannot be inferred either from the text or from the history of the Charter that they have agreed that it is not allowed to give direct effect to Article 6(4). In view of this state of affairs, only the content of the provision is decisive under Dutch law: does it oblige the Dutch legislature to enact national rules of a given content or scope or is it of such a kind that the provision can simply function as law in the national legal order?[22]

On the basis of these criteria the Supreme Court held that Article 6(4) of the ESC had direct effect, arguing that the provision was worded in such a way that it might be invoked in domestic jurisdictions, and that state parties which would leave the application and elaboration of the right to strike to their courts (instead of the legislature) did not violate the Charter. Although this ruling greatly enhanced the possibilities for the courts to attribute direct effect to treaty provisions, they continued to regard treaty provisions as either having or not having direct effect—*tertium non datur*. Direct effect was treated as a switch that was turned on or off. This binary approach did not necessarily imply that courts could not take a treaty provision into account if the switch was turned off. In such a case it was still possible to construe or apply national law in light of the treaty obligations of the State (see Sect. 4), but a provision which was denied direct effect could not itself be applied by the courts, nor render primary or subordinate legislation inapplicable, regardless of the context in which the provision was invoked.

Until very recently, the binary approach has been dominant in Dutch case law. This did not even change after the 1983 amendment of the Constitution, although the legal history again provided leads for a fundamentally different approach.[23] That year, the Constitution underwent a general revision. On this occasion, the articles on international relations were smoothed over and shortened, but their substance was mainly left untouched. Some Members of Parliament had proposed to extend the 'supremacy clause' to all provisions of treaties and of decisions of international organisations (i.e. to remove the limitation to provisions that were binding on

[20] Fleuren 2004, at 245–259.

[21] *NV Nederlandse Spoorwegen v Vervoersbond FNV* et al., Hoge Raad, Judgment, No. 12698, NJ 1986, No. 688 (English translation: NYIL (1987) pp. 389–397), 30 May 1986 ('*Spoorwegstaking*').

[22] *Spoorwegstaking*, op. cit., para 3.2. The translations in this contribution are from the author.

[23] Fleuren and Viering 2001.

everyone),[24] because they feared that otherwise there would grow a deepening gulf between the case law of the European Court of Justice (ECJ) on the direct effect of Community law on the one hand, and the case law of the Dutch courts on the direct effect of international law provisions which did not belong to Community law on the other.[25] Dutch courts have accepted the rulings of the ECJ on the direct effect and supremacy of Community law (presently EU law) within the jurisdictions of the Member States from the very beginning. But these Members of Parliament were afraid that the courts would give (under the influence of the ECJ) a broad interpretation to the concept of direct effect when it came to (primary or secondary) provisions of Community law and (under the influence of the wording of the 'supremacy clause') a more narrow interpretation of this concept when it came to provisions of 'traditional' international law. Only after the Government had assured the Parliament that there was no reason to fear that such a discrepancy would materialize and had more or less invited the courts to consider the judgments of the ECJ on the concept of direct effect as a source of inspiration in cases in which they had to rule on the direct effect of 'traditional' international law,[26] the said Members of Parliament withdrew their proposal to rephrase the 'supremacy clause' in such a way that it would no longer be limited to the review of domestic legislation against international law provisions which may be binding on everyone.[27]

In fact, history proved the Members of Parliament right. In the course of time, the ECJ has adopted a flexible approach to the question of direct effect. The well-known criteria whether a provision of EU law is 'unconditional' and 'sufficiently precise' are not applied in a binary, but in a relative or contextual manner. According to this approach a provision of EU law that provides no suitable basis for claiming individual or subjective rights may nevertheless have direct effect in the sense that it can be invoked by litigants before the national courts in order to prevent the application of domestic legislation that is inconsistent with this provision. Therefore, the answer to the question whether a provision of EU law has direct effect may very well depend on the result a litigant wants to achieve by relying on this provision.[28]

Until recently, the case law of the ECJ had a rather limited impact on the way the Dutch courts used to deal with the effects of international law provisions (not belonging to EU law) within the Kingdom of the Netherlands. Now and then a court payed lip service to the two criteria of 'unconditional' and 'sufficiently precise' provisions when it had to deal with the question of whether a treaty provision had direct effect or not, but nevertheless adhered to an binary approach. After the

---

[24] Kamerstukken II 1979/80, 15 049 (R 1100), No. 14. Cf Handelingen II 1979/80, p. 4436.

[25] Kamerstukken II 1978/79, 15 049 (R 1100), No. 6, pp. 13–15; Kamerstukken II 1979/80, No. 9, pp. 6–7; Handelingen II 1979/80, pp. 3912–3913, 4436.

[26] Handelingen II 1979/80, p. 4093. Cf Handelingen II 1979/80, pp. 4431, 4436; Kamerstukken I 1980/81, 15 049 (R 1100), No. 19, p. 3; Handelingen I 1980/81, p. 241.

[27] Handelingen II 1979/80, p. 4436.

[28] Prechal 2000 still provides one of the best analyses of the way the ECJ deals with the question of the direct effect of provisions of EU law.

constitutional revision of 1983, some administrative courts have actually experimented with a contextual approach, inter alia with respect to the right to fair wages and equal remuneration for work of equal value embodied in Article 7(a)(i) of the International Covenant on Economic, Social and Cultural Rights.[29] But these experiments died down after the Supreme Court ruled in 1990 that this provision was not binding on everyone and thus implicitly confirmed its adherence to a binary approach.[30] This judgment caused the Central Appeals Court (*Centrale Raad van Beroep*), i.e. the appeal court for public service and social security matters, to abandon its contextual approach to Article 7(a)(i) and to confirm the ruling of a lower court that Article 7 in its entirety lacked direct effect.[31] However, in 2007 the Central Appeals Court mitigated its position again and no longer ruled out that Article 7(a)(i) could have direct effect.[32] The Court explicitly referred to the General Comment No. 3 (1990), in which the Committee on Economic, Social and Cultural Rights had specified a number of provisions of the International Covenant on Economic, Social and Cultural Rights which it considered 'to be capable of immediate application by judicial and other organs in many national legal systems'.[33]

Another development that prompted a revival of the contextual approach was related to the Charter on Fundamental Rights of the European Union, which had become binding on the date that the Lisbon Treaty entered into force, i.e. 1 December 2009. Persisting in a binary approach may easily have led to the awkward situation that a court would have had to give direct effect to a provision of the Charter, while at the same time denying direct effect to a kindred provision in a human rights treaty. For this reason, the Administrative Jurisdiction Division of the Council of State (*Afdeling bestuursrechtspraak van de Raad van State*), the appeal court for general administrative law matters, issued in 2012 a judgement explicitly dealing with the invocability of both Article 3 of the Convention on the Rights of the Child and the related Article 24 of the EU Charter on Fundamental Rights on the bases of the case law of the ECJ.[34] A few years later, the Supreme Court also turned to a contextual approach that was clearly inspired by the case law of the ECJ.

[29] *Het bestuur van het Academisch Ziekenhuis bij de Universiteit van Amsterdam v X and Y*, Centrale Raad van Beroep (CRvB), Judgment, No. AW 1984/B117-118, Administratiefrechtelijke Beslissingen (AB) 1989, No. 164 (English translation: 21 NYIL 1990, p. 375), 16 February 1989.

[30] *Dirk Hoogenraad v Nederlandse Organisatie voor Wetenschappelijk Onderzoek*, Hoge Raad, Judgment, No. 13831, NJ 1992, No. 636 (English translation: 22 NYIL (1991) p. 376), 20 April 1990.

[31] *J. V. v Dagelijks Bestuur van het Werkvoorzieningschap Zwolle en Omgeving*, CRvB, Judgment, No. WSW 1990/16, Rechtspraak Sociale Verzekering 1992, No. 164, 17 December 1991.

[32] *X v Het dagelijks bestuur van de Intergemeentelijke Sociale Dienst Zuidwest-Fryslân*, CRvB, Judgment, No. 07/1896 WWB, ECLI:NL:CRVB:2007:BB5687, 11 October 2007.

[33] UN Committee on Economic, Social and Cultural Rights (1990) General Comment No. 3: The Nature of States Parties' Obligations, adopted at the Fifth Session of the Committee on Economic, Social and Cultural Rights, 14 December 1990.

[34] *X v Minister voor Immigratie en Asiel*, Afdeling bestuursrechtspraak van de Raad van State (ABRvS), Judgment, No. 201103064/1/V2, ECLI:NL:RVS:2012:BV3716, 7 February 2012.

16.2.3 The Supreme Court's Turn to a Contextual Approach

The Supreme Court has formulated its new approach in a judgement delivered on 10 October 2014, which concerned the lawfulness of exceptions to smoking bans in bars and restaurants. On 27 April 2005, the World Health Organization (WHO) Framework Convention on Tobacco Control had entered into force for the Netherlands.[35] According to Article 8(2) of this Convention, each State Party 'shall adopt and implement [...] effective legislative, executive, administrative and/or other measures, providing for protection from exposure to tobacco smoke in indoor workplaces, public transport, indoor public places and, as appropriate, other public places'. With regard to restaurants and bars, the Netherlands implemented this provision by means of adopting primary and subordinate legislation that obligated all restaurant and café owners to prohibit smoking in their establishments, except for enclosed smoking areas (where no service would be provided). However, in 2011, after a change of government, an Order-in-Council (*Algemene Maatregel van Bestuur*) was issued which excluded owners of small pubs from this obligation, because they may not have the space and financial means to create enclosed smoking areas (and thus there might be a risk of unfair competition).[36] An association of non-smokers instituted civil proceedings against the State, arguing, inter alia, that this relaxation of the smoking ban was in conflict with Article 8(2) of the WHO Framework Convention on Tobacco Control and therefore should not be applied. Referring to the 1986 judgment of the Supreme Court on the direct effect of Article 6(4) ESC, the Court of first instance ruled that the provisions of the WHO Framework Convention lacked direct effect in the Netherlands, because they were not phrased in such a way that they may simply function as law in the national legal order.[37] However, the Court of Appeal argued that a treaty provision that has to be implemented by means of domestic legislation may nevertheless have direct effect, for instance if the result that has to be achieved by the domestic legislation is defined in the treaty provision in a clear and unconditional manner. The Court of Appeal concluded that Article 8(2) had direct effect in regard to the obligation to adopt effective legal measures against the exposure to tobacco smoke in indoor public places and that therefore the exceptions for small bars were unlawful and non-binding.[38] The Supreme Court upheld the judgment of the Court of Appeal, but

---

[35] Tractatenblad (Treaty Series) 2005, No. 72.

[36] Staatsblad (Bulletin of Acts and Decrees) 2011, No. 337.

[37] *Nietrokersvereniging CAN v Staat der Nederlanden*, Rechtbank Den Haag (District Court The Hague), Judgment, No. 406327/ HA ZA 11-2623, ECLI:NL:RBSGR:2012:BW6789, 16 May 2012.

[38] *Nietrokersvereniging CAN v Staat der Nederlanden*, Hof Den Haag (Court of Appeal The Hague), Judgment, No. 200.111.618/01, ECLI:NL:GHDHA:2013:BZ4871, 26 March 2013.

did not overtly dissociated itself from the reasoning of its 1986 judgment.[39] To begin with, the Supreme Court stated that the question whether a treaty provision has direct effect within the meaning of Articles 93 and 94 of the Constitution has to be answered through an interpretation of the treaty provision, which has to be given in conformity with the Articles 31–33 of the Vienna Convention on the Law of Treaties. Unless it follows from the text and the history of the treaty that its parties did not want the provision to be given direct effect, the content of the provision is decisive:[40] the provision has direct effect in so far as it may be applied as law in the context in which it has been invoked. Even if the provision leaves it to the discretion of each state party to decide which measures it considers appropriate to implement the provision, this does not necessarily mean that it lacks direct effect. If a treaty provision defines the result that it aims to achieve in the domestic jurisdiction in an unconditional and sufficiently precise manner, it does not lack direct effect merely because it is up to the legislature or other public authorities to choose the measures they deem fit to implement the provision. Applying this reasoning to Article 8(2) of the WHO Framework Convention, the Supreme Court concludes that the obligation embodied in this provision is at least unconditional and sufficiently precise in the sense that it opposes legislation that excludes small cafés from the smoking ban. The Supreme Court acknowledged that the State should be allowed a reasonable time period for the implementation of Article 8(2). However, in this case, the State had initially complied with the provision, so that the need for an implementation period could not justify adopting legislation that was inconsistent with the treaty obligation at hand.

Evidently, the reasoning of the Supreme Court is inspired by the case law of the ECJ on the direct effect of EU law, especially of EU directives. It is hard to find judgments of the ECJ in which this court has denied the right of litigants to rely on provisions of a directive against a Member State which has not or not correctly implemented the directive in time, in order to preclude the application of national (legislative or administrative) measures which are inconsistent with these provisions. Sometimes the ECJ even simply tests whether the contested domestic measures have exceeded the Member State's discretion, without explicitly examining the unconditionality and degree of precision of the relevant provision of EU law.[41] It remains to be seen whether Dutch courts will develop a similar line of reasoning when dealing with conflicts between Dutch law and provisions of 'traditional' treaties and decisions of international organisations. In any case, the *Smoking ban* judgment of the Supreme Court is an important start, that ties in with the legal history of both the 1956 and 1983 amendments of the Constitution.

---

[39] *Staat der Nederlanden v Nederlandse Nietrokersvereniging CAN*, Hoge Raad, No. 13/02931, ECLI:NL:HR:2014:2928, 10 October 2014 ('*Rookverbod*').

[40] I take this to be the meaning of the first sentence of para 3.5.2.

[41] Prechal 2000; Fleuren and Viering 2001, at 110–115; Kapteyn 2008, at 528–529; De Witte 2011, at 332.

In this new approach of the Dutch courts, the extent to which a treaty provision may have direct effect depends on the extent to which this provision imposes limits on the discretion of the state parties. In particular, when a provision is cast in vague terms, it may be difficult to establish these limits. Yet, in the course of time, the meaning of terms that initially were vague may become more specific as the provision is interpreted, applied or otherwise taken into account by international and national bodies. In this respect, another trend in the case law of Dutch courts calls for attention, namely the increasing impact of opinions, recommendations, general comments and other non-binding instruments of international (supervisory) bodies. These instruments may be very helpful for national courts in cases in which they have to rule on the limits that a treaty provision entails for the state parties and thus on the extent that this provision may have direct effect in the case under consideration.

16.3 International Soft Law

The constitutional articles on the legal force and supremacy of self-executing provisions of international law within the Kingdom of the Netherlands only apply to treaties and decisions of international organisations that are binding upon the Kingdom (and are applicable to the whole Kingdom or to one or more of its parts). Non-binding international instruments (international soft law) cannot have direct effect nor can they set aside domestic legislation. For this reason, for example, none of the provisions of the Universal Declaration of Human Rights create rights that individuals may enforce before Dutch courts.[42] A claim or plea that is based on an international instrument that has no legal force for the Kingdom of the Netherlands may simply be dismissed by a court with a reference to its non-binding character.[43] That being said, it should be noted that, in recent years, opinions and recommendations, in particular from human rights bodies that have been established to supervise the compliance of States Parties with human rights treaties, are frequently taken into account by Dutch courts when they have to construe and apply those treaties.[44] A leading judgment on this matter was delivered by the Central Appeals

[42] *X v Staatssecretaris van Financiën*, Hoge Raad, Judgment, No. 21769, NJ 1985, No. 247 (English translation: 17 NYIL (1986) p. 253), 7 November 1984.

[43] See, e.g., *X v Staatssecretaris van Veiligheid en Justitie*, ABRvS, Judgment, No. 201011330/1/H3, ECLI:NL:RVS:2011:BQ8830, 22 June 2011, para 2.4.1; *Minister van Buitenlandse Zaken v X* et al., ABRvS, Judgment, No. 201301105/1/V1, ECLI:NL:RVS2014:923, 12 March 2014, para 6.1.

[44] For an in-depth study of the status of non-binding decisions of human rights treaty bodies and the various ways in which they are dealt with by Dutch courts, see Gerards 2016. For responses by Dutch politicians to these decisions, see Krommendijk 2015. A comparative analysis of the ways in which informal international instruments may be taken into account by domestic courts is provided by Kanetake and Nollkaemper 2014.

Court in 2006, in which it had to rule on the weight it should attach to views of the Human Rights Committee (CCPR) on individual complaints concerning a violation of the International Covenant on Civil and Political Rights (ICCPR). After stressing that these views are strictly speaking non-binding, it added that 'generally opinions of an international committee in the field of human rights should be considered as authoritative' and that courts should only depart from such an opinion 'if this can be justified by compelling reasons'.[45] How this approach to the status of opinions and recommendations of international human rights bodies may be used to clarify the meaning of treaty provisions in order to give them direct effect in the case at hand may be illustrated by a recent judgment that was delivered on 23 September 2016 by a court of first instance, the District Court Midden-Nederland. In the years between 2004 and 2008, Dutch social security laws had not provided for maternity leave benefits for self-employed women (because it was not considered a responsibility of the State to provide self-employed people with such benefits). In the past, courts had refused to rule that this situation was incompatible with Article 11(2)(b) of the Convention on the Elimination of All Forms of Discrimination against Woman (CEDAW). According to this provision, State Parties shall take appropriate measures to introduce maternity leave with pay or with comparable social benefits without loss of former employment, seniority or social allowances. The ruling of lower courts that this provision did not have direct effect was upheld by the Supreme Court. The Supreme Court recalled the criteria it had put forward in its judgment of 30 May 1986 mentioned above, adding the importance of the question whether the provision under consideration is unconditional and sufficiently precise in order to be applied by the courts. This lip service to the case law of the ECJ did not prevent the Supreme Court from concluding that Article 11(2)(b) was not suited for direct application by domestic courts, without paying any attention to the context in which the provision was invoked.[46] However, some of the plaintiffs filed a complaint under the Optional Protocol to the CEDAW, which were decided upon by the Committee on the Elimination of Discrimination Against Woman on 17 February 2014. According to the views of the Committee, the Netherlands had indeed violated Article 11(2)(b) of the Convention. Furthermore, in its considerations the Committee recalled its view that this provision was directly applicable.[47] In its judgement of 23 September 2016, the District Court Midden-Nederland had to rule in a case in which one of the women whose complaint was upheld by the Committee claimed maternity leave benefit because she had given birth in 2005. Feeling encouraged by the views of the Committee, the District Court made full use of the new approach that was developed by the Supreme Court in the *Smoking ban* case. The assertion of the Government that the provision only applied to women in

[45] *X v Raad van bestuur van de Sociale verzekeringsbank*, CRvB, Judgment, No. 03-3332 ANW, ECLI:NL:CRVB:2006:AY5560, 21 July 2006.

[46] *Stichting Proefprocessenfonds Clara Wichmann et al. v Staat der Nederlanden,* Hoge Raad, Judgment, No. 09/04671, ECLI:NL:HR:2011:BP3044, 1 April 2011.

[47] *Elisabeth de Blok* et al. *v The Netherlands*, Committee on the Elimination of Discrimination against Women, views, Communication No. 36/2012, 17 February 2014.

paid employment and therefore not to self-employed women, had been dismissed by the Committee. In the past, uncertainty on this matter may well have contributed to the denial of direct effect. This uncertainty now being removed by an authoritative body in regard to the interpretation of the Convention, the District Court ruled that Article 11(2)(b) had direct effect in the context of the case under consideration, and that the woman in question had a claim under the 2008 Maternity Allowance for the Self-Employed Act (*Wet zwangerschaps-en bevallingsuitkering zelfstandigen*).[48] The benefits agency should have disapplied the clause in this Act that excluded self-employed women that had given birth before the date on which the Act had become effective.[49] It may be noted that the judgment thus confirms that, according to Dutch constitutional law, self-executing treaty provisions not only have to be applied and given supremacy over national law by the courts, but also by administrative bodies.[50]

16.4 Treaty-Consistent Interpretation and Application of National Law

According to a well-accepted principle in legal doctrine, a State or its legislature should not be presumed to have intended to violate international law. A corollary of this presumption is that, as far as possible, domestic law must be construed and applied in such a way that a conflict with international law is avoided. This is the rationale behind the so-called technique of consistent interpretation. In 1919 this rationale was already formulated by the Dutch Supreme Court:

> It certainly cannot be assumed that the Dutch legislature should in any Act have deviated unilaterally and high-handedly from that which has been agreed upon in a ratified treaty with a foreign power, unless the text of the act compels this assumption.[51]

---

[48] Staatsblad 2008, No. 192.

[49] *X v Raad van bestuur van het Uitvoeringsinstituut werknemersverzekeringen*, Rechtbank Midden-Nederland, Judgment, No. UTR 15/5247, ECLI:NL:RBMNE:2016:5113, 23 September 2016.

[50] *X and Y v Directeur van het Landelijk Bureau Inning Onderhoudsbijdragen*, ABRvS, Judgment, No. 201109886/1/A2, ECLI:NL:RVS:2012:BX4660, 15 August 2012, para 2.4.2; *X* et al. *v Burgemeester van Amsterdam*, ABRvS, Judgment, No. 201406757/1/A3, ECLI:NL:RVS:2014:4117, 12 November 2014 ('*Sinterklaasintocht*'), para 6.3; *X v Raad van bestuur van de Sociale Verzekeringsbank*, Rechtbank Gelderland (District Court Gelderland), Judgment, No. AWB 15/3803, ECLI:NL:RBGEL:2016:3970, 19 July 2016 (with references to parliamentary documents in which the view that Article 94 Const. has to be observed by both the courts and administrative authorities is endorsed by the Government).

[51] *Grenstractaat Aken*, op. cit.

The consequence of this assumption was spelled out by the Supreme Court in a 1990 judgment: the Dutch courts 'should, as far as possible, construe and apply Dutch law in such a manner that the State complies with its treaty obligations'.[52] In this formulation, no distinction is made between treaty obligations that have direct effect and other treaty obligations. Furthermore, it has to be stressed that 'Dutch law' is evidently a very wide notion, including primary and subordinate legislation, principles of law, customary law as well as discretionary powers of administrative authorities. A logical conclusion from these considerations would be that an affirmative answer to the question of whether a treaty provision has direct effect is only necessary in cases in which a violation of this provision cannot be avoided by a treaty-consistent interpretation and application of written and unwritten legal rules, principles of law and discretionary powers. A court that endorses this conclusion only has to deal with the question of direct effect if there are not enough leads in domestic law to comply with the provision by means of the technique of harmonious interpretation and application.[53] The District Court of The Hague has made full use of this insight in its prominent *Urgenda* judgment of 24 June 2015.[54] In this case on climate change, the provisions of the UN Climate Convention were denied direct effect, but this did not stop the court from taking the goals and principles that are laid down in the Convention into account in its ruling on the question of whether the State was taking enough measures to reduce the emissions of greenhouse gases. Applying domestic principles and doctrines of tort law, the court ordered the State to speed up its efforts and to make sure that, by the end of 2020, the annual emissions of greenhouse gases in the Netherlands will be reduced by at least 25% compared to the level of emissions in 1990.

16.5 Epilogue

In the case law of the ECJ the doctrines of direct effect and consistent interpretation are supplemented by the doctrine of state responsibility. In the event a Member State has failed to implement a provision of EU law which—if implemented correctly—would have resulted in the creation of individual rights, but at the same time lacks direct effect in the sense that the domestic courts cannot remedy this omission by applying the provision itself, the Member State may nevertheless be held responsible before the domestic courts for a breach of EU law and be ordered to pay

[52] *T.S.M. Compagnie d'Assurance Transports v Geisseler Transport A.G.*, Hoge Raad, Judgment, No. 13997, NJ 1992, No. 107, 16 November 1990, para 3.2.3.

[53] Fleuren 2004, at 372–374; Fleuren 2010, at 259–261; Gerards and Fleuren 2014, at 229–230.

[54] *Stichting Urgenda v Staat der Nederlanden*, Rechtbank Den Haag, Judgment, No. C/09/456689/HA ZA 13-1396, ECLI:NL:RBDHA:2015:7145 (Dutch) and ECLI:NL:RBDHA:2015:7196 (English translation), 24 June 2015. See especially para 4.43, which seems to be inspired by Bovend'Eert et al. 2009, Article 93, note 6 (Fleuren). An English-language analysis of the court's reasoning is provided by De Graaf and Jans 2015.

damages.[55] A similar doctrine with regard to 'traditional' international law has not (yet) emerged in Dutch case law.[56] A claim that is merely based on state responsibility for violating an international law provision that is lacking direct effect will be dismissed. At the same time it should be noted that there have been cases in which the Supreme Court has accepted state responsibility while remaining silent on the question of whether the international law provision that was not complied with by the public authorities had direct effect or not.[57] Whether these judgments will one day prove to have been forerunners of an assimilation of the Dutch doctrine on state responsibility with its counterpart in EU law, has to be awaited. But it is undeniable that the Dutch case law on the (direct or indirect) invocability of treaty provisions is taking fresh directions that will open up new horizons.

References

Alkema EA (2011) Netherlands. In: Shelton D (ed) International Law and Domestic Legal Systems - Incorporation, Transformation, and Persuasion. Oxford University Press, Oxford, pp 407–428

Bovend'Eert PPT et al (2009) Grondwet voor het Koninkrijk der Nederlanden: Tekst & Commentaar, 3rd edn. Kluwer, Deventer

Brouwer JG (2005) National Treaty Law and Practice: The Netherlands. In: Hollis DB, Blakeslee MR, Ederington LB (eds) National Treaty Law and Practice - Dedicated to The Memory of Monroe Leigh. Martinus Nijhoff Publishers, Leiden, pp 483–536

de Graaf KJ, Jans JH (2015) The Urgenda Decision: Netherlands Liable for Role in Causing Dangerous Global Climate Change. Journal of Environmental Law 27:517–527

de Witte B (2011) Direct Effect, Primacy and the Nature of the Legal Order. In: Craig P, de Búrca G (eds) The Evolution of EU Law. Oxford University Press, Oxford, pp 323–362

Fleuren JWA (2004) Een ieder verbindende bepalingen van verdragen. Boom Juridische Uitgevers, The Hague

Fleuren JWA (2010) The Application of Public International Law by Dutch Courts. Netherlands International Law Review 57:245–266

Fleuren JWA, Viering MLWM (2001) Rechtstreekse werking en een ieder verbindende kracht: Europese inspiratie voor de nationale rechter? In: Bovend'Eert PPT, Fleuren JWA, Kummeling HRBM (eds) Grensverleggend staatsrecht: Opstellen aangeboden aan Prof. mr. C.A.J.M. Kortmann. Kluwer, Deventer, pp 101–138

Gerards JH (2016) De rechtskracht van niet-bindende uitspraken van verdragscomités op het terrein van de grondrechten. VAR-reeks 156:11–85

---

[55] *Francovich and Others v Italian Republic*, ECJ, Judgment, Joined Cases C-6/90 and C-9/90, ECR I-5357, 19 November 1991 ('*Francovich*'); *Dillenkofer and Others v Federal Republic of Germany*, ECJ, Judgment, Joined Cases C-178/94, C-179/94, C-188/94, C-189/94 and C-190/94, ECR I-4845, 8 October 1996 ('*Dillenkofer*').

[56] Cf *Staat der Nederlanden v X* (ECLI:NL:HR:2015:2723), op. cit.

[57] *Abdellah Medjahri v Staat der Nederlanden*, Hoge Raad, Judgement, No. 13 830, AB 1994, No. 10, 11 June 1993 ('*Roosendaal-methode*'); *Staat der Nederlanden v X* et al., Hoge Raad, Judgment, No. 11/01153, ECLI:NL:HR:2012:BW5328, 21 September 2012.

Gerards J, Fleuren J (2014) The Netherlands. In: Gerards J, Fleuren J (eds) Implementation of the European Convention on Human Rights and of the Judgments of the ECtHR in National Case-law: A comparative analysis. Intersentia, Cambridge, pp 217–260

Kanetake M, Nollkaemper A (2014) The Application of Informal International Instruments Before Domestic Courts. The George Washington International Law Review 46:765–807

Kapteyn PJG (2008) The Application and Enforcement of Community Law in the National Legal Systems. In: Kapteyn PJG et al (eds) The Law of the European Union and the European Communities, 4th edn. Kluwer Law International, Alphen aan den Rijn, pp 511–574

Krommendijk J (2015) Between Pretence and Practice: The Dutch Response to Recommendations on International Human Rights Bodies. Netherlands Yearbook of International Law 46: 421–438

Nollkaemper A (2009) The Netherlands. In: Sloss D (ed) The Role of Domestic Courts in Treaty Enforcement - A Comparative Study. Cambridge University Press, Cambridge, pp 326–369

Prechal S (2000) Does Direct Effect Still Matter? Common Market Law Review 37:1047–1069

Shelton D (ed) (2011) International Law and Domestic Legal Systems - Incorporation, Transformation, and Persuasion. Oxford University Press, Oxford

Sloss D (ed) (2009) The Role of Domestic Courts in Treaty Enforcement - A Comparative Study. Cambridge University Press, Cambridge

Table of Cases*

INTERNATIONAL

Ad Hoc Arbitration

Court of Justice of the European Union

* The Table of Cases was compiled by Ms C.C. Diepeveen, Middelburg, The Netherlands, e-mail: cdiep@zeelandnet.nl

M. Kuijer and W. Werner (eds.), *Netherlands Yearbook of International Law 2016*, Netherlands Yearbook of International Law 47,
DOI 10.1007/978-94-6265-207-1

NATIONAL

Belgium

Court of Cassation
Yahoo v. Belgium, 1 December 2015, 158 n55, 169 n103

Canada

Supreme Court
Libman v. The Queen, 10 October 2015, 62 n68

France

Tribunal de Grande Instance de Paris
LICRA v. Yahoo France, 22 May 2000, 157 n55

Germany

Administrative Court of Cologne
In re Duchy of Sealand, Case No. 9 K 2565/77, 3 May 1978, 24 n24

Bundesgerichtshof (Federal High Court)
Arzneimittelwerbung im Internet, 30 March 2006, 158 n55
Persönlichkeitsverletzungen durch ausländische Internetveröffentlichungen, 2 March 2010, 158 n55

Italy

Constitutional Court
Re Hartmann and Pude, 71 ILR 258, 18 April 1967, 24 n25

Court of First Instance of Rome
Thome Guadalupe v. Associazione Italiana di S. Cecilia, 8 ILR 151, 27 February 1937, 32 n72

Netherlands

Supreme Court
Abdellah Medjahri v. Staat der Nederlanden (Roosendaal-methode), 11 June 1993, 392 n56
Criminal proceedings against Desi Bouterse, 18 September 2001, 381 n14
Criminal proceedings against X, 8 July 2008, 381 n14
Dirk Hoogenraad v. Nederlandse Organisatie voor Wetenschappelijk Onderzoek, 20 April 1990, 385 n30

United States

Supreme Court

United States Court of Appeals

District Court for the Southern District of New York

Index[*]

[*] The Index was compiled by Ms C.C. Diepeveen, Middelburg, The Netherlands, e-mail: cdiep@zeelandnet.nl

M. Kuijer and W. Werner (eds.), *Netherlands Yearbook of International Law 2016*, Netherlands Yearbook of International Law 47,
DOI 10.1007/978-94-6265-207-1

U

MIX
Papier aus verantwortungsvollen Quellen
Paper from responsible sources
FSC® C105338

If you have any concerns about our products,
you can contact us on
ProductSafety@springernature.com

In case Publisher is established outside the EU,
the EU authorized representative is:
Springer Nature Customer Service Center GmbH
Europaplatz 3, 69115 Heidelberg, Germany

Printed by Libri Plureos GmbH
in Hamburg, Germany